THE ROUTLEDGE COMPANION PHILOSOPHY OF RACE

For many decades, race and racism have been common areas of study in departments of sociology, history, political science, English, and anthropology. Much more recently, as the historical concept of race and racial categories have faced significant scientific and political challenges, philosophers have become more interested in these areas. This changing understanding of the ontology of race has invited inquiry from researchers in moral philosophy, metaphysics, epistemology, philosophy of science, philosophy of language, and aesthetics.

The Routledge Companion to Philosophy of Race offers in one comprehensive volume newly written articles on race from the world's leading analytic and continental philosophers. It is, however, accessible to a readership beyond philosophy as well, providing a cohesive reference for a wide student and academic readership. The Companion synthesizes current philosophical understandings of race, providing 37 chapters on the history of philosophy and race, as well as how race might be investigated in the usual frameworks of contemporary philosophy. The volume concludes with a section on philosophical approaches to some topics with broad interest outside of philosophy, like colonialism, affirmative action, eugenics, immigration, race and disability, and post-racialism.

By clearly explaining and carefully organizing the leading current philosophical thinking on race, this timely collection will help define the subject and bring renewed understanding of race to students and researchers in the humanities, social science, and sciences.

Paul C. Taylor is Professor of Philosophy and African American Studies at the Pennsylvania State University, where he also serves as Associate Dean for Undergraduate Studies. Professor Taylor received his Bachelor's Degree in Philosophy from Morehouse College, a Master's Degree in Public Administration from the Kennedy School of Government at Harvard University, and his Ph.D. in Philosophy from Rutgers University. He has written three books, including *Black Is Beautiful: A Philosophy of Black Aesthetics* and *On Obama*, and is one of the founding co-editors of the journal *Critical Philosophy of Race*.

Linda Martín Alcoff is Professor of Philosophy at Hunter College and the CUNY Graduate Center, and Visiting Research Professor at Australian Catholic University. She was president of the American Philosophical Association, Eastern Division, for 2012–2013. Her books include *The Future of Whiteness* and *Visible Identities: Race, Gender and the Self*.

Luvell Anderson is Assistant Professor of Philosophy at the University of Memphis. Before coming to Memphis, he was Alain Locke Postdoctoral Fellow at Pennsylvania State University. His research lies principally in philosophy of language, philosophy of race, and aesthetics. He has published articles on the semantics of racial slurs and on racist humor. Professor Anderson's current writing projects include analyzing the linguistic underpinnings of racial humor, investigating the ways power interacts with our interpretative practices, and attempts to construct viable strategies for bridging certain racially motivated divides that foster miscommunication.

Routledge Philosophy Companions

Routledge Philosophy Companions offer thorough, high quality surveys and assessments of the major topics and periods in philosophy. Covering key problems, themes and thinkers, all entries are specially commissioned for each volume and written by leading scholars in the field. Clear, accessible and carefully edited and organized, *Routledge Philosophy Companions* are indispensable for anyone coming to a major topic or period in philosophy, as well as for the more advanced reader.

Recently published:

The Routledge Companion to Philosophy of Race
Edited by Paul C. Taylor, Linda Martín Alcoff, and Luvell Anderson

The Routledge Companion to Feminist Philosophy
Edited by Ann Garry, Serene J. Khader, and Alison Stone

The Routledge Companion to Philosophy of Social Science
Edited by Lee McIntyre and Alex Rosenberg

The Routledge Companion to Sixteenth Century Philosophy
Edited by Benjamin Hill and Henrik Lagerlund

The Routledge Companion to Free Will
Edited by Kevin Timpe, Meghan Griffith, and Neil Levy

The Routledge Companion to Philosophy of Medicine
Edited by Miriam Solomon, Jeremy R. Simon, and Harold Kincaid

The Routledge Companion to Philosophy of Literature
Edited by Noël Carroll and John Gibson

The Routledge Companion to Islamic Philosophy
Edited by Richard C. Taylor and Luis Xavier López-Farjeat

The Routledge Companion to Virtue Ethics
Edited by Lorraine Besser-Jones and Michael Slote

The Routledge Companion to Bioethics
Edited by John Arras, Rebecca Kukla, and Elizabeth Fenton

The Routledge Companion to Hermeneutics
Edited by Jeff Malpas and Hans-Helmuth Gander

The Routledge Companion to Eighteenth Century Philosophy
Edited by Aaron Garrett

For a full list of published Routledge Philosophy Companions, please visit www.routledge.com/series/PHILCOMP

Forthcoming

The Routledge Companion to Thought Experiments
Edited by Michael T. Stuart, Yiftach Fehige and James Robert Brown

THE ROUTLEDGE COMPANION TO PHILOSOPHY OF RACE

Edited by
Paul C. Taylor, Linda Martín Alcoff,
and Luvell Anderson

NEW YORK AND LONDON

First published 2018
by Routledge
52 Vanderbilt Avenue, New York, NY 10017

and by Routledge
2 Park Square, Milton Park, Abingdon, Oxon, OX14 4RN

First issued in paperback 2020

Routledge is an imprint of the Taylor & Francis Group, an informa business

© 2018 Taylor & Francis

The right of Paul C. Taylor, Linda Martín Alcoff, and Luvell Anderson to be identified as the authors of the editorial material, and of the authors for their individual chapters, has been asserted in accordance with sections 77 and 78 of the Copyright, Designs and Patents Act 1988.

All rights reserved. No part of this book may be reprinted or reproduced or utilised in any form or by any electronic, mechanical, or other means, now known or hereafter invented, including photocopying and recording, or in any information storage or retrieval system, without permission in writing from the publishers.

Trademark notice: Product or corporate names may be trademarks or registered trademarks, and are used only for identification and explanation without intent to infringe.

Library of Congress Cataloging-in-Publication Data
A catalog record has been requested for this title

ISBN 13: 978-0-367-65998-1 (pbk)
ISBN 13: 978-0-415-71123-4 (hbk)

Typeset in Goudy Std
by Apex CoVantage, LLC

Printed in the United Kingdom
by Henry Ling Limited

CONTENTS

List of Illustrations   ix
Contributors   x
Acknowledgments   xv
Introduction   xvii

PART I
History and the Canon   1

1 Critical Philosophy of Race and Philosophical Historiography   3
ROBERT BERNASCONI

2 Of Problem Moderns and Excluded Moderns: On the Essential Hybridity of Modernity   14
OLÚFẸ́MI TÁÍWÒ

3 Kant on Race and Transition   28
FRANK M. KIRKLAND

4 Hegel on Race and Development   43
FRANK M. KIRKLAND

5 Heidegger's Shadow: Levinas, Arendt, and the Magician From Messkirch   61
JONATHAN JUDAKEN

6 Race-ing the Canon: American Icons, From Thomas Jefferson to Alain Locke   75
JACOBY ADESHEI CARTER

7 At the Intersections: Existentialism, Critical Philosophies of Race, and Feminism   88
KATHRYN T. GINES

8 Critical Theory: Adorno, Marcuse, and Angela Davis   102
ARNOLD L. FARR

CONTENTS

9 Post-structuralism and Race: Giorgio Agamben and Michel Foucault 113
LADELLE MCWHORTER

PART II
Alternative Traditions 125

10 Rights, Race, and the Beginnings of Modern Africana Philosophy 127
CHIKE JEFFERS

11 Africana Thought 140
LEWIS R. GORDON

12 Theorizing Indigeneity, Gender, and Settler Colonialism 152
SHELBI NAHWILET MEISSNER AND KYLE WHYTE

13 The History of Racial Theories in China 168
FRANK DIKÖTTER

14 Racism in India 181
ANIA LOOMBA

PART III
Metaphysics and Ontology 201

15 Analytic Metaphysics: Race and Racial Identity 203
JORGE J. E. GRACIA AND SUSAN L. SMITH

16 American Experimentalism 216
HARVEY CORMIER

17 Phenomenology and Race (or Racializing Phenomenology) 233
GAIL WEISS

PART IV
Epistemology, Cognition, and Language 245

18 Epistemic Injustice and Epistemologies of Ignorance 247
JOSÉ MEDINA

19 Implicit Bias and Race 261
MICHAEL BROWNSTEIN

CONTENTS

20 The Mark of the Plural: Generic Generalizations and Race   277
DANIEL WODAK AND SARAH-JANE LESLIE

21 Psychoanalysis and Race   290
KELLY OLIVER

PART V
Natural Science and Social Theory   303

22 Race and Biology   305
RASMUS GRØNFELDT WINTHER

23 Eugenics   321
CAMISHA RUSSELL

24 Framing Intersectionality   335
ELENA RUÍZ

25 Canonizing the Critical Race Artifice: An Analysis of Philosophy's Gentrification of Critical Race Theory   349
TOMMY J. CURRY

PART VI
Aesthetics   363

26 Race-ing Aesthetic Theory   365
MONIQUE ROELOFS

27 Joking About Race and Ethnicity   380
STEPHANIE PATRIDGE

28 Anti-black Racism: The Greatest Art Show on Earth   391
JANINE JONES

PART VII
Ethics and the Political   403

29 Racism   405
LUC FAUCHER

30 On Race and Solidarity: Reconsiderations   423
LUCIUS TURNER OUTLAW (JR.)

31	Race, Luck, and the Moral Emotions SAMANTHA VICE	446
32	Racism and Coloniality: The Invention of "HUMAN(ITY)" and the Three Pillars of the Colonial Matrix of Power (Racism, Sexism, and Nature) WALTER D. MIGNOLO	461
33	White Supremacy CHARLES W. MILLS	475

PART VIII
Politics and Policy 489

34	On Post-racialism: Or, How Color-Blindness Rebranded Is Still Vicious RONALD R. SUNDSTROM	491
35	Philosophy of Race and the Ethics of Immigration JOSÉ JORGE MENDOZA	507
36	Mixed-Race JARED SEXTON	520
37	Racism, State Violence, and the Homeland FALGUNI A. SHETH	539

Index	549

ILLUSTRATIONS

Figures

19.1–4	Implicit Association Test	262
22.1	"Schematic world map of the 'flow' of microsatellite alleles"	309
22.2	The amount of heterozygosity of each of approximately 40 worldwide populations diminishes as a function of their respective distance, along (approximate) migration routes, from Addis Ababa	310
22.3	High correlation between pairwise F_{ST} and pairwise geographic distance of worldwide populations	312
24.1	The intersectional model of identity	342
26.1–2	Kara Walker, Installation view: *At the behest of Creative Time Kara E. Walker has confected: A Subtlety, or the Marvelous Sugar Baby, an Homage to the unpaid and overworked Artisans who have refined our Sweet tastes from the cane fields to the Kitchens of the New World on the Occasion of the demolition of the Domino Sugar Refining Plant, 2014*	370
26.3	Kara Walker, *The moral arc of history ideally bends towards justice but just as soon as not curves back around toward barbarism, sadism, and unrestrained chaos, 2010*	372
32.1	Ren	468

Table

22.1	Allele frequencies of three distinct genes across continental regions	311

CONTRIBUTORS

Robert Bernasconi is Edwin Erle Sparks Professor of Philosophy and African American Studies at the Pennsylvania State University. He is the editor of *Race* and, with Tommy Lott, *The Idea of Race*. He has published more than twenty-five volumes of primary literature on the history of the concept of race and is one of the founding editors of the journal *Critical Philosophy of Race*.

Michael Brownstein is Assistant Professor of Philosophy at John Jay College of Criminal Justice (CUNY). His articles on the metaphysics of implicit attitudes, moral responsibility for biased actions, skill and knowing-how, and the ethics of spontaneity have appeared in journals such as *Noûs, Synthese, Philosophical Studies, Mind and Language*, and *The Stanford Encyclopedia of Philosophy*.

Jacoby Adeshei Carter is Associate Professor of Philosophy at John Jay College of Criminal Justice (CUNY). Carter is Director of the Alain Leroy Locke Society and the co-editor of *Philosophic Values and World Citizenship: Locke to Obama and Beyond*. He is also the author of *African American Contributions to the Americas' Cultures: A Critical Edition of Lectures by Alain Locke*.

Harvey Cormier is Associate Professor of Philosophy at Stony Brook University. He is the author of a book on William James's theory of truth, *The Truth Is What Works*. He has also researched Cornel West's Marx-influenced criticisms of James; Nietzsche on freedom and selfhood; and the film *2001: A Space Odyssey* as a work of modernist art.

Tommy J. Curry's work spans philosophy, jurisprudence, Africana studies, and gender studies. Though trained in the American and continental philosophical traditions, Curry's primary research interests are in critical race theory and Africana philosophy. Currently his research focuses on the linking the conceptualization of ethics found in the Belmont Report to civil rights and social justice paradigms.

Frank Dikötter is Chair Professor of Humanities at the University of Hong Kong. He has published widely on the history of modern China and is the author, most recently, of a *People's Trilogy*, which uses party archives to illustrate the impact of communism on everyday life under Mao. He is also the author of *The Discourse of Race in Modern China*.

Arnold L. Farr received his Ph.D. in philosophy from the University of Kentucky in 1996, where he currently teaches. He is a co-author and co-editor of *Marginal Groups*

CONTRIBUTORS

and Mainstream American Culture. In 2009 he published *Critical Theory and Democratic Vision: Herbert Marcuse and Recent Liberation Philosophies.*

Luc Faucher is Full Professor in the Department of Philosophy of the Université du Québec à Montréal. His research interests include philosophy of cognitive sciences, philosophy of race, and philosophy of psychiatry. He has published papers in *Philosophy of Science, Philosophy of Social Sciences, Journal of Social Philosophy,* and the *Monist,* among others.

Kathryn Gines's primary research and teaching interests lie in continental philosophy, Africana philosophy, black feminist philosophy, and critical philosophy of race. Gines is the author of *Hannah Arendt and the Negro Question,* co-editor of an anthology titled *Convergences: Black Feminism and Continental Philosophy,* and one of the founding editors of the journal *Critical Philosophy of Race.*

Lewis R. Gordon is Professor of Philosophy and Africana Studies at the University of Connecticut, Storrs; European Union Visiting Chair in Philosophy at Université Toulouse Jean Jaurès, France; and Nelson Mandela Distinguished Visiting Professor at Rhodes University, South Africa. His books include *Existentia Africana, Disciplinary Decadence, An Introduction to Africana Philosophy,* and with Jane Anna Gordon, *Of Divine Warning: Reading Disaster in the Modern Age.*

Jorge J.E. Gracia holds the Samuel P. Capen Chair in Philosophy and is State University of New York Distinguished Professor. Gracia is the author of 20 books and over 250 articles published in the United States, Europe, Latin America, and China. Particular honors include the Findlay Prize for his book *Individuality* and the Aquinas Medal from the American Catholic Philosophical Association.

Chike Jeffers is Associate Professor of Philosophy at Dalhousie University. He specializes in Africana philosophy and philosophy of race, with broad interests in social and political philosophy and ethics. He is the editor of *Listening to Ourselves: A Multilingual Anthology of African Philosophy* and is currently completing *Du Bois,* his first single-authored book.

Janine Jones is Associate Professor of Philosophy at the University of North Carolina, Greensboro. She is interested in how the entanglement of imagination, language, perception, and power constructs social realities. She is a co-editor of *Pursuing Trayvon Martin: Historical Contexts and Contemporary Manifestations of Racial Dynamics,* in which her piece "Can We Imagine *This* Happening to a White Boy?" appears.

Jonathan Judaken is the Spence L. Wilson Chair in the Humanities at Rhodes College in Memphis. He is the author of *Jean-Paul Sartre and the Jewish Question: Antiantisemitism and the Politics of the French Intellectual.* His most recent book, *Situating Existentialism: Key Texts in Context,* was co-edited with Robert Bernasconi.

Frank M. Kirkland is Associate Professor of Philosophy at Hunter College and the Graduate Center (CUNY). He has published articles on Kant, Hegel, and Husserl;

Douglass, Du Bois, Hegel, and the Haitian Revolution; and the theme of modernity and intellectual life in the African diaspora. He is currently at work on a book titled *Hegel's Idealism and the Black Atlantic Tradition*.

Sarah-Jane Leslie is the Class of 1943 Professor of Philosophy, the Director of the Program in Linguistics, and the Founding Director of the Program in Cognitive Science at Princeton University. She is the author of numerous articles in philosophy and psychology that have been published in journals such as *Science*, *PNAS*, *Philosophical Review*, and *Noûs*.

Ania Loomba is Catherine Bryson Professor of English at the University of Pennsylvania. She is the author of *Shakespeare, Race, and Colonialism*, *Colonialism—Postcolonialism*, and *Gender, Race, Renaissance Drama*, as well as numerous articles on early modern studies, race, colonial histories, and feminism. Her latest book, a study of radical and communist women in India is forthcoming from Routledge in 2018.

Ladelle McWhorter is the author of *Bodies and Pleasures: Foucault and the Politics of Sexual Normalization*, *Racism and Sexual Oppression in Anglo-America: A Genealogy*, and more than three dozen articles on Foucault, Bataille, Irigaray, and race theory. She holds the Stephanie Bennett-Smith Chair in Women, Gender, and Sexuality Studies at the University of Richmond.

José Medina is Walter Dill Scott Professor of Philosophy at Northwestern University. His articles have appeared in journals such as *Critical Philosophy of Race*, *Inquiry*, *Metaphilosophy*, *Philosophical Studies*, *Philosophy and Social Criticism*, and *Social Epistemology*. His books include *Speaking From Elsewhere* and *The Epistemology of Resistance*, the latter of which received the North American Society for Social Philosophy Book Award.

Shelbi Nahwilet Meissner is a doctoral student in the Department of Philosophy at Michigan State University and a graduate affiliate of American Indian and Indigenous Studies. Her research interests include American Indian and Indigenous philosophy, philosophy of language, and feminist epistemology.

José Jorge Mendoza is Assistant Professor of Philosophy at the University of Massachusetts, Lowell, and is a co-editor of *Radical Philosophy Review*. His areas of specialization are moral and political philosophy, philosophy of race, and Latin American philosophy. He is the author of *The Moral and Political Philosophy of Immigration: Liberty, Security, and Equality*.

Walter D. Mignolo is Director of the Institute for Global Studies in Humanities, William H. Wannamaker Professor of Literature and Romance Studies, and Professor of Cultural Anthropology at Duke University. He is the author of *The Idea of Latin America*; *Local Histories/Global Designs: Coloniality, Subaltern Knowledges, and Border Thinking*; and *The Darker Side of the Renaissance: Literacy, Territoriality and Colonization*.

Charles W. Mills is Distinguished Professor of Philosophy at the Graduate Center (CUNY). He works in the general area of oppositional political theory and is the

CONTRIBUTORS

author of six books, most recently *Black Rights/White Wrongs: The Critique of Racial Liberalism*.

Kelly Oliver is W. Alton Jones Professor of Philosophy at Vanderbilt University. She is the author of 15 scholarly books, of which perhaps the best known is *Witnessing: Beyond Recognition*. Her work has been translated into seven languages. Most recently, she has published two novels in the *Jessica James, Cowgirl Philosopher* mystery series.

Lucius Turner Outlaw (Jr.) is Professor of Philosophy, African American and Diaspora Studies, and Human and Organizational Development at Vanderbilt University. He is the author of *On Race and Philosophy* and *Critical Social Theory in the Interest of Black Folks*, among other writings.

Stephanie Patridge is Professor of Philosophy at Otterbein University. She is a co-editor of *Aesthetics: A Reader in Philosophy of the Art* (forthcoming). She is the author of numerous articles on ethical assessment in imaginative contexts. Her work often focuses on issues of race and gender.

Monique Roelofs is Professor of Philosophy at Hampshire College. She is the author of *The Cultural Promise of the Aesthetic* and editor of "Aesthetics and Race," a special issue of *Contemporary Aesthetics*. Roelofs currently is completing two books, *Arts of Address: How We Relate to Language, People, Things, and Places* and *Aesthetics, Address, and the Making of Culture*.

Elena Ruíz is Assistant Professor of Philosophy and Global Studies at Michigan State University. Her work examines the philosophical foundations of violence, structural oppression, and theories of harm in the context of violence affecting women and marginalized populations in the global South. Her work has appeared in *Hypatia*, *Feminist Philosophy Quarterly*, and *Human Studies*, among other places.

Camisha Russell is Assistant Professor of Philosophy at the University of Oregon. Her first book, *The Assisted Reproduction of Race: Thinking Through Race as a Reproductive Technology* (forthcoming), explores the role of race and racial identity in assisted reproductive technologies. She has held several fellowships, including most recently the Riley Postdoctoral Fellowship at Colorado College (2015–2017).

Jared Sexton teaches African American Studies at the University of California, Irvine. He is the author of *Amalgamation Schemes: Antiblackness and the Critique of Multiracialism* and various articles and essays on contemporary political and popular culture.

Falguni A. Sheth is Associate Professor in the Department of Women's, Gender, and Sexuality Studies at Emory University. Her books include *Race, Liberalism, and Economics*, co-edited with David Colander and Robert E. Prasch, and *Toward a Political Philosophy of Race*. Sheth is an organizer of the California Roundtable for Philosophy and Race.

Susan L. Smith is Director of the Social Science Interdisciplinary Degree Programs at the University at Buffalo. Smith's research focuses on metaphysics and race as well as genetics and ethics. She currently serves on the advisory board of the University at Buffalo Genomics, Education, and the Microbiome (GEM) Community of Excellence.

Ronald R. Sundstrom is Professor of Philosophy and a member of the African American Studies and Critical Diversity Studies programs at the University of San Francisco. His areas of research include race theory, political and social theory, and African American philosophy. He is the author of *The Browning of America and the Evasion of Social Justice*.

Olúfẹ́mi Táíwò is Professor of African Political Thought at Cornell University's Africana Studies and Research Center. His research interests include philosophy of law, social and political philosophy, Marxism, and African and Africana philosophy. Táíwò is the author of *Legal Naturalism: A Marxist Theory of Law*, *How Colonialism Preempted Modernity in Africa*, and *Africa Must Be Modern: A Manifesto*.

Samantha Vice is Professor of Philosophy at the University of the Witwatersrand. She works in moral and social philosophy. She has co-edited volumes on ethics and film, the ethics of aging, and the work of John Cottingham, and has published papers on beauty, goodness and evil, cynicism, the meaning of life, and the work of Iris Murdoch.

Gail Weiss is Professor of Philosophy at George Washington University and General Secretary of the International Merleau-Ponty Circle. She is the author of two monographs: *Refiguring the Ordinary* and *Body Images: Embodiment as Intercorporeality*. Her research investigates specific issues related to human embodiment, drawing upon recent work in feminist theory, critical race theory, and disability studies.

Kyle Whyte holds the Timnick Chair in the Humanities at Michigan State University, where he is also Associate Professor of Philosophy and Community Sustainability. His research, teaching, training, and activism address moral and political issues concerning climate policy and Indigenous peoples and the ethics of cooperative relationships between Indigenous peoples and climate science organizations.

Rasmus Grønfeldt Winther is Associate Professor of Philosophy at the University of California, Santa Cruz. He co-edited a special issue on "Genomics and Philosophy of Race" that appeared in *Studies in the History and Philosophy of Science, Part C*, and his book *When Maps Become the World* is forthcoming.

Daniel Wodak is Assistant Professor of Philosophy at Virginia Tech, where he is also affiliated with the Program in Philosophy, Politics, and Economics. Much of his work concerns the intersection between moral and social norms. His work has been published in *Philosophical Studies*, *Oxford Studies in Metaethics*, and *Philosophical Compass*.

ACKNOWLEDGMENTS

This volume would not exist were it not for the support and involvement of a great many extraordinary people. We will offer four words of thanks here from the editors as a team, and then a few words apiece from each individual editor.

We would first like to thank the remarkable editorial team at Routledge for making this volume possible. We have to begin with Andrew Beck, whose interest in the project, patience in seeing it through to completion, and many good ideas were essential to helping us get to this point. Andy's editorial assistants Vera Lochtefeld and, before her, Elizabeth Vogt were islands of stability and reassurance in a roiling sea of deadlines and details. We are grateful for their help and guidance.

Second, we have to thank the indefatigable Edith Gnanadass. Dr. Gnanadass began work on the project as Paul C. Taylor's editorial assistant, but soon came to play a larger role, equal parts journal managing editor and air traffic controller. Edith kept us on a single, unified track when we were in danger of racing off in three (or more) different directions. What's more, she did the same for our contributors during the delicate early and middle stages of the project, and she did it all with unfailing good humor. We were very sorry when she had to go, but thrilled we had the chance to work with her.

Third, we absolutely have to thank Toyin Ojih Odutola (and her representatives at the Jack Shainman Gallery) for allowing us to use a piece of her astonishing art for our cover image. The power of Odutola's work outstrips our ability to capture it in words, which may be why *Aperture* asked an award-winning poet to give it a try. Claudia Rankine describes the work like this:

> Toyin Ojih Odutola's drawings engage, destroy, highlight, and ultimately privilege a new grammar for blackness. Using black ballpoint, graphite, pastel, and charcoal, Odutola subordinates representation and fact telling to mark making and open-ended image construction. Before a face becomes a face, for example, we take in its shapes, tonality, and lines. . . . Historically, in a narrow read, blackness becomes unilaterally a signifier of race. But in Odutola's work, race is there or it is not there, but its presence is never without our perceptions and projections.
>
> (Claudia Rankine, "A New Grammar for Blackness,"
> *Aperture* 223 [Summer 2016], 66)

Could there be a better way to open a set of philosophical reflections on race than with an image like this?

Finally, we want to thank the contributors. This volume, as edited volumes are wont to do, occasionally put its editors in mind of that reliable old metaphor, herding cats.

ACKNOWLEDGMENTS

But as any cat will tell you, in the Nietzschean spirit that defines the general run of felinity, being herded is not a fit occupation for original and independent spirits. We have had the privilege of working with thirty-nine brilliant thinkers, thinkers whose originality and independence inform the profound enactments of philosophical race theory that make up this book. We are grateful to them for signing on to the project, and for their patience as we worked to find a mode of direction and coordination appropriate to independent spirits.

Linda Martín Alcoff: I would like to thank my three department chairs at Hunter College who, during the long course of this book, have helped me in numerous ways: Frank Kirkland, Laura Keating, and Omar Dahbour. I owe a special debt to Frank for hiring me to this wonderful department, and also for the experience of team teaching a graduate seminar on the Critical Philosophy of Race at the CUNY Graduate Center. His high political and intellectual standards continue to be an inspiration. I also want to thank my entire family, especially my husband Larry and sons Sam and José, for their loving support and ongoing enthusiasm for my work. And I'd like to thank all of our contributors who gave generously of their limited time to help us in the endeavor to assemble and expand this area of philosophical work. To Paul and Luvell, all I can say is, *mil gracias por todos*.

Luvell Anderson: I would like to thank my co-editors for letting little old me tag along and hang out with the big kids. I definitely gained a lot from their wisdom and insight. I am also grateful to my colleagues at the University of Memphis for their support. Finally, I am especially thankful to Verena Erlenbusch for letting me run ideas by her and for extensive feedback.

Paul C. Taylor: I would like to thank Maya Stainback, who succeeded Dr. Gnanadass as my research assistant and helped keep the project moving forward for a year. Dr. Stephanie Scott provided invaluable assistance as we transitioned from commissioning and coaxing individual papers into being to turning the individual papers into a submission-ready manuscript. Dr. Tamara Nopper provided similar help, with her usual keen eye and with an unusually quick turnaround (in response to an unconscionably late request for help). The Pennsylvania State University provided helpful research support, and colleagues like Anika Simpson, Anne Eaton, Charles McKinney, Mark Jefferson, and Charles Peterson provided essential moral and intellectual support. Nearly most of all, my co-editors were a joy to work with, and repeatedly justified my original thought that taking on this project would be a pleasant undertaking as well as a useful contribution to the discipline. Finally, and truly most of all, I want to thank my family, my wife Wilna and my children, John and Julia, for giving me the time and space to do this work, and for giving me reasons and opportunities to pull away from the work and recharge, and to remember what the stakes of the work really are.

INTRODUCTION

There is no more complex and thorny topic for philosophical investigation than the topic of race. Nor is there one with more real-world relevance. This book provides a definitive guide to the burgeoning subfield of philosophy that focuses on racial phenomena.

The philosophy of race obviously has at its core a number of important debates in ethics and political philosophy, but the field is not exhausted by these subjects. There are the familiar discussions of, for example, the definition of racism and the justifiability of anti-racist policy initiatives such as affirmative action and reparations. But there are also the discussions of race in relation to aesthetics, language, epistemology, cognition, and the philosophy of science. Perhaps most challenging for many philosophers, the field has also opened up vigorous debates in the history of philosophy, and pushed for a reformation of the standard canon.

This volume brings together chapters on all of these topics by a diverse set of scholars, representing a variety of metaphilosophical perspectives. The result is a comprehensive image of the field that offers a bracing challenge to the distressingly widespread modes of philosophical complacency that have been content to rely on inadequate sources and falsely universal claims. Taking race seriously, in philosophy as in other precincts of inquiry and activity, implicates a variety of normative, interpretive, ontological, and epistemological questions, and raises the stakes of engaging those questions responsibly.

The remainder of this introduction will set the stage for the work of this volume, and will do so in two steps. First, it will explore the question of how to refer to the enterprise the volume introduces, and the related question of why this matters. Then it will plot out the various sections of the volume, and provide short glimpses of the work that each contribution aims to do.

Philosophy of Race, or *Critical* Philosophy of Race?

Many of the participants and consumers of this volume will think of it as an exercise in the "critical" philosophy of race. The prevalence and plausibility of this label require some comment, especially in light of our decision to refuse it. Simply put, one might describe this volume in that way, but one needn't do so, and there are reasons not to do so, and, in any case, insisting on a wholesale embrace or refusal of the label is inessential to the work we mean to do here.

On the one hand, insisting on the critical dimension of philosophical race theory is a way of signaling that the *meaning* of race is very much under ongoing contestation, to such a degree that the advisability of using the term remains in question. Academic philosophers, scholars in other fields, and people outside the academy all still disagree with each other about what, if anything, "race" refers to, and about whether anyone is justified, ethically or epistemologically, in using the term. By the 1990s there was nearly a complete consensus among biologists around two propositions. The first was that the folk concept of race had no biological correlate, the claims of the high modern race "sciences" of craniometry and the rest notwithstanding. And the second was that the continued use of the race concept required ignoring or actively refusing the evidence of good science. This consensus led many, both scientists and non-scientists alike, to argue for the abandonment of race-talk and the abolition of racial practices. But this eliminativist turn inspired many political philosophers, social theorists, and others to dissent, and to argue that the concept of race tracks important social realities, irrespective of its claim on the attentions of natural scientists. Eventually, to make matters worse for the eliminativist, the consensus in the natural sciences eroded, as philosophers of biology and others developed new, non-racist ways to argue that the socially recognizable concept of race does refer to a biological kind.

Contemporary philosophical race theory might be critical, then, in the sense that it refuses both the easy embrace and the quick refusal of race-thinking. White supremacist race "science" fails, as do the ethicopolitical and cultural frameworks that grew up around it. But the knee-jerk eliminativism that takes this failure as its primary subject matter and justification is also unsatisfying. Race matters, *pace* the eliminativist; but it matters in complicated ways, *pace* the nineteenth-century racist. So the question of whether the term "race," however variably defined, refers to anything "real," however variably defined, is very much an open one, and one we seek to take up in this volume.

The philosophy of race might be critical also in a second sense, though. In this sense, it might be an expressly philosophical mode of, or companion to, the specific tradition of legal theory and analysis that goes by the name of "critical race theory," or CRT. Perhaps better, critical philosophy of race, or CPR, might be a philosophical contribution to the growing body of work in a variety of fields that adopts the original spirit of the legal enterprise. The "critical" in these formulations plays something like the role it plays in "critical social theory," which names "a social theory critical of present forms of domination, injustice, coercion, and inequality."[1]

Much of what appears in this volume will clearly adopt this critical spirit, but not all of it will do so. Some of our contributors will aspire to this spirit in ways that might not register as sufficiently critical to others, while still others may refuse this aspiration altogether. Mapping the conceptual terrain that concepts like "race" and "racism" inhabit, or teasing out the metaphysical implications of one approach or another, may not involve directly criticizing "present forms of domination." It might support or inform such criticism, but it is not identical with this critical work.

To sum up: our contributors and readers may have different views about what it takes for race theory in philosophy to earn the label, "critical." Perhaps it is enough to refuse the consolations of crude racialism and of hasty anti-racialism. Perhaps a particular mode of expressly political engagement is necessary. Or perhaps still more is required. Settling this question is not essential to the work of this volume; and peremptorily stipulating to an answer might foreclose lines of inquiry—like the one that Tommy Curry explores in Chapter 25—that are part of the subject matter of the field we mean to introduce. Consequently, we will use the more ecumenical label "philosophy of race" to frame this project.

INTRODUCTION

The Plan for the Volume

We have divided the volume into eight parts, each broadly organized around the way race theory inflects a major subfield or set of related subfields in philosophy. One could of course divide the field differently, into more or fewer or in any case different parts. We have chosen this way of circumscribing the topic because it tracks, more or less, certain familiar ways of mapping the terrain of professional philosophy, and because it seems to strike the right balance between granularity and generality. We are under no illusions that this mapping of the field is definitive, or that the boundaries we've set up are impermeable or immutable.

Part I: History and the Canon

Perhaps the most contentious question in philosophical race theory is at the heart of the area with which we begin the volume: can the philosophy of race, practiced in the right sort of critical spirit, challenge philosophy itself not simply to expand or open its doors, but to change its self-understanding and its methods of work? The need for change is made clear by new work of scholars in the history of philosophy, especially in regard to the modern European philosophical canon, which many of us take not just as our shared lineage but also as the model for ongoing philosophical work. How can we reconcile the great liberal and skeptical traditions that emerged in this period with the quite illiberal and uncritically racist arguments that we find work in the writings of such great thinkers as Locke, Hume, Kant, and Hegel?

How should we assess our shared philosophical history, our standard canons, and their legacy? These questions are germane to every philosophical tradition starting with modern European thought (early, middle, and late) as well as critical theory, existentialism, post-structuralism, and pragmatism. It is not at all difficult to find the topic of race, racism, racial oppression, and race-based forms of colonialism treated by numerous modern European and US philosophers working in these traditions. Yet, the racist arguments in philosophical texts were until recently passed over unexamined, taken to be trivial and obviously irrelevant. Robert Bernasconi argues that the attachment to ahistorical, decontextualized methods of interpretation that could justify ignoring racist passages was actually a form of self-defense, because the racism of the moderns challenges philosophy's understanding of itself in a fundamental way. In actuality, as Olúfẹ́mi Táíwò shows here, the modern European intellectual tradition provided white supremacy and European colonialism with some valuable frameworks and concepts. This canon is in truth an invaluable resource for understanding how the West justified genocide, land annexation, slavery, and colonialism.

Exposing the racism of the modern European canon has raised new methodological questions about interpretation that have generated a productive reinvigoration in the field of the history of philosophy. These questions concern not only historians of philosophy but also those of us who draw arguments and ideas, as well as political inspiration, from Hume, Kant, Hegel, Marx, or others. Can the work of such figures be recruited, without peril, for current anti-racist liberatory projects? It is clear that there are more than negative lessons to be gained from the modern canon since it also contains conflict and contestation over ideas about human differences and moral universalism. Frank Kirkland argues here that the modern tradition stages a productive debate between the affirmation of individuals versus the affirmation of groups, and continues to provide resources for ongoing philosophical work on questions of oppression. We have included here two papers from Kirkland offering original interpretations of Hegel and Kant, the subject of much current debate. Without in any way excusing their racism, what these papers offer is an analysis of the complex and polyvalent legacy of these major modern thinkers, suggesting that some of their concepts, carefully interpreted, could be put to anti-racist use.

Hence, the legacy of Western philosophy in regard to race and racism is a more complicated question than might initially be thought, and is explored in the remainder of the chapters in this part. What may appear to be universal ideals, conditions of human existence, or critical methods of analysis often turn out to be limited and specific to European history or certain population groups. Jacoby Carter shows how the gender and race exclusivity of the canon of American philosophy, or pragmatism, hampered its capacity to answer the questions thinkers posed as well as restricting the scope of questions. He also explains the difficulty of correction: how does one take a social theory that ignores issues of diversity and oppression and revise it so that these take, as they must, a central place?

Existential phenomenology had universal aspirations as an account of the fundamental conditions of human experience, yet it too drew initially from quite limited explorations of lived experience. Kathryn Gines holds that existentialism has been "expanded, enhanced, and enriched by the existential insights of a broader range of philosophical figures," and shows how the augmentation of existential work has corrected some of the tradition's false universals. Jonathan Judaken considers the particular case of Heidegger, who pursued a thorough deconstruction of the tradition of Western metaphysics even while his work was persistently Eurocentric in its focus and its formulation of problems. It is unquestionable nonetheless that Heidegger and the existentialist tradition he spawned gave rise to radical approaches to ethics and politics in, for example, the work of Sartre, Beauvoir, Arendt, and Levinas among others. Both Judaken and Gines consider the thorny question of how far this radical tradition can take us in relation to racial oppression.

The critical theory that developed out of the Frankfurt School offered a radical analysis of the appeal of authoritarianism, the cultural reproduction of capitalism, and the distorting effect of positivism on the social sciences, yet its lack of engagement with racism or colonialism limited its explanatory value. Arnold Farr argues here that the work of Marcuse and, in particular, Angela Davis shifted focus and sought to enhance our critical theory's understanding of social groups and social movements. This had productive results, leading to a reassessment of the possibilities, and strategies, of social change. He argues that Davis needs to be understood as a major figure in this tradition.

Post-structuralism was another important trend of twentieth-century European radical philosophy that, despite its Eurocentrism, is taken by many today to provide a new and better approach to social and political analysis, better certainly than the modern liberal tradition. Ladelle McWhorter considers this claim in relation to two of the most influential figures—Agamben and Foucault—and the potential applications of their work to race. She argues that Agamben's ahistorical conceptualizations pose serious obstacles for his capacity to shed light on such issues as the oppression of indigenous groups, but that Foucault's more historically embedded approach to philosophical argumentation has greater potential applicability.

INTRODUCTION

Part II: Alternative Traditions

The work of engaging with the mainstream philosophical canon will have to continue for some time, but there also needs to be more attention and study given to non-mainstream or alternative philosophical traditions. Numerous non-European-based traditions are still neglected in too many departmental core curricula, so that students can achieve Ph.D.s without having read a single text from Africa, Latin America, Asia, or the Middle East. The arbitrariness of these exclusions raises meta-epistemological questions about how the rigorous norms of justification and of knowledge debated through the history of Western philosophy could be so poorly applied within our own house. The obvious pattern of exclusion demands an analysis of how race has affected and distorted the "standard" formulation of topics and issues and arguments.

Chike Jeffers's essay here provides a new history of the tradition of modern philosophy by tracing it through the seventeenth-century African philosopher Zera Yacob as well as later thinkers such as Anton Wilhelm Amo, Lemuel Haynes, and Quobna Ottobah Cugoano. Rationalism and natural rights, as it turns out, were not ideas or intellectual trends unique to Europe and in fact constitute the historical grounds of the tradition of modern African philosophy. As Lewis Gordon shows, an original tradition of Africana philosophy has also emerged in the diasporic conditions of displacement, racialization and slavery, and this tradition was from the beginning necessarily meta-theoretical. Since it emerged from an experience of forced alienation from European modernity, it could not but reflect skeptically and critically on the liberatory concepts that emerged in that modernity. As he explains, Africana philosophy has begun to diagnose the essential nonrelationality of European subject formation, and as an antidote, has argued for the need to affirm an inherent openness of the category of the human.

Modern European conceptions of racial identity influenced the way in which diverse cultural, ethnic and national groups around the world were described and categorized. In effect, the racial imaginary came to mediate all other notional approaches to human difference. This process took different forms as it encountered and engaged with existing modes of self-identity and group differentiation. Europeans were not the only agents in these encounters, nor did they did succeed at obliterating prior meaning systems.

Shelbi Nahwilet Meissner and Kyle Whyte explore the concept of indigeneity in relation to race, and argue that indigeneity's operable meaning in the Americas has always been more fluid in ways that the biological and/or visual approaches to race cannot quite accommodate. The idea of indigenous identity itself did not exist prior to settler colonialism. Some indigenous peoples, for example, identified mostly by clan or region. The concept of indigeneity, then, is an historical effect of colonialism and a product of racism, but today it is also a counter to racial discourse. Meissner and Whyte explore how, under colonialism, lineage became central to the identification of indigenous peoples, imposing Western-style patriarchy and excluding non-heterosexist forms of individual identity and family formation.

The spread of Western concepts of race to China in the late nineteenth century produced a similar clash with existing ideas and practices, but also became coopted for new uses. Frank Dikötter explains that the influence of race had to do not only with its colonial imposition but its association at the time with science and modernity as a credible way to divide human groups. There was already a long tradition of colorism in China, favoring fair skin, and in the encounter with Europe a ranking system was further developed based on differences of hue. There were two other ways in which Western ideas of race were coopted: some reformers took it up as a way to imagine a pan-racial Asian identity that could be united and turned against European colonialism, while others developed hierarchies that placed "white" and "yellow" races superior to the darker peoples of the earth.

In India there existed long-standing hierarchies correlated to identity designations determined by lineage, but the question of precisely how the ancient concept of "caste" relates to the concept of race continues to animate theorists today. Here Ania Loomba argues that South Asians, even nationalists, effectively accepted and reproduced European racial hierarchies with some modifications. The Western concept of race was not imposed on a blank slate or on a culture devoid of identity based forms of ranking. She shows that there are both commonalities and differences between the ancient Indian modes of defining group difference and the European practices.

Part III: Metaphysics and Ontology

Attempting to relate the concept of race to the ancient philosophical pursuit of the nature of being, captured in metaphysics and ontology, may seem to involve a category mistake. Metaphysics and ontology aim to describe "first things," the fundamental building blocks of reality, transcendent of any given historical epoch or social milieu. Yet race, as most today attest, is radically context-dependent, if it is anything, to such a degree that it is easy to find people arguing that it is a modern, Western invention, a social construct reliant on nothing more fundamental than our contingent and changing social practices. What's more, it is not uncommon to find the impulse to assign race a deeper meaning in the structure of the cosmos, to think of it, say, as a natural kind or a Platonic Form, tracking fascist or otherwise ethically distressing tendencies.

However, a broader understanding of the traditional questions in metaphysics and ontology allows us to treat race as a perfectly legitimate category to analyze. For one thing, metaphysical inquiry aims to help us understand the way in which reality is carved up and represented, and this aim dovetails neatly with one of the central functions of the race concept: to identify the conditions under which and respects in which individual persons and human populations interestingly differ from each other. Even further, we might argue that it is critically important in racialized contexts to ask a core metaphysical question: to what, exactly, does "race" refer?

Jorge Gracia and Susan Smith provide a helpful overview here of work by analytic philosophers on the concept of race over the last few decades. As with any analytic project of inquiry, the inquiry into race seeks to clarify the meaning of the concept and determine whether it refers to anything real, and if so, to what. Their summary of positions covers both those who argue that a close analysis will reveal no "there" there, and that we should henceforth cease and desist using the term, as well as those who offer a conceptual reconstruction of the category that attempts to make it philosophically respectable and politically benign or even helpful.

Harvey Cormier considers how the American pragmatist tradition fared in this inquiry. He looks carefully into the work of both James and Du Bois on race, and argues that each applied an experimentalist approach with an open-ended view about the future viability of the concept. James took human groups in general to be "willed and hopeful social experiments," or social constructs but with collective agency and intentionality. For Du Bois, the question of race centered around the issue of the historical legacy that created the category, and the wisdom of carrying this history forward. Hence, the experimentalism of the pragmatists instructed the agents involved in social construction to consider the effects of doing things one way rather than another, as well as possible unintended consequences. The question of race then shifts from "what is?" to "what if?"

A third approach to ontology is developed in Gail Weiss's contribution here, through an elaboration of Fanon's phenomenological approach to an existential ontology of racial embodiment. Fanon rejected the possibility of giving a pure phenomenological description of blackness separated from the political context in which such questions arise. Rather, as she argues, his work helped to denaturalize the natural attitude. Yet Fanon brilliantly showed how a phenomenological account could reveal dimensions of lived experience impossible to account for in more objectivist, empirical approaches. Weiss highlights also the political importance of Fanon's "corrective descriptions of social reality that present it as it truly is, not as we might wish it could be."

Part IV: Epistemology, Cognition, and Language

This volume presupposes the thought that the contemporary world faces a number of difficult and pervasive race-related challenges. But not everyone agrees with this assessment. For many, the issues of race and racism are too easily overblown, especially in the contemporary academy. In this view, race matters only when racism is a problem, and "real" racists constitute only a minute, fringe segment of society. In addition, many believe that race is not a strong determinant of one's prospects in life, and that claims to the contrary, and the racial tensions these claims promote, are the result of media instigation.

The entries in this part may rebut this declensionist account of the significance of race more effectively for some audiences than even the more familiar arguments about racial injustice and oppression. Philosophical research into the effects of race on our epistemic, cognitive, and linguistic practices, on our practices of knowing, judging, communicating, and subject formation, show that race affects human life in deep, intense, and abiding ways, ways that go to the heart of human experience and social intercourse as such. The philosophy of language in particular has seen an exciting spike in work on racist speech, on how to define and delimit racism, as well as on how to understand the meanings and morality of racist humor, among other topics. Similarly, epistemology has been both challenged and invigorated by new accounts of implicit bias and epistemic injustice that have raised new questions about how we should define, and how we might achieve, justification as well as epistemic responsibility.

In relation to the effects of race on cognition, Michael Brownstein points out that while explicit prejudice seems to have lessened, social inequity and racial tension persist, raising the question of how to account for this apparently discordant situation. The notion of implicit bias has been proffered as one explanation, and here Brownstein explains what exactly it is for an attitude to be implicit. Some have defined it by either appealing to the notion of automaticity (i.e., controlled or automatic processes) or unconsciousness. Brownstein sees these more as *conditions* under which implicit attitudes operate rather than features that demarcate implicitness and explicitness. Rather than attitudes that are mainly automatic or largely unavailable to introspection, implicit attitudes "reflect complex yet validity-inapt processes of enculturation." Thus, according to Brownstein, tests of implicit bias "reveal our arational attitudes."

Race is also pervasive in our language. Daniel Wodak and Sarah-Jane Leslie discuss the significant and pernicious role generic generalizations such as "Blacks are unreliable. You can't count on them," play in our discourse and racial relations. For Wodak and Leslie, such racial generics communicate complex, false, and pernicious information (i.e., that one group is essentially different from another) and that this explains the presence of the negative property attributed in the generic. Further, this false information is often viewed as a natural and immutable feature of the world. Uses of generics "contribute to the very construction of the racial categories that divide 'us' from 'them'."

Kelly Oliver takes up the question of the effects of oppression and social exclusion in subjectivity and psychic formation. Utilizing theorists such as Fanon and Lacan, Oliver investigates the role of social context in the formation of subjectivities, advancing beyond what she sees as Freud's focus primarily on the individual. Oliver argues that we must engage with the effects of unconscious desires on our actions. As she writes, failing to make manifest unconscious motives risks "repeating racism rather than understanding and overcoming it."

Lastly, not only does race have significant effect on our cognition, language, and subject formation, we also see its effects in our epistemic practices. José Medina illustrates some of these effects in his discussion of active ignorance and epistemic injustice. The conditions of racial oppression have fostered "epistemologies of ignorance," that is, epistemic practices that "protect the voices, meaning, and perspectives of some by silencing the voices, meanings, and perspectives of others." Mechanisms of active ignorance work to shield would-be knowers from honest engagements with social realities that would disturb their jaundiced views.

Part V: Natural Science and Social Theory

It is a short step from studying race in relation to reality, experience, inquiry, and sociality, as in Parts III and IV, to studying race in relation to the modes of inquiry that purport to unveil the natural and social worlds. Part V offers a selection of perspectives on race in natural science and in social theory. Key concepts under consideration here include intersectionality, biological racialism, eugenics, and critical race theory itself.

The concept of intersectionality has emerged as a critical tool in understanding the nature of racial oppression, and is offered as a corrective to some accounts that provide too monolingual a lens. In her essay here Elena Ruíz distinguishes between *operative intersectionality* and *feminist intersectionality*. Recent criticisms of intersectionality that charge it with essentializing identities or other failures apply to the former but not the latter version. Operative intersectionality emerged due to an academic mainstreaming of the concept, a cooptation that separated the concept from its original purpose (i.e., as a tool for highlighting the unique experiences of oppression by Black women). This original purpose is found in the proto-intersectionality of Black feminists like Maria Stewart, Ida B. Wells, Anna Julia Cooper, Sojourner Truth, and others. Ruíz calls for a reframing of intersectionality through a process of academic decolonization in order to recover some of the concept's liberatory features.

INTRODUCTION

Camisha Russell explores the shared epistemic space of race, heredity, and eugenics with an eye towards answering the following question: "Can we have a eugenics project free from or purged of racism?" Proponents of a contemporary "non-racial" eugenics program see benefits in the use of reproductive and reprogenetic technologies, according to Russell, for timely interventions with "natural" processes that impeded productivity, efficiency, and industry. Even if new eugenicists disavow biological race, Russell contends there are at least three reasons to continue evaluating new eugenic programs with respect to race and racism: (1) racist projects of the old eugenics did not disappear with WWII; (2) we can reasonably expect access to eugenic technologies and the benefit of eugenic programs to be affected by current racial inequalities; and (3) even if the technologies were fully accessible, their use risks creating biogenetic distinctions that serve as the basis for the creation of new "races" and accompanying racisms.

Rasmus Grønfeldt Winther discusses the metaphysics of race in the chapter, "Race and Biology." Metaphysical theorizations of race take place at the biogenomic, biological, and social levels, and Winther lists four questions that must be distinguished in such theorizations: (1) The "biogenomic race" question: Is there genetic structure in human populations and what is it? (2) The "semantic" question: Does the genetic structure correspond to extant designations of populations or kinds, in different languages? (3) The "biological race" question: Does the genetic structure correspond to significant genetically based differences for socially important variables? (4) The "social race" question: Are there racialized social kinds? After laying out the landscape, Winther concludes that human genetic variation displays strong overlap both across continental regions and within continents.

Tommy Curry, for his part, advances the discussion that we started earlier in this introduction, on whether philosophy has earned the "critical" in "critical philosophy of race." Curry vigorously takes mainstream philosophical race theory to task for what he sees as a misleading and obscurantist effort to wrap itself in the mantle of critical race theory. Curry insists on the sociological and political contexts of philosophical research, and argues that the apparent uptake of CRT in the predominantly white field of philosophy has produced work that abandons the radical vision inherent in the work of CRT icons like Derrick Bell, while also concealing the contributions and originality of black emancipatory intellectual traditions.

Part VI: Aesthetics

Race theory has approached the mainstream of contemporary professional philosophy in large part because of the discovery that it was possible to bring the tools of "hard" philosophy to bear on racial phenomena. This meant focusing on metaphysics and epistemology for some, existential phenomenology for others, and language for most. But for too many this discovery enabled a detour around the axiological questions that give racial phenomena their claim on the attentions of non-philosophers. These axiological questions never went away even in philosophy, of course, and have in recent years seen a resurgence of interest. Parts VI through VIII reveal the fruitfulness and importance of these axiological investigations from a variety of directions and metaphilosophical orientations.

Part VI explores the aesthetic dimensions of racial phenomena. Monique Roelofs sets the stage with a discussion of the ways in which, and the degree to which, taking race seriously means rethinking the work of aesthetic theory. She develops the thought that race and aesthetics have historically been intertwined in deep, abiding, and routinely problematic ways—in interlocking processes of what she calls "aesthetic racialization" and "racialized aestheticization." After locating these processes in the work of canonical figures like Kant, she turns to the alternative frameworks provided by newer figures like Fanon, Spivak, and Kara Walker. Finally, she explores the implications of adopting a critical race feminist aesthetics for the study of standard topics in aesthetic theory, such as pleasure, experience, and aesthetic concepts.

Patridge follows out the connections between race and aesthetics in the direction of another core topic in philosophical aesthetics, the study of humor and jokes. She first considers the various conditions—causal, motivational, and contextual—under which telling or enjoying a joke might count as racist. She then closes by rejecting the claim that applying categories like "racist" to putatively inconsequential phenomena like jokes devalues the category and limits its ethical and discursive force.

Janine Jones closes this part by developing the thought that aesthesis a central mechanism in the reproduction and maintenance of racial bias and hierarchies. Focusing in particular on the production, maintenance, and promotion of specifically anti-black animus, Jones uses Roelofs's account of the interlocking processes of racialization and aestheticization to show that these processes often work together to mask or even promote racial bias and racist violence. In Jones's view, the processes are so tightly woven together in experiences laden with immediate meaning that we can speak of race and its productions—productions like the fanciful, mythic characters that at crucial, tragic moments stand in for people like Trayvon Martin, Michael Brown, and Renisha McBride—as works of art in their own right.

Part VII: Ethics and the Political

Part VII picks up the emphasis on ethics and politics that pervades the discussion of racialized aesthetics and refines it further into an interrogation of a variety of specific subjects. The essays by Outlaw and Vice explore the implications of race-thinking for hoary topics in ethics and political theory: solidarity and virtue. Faucher and Mignolo, by contrast, take up subjects that are newer to philosophers: racism and coloniality.

Samantha Vice asks how moral agents in racialized contexts can inhabit those contexts virtuously. Focusing in particular on the ethical challenges of whiteness in settings shaped by white supremacy, she argues for the importance of racialized subjects taking responsibility for the selves they become, the potential offsets of moral luck notwithstanding. This inquiry not only offers resources for resisting the temptation either to demonize or absolve agents racialized as white, with no more subtle ethical options between these; it also yields general insights into the relationships between racial identity, luck, and responsibility, insights that are, *mutatis mutandis*, generalizable to agents who are racialized differently.

Lucius Outlaw traces racial solidarity to its roots in human sociality as such. His aim is to assemble resources for an account of solidarity that depict it not as a dangerous invention of political technique but as an outgrowth of humankind's essentially social nature. To the extent that sociality is essential the condition of the human, and has been advantageous to the persistence and development of humankind, the impulse to treat it as necessarily problematic and to reflexively set aside either our solidaristic impulses or our racial projects should thereby be weakened.

Luc Faucher aims to refine the concept of racism, and to understand just how much refinement is possible and why. The philosophical literature on racism, he argues, merely appears to explore a single topic. Different authors discuss different things using the same term, and range so widely in the process that they lose sight of the real issue: the constellation of more or less related moral ills that we use this single term to denote. Recognizing the ineliminable variety of meanings we attach to the term would allow us to look past the term, and past arguments about criteria for applying the term, and focus on the ills themselves.

For his part, Walter Mignolo seeks to restore the phenomenon of racism to its roots in the "logic of coloniality." For Mignolo, racism is not a stand-alone concept or moral problem but a manifestation of deeper dynamics, dynamics that also produce the categories and distinctions that modern societies have articulated in terms of sexuality and nature. Charles Mills's chapter on white supremacy also turns our attention to the wider dynamics that frame the various ills that "racism" is meant to denote. After teasing out and working through five key features that distinguish white supremacy as a social system, he argues that the capacity to discern and theorize this system can be a vital resource not just for philosophical race theory but also for social and political philosophy more broadly.

Part VIII: Politics and Policy

Part VIII focuses even more narrowly on a particular dimension of racial axiology. At the same time, though, it opens more directly onto the world that philosophy seeks to illuminate. The chapters in this part examine several specific developments in racial politics that became particularly concerning for scholars, activists, and others around the turn of the twenty-first century.

Sundstrom's essay on the limits of postracialism and color-blindness serves useful mapping and critical functions. He identifies different approaches to the idea of postraciality and locates them relative to the idea of color-blindness. Then he argues that these ideas problematically promote both epistemic and moral callousness—blinding moral agents to salient aspects of their environments as well as to the value and, too often, the suffering of their fellows.

José Jorge Mendoza attempts to stage a mutually productive encounter between philosophical studies of immigration and philosophical race theory. He points out that these fields have largely remained at a strange remove from each other, with each engaging the concerns of the other only partially or superficially. But taking race seriously in the context of immigration policy yields an argument for limiting state discretion that we might otherwise overlook.

Jared Sexton insists on a critical orientation to the question of mixed-race identity, an orientation that restores it to its relationships to history and power. He refuses the thought that simply deviating from the rule of hypodescent makes mixed-race identity automatically or necessarily radical. In its place he challenges multiracial and critical mixed race studies to refuse the artificial distinction between their inquiries and the work of black studies.

INTRODUCTION

Falguni Sheth closes the volume with a provocative rumination on the limits of the racial contract idea for theorizing state violence. The racial contract idea is too easily limited to the divide between white and non-white, and as a result can fail to track some vital contemporary currents in racial politics. The politics of security and of immigration in particular reveal that a kind of multicultural white supremacy has emerged, relying on ideologies and technologies that the idea of the homeland captures more effectively than the idea of the racial contract.

Note

1   Stephen Best. (1995) *The Politics of Historical Vision: Marx, Foucault, Habermas*. New York: Guilford, p. xvii.

Part I
HISTORY AND THE CANON

1
CRITICAL PHILOSOPHY OF RACE AND PHILOSOPHICAL HISTORIOGRAPHY

Robert Bernasconi

Introduction

One of the major areas within critical philosophy of race that so-called mainstream philosophers have found increasingly hard to ignore has been philosophical historiography. This is not only because it puts into question from the perspective of the history of racism the high regard in which some of the main figures of the philosophical canon are held. It also represents a challenge to the discipline's self-image and to the way the philosophical canon is conceived. That numerous white philosophers within modernity made racist comments is no surprise to anyone familiar with the pervasiveness of such ideas, but it is troublesome to find that mainstream philosophers today still often use that very pervasiveness to dismiss out of hand concerns about the degree to which so many of the canonical figures of Western philosophy played a significant role in the spread of racist ideas, including expressing support for slavery and the slave trade.

The work of investigating any historical philosopher to determine the extent to which their work is implicated in the history of racist ideas is not an easy one, because it goes far beyond collating compromising quotations from their writings. To pass judgment on the extent to which the racist statements of any given philosopher were original or extreme in the context in which they were made, one needs a broad historical knowledge of the period, including familiarity with what the philosopher in question could or should have known. Furthermore, the task of determining the extent to which their racist views contaminated other aspects of their philosophy calls for speculative judgment, and involves a departure from the way mainstream historians of philosophy have tended to practice their craft since the end of the Second World War.

The dominant tendency of historians of philosophy from the 1950s through at least the 1970s was to focus on reformulating and improving arguments rather than on establishing the original meaning of those arguments based on a study of the context in which they were first developed or the novelty of the concepts employed. This was because that generation had inherited a uniquely narrow conception of philosophy. Under the burden of establishing that they were genuine philosophers under this new restricted sense of the discipline, some historians of philosophy compromised their integrity as historians. This has been changing but it is still the case that, for example, students accustomed to hearing questions being asked about the racial views of early American presidents can find their inquiries about the racial views of canonical philosophers dismissed as irrelevant. On this model all that is supposed to matter are those doctrines that are supposed to represent the core of any given philosopher's thought, even though it is widely known that what is thought to belong to the core of any given philosopher frequently changes across time (Bernasconi 2003a).

Although the questions addressed by critical philosophers of race to the works of canonical philosophers and the way the ideas of those philosophers tend to be presented has led, for example in the case of Kant, to more genuinely historical approaches to the history of philosophy, larger questions about the contribution of canonical philosophers to the spread of racist practices remain by contrast largely undeveloped. An especially egregious example of this is the tendency of historians of modern political philosophy to ignore the role of canonical philosophers in the defense of slavery and their failure to pose the question of why they played at best only a minor role in the history of its abolition. Given the prominence in Europe during the eighteenth century of the debate about the legitimacy of slavery, one might expect it to be equally prominent in historical surveys of the period, especially as the debate led to what could be described as an ethical invention insofar as almost nobody put the institution of slavery as such in question during the previous century, whereas by the end of that time hardly anybody in Europe was willing to defend it. The question of why no canonical philosopher of the eighteenth century seems to have been at the vanguard of the slavery debate raises a further question as to why philosophers today still largely resist demands to expand the canon of political philosophy beyond the list that was established over 200 years ago and continue to exclude those voices that were insistent on its abolition.

Of all the disciplines within the humanities, philosophy has been the most reluctant to entertain a debate about the canon or even, with a few exceptions, ask the question of how the canon came to take on the form it did. The exclusivity accorded to the Western philosophical canon over the last two centuries, the sense that accompanies it of a precious heritage to be protected and not diluted, has served to relegate all forms of non-Western philosophy to the margins and the task of challenging its hegemony is a further task associated with the critical philosophy of race, especially because there is growing evidence that racism shaped the formation of the canon and served to sustain it (Bernasconi 1997).

Perhaps no book has been as influential within critical philosophy of race as Charles Mills's *Racial Contract*, and it is a book with a historical basis (Mills 1999). Nevertheless, not all critical philosophers of race are committed to the idea that a rigorous study of the history of racism is a major component of the discipline. The more detailed examination of these issues that follows, in addition to introducing some of the major issues, attempts to make the case that philosophical historiography is indispensable to critical philosophy of race. I treat in turn (1) philosophy's relation to the history of the concepts of race and racism, (2) its relation to the writing of the history of racism, (3) its relation to the debate about slavery, (4) the racism of canonical philosophers, and (5) the debate about the philosophical canon.

Philosophy and the History of the Concepts of Race and Racism

The term *race* and the much later term *racism* both have complicated histories that are still not fully documented. Knowledge of the history of these terms is important for critical philosophers of race, not least because there has been a tendency to focus on only a narrow portion of the history of racism, highlighting such ideas as the elusively biological conception of race, racial essentialism, and the claim that the so-called four or five main races alone should properly be called races. Far from constituting the historical core of racism these three ideas came to prominence relatively late largely as a result of an initiative of the Boasian school of anthropology, an initiative that came to fruition in the UNESCO Statement on Race prepared in 1950 by Ashley Montagu under the auspices of its Director-General, Julian Huxley (UNESCO 1971: 30–35).

The first use of the concept of race in its modern sense as a division between peoples is conventionally attributed to an essay by François Bernier, a student of Pierre Gassendi, in 1684, but he primarily conceived of it as a geographical concept as the title indicates: "A New Division of the Earth, According to the Species or Races of Men Who Inhabit It" (Bernier 2000). Scholars debate whether one should attribute the first rigorous definition of race as a scientific concept to Buffon or Kant or to some third person (Bernasconi 2001; Doron 2012). According to Kant, "the concept of race is: the class distinction of animals of one and the same line of descent in so far as it is invariably heritable" (Mikkelsen 2013: 136). That is to say, for Kant racial characteristics were inheritable characteristics, and to the extent that we judge that to be decisive to the meaning of race, then Kant introduced the scientific account of race two years before Buffon (Bernasconi 2015: 101–102).

It was in the mid-nineteenth century that the concept of race passed from prominence to dominance, and this was at the time when race came to be seen through the lens of history rather than biology or natural history (Bernasconi 2010). For Joseph-Arthur Gobineau and Robert Knox, race was everything (Gobineau 1915: xiv; Knox 1850: v). To be sure, throughout the nineteenth century the term "race" was a very fluid concept often used as a synonym for "people." The opening pages of W.E.B. Du Bois's "Conservation of Races" from 1897 reflect the dominant usage of the time, where race is only "generally of common blood or language" whereas it is "always of common history, traditions and impulses" (Du Bois 2000: 110). He was reporting the fact that at that time it was history more than biology that dictated how the word should be used. The exclusively biological concept of race is a product of the twentieth century. The UNESCO Statement on Race recommended that the term "race" should be the exclusive preserve of biologists and that everyone else should use the concept of ethnicity instead. This proposal to abandon the term "race" in favor of ethnicity had its source in a book from 1935 by Huxley and Haddon with the dubious title *We Europeans* (Huxley and Haddon 1935: 108). Behind this recommendation was the separation of cultural anthropology from physical anthropology that had been accomplished only in the first half of the twentieth century, most notably among Franz Boas's students. In 1911 Boas deployed statistics in an effort to separate the influence of heredity from that of environment in a way that would endow the distinction between nature and culture a force within discussions of race that Lamarkianism had denied it (Bernasconi 2011c). The implications of this distinction were not clear all at once. Indeed, for some time Boas continued to believe there was a correlation between the physical conditions of a body and the fundamental traits of the mind within that body (Stocking 1982: 191). However, the ultimate achievement of the Boasian school was the idea that if race would be declared by edict to be exclusively a biological concept, then racism (understood as the attribution to someone of moral and mental characteristics on the basis of their biological race) was an epistemological error, not simply because the correlation between moral characteristics and physical characteristics was unproven, but because biologists had failed to establish a sustainable biological definition of race. To be sure, there were historically forms of racism that drew heavily on science, and other established forms of racism that turned to science for support, but not all forms of racism relied on racial science. Indeed, laws defining race in the United States only rarely followed the best scientific knowledge of the time.

Second, in spite of the fact that Kant contributed to the development of a scientifically based racial essentialism by lending support to the idea that racial characteristics were heritable and permanent, one cannot attribute a strict racial essentialism to Kant because of the status of the study of natural history (as opposed to natural description) in his work. Blumenbach, who is often referred to as the father of racial science, had an approach more typical of the time: in 1795 in the third edition of *On the Natural Variety of Mankind*, Blumenbach still maintained that there were no essential divisions between the five main human varieties; they formed a continuum (Blumenbach 1865: 264). It was only with the rise to dominance of polygenesis in the second half of the nineteenth century, first in the United States and then in France with anthropologists like Paul Broca, that a scientific racial essentialism became widespread (Loring Brace 2000: 239). Racial stereotyping in the sense of attributing a strong tendency for certain populations to behave in certain specific ways remains widespread, but strict scientifically understood racial essentialism was always relatively rare, and so attempts to combat it are important but leave much racism untouched.

Third, the identification of four or five main races is a long-standing tendency but the idea that the only proper usage of the term *race* was in reference to them is more recent and suited the North American context in which it was important for white people to form a coalition to maintain their dominance. Its role in doing so is confirmed by the way the range of whiteness frequently expanded to serve this purpose. By contrast, the European tendency was to multiply the number of races both because it reflected national histories and because it served to divide colonized peoples in order to better rule them. The idea that the proper use of the term race is restricted to the main races has, like the other two ideas considered here, distorted the writing of the history of racism especially when it is imagined that racism is limited to discriminating against someone on account of their race.

The first uses of the term *racism* are in French and date back to the end of the nineteenth century (Taguieff 2001: 82–96). Racism was not seen as something evil but as a step on the way to internationalism, as nationalism had been earlier (Malato 1897: 47). In the 1920s the French began opposing "racism" to universalism, where "racism" was largely understood as a scientific doctrine associated with the Germans. This was also the dominant sense "racism" had when in the late 1930s the word was introduced into English and was quickly adopted by the Boasian school of anthropology and the Chicago school of sociology (Bernasconi 2014: 8–12). According to Ruth Benedict, "racism is the dogma that one ethnic group is condemned by nature to congenital inferiority and another group is destined to congenital superiority" (Benedict 1942: 97).

The advantage of this and other narrow accounts of racism to its proponents at that time was that it could readily be applied to some of the more prominent Nazi racisms without obviously compromising the racial institutions within the European colonies, the United States, and South Africa (Benedict 1942: 126; Dubow 1995: 277). As Oliver Cromwell Cox, a Trinidadian-American sociologist trained at the University of Chicago observed, anti-Black racism in the United States was "only a symptom of a materialistic social fact" (Cox 1944: 452). In the same vein Stokely Carmichael and Charles V. Hamilton subsequently introduced the idea of "institutional racism" (Carmichael and Hamilton 1967: 4).

Philosophy and the History of Racism

In this section, I will outline the potential contribution of critical philosophy of race to an understanding of the history of racism. Whereas critical race theory, which has its roots in legal studies, has tended to focus on laws and cases brought under those laws to illuminate historical forms of racism in their specific contexts, philosophers have tended to look more at the history of the concept of race itself and the racial science which gave legitimacy to new ways of thinking about race. However, critical philosophy of race also has the potential to use its resources to introduce new ways of conceptualizing the history of racism, much as Michel Foucault's brief remarks linking biopolitics to racism (Foucault 2003: 254–263) did for a generation of philosophers (e.g., McWhorter 2009). Rewriting the history of racism has been one of the most effective ways of contesting the narrow definition of racism promoted by the Boasian school and the histories of racism written on its basis.

The historian Francisco Bethencourt provides a useful point of contrast. He takes account of race-based systems of slavery and racialized colonialism and on their basis argues that racism preceded theories of race (Bethencourt 2013: 368). He also shows that, because racism is not cumulative or linear it has "assumed different forms shaped by specific conjunctures," one should talk about *racisms* in the plural (Bethencourt 2013: 373). His argument that the distinction between nature and culture from the 1950s distorts the history of racism can be seen as an attack on the Boasian approach to the history of racism (Bethencourt 2013: 150).

Philosophers and the Debate About Slavery

The history of political philosophy within modernity is still often taught according to an agenda set in the nineteenth century among a class of people for whom freedom had more to do with the priority of property rights than the fight against slavery. Indeed, if one relied solely on textbooks of political philosophy one would have no idea how prominent the issue of the legitimacy of slavery was to political discussions throughout the period 1750 to 1865. Furthermore, many specialists appear to be indifferent to the question of what the philosophers on whom they specialize had to say on the issue, as if their contributions to this debate should be entirely irrelevant to our assessment of their philosophies, even their ethics.

Until relatively recently philosophers have paid close attention only rarely and in passing to the views on slavery held by canonical philosophers. Discussions of Aristotle's views on natural slavery announced in the *Politics* offer the clearest exception to this neglect, but, even so, it is not always acknowledged that appeals to Aristotle's claims about slaves by nature played a major role in the early history of modern slavery and especially in the debate between Las Casas and Ginés de Sepúlveda (Hanke 1959: 14–17, 44–61). Earlier, in 1537, Pope Paul III in *Sublimis Deus* condemned the slavery of "Indians and other peoples," but by the seventeenth century this had been forgotten (Panzer 1996: 81). The fact that in 1576 Jean Bodin criticized the alleged naturalness of slavery (Bodin 2009: 56–59) makes all the more pressing the question of why, as Russell Jameson's study of Montesquieu shows, during the eighteenth century there were no extended attacks on slavery as an institution (Jameson 1911). Even Montesquieu, who 175 years after Bodin was the next canonical philosopher to offer a sustained attack on slavery, is rarely studied for his contributions to the understanding of this issue, albeit this is because of the somewhat ambiguous way in which he addressed the topic which managed to confuse some readers (Montesquieu 1989: 246–263).

In the seventeenth century philosophical discussions of slavery by Hugo Grotius, Samuel von Pufendorf, and John Locke, among others, were largely limited to addressing the questions of who could legitimately be enslaved, whether slavery was hereditary, and how slaves should be treated. Although Locke rejected hereditary slavery, the power he gave to a master in his dealings with a slave was unprecedented among philosophers: according to *Two Treaties of Government*, the master had "Absolute, Arbitrary Power of another, take away his Life, when he pleases" (Locke 1994: 284). It is hard to believe that this account was not in part an attempt to justify retrospectively a similar provision that Locke as a co-author included in *The Fundamental Constitution of Carolina*, where we read that "Every Freeman of Carolina shall have absolute power and authority over his *Negro Slaves*, of what Opinion or Religion so ever" (Locke 1739; 15. See Armitage 2013: 90–113). One gets a clearer perspective on Locke's extreme racism if one contrasts it with the more enlightened work of his close friend, James Tyrell, who is all but totally ignored today (Tyrrell 1681: 105; Bernasconi 2011a).

Recent research suggests that Francis Hutcheson, David Hume, Adam Smith, John Millar, and Adam Ferguson, the philosophers of the Scottish Enlightenment who are most associated with criticisms of slavery, lacked engagement with the problem of resolving the very real problem of slavery in British society (Doris 2011b). In the context of his refutation of David Hume's remarks on the inferiority of Negroes, James Beattie, addressing "Britons," pleaded: "Let it never be said, that slavery is countenanced by the bravest and most generous people on earth; by a people who are animated with that heroic passion, the love of liberty, beyond all nations ancient or modern" (Beattie 1774: 467–468). Nevertheless, Beattie lacked the courage to join the campaign against it (Doris 2011a). William Paley had no such qualms (Paley 1792), and in the preface to *The Principles of Moral and Political Philosophy* he gave Ferguson as an example of a philosopher who, while expressing opposition to slavery in principle, deployed a "sententious, apothegmatizing style" in order to conceal the implications of these argument from their readers (Paley 1785: vi). Nevertheless, while looking forward to a gradual emancipation of the slaves he did not himself condemn slavery on principle (Paley 1785: 195–198). Philosophers rarely cite these failures and it allows them to ignore the contributions of figures like Olaudah Equiano, Ottobah Cugoano, Thomas Clarkson, Granville Sharp, and Condorcet. If contemporary moral philosophy has an interest in overcoming deep-seated prejudices and using arguments to change people's behavior, one might think that the ethical invention whereby an institution widely regarded as natural was overturned in a generation would attract more interest and that the thinkers who helped bring about this transformation would be studied by them.

The almost complete disregard by academic philosophers for this debate which saw Europeans reject first the slave trade and then slavery is clearly on display in their lack of interest in the fact that Kant publicly defended the enslavement of Africans in 1788 on racist grounds and the confessions that disqualify some of those who do discuss it (Mikkelsen 2013: 344–345). Pauline Kleingeld has shown that Kant, in some unpublished notes from the mid-1790s, criticized "the trade in Negroes" as a violation of their cosmopolitan right (Kleingeld 2007: 587). This modification of his views is undoubtedly significant, but whether it means that Kant abandoned every aspect of his earlier racism can be contested, especially as Kant nowhere publicly disowned his earlier views (Bernasconi 2011b). This was at a time when, at least in Europe, defenders of slavery were largely restricted to claiming that it was impractical to abolish it in the short term.

There are, then, questions about why canonical philosophers, equipped as they were with the same moral theories that are still promoted by philosophers today, did not come out against slavery and the slave trade; why these philosophers are still regarded as canonical in areas where they were clearly deficient compared with other thinkers who are still ignored in philosophical circles; and, above all, why philosophers today tend to be so quick to dismiss these questions when they are raised. Pursuit of these questions inevitably leads to questions about the reactionary character of philosophy. In the eighteenth century university philosophers taught by rehearsing old arguments drawn from canonical texts, and this still happens today. This would be more defensible if there was a willingness to revise the canon by including the voices of the oppressed.

Addressing the Racism of Canonical Philosophers

The racism of such canonical figures of Western philosophy as, for example, Hume, Kant, Hegel, Nietzsche, and Heidegger is now well documented, even if it is only in the case of the last-named of these that much attention has been given to the proposal that his views were sufficiently outrageous to warrant him from the rank of philosophy altogether (Faye 2009: xxv, 316). A more nuanced approach to this problem was exemplified by Emmanuel Levinas who, while recognizing that the climate of Heideggerian philosophy had to be abandoned, considered that one should leave it only for a philosophy that was pre-Heideggerian (Levinas 2001: 19).

The interrogation of past philosophies in this way is nothing new, even if we look beyond the questionable precedent of critics combing through endless pages to locate a few incriminating remarks that would identify their targets as heretics or atheists. Already in 1794, a young Jew, Saul Ascher, on reading Fichte's essay on the French Revolution with its vicious polemic against the Jews, identified a new form of Jew-hatred arising from the new secular universalism of Kantian philosophy (Fichte 1964). The dominant form of prejudice against the Jews until that time was sustained by Christianity and consisted largely in a series of calumnies directed against them. Many of these prejudices were documented by Johann Andreas Eisenmenger in *Judaism Revealed* (Eisenmenger 1711). So, when exposing Fichte, Ascher called his essay *Eisenmenger the Second* (Ascher 1794). Ascher did not target Kant in this essay, but he might well have done so had he known that Kant in his lectures on ethics had adopted for himself Fichte's account of the Jews as enemies of cosmopolitanism when he wrote that among the Jews "all estimation for other men, who are not Jews, is totally lost" (Kant 1997: 406).

Richard Popkin was among the first scholars in recent time to explore the question of the role of philosophers in the development of racism (Popkin 1974). He drew attention to Isaac La Peyrère, an early proponent of polygenesis (see also Popkin 1987), and the racist remarks of David Hume (see also Immerwahr 1992). Popkin already recognized that the question of whether certain ways of philosophizing lend themselves more readily to racism than others is more important than documenting the racist remarks of canonical philosophers. Before him, in 1933, Eric Voegelin also attempted to explore how the ideas of Leibniz, Kant, and Herder might have contributed to the birth of the modern idea of race (Voegelin 1998). Harry Bracken argued that empiricism was more amenable to racism (and sexism) than rationalism (Bracken 2002: 122–127). There is also a question as to which styles of reasoning impede insight into forms of racism. For example, Jean-Paul Sartre's criticisms of analytical reasoning in *Search for a Method* for its tendency to reduce considerations of class to individuals could be extended to include race (Sartre 1963: 3–6, 91–100). Similar considerations suggest that dialectical reasoning is better equipped to identify and sustain forms of institutional racism (Bernasconi 2012).

The Construction of the Philosophical Canon

Literature departments have revised the literary canon, and historians of art effect and reflect changes in taste, but mainstream philosophers tend to treat the philosophical canon as if it were set in stone. It serves as the rock to which contemporary mainstream philosophy clings as it tries to retain its integrity against what it conceives as "external" challenges. Feminist philosophers are all too familiar with this kind of resistance to their efforts to expand the canon and extend the range of issues considered worthy of philosophical examination. There are signs that the list of those considered worthy of philosophical consideration is being expanded when it comes to the study of twentieth-century European philosophy, so that Frantz Fanon is sometimes given a place. However, the more common practice is to restrict changes to the introduction of specialized courses in, for example, African American philosophy or critical philosophy of race, and these are the only contexts in which students are likely to be exposed to figures like Frederick Douglass, W.E.B. Du Bois, and Anna Julia Cooper.

There is a long and complex story to be told about how the canon came to take the shape it did and at the moment that story is only known in part (for example, Kuklick 1984). Here I am concerned only with the racial aspect of the formation of the canon. It was only at the end of the eighteenth century that Western philosophy decisively claimed for itself a hegemonic role within the academic teaching of philosophy. To be sure, René Rapin in 1671 and 1676 paid lip service to the convention of beginning histories of philosophy with Oriental philosophy while indicating his conviction that the Greeks were the first to do philosophy properly (Rapin 1706: vol. 1, 328–331, vol. 2, 348–351). Pierre Coste took a similar attitude toward oriental philosophy in the anonymous brief history of philosophy introduction in 1690 into the second edition of Pierre-Sylvain Regis' *Cours entier de Philosophie*, but his account was less a history than a celebration of the philosophy of his own century (Coste 1691). Nevertheless, for most of the eighteenth century the ideas of, for example, the Chaldeans, Babylonians, Hebrews,

Persians, Indians, Phoenicians, and Egyptians, were included in histories of philosophy (Piaia 2011). The foremost historian of philosophy of the century, Jacob Brucker, in 1744 included under the title "Exotic Philosophy" a discussion of the so-called Malabars (primarily the Tamils), the Chinese, the Japanese, and the Canadians (or Native Americans) (Brucker 1742: 1–277). To be sure, Brucker was not especially sympathetic to the so-called barbarian and exotic philosophies that he described, but he did not exclude them from the outset as usually happened by the end of the eighteenth century. There are multiple reasons why this change was brought about, but Peter Park has shown the role of racism in the construction of philosophy as Western at the end of the eighteenth century and has highlighted in particular the role of Christoph Meiners of Göttingen in this process (Park 2013: 76–82; see also Bernasconi 2003b).

Philosophy as a practice is unlikely to disappear, but whether philosophy deserves to survive as an academic discipline depends in large part on whether it is willing to confront its past and be more expansive in future. This kind of challenge is one that every institution is in the process of facing, but whereas one would expect philosophy to be at the forefront of such efforts at self-examination, there has so far been extraordinary resistance to doing so.

References

Armitage, D. (2013) *Foundations of Modern International Thought*, Cambridge: Cambridge University Press.
Ascher, S. (1794) *Eisenmenger der Zweite*, Berlin: Hartmann.
Beattie, J. (1774) *An Essay on the Nature and Immutability of Truth*, 4th edition, Edinburgh: William Creech.
Benedict, R. (1942) "A Natural History of Racism," in *Race and Racism*, London: Routledge, pp. 96–140.
Bernasconi, R. (1997) "Philosophy's Paradoxical Parochialism: The Reinvention of Philosophy as Greek," in K. Ansell-Pearson, B. Parry, and J. Squires (eds.), *Cultural Readings of Imperialism*, London: Lawrence and Wishart, pp. 212–226.
———. (2001) "Who Invented the Concept of Race? Kant's Role in the Enlightenment Construction of Race," in R. Bernasconi (ed.), *Race*, Oxford: Blackwell, pp. 11–36.
———. (2003a) "'Will the Real Kant Please Stand Up?' The Challenge of Enlightenment Racism to the Study of the History of Philosophy." *Radical Philosophy* 117: 13–22.
———. (2003b) "With What Must the History of Philosophy Begin? Hegel's Role in the Debate on the Place of India within the History of Philosophy?" in David A. Duquette (ed.), *Hegel's History of Philosophy*, Albany: State University of New York Press, pp. 35–44.
———. (2010) "The Philosophy of Race in the Nineteenth Century," in D. Moyar (ed.), *The Routledge Companion to Nineteenth Century Philosophy*, London: Routledge, pp. 498–521.
———. (2011a) "Proto-Racism. Carolina in Locke's Mind," in I. Wigger and S. Ritter (eds.), *Racism and Modernity*, Vienna: Lit, pp. 68–82.
———. (2011b) "Kant's Third Thoughts on Race," in S. Elden and E. Mendietta (eds.), *Reading Kant's Geography*, Albany: State University of New York Press, pp. 291–318.
———. (2011c) "Race, Nature, Culture," in Paul Taylor (ed.), *The Philosophy of Race*, Vol. 1, New York: Routledge, pp. 41–56.
———. (2012) "Racism Is a System: How Existentialism Became Dialectical in Fanon and Sartre," in S. Crowell (ed.) *The Cambridge Companion to Existentialism*, Cambridge: Cambridge University Press, pp. 342–360.
———. (2014) "Where Is Xenophobia in the Fight Against Racism?" *Critical Philosophy of Race* 2, no. 1: 5–19.
———. (2015) "Silencing the Hottentots. Kolb's Pre-Racial Encounter with the Hottentots and Its Impact on Buffon, Kant, and Rousseau." *Graduate Faculty Philosophy Journal* 35, nos. 1–2: 101–124.

Bernier, F. (2000) "A New Division of the Earth," in R. Bernasconi (ed.), *The Idea of Race*, Indianapolis: Hackett, pp. 1–7.
Bethencourt, P. (2013) *Racisms: From the Crusades to the Twentieth Century*, Princeton: Princeton University Press.
Blumenbach, J.F. (1865) *The Anthropological Treatises*, ed. T. Bendyshe, London: Longman, Green.
Bodin, J. (2009) *On Sovereignty: Six Books of the Commonwealth*, trans. M. Tooley, np: Seven Treasures.
Bracken, H.M. (2002) *Descartes*, Oxford: One World.
Brucker, J. (1742) *Historia Critica Philosophiae a Mundi Incunabulis*, Vol. 1, Leipzig: Breitkopf.
Carmichael, S. and Hamilton, C. (1967) *Black Power*, New York: Vintage.
Coste, P. (1691) "Discours sur la philosophie," in Pierre Silvain Regis (ed.), *Cours entier de Philosophie*, Vol. 1, Amsterdam, Hugvetan.
Cox, O. (1944) "The Racial Theories of Robert E. Park and Ruth Benedict." *Journal of Negro Education* 13, no. 3: 452–463.
Doris, G. (2011a) "An Abolitionist Too Late? James Beattie and the Scottish Enlightenment's Lost Chance to Influence the Slave Trade Debate." *Journal of Scottish Thought* 2, no. 1: 83–97.
———. (2011b) *The Scottish Enlightenment and the Politics of Abolition*, Ph.D. diss., University of Aberdeen.
Doron, C.-O. (2012) "Race and Genealogy: Buffon and the Formation of the Concept of 'Race'." *Humana. Mente: Journal of Philosophical Studies* 22: 75–109.
Du Bois, W.E.B. (2000) "The Conservation of Races," in R. Bernasconi (ed.), *The Idea of Race*, Indianapolis: Hackett, pp. 108–117.
Dubow, S. (1995) *Scientific Racism in Modern South Africa*, Cambridge: Cambridge University Press.
Eisenmenger, J.A. (1711) *Entdecktes Judenthum*, Königsberg: n.p.
Faye, E. (2009) *Heidegger. The Introduction of Nazism Into Philosophy*, New Haven: Yale University Press.
Fichte, J.G. (1964) *Beitrag zur Berichtigung der Urteile des Publikums über die Französischen Revolution* in *Gesamtausgabe der Bayerischen Akademie der Wissenschaften*, eds. R. Lauth and H. Jacob, Stuttgart-Bad Cannstatt: Frommann, Vol. 1, pp. 203–404.
Foucault, M. (2003) *Society Must Be Defended*, New York: Picador.
Gobineau, A. (1915) *The Inequality of Human Races*, London: William Heinemann.
Hanke, L. (1959) *Aristotle and the American Indians: A Study in Race Prejudice in the Modern World*, Chicago: Henry Regnery.
Huxley, J. and Haddon, A. (1935) *We Europeans*, London: Jonathan Cape.
Immerwahr, J. (1992) "Hume's Revised Racism." *Journal of the History of Ideas* 53: 481–486.
Jameson, R.P. (1911) *Montesquieu et l'esclavage*, New York: Lennox Hill.
Kant, I. (1997) *Lectures on Ethics*, trans. P. Heath, Cambridge: Cambridge University Press.
Kleingeld, P. (2007) "Kant's Second Thoughts on Race." *Philosophical Quarterly* 57: 173–292.
Knox, R. (1850) *The Races of Men*, London: Henry Renshaw.
Kuklick, B. (1994) "Seven Thinkers and How They Grew: Descartes, Spinoza, Leibniz; Locke, Berkeley, Hume; Kant," in *Philosophy in History*, eds. R. Rorty, J. Schneewind, and Q. Skinner, Cambridge: Cambridge University Press, pp. 125–139.
Levinas, E. (2001) *Existence and Existents*, trans. A. Lingis, Pittsburgh: Duquesne University Press.
Locke, J. (1739) "The Fundamental Constitutions of Carolina," in A. Collins (ed.), *A Collection of Several Pieces of Mr. John Locke*, London: Francklin, pp. 1–16.
———. (1994) *Two Treatises of Government*, Cambridge: Cambridge University Press.
Loring Brace, C. (2000) *Evolution in an Anthropological View*, Lanham: Rowman & Littlefield.
Malato, C. (1897) *Philosophie de l'anarchie (1888–1897)*, Paris: P.-V. Stock.
McWhorter, L. (2009) *Racism and Sexual Oppression in Anglo-America*, Bloomington: Indiana University Press.
Mikkelsen, J. (ed.) (2013) *Kant and the Concept of Race*, Albany: State University of New York Press.
Mills, C. (1999) *The Racial Contract*, Ithaca: Cornell University Press.
Montesquieu (1989) *The Spirit of the Laws*, Cambridge: Cambridge University Press.
Paley, W. (1785) *The Principles of Moral and Political Philosophy*, London: R. Faulder.

———. (1792) *Recollections of a Speech Upon the Slave Trade*, Carlisle: F. Jollie.
Panzer, J. (1996) *The Popes and Slavery*, New York: Alba House.
Park, P.K.J. (2013) *Africa, Asia, and the History of Philosophy*, Albany: State University of New York Press.
Piaia, G. and Santinello, G. (2011) *Models of the History of Philosophy*, Vol. 2, Dordrecht: Kluwer.
Popkin, R. (1974) "The Philosophical Bases of Modern Racism," in C. Walton and J. P. Anton (eds.), *Philosophy and the Civilizing Arts*, Athens: University of Ohio Press, pp. 126–165.
———. (1987) *Isaac La Peyrère (1596–1976)*. Leiden: Brill.
Rapin, R. (1706) *The Whole Critical Works of Monsier Rapin in Two Volumes*, London: Bonwicke.
Sartre, J-P. (1963) *Search for a Method*, New York: Alfred A. Knopf.
Stocking, G. (1982) *Race, Culture, and Evolution*, Chicago: University of Chicago Press.
Taguieff, P.-A. (2001) *The Force of Prejudice*, trans. H. Melehy, Minneapolis: University of Minnesota Press.
Tyrrell, J. (1681) *Patriarcha non monarcha*, London: Richard Janeway.
UNESCO. (1971) *Four Statements on Race*, Paris: UNESCO.
Voegelin, E. (1998) *The History of the Race Idea: From Ray to Carus*, trans. R. Hein, Baton Rouge: Louisiana State University Press.

2

OF PROBLEM MODERNS AND EXCLUDED MODERNS

On the Essential Hybridity of Modernity*

Olúfẹ́mi Táíwò

The modern archives of the Euro-American philosophical tradition are not, generally speaking, kind to "the Rest of Us," apologies to Chinweizu (1975). If you are, like me, African-descended, racially typed "black," some of whose forebears were enslaved, most of whom are ex-colonized, but who possess a modicum of historical consciousness, reading, teaching, and writing about the leading lights of those archives cannot but be a fraught engagement, indeed.

There is a simple reason why our engagement with the canons of Euro-American philosophy is fraught with anxiety, resentment, self-doubt, and on occasion, sheer anger. This tradition, embodied in the works of its most influential thinkers, has furnished global white supremacy with its theoretical birth certificate, its philosophical credentials, and a long history of the sheer denial of the basic humanity of African-descended humans or, at the least, casting some serious doubt on our full membership in the human family.

However it is conceived, few now deny that racism is a standard feature of modern Euro-American philosophy, especially when it comes to its canonical thinkers. The only issue in debate is to establish the significance of race and racism in the philosophical output of the canonical thinkers. There are diverse approaches in the literature to this issue. There are those who argue that racism is basically incidental to and somewhat tangential to the philosophies. In other words, the integrity of the ideas and the philosophical systems that populate the tradition is not mortally, if at all, affected by the racism that many critics have identified. Others insist that racism plays a role in constructing their philosophical offerings and is, therefore, inseparable from their philosophies (see Valls 2005 for a representative collection).

The racism of modern Euro-American philosophy is not incidental. Given how much global white supremacy draws upon philosophy for its justification and much of its plausibility, especially in the popular imagination—pseudo-science[1] does the rest in this respect—it is not quite plausible that we should focus on the theories and systems and ignore the racism. Simultaneously, I have serious difficulty with the claims often made by critics that (1) racism colors the canon's philosophies and (2) the philosophers/philosophies are racist. It is easier to grant the plausibility, veracity even, of these claims than it is to pin down what these claims mean and, more importantly, what they entail for our responses to them.

The claim that the philosophies are racism-inflected does not mean that the validity of their core arguments is diminished or otherwise undermined. This is not controversial. Furthermore, I am sure that however much the soundness of their arguments is adversely impacted by their racism, it is not the case that whatever truth their assertions contain is thereby extirpated. Above all, their racism has for the most part not been construed to require us to stop teaching them in our classes at all levels.

This last point has especial resonance for African-descended philosophy teachers. Unfortunately, I have to report that I have been unimpressed by what is on offer in much of the discussion of the questions identified above. Let me illustrate the point under review here. Several years ago, an African American student of mine reported to me what happened in an ethics class she was in, taught by a Caucasian American colleague. She had interjected into a class discussion the role, both as an investor and as a theoretical enabler, in the European slave trade and New World slavery played by John Locke. My colleague peremptorily shut down any possibility of an examination by the class of this line of inquiry by firmly proclaiming that Locke's personal behavior, including his investment choices, had no relevance to that ethics class. Obviously, my colleague also was convinced that his endorsement of slavery did not in any manner whatsoever impact his universalist proclamations in the *Two Treatises on Government*.[2] I would not be surprised if my then colleague remains typical when it comes to teaching Locke and modern philosophers in many of our philosophy departments at present. I do not know of many philosophy programs where we routinely explore such connections as standard approaches to teaching canonical or even "lesser" thinkers.

Let us instead substitute an African-descended professor in a similar class with the same query raised by a student of whatever epidermal inheritance. It is not clear to me that we can assume that this professor would have reacted differently. I know that this may sound counterintuitive to some, but I do not think that it is implausible.[3] Indeed, we must stop thinking that the sheer descent from African roots immediately inclines one towards being an anti-racist warrior. Additionally, one could be an anti-racist warrior while, simultaneously, sharing the premises that racist arguments are built upon. Many in the analytic philosophy tradition fall into this category. This possibility is hardly ever entertained in much of the literature on philosophy and race. I shall be making more of this later in this essay.

Given that, historically, big or small, accidental or deliberate, much of the modern inflection of the Euro-American philosophical canon has very little that is positive, tasteful, or nice to say about African-descended peoples and cultures, what are we to do when we have to teach these same materials? This is where the difficulty I earlier spoke about comes into clear relief. When we, as we routinely do, establish the racism of the canon, what do we do next? This question applies to all who acknowledge the racism of the canon. It is much more poignant for us, African-descended workers in philosophy's vineyard, who nonetheless have to work with this tarnished inheritance.

In the rest of this chapter, I respond to this question from a vantage point that departs fundamentally from the dominant responses to the question abroad in much of the literature. Generally speaking, the identification of the racism of the canonical thinkers and their texts in the modern Euro-American philosophical tradition is why we consider these thinkers "problem moderns." What makes these thinkers and their ideas problematic?

It will not be wide of the mark to say that the canonical modern thinkers were embodiments, both literally and figuratively, of epochal hypocrisy. At the same time that they were putting together the modern template for freedom, they were forging the theoretical manacles for racialized chattel slavery that was unprecedented in the history of humanity and has had no peers anywhere else in the world since then. They have been shown to be adept at holding inconsistent positions even while they presented themselves as paragons of logical rigor (Popkin 1984). After all, it is on account of their much-heralded claim to primary, if not sole, ownership of reason that they dismissed our forebears as devoid of it and, therefore, of basic humanity, too. They were not beyond proclaiming falsehoods dressed with the patina of a pseudo-science[4] when it came to the human nature of those that they subjugated, imperialized, and dehumanized as a way of justifying their inhumane treatment of their victims. They globalized their local and universalized their provincialism while denying the capacity of the Rest of Us to capture and represent the universal in our own corners of the human experience (Táíwò 1998). Finally, they were not above making their claims true by fiat.

How have we responded to the phenomena associated with the problem moderns that I just iterated? This is where this essay proposes to chart a different path. Some distinctions are in order. We must separate different sets of responses. One set is made up of the responses of their own contemporaries. An example would be James Beattie's response to David Hume or the Immanuel Kant vs. J.G. von Herder exchange (Eze 1997: chapters 3 and 5). The other set is made up of the critical literature that has built up since the original writings were first published. Here we include ongoing debates and controversies regarding the tarnished inheritance and its implications for all who have to work with it either in agreement or in opposition, or even in indifference (Valls 2005; Bernasconi and Lott 2000; Bernasconi 2001; Popkin 1980).

Among the latter responses, there are further subcategories. We argue with and seek to refute the principal claims of the canonical texts and thinkers. This is the most diffuse response in the literature. I will show, presently, why it is also quite problematic and severely limited. Then there are the debates and controversies among the critics themselves: for example, whether Emmanuel C. Eze overstated his case for the centrality of racism in the construction of Enlightenment philosophy, or whether Charles W. Mills somehow misjudged Kant with the former's appropriation of the idea of sub-personhood as a trope for laying bare Kantian racism and its impact on his transcendental philosophy (Valls 2005).

Unfortunately, all the responses, however far back we go, to the problem moderns have been vitiated by something for which I suggest a recovery of an idea going back to Francis Bacon: idolatry. Although it would be too much to say that we are captive to "false notions," I surely want to argue that our relation to the canons of the Euro-American philosophical tradition and, more specifically, our handling of the problem moderns and their tarnished legacy have fallen victim to one of the class of idols that Bacon long ago lamented had taken "possession of the human understanding and [had] taken deep root therein" (Bacon 1939: 34).

In *Novum Organum*, Bacon indicated that he parted ways with sceptics "who have denied that certainty could be attained at all" and asserted "simply that nothing can be known" even as he agreed with them that "not much can be known in nature by the way which is now in use" (Bacon 1939: 34). He instead wanted to identify the obstacles to genuine knowledge in nature and clear them as a prerequisite to attaining knowledge. He called these obstacles "idols." He identified four such idols: "There are four classes of idols which beset men's minds. To these for distinction's sake I have assigned names,—calling the first class *Idols of the Tribe*; the second, *Idols of the Cave*; the third, *Idols of the Marketplace*; the fourth, *Idols of the Theater*" (Bacon 1939: 34). In ways similar to those identified by Bacon, our reaction to and, by extension, appreciation of the problem moderns are obscured by some contemporary analogues of the idols. I am suggesting that our philosophical understanding at the present time is afflicted with the equivalent of the "Idols of the Theater."

I mentioned earlier that both Hume and Kant, in varying degrees of acknowledgment, responded to some of their contemporaries' rejoinders to their arguments. But they did not do this with all or most of their contemporary interlocutors. Nor did others throughout the modern period make a habit of acknowledging, much less responding to those they consider unworthy interlocutors. I mention this because till now contributors to the discussions have been selective in their culling of what in the available literature they are willing to engage. Meanwhile, as the tradition was constructed and handed down to us, some unwritten criteria emerged regarding who was worthy of being read and responded to. In the last century, the professionalization and academicization of philosophy, the installation of a hierarchy of honorifics, and the star system have crystallized into the implantation of different forms of idolatry in our relationship to the canon.

I would like to suggest that the philosophy scene can be analogized to Bacon's theater teeming with its own, resident idols. According to Bacon,

> Lastly, there are idols which have immigrated into men's minds from wrong laws of demonstration. These I call Idols of the Theater; because in my judgment all the received systems are but so many stage-plays, representing worlds of their own creation after an unreal and scenic fashion. Nor is it only of the systems now in vogue, or only of the ancient sects and philosophies, that I speak: for many more plays of the same kind may yet be composed and in like artificial manner set forth; seeing that errors the most widely different have nevertheless causes for the most part alike. Neither again do I mean this only of entire systems, but also of many principles and axioms in science, which by tradition, credulity, and negligence have come to be received.
> (Bacon 1939: 35)

I do not fully describe here the analogy between philosophy and Bacon's theater. One thing is clear, though. Philosophy, academic and professional, mimics a theater in several significant respects. The different systems, movements, trends, sects even in philosophy can be assimilated into "so many stage-plays" created by diverse thinkers all filling their plays with equally diverse "laws of demonstration" or, in the present case, modes of discourse and standards for assessing the quality of proficiency in them. Whether it is the analytic or the continental tradition, whether it is British empiricism or French existentialism, phenomenology or positivism, each can be assimilated to different "received systems" "representing worlds of their own creation after an unreal and scenic fashion." And when Bacon spoke of "many more plays of the same kind" being "composed and . . . set forth," we have contemporary versions in new systems like post-modernism, post-structuralism or postcolonial studies that have emerged with little different blinker regarding racism from those of the old "received systems." Newer generations of actors are socialized into these systems and have thereby their respective idols, old and new, implanted in their minds. Errors, mischaracterizations, invalidities, and so on not only multiply, but each successive generation gives new leases on life to old crudities. Nowhere is this more prevalent than in how different generations in modern Euro-American philosophy have converged on how to treat the issue of the problem moderns.

I argue that the critiques of the racism of the philosophy canon have been vitiated by the idols of philosophy's theater. It is why we keep talking endlessly about the racism but never seem to find a way to get beyond it to real changes that might begin to indicate fresh paths to reducing their impact on the very way we frame the problems that we find with them. Everyone possessed of the idols of philosophy's theater takes her cue from the same tarnished canon respecting what should count as philosophy, who deserves to be read, whose arguments are worthy of rejoinders, and so forth. It is why it almost seems as if pedigree tops everything. And this, as I show in a moment, is as true for critics of the problem moderns as it is for their supporters. For us to see how this is so, how the idols prevent us from breaking free from the limits imposed by the many "systems now in vogue," "the many axioms and principles which by tradition, credulity, and negligence have come to be received," we need to introduce another category of moderns: *the excluded moderns*.

Excluded moderns are those real and putative victims of modernity who, simultaneously, embrace modernity and enact their "*J'accuse*" from very firm, immanent modern vantage points. Both the canon and those who continue to work with it have had a problem dealing with global African responses to the tarnished legacy of the Enlightenment. Just as the Enlightenment thinkers who populate the canon wrote as if no African before or contemporaneous with them had written on the perennial problems of philosophy or even on the issue that agitated the problem moderns, especially on the idea of freedom, many of us writing in our time, too, write as if it is forbidden that an African or a thinker of African descent might actually seek deliberately to embrace modernity and adopt its framework for making sense of the world. This is where the idolatry of the tradition comes into very clear relief. Everybody talks about the victims of philosophy's racism. And defenders of the victims are very prominent in the discourse of modernity. But, and this is the problem, even we who are descended from the victims and continue to be victimized by modernity are dominated by philosophy's idols.

Here is why. Let us recall what makes some moderns problematic. They deny that Africans and their descendants are unproblematic members of the human race. They insist that even if Africans are, they are of such an inferior character that their status as moral beings is easily trumped by the superior endowments of other groups. Most important, they contended that Africans did not possess Reason, a singular constituent of modern humanity, and if they did, it was of such poor quality that their kind had not contributed anything significant to human civilization. The moderns were quite consistent in their behavior. Primarily, they could not even be bothered to do due diligence and provide evidence for these obviously empirical claims. When any evidence was adduced of African intelligence, they were quick to dismiss such, the most notorious being Hume's dismissal of a rumored Jamaican genius and Thomas Jefferson's cursory dismissal of Phyllis Wheatley's poetic gifts (Eze 1997: chapters 3 and 8; Popkin 1984). This partly explains all the hyperventilation about the effects on reason of nearness to the equator, living in the tropics, and suchlike that back then dominated the European discourse of philosophical anthropology. Be that as it may.

Are the victims of this philosophical libel as monolithic as the literature on philosophy and race seems to regard them? Are they the mute, inert, if not absent, presences that the literature would seem to think they were? We must answer both questions in the negative. Yes, Kant is welcome to think that black and stupid go together. The same goes for Hume. But what happens when we stop privileging Kant and Hume, stop trying to convince them that they are wrong on the basis of their logic alone? I would not like to be misunderstood. Indeed, were we to take seriously the illogicalities of the canon's thinkers on this score, we would long ago have done what, I point out later, should be done with them: show them as brilliant examples of how not to think about, much less make a case for inferiority, as did the late Richard H. Popkin (1984). I take it that a non sequitur does not become acceptable just in case it is advanced by Kant or Hume.

It is not in dispute that African-descended victims were never quiescent nor inert presences even as the tradition was being constituted. However isolated, there were living, breathing, writing refutations of the claims being made about black people.[5] Many of them not only criticized the insults that were bandied about respecting their race's intellectual abilities, they embraced modernity and sought to remake their lives—personal and public—as well as, in some cases, their societies in the modern style. This embrace was not without difficulties for them and these difficulties have probably shaped our own responses to them. I am talking of those African-descended thinkers who accepted that black people had fallen behind in the civilization race and embracing modernity and its tenets offered the quickest route to regaining their footing and making Africans walk again with other races in the march of civilization.[6]

No, they were no dopes. Nor were they self-haters. They definitely, resolutely and vociferously denied that African backwardness was either divinely ordained or secured by nature. There were others among them who never accepted that Africa was ever backward even if they accepted that Africa's progress had been arrested by Europe's regime of aggression and rapine against the continent.[7] Their standpoint was similar to that of Antonio Gramsci in his analysis of the backwardness of southern Italy or V.I. Lenin's of Russia respecting the slow development of capitalism there. Quite the contrary, those modern African thinkers were serious historicists, some of the earliest, even if inchoate, social constructionists for whom the backwardness and most other ills of their race, back then, were products of history and a history not separable from the incorporation of and long, active participation in, by Europeans, the heinous Trans-Atlantic Slave Trade.

Many of them were the proto-"Afrocentrists" who were the first to claim ancient Egypt's African identity, and that not merely in a benign geographical sense; for whom Africa was not divisible into all the racist divisions that now rule our discourses: "Black Africa," "Africa proper," "sub-Saharan Africa," "Negro Africa," and so on (Horton 1969 [1868]; Attoh Ahuma 1971). They routinely assumed their place in the universe of thought prevalent in their time and while some of them had to deal with the racial animosity contained in and fueled by the writings that now make up the modern canon by their fellow speakers of modernity-speak, they did not evince any signs that they thought that their philosophical explications came with an asterisk. In other words, they never considered their discourse to be external to the canon. They never thought that the modern self was a notion that was not capacious enough to accommodate their adaptations of it.

However, because the canonical thinkers did not think anything of their exertions, and, no doubt, we adhere strictly to their line of thinking, the idols of the theater ensure that we, too, think little of their efforts. This includes those of us, African-descended workers, in philosophy. It matters little how much we excoriate Hume, Kant, Hegel, and the rest of them; they remain our preferred interlocutors. We who are excluded are no less ardent adherents of the idols of academic philosophy's theater. Under the influence of this idolatry, we wittingly—and often unwittingly—participate in and help perpetuate the incestuous practices that permeate much of philosophy writing over the centuries, especially since the modern age came into its own. Notwithstanding all the vociferous declarations about objectivity and standards, the facts indicate that both the constitution of the canon and the orientation of those who subscribe to and work within its boundaries exhibit a high degree of tribal consciousness when it comes to what is to be read or taught; and who could feature as an interlocutor.[8]

As a result of this idolatry and its concomitant in-group mentality, even though we consider problematic those who in their original postulations were living embodiments of contradictions, inconsistencies, and the occasional outright falsehoods, were selective in determining who were worthy interlocutors and what ought to be read, made a reputation based on myriad non sequiturs that we, their successors, have either continued to ignore or decided do not have to be refuted, we let them continue to rule the philosophical roost. This in spite of what we are told in elementary logic that pointing out a non sequitur is enough to dismiss the one who affirms it. Rather, it is those that they excluded but whose writings, we now know, rightly belong in the annals of their common discourse that we persistently ignore.

The problem is that the discourse of modernity cannot be neatly divided between the authors and their critics. The excluded moderns seem incongruous to us given the neat schema that we prefer to work with. This explains in part why we do not know what to do with the excluded moderns or how to incorporate them in our discourse and pedagogy. We hardly check into their writings unless the problem moderns and their worshippers deign to address such and, by so doing, indicate that such thinkers are "worthy" interlocutors. We expend more energy trying to reason with the problem moderns and, occasionally, unwittingly offering alibis for their glaring errors and distortions, if not their follies. But we never really breach the walls of the canon by that approach. What is more, under the impact of the idols of the theater, we, too, go along with the exclusions and limit our discussions, even our criticisms, accordingly to those that pass muster as "worthy" interlocutors. I reject this orientation.

It is time to bring the excluded moderns in from the cold. What happens when we take seriously the perorations of the excluded moderns and re-inscribe their contributions into the philosophical discourse of modernity and the records of modern Euro-American philosophy? Given that an important element of the inspiration for this collection is pedagogy, I would like to offer some suggestions on how teaching the canon might be problematized, maybe even improved, by looking from a different vantage point. We have to invest in the excluded moderns and their offerings. Therein lies the path out of idolatry and to genuine knowledge, true portrayal and more correct appreciation of Euro-American philosophy's modern canon.

To begin with, we need to spread the news that the excluded moderns did what the problem moderns said they could not do: have and deploy subjectivity denominated by Reason. Kant was welcome to insist that blacks were sub-persons. But Kant could not stop blacks from proclaiming their personhood, flaunting it and insisting that folks like Kant show them respect. In light of this, although he would withhold recognition from black subjects, within the framework of modernity's own tenets, he would have had to make some serious investment in what Jean-Paul Sartre would in our time call "bad faith". Historically, under chattel slavery, the fact that black slaves were the only "farm implements" that could and did talk back must have occasioned considerable disquiet for their owners. What is more, slaves' insistence on their owners recognizing and respecting certain boundaries, insisting that they, too, deserved promise-keeping from their owners and, ultimately, exercising the prerogative of working for and purchasing their freedom might be a more effective reply to the denial or diminution of African humanity in the canon.

As I have written elsewhere, slaves may actually be better singers of freedom's song than their owners (Táíwò 2010a; James 1963). Those who confronted and often succumbed to the dread of death in order to be free are in reality better exemplars of Hegelian subjectivity that everyone associates with the master. When this is factored into the equation, the articulators of freedom who enjoyed leisure funded by the unpaid labor of African slaves cannot be the only law-making residents of freedom's domain. In a contest it cannot be that we continue to write as if the contest took place in the absence of the other party to the struggle. The color of the contest cannot be named after only one party to it. Historically and sociologically, that would be false. Should it be any less false in philosophy?

That is, our account of the canon's population as well as of who has participated in its constitution must remain essentially incomplete to the extent that we go along with the pretense that modern Euro-American philosophy has been solely constituted by thinkers who look a certain way. It is as if we accept that Euro-American philosophy has not had, among its interlocutors, thinkers who were not Caucasian. If we admit the responses to the fundamental claims of the canonical thinkers by those they described as less than human or inferior to themselves, I do not see how we can escape the judgment that modern Euro-American philosophy was hybrid, creolized, almost the whole time it has existed.

By way of illustration, let us assume that Jefferson was right to doubt that Ignatius Sancho wrote the letters that are attributed to his authorship (Eze 1997: 100).[9] Does that make it okay for us to appear to believe that Jefferson was right that Sancho did not author the letters and, if he was, given the quality of the writing "we are compelled to enroll him at the bottom of the column" of his contemporaries? That is, should we conflate Jefferson's right to express an opinion and the correctness of the content of that opinion? What if, instead, we took seriously the ideas expressed by Sancho and juxtapose them with those of Jefferson respecting the issue of freedom and the wrongness of slavery?

Once they made the language of freedom their own, the slaves, the colonized, our excluded moderns, also set about fashioning the world after their own design. They laid hold of what is true and universal in the writings of the problem moderns and domesticated it while, at the same time, apprehending the universal in their respective provinces (Newman, Rael, and Lapsansky 2001; Equiano 2004 [1789]). And the ability to name the world is a prerogative of rational humans. When slaves appropriated various social forms from their owners, they were no mimics; they *changed* the forms and created new idioms from the original syntaxes: new religious forms, new music genres, new cuisines, and so forth.

The same is true of the colonized when colonialism came on the heels of the abolition of the slave trade and slavery. Africans who accepted modernity wanted to marry the best of their indigenous inheritance with the best of their conflicted legacy from slavery and, later, colonialism. They regarded themselves as peoples who had previously exercised the privilege of leading the world in civilization; some even claimed traditions that made them first peoples in the world.

Why do we not insist, following the lead of black thinkers, that the Cartesian sum is not necessarily white and that when Hume proclaimed his generalization regarding the absence of genius among black people, he fell short of his inductive principles? (see Valls 2005: chapter 7). More importantly, all we need do is take very seriously the history of peoples in different parts of Africa and just simply dismiss, yes, dismiss Hume as an uninformed bigot rather than confer respectability on his rubbish by arguing with it as if there is some way, outside of prejudice, that it might be worthy of another look.

Our excluded moderns did a good job of showing up the hypocrisies, inconsistencies, falsehoods and illogicalities of the problem moderns. I am often stupefied by how often we ignore the yeoman efforts of excluded moderns to reduce the gap between the theory and the reality of modernity. Examples include W.E.B. Du Bois (Sundquist 1996), Paul Robeson (1998), Frantz Fanon (2008), and Aimé Césaire (1972) in our own time. What is even more remarkable is that the excluded moderns prove to be better moderns than their racist problem modern fellows. They were able to distinguish the truth kernel that problem moderns encased in the dross of racism and prejudice from the tribalism that distort their findings. This is why very few of them measure up to the standards of nationalism that global white supremacy evinced and would force on those of us who fight it. That is, they never argued that theirs was the "black" version of truth; they instead contested the claims of problem moderns to being purveyors of truth. They were trying to force their problem modern interlocutors to act as if the latter believed in the principles that were supposed to ground their common efforts in reaching true knowledge in nature.

I supply one example of the kind of entry that is missing. Horton was a shining example of an excluded modern who dismissed many of the favorite arguments that we repeatedly dress up as candidates for refutation, based on very firm modern grounds. He called Hume and his ilk out in 1868:

> I must say a few words on some grave errors in generalization which men of science with restricted observation have arrived at respecting the capacity of progression in the African race. Thus it has been argued that their physical and mental peculiarities have undergone no change since they were first observed by civilized nations. "The type," says Sir George Cornwall Lewis, "is as unchanged as that of the greyhound, since the time of the Romans." Hume, in his Essay on *Natural Characters*, says that "There scarcely ever was a civilized nation of that complexion (negro), nor even any individual eminent either in action or speculation. . . . In Jamaica, indeed, they talk of one negro as a man

of parts and learning, but it is likely he is admired for slender accomplishments, like a parrot who speaks a few words plainly." A witty writer, the late Dr. Knox, of Edinburgh, believes that the races of men, particularly the negro, as they were several centuries ago, still continue to be now; and that despite of Christian influences and other civilizing agencies bearing on their rude and savage character, they will continue to be. Although there might be something suggestive and interesting in this antitheological scientific doctrine propounded in his *Fragment of the Races of Men*; yet still we deprecate in the strongest terms the main points of his arguments.

(Horton 1969 [1868]: 31)

The title of the chapter under review is "False Theories of Modern Anthropologists." And it comes after an opening chapter titled "Description of the Original and Uncivilized State of the Native Tribes." This is why I said above that the excluded moderns shared certain premises with problem moderns without at the same time buying into the latter's pseudo-scientific and bigoted explanatory models. Where Horton saw the history as the place to look, the problem moderns tried to argue for a base in inalterable biology. Even when he bought into the erroneous views that climate mattered in the formation of racial groups, he never allowed that there were any fixed natures where humankind was concerned.

> Now it must be acknowledged that the damaging influences to which the negro race has for centuries been subjected, have not been favourable to the improvement of their condition, nor in any way raising their minds to a higher species of cultivation; trampled under foot by perpetual despotism, enslaved from one generation to another, inhabiting the most wretched hovels that it is possible for humanity to exist in, deprived of every means of education or of witnessing the conquests of arts and science ... can there be the least doubt in the minds of the unprejudiced that their present unimproved condition is the natural sequence of the operation of these powerful re-agents?

(Horton 1969 [1868]: 32)

If the conditions are contingent, they are open to alteration with the appropriate "re-agents," Horton insists. His entire book is a manual of how to go about this regeneration after the "vindication of the race," the other main aim of the text.[10] Contrary to this most scientific manner of proceeding Horton berated Dr. Knox for being fixated on race to an irrational extent.

> True it is that certain peculiarities which are characteristic of a nation can be traceable for generations, however greatly admixture and other external influences may have operated on their general character; but to insist on the broad dogma that no changes have taken place in the races of men, or even animals, as far back as historical evidences can be traced, is to insist on what is opposed to nature; and none but the unreflecting can be carried away by so sweeping a doctrine. Dr. Knox regards everything to be subservient to race; and his arguments are brought forward to show that the negro race, in spite of all the exertions of Exeter Hall, or as his commentators most sneeringly call them, the

"broad-brimmed philanthropy and dismal science school," will still continue as they were. To him, as he says, "Race is everything—literature, science, art—in a word, civilization depends on it. . . . With me race or hereditary is everything, it stamps the man."

(Horton 1969 [1868]: 32)

Of another pseudo-scientist, Dr. Hunt, he wrote:

Of Dr. Hunt we must truly state that he knows nothing of the negro race, and his descriptions are borrowed from the writings of men who are particularly prejudiced against that race; his absurd pro-slavery views, as contained in his pamphlet, would perhaps have suited a century ago; but all true Africans must dismiss them with scorn.

(Horton 1969 [1868]: 33)

One is right to query why much of the debate on race and philosophy manages to proceed without taking seriously what those that I have called excluded moderns have said about the matter from the vantage point of their modern inheritance against those who subverted their shared principles to push odious but often groundless views. This is where the influence of the idols of the philosophy theater might help us make sense of these omissions.

I argue that once we rid ourselves of the idols of the philosophical theater, we immediately see that in offering their ideas to the public, problem moderns were in no position to control who reads them or how they are read. And insofar as African-descended readers could and were willing to pay the price of admission—acquire the relevant skills and resources to gain access to the materials—no one, not even the slave masters, could stop them from offering the world *their* takes on such materials and what frameworks they come to the contents of the canon with. It does not matter much that they have been largely ignored. But the battle had already been joined; the narrative could no longer pretend to any kind of racial purity. The works of the problem moderns can no longer be read innocently of how they have been received by African-descended interlocutors. To that extent, contrary to received wisdom modern philosophy has *always* been hybrid. Its hybridity is essential and inescapable. The exegeses, commentaries, criticisms, and other materials, including those authored by excluded moderns, become essential parts of the record. David Walker's appeal is not incidental to Euro-American philosophy. Nor are Frederick Douglass's reflections on freedom and bondage. They, and others, are an integral part of the record (Newman, Rael, and Lapsansky 2001). Horton's contestations are not external to the tradition; they are integral to it. Their primary interlocutors are not local; they are the framers of the discourse, the ones who affirmed and denied freedom in the same breath; who spoke of but never meant human nature to be truly universal. In short, those who always cheated but hoped that some of their interlocutors, the excluded moderns—the idols already ensured that their fellow race-inflected thinkers would not see anything the matter with their illogicalities—would not notice. They were wrong about the excluded moderns. The only problem arises when we, in our time, fail to take into account the complexity and heterogeneity of that record.

When we take the record as it truly was constituted, we find that the color and composition of the canon begin to alter. This is nothing new. This is what happened when feminists began to fill out the true record of the history of the Euro-American philosophical tradition going back to the ancients. Fortunately, we do not have to strain too much to show that the history of the same tradition has not been constituted by people who look only one way. The modern period is the most afflicted with racial prejudice (Park 2013).

In leaving this record unchallenged, we end up allowing global white supremacy to claim modernity as an exclusively European legacy and an ideological cudgel with which to clobber the Rest of Us into scampering to discover "alternative modernities" in our ever-shrinking localities. We, on the other hand, are content to dismiss modernity as a Eurocentric contraption and one our relationship with which is either as victims or resisters. One consequence of this idolatry is that we completely go along with the exclusion of non-European interlocutors in the discourse of modernity quite a number of whom were not mere mute objects—yes, there were some, especially those objectified by the European thinkers—but also, importantly, speakers of modernity's language who, in some cases, adapted it to their own idioms. Indeed, a serious critical engagement with modernity cannot afford to ignore them. Unfortunately, so far, they have been twice excluded: first, by their European co-speakers of the language, and second, by us, the much-vaunted critics of modernity's discourse. I hope that this piece indicates a useful direction for breaching the walls of modernity. The beginning of wisdom is the acknowledgment of the historicity of modernity and, as a consequence, its essential hybridity: many and diverse are the voices that have contributed to its constitution. Purity is not to be had, nor is it necessary.

For what I have just stated to be done, we must loosen the reins. We must tear down the walls that enclose and isolate the philosophical theater and extend our purview to those sources that our idolatry-driven penchant for pedigree has made us to discount in our attempts at filling out philosophy's record. These include literature, slave narratives, protest pamphlets, theology, religious studies, and so on.

There is ample evidence that the problem moderns did not think that logic and conceptual analyses sufficed for their characterizations of African-descended peoples. They sought to find empirical corroboration for their logical expostulations and arguments. Their writings offered empirical details, facts, history, sociology, and so on, that they were convinced supported and provided much needed confirmation of their cases. This is no longer the case. We now live in a world in which, again, the idols dominate in this respect and they dictate that we come up with ever more sophisticated logic chopping to do a job that requires different sets of tools: fact-checking, alternative formulations, looser boundaries of the universe of discourse, and the products of the excluded moderns.

This, in the final analysis, is for me the only reason to continue to engage the perennial problem of the racism of the canons of the modern Euro-American philosophical tradition. One felicitous by-product of this approach will be the shutting down of the torrent of books and papers that seek to undermine racism mainly, if not solely, by philosophical analysis.

Notes

* I would like to thank Barry Hallen and Grant Farred for crucial interventions in the process of revising the original version of this chapter. This is a better product thanks to their suggestions.
1 Pseudo-science here refers to efforts devoted to showing that African-descended and other peoples designated black in our common discourse are congenitally defective in their mental capacities and,

therefore, are inferior to white people. An appreciable segment of this is to be found in the discourse regarding intelligence quotients (IQ) of different peoples. The pseudo-science of eugenics was foregrounded by the anthropology and biology of the nineteenth century that sought to confirm on respectable scientific grounds what philosophy had given birth to in the eighteenth century. For a more recent treatment of this theme by an African scholar, see Bernard M. Magubane (2007).

2 No doubt there are many ways to understand my colleague's reaction. We may be wrong to assume that the student's question or suggestion did not blindside the teacher. That the teacher did not think that there is a connection does not immediately translate into racism. For the rest, the validity of Locke's arguments is not obviously impacted by his personal behavior. This is what separates modern philosophy's standpoint from that of the ancients regarding the dialectics of knowing and doing. But that is beyond the scope of the present discussion.

3 When I was taught Locke in Nigeria, no less—admittedly back then by Europeans, but nothing has changed since Africans started doing the duty—at both the undergraduate and graduate levels, Locke's participation in the slave trade or the appropriation of native lands was never mentioned. At a conference in 2010 in Accra, Ghana, a young Nigerian philosopher was indignant at my extending the status of philosophers to Kwame Nkrumah, Leopold Sédar Senghor, and Julius Nyerere. He said, "When I think of philosophers, I think of Hume, Kant, and Hegel." He was trained at the doctoral level in Nigeria almost 30 years after my time.

4 See p. 19, for an example of an African thinker making the same judgment of some of what European thinkers were offering in the nineteenth century.

5 Olaudah Equiano lived from 1745 to 1797 while Jefferson lived from 1743 to 1826. They were practically contemporaries and they were writing at the same time, even though one had a totally inauspicious start to his intellectual career and was never as privileged as the other in terms of enabling circumstances for his career, such as it was. Most importantly, one was a slave who bought his freedom and the other was a slave owner. It is curious that neither Eze nor Magubane thought it fit to include any excerpts from Equiano's or any other African thinker's writings in their respective works. There is no reason to speculate on why this choice was made, but I suggest that, unless we decide that Equiano could not have been a philosopher or that his refutations of the racism of the likes of Jefferson do not pass muster as philosophy, the ideas belong together and readers of the canon will be better served by knowing that thinkers of African descent did not wait till their location in Euro-American academies in the twentieth century to challenge the inconsistencies and crudities of the Euro-American philosophical canon. Similar things can be affirmed of Ignatius Sancho, who lived and wrote from 1720 to 1789. Apparently, from the existing literature, Popkin's (1984) point on this same score has not gained much traction with subsequent commentators.

6 On the American side, such was their acceptance of and adherence to modernity as the template for reordering their world that many African American thinkers of the nineteenth century have been lumped together with the ranks of Western imperialists in Africa. See Tunde Adeleke (1998). In West Africa, their ranks included Philip Quaque, Samuel Ajayi Crowther, James Africanus Beale Horton, and S.R.B. Attoh Ahuma. For a discussion of these "apostles of modernity," see Olúfẹ́mi Táíwò (2010b).

7 A very good example is William Essuman Gwira Sekyi, also known as Kobina Sekyi. In the early part of the twentieth century, he was a member of the Aristotelian Society in the United Kingdom.

8 I am often amused by how much even the new movements incarnate these idols in their new systems when it comes to who they think deserves to be admitted into their discourses. As a colleague loves to ask: were there no intellectuals of African descent in France, or why is there no hint of them in the latest mode of French philosophizing that has crossed the pond to the United States?

9 Contrast this with the indictment of slavery and its operations in Equiano (2004 [1789]). It is doubtful that he was ever interested in evidence. Hume's example is instructive in this respect. According to Popkin (1984), "Hume did not look into the facts in the case. He managed to avoid taking cognizance of the facts that disproved his claim, even though he knew of at least some of them" (p. 66).

10 Horton had more positive things to say about some indigenous cultures in West Africa regarding their preparedness for modern governance based on the advanced nature of their indigenous modes of governance. See Part II: "African Nationality" in the book for some significant insights that bear relevance even now.

Further Reading

Howard Brotz, ed. *African-American Social and Political Thought* (New Brunswick: Transaction, 1999) is a very good collection of original materials from African American excluded moderns. Toni Morrison, *Playing in the Dark: Whiteness and the Literary Imagination* (New York: Vintage, 1993) makes the argument that one cannot read American literature as represented in its canons without acknowledging how the literature is inseparable from the African American experience that helped to define it, with which it has been in conversation from the very beginning, and one which remains the foil against which white imagination has pretended to define the universal. I have made essentially the same argument for the formation of the modern canon in Euro-American philosophy. J. Ayodele Langley, ed. *Ideologies of Liberation in Black Africa: 1856–1970* (London: Rex Collings, 1979) has an introduction by the editor that situates the materials in it in the annals of modernity from the African-descended contributors to modern thought.

References

Adeleke, Tunde. (1998) *UnAfrican Americans: Nineteenth Century Black Nationalists and the Civilizing Mission*, Lexington: University Press of Kentucky.
Attoh Ahuma, S.R.B. (1971) *The Gold Coast Nation and National Consciousness*, London: Frank Cass.
Bacon, Francis. (1939) "Novum Organum," in Edwin A. Burtt (edited and introduced), *The English Philosophers From Bacon to Mill*, New York: Modern Library.
Bernasconi, Robert. (ed.) (2001) *Race*, Malden: Blackwell.
Bernasconi, Robert and Tommy L. Lott. (2000) Edited with Introductions. *The Idea of Race*, Indianapolis: Hackett.
Césaire, Aimé. (1972) *Discourse on Colonialism*, New York: Monthly Review Press.
Chinweizu. (1975) *The West and the Rest of Us*, New York: Vintage.
Equiano, Olaudah. (2004 [1789]) *The Interesting Narrative of the Life of Olaudah Equiano, or Gustavus Vasa, the African. Written by Himself*, ed. Joanna Brooks. N.p.: R.R. Donnelley & Sons.
Eze, Emmanuel Chukwudi. (ed.) (1997) *Race and the Enlightenment: A Reader*, Cambridge, MA: Blackwell.
Fanon, Frantz. (2008) *Black Skin, White Masks*, trans. Richard Philcox, New York: Grove Press.
Horton, James Africanus Beale. (1969 [1868]) *West African Countries and Peoples*, Edinburgh: University Press.
James, C.L.R. (1963) *The Black Jacobins: Toussaint L'Ouverture and the San Domingo Revolution*, New York: Random House.
Magubane, Bernard M. (2007) *Race and the Construction of the Dispensable Other*, Pretoria: University of South Africa Press.
Newman, Richard, Rael, Patrick, and Lapsansky, Philip. (eds.) (2001) *Pamphlets of Protest: An Anthology of Early African-American Protest Literature, 1790–1860*, New York: Routledge.
Park, Peter K.J. (2013) *Africa, Asia, and the History of Philosophy: Racism in the Formation of the Philosophical Canon, 1780–1830*, Albany: State University of New York Press.
Popkin, Richard H. (1980) "The Philosophical Bases of Modern Racism," in Richard A. Watson and James E. Force (eds.), *The High Road to Pyrrhonism*, San Diego: Austin Hill Press.
———. (1984) "Hume's Racism Reconsidered." *Journal* 1, no. 1: 61–71.
Robeson, Paul. (1998) *Here I Stand*, Boston: Beacon Press.
Sundquist, Eric J. (ed.) (1996) *The Oxford W.E.B. Du Bois Reader*, New York: Oxford University Press.
Táíwò, Olúfẹ́mi. (1998) "Exorcising Hegel's Ghost: Africa's Challenge to Philosophy," in "Religion and Philosophy in Africa," *African Studies Quarterly*, 1, no. 4 www.africa.ufl.edu/asq/v1/4/2.pdf.
———. (2010a) "'The Love of Freedom Brought Us Here': An Introduction to Modern African Political Philosophy." *South Atlantic Quarterly* 109, no. 2 (Spring): 391–410.
———. (2010b) *How Colonialism Pre-empted Modernity in Africa*, Bloomington: Indiana University Press.
Valls, Andrew. (ed.) (2005) *Race and Racism in Modern Philosophy*, Ithaca: Cornell University Press.

3

KANT ON RACE AND TRANSITION

Frank M. Kirkland

Introduction

To be judged "not by the color of their skin, but by the content of their character." These words are part of a speech, delivered majestically by Martin Luther King Jr. to upwards of 400,000 people on August 28, 1963. They are part of his anaphoric use of "I have a dream . . ." to refer, in this case, to the future of his then four young children. Most do not know, however, that the lion's share of King's speech, proffered in front of the Lincoln Memorial in Washington, DC, for the famous "March on Washington for Jobs and Freedom," consisted of three parts. The first was a sharply candid admonition concerning the long-standing vicious harms of politically sanctioned racial segregation of and its harmful economic repercussions on black people generally in the United States. The second was a somber warning to black people that white backlash and further agony, subsequent to the "March," would needs be undergone, stemming from the civic and moral protest against these detriments for the sake of basic civil rights and economic fairness. The third part of the speech was an inspiring peroration to a future redeemed in the aftermath of such extensive suffering. The anaphoric use of "I have a dream . . ." is found in this third and final section of the speech. King's speech, originally untitled, which could have just as well been called, say, "What Must Our Continued Struggle for Freedom Purchase?," came to be called "I Have a Dream."

America's public naming of King's speech as "I Have a Dream" has an unintended consequence worth mentioning. The first two parts of the speech vanish in the mind of the American public, as if its third part stands alone. More importantly, the gist of King's whole speech becomes in the mind of the American public only about "having the dream" that all God's children, not just King's, shall be judged "not by the color of their skin, but by the content of their character." However, despite the public's commemoration of King's speech solely in terms of its celebrated adage, the *meaning* of that famous refrain in the public's mind has been rather a hotly contested matter.

Broadly speaking, there are two competing views. We shall deal only with the first view here.[1] On the first view, King's phrase means that we must (i) *cease pre-judging* people by their skin color or race and (ii) *begin judging* them solely by the substance of their character. By so judging, we gauge the strength of their character in terms independently of the emotional pull of their racial attachments and commitments and give moral credit to actions done and beliefs held from their sense of duty and responsibility alone. The strength and "content of their character" would presuppose that attaching racial content to moral commitments is wrong and oppressive, and that human fidelities, neutral to race, blind to color, flourish, a state of affairs, many think, King himself endorsed. The obligations stemming from (ii) would trump all considerations involving race, among other emotional attachments and commitments, and enable a "radically non-racial humanism concerned with forms of human dignity that race-thinking undoes or strips away"[2] Judging people solely by the "content of their character" is the moral thing to do without exception; pre-judging them by their race is immoral without exception.[3]

I seek to examine the philosophical salience of Kant on the race-concept ("race") and, if any, on the contending views of the meaning of the famous saying of King's "I Have a Dream" speech. In broad strokes, the first view appears to represent a Kantian stance by affirming that we ought to judge people based solely on the "content of their character" full stop. It would be regarded as Kantian, because our judging ought to necessarily and sufficiently put out of play contingent/arbitrary attachments and factors, in this case racial ones, in assessing the content of a person's character.

Now in saying these things, I am neither expressing nor implying that King had read or was reliant on Kant's thought for the whole or any part of his 1963 speech. Over the course of my essay, I shall, in passing, make claims that the philosophy of Kant, construed concisely, can be brought to bear respectively on the first view of the meaning of King's refrain. But, in the main, my essay, more importantly, makes and seeks to demonstrate two proposals. First, the philosophy of Kant, concisely framed, can show the manners in which *normative* import can extend to the race-concept. Normatively Kant did have "second thoughts" on "race" through his conception of "*transition*." Second, the philosophy of Kant can serve to justify (i) and (ii) in King's refrain, as "transitionally" (Kant) *related*, not as *self-standing alternatives*. Neither proposal is entertained in the literature. Furthermore my claim does not and will not preclude a discussion of Kant's controversial racial chauvinism[4], a discussion which has, in various ways, already been put forward in a variety of philosophical venues. Still although "race" may carry normative weight on the basis of Kant's philosophy, which can be brought to bear on the first view of King's speech, it prompts two points.

First, contrary to the attitudes of many scholars of Kant to ignore his racial chauvinism, my claim will *not* involve defending, let alone implying, that Kant's racial chauvinism is to be discounted in and by his own philosophy. My claim should *not* be taken as an apologetic for dispensing with or disregarding his racial chauvinism. Second, contrary to critics of Kant on racial matters, I will *not* endorse or suggest that charting his racial chauvinism sufficiently thwarts his philosophy from denying (1) that enactments of people racially characterized are representative of inferior or superior intellectual and moral competences derived from the invariant "substance" of physiological attributes. Demonstrating my claim requires a concise perspective on his thought, not an apologetic of his core commitments discounting his racial chauvinism and not a chronicling of that chauvinism as if it amply showed his philosophy to be "inconsistently universal or consistently inegalitarian."[5]

Kant on Race and Transition

As I mentioned earlier, it is not unusual, indeed it is rather commonplace, to render the meaning of King's speech along an orthodox Kantian line on which pre-judging people on the "core" of their racial attributes (visible and heritable physiological features) is treating them as not having any estimable worth, while judging people on the import of their character is an obligation to respect them as having inestimable worth. The former would be prejudicial, deleterious to the integrity of the moral practice of the latter. In doing so, we subject King's anaphoric refrain to Kant's "rigorism," i.e., with respect to morally pertinent actions, judgments, and character involving race, there is no middle position. Either I treat the disposition of others in a race-specific cum racist fashion and, hence, in a (supposedly) morally inimical way, or I treat the disposition of others in a virtuously race-neutral fashion[6] and, hence, in a morally integral way.

The problem with the aforementioned position, however, is that whereas King could endorse, supposedly on Kantian grounds, *only* the race-neutral evaluation of people's disposition as morally significant, Kant himself endorses *both* the race-specific and race-neutral appraisals. At face value, Kant's rigorism would be put out of play not by the standard objections to it, but by his own accounts on race. Kant could likely regard the race-neutral appraisal of people's character as morally worthwhile, but he would likely not consider the race-specific treatment of people's character as morally detrimental, since such a treatment would, in his eyes, rely on a scientific certification of "race." That certification would leave in place an *extra-moral yet rational incentive* (hypothetical imperative) to accept the treatment as morally permissible. There would be nothing prejudicial, on scientific grounds, in such treatment to moral practice. We have thus entered the thicket that is Kant's own racial theory.

Kant is regarded as providing the original formulations of the modern notion of "race."[7] Generally speaking, he makes the following points. The modern concept of "race" is an empirical one, framed necessarily to describe and explain "scientifically," not "manifestly," the diversity of people in the world.[8] As an empirical concept, "race" would be regarded as warranted in acquiring sense and reference within experience. It would receive such warrant from what Kant calls an "empirical deduction" which addresses the *quid facti* status of "race." Its objective employment in judgment would be dependent on experience scientifically corroborated. But "race" does not acquire its warrant from a "transcendental or non-empirical deduction," addressing the *quid juris* status of a concept, since "race" does *not* possess such a status. If it were to have one, its objective employment in judgment would be rightly entitled to serve as an epistemic condition of experience.[9]

As an empirical concept, "race" would consist of "marks," *intensionally* distinguishing and individuating it from other concepts such as, in this case, "species," "variety," and "breed." Furthermore its specificity would establish *extensionally* the introduction of different populations ("differentia") such as, in this instance, "white," "black," "brown," "red," "yellow," and so forth, which can be arranged hierarchically, invariantly, as a matter of nature through what Kant postulates as imperceptible "germs" (*Keime*). Kant's postulate of "germs" allows "race" to serve as a phenomenal expression of an empirical character based on an imperceptible predisposition enabling "race's" empirical reality to track it scientifically. Such a character could be tracked from the appearances in which "race" is postulated and thereby, insinuate at least, a predisposition to act or behave on the grounds of maxims serving racial cum racist ends. Hence, through his postulate of "germs," Kant's empirical race-concept would admit to a racist (not exclusively a racialist) conception as well.

This portrayal answers, for example, the question of the late Emmanuel Eze whether "race" is "transcendental." The answer is categorically "no." Kant would not be trying to establish that the objective use of the race-concept in experience is entitled by right to operate as an epistemically normative pre-condition of experience. He rather tries to establish that the objective use or empirical reality of the race-concept in experience can be certified scientifically. This point marks his writings on "race." The race-concept would not be involved in governing Kant's philosophical examination of the a priori parameters of theoretical reason in and of experience. Instead it would be governed by them. But the validity of "race" as an empirical concept is something Kant would be trying to demonstrate, that is, attempting to corroborate its use in experience by experience scientifically, not attempting to seek its use in experience as something entitled a priori or normatively by right. If the scientific demonstration were *successful*, "race" would have objectively cognitive content certified scientifically of its empirical reality and would fall under the purview of what Kant calls a "judgment of experience."

This point, however, sets problems for Kant because, if the scientific demonstration is *unsuccessful*, "race" could not be an empirical but, what he would call, a "usurped" (*usurpierte*) or pseudo-concept.[10] The race-concept may be "manifestly" used in experience, but could not be construed as possibly credentialed by experience scientifically. To be clear, Kant never expressly claimed or argued that "race" was a pseudo-concept and, therefore, never referred to the science of race as pseudo-science, as is the case today. Otherwise "race" would not even have *quid facti* status. Indeed if he were to deny it such status, it would then be legitimate to claim that Kant could underwrite in full the *first version* of the anaphoric refrain of King's "I Have a Dream" speech. Yet, for Kant, the possibility that "race" could *not* receive scientific validation as an empirical concept would *not* rule out per se the race-concept. The *quid facti* status of "race" could be regarded as a matter dependent on our *presumption* about nature as purposive, entitled by right under the purview of what Kant calls a "judgment of taste" as well as its impact on the judgment of others.

Briefly this would signify that the race-concept could admit of a transcendental or non-empirical deduction of its *quid facti* status by demonstrating the legitimacy of our presumption of nature's purposiveness reflected in judgments of taste. "Race" would be *neither* a matter of taste *nor* a matter rightfully entitled to be used, because Kant did not believe that nature itself was purposively ordered to be *necessarily suitable* for our objectively cognitive or scientific needs and demands. Rather it would be a matter for a judgment of taste, wherein "race" (a) would bear aesthetically appealing "common sense" (*Gemeinsinn*, not *gemeinen Menschenverstand*)[11] not bound to its conceptual intension and extension, (b) would occasion an estimation of its aesthetic appeal to our *presumption* of a purposive and non-doctrinal conception of nature, and (c) would license only what others ought to find "exemplary" or communicable about "race" without cognitively determining or scientifically credentialing its truth value and empirical reality. Racist ends *may still* appear and proliferate; they also *may not*. But, as matters of judgment of taste, they would be *without* cognitive or scientific guarantee in either instance.

If we take "race" to have a "common sense" and express it as estimation of a shareable taste coinciding with our open-ended yet rightful presumption of nature as "purposive without a purpose,"[12] then the possibility is open that "race" could be involved in empirical inquiry, but whose scientific credential would *not* be an explicitly sought or guaranteed desideratum in or of such inquiry.[13] That is to say, "race" can be assumed

(a) to occasion an endeavor or project to judge or appraise in a manner purposively amenable to our cognitive ends, whatever they may presently or eventually be, without such a project needing or dictating in advance a specific purpose or end, and (b) to be oriented by that endeavor's open-ended and disinterested capacity to share "race's" sense as anyone else would.

Thus even the lack of success to demonstrate that and how the objective employment of "race" *judgmentally or cognitively in experience* acquires its empirical reality scientifically would *not* foreclose a *non-empirical deduction* of a *judgment of taste* regarding "race" wherein the *quid facti* status of "race" could be justified or rightly entitled by our presumption of nature as purposive to allow for both its "common sense" and its appraisals of what ought or ought not to be sentiments toward it.[14]

So Kant's writings in support of the race-concept, for example, in his 1775 and 1785 essays, "Of the Different Races of Human Beings" (DRHB) and "Determination of the Concept of a Human Race" (DCHR), respectively,[15] can be characterized as Kant's attempt to show "race" as an objectively employable empirical concept and thus tacitly, at least, a challenge to the belief that "race" would be a pseudo-concept.[16] In contrast, his 1788 essay, "On the Use of Teleological Principles in Philosophy" (OUTPP),[17] does not exclusively delineate whether the race-concept could be objectively employable in empirical settings (in nature, even human nature), but entertains whether the ends that concept serves, *whatever they may be*, can be rightly assumed in a judgment of taste to exhibit necessarily a licit plausibility in them. In OUTPP, Kant affirms our entitlement to *assume* in such a judgment the empirical reliability of *either* racial cum racist *or* just solely racial ends that "race" could purposively satisfy, but without prior attestation that it does.[18] But, in that same essay, he *also* avows our entitlement to anticipate and judge freely, rationally, and unconditionally that those ends, purposively assuming their empirical reliability, are under moral projects and the law of freedom, and thus ought be *neither* worthy to pursue morally nor sufficient to promote objectively.[19]

Besides intimating that "race" may *not* be restricted exclusively to its scientifically credentialed determination, given that our varied appraisals of it may be in accord with our rightful assumption to approach nature as if it were purposively open-ended rather than as if it were not, there is another point that OUTPP considers that DRHB and DCHR do not. Kant alludes to the manner that "race" as a matter for a judgment of taste and the purposiveness of nature rightly presumed in such judgment ought to be subject to the demands of morality and that those demands ought to be realized in this world. Although I cannot here elaborate on the details, ramifications, and nuances of this point in a fuller way, it is important, I believe, to acknowledge that this point gives Kant pause, raises "second thoughts"[20] for him, about the race-concept.

Indeed Kant could underwrite King's anaphoric refrain concerning the dream of people judging someone by the color of their skin turning one day toward judging someone by the content of their character. But whereas for King this turn is a matter longed for in a "dream," it would be, for Kant, a matter of what he calls the "transition (*Übergang*) from nature (wherein "race" would be either be cognitively used as scientifically credentialed or would be rightly presumed to have common sense without objectively cognitive contribution or truth value) to freedom (wherein "race" ought *not* be effectuated in our moral demands on this world)." Although this "transition" is not a "dream" for Kant, it is still very problematic for him.

Kant does not provide a uniformly distinct explication of both the notion of "transition" and the manner it is to be comprehended. In the *CPR*, "transition" is that in which the concepts of nature and of freedom are *conceived* as connected within the *single* jurisdiction of reason itself.[21] In the *Critique of Practical Reason* (*CPrR*), "transition" leads to the achievement extending the employment of a priori concepts legitimately to noumena or ideals, *not solely to phenomena*, to enable hope in such ideals to incentivize morality.[22] But the explication which appears to prevail ultimately in his thought is "transition," found in *CPJ*, as the "bridge" or conduit over the "immense gulf" between *two* conceptual jurisdictions, that of nature and that of freedom.[23] There is this "immense gulf," because neither conceptual jurisdiction is derivable from the other. But both rightfully cover the same terrain or empirical reality, which encompasses *all objects of possible experience, inclusive of all objects that ought or ought not to be effectuated in possible experience*.

There must be some kind of compatibility with each other. Kant, however, would never affirm that nature's conceptual jurisdiction stems from that of freedom. Yet most contemporary philosophers would argue, contra Kant, that freedom's conceptual jurisdiction is compatible with that of nature, thereby naturalizing freedom and rendering it empirically conditioned. How then do these two conceptual jurisdictions cover the same possible experience or empirical reality without conflicting with or hampering each other? The answer for Kant would be—only if what should be moral ends, circumscribed by the conceptual jurisdiction of freedom, not by that of nature, are obtained and ensured in this world. What does all this have to do with the race-concept?

Kant offers DRHB as the account of the empirical reality of the race-concept, relying on hypotheses correlating the diversity of racial populations, given the unity of the human species, to geo-climatic areas around the globe. DCHR gives, on the other hand, a treatment of the empirical reality of the race-concept, defending it on grounds of monogenetic causes, subject to laws of nature, to explain the diversity within the unity of the human species. The difference between them is, for Kant, better scientific certification of the empirical reality of "race" in the latter rather than in the former essay. Still the racial cum racist ends would be served by that concept in both essays, would be empirically conditioned, and thus would be subject to nature's conceptual jurisdiction. Therefore, a "transition" to the concept of freedom, as found in *CPR*, could admit to the *conceivability* of "race" as innocuous/inessential to human practices and morality in the long run for the human species, but *not* to its possible employment as incidental in empirical reality. This sense of "transition," apropos to "race," would not be fitting to King's anaphoric refrain, because the refrain would speak to the *possible employment* of "race" as inessential to the consideration of a person's character in empirical reality, but never solely to "race's" *conceivability* as inessential.

Kant's essay, "Idea for a Universal History with a Cosmopolitan Aim," would, for example, deny that the empirical reality of "race" is subject to the conceptual jurisdiction of freedom (not to that of nature), but would affirm that the conceivability of cosmopolitanism is supportive of a hopefulness that nature could gradually, albeit unnoticeably, perhaps providentially, over the long haul be amenable to "race" becoming nugatory to human practices and morality.[24] The "cosmopolitan aim" becomes one of a number of conceivable moral ideals worthy of praise and appreciation for which to hope, but without justifying what motivates practical employment of such ideals to future prospects in possible experience, despite nature's contribution to our "unsociable sociability."[25] The "transition" here, pertinent to "race," could be in sync with King's refrain, *only if* King were to hold that consideration of a person's character, in which "race" were inessential, would be a moral state of affairs for which *only* hoping (or dreaming) it would be significant.

As I stated above, the sense of "transition" in OUTPP (and later in *CPJ*) is different from the two senses above and prevails in Kant's thought on "race." Kant distinguishes ends of nature and of freedom, but each set is directly related to reason generally. He further distinguishes them by referring to the former as empirically conditioned whereby "race" together with racial cum racist ends are elements over which the conceptual jurisdiction of nature holds sway. He refers to the latter as belonging to a "doctrine of practically pure ends," that is, morality and its demands, necessarily presupposing objective reality in this world for what they ultimately, universally, and *unconditionally* prescribe.[26] But, *for the first time*, Kant is arguing for the necessary possibility of the conceptual jurisdiction of freedom, which holds sway over morality and its demands, and which would have *rational and unconditional moral influence* over empirically *conditioned* items, such as "race" and its racial cum racist ends, and enjoining them to it.

This sense of "transition" is the strongest version Kant proposes which could underwrite King's anaphoric refrain. Here Kant would be affirming that, say, empirically conditioned racial cum racist ends ought to be unconditionally subject to and influenced by morally motivated demands realized in this world. The move from considering a person on the basis of the "color of her skin" to considering a person's character not just independently of "race" and its aforementioned ends, but motivationally by morally reasoned demands *not* to do so, would be characteristic of the meaning of King's refrain under its "first view." But this sense of "transition" still would pose problems for Kant.

Again, for Kant, under this sense of "transition," freedom's conceptual jurisdiction neither stems from nature's conceptual jurisdiction nor should be subordinate to it. Rather it must be possible that its rational and unconditional moral influence ought never be proscribed or mitigated by the ends under nature's jurisdiction to render actions or pursuits based on such influence impossible. It is not unusual to think that what Kant calls "culture" conveys the third sense of "transition" from nature to freedom described immediately above. Kant refers to "culture" as the capacity of the human species to produce *freely* chosen ends with *skill*, that is, *aptly* setting and using purposes on the effects of nature which cannot be discovered or found in nature, and with *discipline*, that is, *freely* setting and using purposes without the compulsion of desires and thus without passions dictating choice. "Culture" would allow for freedom *only* to be exercised *not* in virtue of the power of passions, but in virtue of its power to set ends aligned with the purposiveness of nature presumed in judgments of taste. As a consequence, "culture" could allow for racial cum racist ends, freely chosen, that "race" could presume to satisfy purposively, but without objective confirmation that it does. But, on the grounds of this consequence alone, it could *not* set ends worthy to dispute morally or to contest sufficiently, could *not* set ends that should unconditionally challenge in a rationally moral way freely chosen, yet purposively assumed, racist ends. So it could *not* convey or express the third sense of "transition," through which the moral valence of the conceptual jurisdiction of freedom on possible experience ought to be compelling.

"Culture" could allow one to be progressively civilized, but not progressively moral, having standards of moral evaluation, yet incapable of generating the unconditionally motivational factor needed to undo to the contrary, in this instance, racist ends on the basis of the standards. This general scenario has led Thomas McCarthy to claim rather smartly that Kant's "culture" could yield a civilization that is itself along the lines of what Walter Benjamin called a politically expedient "monument to barbarism."[27] It would not be today unusual to call it a politically expedient "monument to white supremacy."

The issue raised here, however, is that Kant is aware of the difficulty surrounding the practical employment of moral demands against "race" and its aforementioned racist ends, since the success of this employment entails only that effectuating such moral demands in this world ought not be impossible, not that they are guaranteed. This situation, in my mind, provokes Kant's "second thoughts" on "race." But his "second thoughts" on "race" are *not* what Pauline Kleingeld refers to as Kant's "radically revised views"[28] on "race." She cites as evidence for these "revised views" (a) Kant's silence on racial hierarchy; (b) his increasing egalitarianism regarding race; (c) his extension of juridical status to non-whites; (d) his articulated prohibition of colonialism for the sake of cosmopolitan aims; (e) his rejection of consequentialist justifications for colonialism; and (f) his condemnation of chattel slavery, all of which represents a moral constraint on the behavior of European nations and all presented in various places exclusively in his post-1790 writings.[29]

But Kleingeld's thesis and her evidence cited to support it turn on a mistake. She attests that in his post-1790 writing, "Toward Perpetual Peace," (a) Kant regards nature as having "organized the earth in such a way that humans can and will live everywhere . . . [using] the surface of the earth for interacting peacefully."[30] Further she affirms that (b) Kant "envisages a world in which people of different colors and on different continents establish peaceful relations with each other that honor the normative principles laid down in his exposition of cosmopolitan right."[31] Regarding (a), Kant would have to presume that nature organizes purposively in that way, not claim that it does so. Regarding (b), Kant does envisage such a world, but the issue for him is the realization of such a world under the laws of freedom and ends of morality.

In effect, Kleingeld misses two points. She fails to grasp that the purposiveness of nature is attributed to our presumption about nature, not to nature itself, which can aid in reconfiguring "race" in an open-ended way. Indeed it still would leave in one piece the racist ends "race" serves, but it would open that concept to serve non-racist ends with neither cognitive nor objective import. She also fails to grasp that the ultimate issue for Kant would *not* be envisaging (conceiving or presuming) a post-and non-racial cum racist world subject to moral requirements, but would be raising matters of such a world's realizability, that is, the *effectuation* of those requirements on the sensible world. In short, Kleingeld affirms Kant's "second thoughts" on "race" independently of or without grasping the significance of "race's" alteration specifically under Kant's notion of the third or post-1788 sense of "transition."

Kant's "second thoughts" then would *not* be "radically revised" ones. They rather would be *reservations regarding the impact of earlier thoughts on "race" in light of the impact of later or different ones on it, specifically what the thought of effectively realizing the moral purge of "race" and its ends ought to have on them in the sensible world.* As I stated above, Kant never regarded "race" as a pseudo-concept and never regarded its science as pseudo-science, as we do today. This concept and the racist ends it served remained intact and in force under Kant's conceptual jurisdiction of nature and were never recanted or repudiated. Only the concept, not the racist ends, was revised for the sake of a better scientific account, but within that jurisdiction. The shift to the conceptual jurisdiction of freedom, however, subjects "race" to a different account, in which it is at first conceivable, then hoped, that its meaning is rendered nugatory and its racist ends are expunged in the face of moral requirements. But Kant's notion of "race" under the conceptual jurisdiction of nature would still be in play, despite conceiving of and hoping for its conceptual insignificance and moral removal, unless there is such removal of it and its ends effectively in the sensible world. The evidence Kleingeld cites does speak to moral ends, conceived of and hoped for, within the conceptual jurisdiction of freedom, *but not to moral ends ultimately having to be effectively realized in this world under that conceptual jurisdiction*. Given that each jurisdiction has its own integrity, "race" and its racist ends would be in play, unless de-certified scientifically in this world *and* effectively removed morally in this world. In that light, Kant could not count, in his day, on the former happening in this world, but could only promote that the latter should.[32]

Kantian Postscripts

Still everything stated so far still would give pride of place to Kleingeld's thesis generally. But it would not do so to the views of her critics such as Robert Bernasconi and Charles Mills, who have basically argued that "race" and its racist ends are intact and in force *throughout* Kant's philosophy. Their thesis would deny not only the validity of Kant having "second thoughts" on "race" but, more importantly, the validity of placing Kant's "second thoughts" on "race" in the context of his notion of "transition," for which I have argued.

Bernasconi's recent critical response to Kleingeld's essay takes the position that Kant's cosmopolitanism is not an "antidote" to the racial cum racist ends of "race," but rather the "natural accompaniment" to them.[33] Kant's so-called second thoughts and "silence" on "race" in his post-1790 writings supposedly relies on the belief that cosmopolitanism is an antidote to the aforementioned ends of "race." Yet, for Bernasconi, Kant's cosmopolitanism accompanies racism, not as a necessary possibility like the "I think" accompanying all one's representations, but as a belief that they were naturally concomitant with each other. This serves as evidence for Bernasconi to make the rather historically positivist claim that Kant and those of his times had differences from contemporary philosophers, who would regard cosmopolitanism as remedial to, not as coexisting with, racism. Thus, on this point, Bernasconi is critical of Kleingeld for both believing that the ends of Kant's moral philosophy trump racial cum racist ends and imposing sentiments about cosmopolitanism divergent from those of his times, all aimed solely to rescue Kant's reputation from the charge of racism rather than to acknowledge his continuous acceptance of it.

But Bernasconi's response misses the mark. First, cosmopolitanism's accompaniment with racism would not be a historically positivist affair, but would be a matter pertinent to Kant's thought. Consistent with what I earlier stated, that accompaniment would be possible for Kant, on the condition that the ends of civilization were a matter of "skill" and "discipline" alone, not a matter of the times. If so, it would rely on freedom solely as the setting of *empirically conditioned ends*, consistent with allowing them to be realized in this world for the sake of political expediency, rather than as the setting of *empirically unconditioned ends*, enabling them to be realized in this world for the sake of morally political obligation.[34] Second, Kant's cosmopolitanism would thus legitimately serve as antidote to racism on morally political grounds, not as attendant to it on politically expedient ones. Kleingeld regards cosmopolitanism as (1) a morally conceivable end designed as the antidote to racism or (2) a morally conceivable end whose purpose is that for which the foreclosure of racism is to be hoped. She leaves out cosmopolitanism as (3) a morally remedial end designed toward the elimination of racism, which ought to be effectuated in this world. Her problem then would be simply *neglecting an alternative* Kant could necessarily take. Bernasconi's problem, however, is *regarding all three stances as out of the question* in Kant's thought, favoring a historically positivist and politically expedient stance toward Kant's cosmopolitanism rather than trying to extend the cosmopolitan commitments Kant would have toward morally foreclosing racism, to those commitments he must have toward such moral foreclosure.

Kleingeld does not include, therefore, the aforementioned third point in her "second thoughts" on "race." But Bernasconi does not affirm any of them. This would suggest that while Kleingeld would, in part, embrace, with respect to "race," Kant's attempt to "bridge" or "transition" the "vast gulf" or dualism between what is experienced according to laws of nature circumscribed within theoretical reason and what ought to be experienced according to laws of freedom circumscribed within practical reason, Bernasconi would not. The consequence of his position would not be a denial of this dualism, but it would be a denial of Kant's attempt to find compatibility between the two without reducing one to the other or, as Allen Wood has claimed, a "compatibility of compatibilism and incompatibilism"[35] as well as the *incompatibility between freedom empirically conditioned and empirically unconditioned.* "Race" and the racial cum racist ends it serves originate in experience, and their objective reality is sought there scientifically, circumscribed within nature's conceptual jurisdiction or theoretical reason. They would still be in force circumscribed within an empirically conditioned freedom. Since Bernasconi does *not* abide by Kant's sense of "transition," freedom's conceptual jurisdiction (practical reason) can be distinctly maintained, but plays no role, has no influence, and ought not to have one on "race" other than its empirically conditioned and less than subsidiary impact in and on experience. So Kant's position on "race" would not change, would not be subject to "second thoughts," because it is not and cannot be *unconditionally* changed by practical reason.[36]

This is the line of argument undergirding Mills's faultfinding views of Kant and his sympathizers on "race." He shares with Bernasconi two things—the idea of "transition" has no place in their thought and that Kant's position on "race" is unalterable and holds the field philosophically, scientifically, morally, and politically throughout. But there is a difference between the two of them. Bernasconi would uphold Kant's distinction between theoretical and practical reason, but deny the unconditional effectiveness of the latter on the former's explanatory and justificatory hold on "race." Mills denies *both* Kant's distinction *and* the possibility that practical reason's effectiveness against "race" ought and must be empirically unconditioned.

Unflinchingly Mills gives way and sway to the noted intellectual historian, Jonathan Israel, and his interpretation of Kant's racial views, expressed in his three-volume work on the Enlightenment. Allow me to quote Mills in full.

> Kant's racial views . . . are emphatically not to be partitioned off from his ethico-political diagnoses and prescriptions but rather to be seen as an integral

part of his thought—*Kantianism simpliciter* that needs to be situated within the global context of the times of fierce pro- and anti-imperialist debate and recognized as theoretically important. *They are not, for Israel—nor, in my opinion, should they be for us—denizens of separate intellectual worlds, the empirical/subtheoretical/quirky and the abstract/principled/important, but the same world.*[37]

Uniformity and continuity of Kant's racial cum racist views not just across his writings but, more importantly, across theoretical and practical reason to dispel the difference in their conceptual jurisdictions, constitute "*Kantianism simpliciter*," which can for Mills serve as a theoretically connecting tissue to the capacious manifold of forays engaged in using "race" and its racist ends around the globe historically and presently. For example, this point allows Mills to tether Kant's racial views to the notion of "Untermenschen" and the so-called ethic of Nazism. And since Kant's difference between theoretical and practical reason has been melded into "*Kantianism simpliciter*," Mills thus commits Kant's philosophy significantly to the effectuation of "race" and its racial cum racist ends without "transition" and reason's jurisdictional difference. Indeed no Kantian would accept such a conclusion. But there may be plausibility for such in Kant himself.

Minimally the credibility of "*Kantianism simpliciter*" would rest on four factors. (1) The objective reality of "race" would have to consist in the explanation of skin color (via "germs") as "unfailingly hereditary."[38] (2) Racial heredity would have to enable or be conjoined with both "pathological necessitation" and "pathological affection" of a human will.[39] (3) An empirically conditioned will would have its freedom pathologically *affected* by sensibly empirical motives. On the other hand, an empirically conditioned will, pathologically *necessitated* by them, could *only* sense an impulse to do *x*, but *never* conceive of itself as free to do so. (4) Freedom as empirically unconditioned may be rationally conceivable for a pathologically affected will, *but impoverished, insufficient or neutral to be motivated unconditionally for it*, to derive conclusions of what morally ought to be done and effectuated. Points 1–3 would make possible a racially necessitated will for which freedom would be inconceivable, and "Untermenschen" could be designated. They would also make possible an ethic establishing that which ought to be the case racially is dictated sufficiently by what is necessitated racially. A so-called ethic of Nazism or, more broadly, what Mills has called "Herrenvolk Ethics"[40] has been formulated in this manner. Point 4 indicates a conception of freedom, for which a pathologically necessitated will does not, cannot, and ought not to be motivated morally at all. Although a pathologically affected will does not, it could and ought to be unconditionally motivated morally for the sake of being effective morally. Without a notion of "transition," the landscape, which point 4 indexes, is impossible to enter, let alone entertain, for "*Kantianism simpliciter*."

Bernasconi, Larrimore, and Mills all deny that which would spur Kant to have "second thoughts" on "race"—the "transition" to the conceptual jurisdiction wherein freedom can be regarded rationally as morally motivating and effectuating unconditionally the repudiation of "race" and its racist ends in this world. Kant, as I stated earlier, never recants, but sustains, his affirmation of the empirical reality of "race" scientifically, and that fuels the belief among them that freedom's conceptual jurisdiction over "race" and its ends is either non-existent to (Mills) or subsidiary to (Bernasconi/Larrimore) or ineffective in relation to (Bernasconi/Larrimore) nature's conceptual jurisdiction over it and its ends in the sensible world. But that is their mistake. Kant's affirmation by itself forecloses neither the distinction between "nature" and "freedom" nor the crossover from one to the other. Despite my criticism, Kleingeld affirms a sense of "transition" necessary to spur Kant to have "second thoughts" on "race." His "second thoughts" are not as strong as she proposes ("radical revisions"). But they still are reliant on the crossover to and the impact of freedom's conceptual jurisdiction over "race," in which "race" and its racist ends ought to be effectively eliminated morally in this world, even if they are not effectively eliminated scientifically in this world. King would have had an advantage over Kant with the ascendancy of the scientific elimination of "race" during his times. Still, reading King's refrain may have an undercurrent reliant on Kant, when read as calling for the realization of judging the content of character on moral grounds unconditionally rather than pre-judging it on biologically physical grounds.

Notes

1 The second view shall be addressed in the chapter "Hegel on Race and Development" in this volume.
2 A proponent of this view would be Paul Gilroy, who claims that "Dr. Martin Luther King, Jr. . . . was fond of pointing out that race-thinking has the capacity to make its beneficiaries inhuman even as it deprives its victims of their humanity." See his *Against Race* (Cambridge: Harvard University Press, 2000), 15, 17.
3 It should be noted that King's claim has African American religious antecedents first identified by W.E.B. Du Bois. In the final chapter of *The Souls of Black Folk*, "On the Sorrow Songs," Du Bois remarks that those songs conveyed the hopeful message that "men will judge men by their souls, not by their skins." King's claim under the first view would be in sync with the sorrow songs' message. Du Bois himself does not disavow the message, but raises questions about its possible fulfillment. See *The Souls of Black Folk* in *Du Bois Writings*, edited by Nathan Huggins (New York: Library of America, 1980), 544.
4 For representative, albeit not exhaustive, discussions on Kant's racism, see Robert Bernasconi's "Who Invented the Concept of Race?—Kant's Role in the Enlightenment Construction of Race" in *Race*, ed. Robert Bernasconi (Oxford: Blackwell, 2001), 11–36, and "Kant as an Unfamiliar Source of Racism" in *Philosophers on Race*, ed. Julie K. Ward and Tommy L. Lott (New York: Oxford University Press, 2002), 145–166; Emmanuel Chukwudi Eze, "Race: A Transcendental?" in his *Achieving Our Humanity: The Idea of the Postracial Future* (New York: Routledge, 2001), 77–111; Thomas E. Hill and Bernard Boxill, "Kant and Race," in *Race and Racism*, ed. Bernard Boxill (New York: Oxford University Press, 2001), 448–471; Pauline Kleingeld, "Kant's Second Thoughts on Race," *Philosophical Quarterly* 57, no. 229 (2007): 573–592; Charles Mills, "Kant's Untermenschen" in *Race and Racism in Modern Philosophy*, ed. Andrew Valls (Ithaca: Cornell University Press, 2005), 169–193, and "Kant and Race, Redux" in *Graduate Faculty Philosophy Journal* 35, no. 1–2 (2014): 125–157.
5 See Kleingeld, "Kant's Second Thoughts on Race," 582–586.
6 Since "race-neutrality" or even "race-eliminativism" is not analytically or by definition "virtuous," I suspect, even for King, it would be significant to establish or discover how it acquires its, say, "virtuousness."
7 See Bernasconi, "Who Invented the Concept of Race? Kant's Role in the Enlightenment Construction of Race"; Mark Larrimore, "Antinomies of Race: Diversity and Destiny in Kant" in *Patterns of Prejudice* 42, no. 4–5 (2008): 341–363, hereinafter cited as Larrimore.
8 For the distinction between the "scientific" and the "manifest" image of man and world, see Wilfrid Sellars, "Philosophy and the Scientific Image of Man" in his *Science, Perception and Reality* (London: Routledge & Kegan Paul, 1963), 1–41. In short, but not in full, the "manifest" image refers to the framework in which human beings come to the awareness of themselves as human beings in context and as reliant on contextually based correlational "procedures" for items perceived and for items introspected. The

"scientific" image refers to the framework of postulating imperceptible items for explaining correlations among perceptible items and whose sustained presence is derived from the success of theory construction based on such postulations.

9 See Henry E. Allison, *Kant's Transcendental Deduction: An Analytical-Historical Commentary* (New York: Oxford University Press, 2015), 181–196. For those unfamiliar with Kant, he does not use "deduction" as an argument whose conclusion follows logically, necessarily, from its premises. Rather, it is being used as an argument seeking to establish rightful entitlement to the ownership of property, demonstrating that such entitlement is neither grounded on physical possession/use of property nor grounded on how said possession was obtained, but grounded on the juridical distinction between "mine" and "thine." Kant takes "deduction" to argue for the difference between (a) the entitlement of concepts' use, because their validity is indispensable to and non-circumventible by what counts as a real possibility of experience and (b) the use of concepts by virtue of possession, because their validity is reliant on and acquired from real experience. A priori concepts make up the former, thereby holding *quid juris* status; empirical concepts make up the latter, thereby holding *quid facti* status.

10 Allison, *Kant's Transcendental Deduction*, 182. Allison is referring to passages from A84–87/B117–119 in Kant's *Critique of Pure Reason*, trans. Paul Guyer and Allen Wood (Cambridge: Cambridge University Press, 1997), hereinafter cited as *CPR*.

11 See Immanuel Kant's *Critique of the Power of Judgment*, trans. Paul Guyer and Eric Matthews (Cambridge: Cambridge University Press, 2001), 122–124, sec. 20–22 and 174–175, sec. 40, hereinafter cited as *CPJ*. *Gemeinsinn* as "common sense" refers to common meaning about "x"; *gemeinen Menschenverstand* as "common sense" refers to a common yet non-intellectual orientation or state of mind towards "x."

12 *CPJ*, 105, sec. 10.

13 For example, Alain Locke would strongly deny even the possibility that "race" could be scientifically credentialed, despite the history of attempts to do so. But, I think, he would affirm the actuality that "race" is aesthetically branded in appraisals that value it favorably, a prospect he would take further and seek to confirm, unlike Kant. See his "The Theoretical and Scientific Conceptions of Race" and "The Political and Practical Conceptions of Race" in his *Race Contacts and Interracial Relations: Lectures on the Theory and Practice of Race*, ed. Jeffrey C. Stewart (Washington, DC: Howard University Press, 1992).

14 Be mindful that *neither* "race's" use *nor* the assumption of its shareable "common sense" in our sentiments affirming it currently (and previously for a long time) has acquired empirical credentials scientifically or rightful entitlement legally and morally. These points, however, do not prevent further attempts to seek scientific validation in "race's" use, albeit now very rarely, or to presume, rather frequently, that there is something legitimate in the assumption of its alleged "common sense." Still it is significant to recognize that, during Kant's time, its scientific certification and rightful entitlement legally and morally were both often employed and presumed.

15 For these essays, see Immanuel Kant, *Anthropology, History, and Education*, ed. Günter Zöller and Robert B. Louden (Cambridge: Cambridge University Press, 2007), 82–98 and 143–159, respectively, hereinafter cited as *Anthro, Hist, Educ*.

16 In contrast to an empirical one, a pseudo-concept would be a representation formed to *generalize* through *association* of items, *without* bona fide "manifest," "scientific," or a priori credentials, about "x." It would *not* be a representation formed to *universalize* through *comparison* of patterns or schemata, governing both the apprehension of those items and the abstraction from their differences, about "x."

17 For this essay, see *Anthro, Hist, Educ*, 192–218.

18 To make this point clearer, ask the following question: What is the difference, *as a matter of a judgment of taste*, between ascertaining that a young black girl's possession of a black doll rather than a white one is *deleterious* to her well-being and, on the other hand, a young black girl's possession of a fictional book about black girls and their adventures rather than white boys and theirs is *beneficial* to her? To be sure, the science of psychology can step in to investigate each scenario to establish its cognitive or objective truth value. But the communicability of the common sense of each would remain in force for Kant regardless of the scientific results, unless those results were to "feedback" into and "saturate" the common sense of one or the other.

19 *Anthro, Hist, Educ*, 217. "Morality is destined to realize its [doctrine of practically pure] ends in the world, not neglecting their possibility in the world, securing the objective reality of [the aforementioned doctrine of] ends such that the doctrine prescribes as to be effectuated in the world."
20 On this issue, I'm in general agreement with Kleingeld. My difference with her resides in what motivates Kant to have "second thoughts" on the race-concept and what those "second thoughts" mean for him. See Kleingeld, "Kant's Second Thoughts on Race."
21 See CPR, A339/B386.
22 See Immanuel Kant, *Critique of Practical Reason*, trans. Mary Gregor (Cambridge University Press, 2008) 5–6, 5: 6–7, hereinafter cited as CPrR.
23 See CPJ, 63. Unlike the conceptual jurisdiction of nature, from which neither transition to nor influence on the conceptual jurisdiction of freedom can be had in Kant's thought, "the latter [jurisdiction] *should* have an influence on the former, namely the concept of freedom should make the end that is imposed by its laws real [or effective] (*wirklich*) in the sensible world; and nature must [as a consequence therefrom] be able to be presumed in such a way that the lawfulness of its form is at least in agreement with the possibility of the ends that are to be realized in it in accordance with the laws of freedom."
24 See *Anthro, Hist, and Educ*, 107–120.
25 *Anthro, Hist, and Educ*, 111.
26 *Anthro, Hist, and Educ*, 217.
27 See Thomas McCarthy, "Kant on Race and Development," in his *Race, Empire, and the Idea of Human Development* (Cambridge, MA: Cambridge University Press, 2009), 61.
28 Kleingeld, "Kant's Second Thoughts on Race," 586.
29 Kleingeld, "Kant's Second Thoughts on Race," 587–588.
30 Kleingeld, "Kant's Second Thoughts on Race," 589.
31 Kleingeld, "Kant's Second Thoughts on Race," 589.
32 For over a century, the former has happened, but the latter has remained rather entangled under this Kantian view.
33 See Robert Bernasconi's "Kant's Third Thoughts on Race" in *Reading Kant's Geography*, ed. Stuart Elden and Eduardo Mendieta (Albany: SUNY Press, 2011), 295–296.
34 See Immanuel Kant, "Toward Perpetual Peace: A Philosophical Project" in *Practical Philosophy*, trans. Mary Gregor (Cambridge: Cambridge University Press, 1999), 344–347, hereinafter cited as TPP.
35 See Allen Wood, "Kant's Compatibilism" in *Self and Nature in Kant's Philosophy*, ed. Allen Wood (Ithaca: Cornell University Press, 1984), 74.
36 Larrimore's excellent work on Kant's racial views also succumbs to this criticism. Larrimore clearly understands that "race" as an essential part of the *physical-anthropological* investigation of what "nature makes of man" becomes, in Kant's post-1790 writings, an essential part of the *pragmatic-anthropological* investigation of, as Larrimore puts it, "what man can and should make of himself." This is noteworthy for two reasons. He (1) omits an important part in the latter quote and, in so doing, (2) construes "race" under an empirically conditioned sense of freedom and rationality. Kant's latter quote actually states, "what man as a *free agent makes*, or can and should make, of himself." Larrimore's omission would concede Kant regarding "race" and the racial cum racist ends it serves as having a necessary hand in what man freely makes of himself, which would be empirically conditioned. For Kant, what man makes, or can and should make, of himself as a free agent would involve being motivationally primed rationally *not* to act or believe in ways "race" and its ends are determined and executed in this world. The issue—the effectuation of that point—cannot be entertained by Larrimore, since it is not on the table. See Larrimore, "Antinomies of Race," 357–363.
37 See Mills, "Kant and Race, Redux," 137–138 (my emphasis).
38 See *Anthro, Hist, and Educ*, 151.
39 See CPR, A534/B562 and A802/B830.
40 See Charles Mills, "White Right: The Idea of a *Herrenvolk* Ethics" in his *Blackness Visible: Essays on Philosophy and Race* (Ithaca: Cornell University Press, 1998), 139–166.

References

Allison, Henry E. (2015) *Kant's Transcendental Deduction: An Analytical-Historical Commentary*. New York: Oxford University Press.
Bernasconi, Robert. (2001) "Who Invented the Concept of Race?—Kant's Role in the Enlightenment Construction of Race," in Robert Bernasconi (ed.), *Race*. Oxford: Blackwell, pp. 11–36.
———. (2002) "Kant as an Unfamiliar Source of Racism," in Julie K. Ward and Tommy L. Lott (eds.), *Philosophers on Race*. New York: Oxford University Press, pp. 145–166.
———. (2011) "Kant's Third Thoughts on Race," in Stuart Elden and Eduardo Mendieta (eds.), *Reading Kant's Geography*. Albany: State University of New York Press, pp. 291–318.
Du Bois, W.E.B. (1980) "The Souls of Black Folk," in Nathan Huggins (ed.), *Du Bois Writings*. New York: Library of America, pp. 357–547.
Eze, Emmanuel Chukwudi. (2001) *Achieving Our Humanity: The Idea of the Postracial Future*, New York: Routledge.
Gilroy, Paul. (2000) *Against Race*. Cambridge, MA: Harvard University Press.
Hill, Thomas E., and Bernard Boxill. (2001) "Kant and Race," in Bernard Boxill (ed.), *Race and Racism*, New York: Oxford University Press, pp. 448–471.
Kant, Immanuel. (1997) *Critique of Pure Reason*, trans. Paul Guyer and Allen Wood. Cambridge: Cambridge University Press.
Kant, Immanuel. (1999) "Toward Perpetual Peace," in *Practical Philosophy*, trans. Mary Gregor. Cambridge: Cambridge University Press, pp. 311–352.
———. (2001) *Critique of the Power of Judgment*, trans. Paul Guyer and Eric Matthews. Cambridge: Cambridge University Press.
———. (2007) *Anthropology, History, and Education*, eds. Günter Zöller and Robert B. Louden. Cambridge: Cambridge University Press.
———. (2008) *Critique of Practical Reason*, trans. Mary Gregor. Cambridge: Cambridge University Press.
Kleingeld, Pauline. (2007) "Kant's Second Thoughts on Race." *Philosophical Quarterly* 57, no. 229: 573–592.
Larrimore, Mark. (2008) "Antinomies of Race: Diversity and Destiny in Kant." *Patterns of Prejudice* 42, no. 4–5: 341–363.
Locke, Alain. (1992) *Race Contacts and Interracial Relations: Lectures on the Theory and Practice of Race*, ed. Jeffrey C. Stewart. Washington, DC: Howard University Press.
McCarthy, Thomas. (2009) *Race, Empire, and the Idea of Human Development*. Cambridge: Cambridge University Press.
Mills, Charles. (1998) "White Right: The Idea of a *Herrenvolk* Ethics," in *Blackness Visible: Essays on Philosophy and Race*. Ithaca: Cornell University Press, pp. 139–166.
———. (2005) "Kant's Untermenschen," in Andrew Valls (ed.), *Race and Racism in Modern Philosophy*. Ithaca: Cornell University Press, 169–193.
———. (2014) "Kant and Race, Redux." *Graduate Faculty Philosophy Journal* 35, no. 1–2: 125–157.
Sellars, Wilfrid. (1963) *Science, Perception and Reality*. London: Routledge & Kegan Paul.
Wood, Allen. (1984) "Kant's Compatibilism," in Allen Wood (ed.), *Self and Nature in Kant's Philosophy*, Ithaca: Cornell University Press, pp. 73–101.

4
HEGEL ON RACE AND DEVELOPMENT

Frank M. Kirkland

Introduction

Previously, among other things, I argued that Kant's philosophy could serve as a warrant justifying the *first* view of King's famous phrase in his 1963 "I Have a Dream" speech, wherein we must (i) *cease pre-judging* people by their skin color or race and (ii) *begin judging* them solely by the substance of their character.[1] By so judging, we gauge the strength of their character in terms independently of the physiologically racial qualities and the emotional attachments thereto and instead give moral credit to actions done and beliefs held from their sense of duty and responsibility alone. The strength and "content of their character" would presuppose that attaching racial content to moral commitments is wrong and oppressive, and that human fidelities, neutral to race, blind to color, flourish, a state of affairs to which King himself is aligned. But there is a competing *second* view to which King is also aligned.

On the second view, King's speech does entail (i) full stop, but (ii) only to some extent. I say "to some extent" because, on this view, judging people by the "content of their character" would *not* foreclose judging them by their race, especially when judging people this way is done to acknowledge and affirm the socio-cultural and historical importance of whom and what they have or may become for social life (not to pre-judge, ascribe and derive the inferiority/superiority of their intellectual and moral competences from an invariant "substance" of their physiological features). If judgments about character or disposition were conducted wholly in race-neutral fashion and, hence, separated and inoculated from socio-cultural and historical factors pertinent to race, then judging people's character in this manner would appear to leave the strength or "content of character" problematically unrelated to some social and institutional life wherein race is morally or ethically salient.[2] As morally relevant, judging people by race can entail subjecting oneself to a norm with motivational pull and to heeding a kind of reason with discursive weight.

Despite his "I Have a Dream" speech, King was not wholly adverse to this second view. Indeed, in his 1967 text, *Where Do We Go From Here: Chaos or Community?*,[3] King emphatically praised the idea of "Black Power" for its moral affirmation of black self-determination and black self-regard, enabling black people "to sign with the pen and ink of assertive selfhood [their] own emancipation proclamation."[4] Yet, in the very same text, he strongly criticized that idea as ultimately conveying a "black nihilistic philosophy of despair."[5] Is a contradictory message on King's part being conveyed in this 1967 text? I shall not address this matter here.

Rather I seek to examine the philosophical salience of Hegel on the race-concept ("race") and, if any, on the contending views of the meaning of King's "I Have a Dream" speech. The second view appears to represent a Hegelian stance by affirming that we may judge people based on factors and attachments, such as racial ones, if and when they count as shareable reasons to assess and acknowledge another. It would be deemed Hegelian, because only under certain social arrangements and historical circumstances can we judge taking such factors and attachments as ethically salient reasons in considering and recognizing the content of a person's character.

Now in saying these things, I am *neither* expressing *nor* implying that King had read or was reliant on Hegel's thought for the whole or any part of his 1963 speech or 1967 text. I shall, in passing, make claims that the philosophy of Hegel can be brought to bear respectively on the second view of the meaning of King's refrain. But, in the main, this chapter makes and seeks to demonstrate two proposals. First, the philosophy of Hegel, concisely framed, can show the manners in which *normative* import can extend to the race-concept. Normatively Hegel's idealism does entitle, through his notion of "development," non-white people and their achievements to be construed historically within a normative framework. It does not support characterizing them as perennially unhistorical in an empirically tropistic context. Second, the philosophy of Hegel can serve to justify (i) and (ii) in King's refrain, as "developmentally" related, not as *self-standing alternatives*. Neither proposal is entertained in the literature. Furthermore my claim does not and will not preclude a discussion of Hegel's[6] controversial racial chauvinism, a discussion which has already been put forward in a variety of philosophical venues. Still, although "race" may carry normative weight on the basis of Hegel's philosophy, which can be brought to bear on the second view of King's speech, it prompts two points.

First, contrary to the attitudes of many scholars of Hegel to ignore his racial chauvinism, my claim will *not* involve defending, let alone implying, that Hegel's racial chauvinism is to be discounted in and by his own philosophy. My claim should *not* be taken as an apologetic for dispensing with or disregarding his racial chauvinism. Second, contrary to critics of Hegel on racial matters, I will *not* endorse or suggest that charting his racial chauvinism sufficiently thwarts his philosophy from denying (1) that enactments of people racially characterized are representative of inferior or superior intellectual and moral competences derived from the invariant "substance" of physiological attributes and (2) that black people are *not* historically expressive full stop. Demonstrating my claim requires a concise perspective on his thought, and neither an apologetic of his core commitments discounting his racial chauvinism nor a chronicling of it.

Hegel on Race and Development

The charge of racial chauvinism has been long-standing and still resonates against Hegel's philosophy and against the claims of others which reverberate with the racial chauvinism attributed to him.[7] Hegel's racism strongly resounds especially in the popular mind. If so, how could it even be possible to consider Hegel's philosophy, given the hoary yet legitimate charge of racial chauvinism attached to it, as underwriting what is the complex and complicated second version of the meaning of King's anaphoric refrain?[8] As we shall see, Hegel brings his own complexity to the race-concept as well as to King's refrain.

Regarding "race" and its racial cum racist ends, both in general and to blacks in particular, Hegel is best known by his claim that the indigenous inhabitants of Africa "do not have history in the true sense of the word."[9] Most believe that (1) Hegel's claim is based on his racial chauvinism and/or (2) the recent scientific and historiographical research on Africa has repudiated the claim's veracity. The former is, in some sense, true, about which more will be said below. Surprisingly, on the other hand, the latter is false, because Hegel's claim presupposes (a) an idealism whose *normative* benchmark distinguishes peoples who are "world historical" from those who are not and (b) some reflexive awareness on how and why that benchmark is met. Let me examine the latter stance first, due to its complexity.

For Hegel, that normative benchmark is the "idea of freedom" in spirit's self-conscious development. Self-consciously satisfying that benchmark, Hegel believes, is determinate of history's "purposive movement," is specific to the developmental advance of the "idea of freedom" for the sake of world history as reflected in certain cultural geographies and discerned in a certain kind of philosophical idealism. Hegel's normative benchmark is the criterion on which his claim that Africa's lack of history turns, and it is set within a peculiar kind of idealism through which the empirical evidence on Africa, even evidence obtained in the twentieth century through archaeological research and new historiographical methods,[10] must be gauged in terms of "spirit's self-determination in time under the idea of freedom." This means that Hegel denied Africa's historical relevance *normatively* and could do so even if it were affirmed scientifically.

Hegel would not deny the importance and development of the empirical sciences per se.[11] Their scientific significance in picking out and identifying those facts rendering Africa's reality as *unhistorical*, during Hegel's time, would be acceptable to him. But so would it be acceptable to him, given the past 75 years to the present, that their scientific significance has confirmed Africa's reality as *historical*. Nonetheless his idealism can affirm either side because, on its own grounds, Hegel would deny that, how, and why what is scientifically picked out and identified as evidence of, say, Africa's unhistorical or historical reality is normatively responsible for or normatively prohibits Africa from being considered as historical.

In short, his idealism would be untroubled by the outcomes and findings of the empirical sciences. Outside his idealism's normative benchmark, history is that solely elicited by what the empirical sciences and their methods deliver veridically about events as independent matters of fact or as some kind of causal outcome in their contact, in this case, with Africa's past. Inside it, such history is not rejected. However, for Hegel, it must be primarily reliant on people freely trying to give and share reasons for events they enact and discern themselves within an intersubjective context or a "cultural geography" whose norms sustain thinking and acting freely in an ongoing manner and govern such reasons even as they change and develop.

Some of these new historiographical methods would enable a comparison of, say, Africa's material development, environment, and resources with parallel information from other regions of the world, other populations. An example of such a comparison would be just what Jared Diamond did 20 years ago with extraordinary skill in his best-selling book *Guns, Germs, and Steel*, whose thesis he smartly encapsulated in his prologue: "History followed different courses for different peoples because of differences among peoples' environments, not because of biological differences among peoples themselves."[12]

If plied to Africa, Diamond's claim would place the movement of history in accord with persistently long-term environmental factors, but not with the "idea of freedom." Africa's history would not be construed as a purposive (Hegelian) movement of knowing and acting under the norm of freedom, but would rather be construed as a nonpurposive (Braudelian) movement of the "long (material) duration" (*la longue durée*) with which Diamond's conception of history would be largely consistent.[13] Hegel does not and would not deny that history followed different courses for different peoples because of the different long-term impact of varying geographic, climatic, and demographic constraints. But for the sake of the aforementioned normative benchmark and its resolution of how and why it is met or not, he needs rather to show that history, as a purposive movement, can follow different courses for different people because of the varying degrees, not of the uniformity, to which people developmentally frame their own cognitive and practical orientations under the idea of freedom.[14] What enables Hegel to take this position is his notion of "natural spirit."

Hegel's idealism leads him to characterize Africans, as he does all other peoples, in terms of "natural spirit," and this means the following. Indeed Africans are sentient human beings (in Kant's language, "pathologically affected beings") subject to the imperatives stemming from nature. But, at the same time, they take on those imperatives in a manner, if not eliminating them (at this stage), at least mitigating their immediate impact on them. Their initial steps lead to a position wherein the invocation of nature as a reason or warrant for an enactment gradually stops being cognitively or ethically appropriate for or useful to them. But they also lead to a position wherein reasons gradually represent improved successes of Africans justifying their enactments *without* recourse to nature. Since Hegel refers to Africans as "rational" by virtue of their "mastery of nature" via religion,[15] they would have to engage in enactments which can incrementally downplay the cognitive or ethical appropriateness of invocations of nature as reasons or warrants, and which simultaneously can upgrade incrementally the caliber of reasons or warrants in terms of what is proffered freely on their behalf to "master" nature progressively without reliance on nature.[16]

As Robert Pippin has claimed,[17] natural spirit refers to Hegel's incipient non-dualist position or compatibilism. It is, on the one hand, the sentience of spirit and, on the other, the impetus of spirit, wherein spirit gradually yet progressively (a) undoes, as a source of justification and truth for cognitive and ethical enactments, the natural determinations or sentience attached to them. In so doing, it (b) proceeds freely to sustain, ultimately in an ongoing way, the justification and truth of them as its own accomplishments and recognized as such. The full-fledged development of spirit is a people's self-developing and ongoing historical accomplishment, which reflects (a) an *ever-decreasing reliance* of its enactments, responsiveness to reasons, and self-understanding on invocations or appeals to nature's imperatives or explanations based on nature and (b) an *ever-increasing and, ultimately, ongoing reliance* of them on the self-enacted sanctioning and reflective approval of the reason-giving and reason-sharing influence pertaining to them.[18]

Failure to recognize this point, I believe, is the unavoidable mistake that is pervasive in the argument using scientific advancement and realism pertinent to Africa to criticize Hegel's *normative, not empirical* claim that Africa has no history. It is a mistake believing or expecting (1) that Hegel's claim is empirical and (2) that history elicited in the former sense provides the independent "truth maker" as the remedy to Hegel's claim.[19] Even though the former sense empirically would either confirm or disconfirm Africa's lack of historical status, it would also render moot or illusory the idea that the enactments and discernments of Africans were, at least in part, freely undertaken, leaving the impression, if not certifying, that their enactments and discernments, their cognitive and practical orientations, were more tropistic than not.

For Hegel, history elicited in the normative sense is history "in the true sense of the word," is "the record of spirit's efforts to achieve knowledge of what it is in itself, i.e., freedom" and "hence knowledge of freedom as its sole purpose."[20] It is then spirit's account of how a certain conception of freedom comes to be significantly widespread and extensively significant in its own development. This is what Hegel's conception of history is about. Its course can be briefly construed as that wherein a people knew and lived through their enactments that only *one* was free, to a people who knew and lived through their enactments *some* were free, to a people who knew and lived through their enactments that *all* are free in an ongoing manner.[21]

Like Kant, Hegel distinguishes the conceptual jurisdiction of nature from that of freedom wherein, according to Hegel, "spirit" receives its significance and to which it is identified. But, unlike Kant, Hegel does *not* argue that they are irreducible, that a transition from one to the other needs be made, and that the moral demands subject to the latter jurisdiction ought to be effectuated in this world. Rather Hegel concedes that they cannot be reducible to each other as long as spirit differentiates itself and progressively continues to do so away from the conceptual jurisdiction of nature such that moral demands under its own jurisdiction *ought* to become effectuated, not ultimately, but *developmentally* in this world.

Hegel claims that Africans are "enmeshed in natural spirit."[22] Such a claim is not a racial disparagement of them.[23] Africa's indigenous or diasporic populations cannot be regarded as naturally unable of or ontologically contrary to this self-development, as most are prone to say,[24] as if the impetus of spirit is permanently absent in African peoples. Rather their self-development under both (a) an *ever-decreasing reliance* of its enactments and responsiveness to reasons on appeals to nature's imperatives or explanations based on nature and (b) an *ever-increasing and, ultimately, ongoing reliance* of them on the reason-giving and reason-sharing influence pertaining to them is not fully in effect. It is not fully actualized in their practices or enactments, and is still provisionally reliant, at least in part, on making reference to nature's imperatives as a warrant for explaining their practices and enactments.

Africans then are regarded as without historical relevance in Hegel's idealism, because their enactments, responsiveness to reasons, and self-understanding, for the time being, lead back, more often than not, to their warrant of them in terms of appeals to nature, to their warrant of them as more "naturalistic" than not. Their enactments and discernments discount, in Hegelian parlance, their *"negative relation"* to their own appeal to nature, to their own natural spirit, a "negative relation" that Hegel regards as an incipient expression of freedom. Consequently, in the context of Hegel's idealism, Africa as a cultural geography "vanishes" from history in the normative sense, but not necessarily in the empirical one. Within his idealism, Hegel could concede the former while affirming the latter. So Africans would have a history, empirically and scientifically so, but *not* normatively so, that is, as people acting fully under the idea of freedom.

Thus we have jumped from the frying pan into the fire. We have shown that Hegel's claim that "Africa is unhistorical" *cannot* be an empirical one. He is not claiming that being unhistorical is that which Africa empirically is. But that now puts us in the position to see that Hegel's claim that "Africa is unhistorical" is normative. He is claiming that "Africa is what it must and should be, viz., unhistorical." Does that mean that there cannot be constitutively and regulatively any experience and rationality of the indigenous inhabitants of Africa and those of its diaspora to delineate in terms of the idea central to Hegel's idealism, namely, people thinking and acting under the "idea of freedom?" If so, there is at least one thing for certain—King's anaphoric refrain could *never* have Hegel's idealism as a possible warrant.

But since I am of the mind that Hegel's idealism can serve as a possible warrant for King's refrain, the question to ask is how should the relation of Hegel's philosophy to "race" generally, to blacks particularly, be ascertained? A conclusion different from the prior one needs be reached, a conclusion Hegel himself never made, but a conclusion which Hegel's idealism could embrace, which would affirm that blacks *do not and ought not "vanish"* from history in the normative sense. To make this point, we need to return to Hegel's conception of "natural spirit" as his explicit entry into "race."

We have shown "natural spirit" to be that wherein spirit is increasingly less susceptible to treating its reasons and cognizance of them as effects, signs, or sets of natural causes or inclinations and increasingly more reliant on its reasons and cognizance of them as stemming from its own developmental orientation and away from nature as an explanatory source. This point emphasizes *that and how* spirit is differentiated from nature. But there is another point of emphasis. The spiritual differentiation from nature is *variable, not uniform*, when it is employed in terms of the *degree and extent* to which spiritual differentiation from nature occurs at any given time. *Hegel uses the degree and extent to which such differentiation occurs to distinguish human groups racially, ethnically, and geographically in a cultural sense.*[25]

Regarding this second point of emphasis, Hegel is *not* making a case for the possible belief that some relatively fragile sense of freedom is subordinate to some weighty determinism in force, as can be practically found, but not morally endorsed, say, in Kant. Rather Hegel is trying to make a case for how this normative idea of freedom is pertinent to the manifestation of "race" as something *achieved*, even progressively so, and as something *neither* constantly naturalized *nor* necessarily expunged morally. And Hegel attempts to demonstrate this point by referring to "natural spirit" in terms of "racial differentiation or variety," in short, Hegel's racialism.[26]

Most contemporary philosophers have come to understand, through K. Anthony Appiah, racialism as a doctrine to be dismissed or a doctrine that ought *not* to be tightly embraced.[27] It is, for Appiah, the doctrine that

> there are heritable features, possessed by members of our species, that allow us to divide them into a small set of races in such a way that all the members of these races share certain traits and tendencies with each other that they do not share with members of any other race.[28]

In short, it is the doctrine affirming the existence of races, a doctrine, Appiah maintains, is false. Appiah's contention is that, under racialism, the "traits and tendencies" definitive of a racial singularity constitutes the singularity's "racial essence." What this means is that the visibly natural morphological features of a singularity are not simply inessential and contingent, but racially indispensable and constant features, establishing them as the essential and necessary racial differences among singularities, not as the ancillary and superficial attributes they are. Consequently the constancy of the racial features of each singularity is the perennially ontological order and reality a singularity racially ensouls and embodies. And Hegel, according to Appiah, is among those who had subscribed to this false doctrine.[29]

Although Hegel subscribes to racialism, he would not need to be wedded to Appiah's account of it. Appiah's account requires that "race" refers to an animal organism comprising of singularities already distinguished from and opposed to each other, all subject to the same human genus, but each differentiated by its own racial essence. There would then be a given variety of races each essentially instantiated by its own racial type. Hegel's account, on the other hand, would require that "race" refers to an animal organism, but whose singularities, subject to the same human genus, are the differential outcomes of each singularity's impetus for distinguishing itself from another through its habits, dispositions, and location as well as coming to recognize this act of distinguishing as its own.[30] There would then be a distinctive variety wherein racial singularities are not tokens or instantiations of racial type, but unique racial singularities. Nowhere do Hegel's account of racialism and its variety of racial singularities embrace or entail a racial essence for defining the singularity of a racial group.

Racial singularities sustain "race," for Hegel, as "natural spirits" (*Natürgeister*),[31] movements of spirit discernible in natural and geographical limits, limits that mark the degree in which "race" is connected to the variable development of racial singularities minimally or not. They are groups of sentient, human beings, the variety of which is manifest geographically and the identities of which are differentially conveyed less by some particular sentient feature(s) that marks them essentially than by particular accomplishments conveyed in their distinctive habits, rituals, and socialized emotional dispositions. Despite their sentience, they manifest the degree and extent each develops, i.e., "spiritually" distances its accomplishments (habits, rituals, emotional dispositions) as responses to nature's imperatives. For Hegel, it is the accomplishments of this development that differentiate and diversify across racial singularities and within them, differentiating and diversifying what counts as "race" in terms of singularities freely expressing a concept that cannot but motivate its realization in a context leading to all being free in ongoing fashion. In short, in comparison to Kant, racial singularities, without "natural spirit," would have natures, but would not have histories.

Hegel does believe that racial singularities develop differently, unevenly, and to different degrees over time. Nowhere does Hegel argue for the equality of them; nowhere does his idealism embrace this view. Yet we should not confuse Hegel's views on the comparative levels of development among racial singularities with the stages of development themselves. The developmental stage of any given racial singularity must be variable. A racial hierarchy may be rigid but, by virtue of any racial singularity's accomplishments ("movement of spirit"), the stages of development cannot be and, to that extent, the hierarchy cannot be constantly in stasis. In short, a racial group's development cannot be fixed. If this were to hold, even Hegel's idealism would have to allow that all human beings, including Africans, are sufficiently able to develop the impetus of spirit further away from nature's course.

That is to say, if dark skin color, a certain physiognomy, and a geographical location in equatorial Africa are fixed characteristics, physiologically and geographically, they are not evidence of a fixed and unalterable boundary to a racial singularity's enactments and its capabilities to advance with reason its enactments even further from nature's imperatives under the auspice of freedom. Although Hegel himself compromises this view, his argument for this position is to be found in his discussion of what he calls "peoples," "nations," or "national spirits" (*Nationgeister*),[32] what I believe we would call today "ethnicities," that is, culturally organized groups within races each minimally bearing some political aim grounded in the cultivated relevance of their habits and dispositions.

Some have contended that, for Hegel, this suggests a move from racial differentiation (difference/diversity across racial singularities) to ethnic differentiation (difference/diversity within them), a contention Bernasconi holds valid. Indeed, Bernasconi maintains that this move allows Hegel to displace "race" with "people," enabling Hegel to remove Africans (as well as other peoples of color) from any connection to history.[33] As Bernasconi recognizes, Hegel denies any connection of the idea of different "peoples" to Africa, claims the diversity of peoples is absent in "Africa proper," while affirming both the connection of this idea to Europe and the diversity of peoples within it. In short, Hegel regards Africa totally and solely as a racialized continent wherein Africans are, in Hegel's words, an "undifferentiated and concentrated unity."[34] Calling all blacks or Africans "negro," without any reference to ethnicities or to "national spirits," is the case in point as well as compromising, to say the least, the pertinence of "natural spirit" to Africa and its diaspora.

As a consequence, Bernasconi ascribes a chauvinistic "racial basis" to Hegel's notion of world history, excluding all but Caucasians from being historical subjects in the full sense, insofar as only Caucasians can be characterized in terms of peoples.[35] He notes that Hegel states, "the philosophy of history has the world-historical significance of *peoples* as its subject matter."[36] The allusion is that "peoples" have such significance, not races, and seems to confirm the aforementioned suggestion that ethnic differentiation (*national spirit*) displaces racial differentiation (*natural spirit*) at the level of history. So not only does Bernasconi give very little credence to the idea of freedom, affirmed in Hegel's idealism, as a normative benchmark for assessing a racial singularity's contribution to world history. But he also takes seriously Hegel's employment of the displacement of "race" as a necessary criterion for ascribing such a singularity's contribution to and role in world history as well as its members' enactments under the idea of freedom. Any singularity construed without this displacement of "race" cannot be construed ethnically and under that idea. As a consequence, "race" cannot be historically significant.

However, Bernasconi misses a major point. Hegel goes further in the aforementioned quotation concerning history and peoples. "If we take 'world history' in its broadest sense, such significance will be the highest development achieved by the original disposition of the national character, the most spiritual form achieved by the *natural spirit dwelling within nations*."[37] Natural spirits (races) are not displaced. They are still operative in "peoples." Nations are fused with natural spirit and thereby still "racialized." Races and ethnicities, natural and national spirits, overlap each other.

As "ethnicized," a race may differentiate or diversify into a number of ethnicities or "peoples."[38] Ethnicities of a racial singularity differentiate from each other, cultivating the degree and the extent to which each incrementally advances its rationality further from natural imperatives under the auspice of freedom. Ethnicities, each with distinct yet deep habits of heart, of mind, of body, may belong to the same racial singularity. But, since the achievements obtained by an ethnicity in the "movement of spirit" vary in each racial singularity, there is variability in stages of development. Stages of development would vary within different ethnicities of a racial singularity *and* across the ethnicities of different racial singularities. Although Hegel himself delineates neither with respect to Africa, nothing precludes his idealism from doing so.

"Race" then does not appear to be displaced by the notion of "people" in Hegel's idealism. Again "race" does not refer to a sentient group which simply embodies its nature and geographical habitat as an immediate response to nature's imperatives. It refers rather to a sentient group defined by (a) a way of being habitually disposed, not immediately responsive, toward the appropriateness of something naturally or geographically influential and (b) members' openness to the variety in taking up this way of being habitually disposed and thereby being responsive, each in their own specific way, to the relevance of these natural and geographical influences in representing what members do. There is no (a) without (b) and vice versa.

But neither (a) nor (b) are immediately natural responses to natural stimuli or steps in the natural maturation of a sentient being toward its natural end. Otherwise they would be in the service of natural processes significant to the species' perpetuation. Expressing a "negative relation," they rather lend themselves, at least minimally, to rising above such processes, to (c) being understood as self-ascriptions, in the sense of commitments to be acknowledged (by both oneself and others), and open to further development over time (even to the point of being challenged and revised if unsuccessful in the interim.) The "movement" of (a) through (c) conveys the cultivated differentiation of spirit from natural spirit, a cultivated differentiation incrementally reflecting spirit's own autonomous outcome and embodied in ethnicized races historically and gradually reflecting the degree and magnitude of this cultivated outcome in different ethnicized races historically.

As an ethnicized racial singularity then, black "people" would be neither naturally precluded in full from that "movement" of historically expressing its cultivated difference gradually from nature nor would they be historically precluded in full by the degree and extent it carries out this cultivation. They would be "spiritually" limited pro tem or "spiritually" ongoing in that "movement." Their cultivated difference would have to be in some magnitude and in some variably qualitative way part of the historical narrative of spirit, and the degree and extent of carrying out that cultivation would be open incrementally to expression in that historical narrative.

Hegelian Postscripts

Most Hegel scholars such as Alfredo Ferrarin, Robert Pippin, and Michael Wolff[39] have focused their scholarly attention exclusively on natural spirit's first sense, in which it is employed in terms of *that and how* spirit is differentiated from nature, but *not* on its second sense, in which it is employed in terms of the *degree and extent* to which spirit is differentiated from nature. It is its second sense wherein Hegel distinguishes human groups racially and geographically. This is why Hegel's racialism is non-existent in their otherwise very thoughtful analyses.

Most critics of Hegel's intellectual treatment of racially non-white "peoples" of color believe the non-existence of Hegel's racism in the discourse of current Hegel scholarship reveals the indifference of Hegel scholars to this matter, to their silence on it, since Hegel scholars do not regard his treatment of it as having any resonance, one way or the other, on Hegel's philosophy generally. But, with the exception of Allegra de Laurentiis and Michael Hoffheimer, they do not focus either on natural spirit at all or on Hegel's racialism as stemming from the second sense of natural spirit. Or, as most do, they identify automatically Hegel's racialism with his racial chauvinism. This is why it is not unusual for critics to claim that Hegel regards Africans as so immersed in nature that its spiritual impetus and cultivation never get off the ground, so to speak, or are non-existent. Rather than take, on the basis of natural spirit, the variable degree and extent of Africans' cultivated differentiation from nature as a limited pro tem spiritual accomplishment yet open to an incrementally normative development historically, they are taken exclusively as invariant natural attributes, as natural and physically geographical determinations, of Africans full stop. And this position serves as the basis for the contention, falsely in my mind as I have argued above, that Africans were without any real (empirical) history in Hegel's philosophy.

So Hegel scholars have revealed the importance of "natural spirit" to Hegel's idealism without assessing the racialism attached to it; critics of Hegel have drawn out the racial chauvinism in Hegel's racialism without examining "natural spirit" as that to which Hegel's racialism belongs. Each side emphasizes one sense of it the other neglects, despite the philosophical commitment in his idealism to both senses. I have, to the contrary of each side, assessed both notions and their importance.

Again Hegel's first sense of "natural spirit" is employed in terms of *that and how* spirit is differentiated from nature. His second sense is employed in terms of the *degree and extent* to which spirit is differentiated from nature. He uses that second sense to distinguish human groups racially and geographically. This is the source for the charge of Hegel's racism, although those who make this charge against Hegel rarely, if ever, mention "natural spirit," let alone understand it. Hegel wants, I believe, to claim that the greater or lesser the degree and extent spirit is differentiated away from nature expresses how great or less the strength of a group's *incipiently rational motivation, not natural capacity,* to comprehend or enact what counts as objective, moral, and desirable under the idea of freedom. But, to the contrary, Hegel's remarks on this second sense of "natural spirit" leaves his critics with the strong belief that the degree and extent to which a group "spiritually" differentiates or distances itself from nature are reliant on the natural racial kind and geographical features of the group. As a consequence, the degree and extent of the group's spiritual differentiation away from nature are, for Hegel's critics, *less an accomplishment and more an attribute* of the group, thus undermining his conception of spirit itself.

Contrary to Hegel scholars, I am neither stating nor implying that Hegel's racialism or racial chauvinism is irrelevant to Hegel's enterprise as a whole. Contrary to Hegel critics, I am neither stating nor implying that registering Hegel's racial chauvinism is sufficient to prevent Hegel's idealism from holding the field against the positions that African enactments are representative of invariant natural attributes or they are not historically expressive, even minimally so.

What has been done so far is more fully flesh out and finely adjust the sense of "natural spirit" in terms of "racial variety" or Hegel's "racialism." In so doing, an argument can be credibly made, supported by Hegel's idealism, that, under the auspice of freedom, Africans are ethnically differentiated; that they advance incrementally, in varying degrees, not just their habits and social dispositions as well as their cognizance of them within reason from nature's imperatives, but also advance incrementally beyond their habits and the sedimentation of the acquired positivity of ethno-racial membership. The conceptual space has now been cleared for elaborating on Africa's history, but now in terms of satisfying in full Hegel's normative benchmark—spirit's self-determination in time under the auspice of freedom. A form of African life, in which only one, and no other, is free, gives way to another form of African life, in which ultimately one is and thereby all are free in ongoing fashion, namely, that which motivated, for example, the Saint Domingue Revolution (SDR).[40]

The impact of Kant's notion of "transition" on "race" is quite different from that of Hegel's concept of "development" (*Entwicklung*) on it. In Kant's philosophy, "race" and its purported racist ends are matters whose empirical reality reliant on scientific certification is subject to the conceptual jurisdiction of nature. But his "transition" to the conceptual jurisdiction of freedom makes their reality and credential as (a) conceivably irrelevant to the moral demands of the species, or (b) hopefully quashed in their moral foreclosure, or (c) effectively eliminated in this world guided by what morality proclaims what ought to be done. With the "transition" to the conceptual jurisdiction of freedom, in short, "race" and its racist ends are to be morally expunged categorically. This is why, as stated above, Kant's philosophy could underwrite the first view of King's refrain via (b) or (c).

With Hegel, on the other hand, "race" and its purported racist ends are matters of spirit, meaning that their explanatory impact would fall increasingly less under the conceptual jurisdiction of nature. They rather would be open to revision developmentally under the conceptual jurisdiction of freedom by which spirit is entailed. This means, to make a very long story very short, the following. The intelligibility of "race" is increasingly *not* dependent, at least in large part, on "race's" acquisition of empirical reality and/or scientific certification, thereby justifying the first-order truth of the natural place in the hierarchy it attaches to and sets as the natural end of a group. Rather it is increasingly dependent on the propriety of being subject to self-conscious warrant to enable and sustain with reason what counts as its first-order truth, especially when what counts periodically peters out, is from time to time no longer motivationally effective. An ethno-racial singularity is developed by the conditions of an individual's degree of attachment to what counts as "race" in ongoing, not repetitive, ways expressive of the caliber of reasons shared in a context wherein one is free, and thereby all are free. Admittedly these remarks sound theoretically flamboyant, especially (a) since Hegel's notion of "development" appears to be nothing more than a dab of blush when plied to Africa and its diaspora, and rather flaccid, especially (b) since Hegel never expressly made them.

Sylvia Wynter tags the consequences of what could be called Hegel's theoretical histrionics in her well-known essay, "Is 'Development' a Purely Empirical Concept or Also Teleological?: A Perspective From 'We, the Underdeveloped.'"[41] She argues that the notion of development is culturally specific, not culturally neutral, whose genesis and structure are subject to the "Western epistemological order," in which an understanding of African "traditional system of thought" would remain entrapped. Briefly the strategies of development implemented today to remedy Africa's long-standing and ever-deepening economic and ecological crisis, she contends, have been and still are reliant primarily on that epistemological order. According to Wynter, given this crisis, Africa and its diaspora have been called upon, time and again, to acquiesce to both "development" along material (empirical) and normative (teleological) lines they do not and would not prescribe for themselves. For Wynter, such has been their history, both in empirical and in normative terms.

The consequence of such acquiescence is that Africa and its diaspora are made to experience themselves as the "*massa damnata* (those not elected for salvation),"[42] always coupled to the narrative of "development" as "we, the underdeveloped." In effect, Wynter is highly incredulous of "development" at work along material lines (modernization) and development at work in over-ambitious philosophies of history with their affirmation of "faith in uninterrupted progress" as the horizon for human beings, especially for those of African descent.

Although a more sophisticated analysis of Wynter's essay cannot be presented here, it is clear that her skepticism to "development" would extend toward Hegel's, given its emphasis on progress. But there are a number of points that must be kept in mind regarding Hegel's conception of "development." First, Hegelian "development" is *not* natural maturation or growth to a natural end state, because it is operative only in spirit. Second, it is *not* advancement to an end state of perfection or to something utopian, materialist or otherwise, because of the indeterminacy surrounding perfection. Third, it is *not* eschatology leading to a divine end state, involving some dramatic transcendent incursion consummating the history of the world from the outside, because it proceeds arduously, gradually and internally via the giving and sharing of reasons, if not struggles.

As Hegel puts it, "development in the spiritual world is at once a hard and unending struggle with itself... hard and strenuous labor on itself."[43] A retrospective dimension is to be had in Hegel's conception of "development." It is found neither in Wynter's skeptical account nor in the three aforementioned conceptions. Her account and those conceptions do not tally "development's hard and strenuous labor on itself." What people of African descent as ethno-racial singularities thought, desired, and did, and why they thought, desired, and did it in the face of colonialism or enslavement and their aftermaths, would be outcomes of "development" for Hegel only *following* their grasp and reconstruction of what they were dedicated to enacting, recognized or unrecognized, as their thoughts, desires, and deeds. Those oppressive institutions can never be justified, given their real historical role in the impediment to the human self-development and material development of people of African descent. But they may not preclude for Hegelian "development" other institutions consistent with people of African descent being free *if and only if* that consistency is ever defended in a manner wherein even the assumption, not just the claim, of privilege and disparity is non-existent and not in force.[44] "Race" is reconstructed as it "develops" not as a concept to be made empirically real or factually true, but as a concept to be made normatively fulfilling with good, salient reasons.[45]

What spirit counts as a first-order truth objectively, obligatorily, and desirably not only can be unsuccessful as models of experience, but its effort to abide these models can reveal only in retrospect its periodic incapability to sustain the ongoing alteration of them and their authority. Hegel's idealism admits that the ongoing alteration, not the constant reauthorization by nature or positivity, of what is counted by a people (or an ethno-race) can be regarded as yielding better outcomes of what counts than those of and in previous periods of time. But what this signifies is that a great number of matters that could count do not. This would be due not *solely* because of what has happened to people (ethno-racial singularities), or what people do not consider or comprehend or have not considered or comprehended, but inclusively because of what people have not let themselves consider or comprehend for the time being.

The ongoing alteration of what people count can be sustained only when each and all as individuals are free, ubiquitously recognized by other free individuals, and hence set in a context which abides the flourishing of such self-determination and recognition. In Hegel's idealism, "change [or alteration of what counts] is [not progress, but] a form of progress"[46] to and for the sake of freedom. History becomes the sequence of such changes to a stage wherein alteration of what counts is an unending affair, because what counts as reasons at any period can peter out or cannot be sustained. "Race" as a bona fide concept of spirit can both give way incipiently and give sway ultimately to ongoing revisions of reasons salient to individuals to acknowledge and evaluate the relation of its content to character under normatively historical conditions. That relation is attendant to ethno-racial singularities pertinent to the development of a "spiritual" or socially constructed life in which all are free. The second version of King's anaphoric refrain would find support in this Hegelian idealistic point.[47]

Let me end this chapter with my paraphrase of a claim by Michel Foucault. In his 1970 installation to the chair of "History and Systems of Thought" at the Collège de France, he did two things in his "Inaugural Lecture." He (a) dedicated it to the noted French Hegelian and existentialist Jean Hyppolite, despite his own anti-Hegelianism and anti-existentialism, and (b) criticized the philosophical position most prominent in France at the time—structuralism—despite what was alleged to be his attachment to and sentiments for it. My paraphrase thereof indexes below a philosophical position prominent at this moment.

Most people working in critical race theory or Africana Philosophy "flee or dismiss Hegel [and Kant]" because of the disparaging and disconcerting remarks [both have] made about peoples of color or because of a customary indifference to them as philosophers. "But truly to escape Hegel [and Kant would] involve an exact appreciation of the price we have to pay to detach ourselves from [them.]" "The appreciation of this price [would] assume that we are aware of the extent to which Hegel [and Kant], insidiously perhaps, [are] close to us; it [would] imply knowledge, permitting us to think against Hegel [and Kant]. . . . We [would] have to determine the extent to which our anti-Hegelianism [and anti-Kantianism are] possibly [each one's] tricks directed against us, at the end of which [they] stand, motionless, waiting for us."[48]

Notes

1 The first view is addressed in the chapter "Kant on Race and Transition" in this volume.
2 A proponent of this view would be Cornel West who, in arguing against the "pitfalls of racial reasoning" (pseudo-authenticity, closing-ranks mentality, male subordination of women), still makes a case for a "prophetic moral reasoning" wherein *"the moral content of a mature black identity* [coincides with] accenting the crucial role of coalition strategy in the struggle for justice and promoting the *ideal of black cultural democracy.*" See his *Race Matters* (Boston: Beacon Press, 1993), 31 (my emphasis).
3 See Martin Luther King Jr., *Where Do We Go From Here: Chaos or Community?* (Boston: Beacon Press, 2010), 23–69.
4 King, *Where Do We Go From Here*, 44.

5 King, *Where Do We Go From Here*, 46–47.
6 For representative discussions on *Hegel's racialism*, see Robert Bernasconi, "With What Must the Philosophy of World History Begin? On the Racial Bias of Hegel's Eurocentrism," *Nineteenth-Century Contexts* 22 (2000): 171–201; Allegra de Laurentiis, "Race in Hegel: Text and Context," in *Philosophie Nach Kant: Neue Wege zum Verstandnis von Kants Transzendental- und Moral-Philosophie*, ed. Mario Egger (Berlin: DeGruyter, 2014), 591–624; Michael Hoffheimer, "Race and Law in Hegel's Philosophy of Religion," in *Race and Racism in Modern Philosophy*, ed. Andrew Valls, 194–216 (Ithaca: Cornell University Press, 2005) and "Hegel, Race, Genocide" in *Southern Journal of Philosophy* 39 (2001): 35–62; Frank M. Kirkland, "Hegel and the Saint Domingue Revolution—Perfect Together?: A Review of Susan Buck-Morss' *Hegel, Haiti, and Universal History*," *Logos: The Journal of Modern Society and Culture* (online) 11, no. 2–3 (2012): n.p.; Patricia Purtschert, "On the Limit of Spirit: Hegel's Racism Revisited," *Philosophy & Social Criticism* 36, no. 9 (2010): 1039–1051.
7 See the speech of the recently former president of France, Nicolas Sarkozy, titled "Dakar Speech," July 26, 2007. For critical responses to the speech, see Makhily Gassama, ed., *L'Afrique répond à Sarkozy* (Paris: Philippe Rey, 2008).
8 The discussion in this essay will be conveyed from the vantage point of Hegel's idealism and not *exclusively* from his "Geographical Basis of World History" as is usually done. It will attend to his conception of "natural spirit," on which his discussion about Africa and its diaspora should turn.
9 Georg Wilhelm Friedrich Hegel, *Lectures on the Philosophy of World History: Introduction*, trans. Hugo Barr Nisbet (Cambridge: Cambridge University Press, 1975), 190, hereinafter cited as *LPWH*.
10 Jan Vansina, *De la tradition orale: essai de method historique* (Tervuren: Mémoire no. 36 du Musée Royal de l'Afrique Centrale, 1961); Basil Davidson, *Africa in History*, rev. ed., (New York: Simon & Schuster, 1995); John Thornton, *Africa and Africans in the Making of the Atlantic World, 1400–1800* (Cambridge: Cambridge University Press, 1992); Jacqueline Ki-Zerbo, ed., *General History of Africa, Vol. I: Methodology and African Prehistory* (Berkeley: University of California Press, 1981); Roland Oliver and Brian Fagan, *Africa in the Iron Age* (Cambridge: Cambridge University Press, 1975); Thurstan Shaw et al. (ed.), *The Archaeology of Africa: Foods, Metals, and Towns* (New York: Routledge, 1993); David Phillipson, *African Archaeology* (Cambridge: Cambridge University Press, 1993); Joseph H. Greenberg, *The Languages of Africa* (The Hague: Mouton, 1966); John Reader, *Africa: Biography of the Continent* (New York: Knopf, 1998).
11 See Georg Wilhelm Friedrich Hegel, *The Encyclopedia Logic*, trans. T. F. Geraets, W. A. Suchting, and H. S. Harris (Indianapolis: Hackett, 1991), 33, sec. 9. Furthermore, Hegel would not speak against any empirical science supporting the race-concept.
12 Jared Diamond, *Guns, Germs, and Steel* (New York: Norton, 1997), 25.
13 Fernand Braudel, *Civilisation matérielle et capitalisme* (Paris: A. Colin, 1967), 17.
14 For another position regarding geographical influence and the idea of freedom, see David Harvey, *Cosmopolitanism and the Geographies of Freedom* (New York: Columbia University Press, 2009).
15 Hegel, *LPWH*, 179. "Man knows only himself and his opposition to nature, and this is the *sole* rational element which the African peoples recognize. They acknowledge the power of nature and attempt to raise themselves above it."
16 Whereas Kant would characterize these enactments under "skill" and "discipline," still empirically conditioned and dependent on naturalized freedom, Hegel would characterize them as outcomes stemming from a need to decrease dependence on nature and a motivation to refine such a need freely and increasingly.
17 See Robert Pippin, "Naturalness and Mindedness: Hegel's Compatibilism," *The European Journal of Philosophy* 7, no. 2 (1999): 194–212. See a similar, but more expansive, essay in his *Hegel's Practical Philosophy: Rational Agency as Ethical Life* (Cambridge: Cambridge University Press, 2008), 36–64.
18 See Georg Wilhelm Friedrich Hegel, *Philosophy of Subjective Spirit, Vol. 1* (with German text), trans. and ed. M. J. Petry (Dordrecht: D. Reidel, 1978), 7, hereinafter cited as *PSS, Vol. 1*. "These are the two aspects [of spirit's impetus]. Yet if we inquire into what spirit is, the direct answer is that it is this movement, this process of moving straight away from, freeing itself from nature" (translation altered; my addition).

19 This failure can also be found both in arguments using anti-racism and in arguments affirming the existence of material and civilizational advancement in Africa to criticize Hegel's claim.
20 Hegel, LPWH, 54–55.
21 Hegel, LPWH, 54–55.
22 Hegel, LPWH, 190.
23 An example of Hegel's racially disparaging remarks would be the following:

> [M]an as we find him in Africa has not progressed beyond his immediate existence... All our observations of African man show him as living in a state of savagery and barbarism, and he remains in his state to the present day. The negro is an example of animal man in all his savagery and lawlessness, and if we wish to understand him at all, we must put aside all our European attitudes. We must not think of a spiritual God or of moral laws; to comprehend him correctly, we must abstract from all reverence and morality, and from everything we call feeling. All this is foreign to man in his immediate existence, and nothing consonant with humanity is to be found in his character.

See Hegel, LPWH, 177. In Kantian language, Africans would be "pathologically necessitated," not "pathologically affected," racially in Hegel's eyes. But these remarks do not even allude to characterizing Africans in terms of "natural spirit."

24 Representative of this view, but in a sophisticated way, is the impressive work by Michel-Rolph Trouillot, *Silencing the Past: Power and the Production of History* (Boston: Beacon Press, 1995), 72–95, hereinafter cited as Trouillot. See also Pierre-Franklin Tavares, "La Conception de l'Afrique de Hegel comme critique" ["Hegel's Conception of Africa: A Critique"], *Chemin Critiques* 2, no. 2 (1991): 153–166.

25 These two points connect "race's" natural spirit to the recent spate of, say, "bio-social" or social-natural accounts of "race," which either correlate social categorization of "race" to the geo-histories of breeding populations or give biological content to "race's" social categorization. But whereas bio-social accounts address *ontologically* how and why "race's" social categorization must be attached to biological genealogy or to biological content for scientific utility or medical purposes in examining peoples or their members, natural spirit addresses *normatively* how and why "race's" social categorization must "increasingly *not* rely on" (Hegel) or "infinitely transcend" (Du Bois) that attachment for the sake of explaining its differences in terms of its achievements as outcomes of freedom. For such "bio-social" accounts, see Philip Kitcher, "Does 'Race' Have a Future?," *Philosophy and Public Affairs* 35, no. 4 (2007): 293–317 and Quayshawn Spencer, "What 'Biological Racial Realism' Should Mean," *Philosophical Studies* 159, no. 2 (2012): 181–204. In examining social-natural accounts, Paul Taylor addresses *pragmatically* ethno-racial singularities (distinguishing racial groups from racial breeding populations) in terms of having "we-intentions." The question to Taylor, under Hegelian lights, would be—to what extent? See Paul Taylor, *Race: A Philosophical Introduction* (New York: Polity Press, 2003), 103–104. An earlier work that *phenomenologically* addressed the "bio-sociality" of "race" is Lucius Outlaw's *On Race and Philosophy* (New York: Routledge, 1996).

26 See Georg Wilhelm Friedrich Hegel, *Philosophy of Subjective Spirit*, Vol. 2 (with German text), trans. and ed. M. J. Petry (Dordrecht: D. Reidel, 1978), 44–83, § 393–394, hereinafter cited as PSS, Vol. 2.

27 For racialism's dismissal, see Kwame Anthony Appiah, "Racisms," in *Anatomy of Racism*, ed. David Theo Goldberg (Minneapolis: University of Minnesota Press, 1990), 4–5; in contrast, for its needed slackening, see "Race, Culture, Identity: Misunderstood Connections" in Kwame Anthony Appiah and Amy Gutmann's *Color Conscious: The Political Morality of Race* (Princeton: Princeton University Press, 1998), 104.

28 Appiah, "Racisms," 5.
29 Appiah, "Racisms," 5.
30 See Hegel, PSS, Vol. 2, 44–93, §§ 393–395.
31 Hegel, PSS, Vol. 2, 44–49, § 393.
32 Hegel, PSS, Vol. 2, 64–67, § 394.
33 Bernasconi, "With What Must the Philosophy of World History Begin? On the Racial Basis of Hegel's Eurocentrism," 187–188.

34 Hegel, *LPWH*, 177.
35 Bernasconi, "With What Must the Philosophy of World History Begin?," 171.
36 Hegel, *PSS, Vol. 2*, 67, § 394.
37 Hegel, *PSS, Vol. 2*, 67, § 394.
38 On this point, Hegel would appear to have something in common with both Linda Martín Alcoff and David Theo Goldberg, who themselves prefer the notion "ethnorace" rather than "race." The difference, however, between Alcoff and Goldberg, on the one hand, and Hegel, on the other, is that the former takes seriously, albeit does not affirm, the idea that "race" refers to visible physiological markers and "ethnicity" refers to matters of cultural identity. Alcoff and Goldberg subscribe to "ethnorace" to reconcile problems produced by the difference between the referents of the two notions. For Hegel, a race cannot be understood without ethnicity and vice versa. Both are matters of spirit. There is no immediate difference between the notions' referents to reconcile, because the two notions mediate each other. For Hegel, the intelligibility of one requires the intelligibility of the other. See Linda Martín Alcoff, *Visible Identities: Race, Gender, and the Self* (Oxford: Oxford University Press, 2006), 246 and David Theo Goldberg, *Racist Cultures: Philosophy and the Politics of Meaning* (Oxford: Blackwell, 1993), 74–77.
39 See Alfredo Ferrarin, *Hegel and Aristotle* (Cambridge: Cambridge University Press, 2001), 234–283; Pippin, "Naturalness and Mindedness"; and Michael Wolff, *Das Körper-Seele-Problem: Kommentar zu Hegel, Enzyklopädie (1830) § 389* (Frankfurt: Klostermann, 1992). An exception may be Terry Pinkard, who appears *not* to discount the second sense. See his *Hegel's Naturalism* (New York: Oxford University Press, 2012), 64–68 and 81–82 n.55.
40 For a view expressing the impossibility of such a conceptual space for the enactment of the SDR under Hegelian auspices, besides Trouillot, *Silencing the Past*," 97, see Susan Buck-Morss, *Hegel, Haiti, and Universal History* (Pittsburgh: University of Pittsburgh Press, 2009) and Pierre-Franklin Tavares, "Hegel et Haiti ou le silence de Hegel sur Saint-Domingue" ["Hegel and Haiti—Or Hegel's Silence on Saint-Domingue"] in *Chemin Critiques* 2, no. 3 (1992): 113–131. For a view expressing, contrariwise, the possibility thereof, see Frank M. Kirkland, "Hegel and the Saint Domingue Revolution—Perfect Together?: A Review of Susan Buck-Morss' *Hegel, Haiti, and Universal History*."
41 Sylvia Wynter, "Is 'Development' a Purely Empirical Concept or also Teleological?: A Perspective from 'We the Underdeveloped,'" in *Prospects for Recovery and Sustainable Development in Africa*, ed. A. Y. Yansané (Westport, CT: Greenwood Press, 1996), 297–316.
42 Wynter, "Is 'Development' a Purely Empirical Concept or also Teleological?," 305.
43 Hegel, *LPWH*, 127.
44 For a position that may be contrary to the one above, but still would respect the importance of some kind of Hegelian development on the African continent, see the excellent book by Olúfẹ́mi Táíwò, *How Colonialism Preempted Modernity in Africa* (Bloomington: Indiana University Press, 2010).
45 Again this conclusion is not drawn from Hegel himself. But it is responsive to two claims made by Hegel. First, it is important to keep Hegel's famous, albeit elusive, remark in mind—"philosophy's task is to be its own time comprehended in thoughts"—when philosophically commenting on "race." Second, this point becomes more important when it is recognized that Hegel, in his *LPWH* (190), stated that he would forgo historical diagnosis of the Americas, because spirit's long and hard developmental work had not yet taken hold. For us, that would mean developmental work on "race" had not been done. Hegel passed away in 1831, so it would be quite simple to conclude that Hegel proffered nothing like what I attribute to his idealism. But it can be argued that the "spiritual" development of "race" in the Americas was picked up by and took off from the works of Antenor Firmin, Anna Julia Cooper, W.E.B. Du Bois, Alain Locke, and C.L.R. James, indeed less so with Firmin's positivist anthropology, Cooper's feminist social epistemology, and Locke's critical pragmatism and more so with Du Bois' historically interpretive sociology and James' theoretically concomitant avowal of the importance of Hegel's dialectic and allegiance to Marxian theory for peoples of color and their histories. Examining the Black Atlantic intellectual tradition for ascertaining and seeking to complete a comprehension of "race" through, not against, Hegel is a topic for another essay.

46 Hegel, *LPWH*, 128 (my additions).
47 Although it cannot be done here, Hegel's notion of spirit and its specific form of development can be regarded as a *strong* precursor to and *stronger* in comparison with the notion of "social construction." "Social construction" is construed and pursued in terms of how we have acquired or been taught the social conventions by which the objectivity, propriety, and desirability of "*x*" is thought and acted upon. Spirit, on the other hand, is that which construes and pursues in thought and action "*x*" on the basis of freely expressed and shared reasons in the face of the grounds of "*x*" collapsing or expiring with no guarantee (metaphysical, natural, or conventional) to uphold the objectivity, propriety, and desirability of "*x*" other than the caliber of reasons to sustain or innovate them effectively.
48 Michel Foucault, *L'ordre du discours* (Paris: Éditions Gallimard, 1971), 74–75. See also Michel Foucault, "The Discourse on Language," in his *Archaeology of Knowledge*, trans. Rupert Swyer (New York: Pantheon Books, 1972), 235 (my additions; translation altered).

References

Alcoff, Linda Martín. (2006) *Visible Identities: Race, Gender, and the Self*, Oxford: Oxford University Press.
Appiah, Kwame Anthony. (1990) "Racisms," in David Theo Goldberg (ed.), *Anatomy of Racism*, Minneapolis: University of Minnesota Press, pp. 3–17.
———. (1998) "Race, Culture, Identity: Misunderstood Connections," in Kwame Anthony Appiah and Amy Gutmann (eds.), *Color Conscious: The Political Morality of Race*, Princeton: Princeton University Press, pp. 30–104.
Bernasconi, Robert. (2000) "With What Must the Philosophy of World History Begin? On the Racial Bias of Hegel's Eurocentrism." *Nineteenth-Century Contexts* 22: 171–201.
Braudel, Fernand. (1967) *Civilisation matérielle et capitalisme*, Paris: A. Colin.
Buck-Morss, Susan. (2009) *Hegel, Haiti, and Universal History*, Pittsburgh: University of Pittsburgh Press.
Davidson, Basil. (1995) *Africa in History*, revised edition, New York: Simon & Schuster.
de Laurentiis, Allegra. (2014) "Race in Hegel: Text and Context," in Mario Egger (ed.), *Philosophie Nach Kant: Neue Wege zum Verstandnis von Kants Transzendental- und Moral-Philosophie*, Berlin: DeGruyter, pp. 591–624.
Diamond, Jared. (1997) *Guns, Germs, and Steel*, New York: Norton.
Ferrarin, Alfredo. (2001) *Hegel and Aristotle*, Cambridge: Cambridge University Press.
Foucault, Michel. (1971) *L'ordre du discours*, Paris: Éditions Gallimard.
———. (1972) "The Discourse on Language," in Michel Foucault (ed.), *The Archaeology of Knowledge*, trans. Rupert Swyer. New York: Pantheon Books, pp. 215–238.
Gassama, Makhily. (ed.) (2008) *L'Afrique répond à Sarkozy*, Paris: Philippe Rey.
Goldberg, David Theo. (1993) *Racist Cultures: Philosophy and the Politics of Meaning*, Oxford: Blackwell.
Greenberg, Joseph H. (1966) *The Languages of Africa*, The Hague: Mouton.
Harvey, David. (2009) *Cosmopolitanism and the Geographies of Freedom*, New York: Columbia University Press.
Hegel, Georg Wilhelm Friedrich. (1975) *Lectures on the Philosophy of World History: Introduction*, trans. Hugo Barr Nisbet, Cambridge: Cambridge University Press.
———. (1978a) *Philosophy of Subjective Spirit*, Vol. 1 (with German text), trans. and ed. M. J. Petry. Dordrecht: D. Reidel.
———. (1978b) *Philosophy of Subjective Spirit*, Vol. 2 (with German text), trans. and ed. M. J. Petry. Dordrecht: D. Reidel.
———. (1991) *The Encyclopedia Logic*, trans. T. F. Geraets, W. A. Suchting, and H. S. Harris, Indianapolis: Hackett.
Hoffheimer, Michael. (2001) "Hegel, Race, Genocide." *Southern Journal of Philosophy* 39: 35–62.
———. (2005) "Race and Law in Hegel's Philosophy of Religion," in Andrew Valls (ed.), *Race and Racism in Modern Philosophy*. Ithaca: Cornell University Press, pp. 194–216.
King, Martin Luther, Jr. (2010) *Where Do We Go From Here: Chaos or Community?* Boston: Beacon Press.

Kirkland, Frank M. (2012) "Hegel and the Saint Domingue Revolution—Perfect Together? A Review of Susan Buck-Morss' *Hegel, Haiti, and Universal History.*" *Logos: The Journal of Modern Society and Culture* (online) 11, nos. 2–3: n.p.

Kitcher, Philip. (2007) "Does 'Race' Have a Future?" *Philosophy and Public Affairs* 35, no. 44: 293–317.

Ki-Zerbo, Jacqueline. (ed.) (1981) *General History of Africa, Vol. 1: Methodology and African Prehistory*, Berkeley: University of California Press.

Oliver, Roland, and Fagan, Brian. (1975) *Africa in the Iron Age*, Cambridge: Cambridge University Press.

Olúfẹ́mi, Táíwò. (2010) *How Colonialism Preempted Modernity in Africa*, Bloomington: Indiana University Press.

Outlaw, Lucius. (1996) *On Race and Philosophy*, New York: Routledge.

Phillipson, David. (1993) *African Archaeology*, Cambridge: Cambridge University Press.

Pinkard, Terry. (2012) *Hegel's Naturalism*, New York: Oxford University Press.

Pippin, Robert. (1999) "Naturalness and Mindedness: Hegel's Compatibilism." *European Journal of Philosophy* 7, no. 2: 194–212.

———. (2008) *Hegel's Practical Philosophy: Rational Agency as Ethical Life*, Cambridge: Cambridge University Press.

Purtschert, Patricia. (2010) "On the Limit of Spirit: Hegel's Racism Revisited." *Philosophy & Social Criticism* 36, no. 9: 1039–1051.

Reader, John. (1998) *Africa: Biography of the Continent*, New York: Knopf.

Sarkozy, Nicolas. "Dakar Speech." *Speech*, July 26, 2007.

Shaw, Thurstan, Sinclair, Paul, Andah, Bassey, and Okpoko, Alex (ed.). (1993) *The Archaeology of Africa: Foods, Metals, and Towns.* New York: Routledge.

Spencer, Quayshawn. (2012) "What 'Biological Racial Realism' Should Mean." *Philosophical Studies* 159, no. 2: 181–204.

Tavares, Pierre-Franklin. (1991) "La Conception de l'Afrique de Hegel comme critique" ["Hegel's Conception of Africa: A Critique"]. *Chemin Critiques* 2, no. 2: 153–166.

———. (1992) "Hegel et Haiti ou le silence de Hegel sur Saint-Domingue" ["Hegel and Haiti—Or Hegel's Silence on Saint-Domingue"]. *Chemin Critiques* 2, no. 3: 113–131.

Taylor, Paul. (2003) *Race: A Philosophical Introduction*, New York: Polity Press.

Thornton, John. (1992) *Africa and Africans in the Making of the Atlantic World, 1400–1800*, Cambridge: Cambridge University Press.

Trouillot, Michel-Rolph. (1995) *Silencing the Past: Power and the Production of History*, Boston: Beacon Press.

Vansina, Jan. (1961) *De la tradition orale: essai de method historique*. Tervuren: Mémoire no. 36 du Musée Royal de l'Afrique Centrale.

West, Cornel. (1993) *Race Matters*, Boston: Beacon Press.

Wolff, Michael. (1992) *Das Körper-Seele-Problem: Kommentar zu Hegel, Enzyklopädie (1830)*, Frankfurt: Klostermann.

Wynter, Sylvia. (1996) "Is 'Development' a Purely Empirical Concept or also Teleological? A Perspective From 'We the Underdeveloped,'" in Aguibou Y. Yansané (ed.), *Prospects for Recovery and Sustainable Development in Africa*. Westport, CT: Greenwood Press, pp. 297–316.

5

HEIDEGGER'S SHADOW

Levinas, Arendt, and the Magician From Messkirch

Jonathan Judaken

We gave Heidegger the nickname "the little magician from Messkirch." . . . His lecture technique consisted in building up an edifice of ideas, which he then proceeded to tear down, presenting the spellbound listeners with a riddle and then leaving them empty-handed.
                                                                Karl Löwith (2001: 34–35)

To treat Martin Heidegger, Emmanuel Levinas, and Hannah Arendt together on the topic of race is to tell a family story. All family histories, especially those about race, are about legacies and inheritance. Heidegger was not only Arendt's and Levinas's professor, but their key intellectual influence, impacting their lives as well as their philosophy. When Heidegger publically sided with Nazism, they were upended. This chapter considers how Levinas and Arendt both thought within but also sought to move beyond "Heidegger's shadow": his tutelage, his approach to the Western metaphysical and philosophical tradition, and his support of Nazism.

Heidegger's "Hitlerism," to use Levinas's formulation, was undergirded by the legacy of the German *völkisch* tradition, which was framed by a specific ethnocentric and Eurocentric trajectory. Rejecting Heidegger's *völkisch* thought and his ethnonationalism, Arendt and Levinas nonetheless shared his Eurocentrism. This caused them at times to get lost in his shadow, tripping like Dante in a dark wood, repeating racial stereotypes and typecast racial tropes. But Heidegger also opened a new path in philosophy that sought a destructuring (*Destruktion*) of Western metaphysics. This helped spur Levinas and Arendt to confront the heritage of Western race thinking. Levinas's ethical project focused on the infinite responsibility for the Other, violated by the racism immanent in Western thought. Arendt historicized the stream of modern European ideas and institutions linking anti-Semitism, imperialism, totalitarianism, and genocide. This chapter traces the intellectual legacies of Heidegger, Levinas, and Arendt by mapping how scholars have addressed the debates about Hitlerism, race and racism, Jews and Judeophobia, the Holocaust and genocide, and the ethics and politics in their work.

JONATHAN JUDAKEN

Racing Heidegger's Shadow

The shadow of Heidegger's relationship to Nazism haunts the scholarship of his views on race. This is because in April of 1933, shortly after Hitler's assumption of the chancellorship and amid the political restructuring of education, Heidegger maneuvered to obtain the post of rector of the University of Freiburg. He was elected to the position on April 21 and delivered his Rectoral Address on "The Self-Assertion of the German University" on April 27. It was replete with references to the *Führerprinzip* couched in some of his philosophical formulations (Heidegger 2003 [1933]: 2–11). In May 1933, Heidegger sent a telegram to Hitler expressing solidarity with the recent *Gleichschaltung* legislation that promised to align the university with the official policies of the Third Reich. This included enforcing the anti-Semitic laws that banned Jews from all government service, including university life. Known as the Baden Decree, it was implemented to purge the "Jewification of the Universities." It meant that Edmund Husserl, the founder of phenomenology and Heidegger's benefactor, was now removed as professor emeritus, forbidden from even using the university library. He was one among 1,600 Jewish professors expunged. Commenting on this in a letter to Karl Jaspers, Arendt noted painfully, "I cannot but regard Heidegger as a potential murderer" (Arendt and Jaspers [1992]: 48). She and Levinas were at once "distraught, and philosophically instigated by Heidegger's Nazi turn" (Moyn 1998: 23).

Heidegger's Nazi turn, however, requires us to separate a set of overlapping themes: Heidegger's views on race, his *völkisch* thought, and the relationship between his philosophy and National Socialism. The latter debate has become known as "the Heidegger Affair" and has gone through several waves. The issue was first deliberated in France in 1946 and 1947 in *Les Temps modernes*, and then in more scattered discussions from 1948 to 1987 (Kleinberg 2012: 386–413). It became a major affair in France in the immediate aftermath of the publication of Victor Farías' dossier *Heidegger et le nazisme* in 1987. Farías's text was responded to between October 1987 and May 1988 with the publication of a series of books on the topic by some of France's most prominent philosophers: Jean-François Lyotard, Luc Ferry and Alain Renaut, Jacques Derrida, Pierre Bourdieu, Philippe Lacoue-Labarthe, and in a flurry of subsequent radio and television programs and magazine and journal articles in France and internationally (Wolin 1988; Sheehan 1988; Rockmore 1995). More recently, Emmanuel Faye published the most extreme indictment yet of Heidegger, *L'introduction du nazisme dans la philosophie: Autour des séminaires inédits de 1933–1935* (Faye 2009). Faye insists that Heidegger's Nazism infuses all of his philosophy and that there is consequently nothing redeemable in his thought. The latest cascade of considerations has resulted from the publication of Heidegger's *Schwarze Hefte*, or "Black Notebooks," his handwritten reflections penned in small black diaries (Trawny 2014; Wolin 2014; Gordon 2014; Faye 2014).

Heidegger's relationship to Nazism is no less complicated than Nazi views on race. The problem with much of the literature on race and the Nazis of which the debates about Heidegger are a part is that often Hitler's statements in *Mein Kampf* and elsewhere are taken as the template for this discussion. Hitler claimed that all of life was a struggle for existence governed by rigid biological laws, where victory depended upon racial purity, and the rootless Jew was the personification of evil. But following in the footsteps of the pioneering scholars of Nazi culture like Fritz Stern (1961) and George Mosse (1981 [1964]), intellectual historians including Anson Rabinbach and Sander

Gilman have noted the pliability and broad range of positions articulated in the name of race and the *Volk* by adherents to one version or another of Nazi ideas:

> Nazi ideology had its roots in a broad array of *völkisch*, anti-Semitic, and pseudo-scientific ideas put forward during the nineteenth century, including social Darwinism, eugenics, pan-Germanism, Aryan mysticism, and extreme nationalism. But it never developed a consistent or officially prescribed doctrine.... Despite Hitler's frequent claim that "National Socialism is a worldview," even the leading ideologues of the movement—like Rosenberg, Krieck, Goebbels, and Hitler himself—showed little consensus about what this worldview encompassed.
>
> (2013: 107)

Race talk was consequently central to the Nazi message, but what anchored this message was variable, veering from biology to religion to more diffuse notions of spirit or cultural essence. There was a malleability and plasticity to notions of *Volk* and *Rasse* that were contested, sifted, reassessed, and rearticulated in the process of defining the national community (*Volksgemeinschaft*). Judeophobia functioned within this toxic mix as what Shulamit Volkov (1978) famously designated "a cultural code": the conspiratorial anti-type to the *Volk*, embodying the rootless foreigner and the exploitative, materialist, and threatening shadow of modernity. What was key for the Nazis was that *Volk* and race were the terms in which the discussion of identities were deliberated because it was as such that the Nazi racial state extended its power. It was less important to the Nazis that a fixed definition of race coagulated.

Heidegger's letters, diaries, speeches, essays, and lectures have to be understood in this broader frame, as well as within the philosophical debates of the era. Even before the Black Notebooks, we knew of Heidegger's Judeophobia and his use of *völkisch* idioms. In 1929, for example, he had penned a letter to Victor Schwoerer, director of the Bureau of Universities of the Ministries of Public Education, in which he noted:

> We are confronted by a crucial choice: Either to infuse, again, our German spiritual life with genuine indigenous forces and educators, or to leave it at the mercy, once and for all, of the Jewish contamination [*Verjudung*], both in a larger and a narrower sense.
>
> (2003: 1)

He concluded by saying how he took great pleasure "in seeing my work deeply rooted in our native soil" (Heidegger 2003 [1929]: 1). The example is pointed since Jewification (*Verjudung*) and rootedness were the two key antipodes of *völkisch* thought.

The Black Notebooks now show more clearly than ever that "during the 1930s and 1940s Heidegger was wholly obsessed with Bolshevism, National Socialism, and the ignoble actions of 'World Jewry' (*Weltjudentum*), as represented by Western powers such as England and the United States" (Wolin 2014: 40). They are replete with the stock and trade of anti-Semitic stereotypes. Heidegger notes, for instance:

> Contemporary Jewry's ... increase in power finds its basis in the fact that western metaphysics—above all, in its modern incarnation—offers fertile ground for the dissemination of an empty rationality and calculability, which in this

way gains a foothold in "spirit," without ever being able to grasp from within the hidden realms of decision.

(Wolin 2014: 42)

He jots elsewhere that "the tenacious aptitude for calculating and profiteering and intermingling, upon which the worldlessness of Jewry is founded" contributes to the hidden form that "machination" (*Machenschaft*) takes in modernity (Gordon 2014). As Adorno explained about how stereotypes work in *The Authoritarian Personality*, "Jewry" functions in the Black Notebooks as the personification of the targets of Heidegger's thinking—Western metaphysics, calculative rationality, technology, and capitalist modernity—serving as the progenitors of those values in the nation-states that competed with Germany.

While his reign as a Nazi official ended when he resigned as rector in April 1934, Heidegger still continued to end classes by saluting Hitler, proclaimed "the inner truth and greatness of the movement" in 1935, and he remained in the Nazi party until 1945. But to understand what this meant to him in terms of Nazi racial politics, we can turn to his lectures to gain a clearer sense of his public position on *Rasse* and *Volk* in this period. Robert Bernasconi's "Heidegger's Alleged Challenge to the Nazi Concepts of Race" is a good guide because he provides an attentive reading of Heidegger's shifting position alongside the work of other Nazi philosophers writing on the topic (Bernasconi 2000). In elucidating Heidegger's position, Bernasconi also critiques past scholarship, including works by Julian Young, Pascal David, Berel Lang, and Tom Rockmore. He does so by focusing on the debate about the relevance of Heidegger's lack of "biologism": the fact that Heidegger did not subscribe to a biologically based understanding of race. This focus, Bernasconi shows, occludes a more finely grained understanding of Heidegger's position on race, one attuned to how it reverberated in the lecture halls and in the philosophical debates of the Nazi period.

For Bernasconi, Julian Young's book *Heidegger, Philosophy, Nazism* (1997) stands in a long line of Heidegger's apologists who separate Heidegger's politics and prejudices from his philosophy. Young's defense of Heidegger's racism maintains that because Heidegger was critical of biological racism, and since racism is always biological, Heidegger was no racist. To Young, "spiritual racism" is a self-contradiction. Young's dualism thus pulls apart biology and spirit to serve his *apologia*; the racial and the spiritual are separated further in Pascal David's defense of Heidegger where he "dissociates Heidegger's conception of *Volk* from that of race by identifying it as spiritual" (Bernasconi 2000: 53).

Bernasconi next considers Berel Lang and Tom Rockmore, who each agree that Heidegger may have critiqued biological racism, but that he still adhered to what Lang terms "metaphysical racism" (1996). Through a reading of Heidegger's lectures on Nietzsche in the late 1930s, Bernasconi suggests three things. First, that Lang's concept of "metaphysical racism" is derived from Nietzsche's work. Second, "Heidegger's lectures on Nietzsche are the main site of Heidegger's public confrontation with the extreme forms of Nazi racial thought in the late 1930s" (2000: 57). In these lectures, Heidegger sought to go beyond the appropriations of Nietzsche by Social Darwinian and racist Nazi philosophers who used Nietzsche to justify racial hygiene and eugenics, most perniciously Alfred Baeumler. In doing so, Heidegger was critical of one important philosophical strand of Nazi racism. Third, Bernasconi reminds readers that for Heidegger, Nietzsche was the culmination of Western metaphysics. Bernasconi provocatively suggests that race thinking likewise is an aspect of Western metaphysics, which remains a problem yet to be overcome, and that perhaps Heidegger's critique of Western metaphysics can be bent in this direction.

Sonia Sikka's chapter "Heidegger and Race" in *Race and Racism in Continental Philosophy* (2003) adds a cautionary caveat to Bernasconi's arguments. Sikka concurs that Heidegger's views on race were not congruent with the picture we get of Hitler's biologism in *Mein Kampf* or in the Social Darwinian philosophical racists like Baeumler. She discusses Heidegger's lectures on "Logic as the Question Concerning the Essence of Language" in 1934, Heidegger's lectures on Holderlin in 1934–1935, and on Nietzsche in 1936. She confirms Bernasconi's (and Heidegger's own retrospective claims) that in these lectures one sees a progressive critique of National Socialist biological racism. This much of Heidegger's own story about his relationship to the Nazi movement holds up (Heidegger 2003 [1966]).

But contra Bernasconi, she maintains that Heidegger's reading of Nietzsche was congruent with some Nazi appropriations, since Heidegger had an essentialist conception of the German *Volk*, a claim that Bernasconi has responded to in his most recent take on these issues (Bernasconi 2010). Sikka details how Heidegger dovetails with certain strands of *völkisch* ideology: always insisting on the unity of the *Volk* and using the language of landscape, heritage and destiny as categorical for thinking about the historical/cultural formation of peoples, which Heidegger consistently thought of as unitary. Sikka thus neatly synthesizes Heidegger's views on race:

> In sum, while Heidegger did not support, and indeed opposed, any biologically based concept of race, he held a strong view of the unity and identity of every particular *Volk*. This view included the idea that each people has a single, unique character and destiny and a set of obligations rooted in that character and destiny.
>
> (2003: 87–88)

Sikka concludes that there is nothing intrinsically racist about Heidegger's *völkisch* thought: he didn't ever place groups into a hierarchy and argue that some were superior, only that some had a unique mission and that the Germanic mission was tied to its language and its role within the history of Europe, which linked the Germans and Greeks. She maintains this view was Eurocentric and it could feed cultural racism, but it need not.

While this is true, reinserted into its political context, it did. Steven Ashheim (1992) indicates this in his masterly reception history *The Nietzsche Legacy in Germany, 1890–1990*. Aschheim maintains that when Karl Löwith first penned "The Political Implications of Heidegger's Existentialism," which is what sparked the whole Heidegger Affair in its first incarnation in 1946, he indicated what intellectual historians like Aschheim have repeatedly insisted upon: "the perception of decline and impending European catastrophe . . . was not an idiosyncratic Heideggerian whim, but part and parcel of the post-1914 radical-right stock-in-trade, integral to the conservative revolutionary mentalité" (Ashhheim 1992: 264). Understanding Heidegger's views on race entails situating Heidegger within this *mentalité* of which he was a part, and retracing how it played out in the Nazi era. It is as such that we can understand his political choices, but also central aspects of his *Technikkritik* (his critique of modern technology), his criticism of calculative rationality, and his condemnation of capitalist modernity. *Völkisch* thought had long identified these traits with Jewish attributes. This *völkisch* tradition could abjure biologism all it wanted, but within the Nazi state its cultural racism was one strand that legitimated Nazi state policy on the Jewish question.

Levinas After Heidegger's Hitlerism

As Jewish students of Heidegger, Levinas's and Arendt's views on race are usefully understood as studies in the "anxiety of influence." As Richard Wolin maintains in *Heidegger's Children*, his "children sought to philosophize *with Heidegger against Heidegger*, thereby hoping to save what could be saved, all the while trying to cast off their mentor's long and powerful shadow" (2001: 7–8). The literature on Levinas bears out this burden. Now entering its third generation, the first commentators were elucidators, translating and trying to understand Levinas's notoriously difficult formulations (Drabinski 2011: xiv–xv). Levinas worked within the phenomenological tradition set by Husserl and Heidegger to establish the key axioms of his own philosophy, which from his earliest postwar writings to his final work concern the question of alterity (Otherness): existence as confronting the alterity of Being as horror; time as alterity; God as alterity; and most centrally the other person as irremediably Other (*autrui*), but whose existence demands hyperbolic responsibility, which is constitutive of the Self.

A second generation of scholars, animated by the early analysis of Levinas's work by Derrida, concentrated on the questions of the alterity of language, and the gender of Levinas's Other. They also sought to understand Levinas's relationship to Heidegger's thought, as well as Levinas's Jewish writings in relation to his phenomenological work (Morgan 2007). The present generation of scholars has drawn attention to this relationship from a new angle, by explicitly considering Levinas's views on race. Bernasconi (2005) first teased out the problem in another seminal article titled "Who Is My Neighbor? Who Is the Other? Questioning 'the Generosity of Western Thought.'"

Originally published in 1992, this was a groundbreaking analysis of Levinas's views on race, since Bernasconi framed the issue in terms of the relationship between ethnics and ethics in Levinas's thought. To appreciate the stakes of this discussion it is useful to revisit the text where Levinas marks his break with Heidegger: "Reflections on the Philosophy of Hitlerism" (1990b [1934]). While Heidegger's name is unmentioned in the original, it is clearly signaled in Levinas's "Prefatory Note" that accompanied the English translation in 1990:

> The source of the bloody barbarism of National Socialism lies not in some contingent anomaly within human reasoning, nor in some accidental ideological misunderstanding . . . [but rather by] the essential possibility of *elemental Evil* into which we can be led by logic and against which Western philosophy had not sufficiently insured itself. This possibility is inscribed within the ontology of a being concerned with being . . . to use the Heideggerian expression.
>
> (1990b: 63)

In "Reflections on the Philosophy of Hitlerism," Levinas subverts Heidegger's own effort to exit from Western metaphysics via ontology. He insists instead upon an ethical impulse at the foundation of "Western civilization"—an impulse that he identifies with

Judaism—and that the philosophy of Hitlerism sought forcibly to eliminate. For Levinas, Hitlerism was a product of an autoimmune deficiency syndrome within "Western civilization," that needed to (re)connect to ethics as its first principle.

Levinas maintains that Hitlerism sought to snuff out this Jewish impulse by radicalizing the materialism of the Enlightenment. National Socialism picked up on an insight of Socialism, which was an extension of Enlightenment principles, but located it within the Nazi vision of *völkisch* nationalism. The body was now firmly fixed in nature, and seen to determine psychological life, our temperament, our activities, and our feelings of identity. Spiritual strivings were themselves located in the body, the blood, heredity. Race determined nature, which defined destiny. As such, Levinas concluded "Reflections on the Philosophy of Hitlerism" by stating, "It is not a particular dogma concerning democracy, parliamentary government, dictatorial regime, or religious politics that is in question. It is the very humanity of man" (1990b: 71). Unfurling the full significance of this last line would preoccupy the rest of his life. But as early as 1934, he maintained that Hitlerism revealed a problem constitutive of "Western civilization," whose currents were either congruous with National Socialism or constitutionally immune to adequately confronting its racism.

Bernasconi's article probes whether the Other in Levinas's thought is a figure for pure transcendence or whether Levinas's concept cross-circuited with figures of Jews and Judaism, as well as his understanding of anti-Semitism, which he universalizes, as he does in "Reflections on the Philosophy of Hitlerism." Another good example of this universalization is his dedication to *Otherwise Than Being or Beyond Essence* (1981 [1974]): "To the memory of those who were closest among the six million assassinated by the National Socialists," wrote Levinas, "and of the millions on millions of all confessions and all nations, victims of the same hatred of the other man, the same antisemitism." Considering a number of texts that stretch from 1934 to 1974, Bernasconi interrogated Levinas's views on race by considering whether he reiterated the abstract humanism and claims to colorblindness that legitimated the French Third Republic's defense of colonial expansion. He also considers the tensions between Levinas's critique of Western philosophy in works like *Totality and Infinity* and *Otherwise Than Being* with Levinas's simultaneous celebration of Western culture in some of his other writing. In *Totality and Infinity*, Levinas argued that Western philosophy has a long history of totalizing thought, subsuming difference within a totalitarian and imperial gaze. But in a set of short articles and interviews, like "Meaning and Sense" (1964) among many others, Levinas celebrated Western culture's ability to understand other cultures better than they could understand themselves. This point has become a key bone of contention among scholars.

A decade after Bernasconi's article, in a section of his *Levinas and the Political* titled "Threatening Others," Howard Caygill laid out some of the key signposts for Levinas's slips on racial Others that portended a clear problem in his views on race and their links to "Western civilization." These stopping points have now become the key focus of scholars rethinking Levinas's work from a decolonial or postcolonial perspective (Caygill 2002). In a cluster of statements, Levinas set in opposition "Afro-Asiatic Civilizations and Western Tradition" (Lin 2008). Caygill (2002) terms Levinas's "Dialectics and the Sino-Soviet Quarrel" (1960) his "ugliest and most disturbing published work." It was written in the context of the Sino-Soviet split in the 1960s. In it, Levinas urges that "Russia" (not the Soviet Union, which was the state involved at the time) should ally with Europe, and defend itself against Asia. In a line that damns the text, Levinas writes "The yellow peril! It is not racial, but spiritual. Not about inferior values but about a radical strangeness, strange to all the density of its past, where no voice with a familiar inflection comes through: a lunar, a Martian past" (1994: 108). Asia is here consigned to an orientalist alterity.

The statement was not a one-off. In "Jewish Thought Today," an essay from 1961 included in *Difficult Freedom*, a collection of his Jewish writings, he stipulates as one of the three factors shaping Jewish philosophy, "the rise of countless masses of Asiatic and underdeveloped peoples. . . peoples and civilizations who no longer refer to our holy history, for whom Abraham, Isaac and Jacob no longer mean anything" (Levinas 1990a: 165). In "Beyond Dialogue" from 1967, Levinas called for Judeo-Christian solidarity in the face of the "innumerable masses advancing out of Asia. In the eyes of these crowds who do not take holy history as their frame of reference, are we Jews and Christians anything but sects quarrelling over the meaning of a few obscure texts" (Levinas 1999: 83). Strung together this mesh of statements evinces a nasty tendency to reiterate the formulas of Eurocentrism and orientalism, statements that are echoed in interviews.

The work of John Drabinski and Nelson Maldonado-Torres are indicative of the new current of scholarship on Levinas probing the tension between his critique of Western thought and his Eurocentrism. In a historiographic article, "Levinas's Hegemonic Identity Politics, Radical Philosophy, and the Unfinished Project of Decolonization" (2008) Maldonado-Torres rips into the Levinas cognoscente. He targets scholars who refuse to slam Levinas's Judeocentrism, his Zionism, and his Eurocentrism, which he treats as congruent.

Maldonado-Torres nonetheless draws on Levinas's critique of European hegemonic thought as imperial and totalizing: "Levinas articulates his critique," he writes, "in terms of the primacy of being, power, the ego, conflict, self-preservation, and war, all of which can be useful in understanding colonization" (Maldonado-Torres 2012: 86–87). This is a point he enlarges in *Against War* (2008). But he is critical of Levinas, insisting that his Eurocentrism does not permit "the geography of reason" to shift into alignment with the global South, something made possible by thinkers like Enrique Dussel and Frantz Fanon, whom he triangulates with Levinas to forge his argument in *Against War*.

In *Levinas and the Postcolonial: Race, Nation, Other*, John Drabinski elaborates the point. Drabinski argues that Levinas's radical responsibility to the Other as the core of his work is "critical for thinking in a postcolonial context." However, he also argues that Levinas's philosophy must be "uncoupled" from his "problematic conception of Europe." For Drabinski, it is "Levinas's concern with the meaning and future of Judaism" that "seals his work, especially with its Europeaness, in the particularity of a geography of ideas" (Drabinski 2011: x–xii). Like Maldonado-Torres, he maintains that links between Judeocentrism, Eurocentrism, and Zionism delimit Levinas's thought.

Oona Eisenstadt and Santiago Slabodsky push back on Maldonado-Torres and Drabinski and their new trinity. They insist that Levinas's reflections on Judaism can be and were marshaled as part of a decolonial critique. In his "Emmanuel Levinas's Geopolitics: Overlooked Conversations Between Rabbinical and Third World Decolonialisms," Slabodsky concurs that Levinas's "pre-1970s writing does not appear to qualify Levinas as anything other than a partisan of Eurocentrism." But Slabodsky maintains that beginning in the mid-1970s, there is "strong textual evidence of Levinas's growing openness to decolonial thinking" (2010: 148), a point he elaborates in *Decolonial*

Judaism: Triumphal Failures of Barbaric Thinking (2014). Eisenstadt also assents with the critiques of Levinas's Eurocentrism, but nuances them by showing that "it might help to remember that the reason Levinas admires Europe is because he sees its culture as the one most open to self-criticism." European philosophy not only rationalized racism, she explains, but also spoke to Europe's "historical failings," serving as its "bad conscience." Or as Levinas puts it, some European thought pits "Europe against Europe" (Eisenstadt 2012: 45–46). Eisenstadt demonstrates how Levinas, too, can be used to think against himself in this way. She concludes that Levinas's Eurocentrism "is at odds with a better Levinas . . . the potentially anti-Eurocentric openness to alterity that we find as the main thrust of his thinking" (Eisenstadt 2012: 51).

The core of Levinas's philosophy was the project to deconstruct Western metaphysics and with it the reduction of the human Other in race thinking. What Eisenstadt claims about Levinas's Eurocentrism can be repeated *mutatis mutandis* about his Zionism. Levinas's Jewish writings particularize and ethnicize what he elsewhere articulates in phenomenological and ontological categories. Jews and anti-Semitism were his "optic" through which he viewed more universally the problem of alterity. In each case, the face of the Other who demands a response and thus calls us to our responsibility stands as a critique of the efforts in the West to petrify or assimilate or eviscerate alterity, including in Levinas's own thought, where one finds those "threatening Others" who he identified as opposing a Judeo-Christian, Western heritage, itself somewhat reified.

Race Thinking and Racism in Arendt

Levinas and Arendt were twin critics of the stream of Western history that resulted in totalitarianism, racism, empire, anti-Semitism, and genocide. Robert Eaglestone makes this case in a short article subtitled "Arendt and Levinas After Heidegger": "Arendt's and Levinas's work complement each other: while Arendt's work 'looks out,' as it were to the effects of the subterranean stream, Levinas's 'looks in' to explain and critique its internal dynamic" (Eaglestone 2007: 206). Despite the differences of emphasis—Arendt's focus on politics, Levinas's emphasis on ethics; their competing interpretations of Heidegger; and their different views on Israel—Eaglestone usefully maintains that each sought to "reframe" the Heideggerian legacy that led to Heidegger's Nazism, Judeophobia, and *völkisch* ethno-nationalism. What Eaglestone does not explore is that like Levinas, Arendt also tripped over tropes that shadow Heidegger's Eurocentrism.

Eaglestone's essay was part of a collection edited by Richard H. King and Dan Stone, *Hannah Arendt and the Uses of History: Imperialism, Nation, Race and Genocide*, which serves as an excellent starting point for understanding the developments in scholarship on Arendt's contributions and limitations for the critical philosophy of race. Indeed King and Stone's "Introduction" takes readers through the historiography. Arendt's *The Origins of Totalitarianism* was a touchstone text when it appeared in 1951. Her masterpiece is a genealogy of totalitarianism divided into three parts, "Antisemitism," "Imperialism," and "Totalitarianism." The three parts are roughly chronological but overlap. Anti-Semitism was the dark side of the Enlightenment; Germanic pan-movements—the apex of ethno-nationalism—and European imperial expansion reach across the nineteenth century; and totalitarian movements belong to the twentieth century. She traces the increasing ferocity in the totalitarian features that reached their apogee in the death camps and the gulag archipelago. Her work examines the connections between anti-Jewish and colonial racism that produced the ideology and terror apparatus of totalitarian regimes. If *Origins* defined her early career, by the time of her death in 1975, however, Arendt was read more as a "normative theorist of politics, action, and participatory freedom, of the public-private (in Arendt's terms the political-social) question, and of the problem of political judgment" raised by her books *The Human Condition* (1958) and *On Revolution* (1963) rather than by the issues considered in *The Origins of Totalitarianism*.

But starting with Ron H. Feldman's 1978 collection of Arendt's Jewish essays, *The Jew as Pariah*, and followed by Elizabeth Young-Bruehl's magisterial biography, *Hannah Arendt: For Love of the World* (1982), a new generation of scholars came to appreciate the depth and breadth of Arendt's engagement with Jewish history, Zionism, the State of Israel, and anti-Semitism, and to debate Arendt's understanding of these issues (Feldman 1978; Arendt 2007; Young-Bruehl 1982). The same period gave rise to Shiraz Dossa's breakthrough 1980 essay, "Human Status and Politics: Hannah Arendt on the Holocaust," which akin to the scholarship on Levinas raised the "ethnocentric strain" in Arendt's thought by considering how she parroted primitivism in her depictions of colonized sub-Saharan Africans in *The Origins of Totalitarianism* (Dossa 1980). One instance of this was Arendt's reading of Joseph Conrad's *Heart of Darkness*, a work charged most famously by Chinua Achebe as racist, as the "most illuminating work on actual race experience in Africa" (Arendt 1973: 185). George Kateb's brief account "On Racism in Africa" in his *Hannah Arendt* quickly quashed Dossa's insight by insisting that Arendt did not share European colonial and racial attitudes; she merely sought to describe the effects of their racism. Kateb (1983: 61–63) thereby inaugurated what has emerged as an ongoing problem in treatments of Arendt's writing: how to pull apart her descriptions of others' work from her own perspective.

The 1990s saw a deepening rift around these interpretative issues. Anne Norton (1995) pointed not only to Arendt's attitudes toward Africans, but toward African American activists in Arendt's "Reflections on Little Rock," as further evidence of her deprecation of blacks. Agreeing with Dossa and Norton was Hannah Pitkin who stated that Arendt "simply shares the European prejudice against so-called primitive culture as somehow less cultured or more natural—in a pejorative sense—than the European" (1993: 293). Seyla Benhabib's response was similar to Kateb's earlier, indicating that these positions were reductive of Arendt's views (1999: 83).

The rise of postcolonial theory and the critical philosophy of race opened the floodgates of critique. Kathryn Gines's book *Hannah Arendt and the Negro Question* is the most developed account among those critical of Arendt's racial politics. Gines develops four key arguments: that (1) Arendt sees the "Negro question as a Negro problem rather than a white problem"; (2) "Arendt's analysis of the Jewish question has implications for her analysis of the Negro question, but Arendt does not readily connect the two"; (3) Arendt does not recognize that "anti-Black racism (like Jew hatred) is a political phenomenon"; and (4) "Arendt's representational thinking and judgment are flawed and further inhibit her understanding of the Negro question" (2014: 2–3). The arguments made by scholars like Gines also have their respondents, however, with Arendt's "Reflections on Little Rock" as the crucial contested text in the scholarly melee (Klausen 2010; Cole 2011; Locke 2013).

In "Reflections on Little Rock," Arendt decried the politicization of schools as the front line of the civil rights struggle on the basis of a set of categorical distinctions central to her theorizing of Republican models of political participation: the private, the social, and the political. If politics demands equality as its sine qua non, within the social realm discrimination is permitted and it often takes priority over equality, she maintained. Arendt decried the public legislation of social discrimination that was the foundation of Jim Crow segregation. But she insisted that children should not bear the burden of correcting the "original crime in America's history," and maintained that forced integration of schools was wrong. She also defended states' rights as an important principle since it is core to the checks and balances of American Republicanism. In her letter responding to the critics of her article (Arendt 1959), she speaks to American Negro parents in a superior tone that anticipated the row caused by her haughtiness in *Eichmann in Jerusalem*, the text that remains a lightning rod in critiques of Arendt's views on Jews.

Parallel to the most recent work on Levinas, a slate of scholars inspired by postcolonial theory have moved beyond the dichotomies among the Arendt connoisseurs to deploy her work as a site for connecting the histories of anti-Semitism, racism, colonialism, Nazism, and genocide. These scholars include Paul Gilroy, Aamer Mufti, Mark Mazower, Richard King, Maxim Silverman, Griselda Pollock, Sarah Casteel, Marc Caplan, Anna Guttman, and Isabelle Hesse. To get a sense of this literature, I will just reference the work of Michael Rothberg and Bryan Cheyette. Both Rothberg's *Multidirectional Memory: Remembering the Holocaust in the Age of Decolonization* (2009) and Cheyette's *Diasporas of the Mind: Jewish and Postcolonial Writing and the Nightmare of History* (2013) ask us to reconsider the links of both anti-Semitism and anti-Black racism with empire and to reexamine the connections between instances of oppression and calls for liberation.

Multidirectional Memory makes the case for a "'decolonized' Holocaust memory" that is capable of addressing the "shared histories of racism, spatial segregation, genocide, diasporic displacement, [and] cultural destruction" (Rothberg 2009: 23). Rothberg's reading of Arendt acknowledges what critical philosophers of race have said about her work on Africans and Americans of African descent. He bears in mind how she recapitulates the primitivism that Conrad applied to Africans in *Heart of Darkness*. But in addressing this, Rothberg brings Arendt into dialogue with Aime Césaire's *Discourse on Colonialism*, ultimately reassessing the limits in Césaire's account of the genocide of European Jewry in an Arendtian vein. Cheyette, like Rothberg, valorizes the risk of Arendt's "metaphorical thinking" that finds "similarities in dissimilarities" (2013: 6). Both are cognizant of the blindnesses and insights of Arendt's thought. For Cheyette, the pariah/parvenu distinction that she develops in her writing on Jews, "confines the Jewish diaspora to good/bad Jews, which is merely a continuation of prewar racial discourse. Equally problematically, Arendt applies the pariah/parvenu distinction to the civil rights campaign to desegregate schools in the American South" in "Reflections on Little Rock." She thereby displaces "her experience of the failed social assimilation of European Jewry onto the black/white 'racial divisions' in the United States" (Cheyette 2013: 13–14). But if these are the hazards of Arendt's metaphorical thinking, the advantage of her thought is its experiment in comprehending the connections between Judeophobia, Negrophobia, colonialism, "racial imperialism," genocide, and totalitarianism.

Ultimately, the critical philosophy of race must interrogate the intersections within Western civilization that link together the cultural histories of anti-Semitism and other forms of racism. Levinas and Arendt each took us down this path, following a trail indicated by Heidegger in his effort to reevaluate Western metaphysics. Levinas and Arendt each sought to move beyond Heidegger's shadow by reconsidering the dead ends of his intellectual legacy. While all three left us at a crossroads along the way, failing to interrogate persisting racial tropes in their own work, they also each offered methodological and conceptual resources that remain invaluable for undoing racism. Heidegger's *Destruktion* of Western metaphysics opened the tradition of deconstructive critique, which in the critical philosophy of race has targeted "metaphysical racism" and the semiotics of racial stereotyping. Levinas sought to step beyond Heidegger's shadow by radicalizing the immanent critique of Western thought and culture, often from the vantage of Jews as Europe's primary internal Other. His insistence on "ethics as first philosophy" perpetually demands our responsibility to respond to all Others in their fragility and vulnerability as the basis of every philosophy worthy of the name, since the discipline claims the love of wisdom and justice but can only fulfill its mission if it embraces the wisdom of love. And Arendt's historical genealogy of the effects of Western civilization on the cultures it sought to colonize, to appropriate, expropriate, enslave, and exploit helps to connect critical approaches often treated disparately, showing how racial logics join Judeophobia and Negrophobia with other forms of racism and subjugation. These connections are key if we are ever to correct the harms of racial injustice.

References

Arendt, H. (1973) *The Origins of Totalitarianism*, San Diego: Harcourt Brace Jovanovich.
———. (2000 [1959]) "Reflections on Little Rock," in P. Baehr (ed.), *The Portable Hannah Arendt*, New York: Penguin, pp. 231–246.
———. (2007) *The Jewish Writings*, eds. J. Kohn and R. H. Feldman, New York: Schocken.
Arendt, H. and Jaspers, K. (1992) *Correspondence, 1926–1929*, New York: Harcourt Brace Jovanovich.
Ashheim, S. (1992) *The Nietzsche Legacy in Germany*, Berkeley: University of California Press.
Benhabib, S. (1999) *The Reluctant Modernism of Hannah Arendt*, Thousand Oaks: Sage.
Bernasconi, R. (2000) "Heidegger's Alleged Challenge to the Nazi Conception of Race," in J. E. Faulconer and M. A. Wrathall (eds.), *Appropriating Heidegger*, New York: Cambridge University Press, pp. 50–67.
———. (2005) "Who Is My Neighbor? Who Is the Other? Questioning 'the Generosity of Western Thought'," in C. Katz and L. Trout (eds.), *Emmanuel Levinas: Critical Assessments of Leading Philosophers*, New York: Routledge, pp. 5–30.
———. (2010) "Race and Earth in Heidegger's Thinking During the Late 1930s." *Southern Journal of Philosophy* 48, no. 1: 49–66.
Caygill, H. (2002) *Levinas and the Political*, New York: Routledge.
Cheyette, B. (2013) *Diasporas of the Mind: Jewish and Postcolonial Writing and the Nightmare of History*, New Haven: Yale University Press.
Cole, D. (2011) "A Defense of Hannah Arendt's "Reflections on Little Rock'," *Philosophical Topics* 39 (Fall): 21–40.
Dossa, S. (1980) "Human Status and Politics: Hannah Arendt on the Holocaust." *Canadian Journal of Political Science* 13: 309–323.
Drabinski, J. (2011) *Levinas and the Postcolonial: Race, Nation, Other*, Edinburgh: Edinburgh University Press.
Eaglestone, R. (2007) "The 'Subterranean Stream of Western History': Arendt and Levinas After Heidegger," in R. H. King and D. Stone (eds.), *Hannah Arendt and the Uses of History: Imperialism, Nation, Race, and Genocide*, New York: Berghahn Books, pp. 205–216.

Eisenstadt, O. (2012) "Eurocentrism and Colorblindness." *Levinas Studies* 7: 43–62.
Farías, V. (1989 [1987]) *Heidegger and Nazism*, Philadelphia: Temple University Press.
Faye, E. (2009) *Heidegger: The Introduction of Nazism Into Philosophy in Light of the Unpublished Seminars of 1933–1935*, New Haven: Yale University Press.
———. (2014) "La 'vision du monde' anti-Semite de Heidegger à l'ombre de ses *Cahiers noirs*," in E. Faye (ed.), *Heidegger: le sol, la communauté, la race*, Paris: Beauchesne, pp. 307–327.
Feldman, R. H. (1978) *The Jew as Pariah: Jewish Identity and the Modern Age*, New York: Grove.
Gines, K. T. (2014) *Hannah Arendt and the Negro Question*, Bloomington: Indiana University Press.
Gordon, P. E. (2014) "Heidegger in Black," *New York Review of Books* (October 9).
Heidegger, M. (1966) "Only a God Can Save Us: Der Speigel's Interview," in *Martin Heidegger, Philosophical and Political Writings*, ed. M. Stassen, New York: Continuum.
———. (2003) "Letter to Victor Schwoerer," in *Philosophical and Political Writings*, ed. M. Stassen, New York: Continuum, p. 1.
———. (2003) *Philosophical and Political Writings*, ed. M. Stassen, New York: Continuum, pp. 2–11.
Kateb, G. (1983) *Hannah Arendt: Politics, Conscience, Evil*, Oxford: Oxford University Press.
Klausen, J. C. (2010) "Hannah Arendt's Antiprimitivism," *Political Theory* 38 (June): 394–423.
Kleinberg, E. (2012) "The 'Letter on Humanism': Reading Heidegger in France," in J. Judaken and R. Bernasconi (eds.), *Situating Existentialism: Key Texts in Context*, New York: Columbia, pp. 386–413.
Lang, B. (1996) *Heidegger's Silence*, Ithaca: Cornell University Press.
Levinas, E. (1964) "Meaning and Sense" in *Collected Philosophical Papers*, trans. Alphonso Lingis. Dordrecht: Martinus Nijhoff, pp. 75–107.
———. (1981 [1974]) *Otherwise Than Being, or Beyond Essence*, trans. A. Lingis, Pittsburgh: Duquesne University Press.
———. (1990a) *Difficult Freedom: Essays on Judaism*, trans. S. Hand, Baltimore: Johns Hopkins University Press.
———. (1990b) "Reflections on the Philosophy Hitlerism," *Critical Inquiry* 17 (Autumn): 62–71.
———. (1994) "Dialectics and the Sino-Soviet Quarrel," in N. Poller (trans.), *Unforeseen History*, Chicago: University of Illinois Press, pp. 107–109.
———. (1999) *Alterity and Transcendence*, New York: Columbia University Press.
Lin, M. (2008) "All the Rest Must Be Translated: Levinas's Notion of Sense." *Journal of Chinese Philosophy* 35: 599–612.
Locke, J. (2013) "Little Rock's Social Question: Reading Arendt on School Desegregation and Social Climbing." *Political Theory* 41: 533–561.
Löwith, K. (1993) "The Political Implications of Heidegger's Existentialism," in R. Wolin (ed.), *The Heidegger Controversy: A Critical Reader*, Cambridge, MA: MIT Press, pp. 167–185.
Maldonado-Torres, N. (2008) *Against War: Views From the Underside of Modernity*, Chapel Hill: Duke University Press.
———. (2012) "Levinas's Hegemonic Identity Politics, Radical Philosophy and the Unfinished Project of Decolonization." *Levinas Studies* 7: 63–94.
Morgan, M. L. (2007) *Discovering Levinas*, New York: Cambridge University Press.
Mosse, G. (1981 [1964]) *The Crisis of German Ideology: Intellectual Origins of the Third Reich*, New York: Schocken.
Moyn, S. (1998) "Judaism Against Paganism: Emmanuel Levinas's Response to Heidegger and Nazism in the 1930s," *History and Memory* 10 (Spring): 25–58.
Norton, A. (1995) "Heart of Darkness: Africa and African Americans in the Writings of Hannah Arendt," in Bonnie Honig (ed.), *Feminist Interpretations of Hannah Arendt*, University Park: Penn State University Press, pp. 247–262.
Pitkin, H. F. (1993) *The Attack of the Blob: Hannah Arendt's Concept of the Social*, Chicago: University of Chicago Press.
Rabinbach, A. and Gilman, S. L. (eds.). (2013) *The Third Reich Sourcebook*, Berkeley: University of California Press.
Rockmore, T. (1995) "On Heidegger and Contemporary French Philosophy," in *Heidegger and French Philosophy: Humanism, Antihumanism and Being*, London: Routledge, pp. 126–147.

Rothberg, M. (2009) *Multidirectional Memory: Remembering the Holocaust in the Age of Decolonization*, Stanford: Stanford University Press.
Sheehan, T. (1988) "Heidegger and the Nazis," *New York Review of Books* 35 (June 16).
Sikka, S. (2003) "Heidegger and Race," in R. Bernasconi and S. Cook (eds.), *Race and Racism in Continental Philosophy*, Bloomington: Indiana University Press, pp. 74–97.
Slabodsky, S. (2010) "Emmanuel Levinas's Geopolitics: Overlooked Conversations Between Rabbinical and Third World Decolonialisms." *Journal of Jewish Thought and Philosophy* 18: 165–174.
———. (2014) *Decolonial Judaism: Triumphal Failures of Barbaric Thinking*, New York: Palgrave Macmillan.
Stern, F. (1961) *The Politics of Cultural Despair: A Study in the Rise of the Germanic Ideology*, Berkeley: University of California Press.
Trawny, P. (2014) *Heidegger und der Mythos judischen Weltverswörung*, Frankfurt: Klostermann.
Volkov, S. (1978) "Anti-Semitism as a Cultural Code." *Leo Baeck Institute Yearbook* 23: 25–46.
Wolin, R. (1988) "The French Heidegger Debate," *New German Critique* 45 (Fall): 135–161.
———, ed. (1993) *The Heidegger Controversy: A Critical Reader*, Cambridge, MA: MIT Press, pp. 2–11.
———. (2001) *Heidegger's Children: Hannah Arendt, Karl Löwith, Hans Jonas, and Herbert Marcuse*, Princeton: Princeton University Press.
———. (2014) "National Socialism, World Jewry, and the History of Being: Heidegger's Black Notebooks," *Jewish Review of Books* (Summer): 40–45.
Young, J. (1997) *Heidegger, Philosophy, Nazism*, New York: Cambridge University Press.
Young-Bruehl, E. (1982) *Hannah Arendt: For Love of the World*, New Haven: Yale University Press.

6

RACE-ING THE CANON

American Icons, From Thomas Jefferson to Alain Locke

Jacoby Adeshei Carter

Introduction

The American racial canon does not lie in some pristine past waiting to be discovered. Instead, the canon is what it has been made to be; which has in part to do with what its contributors have intended it to be, though it is not exclusively that, in part to do with what it has and is currently understood to be, and in part to do with what its current interpreters and contributors both understand and intend it to be in the future. Canons are in a sense a codification of an intellectual tradition. In this regard they share with intellectual traditions the fact of being constructions; that is, canons do not exist ready-made. To be sure, there need be no prevailing consensus on any of these points, which is to say that canons are as much contested as they are constructed.

The driving idea of this chapter is to discuss how a serious consideration of race reorients us to questions of canonicity in regard to American philosophy generally, and pragmatism specifically. Canons may just be obstacles, inevitable traps that get in the way of a deeper sense of engagement with the thought and work of figures or traditions that might be fruitfully investigated. No presumption has been made regarding the value of canonizing. It is to be hoped that the critical reflection on the enterprise offered here in the limited context of racializing a canon will help to clarify the drawbacks and potential usefulness of canonical constructions. Emphasizing canons allows one to focus on the consequences of taking race seriously for understanding central figures and their work. It opens the possibility for a critical perspective on putative canons and novel ideas for the construction of new canons, particularly, one that focuses on the philosophy of race. A plausible assumption is that two things happen: the canon's content looks rather different, and one comes to a different understanding of the existing canonical figures. To that end, this chapter will not be a recounting of what all of the canonical figures thought about race, but what happens to American philosophy (and pragmatism) when one takes racialism seriously, does not forgive bigoted intellectuals their racism, and insists on the inclusion and centrality of intellectuals previously excluded from the canon. American philosophy is not usefully defined in the geographic and state-centric sense of philosophy done in the United States. American philosophy names a number of traditions, schools, and camps. Pragmatism is one such tradition. At times pragmatism is the focus of this chapter; at others, the scope extends beyond pragmatism.

One approach to criticizing and reconstructing canons is to do so from the perspective of those excluded from them. That is the approach of this chapter. It aims to criticize the pragmatist and American racial canons from the standpoints of African descendant intellectuals. That is, Afrodescendant intellectuals in the United States are taken as representative of, and an entry point for, a broader anti-racist and decolonial set of traditions that offer crucial critical perspectives on the canon. This could of course be done from the perspective of other racialized and marginalized populations in the United States, for example, Asian American or Indigenous Americans. Afrodescendant people in the United States provided, arguably, the most well-thought out and well-articulated theories of race and racism, and the most thoroughly scathing criticism of white supremacist canons of any racial group in the United States. The perspective taken here does not assume that race is equivalent to blackness, nor does it assume a black/white binary. It does, however, proceed on the assumption that Afrodescendant people in the United States offer a uniquely insightful critical perspective on canonical construction—one with far-reaching implications.

The American racial canon is missing what every good canon needs: a lively active oppositional set of communities of inquiry. The American race canon historically excluded the very oppositional authorities that would have had the most theoretically corrective effect on its production. This exclusion was predicated merely on the race of those potential contributors. The history of race thinking in the United States has gone from naïve attempts to express the xenophobic sentiments of an imperialist culture, to putative religious accounts of human difference, to pseudo-scientific biological views of race, to semi-intellectual racialism, to staunchly recalcitrant racism, finally beginning to yield in the latter twentieth and early twenty-first centuries to a non-biological constructionist racial conception.

The American canon has also not dealt honestly with its own entanglement with the popular rather than theoretical conception of race (Locke 1990). Its architects have tried to proffer as pure science the rationalization of historical cultural bias and prejudice. Every black racial theorist in the history of the United States has inveighed against the intellectual shortcomings of pseudo-scientific accounts of race of their respective days, but the long history of marginalization of their scholarship has served as a bulwark against engagement with the critical perspectives of black men and women, and reified the insular chauvinism of white theorists. American philosophy has not re-oriented itself with an eye towards the centrality that racism has had in the construction and projection of America as a distinct cultural enterprise or an empire.

Presumably, a larger more diverse community of inquiry will likely strengthen a canon. Among other things, a diversity of critical theoretical perspectives, critical evaluation of theories and attempts to defend them against such criticism, the introduction of novel theories and concepts that better explain observed phenomena, are commonly understood as methods for advancing knowledge. However, the historical exclusion from the American canon of non-white male inquirers and communities of inquiry has resulted in a theoretically weaker canon than might have otherwise existed. It is weaker in at least two ways. First, in that it is simply missing informed rigorous theoretical conceptions produced by non-white men and women. Second, that even as this historical exclusion is beginning to be addressed the tendency of contemporary scholars is to interpret the thought of those now finding inclusion in the canon either as ancillary to the thought of white canonical figures or in terms of contemporary philosophical thought; rather than through the theoretical frameworks of previous historical periods. Despite enlarging the canon somewhat, this still happens today, and the result is that the history of philosophical thought about race in the United States has developed largely along two different paths.

Lacunas, Derelictions, and Under-Specialization: Two Unreconciled Racial Strivings

It has been argued that African American philosophy faces a dereliction crisis. One meaning of dereliction is dilapidation; falling into a state of ill repair. Another is the shameful failure to meet one's responsibilities and obligations especially in a professional capacity. There is a tendency in American philosophy, very pronounced in pragmatism, to understand and characterize, explicitly or implicitly, the thought of African American philosophers as the mere extension of canonical white philosophers to issues of race and racism, or the experiences of African descendant peoples in the Americas (Curry 2011a). African American peoples are regarded as the subjects of experiences to which European and Anglo-American philosophies can be applied (Gordon 2000). The subject matter of philosophical reflection, the concrete experiences are black. The theoretical frameworks through which those experiences are given philosophical meaning are white, even when articulated by black people.

American philosophy is dilapidated by this derelictical crisis because it undermines the full articulation, comprehension, and appreciation of genuinely novel philosophical contributions of Afrodescendant peoples. The unprecedented, uniquely critical and radically alternative products of African American thought are not understood or studied as such. It ought not to escape attention that (African) American philosophy is in a state of dilapidation because academic philosophers have been derelict in their intellectual responsibilities. Some philosophers have read canonical figures unstudied in race theory into debates where they are out of place, and neglected a rich tradition of well-studied scholarship on race. Others have failed to express the appropriate indignation at such an unjustifiable intrusion and seemingly purposeful negligence. One form that this dereliction takes is mistaken, incomplete, and misleading canonization.

Arguably, the more interesting focus of this chapter is not so much on racing or racializing "the canon" as it is on articulating a view about the canonizing of race theory. The former presupposes both the existence of a discernable canon, and the legitimacy of that canon as representing, in this case, a tradition of thought in the United States. In that sense, racing or racializing the canon is in large part a process of first identifying iconic intellectual figures, and subsequently asking what if anything they thought about race or racism. This can have a number of undesirable results, such as overemphasizing such thinkers' concerns with racial questions; overestimating the contribution of relatively few and insignificant works to the philosophy of race; attempts to explain the apparent derelictions of iconic figures as relatively benign oversights; or efforts to show that recognized canonical figures concerns with other concepts and social problems, were in fact, implicitly concerns about race or racism.

A different approach is offered by the latter alternative; namely, canonizing race theory. A marked difference of this latter approach from the former is that it begins by first asking what are the central and novel theories, concepts, or arguments about race and racism in the United States, and subsequently asks which thinkers articulated them. The primary concern is with philosophizing about race. This approach has the advantage of not making individual figures appear to be more concerned with racial questions than they in fact were; places important and significant work in the philosophy of race in its proper context; and elevates and recognizes key contributions and contributors to the philosophy of race on their own terms. It is important to note that a number of thinkers who may be included by the latter approach were not vying for inclusion in "the canon" (though admittedly some were). Far from seeing themselves as potential members in a US racial canon, many in fact understood their work as being in opposition to the sort of scholarship that would likely make up such a collection (see for example Cooper 1998; Delany 2003; Stewart 1987; Walker 2000). One such example is the polemicist abolitionist David Walker.

As David Walker points out in his critique of Thomas Jefferson, white theorists in the United States often underestimate the effects of chattel slavery and social exclusion on the progress of African descendant peoples (Walker 2000: 12–20). Walker takes issue with Jefferson's contention that it was unfortunate that God made some human beings black, where that is understood by Jefferson to mark either a cultural or biological inferiority (Walker 2000: 12). Walker's response on this score is perhaps along the lines Alain Locke had in mind in rejecting the idea that lack of political power and fortune could be correctly explained by supposed cultural or biological inferiority (Locke 1992: 22–24). Walker asserts that African descendant peoples are equal in their endowments to whites, and that both have the same right to be free from enslavement or to enslave the other. Walker contends that it is the greed, thirst for power, and pursuit of profit and material gain, not a biological or cultural superiority, or possession or lack of rights, that motivates whites to enslave blacks (Walker 2000: 14).

Walker sees the need for educating Negro youth to meet the intellectual challenges to their personhood (Walker 2000: 17). Walker maintains that the refutations of white Americans are not enough because as white they embody a certain cultural perspective (that same sort of perspective that one finds on display in Emerson, Addams, and Royce); they, unlike Afrodescendants, cannot write from the perspective of the downtrodden in a white supremacist world. Even white intellectuals such as Emerson and Addams who decry the evils of slavery may hold to problematic racial views, or misunderstand the phenomenon of racism. Moreover, such thinkers may fail to appreciate fully the intellectual and cultural contributions of Afrodescendant peoples (Walker 2000: 16–17).

It is important to Walker's mind that blacks themselves offer a refutation. He writes:

> For let no one of us suppose that the refutations which have been written by our white friends are enough—they are *whites*—we are *blacks*. We, and the world wish to see the charges of Mr. Jefferson refuted by the blacks *themselves*, according to their chance; for we must remember that what the whites have written respecting this subject, is other men's labours, and did not emanate from the blacks.
>
> (Walker 2000: 17)

For one, Walker thinks that blacks themselves must offer a refutation of Jefferson's pronouncements because thorough refutation requires criticism from the perspective of the enslaved (Walker 2000: 17). Moreover, Walker sees the writing of such a refutation itself as an assertion of one's humanity and dignity. This is also why he thinks that such activity cannot be left to whites; for Walker, it seems that the humanity of a people must be claimed and maintained through repeated acts of assertion and confrontation (Walker 2000: 17). Walker is keenly aware of the damage that Jefferson's claims about African descendant peoples has done, and will continue to do when he writes: "Do you believe that the assertions of such a man, will pass away into oblivion unobserved by this people and the world?" (Walker 2000: 17–18).

Walker argues for an existential demonstration of black personhood; an active affirmation of one's humanity manifested through a refusal to be subject to the dehumanizing actions of white Americans (Walker 2000: 30). The difference between Walker and Jefferson is not the call for such demonstration, but Jefferson's "suspicion" that no such demonstration is in the offing, and Walker's unyielding confidence that it is. Already, Walker alludes to a possible way to situate Jefferson into the American race canon; Jefferson gives clear and forceful articulation to the intellectual and cultural challenge facing Afrodescendant peoples in the United States from the perspective of white Americans (Walker 2000: 29–30). Walker's consideration of Jefferson raises another interesting aspect of the American racial canon. It is not only that white intellectuals are included and blacks are not, nor is it simply that white intellectuals are able to determine who is admitted and who is not, but the thought of white intellectuals functions so as to set the terms, the very conditions for the possibility of the inclusion of African descendant voices in the canon. And importantly, their work is able to serve that function regardless of its intellectual warrant; but merely in virtue of being the product of a member of a group believed capable of theorizing, and producing knowledge, relative to the work of members of a group deemed incapable of such pursuits (see for example Curry 2010; Harris 1987, 1988, 1989, 1997, 1999). This is why the mere "suspicions" of a man like Jefferson can become a standard of legitimacy, and a prima facie intellectual hurdle for black thinkers who must first demonstrate that Jefferson's suspicion is false, before they can establish facts about the humanity and potential of African descendant peoples. This is so even when such refutations already exist in the form of the intellectual works of African Americans such as Alexander Crummell and Benjamin Banneker.

Neither pragmatism nor American philosophy is characterized by a deep and abiding criticism of racialization or racial injustice in the United States (or anywhere else in the Americas) (Curry 2010). Preoccupation with meta-philosophical concerns—standards of rigor, what counts as philosophy, and the rules of philosophical inquiry, and so forth—may distance interested philosophers from the substance of race theory. Contemporary philosophers unfamiliar with black intellectual history, opt instead to approach the philosophy of race by extending the thought of revered members of Anglo and European traditions to the subject of race and racism. This is the crux of underspecialization in race theory; it is both a lack of expertise in intellectual traditions that have made race and racism primary concerns, and the attempt to refashion those traditions in accordance with more mainstream philosophical views and philosophers. One is extremely hard-pressed to determine whether contemporary pragmatist or contemporary continental philosophers are most guilty of this particular form of underspecialization (Curry 2010). (The focus here will remain on pragmatism and more will be said on the matter in the next section.) More than the privileged infiltration of Anglo and European descendant philosophers into an area of study in which they cannot reasonably be regarded as specialist, the attempt to make the work of such scholars relevant to race theory obscures the inadequacy and irrelevance of their thinking on race and helps to maintain some rather dubious views about race (Curry 2010).

Emerson offers us an example of how false beliefs about race and races can be compatible with opposition to some forms of racism (Field 2001: 1–3). So we find in an analysis of his writings evidence that opposition to chattel slavery is no bulwark against either racism or false beliefs about race along with a clear example that opposition to slavery need not be rooted in a positive attitude toward peoples of African descent, nor in a desire or willingness to share social, cultural, or democratic living with black people in the United States. Emerson's earlier belief that Negroes were intellectually inferior to whites and that slavery was justifiable if it tended toward the improvement of the enslaved is demonstrably false (Field 2001: 6). There were in fact Negroes of considerable intellect, but what is more, this sort of thinking about race has been responded to by black intellectuals.

While Emerson observed in his journals that specious argumentation could never provide a satisfactory defense of slavery to any reasonable person, not even that realization would help him to avoid the specious argumentation for the natural inferiority of the Negro (Field 2001: 6). Black thinkers such as Fredrick Douglass, Maria W. Stewart, David Walker, Alexander Crummell, Anna Julia Cooper, and Martin R. Delany argued that failure to recognize that slavery was an imposition on the full expression of Negro ability and potential and not a consequence of natural inferiority was an egregious mistake, and that the ability of the Negro to overcome it in many ways is a mark of Negro fortitude and ability (Cooper 1998; Crummell 1995; Delany 2003; Douglass 1995; Stewart 1987; Walker 2000). This marks an important difference between Emerson and David Walker. Walker sometimes has a rather low opinion of those who are in bondage, and certainly thought that continued enslavement was incompatible with human personhood (Walker 2000). Walker, however, distinguished quite carefully between inferiority in consequence of condition, and inferiority in consequence of race (Walker 2000: 9–20).

Pernicious racialism was so ingrained in the intellectual and cultural attitude of white scholars and writers as evidenced by Jefferson, Emerson, Addams and Royce, that any hope of finding in their work an accurate or well-reasoned study of race is at best whimsically nostalgic, and at worst baseless apologetics for undeserving heroes and heroines, or blatant myopia to their numerous theoretical shortcomings, or a misguided attempt to read into past racial theory contemporary conceptions and beliefs about race (Field 2001: 7; see also Curry 2010, 2011b).

Emerson held to the now anthropologically discredited view that race is causally and determinately related to culture (Field 2001: 7; for an alternative view see Locke 1992: 1–19). Emerson held a good deal of disdain for New England abolitionists whom he regarded as sappy moralists lacking in self-reliance (Field 2001: 9). Emerson's view of abolitionists as non-self-reliant "dog-cheap" moralists might have been tempered by the likes of Delany and Walker. Emerson was acquainted with a number of well-known abolitionists and a few of his relations supported the abolitionist's cause more strongly than he, so it was not for want of familiarity with abolitionism that he himself failed to take up the cause.

It was around 1844 that Emerson's views on race began to change (Field 2001: 15). One such change was his recognition that a powerful refutation was needed of the pro-slavery argument. Fortunately, such refutations already existed and had been forcefully called for by Walker in his *Appeal* (Walker 2000). Perhaps what Emerson was on to here was not simply the need for cogent arguments against the institution of slavery; those were already to be had. Emerson became further convinced that fighting slavery required the repudiation of claims of African American inferiority (Field 2001: 15). This need not be the case. One could believe blacks inferior to whites and still maintain that slavery is an unjust institution better abolished than continued. Even in changing some of his false beliefs about race—that the Negro was inferior and the Saxon superior, that race was a precondition for cultural aptitude and intelligence, that the Negro's condition resulted from his own subservient nature—Emerson's later support of abolition was not radical, and failed to issue into any overt plan of action. It was perhaps a theoretical improvement, but made little if any difference in practice.

A non-negligible element of Emerson's anti-slavery stance was opposition to and disdain for the lack of moral fortitude manifested by white New Englanders in the face of attempts by Southerners to defend and preserve the institution of slavery. Perhaps Emerson is a testament to the damaging effect of false beliefs about race on the thought and actions of otherwise reasonable and conscientious people. This makes the role of Afrodescendant peoples in the United States in the canon all the more important. The presence and prescience of their work in the incipient stages of the canons formation provides evidence of African American intellect, their personhood and character, and their active agency in their own plight, and a critical insight on US racial injustice, that is not compromised by the advantages and privileges of membership in the larger white US culture.

It is reasonable to think that Emerson found slavery a grave injustice, incompatible with American principles and values as he understood them, that needed to be abolished, and that he was not committed to a multiracial American future or strongly committed to racial equality. Emerson is proof positive that a white intellectual in the nineteenth century could speak out against slavery, join the abolitionist movement, participate in the Underground Railroad, and still hold false beliefs about race, fail to see a future for America as a racial democracy, and maintain a belief in Saxon racial superiority. And this, all the while he is friends and a close acquaintance to Henry David Thoreau, whose thinking on race matters in the United States was less problematic (McBride 2013; Harris 2002a).

Arguably, Emerson suffered from the epistemic limitations of his particular standpoint. Situated in and embodying a different epistemological perspective, Anna Julia Cooper's pioneering intellectual work, *A Voice From the South*, argues for the importance of black women to black social progress due to the tremendous burdens they are required to shoulder, the importance of education to black social progress, and articulates a theory of race and human value against the prevailing racist view of the worth of black people (Cooper 1998: 53–196). Cooper argued against the prevailing white supremacist view that African descendant people had, and have, nothing of value to contribute to Western civilization (Cooper 1998: 161–187). Perhaps best at articulating the value of speaking from a gendered or racialized perspective is Anna Julia Cooper. She is keen to recognize both the embodied and socially situated position of other writers, as well as her own. An oft quoted passage from *A Voice From the South* makes plain the importance for Cooper of social location to one's thought and praxis. What is often missed is what immediately precedes Cooper's important claim about the situation and role of black women in advancing the cause of the race. It is worth quoting Cooper here at length.

> The late Martin R. Delany, who was an unadulterated black man, used to say when honors of state fell upon him, that when he entered the council of kings the black race entered with him; meaning, I suppose, that there was no discounting his race identity and attributing his achievements to some admixture of Saxon blood. But our present record of eminent men, when placed beside the actual status of the race in America to-day, proves that no man can represent the race. Whatever the attainments of the individual may be, unless his home has moved *pari passu*, he can never be regarded as identical with or representative of the whole.
>
> Only the BLACK WOMAN can say "when and where I enter, in the quiet, undisputed dignity of my womanhood, without violence and without suing or special patronage, then and there the whole *Negro race enters with me.*" Is it not evident then that as individual workers for this race we must address ourselves with no half-hearted zeal to this feature of our mission. The need is felt and must be recognized by all. There is a call for workers, for missionaries, for men and women with the double consecration of a fundamental love of humanity and a desire for its melioration through the gospel; but superadded to this we demanded an intelligent and sympathetic comprehension of the interests and special needs of the Negro.
>
> (Cooper 1998: 63–64)

Properly situating such authors in the American racial canon not only adds to that body of literature the particular location from which African Americans write, but it helps highlight the fact that white authors write from no less embodied, gendered, and racialized a perspective than their African descendant counterparts. More than that, it shows the diversity of perspectives even among African descendant theorists, by demonstrating that no one member of that community is able to speak for every member of the community, even while contending that some members are able to serve as litmus tests for the social plight of the whole. Thinkers such as Delany, Cooper, Walker, and Stewart challenged the normalized white perspective that treats the location of white male theorists as abstract, unembodied, and universal. As Cooper points out, Delany was always keenly aware of his embodiment as a black man, and the ramifications that had both for the character of his thought and his ability and manner of occupying certain spaces. African American writers position us to ask about the American racial canon, not just who are included or excluded, but which perspectives, which theoretical constructions for understanding race and racism in the United States, are able, or unable, to shape our understanding of these things.

There is not a single conception of a canon; this is why issues of their construction, constitution, and legitimacy are so contested. Canons are best conceived as a pluralistic conception. One way to approach the topic is to focus on what the American canon has to say about race. Yet another way is to focus more narrowly on the American philosophical canon's concerns about race. And narrower still would be to canonize works specifically on race.

The American Evasion of the Philosophy of Race?

Canons are not uniformly positive. They are not simply repositories of the best thinking by the best minds. A canon is as often the vindication of a cultural bias, a reification of stereotypes, an amalgam of dogma, or a codification of a forcibly imposed hierarchy, as it is a positive contribution to culture, a reshaping of beliefs, or a critical reflection on the world or culture that produced it. Canons are not a priori or naturally bounded. There is no predetermined way to demarcate a canon; say, nationally, racially, by gender, linguistically, or time period. Rather in choosing any such method of demarcation and construction other beliefs, principles, and importantly, values must be brought to bear on a canon's creation.

Let us first disabuse ourselves of the fictitious belief that pragmatism's canonical white figures—James, Dewey, Addams—had any pressing concern for America's "race problem." And the claim here is twofold. First, that individually and personally, no pragmatist other than Alain Locke, save Cornel West and perhaps Josiah Royce, was seriously concerned with the problems associated with race and racism in America (Curry 2009; Tunstall 2009). Second, the claim is that not only has pragmatism as a school of thought almost completely avoided race as a pressing social concern worthy of conscious ameliorative effort, but that it does not require of its practitioners that they do so as a function of their pragmatism (Carter 2013; Harris 2013, 2002a).

One might ask what it is reasonable to expect in the work of a pragmatist social philosopher on issues of race in the United States. As it turns out, one should expect nothing of note; or perhaps, better, one should expect nothing in stark contrast to the prevailing sentiments about race characteristic of the pragmatist philosopher's own race, class, gender, and social status. The belief that there is something inherent in their pragmatism that would motivate a social agenda or program aimed explicitly at racial justice is unfounded (Carter 2013; Harris 2013, 2002b, 1988). Even were this not the case, we would still be well shy of the contention that pragmatist philosophers ought to be seen as experts on race or race relations in the United States. Furthermore, that a contemporary philosopher's own thinking about race was sparked or influenced by a classical pragmatist, does not make the canonical figures themselves important to, or significantly involved in the theory or philosophy of race. What is more, occupying a place in the canon is not itself an affirmation of the truth or legitimacy of one's position. Some views constitute part of the canon in the negative sense of representing prevalent, but false, theories that needed to be debunked, or representing views once important but now outdated and replaced by better positions.

As telling as an examination of the racial theorizing of major figures in the pragmatist philosophical tradition is for understanding the shortcomings of the US philosophical canon on race, the examination of exchanges between Afrodescendant and white intellectuals in the United States can be even more illuminating. An exemplary instance is the exchange between Jane Addams and Ida B. Wells-Barnett on lynching (Addams 1977; Wells-Barnett 1977). To begin with, Addams is willing to concede to Southerners who support and engage in lynching that they genuinely believe public lynching to be the only effective means of punishing and curtailing the rape or attempted rape of white women by black men (Addams 1977: 24). Moreover, Addams assumes further that Southern whites are convinced that a campaign of public terror is the only way to subdue the underdeveloped Negro (Addams 1977: 24). She later describes the rape of white women as a crime committed by black men against the white race, though she does not describe the lynching of black people as a crime that victimizes the entire black race.

Attention to figures such as Alexander Crummell, Ida B. Wells-Barnett, and W.E.B. Du Bois demonstrates how their white contemporaries' speculative thinking about race is often misguided and under-informed by the actual facts of the case (Crummell 1995: 78–100; Curry 2010). Wells-Barnett and Crummell demonstrate how a lack of familiarity with the facts of Negro life lead to grossly inaccurate estimation of the problems facing black communities (Wells-Barnett 1977: 22–27; Crummell 1995: 85–94). It was Du Bois, of course, who first gave theoretical articulation of the fact that Negro populations are groups who face problems and are not themselves inherently problematic (Du Bois 1995). Addams allows herself to entertain the idea that black men are the problem, and the question then becomes how best to deal with them when they rape white women. Wells-Barnett herself once entertained the idea that lynching was a particularly heinous form of punishment for a particular class of crime until she came to the existential realization that it was not (Curry 2012). In the same way that Cooper earlier illustrated the importance of gender perspectives among African descendant peoples, as it cannot be assumed that the perspective of Afrodescendant men represents the entire race; so too we see here one of the ways in which the perspective of Afrodescendant women can obfuscate the realities black men in the United States sometimes face. Wells, on the other hand, is able to see them as a population that faces a complex problem, and the question becomes, how can African descendant peoples in the United States make themselves safe from the extra-legal terror of lynch mobs? What is important here is the proper alignment of one's perspective or standpoint with the facts.

Wells has an important insight that calls into question the possibility that white commentators on lynching, in particular, but race and racism more generally seem to suffer from some impediment that blinds them to the facts of racial injustice, and inhibits the proper operation of their otherwise estimable intellects (Wells-Barnett 1977: 30). The facts about lynching, Wells points out, were not difficult to come by. Such an easily avoidable mistake is indicative of some more nefarious cause that underlies such a damning blight on such commentaries on America's race problem given that the oversight is so easily avoidable (Wells-Barnett 1977: 30).

A Concluding Note Regarding the Use of Du Bois as a Pragmatist

It is important at this juncture to raise a couple of worries about the use of Du Bois as a pragmatist. There is good reason for scholars to remain unconvinced by attempts to claim that Du Bois was a pragmatist, Paul Taylor's very insightful suggestions regarding what might be useful about thinking of him in that way notwithstanding (Taylor 2004). The possibility of reading Du Bois pragmatically is not denied. Neither is it denied that such reading may prove useful for philosophical projects intended to illuminate either pragmatism or Du Bois. It is reasonable to think that pragmatism might be aided by incorporation of Du Boisian insights, but such likely illuminations are not the only consequences of so reading Du Bois. In terms of his substantive commitments he does not strike many scholars as very pragmatist; few, if any, outside of philosophy read him this way, and it is not the least bit clear that connection with pragmatist figures such as William James shows up prominently in much of his thought. Admittedly, he may at some early point have had some affinity for some of pragmatism's founding figures, but that he was majorly influenced by any of them, or thought of himself as a pragmatist, strikes one as mere wishful conjecture on the part of pragmatists that want to portray the tradition as having been more inclusive than in fact it was.

One could argue that incorporating Du Bois into the pragmatist racial canon provides a window otherwise closed into the problem of race and racism in the United States. It might be thought that the inclusion of Du Bois in the pragmatist canon might mitigate its cooptation by white male supremacist culture. At the very least, reading Du Bois pragmatically in regard to the philosophy of race is lopsided. The benefit is double-sided, perhaps, but unequal. The trouble is that though Du Bois is perhaps further illuminated when read pragmatically, his thought on race is fairly well understandable without it. Whereas pragmatism without the inclusion of figures like Du Bois is almost wholly irrelevant to understanding the phenomenon of race in the United States. But the worry goes deeper than that. One might observe that there are two potential consequences that follow from the pragmatist invocation of Du Bois or any other member of the African American philosophical tradition (with the obvious exceptions of Alain Locke and Cornel West) that are deeply troublesome. First, such invocations set pragmatism up as the standard of legitimacy for the black intellectual tradition, and second, these invocations give pragmatism a legitimacy that it does not deserve.

With regard to the first, attempts to bring Du Bois into the pragmatist fold intentionally or inadvertently situate pragmatism in the privileged epistemological position of legitimizing African American thought and thinkers in the United States. It is as though the primary reason that pragmatists have to take Du Bois or any other aspect of the African American intellectual tradition in the United States seriously is only that it can be shown to be related to pragmatism in some way that it meets the standard of knowledge that pragmatism establishes. One might understand this as a particularly US instantiation of the problem that anti-colonial thinkers like Dussel and Mignolo have in mind when they talk about the geopolitics of knowledge and the geography of knowledge, and Lewis Gordon borrowing from Frantz Fanon has in mind when he writes about the geography of reason. The idea is that one must recognize that knowledge production is sometimes political and cultural, particularly, who can or cannot be a legitimate source of knowledge, and who gets to set the standard for what is to count as knowledge can be deeply culturally embedded and political. One way to think about this in this case is to ask why Du Bois or any Afrodescendant thinker in the United States needs to be associated with pragmatism for a pragmatist to take their thought seriously. This is not a requirement for members of other traditions, like continental philosophy, that pragmatists sometimes consider. No one sees the use or benefit in trying to make Habermas or Sartre out to be pragmatists. You even see pragmatists do this in the case of non-philosophical figures such as President Barack Obama.

The trouble is that intentionally or not, such attempts to situate members of the African American intellectual tradition in the United States within pragmatism sets pragmatism up as a legitimate and legitimizing tradition from which other presumably illegitimate traditions can earn legitimacy through a demonstration of how they can be squared with pragmatism. If something like this is not the unacknowledged underlying assumption, then one wonders why the turn to pragmatism in the first place? If one recognizes the thought of Du Bois or other African American intellectuals in the United States as legitimate in their own right, then what is the *use* of pragmatism? One could just study Du Bois or African American intellectual history in the United States in their own right, much the way they do Habermas, Sartre, or existentialism.

The second worry is that the attempt to include members of the African American intellectual tradition, namely Du Bois, gives pragmatism a legitimacy that it does not merit. The trouble here is that pragmatism is able to claim to be something that it may in fact not be through the inclusion as pragmatists of figures who are not in fact pragmatists. If you include the likes of Du Bois, Martin Luther King Jr., Anna Julia Cooper, and so forth, then pragmatism can claim to be inclusive of perspectives and philosophical approaches they have historically excluded without really being in favor of those things. Moreover, pragmatists are then able to advertise themselves as more pluralistic in their philosophic methodology and orientation, even if the inclusion of alternative perspectives and methodologies is predicated on the ability to portray thinkers and schools of thought as commensurate with pragmatism in the first place.

This relates importantly to an earlier point regarding two differing approaches to race-ing the canon. When one begins with a primary concern for the canon per se, or iconic figures one may be led far afield of the most important work in the philosophy of race. One should not begin out of a fascination with Du Bois as an intellectual icon (though such fascination does have its place); rather one looks to Du Bois when doing work in the philosophy of race because no more sustained, critical, original, or detailed sociological and philosophical analysis of race in the United States is to be found. As regards canon formation, one is then left with an appreciation that canons are not best constructed through the mere subsuming of the African American intellectual tradition in the United States into existing white canons; but rather, through the appreciation of the novelty and expertise of persons outside the traditional canon in their own right and as uniquely situated to contribute much needed perspectives.

Consider for example Martin R. Delany's *Condition, Elevation and Destiny of the Colored People of the United States*. There are within that text considerable pragmatic elements (or significant pragmatic moments)—space will not permit summarizing them here—that would reconcile quite well with aspects of pragmatism. Where perhaps increased caution is authorized is in thinking that where Afrodescendant thinkers have been extremely pragmatic, as they often have been, they were also being pragmatist. Lying back of this claim may be the supposition that pragmatist methodology can be divorced from substantive commitments. If that supposition turns out to be false in regard to the *philosophies born of struggle* that pragmatism seeks to adopt into its canon the rift between pragmatism and the black intellectual tradition may be *substantial*.

References

Addams, J. (1977 [1901]). "'Respect for Law,' *New York Independent* 53 (January 3)," in Bettina Apthecker (ed.), *Lynching and Rape: An Exchange of Views*, New York: American Institute for Marxist Studies, p. 23.

Carter, J. A. (2013) "The Insurrectionist Challenge to Pragmatism and Maria W. Stewart's Feminist Insurrectionist Ethics," *Transactions of the Charles S. Pierce Society* 49, no. 1 (Winter): 54–73.

Cooper, A. J. (1998) *The Voice of Anna Julia Cooper*, eds. C. Lemert and E. Bhan, Lanham: Rowman & Littlefield.

Crummell, A. (1995) *Civilization and Black Progress: Selected Writings of Alexander Crummell on the South*, Charlottesville: University Press of Virginia.

Curry, T. J. (2009) "Royce, Racism and the Colonial Ideal: White Supremacy and the Illusion of Civilization in Josiah Royce's Account of the White Man's Burden," *Pluralist* 4, no. 3: 10–38.

———. (2010) "Concerning the Under-Specialization of Race Theory in American Philosophy: An Essay Outlining Ignored Bibliographic Sources Addressing the Aforementioned Problem." *Pluralist* 5, no. 1: 44–64.

———. (2011a) "The Derelictical Crisis of African American Philosophy: How African American Philosophy Fails to Contribute to the Study of African Descended People." *Journal of Black Studies* 42, no. 3: 314–333.

———. (2011b) "On Derelict and Method: The Methodological Crisis of Africana Philosophy's Study of African Descended People Under an Integrationist Milieu." *Radical Philosophy Review* 14, no. 2: 139–164.

———. (2012) "The Fortune of Wells: Ida B. Wells-Barnett's Use of T. Thomas Fortune Philosophy of Social Agitation as a Prolegomenon to Militant Civil Rights Activism," *Transactions of the Charles S. Pierce Society* 48, no. 8: 456–482.

Delany, M. R. (2003) *Martin R. Delany: A Documentary Reader*, ed. Robert S. Levine, Chapel Hill: University of North Carolina Press.

Douglass, F. (1995). *Narrative of the Life of Frederick Douglass*, New York: Dover.

Du Bois, W.E.B. (1995) *The Philadelphia Negro: A Social Study*, Philadelphia: University of Pennsylvania Press.

Field, P. S. (2001) "The Strange Career of Emerson and Race," *American Nineteenth Century History*, 2, no. 1: 1–32.

Gordon, Lewis. (2000) *Existentia Africana: Understanding Africana Existential Thought*, New York: Routledge.

Harris, L. (1987) "The Legitimation Crisis in American Philosophy: Crisis Resolution From the Standpoint of the Afro-American Tradition of Philosophy," *Social Science Information*, 21, no. 1: 57–73.

———. (1988) "The Characterization of American Philosophy: The African World as a Reality in American Philosophy," *Quest: Philosophical Discussions* 11, no. 1 (June): 25–36.

———. (1989) "The Lacuna Between Philosophy and History." *Journal of Social Philosophy* 20, no. 3 (Winter): 110–114.

———. (1997) "The Horror of Tradition or How to Burn Babylon and Build Benin While Reading A Preface to a Twenty Volume Suicide Note," Republished: John P. Pittman (ed.), *African-American Perspectives and Philosophical Traditions*, New York: Routledge, pp. 94–119.

———. (1999) "Honor and Insurrection," in Bill E. Lawson (ed.), *Frederick Douglass*, Oxford: Blackwell, pp. 227–242.

———. (2002a) "Insurrectionist Ethics: Advocacy, Moral Psychology, and Pragmatism," in John Howie (ed.), *Ethical Issues for a New Millennium: The Wayne Leys Memorial Lectures*, Carbondale: Southern Illinois University Press, pp. 192–210.

———. (2002b) "Prolegomenon to a Tradition: What Is American Philosophy?" in Anne S. Waters and Scott Pratt (eds.), *American Philosophies*, Oxford: Blackwell, pp. 5–6.

———. (2013) "Walker: Naturalism and Liberation," *Transactions of the C. S. Peirce Society*, 49, no. 1 (Winter): 93–111.

Locke, Alain. (1992) *Race Contacts and Interracial Relations*, ed. J. C. Stewart, Washington, D.C.: Howard University Press.

McBride, L. A., III (2013) "Insurrectionist Ethics and Thoreau," *Transactions of the Charles S. Peirce Society*, 49, no. 1: 29–45, Academic Search Complete, EBSCOhost, viewed 14 January 2016.

Stewart, M. W. (1987) *Maria W. Stewart, America's First Black Woman Political Writer: Essays and Speeches*, ed. Marilyn Richardson, Bloomington: Indiana University Press.

Taylor, P. C. (2004) "What's the Use of Calling Du Bois a Pragmatist?," *Metaphilosophy* 35, no. 1/2: 99–114, Academic Search Complete, EBSCOhost, viewed 18 January 2016.

Tunstall, D. (2009) "Josiah Royce's 'Enlightened' Antiblack Racism?," *Pluralist*, 4, no. 3: 39–45.

Walker, D. (2000) *Appeal to the Colored Citizens of the World*, University Park: Penn State University Press.

Wells-Barnett, I. B. (1977 [1901]). "'Lynching and the Excuse for It,' *New York Independent* 53 (May 16)," in Bettina Aptheker (ed.), *Lynching and Rape: An Exchange of View*, New York: American Institute for Marxist Studies, p. 29.

7

AT THE INTERSECTIONS

Existentialism, Critical Philosophies of Race, and Feminism

Kathryn T. Gines

This chapter explores how the idea of existentialism—thought as a method of inquiry and community of inquirers—changes when viewed at the intersections of critical philosophies of race and feminist philosophies. I argue that existentialism as a method of inquiry and community of inquirers is expanded, enhanced, and enriched by the existential insights of a broader range of philosophical figures. The chapter is presented in three sections. "Existentialism as a Method of Inquiry and Community of Inquirers" considers dominant representations of existentialism as European in origin and the ways in which this myopic representation of existentialism is perpetuated in anthologies from the 1950s to 2008. In "Critical Interventions: Expanding the Community and Methods of Inquiry," I highlight the critical interventions to expand existentialism in the US context by Lewis Gordon (and critical philosophies of race) and Margaret Simons (and feminist philosophies engaged with issues of race). This section also explores contacts and influences between figures like Jean-Paul Sartre, Frantz Fanon, Lorraine Hansberry, Richard Wright, Simone de Beauvoir, and Ralph Ellison. In "Existentialism Beyond the Black/white Binary," I take seriously the importance of thinking through existentialism, critical philosophies of race, and feminist philosophies beyond the Black (African American or Africana) and white (European) binary.[1] Toward that end, the final section provides a concise literature review of analyses of existentialism and Latina feminism, Mexican existentialism, and Latin American existentialism. I also provide examples of analyses of existentialism in modern fiction in China, Japan, and India, as well as in the music of Trich Công Són (a Vietnamese singer and songwriter). The chapter contributes to existing secondary literature by diversifying the community of existential inquirers and methods of inquiry beyond European, white, male figures and taking seriously the diverse lineages of existentialism.

Existentialism as a Method of Inquiry and Community of Inquirers

As a method of inquiry, existentialism has often extended beyond myopic boundaries of what counts as "properly" philosophical by explicitly engaging literature, memoir, poetry, art, and other modes of expression. Existentialism examines the idea of existence—the human condition, being, power, agency, freedom, fear, angst, despair, choice, responsibility, subjectivity/inter-subjectivity, authenticity, and so forth. Existential philosophies have called into question (or even rejected) closed philosophical systems and have been more inclined to value the tensions and ambiguities of life and ethics. Jean-Paul Sartre has described existentialism as "a doctrine, which makes human life possible and, in addition, declares that every truth and every action implies a human setting and a human subjectivity" (Sartre 1957: 10). Identifying two versions of existentialism (Christian and atheistic), Sartre explains that both share in common the claim that "existence precedes essence" or that "subjectivity must be the starting point" (Sartre 1957: 13). Simone de Beauvoir describes existentialism as aiming at the goal of preventing the disappointments that arise from false idols and instead focusing on being authentic and the value of living authentically (Beauvoir 2004: 216). She notes that all of our acts have their starting point and source in subjectivity (Beauvoir 2004: 212).

In *The Worlds of Existentialism: A Critical Reader* (1964), Maurice Friedman explains, "Insofar as one can define existentialism, it is a movement from the abstract and general to the particular and the concrete (Friedman 1964: 4). Existentialism is about authenticating one's existence; "it means personal choice, decision, commitment, and ever again that act of valuing in the concrete situation that verifies one's truth by making it real in one's own life—in one's life with man and the world" (Friedman 1964: 9). In *Existentia Africana: Understanding Africana Existential Thought* (2000a), Lewis Gordon notes that "Existentialist philosophy addresses problems of freedom, anguish, dread, responsibility, embodied agency, sociality, and liberation; it addresses these problems through a focus on the human condition" (Gordon 2000a: 7). He adds, "we can regard existentialism—the popularly named ideological movement—as a fundamentally European historical phenomenon. It is, in effect, the history of European literature that bears that name" (Gordon 2000a: 10; 2003: 36).[2]

Following this line of thought, existentialism as a community of inquirers has too frequently been conceptualized (implicitly or explicitly) as exclusively European, white, and male (e.g., focusing on Dostoevsky, Kierkegaard, Nietzsche, Heidegger, and Sartre, among others). Philosophy anthologies and readers, as well as numerous articles, conferences, and syllabi in the US context, (re)present existentialism as predominantly European, white, and male. Put another way, the community of inquirers most frequently associated with existentialism in the Western philosophy canon does not typically include women and/or Black existential writers and thinkers (or other people of color). For example, mid-twentieth century collected editions like Walter Kaufman's *Existentialism From Dostoevsky to Sartre* (1956) includes readings by Dostoevsky, Keirkegaard, Nietzsche, Rilke, Kafka, Ortega, Jaspers, Heidegger, Sartre, and Camus. A book described as introducing existentialism to America, William Barrett's *Irrational Man: A Study in Existential Philosophy* (Anchor Books, 1962), identifies "The Existentialists" as Keirkegaard, Nietzsche, Heidegger, and Sartre. These texts anthologize European (white and/or Jewish) male writers from France, Germany, Russia, Spain, Denmark, and so forth, but there are no women or people of color (e.g, Simone de Beauvoir, Frantz Fanon, Richard Wright, Ralph Ellison, Lorraine Hansberry) in the table of contents.

One of the more comprehensive anthologies from this period (1950s–1960s) is Maurice Friedman's aforementioned *The Worlds of Existentialism: A Critical Reader* (1964). It features more than 50 authors ranging from Sartre, Buber, Frankl, Kierkegaard,

Camus, Tillich, Jaspers, Heidegger, Nietzsche, and Dostoevsky to Rosensweig, Ebner, Berdyaev, Lynd, and Maritain. Friedman criticizes earlier existentialism anthologies (specifically Kaufman's aforementioned) for omitting religious existentialists. He asserts,

> The fact is that there is no one story to tell, and any attempt to reduce existentialism to a single story is an unwarranted oversimplification of a tremendously complex group of interrelated phenomena. Today no mature anthology of existentialism can omit the religious existentialists.
> (Friedman 1964: 11)

The Worlds of Existentialism features not only religious existentialists, but also "important forerunners of modern existentialism, including a number of thinkers who are not properly labeled existentialists but who have marked existentialist strains" such as mystics who "have often made an important contribution to the converging and diverging stream that has issued into this modern movement" of existentialism (Friedman 1964: 5). For Friedman, we cannot limit existentialism to philosophers because literary writers like Franz Kafka are also able to deal with concrete existence and arrive at a unique understanding of it (Friedman 1964: 13). And yet, for all of its inclusions, Friedman's anthology features one woman—Helen Merrell Lynd—and no persons of color. Taking seriously his claim about including religious existentialists, I would add that today no mature anthology of existentialism can omit women and people of color.

One might argue that these anthologies are a product of their time, published before interventions in existentialism from the perspective of critical philosophies of race and feminist philosophies. In some cases such narrow approaches to existentialism anthologies have been slowly changing, in other cases, time seems to have stood still. Examples of more expansive anthologies of existentialism include Linda E. Patrik's *Existential Literature: An Introduction* (2000) which features Dostoyevsky, Sartre, Camus, Beauvoir, Wright, Nietzsche, Kierkegaard, and Kafka. George Cotkin's *Existential America* (2003) is also more inclusive—with sections on "Kierkegaardian Movements," "The Era of French Existentialism," "Realizing the Existentialist Vision" (with a chapter on Richard Wright and Ralph Ellison, Norman Mailer, and Robert Frank), and "Post-War Student and Women's Movement." Gordon Marino's *Basic Writings of Existentialism* (2004) includes sections on Nietzsche, Dostoevsky, Unamuno, Heidegger, Sartre, Beauvoir, Camus, and Ellison. But limited representations of existentialism persist in textbooks and anthologies published in the twenty-first century. For example, *Existentialism: Basic Writings* (2001) edited by Charles Guignon and Derk Pereboom, features Hegel, Kierkegaard, Nietzsche, Heidegger, Husserl, and Sartre. And *On Existentialism* (2008) edited by Mark Tanzer, highlights Nietzsche, Kierkegaard, Heidegger, and Sartre.

Up to this point, I have offered several examples of more narrow conceptions of existentialism as a white and male community of inquirers along with a few more recent attempts to be more inclusive in existentialism anthologies. In the next section I explore critical interventions in existentialism made possible by expanding the community of inquirers and methods of inquiry through critical philosophies of race and feminist philosophy.

Critical Interventions: Expanding the Community and Methods of Inquiry

Lewis Gordon has been a trailblazer in publishing books on existentialism, Blackness and anti-Black racism, such as *Bad Faith and Anti-Black Racism* (1995a), *Existence in Black: An Anthology of Black Existential Philosophy* (1997b), *Her Majesty's Other Children: Sketches of Racism from a Neocolonial Age* (1997a), and *Existentia Africana: Understanding Africana Existential Thought* (2000a).[3] Earlier I noted Gordon's definition of existentialism that emphasized European literature, but he also offers more expansive conceptualizations of existentialism. He explains, "It is clear that, without the contributions of the Africana thinkers, reflections on concerns such as existence, ethics, aesthetics, politics, and human studies exemplify, at best, a false universal" (Gordon 2000a: 40). With this understanding, expanding beyond false universals and taking seriously particularity (and facticity) in existentialism, Gordon considers a far more diverse range of figures to be included in the community of inquirers and methods of inquiry. He offers a broad and expansive range of male *and* female figures contributing to what he calls Africana existential philosophy: Anna Julia Cooper, W.E.B. Du Bois, Frederick Douglass, Ralph Ellison, Frantz Fanon, Toni Morrison, Martin Delany, Maria W. Stewart, William Jones, James Baldwin, Noel Manganyi, Angela Davis, Anthony Bogues, Robert Birt, Bernard Boxill, Tommy Lott, Thomas Slaughter, Percy Mabogo More, Naomi Zack, bell hooks, Joy James, Audre Lorde, and a myriad of others (Gordon 2000a: 7–21, 37–40).

While space will not allow us to explore how all of these figures cited by Gordon have contributed to philosophies of race and existentialism, I will take some time to explore interconnections between a few key figures in existentialism, including Jean-Paul Sartre, Frantz Fanon, Lorraine Hansberry, Simone de Beauvoir, Richard Wright, and Ralph Ellison.

In *Bad Faith and Anti-Black Racism*, Lewis Gordon theorizes race (and racism) existentially, describing the method of his study as a "descriptive ontology" or an "existential phenomenology" (Gordon 1995a: 5). He examines the resources within Sartre's writings for theorizing and combating the phenomenon of anti-Black racism. In *Being and Nothingness* (1943), Sartre identifies race, class, and gender hierarchies in the examples that he gives of being-for-others. Race and physical appearance are presented as "objective characteristics which define me in my being-for-others," and Sartre asserts that although we may assume our being-for-others in infinite ways, we are not able to NOT assume it (Sartre 1956: 671 and 677). Sartre describes this condemnation to freedom (or to choice) as facticity.[4] But Gordon is most interested in Sartre's notion of bad faith.[5] Using what he describes as Sartre's "fundamental insight into the human condition: that whatever we are is not always what we have to be," Gordon analyzes anti-Black racism as a form of bad faith (Gordon 1995a: 6).

Of course, Gordon is also attentive to Fanon's existential insights on anti-Black racism—especially in *Black Skin, White Masks* and *The Wretched of the Earth*, two texts that are very influential on theoretical frameworks of race, racism, violence, and colonialism in the United States (e.g., with the Black Panther Party) and elsewhere. Underscoring both the political and existential aspects of racism, Gordon asserts,

> The relationship between bad faith and antiblack racism results in the following remarkable conclusion: not only does it challenge Fanon's death sentence

on ontological studies of race, but it also challenges the view that existential ontology, as developed in *Being and Nothingness*, is without political distinction.

(Gordon 1995a: 136)

For Gordon, "what is existential about racism is that it is a form of bad faith, which is a phenomenological ontological or existential phenomenological concept" (Gordon 1995a: 135).

Later, in *Her Majesty's Other Children: Sketches of Racism from a Neocolonial Age* (1997), Gordon takes up the intersections of philosophy, existential humanism, race, and racism, along with (neo)colonialism and (post)colonialism. He describes Fanon's philosophy of race as an existential humanism and adds, "His [Fanon's] call for the 'restoration' of humanity makes his existential humanism a form of *revolutionary* existential humanism" (Gordon 1997: 30, emphasis in original). Gordon notes that Fanon offers fundamental assumptions as well as theoretical advances about Western philosophical attitudes. One of the fundamental assumptions is the idea that "racism is a conflict between the self and the Other" and a related theoretical advance offered by Fanon has to do with "the existential reality of oppression" (Gordon 1997: 36). For Gordon, one of Fanon's greatest insights was that articulating the lived experience of the Black required an appeal to sociohistorical reality (Gordon 1997: 144). Gordon adds that this is an insight "at the heart of black existential philosophy," namely, that "existential concepts like anxiety, dread, and despair carry *historical* urgency in black existential thought" (Gordon 1997: 144, emphasis in original).

While Gordon's analysis of race and existentialism in relationship to Sartre, and even more so to Fanon, is often cited, I have seen less attention paid to his discussion of the interconnections between Fanon and Lorraine Hansberry. Among philosophers, the importance of Hansberry as a philosophical figure has been largely overlooked.[6] Gordon observes how both Fanon and Hansberry view race and racism as white constructions that persist in over-determining the lived experience of the Black (Gordon 1997: 159). He notes "ironic similarities" between Hansberry and Fanon worth quoting at length:

> Although the two were six years apart in age and individuals from very different cultures, both were heavily influenced in their early adult years by direct engagement with revolutionary black voices in their communities: Fanon with Aimé Césaire; Hansberry with Paul Robeson and Du Bois. Both produced their first major work in their twenties; Fanon *Peau noire, masques blancs*, at age 26; Hansberry *A Raisin in the Sun* at age 28. Both works were complex explorations of black subjectivity in the face of attempting a dialectical relationship with the White World. (Nearly all of the themes in *Peau noire* emerge in *Raisin*, including the complex relation with negritude that marks a defensive strategy in the struggle for black liberation.) Both delivered important speeches on the role of the black writer in 1959. Both devoted a portion of their last works to the question of violence in a liberation struggle. Both had white spouses who played crucial roles in their literary production. Both were revolutionary humanists. And, as is well-known, both died very young.
>
> (Gordon 1997: 153)

But I would like to take a closer look at Hansberry beyond her similarities to Fanon. More specifically, I am interested in Hansberry's play *Les Blancs*—which takes up issues of race, racism, colonialism, and anti-colonial revolutionary violence (terror/terrorism).

There are several existentialist themes at work in *Les Blancs*, including the gaze, the Other, freedom, responsibility, and authenticity. In "To Be(come) Young, Gay, and Black: Lorraine Hansberry's Existentialist Routes to Anticolonialism" (2008), Cheryl Higashida offers an in-depth analysis of existentialism and existentialist feminism in Hansberry's writings. She describes Hansberry as intertwining anti-imperialist Black leftist politics with post-war European and US existentialism (Higashida 2008: 899), but is careful to note Hansberry's strong critiques of existentialism for sexual and racial othering, individualism, and solipsism, along with its association with despair and apathy (Higashida 2008: 901). Despite her critiques of these aspects of existentialism, Hansberry appreciates Simone de Beauvoir's existentialist feminist insights in *The Second Sex*. Rejecting the gender politics working against Beauvoir, Hansberry asserts, "This writer [Hansberry] would suggest that *The Second Sex* may very well be the most important work of this century. And further that it is a victim of its pertinence and greatness" (Hansberry 1995: 129). Higashida sees affinities between Hansberry's *Les Blancs* and existentialist feminism along with the notion of reciprocal recognition in Beauvoir's *The Second Sex* (Higashida 2008: 905). She argues,

> Hansberry's overt engagement existentialism focused on critiquing its nihilistic and solipsistic articulations of sexual and racial others. However, in countering Genet's vision of anticolonial struggle and its sexual politics, *Les Blancs* invokes ideas of mutual recognition that Hansberry had developed in thinking through gender and sexuality via Beauvoir.
>
> (Higashida 2008: 911)

With Higashida's analysis in mind, I now turn to Beauvoir and Wright.

Gordon made critical interventions into existentialism by articulating Black and Africana existentialisms, and underscoring theoretical connections and insights between figures like Sartre, Fanon, and Hansberry (plus numerous others). Likewise, Margaret Simons is one of the first white feminists to take up feminism, race, and existentialism—specifically connections between Beauvoir and Richard Wright—in her groundbreaking book *Beauvoir and the Second Sex: Feminism, Race, and the Origins of Existentialism* (1999).[7] Simons describes Wright and Beauvoir as holding "a shared concept of the oppressed Other" as well as a similar "focus on the importance of social relations and recognition in the formation of the self" (Simons 1999: 176–177). She adds that both theorists use phenomenological, and I would add existential, descriptions of oppression in an effort to challenge negative stereotypes (Simons 1999: 178).[8] More recently Penelope Deutscher in *The Philosophy of Simone de Beauvoir: Ambiguity, Conversion, Resistance* (2008) has explored influences on Beauvoir's writing on sexism and racism. Describing some influences as important interventions, Deutscher asserts, "Beauvoir's engagement with American racism, and particularly with the analysis of race relations offered by Wright, John Dollard, and [G.] Myrdal constituted, therefore, a decisive intervention into her reflections on relations between the sexes" (Deutscher 2008: 78).

Several biographers have chronicled the interconnections between Wright, Sartre, and Beauvoir—from Wright's writings published in French (often in *Les Temps modernes*), to Sartre's and Beauvoir's separate visits to the United States, to Wright's relocation to France.[9] Taking up the white problem in *The Second Sex*, Beauvoir draws from Wright, Sartre, and Gunnar Myrdal when she argues, "Just as in America there is no black problem but a white one, just as 'anti-Semitism is not a Jewish problem, it's our problem,' *so the problem of woman has always been a problem of men*" (Beauvoir 2010: 148). She references Wright in her description of alterity, explaining,

> American Blacks, partially integrated into a civilization that nevertheless considers them an inferior caste, live it; what Bigger Thomas experiences with so much bitterness at the dawn of his life is this definitive inferiority, this accursed alterity inscribed in the color of his skin: he watches planes pass and knows that because he is black the sky is out of bounds for him.
> (Beauvoir 2010: 311)

Sartre references Wright in *What is Literature?* (asserting "The books of Richard Wright will remain alive as long as the Negro question is raised in the United States," Sartre 1948: 116) and in *Anti-Semite and Jew* (recalling "Richard Wright, the Negro writer, said recently: 'There is no Negro problem in the United States, there is only a White Problem'"; Sartre 1995: 152).[10]

It has been assumed by some that Richard Wright suddenly became an existentialist after relocating to France. Two of Wright's later novels *The Outsider* (1953) and *Savage Holiday* (1954) were written in Europe after Wright became a European (i.e., a French citizen) in 1947. While these novels are thought to be more explicitly existentialist, they were not well received. Beauvoir wrote to Nelson Algren in a personal correspondence, "Dick's Outsider? He can tell a story, but what a meaningless, crazy, stupid story that is—don't you think so?" (Beauvoir 1998; Rowley 2001: 409 and 578). Rowley states that Ellison found Wright's early collection *Uncle Tom's Children* to be better existentialist writing than *The Outsider* (Rowley 2001: 409 and 578).[11] Lorraine Hansberry also wrote a scathing review of *The Outsider* in *Freedom* (April 1953). As Higashida notes, "Hansberry reiterated wider critical views that exilic Wright had applied foreign, inauthentic existentialist tenets to the black American experience—with aesthetically and politically disastrous results" (Higashida 2008: 899). But (as I have argued elsewhere) we must remember that there are existential themes across several of Wright's writings, including his story "The Man Who Lived Underground" (first published in 1942, then reprinted in 1945 and 1961) and his autobiographical *Black Boy* (1945)—both examples of Wright's existential literature published years before his expatriation to Paris (Gines 2011).[12]

Darwin Turner has asserted, "Wright leaned toward existentialism long before the philosophy earned its literary reputation in America and perhaps even before he fully realized the philosophical position which he was articulating" (D. Turner 1984, 164). C.L.R. James describes a conversation with Wright in which Wright explains that he understood the concepts expressed in existentialism *before* reading European existential writings. James recalls Wright pointing to a stack of books by Kierkegaard and saying, "I want to tell you something. *Everything that he writes in those books, I knew before I had them*'" (Cappetti, 2001: 62, emphasis added).[13]

Similarly, we find several existential themes—freedom, choice, responsibility, anguish, alienation, authenticity, subjectivity, inter-subjectivity—in Ralph Ellison's *Invisible Man*.

Michel Fabre suggests that Ellison presents existentialist literature to Wright, citing a 1945 letter in which Ellison writes to Wright:

> I've been reading some fascinating stuff out of France ... Kierkegaard has been utilized and given a social direction by a group who have organized what is called "Existentialist Theater" ... France is in ferment ... Sartre, one of the younger writers, would have no difficulty understanding your position in regard to the left. He writes "Every epoch discovers one aspect of ... the condition of humanity, in every epoch man chooses for himself with regard to others, to love, to death, to the world (Kierkgaardian categories aren't they?)."
>
> (Fabre 1982: 184)

Jerry Gafio Watts and Michel Fabre have both noted that Wright and Ellison often read existentialism and discussed it together. According to Watts, Ellison came to existentialist literature through André Malraux's *Man's Hope* and adds, "Ellison and Richard Wright met often to discuss Unamuno's *The Tragic Sense of Life*" in the 1930s (1994: 55).

In *Existentia Africana: Understanding Africana Existential Thought* (2000), Gordon offers an analysis of Africana existentialist thought as it relates to critical philosophies of race, engaging questions concerning Blackness as a problem as well as mixed race identity. Here Gordon notes, "Sartre stands as an unusual catalyst in the history of Black existential philosophy. He serves as a link between Richard Wright and Frantz Fanon (undoubtedly the twentieth century's two most influential Africana existentialist 'men of letters')" (Gordon 2000: 9). There are connections between Wright and Fanon also worth noting. Aside from the insights of Wright's work that can be seen in *Black Skin, White Masks*, biographer David Macey notes that Fanon wrote a letter to Wright in which Fanon said he was "working on a new study of the 'human breadth' of Wright's novels. He owned, he explained, copies of most of Wright's books, and added: 'I'd greatly appreciate your letting me know the titles of those works I might be ignorant of'" (Macey 2000: 280).[14] Lou Turner has examined connections between Wright and Fanon in more detail in "Fanon Reading (W)right, the (W)right Reading of Fanon: Race, Modernity and the Fate of Humanism" (2003), where he notes that Wright organized the historic First International Congress of Negro Writers and Artists (1956) and invited Frantz Fanon as one of the speakers (L. Turner 2003: 152).[15]

My aims in exploring these contacts and influences are to highlight interesting explorations of existentialism among these figures, as well as to push back on the assumed one-directionality of influence from men to women and/or from white French existentialists to Black existentialists.[16] In the next section I provide a short overview of literature that explores existentialism, critical philosophies of race, and feminist philosophies beyond the Black/white binary.

Existentialism Beyond the Black/white Binary

Important work is being done at the intersections of existentialism, critical philosophies of race, and feminist philosophies beyond the Black/white binary. For example, in "Phenomenological Encuentros: Existential Phenomenology and Latin American & U.S. Latina Feminism" (2006) Mariana Ortega examines existentialist and phenomenological traditions taken up in Latin American feminism. She argues,

> Heideggerian existential phenomenology remains largely ignored by Latin American feminists due to their preference for more Marxist and Sartrean philosophies. But its [Heideggerian existential phenomenology] influence can be felt through the work of thinkiers such as Beauvoir and Irigaray who have had a great impact on Latin American feminists' involvement in political movements and theories.
>
> (Ortega 2006: 45)

Ortega notes that "Inspired by Beauvoir" Graciela Hierro (former coordinator of the Center for Feminist Studies at Universidad Nacional Autónoma de México), "denies the essentialism some attribute to women.... She defends the position that gender is socially constructed and that, consequently, society can provide an education that allows girls and women to occupy spaces other than domestic ones" (Ortega 2006: 51). Ortega also names María Luisa Femenías (Philosophy Department at the Universidad Nacional de la Plata, Argentina), who "analyzes the role of Beauvoir's thought in the development of feminist theories in the later part of the twentieth century . . . [including] Beauvoir's contribution to philosophy and feminism and her critiques against Marxism and Freudian psychoanalysis" (Ortega 2006: 52).[17] Additionally, Ortega highlights the significant import of existentialism, phenomenology, and experience in the scholarship of Latina feminists such as María Lugones, Gloria Anzaldúa, Linda Martín Alcoff, Ofelia Shutte, and Paula Moya.

A few examples of scholarship on Mexican existentialism include Carlos Alberto Sánchez's recent book *Contingency and Commitment: Mexican Existentialism and the Place of Philosophy* (2016).[18] But there are also earlier articles like "The Mexican Existentialism of Solórzano's *Los Fantoches*" (1976) by Katharine C. Richards, in which she examines how existential anguish and a sense of the absurd serve as backgrounds to Carlos Solórzano's play *Los Fantoches*. Foundational contributions to Latin American existentialism are examined by Edwin Murillo in "Existentialism *Avant la Lettre*: The Case of Enrique Labrador Ruiz's *El laberinto de sí mismo*" (2011). He problematizes the marginalization of Latin American contributions to the global cultural phenomenon of existentialism. Murillo explains,

> Historically, Existentialism garnered the immediate attention of critics, as is the case of the work of Luigi Pareyson, Sabino Alonso-Fueyo and Julián Marías, who recognized the precursory involvement of the Spanish philosophers Miguel de Unamuno and José Ortega y Gassett.
>
> (Murillo 2011: 63)

But Murillo also considers figures that have been omitted from these discussions, explaining, "these studies overlooked almost in unanimity the contributions of an entire Latin American contingency composed of Raimundo de Farias Brito, Carlos Astrada and Moisés Vincenzi, to name but these" (Murillo 2011: 63). Offering an example of an overlooked existentialist novel from Latin America, Murillo points to Labrador Ruiz's *Labertino*, "which predates Sartre's *La Nausée* (1938), Camus's *L'Étranger* (1942), Camilo Cela's *La familia de Pascual Duarte* (1942) and Ralph Ellison's *Invisible Man* (1952), the insignias of Existential narratives" (Murillo 2011: 64).

There are also examinations of existentialism in Asian philosophy and literature. For example, in "Elements of Existentialism in Modern Asian Fiction" (1989) Mita

Luz de Manuel explores existential theses and themes in the novels of three modern Asian writiers, Lu Xun of China, Kamala Markandaya of India, and Yasunari Kawabata of Japan. Manuel examines the themes of these novels using insights from Buddhism, Hinduism, and existentialism (making connections with figures like Nietzsche, Camus, Kierkegaard, Marcel, and Dostoyevsky). And in "Death, Buddhism, and Existentialism in the Songs of Trich Công Són" (2007), John Schafer considers the philosophy of life (including Buddhism and existentialism) that is expressed in the music of singer and songwriter Trich Công Són. Of course, these are not exhaustive examples of the diverse lineages of existentialism, but they are intended to help us expand beyond Europe as well as consider expressions of existentialism beyond the Black/white binary.

Conclusion

What does it mean to lay claim to labels like "philosophy" and "existentialism"? Taking up and taking on these labels often involves positive possibilities in tension with potential pitfalls. On the one hand, I refuse to give over reason, rationality, and thinking in general—or philosophy and existentialism in particular—to the continent of Europe and its white descendants (living and dead). On the other hand, I recognize that even in my efforts to expand terms like philosophy and existentialism, or my efforts to trouble disciplinary canons, I remain in a bind—Europe, Europeans, white men (and women) living and dead remain a constant reference point or point of comparison for examining philosophy and existentialism, even from a critical philosophy of race and/or feminist perspective (Gines 2012). Each of the authors cited here faces the same bind. As much as we seek to critique the Western philosophical tradition it seems that we remain entangled within it. This is not a case for abandoning the critiques or the philosophical traditions themselves. Rather, it is an acknowledgement of the existential crisis that often arises when engaging philosophical traditions, even critically. In this chapter I set out to explore existentialism at the intersections of critical philosophies of race and feminist philosophies. Toward that end, I examined how existentialism is expanded and enhanced for the better when we take a broader and more inclusive view of the community of inquirers and methods of inquiry. I would encourage more engagement with existing scholarship on the diverse lineages of existentialism (a small sample of which is represented here), and I look forward to seeing more new scholarship at the intersections of existentialism, critical philosophies of race, and feminist philosophies.

Notes

1 I prefer to keep "Black" and "Blackness" capitalized as African American is capitalized, though I use Black rather than African American throughout because it is a more inclusive term. Also, I prefer to keep "white" in lowercase as an intended disruption of the "norm" (i.e., using either capitals or lowercase letters for both terms). This preference is applied to the text in my own voice, but not to quotes of other texts.

2 For Gordon, the terms *philosophies of existence* and/or *existential philosophies* are more inclusive and go beyond the specifically European manifestation of *existentialism*. I am sympathetic with Gordon's project here and I see the import of his point, but I hesitate to give Europeans intellectual ownership of existentialism in the same way that I resist the idea that philosophy in general is exclusively white or European. I do not think that

KATHRYN T. GINES

Gordon would disagree with me here. It is also worth noting that Gordon's more inclusive terms, existential philosophies or philosophies of existence, are closely aligned with Sartre's account of existentialism, which focuses on concepts like subjectivity, meaning, self-definition, existence, freedom, and responsibility.

3 See also Lewis Gordon, *Fanon and the Crisis of European Man* (New York: Routledge, 1995); "Existential Dynamics of Theorizing Black Invisibility," in *Existence in Black: An Anthology of Black Existential Philosophy*, ed. Lewis Gordon (New York: Routledge, 1997), 69–80; *Fanon: A Critical Reader*, ed. Lewis Gordon, T. D. Sharpley-Whiting, and R. T. White (Oxford: Blackwell, 1996); Lewis Gordon, "Racism as a Form of Bad Faith," in *Newsletter on Philosophy and the Black Experience*, ed. Jesse Taylor and Leonard Harris, *American Philosophical Association Newsletters* 99, no. 2 (2000): 139–141; and Lewis Gordon, "A Short History of the 'Critical' in Critical Race Theory," in *Newsletter on Philosophy and the Black Experience*, ed. Richard Nunan and Jesse Taylor, *American Philosophical Association Newsletters* 99, no. 2 (2000): 151–154.

4 Sartre wrote about American racism in *The Respectful Prostitute* (a play written in 1946, originally titled *La Putain respectueuse*) and "The Oppression of Blacks in the United States" in Appendix II of "Revolutionary Violence" of *Notebooks for an Ethics*, trans. David Pellauer (Chicago: University of Chicago Press, 1992), 561–574, originally published as *Cahiers pour une morale* (Paris: Gallimard, 1983). Additionally, he denounced colonialism and defended anticolonial counterviolence in *Critique of Dialectical Reason: Volume One* [CDR], trans. Alan Sheridan-Smith (New York: Verso, 1991), originally published as *Critique de la raison dialectique* (Paris: Gallimard, 1960); the introduction to Albert Memmi's *The Colonizer and the Colonized*, trans. Howard Greenfield (Boston: Beacon Press, 1991), originally published as *Portrait du Colonisé précédé du Colonisateur* (Corrêa: Buchet/Chastel 1957); and the preface to Frantz Fanon's *The Wretched of the Earth*, trans. Richard Philcox (New York: Grove Press, 1964), originally published *Les damnés de la terre* (Paris: François Maspero, 1961), as well as other essays now collected in *Colonialism and Neocolonialism*, trans. Azzedine Haddour, Steve Brewer, and Terry McWilliams (New York: Routledge, 2001), originally published as *Situations V* (Paris: Gallimard, 1964).

5 Gordon (1999a: 5) explains,

> The core assumptions of bad faith are that human beings are aware, no matter how fugitive their awareness may be, of their freedom in their various situations, that they are free choosers of various aspects of their situations, that they are consequently responsible for their condition on some level, that they have the power to change at least themselves through coming to grips with their situations, and that there exist features of their condition which provide rich areas of interpretive investigation for the analyst or interpreter.

6 I have heard papers on Hansberry by two philosophers (both black women), V. Denise James (at a conference honoring Joyce Mitchell Cook at Yale University in 2015) and Donna Dale Marcano (at a philoSOPHIA Conference at Penn State University in 2014).

7 Elisabeth Spelman's *Inessential Woman: Problems of Exclusion in Feminist Thought* (1998) offers important critiques of white feminism, including figures like Simone de Beauvoir. Simons appreciates these insights but also offers something different by focusing on feminism, race, and existentialism and examining the influences on Beauvoir by Richard Wright and W.E.B. Du Bois. See also Simons, "Beauvoir and the Problem of Racism," in *Philosophers on Race: Critical Essays*, ed. Julie K. Ward and Tommy L. Lott (Oxford: Blackwell, 2002), 260–284.

8 Simons (1999) asserts: "Wright provided a phenomenology of racial oppression to challenge the claims by segregationists that blacks are happy and contented with their naturally inferior place in society, much as Beauvoir, in the second volume of *The Second Sex* (titled *Lived Experience*), relies on a phenomenological description of women's experience to challenge the oppressive stereotypes of popular myths and Freudian psychology" (178).

9 The first issue of *Les Temps modernes* (October 1945) included a French translation of Wright's "Fire and Cloud" (Rowley 2001: 326). *Les Temps modernes* editors Sartre, Beauvoir, Merleau-Ponty, and others continued to feature Wright's writings between 1945 and 1947. A special issue of *Les Temps modernes*' on the United States (1946) featured Wright's "The Early Days in Chicago"—later published in *Eight Black Men* (1961) under the title "The Man Who Went to Chicago." See *Les Temps modernes* 2, no.

11–12 (Août–Septembre 1946). Translations of *Black Boy* (1945) were included in the journal's first six issues in 1947. And they published Wright's "The Literature of the Negro in the United States" and "I Tried to Be a Communist" in 1948. This is also discussed by Simons (1999: 175).

10 Sartre (1995) adds, "In the same way we must say that anti-Semitism is not a Jewish problem; it is our problem" (152). In *An American Dilemma*, Myrdal (1944) makes a similar claim: "The Negro problem is primarily a white man's problem" (669).

11 See also *Conversations With Ralph Ellison*, ed. Maryemma Graham and Amritjit Singh (Jackson: University Press of Mississippi, 1995), 84.

12 Multiple versions of this manuscript were published between 1942 and 1961. It was first submitted as a short novel in December of 1941 to Wright's agent Paul Reynolds, who did not like it (Rowley 2001: 262). Two excerpts of the novel appeared in *Accent: A Quarterly of New Literature* (Spring 1942). The second half of it appeared in *Cross Section: A Collection of New American Writing*, ed. Edwin Seaver in 1944 (New York: L. B. Fischer) and then in *Eight Men* in 1961 (New York: World). For more background, see Michel Fabre, "From Tabloid to Myth: 'The Man Who Lived Underground,'" in *The World of Richard Wright* (Jackson: University of Mississippi Press, 1985), 93–107. For a description and brief analysis of the different variations of the story, see John M. Reilly's "Criticism of Ethnic Literature: Seeing the Whole Story," in *The Society for the Study of the Multi-Ethnic Literature* (Spring 1978), 2–13. Reilly (1978) explains, "Structurally Wright's revisions show him converting a form that might achieve effect as fictional pretense of history (realism) into a philosophically informed tale" (11).

13 Carla Cappetti (2001) asserts that "the philosophical readings encountered by Wright . . . gave him the language for articulating the experience. The experience, however, did not come from books. He lived the experience" (62).

14 Letter dated January 6, 1953.

15 Lou Turner highlights the fact that this would be Fanon's last public speech in France. According to Richard King, the congress "included sixty-eight participants from eight African colonies, five Caribbean islands, India, and the United States, [and] Wright had the unenviable task of mediating between the moderate American delegation and the more radical French-speaking Africans and their Francophone allies." See King's *Race, Culture, and the Intellectuals, 1940–1970* (Washington, DC: Woodrow Wilson Center Press, 2006), 210. The fiftieth anniversary of this historic meeting was sponsored by Henry Louis Gates Jr. and UNESCO and commemorated September 19–22, 2006, in Paris, France.

16 I think we can now put to rest the myth that Beauvoir was a mere follower of Sartre as philosopher in general and/or as an existentialist in particular. See Kate Fullbrook and Edward Fullbrook, *Simone de Beauvoir and Jean-Paul Sartre: The Remaking of a Twentieth-Century Legend* (New York: Basic Books, 1994) and Nancy Bauer, *Simone de Beauvoir, Philosophy, and Feminism* (New York: Columbia University Press, 2001). Concerning the myth that Sartre introduced Richard Wright to existentialism after Wright's visit and relocation to France where he eventually became a citizen (1947), see Gines 2011. Examples of the assumed one-directional influence from white figures to black figures can be found in Robert Bernasconi and David Macey. On the one hand, Bernasconi has noted that Sartre's *Critique of Dialectical Reason* and Fanon's *The Wretched of the Earth* "represents a continuation of existential philosophy," adding "this story has still not been fully integrated into the history of existentialism as it is told in Europe and North America" ("Racism is a System: How Existentialism Became Dialectical in Fanon and Sartre," 343–344). On the other hand, he has read Fanon's *The Wretched of the Earth* as a fulfillment of Sartre's *Critique of Dialectical Reason*. Emphasizing Fanon's intellectual debt to Sartre, he acknowledges,

> I have been criticized for neglecting Fanon's influence on Sartre. . . . However, I still agree with David Macey that there is no direct evidence Sartre was even aware of Fanon until the middle of 1959. And I would add that I am not persuaded that there is any indirect evidence from Sartre's texts before that time that HE had read Fanon either. (Bernasconi, "Fanon's Wretched of the Earth as the Fulfillment of Sartre's Critique of Dialectical Reason," 48, note 18)

17 Stephanie Rivera Burruz has been more critical of Beauvoir and *The Second Sex*. In "At the Crossroads: Latina Identity and Simone de Beauvoir's *The Second Sex*" (*Hypatia* 31, no. 2 [2016]: 319–333),

she argues that the text fails to give an account of the multidirectionality of identity in part because of its reliance on a race/gender analogy along a black/white binary. This approach, Berruzz explains, leave identities at the crossroads between categories of race and gender imperceptible. She offers Latina identity as an intervention in attempting to address this shortcoming. See also Stephanie Rivera Berruz, review of Kathryn T. Gines, *Sartre, Beauvoir, and the Race/Gender Analogy: A Case for Black Feminist Philosophy*, in *Sapere Aude*, Belo Horizonte 3, no. 6 (2012): 504–507. See also Gines 2010 and 2014.

18 See also Andrea J. Pitts (2016) "Carlos Alberto Sánchez: Contingency and Commitment: Mexican Existentialism and the Place of Philosophy." *Human Studies*, 39, no 4: 645–652.

References

Barrett, William. (1962) *Irrational Man: A Study in Existential Philosophy*, New York: Anchor Books.
Beauvoir, S. d., Algren, N., Le Bon de Beauvoir, Sylvie, Reeves, E. G., and Kling, V. (1998) *A Transatlantic Love Affair: Letters to Nelson Algren*, New York: The New Press.
Cappetti, Carla. (2001) "Black Orpheus: Richard Wright's 'The Man Who Lived Underground.'" *MELUS* 26, no. 4: 41–68.
Cotkin, George. (2003) *Existential America*, Baltimore: Johns Hopkins University Press.
de Beauvoir, Simone. (1949) *Le Deuxième Sexe*, Vols. 1–2. Paris: Gallimard.
———. (1959) Simone de Beauvoir to Nelson Algren, March 24.
———. (2004) "Existentialism and Popular Wisdom," in Margaret Simons, Marybeth Timmerman, and Mary Beth Mader (eds.), *Simone de Beauvoir: Philosophical Writings*. Champaign: University of Illinois Press, pp. 199–220.
———. (2010) *The Second Sex*, trans. Constance Borde and Sheila Chevallier, New York: Knopf.
Deutscher, Penelope. (2008) *The Philosophy of Simone de Beauvoir: Ambiguity, Conversion, Resistance*, Cambridge: Cambridge University Press.
Fabre, Michel. (1982) "Richard Wright, French Existentialism, and The Outsider," in Yoshinobu Hakutani (ed.), *Critical Essays on Richard Wright*, Boston: G. K., pp. 182–198.
Fanon, Frantz. (1952) *Peau noire, masques blancs*, Paris: Éditions du Seuil.
———. (1967) *Black Skin, White Masks*, trans. Charles Lam Markmann. New York: Grove Press.
Friedman, Maurice. (1964) *The Worlds of Existentialism: A Critical Reader*, New York: Random House.
Fullbrook, Kate, and Fullbrook, Edward. (1994) *Simone de Beauvoir and Jean-Paul Sartre: The Remaking of a Twentieth-Century Legend*, New York: Basic Books.
Gines, Kathryn T. (2010) "Sartre, Beauvoir, and the Race/Gender Analogy: A Case for Black Feminist Philosophy," in Maria Davidson, Kathryn T. Gines, and Donna Dale Marcano (eds.), *Convergences: Black Feminism and Continental Philosophy*. Albany: State University of New York Press, pp. 35–51.
———. (2011) "The Man Who Lived Underground: Jean-Paul Sartre and the Philosophical Legacy of Richard Wright." *Sartre Studies International* 19, no. 2: 42–59.
———. (2012) "Reflections on the Legacy and Future of Continental Philosophy With Regard to Critical Philosophy of Race." *Southern Journal of Philosophy* 50, no. 2: 329–344.
———. (2014) "Comparative and Competing Frameworks of Oppression in Simone de Beauvoir's *The Second Sex*." *Graduate Faculty Philosophy Journal* 35, nos. 1–2: 251–273.
Gordon, Lewis. (1995a) *Bad Faith and Anti-Black Racism*, Atlantic Highlands, NJ: Humanity Books.
———. (1995b) *Fanon and the Crisis of European Man*, New York: Routledge.
———. (1997a) *Her Majesty's Other Children: Sketches of Racism From a Neocolonial Age*, Lanham: Rowman & Littlefield.
———. (1997b) "Existential Dynamics of Theorizing Black Invisibility," in Lewis Gordon (ed.), *Existence in Black: An Anthology of Black Existential Philosophy*. New York: Routledge, pp. 69–80.
———. (2000a) *Existentia Africana: Understanding Africana Existential Thought*, New York: Routledge.
———. (2000b) "Racism as a Form of Bad Faith." *Newsletter on Philosophy and the Black Experience*, edited by Jesse Taylor and Leonard Harris, *American Philosophical Association Newsletters* 99, no. 2: 139–141.

———. (2000c) "'A Short History of the "Critical" in Critical Race Theory.' In *Newsletter on Philosophy and the Black Experience*, edited by Richard Nunan and Jesse Taylor." *American Philosophical Association Newsletters* 99, no. 2: 151–154.

———. (2003) "African American Existential Philosophy," in Tommy Lott and John Pittman (ed.), *A Companion to African-American Philosophy*. Malden, MA: Blackwell, pp. 33–47.

Gordon, Lewis, Sharpley-Whiting, T.D., and White, R.T. (ed.) (1996) *Fanon: A Critical Reader*, Oxford: Blackwell.

Guignon, Charles, and Derk Pereboom. (2001) *Existentialism: Basic Writings*, 2nd ed. Indianapolis: Hackett.

Hansberry, Lorraine. (1995) "Simone de Beauvoir and The Second Sex: An American Commentary (An Unfinished Essay in Progress)," in Beverly Guy Sheftall (ed.), *Words of Fire: An Anthology of African American Feminist Thought*. New York: New Press.

Higashida, Cheryl. (2008) "To Be(come) Young, Gay, and Black: Lorraine Hansberry's Existentialist Routes to Anticolonialism." *American Quarterly* 60, no. 4: 899–924.

Kaufman, Walter. (1956) *Existentialism From Dostoevsky to Sartre*, New York: Penguin Group.

Luz de Manuel, Mita. (1989) "Elements of Existentialism in Modern Asian Fiction." *Likha* 11, no. 2: 25–42.

Macey, David. (2000) *Frantz Fanon: A Biography*, New York: Picador.

Marino, Gordon. (2004) *Basic Writings of Existentialism*, New York: Modern Library Classics.

Murillo, Edwin. (2011) "Existentialism Avant la Lettre: The Case of Enrique Labrador Ruiz's El laberinto de sí mismo." *Hispanófila* 162: 61–78.

Ortega, Mariana. (2006) "Phenomenological Encuentros: Existential Phenomenology and Latin American & U.S. Latina Feminism." *Radical Philosophy Review* 9, no. 1: 45–64.

Patrik, Linda E. (2000) *Existential Literature: An Introduction*, Belmont, CA: Cengage Learning.

Richards, Katharine C. (1976) "The Mexican Existentialsim of Solórzano's Los Fantoches." *Latina American Literary Review* 4, no. 9: 63–69.

Rowley, Hazel. (2001) *Richard Wright: The Life and Times*, New York: Henry Holt.

Sánchez, Alberto. (2016) *Contingency and Commitment: Mexican Existentialism and the Place of Philosophy*, Albany: State University of New York Press.

Sartre, Jean-Paul. (1956 [1943]) *Being and Nothingness: A Phenomenological Essay on Ontology*, trans. Hazel Barnes, New York: Washington Square Press. Originally published as *L'Être et le néant: Essai d'ontologie phénoménologique*, Paris: Gallimard.

———. (1957) *Existentialism and Human Emotions*, New York: Citadel Press.

———. (1967 [1948]) *What Is Literature?* trans. Bernard Fretchman, New York: Methuen. Originally published as French title—Libraire Galliard.

———. (1995 [1948]) *Anti-Semite and Jew: An Exploration of the Etiology of Hate*, trans. George J. Becker, New York: Schocken Books. Originally published as *Réflexions sur la question juive*, Paris: Editions Morihien.

Schafer, John. (2007) "Death, Buddhism, and Existentialism in the Songs of Trich Công Són." *Journal of Vietnamese Studies* 2, no. 1: 144–186.

Simons, Margaret. (1999) *Beauvoir and the Second Sex: Feminism, Race, and the Origins of Existentialism*, Lanham: Rowman & Littlefield.

———. (2002) "Beauvoir and the Problem of Racism," in Julie K. Ward and Tommy L. Lott (eds.), *Philosophers on Race: Critical Essays*. Oxford: Blackwell, pp. 260–284.

Spelman, Elizabeth. (1988) *Inessential Woman*, Boston: Beacon Press.

Tanzer, Mark. (2008) *On Existentialism*, Belmont, CA: Thomson Wadsworth.

Turner, Darwin T. (1984) "The Outsider: Revision of an Idea," in Richard Mackey and Frank E. Moore (ed.), *Richard Wright: A Collection of Critical Essays*, Englewood Cliffs, NJ: Prentice Hall, pp. 163–171.

Turner, Lou. (2003) "Fanon Reading (W)right, the (W)right Reading of Fanon: Race, Modernity and the Fate of Humanism," in Robert Bernasconi and Sybol Cook (eds.), *Race and Racism in Continental Philosophy*. Bloomington: Indiana University Press, pp. 151–175.

Watts, Jerry Gafio. (1994) *Heroism and the Black Intellectual: Ralph Ellison, Politics, and Afro-American Intellectual Life*, Chapel Hill: University of North Carolina Press.

8

CRITICAL THEORY

Adorno, Marcuse, and Angela Davis

Arnold L. Farr

Critical Theory, Class, and Race

Like most forms of Western philosophy, Frankfurt School critical theory belongs to a literary canon that is completely racialized by the very absence of race. That is, in the Western philosophical tradition white males have been presented as the bearers of philosophical knowledge. It is the white male who best understands and describes the human condition. The absence of race as a serious topic for philosophical discussion in the midst of race-based brutalization of people of African descent produces a discourse that by its very attempt to conceal the centrality of race in Western society makes it all the more visible.

In this chapter I do not plan to offer a critique of racism in philosophy or of the racialized philosophical canon. Indeed, as I have done elsewhere, I will avoid the term racism, as it tends to suggest a conscious commitment to racial animus and discrimination. Instead, my focus is on one movement within Western philosophy that has fallen prey to the *racialized consciousness*—or consciousness that is shaped by racist social structure (Farr in Yancy 2004: 144–145)—perpetuated by traditional Western philosophy. That is, this form of philosophy represents a struggle with itself regarding the role of race in society and in philosophy. This philosophy is Frankfurt School critical theory.

Herbert Marcuse claimed that like Marxism and Marxian theory, critical theory is a historical theory. That is, if the objective of critical theory is to provide a critical theory of society for the sake of liberating the oppressed, then critical theory must always reassess itself in light of historical developments. Therefore, critical theory is not merely a theory about struggle; it is itself a form of struggle. It is a theory that must reinvent itself if it is to respond to the needs of the oppressed. This is precisely what Marcuse's version of critical theory was able to do and Adorno's could not. This is also where Angela Davis plays a major role in reshaping critical theory.

The very context of the development of early Frankfurt School critical theory was limiting. Critical theory began as an inquiry by white male Germans into the problem of gross economic inequality. Hence, early critical theory was driven by class-based inequality and oppression and did not develop as a response to the many other forms of oppression from which a very large portion of the human species suffers. One of the main concerns of the Frankfurt School was the persistence of capitalism even after Marx and many Marxists claimed that the contradictions of capitalism would lead to its destruction. Not only did the Marxist revolution not take place, it was the case that those who would most benefit from revolution of social change were more likely to resist it. Debate about how to explain the persistence of capitalism and various levels of resistance to it informed the direction of the Frankfurt School and its leadership.

The first director of the Frankfurt Institute for Social Research was Kurt Albert, who died in 1922 before the Institute was officially established. His replacement was Carl Grünberg (Jay 1973: p. 9). Grünberg's vision for the Institute was not only framed within the Marxian critique of political economy, it was characterized by a certain deterministic view. According to this view, the economic base determines the development of all other social institutions in capitalist societies. Economic laws shape social life. Understanding social life simply requires understanding the function of these economic laws. This is a view that other members of the Institute questioned. Martin Jay writes:

> The prescription for social explanation offered by Grünberg was not, however, adhered to by the central figures of critical theory; they rejected the idea that all social phenomena were in essence a mere "reflex" of the economic. Likewise a certain optimistic determinism which often found expression in his work, suggesting a progression in the development of social institutions from "the less perfect to the more perfect," was not shared by most of those who later became critical theorists. But the strong emphasis Grünberg placed on historically oriented empirical research, carried out in the context of Marx's insights into political economy, was to become a crucial part of their frame of reference.
> (Held 1980: 31)

Max Horkheimer became the new director of the Institute in 1930 and was officially installed in 1931 after Grünberg's retirement (Jay 1973: 25). Like Grünberg, Horkheimer, at least for his first decade of leadership, attempted to carry out historically oriented empirical research (Abromeit 2011). The key difference between the direction in which Horkheimer took the Institute and Grünberg's direction is that under Horkheimer, emphasis was placed on the role of culture in maintaining and perpetuating capitalism. The Frankfurt School found it necessary to develop a critique of culture that would aid the critique of political economy (Adorno 1991; Marcuse 1969). Although the critique of culture opens the door for a broader critical theory, it remains confined to a critique of political economy and class-based oppression and fails to shed light on other forms of oppression. However, as we will soon see, the theoretical tools developed by critical theory for a critique of economic inequality can also be applied to other forms of oppression. It would be Marcuse and Angela Davis who would expand critical theory in new directions.

Marcuse and New Subjects of Social Change

Within the Marxian or Marxist framework, social change is to be the product of a proletarian revolution or a revolution on behalf on the proletariat. It is the failure of this revolution to materialize that gave birth to critical theory. One of the most important contributions of early Frankfurt School critical theory to social/political theory is the fusion of Marxian social theory and Freudian psychoanalysis. Psychoanalysis would enable members of the Institute to understand the social and psychological mechanisms that prevented the development of revolutionary consciousness in the working class. It would also help them understand the rise of fascism. The empirical studies carried out by the Institute revealed to them the interconnectedness of the individual psyche and certain social and historical developments.

> In its next major empirical project, the 1936 *Studies on Authority and Family*, the Institute would devote more time to historical analysis, as would Horkheimer in his individual explorations of the "anthropology of the bourgeois epoch" in the 1930s. Nonetheless, the study of German workers in 1929 had clearly demonstrated that unconscious character structures played a crucial role in the reproduction of society as a whole, a role that any serious critical theory of society could not afford to ignore. The study had confirmed Fromm's arguments from "The Origins of the Dogma of Christ" that the drives of concrete individuals were bound up in and formed by larger historical and social processes, and that they in turn played a decisive role in the further development of these processes.
>
> (Abromeit 2011: 225)

What the Frankfurt School discovered was that members of the working class had identified with the society that oppresses them. They had internalized the values of that society in such a way that a revolution against that society was unthinkable. The will of the ruling class is internalized and then reinforced by the working class.

A critical theory of society must discover and disclose this process of the internalization of oppressive and alienating values. At this level, Marcuse is in agreement with his Frankfurt School colleagues. It is worth quoting Marcuse at length here. He writes:

> The idea of "inner freedom" here has its reality: it designates the private space in which man may remain "himself" as against the others, with himself in his being with and for others. Now precisely this private space has been invaded and whittled down in the technological reality: mass production and mass distribution claim the *entire* individual, and industrial psychology has long since ceased to be confined to the plant. The manifold processes of introjection seem to be ossified in almost mechanical reactions. The result is, not "adjustment" but *mimesis*: an immediate identification of the individual with his society, and, through his part of society, with the society as a whole. This immediate, "spontaneous" identification (which, according to an influential sociological doctrine, distinguishes "community" from "society") reappears at the stage of high industrial civilization; however, in contrast with the primitive identification with the "community," the new "immediacy" is the product of a sophisticated and scientific process of organization and manipulation. In this process, the "inner" dimension of the mind is whittled down: the dimension in which protest and opposition to the status quo can takes roots, in which the power of negative thinking is at home—Reason as the critical power of negation.
>
> (Marcuse 2001: 53–54)

This passage captures the major thesis of Marcuse's famous book *One-Dimensional Man*. In an interview with Brian Magee, Marcuse takes issue with the claim made by Marx that "the working class has nothing to lose but its chains" (Marcuse in Magee 1978). Marcuse claims that today they have considerably more to lose. He means by this that the system is designed to give the worker enough satisfaction to keep him pacified. It is enough to just have a job. The worker and her employer feel a bond between them because they watch the same TV shows. If the worker and his boss pull for the same football team they identify with each other. Hence, the sharing of trivial interests puts under erasure real important differences in social status between those who benefit from the present order of things and those who are the victims of the present order of things.

Although Marcuse sounds pessimistic from time to time, his work is far from pessimistic. This is what ultimately distinguishes him from Horkheimer and Adorno. What Adorno, Horkheimer, and Marcuse had in common was the awareness that the working class may not develop the kind of critical consciousness that would lead to revolutionary social change. What distinguishes them is that while Horkheimer and Adorno looked no further for revolutionary possibilities, Marcuse never gave up the search for radical subjectivity. Marcuse would also use psychoanalysis to not only examine ways in which critical consciousness is whittled down; he would also use it to look for new possibilities for the development of critical consciousness.

The crucial move made by Marcuse is his reinterpretation of Freud's theory of instinctual repression. In *Civilization and its Discontents*, Freud rightly claims that the development of civilization requires more and more repression. It is as if we are trapped in an oppressive system that leaves no room for emancipation. This attitude is consistent with the kind of critique that the Frankfurt School provides of Western industrial society. Adorno and Horkheimer will talk about the totally administered society, Marcuse will develop a theory of one-dimensional man, and so forth. However, while Freud, Adorno, and Horkheimer never move beyond this pessimism, Marcuse finds the tools for a theory of emancipatory possibilities in Freud's theory. That is, Marcuse will use Freud against Freud. Freud's 1915 essay titled "Repression" reveals that repression can never be complete. The instincts never give up their struggle against the mechanisms of repression. Therefore, it is always possible to develop critical, revolutionary consciousness.

There is no space here for following Marcuse's development and the arguments that he offers. For present purposes it is enough to know that Marcuse was always open to the development of new forms of revolutionary consciousness even if this consciousness did not develop in the working class. The many different forms of repression made possible many forms of resistance. It is this awareness that allowed Marcuse to connect with different social groups who were engaged in emancipatory struggle. Instead of looking to one group for revolutionary activity, Marcuse began to focus on what he called catalyst groups. These catalyst groups are groups of individuals who suffer from various forms of oppression, repression, and domination. As a result of their suffering they develop oppositional attitudes and practices toward the social system that oppresses them. Marcuse uses examples such as the Civil Rights movement, feminism, and student revolts. These sites of opposition provide hope for social change.

From Adorno to Marcuse: Angela Davis, Critical Theory, and Race

The fourth biennial meeting of the International Herbert Marcuse Society was held October 27–29, 2011, at the University of Pennsylvania. On the second day, Angela

Davis delivered the keynote address. Lucius Outlaw offered some reflections on critical theory during our dinner/reception on the final day. Professor Outlaw gave an insightful reflection on what distinguished Marcuse from his colleagues Adorno and Horkheimer. The difference is that Marcuse was a teacher and mentor who was also a student. It was in the activism of his students that Marcuse saw the potential for social change. Although he did not always agree with their tactics, he still took their cause seriously and tried to learn and participate as much as he could. Adorno and Horkheimer, on the other hand, seemed to clash with their activist students. Adorno resisted the application of critical theory to political activism (Farr, Kellner, Lamas and Reitz 2015).

> Adorno continued to refuse the students' request that, as the leading representative of critical theory, he should declare his solidarity with their political goals. It was clear to him that he ran the risk of being used, and he made desperate efforts to preserve his independence as a theoretician.
> (Müller-Doohm 2005: 460)

The fact that Adorno would not declare his solidarity with the students' political goals did not mean that he was unsympathetic. For the most part he agreed with them. However, there were two areas of concern that led Adorno to keep his distance from student protest. First, he was skeptical of the students' understanding of their own situation. That is, how well had they examined the forces that they were up against? How well did they understand the mechanisms of their own oppression? How well did they understand the weapons that were at the disposal of the Establishment? Revolutionary action requires serious theoretical work. Second, Adorno was worried about the premature application of theory to practice. He thought that in the minds of the students, the unity of theory and practice became the dominance of practice. If this is the case, then the theoretician becomes the servant of the activist. Adorno was afraid that he would be forced to conform to the wills of the activists for the sake of activism. If theory is to be correct and helpful, it must be independent.

Marcuse had some of these same worries and did not always agree with student activists. It seemed that Adorno was focused on getting theory right first, while Marcuse allowed theory and practice to work together and inform each other. This view would be reinforced by Angela Davis. Before her study of critical theory Angela Davis was already very political. Her political orientation was forced on her by her social situation. Davis's situation was that of being born in the racially segregated American South where she was forced to experience various forms of dehumanization, brutality, alienation, and so forth. She knew personally the four girls who were killed in Birmingham in 1963 when the 16th Street Baptist Church was bombed by white racists (Davis 2006: 128). Liberation was not just a nice idea or a theoretical concept; it was a necessity.

As a college student Davis was drawn to French literature and philosophy. As she was working toward a degree in French literature, she decided to devote more of her time to philosophy. This would lead to her encounter with the Frankfurt School. Davis had already read Marx at a very young age. Therefore, she was already prepared for Frankfurt School critical theory. Although she encountered Marcuse first while she was studying at Brandeis University, she would journey to Frankfurt to study with Adorno, who had returned to Germany with Horkheimer to reopen the Institute after the war. Marcuse was very supportive of Davis's move to Frankfurt. He believed that it was the best place to get a good philosophical education. However, as the civil rights struggle in the United States intensified, Davis became restless and felt a need to be back home with her people in the struggle. She writes:

> The more the struggles at home accelerated, the more frustrated I felt at being forced to experience it all vicariously. I was advancing my studies, deepening my understanding of philosophy, but I felt more and more isolated. I was so far away from the terrain of the fight that I could not even analyze the episodes of the struggle. I did not even have the knowledge or understanding to judge which currents of the movement were progressive and genuine and which were not. It was a difficult balance I was trying to maintain, and it was increasingly hard to feel a part of the collective coming to consciousness of my people.
> (Davis 2006: 144–145)

Although Adorno had agreed to direct her doctoral dissertation, Davis could not resist the desire to go back to the United States and join the black liberation movement (Davis 2006: 145).

Having decided to leave Germany after two years of study, Davis corresponded with Marcuse who agreed to work with her at his new academic home, the University of California, San Diego. Davis recalls the difference between Adorno and Marcuse as follows:

> Studying with both Adorno and Marcuse allowed me to think early on about the relationship between theory and practice, between intellectual work and activist work. Adorno tended to dismiss intellectual work that was connected with political activism. He argued that the revolution failed, not so much because of problems presenting themselves in the practical implementation of revolutionary theory, but rather because the theory itself was flawed, perhaps even fundamentally flawed. He therefore insisted that the only sure way to move along a revolutionary continuum was to effect, for the present, a retreat into theory. No revolutionary transformation was possible, he said, until we could figure out what went wrong in the theory.
> (Davis 2004a: 316–317)

She continues: "Marcuse, of course, called for a very different relationship between intellectual work and political practice" (Davis 2004a: 317). For Marcuse, social transformation required the cooperation of theory and practice. One could not wait to get theory right first. Right theory developed alongside practice and vice versa. In fact, Marcuse's own theory benefited from his observation of student activism in the '60s and '70s. Marcuse learned from people who were engaged in struggles for liberation the importance of not separating intellectual work from activism. It is here that Marcuse becomes the student of Angela Davis.

What separates Marcuse and Adorno is the ability to empathize with those in struggle. Marcuse learned from the experience of others. Davis says of Adorno: "In Frankfurt, when I was studying with Adorno, he discouraged me from seeking to discover ways of linking my seemingly discrepant interests in philosophy and social activism" (Davis 2005: xi).

Davis felt drawn back to the United States after the formation of the Black Panther Party in 1966. The situation of blacks in the United States created in her a sense of urgency. Unlike Adorno, Marcuse was much more supportive of activism. In the case of Angela Davis and the black struggle for freedom, Marcuse's support was based on his recognition of his own limitations. That is, he knew that he was in no position to fully understand the extent of black suffering. It is here that he learned from Davis; the teacher became the student. In a 1970 letter from Marcuse to Davis, he expresses a type of humility that one would not expect from Adorno. Marcuse admits to being a bit uneasy about introducing the publication of two lectures on Frederick Douglass given by Davis in 1969. He goes on to reflect on his reading of her prospectus for her thesis on Kant. It was in the reading of this thesis that Marcuse began to understand Davis's own attempt to unite theory and practice. He began to understand the urgency of the situation of blacks in the United States.

Marcuse sees in Davis an example of his own critique of abstract philosophical notions of freedom that permeates Western philosophy (Marcuse 2007). Marcuse writes in his letter:

> The abstract philosophical concept of freedom which can never be taken away suddenly comes to life and reveals its very concrete truth: freedom is not only the goal of liberation, it *begins* with liberation; it is there to be "practiced." This, I confess, learned from you! Strange? I don't think so.
> (Marcuse 2005: 49)

Marcuse makes this statement after mentioning what he learned from Davis's lectures on Frederick Douglass. The fight between Douglass and his master, the slave breaker Mr. Covey, is a critical moment because it reveals that freedom has to assert itself in a real, physical form if it is to exist at all. Even the freedom to do theory demands a certain degree of physical freedom. Compare Marcuse's statement to the following statement by Davis:

> We have to talk about a complete and total change in the structures of the society because that's the only way for the concept like academic freedom to remain relevant. We have to go to the streets.
> (Davis 2014: 212)

The point made by Davis and Marcuse is that if there is to be real freedom among human beings then social structures must change so that freedom is possible. A change in social structures demands activism or practice as well as theory. Even the freedom to do theory must be fought for.

In his letter to Davis, Marcuse acknowledges that he and Davis grew up in different worlds and that the world which Davis inhabited was one of violence and cruelty against her people. Her struggle was to make the philosophical concept of freedom a reality that would counter this violence and cruelty. Given the absence of real freedom for blacks in the world inhabited by Davis, it is no mystery that she would try to connect her philosophy (which theorized freedom) to her activism. Marcuse states:

> I feel that no sophisticated explanation is needed to understand how Angela became a black militant, a revolutionary. Precisely because she was a true

"intellectual," precisely because she was a true philosophy student—and because she was a human being, she took seriously what she read in the works.
(Davis 2014: 214)

Critical Theory, Intersectionality, and Angela Davis

Today critical theory still suffers from the appearance of being irrelevant to people of African descent (Outlaw 2005). With the exception of the work by scholars such as Lucius Outlaw, literature on critical theory is still dominated by white males, with the exception of a few white feminists who are a part of what we call third generation critical theorists. Second generation critical theory is dominated by the discourse ethics of Jürgen Habermas, while third generation critical theory is dominated by Axel Honneth's theory of recognition. Neither Habermas nor Honneth adequately theorizes race. For some reason Davis is omitted from histories of critical theory. There are at least two possible reasons for this. First, critical theory, following Adorno, has become bogged down by theory and has sidelined political activism. Second, critical theory has never properly acknowledged the problem of race. Therefore, critical theory reflects the racialized structure of the society that it critiques. My position is that another story must be told if critical theory is to remain relevant. The story of Angela Davis and her engagement with critical theory must be included in the history of critical theory as well as in its future development.

In my view, Angela Davis represents an unrecognized side of Frankfurt School critical theory. As slightly older than Honneth and younger than Habermas, she belongs to a group between second and third generation critical theorists. As a woman and African American, Angela Davis belongs to two groups that have to some degree been overlooked by critical theory. While Habermas and Honneth have given some attention to feminism and their work has been widely used by feminists, their engagement with the struggle of women has been somewhat thin, and their engagement with black people has been even thinner.

Overall, students of critical theory have failed to properly recognize the problem of racism and its centrality in American society and have overlooked Davis and her contribution to critical social engagement (Outlaw 2005). Davis is an example of a critical theory in the interests of black folk as well as in the interests of all oppressed people. Her unique contribution to critical theory is the actual lived unity of theory and practice. We saw earlier Marcuse's praise for Davis's ability to bring the philosophical concept of freedom to life, to give it material existence through political struggle. In addition to uniting theory and practice, Davis also unites a multiplicity of struggles. This is one of her main contributions to critical theory, and it should be a guide for present and future critical theorists, who following Marx's eleventh thesis on Feuerbach, seek to change the world and not merely interpret it.

According to Lucius Outlaw, one of Marcuse's main contributions to a critical theory in the interests of black folk and others was his ability to think in term of the social whole. Thinking in terms of the social whole requires more than theory. While theory is a necessary component, since we are also engaged in a struggle over ideas, it must develop in tandem with practice. That is, theory must always inform and be informed by real concrete struggle for liberation. These struggles take on a multiplicity of forms but they are not disconnected, isolated, self-contained struggles. While each struggle for liberation is against a specific form of oppression which each has its own distinct logic, each form of oppression and its corresponding struggle is a part of a system or network of oppressive mechanisms. For example, we must examine the way in which race-based oppression supports class-based oppression while not being identical to class-based oppression. This holds true in reverse. Marcuse and Davis both seem to embody the view held by Martin Luther King Jr. when he wrote that "Injustice anywhere is a threat to justice everywhere" (King 1986: 290). This is why Davis and Marcuse both advocated a radical transformation of the entire society. This is why Marcuse called for solidarity between all groups who were engaged in a struggle for liberation no matter what form of oppression they struggled against and no matter where that struggle takes place.

The critical theory of Angela Davis is not only informed by Frankfurt School critical theory and Marxism, it is equally and perhaps more informed by real concrete struggles in the street. This includes the civil rights movement, the black power movement, feminism, black feminist thought, prison abolition, and so forth. One of the key ideas that connect Davis to Marcuse's notion of solidarity is the black feminist concept of intersectionality. However, the concept of intersectionality is a bit more complex and goes a bit deeper than the notion of solidarity. The notion of solidarity suggests that various groups engaged in the struggle for liberation support each other in their respective struggles. However, these struggles may still be taken to be separate from each other. If this is the case, then the deep underlying relationship between forms of oppression are never addressed. This allows a fragmentation that hinders the possible success of these movements. In connecting the recent Occupy Movement to other contemporary struggles for liberation, Davis writes:

> The fact that relations among movements—the antiwar movement, the Black movement, the women's movement—were framed as coalitional was indicative of the inability to grasp the organic interrelationships of these issues. Today, many of us effortlessly speak of intersectionality, thanks primarily to the work of women of color feminism. We can conceptualize these issues not as discrete, disconnected issues whose relationship we have to mechanically orchestrate but, rather, as issues that are already in crosshatched, overlaid, intersectional patterns. Class, race, gender, sexuality, ability, and other social relations are not simplistically separate. They can never remain uncontaminated by each other.
> (Davis 2015: 435–436)

The concept of intersectionality has its origins in black feminism (Collins 1998). Black feminism distinguishes itself from what is often called white middle-class feminism by bringing to feminist conversations the issues of race and socio/economic class (Davis 1990: 30). Black feminists criticize those white feminists who have ignored the intersection of gender, race, and class (Davis 1990: 30) Davis, however, takes intersectionality beyond the terrain marked out by most black feminists, as she has engaged issues of war and prison abolition. In a Marcusean way, she has called for the total transformation of our society. Marcuse was aware of and supportive of Davis's call for total social transformation. In some comments made about Davis in 1972, Marcuse seems to highlight Davis's view of intersectionality (Marcuse 2014).

In her publications over the years, Davis has tirelessly demonstrated the connection between the US prison system and gender, class, and race. In a society built on the oppression of certain social groups, the institutions of that society will reflect the goals of the dominant group. This is a point that Marcuse and Davis share. The liberation of individuals demands the liberation of all of our institutions. The project of human liberation must be thorough in its critique of contemporary institutions and their visible and invisible mechanisms of oppression. The concept of intersectionality developed by Davis and other black feminists reflects a refusal to reduce oppression to one sort. Instead, the focus is on the overall social structure that is designed to maintain and perpetuate systems of domination and oppression.

While the critical theory of Angela Davis is informed by Marxian theory and early Frankfurt School critical theory, she has made much broader use of these theoretical tools than others in this tradition. She is one of the few critical theorists who has her focus on the whole social system and the multiple forms of oppression generated by this system. For this reason, it is my view that survival and relevance of critical theory requires a new look at the work of Angela Davis.

References

Abromeit, John. (2011) *Max Horkheimer and the Foundations of the Frankfurt School*, Cambridge: Cambridge University Press.
Adorno, Theodor. (1991) *The Culture Industry*, ed. J. M. Bernstein. New York: Routledge.
Bronner, Stephen Eric. (2002) *Of Critical Theory and Its Theorists*, New York: Routledge.
Collins, Patricia Hill. (1998) *Fighting Words: Black Women & the Search for Justice*, Minneapolis: University of Minnesota Press.
Davis, Angela. (1990) *Women, Culture, & Politics*, New York: Vintage Books.
———. (2004a) "Reflections on Race, Class, and Gender in the USA," in Joy James (ed.), *The Angela Davis Reader*. Malden, MA: Blackwell, pp. 307–325.
———. (2004b) "Unfinished Lecture on Liberation—II," in Joy James (ed.), *The Angela Y. Davis Reader*. Malden, MA: Blackwell, pp. 53–60.
———. (2005) "Marcuse's Legacies," in Douglas Kellner (ed.), *Herbert Marcuse: The New Left and the 1960s*. New York: Routledge, pp. vii–xiv.
———. (2006) *Angela Davis: An Autobiography*, New York: International.
———. (2013) "Critical Refusals and Occupy." *Radical Philosophy Review* 16, no. 2: 425–439.
Davis, Angela, and Marcuse, Herbert. (2014) "Angela Davis and Herbert Marcuse: KPIX Newsclips 1969–1972," in Douglas Kellner (ed.), *Herbert Marcuse: Marxism, Revolution and Utopia*. New York: Routledge, pp. 212–213.
Farr, Arnold. (2004) "Whiteness Visible: Enlightenment Racism and the Structure of Racialized Consciousness," in George Yancy (ed.), *What White Looks Like: African-American Philosophers on the Whiteness Question*. New York: Routledge, pp. 144–145.
Farr, Arnold L., et al. (2013) "Critical Refusals in Theory and Practice: The Radical Praxis of Herbert Marcuse and Angela Davis." *Radical Philosophy Review* 16, no. 2: 405–424.
Feenberg, Andrew. (2014) *Marx, Lukács, and the Frankfurt School*, New York: Verso.
Held, David. (1980) *Introduction to Critical Theory: Horkheimer to Habermas*, Berkeley: University of California Press.
"Herbert Marcuse and the Frankfurt School." International Herbert Marcuse Society. It is in a series on Modern Philosophy by Brian Magee, 2005.
Jay, Martin. (1973) *The Dialectical Imagination: A History of the Frankfurt School and the Institute of Social Research, 1923–1950*, Boston: Little, Brown.

Kellner, Douglas. (1989) *Critical Theory: Marxism and Modernity*, Baltimore: Johns Hopkins University Press.
King, Martin Luther, Jr. (1986) "Letter From Birmingham City Jail," in James M. Washington (ed.), *A Testament of Hope: The Essential Writings of Martin Luther King, Jr.* San Francisco: Harper & Row, pp. 289–302.
Marcuse, Herbert. (1969) "The Affirmative Character of Culture," in *Negations: Essays in Critical Theory*, trans. Jeremy J. Shapiro. Boston: Beacon Press, pp. 65–98.
———. (2001) "The Problem of Social Change in the Technological Society," in Douglas Kellner (ed.), *Herbert Marcuse: Towards a Critical Theory of Society*. New York: Routledge, pp. 35–58.
———. (2005) "Dear Angela," in Douglas Kellner (ed.), *Herbert Marcuse: The New Left and the 1960s*, New York: Routledge, p. 49.
———. (2007) "The Affirmative Character of Culture," in Andrew Feenberg and William Leiss (ed.), *The Essential Marcuse*. Boston: Beacon Press, pp. 201–232.
———. (2007) "Sartre's Existentialism," in Andrew Feenberg and William Leiss (eds.), *The Essential Marcuse: Selected Writings of Philosopher and Social Critic Herbert Marcuse*. Boston: Beacon Press, pp. 128–158.
Müller-Doohm, Stefan. (2009) *Adorno: A Biography*, trans. Rodney Livingstone, Cambridge: Polity Press.
Outlaw, Lucius. (2005) *Critical Social Theory in the Interests of Black Folks*, Lanham, MD: Rowman & Littlefield.
———. (2013) "'Critical Social Theory'—Then and Now: The Personal and the Political in an Intellectual Life." *Radical Philosophy Review* 16, no. 1: 223–235.
Wiggerhaus, Rolf. (1998) *The Frankfurt School: Its History, Theories, and Political Significance*, trans. Michael Robertson, Cambridge, MA: MIT Press.

9
POST-STRUCTURALISM AND RACE
Giorgio Agamben and Michel Foucault
Ladelle McWhorter

Race today is a field of problematization—to use a term of Michel Foucault's. It arises both as what must be thought and as what defies many of the categories and techniques of thought. Its importance is undeniable, and its impacts inescapable, no matter what our particular racial identities happen to be. Yet, race does not confront us as a defineable object with which to grapple; rather, it pervades our situation, seemingly without limit, as ubiquitous disparity, wound, demand, fear, and provocation. Race is where we are and who we are, and where and who we have been all our lives. Yet, it seems untenable—perhaps intolerable.[1]

Whether anything in the writings of Giorgio Agamben or Michel Foucault has value for us as we struggle with how to live in/as/through this field of force relations depends entirely upon where we seek to intervene and what maneuvers we seek to perform. There is no truth in the work of these thinkers—that is, there is nothing in particular in their writings that we *must* know—but there may well be plenty there to help us think, to aid our experiments and strategies.

Accordingly, this chapter is a survey of a range of potential tools. It does not aim for thorough representation of Agamben's or Foucault's ideas about race. Instead, it aims only to consider a few of their concepts' relevance and power for certain sorts of transformative work. The first half of the chapter takes up Agamben's concepts of state of exception, the camp as *nomos*, and *homo sacer*. The second half examines Foucault's normalization and biopower.

Agamben

A state of exception, says Agamben following Carl Schmitt, is established when someone invested with power to do so suspends the law in an effort to preserve the state, nation, or people and, indeed, the law itself. When, for example, in the name of preserving liberty against the threat of terrorist attack a president suspends habeas corpus and allows individuals to be detained indefinitely without trial, we have a state of exception. On its face, a state of exception is paradoxical, a legal suspension of law ushering in a new order that appears, against the background of the order immediately preceding it, as illegality. But it is not illegality; law is simply out of play, so that authorities' actions unfold in a zone of juridical undecidability.

Agamben bases his concept not only on that of Schmitt but also on that of Walter Benjamin, who declared (with horror) that under the Nazi regime a state of exception, which was supposedly established as a response to national emergency, had become no longer an exception but the rule; emergency measures had become normal routine, temporary had become permanent. Agamben, however, extends Benjamin's declaration far beyond the Nazi regime to include, for example, the USA Patriot Act and the US detention center at Guantanamo Bay (Agamben 2005: 3–4). When the state of exception begins to make itself into a permanent arrangement, he maintains, the space that is opened is the camp. "In the camp," he writes, "the state of exception, which was essentially a temporary suspension of the rule of law on the basis of a factual state of danger, is now given a permanent spatial arrangement, which as such nevertheless remains outside the normal order" (Agamben 1998: 169).

Camps are becoming ubiquitous today, whether detention camps for enemy combatants or undocumented immigrants or refugee camps for the millions streaming forth from regions devastated by invasion, civil war, and famine, a fact that prompts Agamben to declare that "the birth of the camp in our time appears as an event that decisively signals the political space of modernity itself" (1998: 174). "The camp . . . is the new biopolitical *nomos* of the planet" (1998: 176). If law is in suspension within the camp, those whose lives unfold there embody the figure of *homo sacer*, the living body set outside the law by sovereign decree, which, as a result, can be killed with impunity but cannot, as Agamben puts it, be sacrificed. Such a life will have, therefore, a death without meaning, to no end; it will be killed (or die of deprivation) simply "as lice" (Agamben 1998: 114).[2]

On a visit to Turkey in 2010, UK Prime Minister David Cameron accused Israel of turning Gaza into a "prison camp." "People in Gaza are living under constant attacks and pressure in an open-air prison," he declared (BBC 2010). Jerome Roos offers Cameron's remarks as reinforcement for Agamben's claim (Roos 2014); according to Roos, the state of exception has globalized and its techniques are routinely shared across borders and regimes. Roos notes, further, that through the Law Enforcement Exchange Program (LEEP), American sheriffs and chiefs of police are routinely sent to Israel to learn militaristic anti-terror techniques (Roos 2014), and since 2004, 12 regional LEEP conferences for police officers have been held in the United States, training more than 9,500 officers from around the country in Israeli techniques (Empowering Law Enforcement, n.d.: 31). Among those so trained were the St. Louis, Missouri, chief of police in February of 2008 (Empowering Law Enforcement, n.d.: 34) and two of the four police forces deployed to Ferguson, Missouri, during the rioting that broke out after Officer Darren Wilson shot and killed Michael Brown, an unarmed 18-year-old African American, in September of 2014 (Roos 2014).

While Roos acknowledges that Ferguson is not Gaza, he does assert that the parallels are close and drawing nearer, and that Agamben's concepts readily apply to both. Ferguson, too, is or at least has been made a zone of legal indistinction, a state of exception. Roos's case is aided by the fact that Agamben himself has suggested that the poor of the third world, whether dispossessed of their land or not, have been effectively abandoned by government to live without protection of law.[3] A "camp," it seems, need not be physically cordoned off from the domain of legality that surrounds it as a prison must be; it must only be a kind of ghetto. That being the case, Roos asserts,

> Today, the ghettos of Detroit and the outer neighborhoods of St Louis, like the townships of Johannesburg and the favelas of Rio de Janeiro, increasingly take on the form of open-air prison camps, in which the police permanently act as temporary sovereign, and in which poor blacks—and male youths in particular—are simply considered free game for the racist fantasies of white officers.
>
> (Roos 2014)

Silvia Grinberg makes similar use of Agamben's concepts of the camp, the state of exception, and *homo sacer* in her analysis of Buenos Aires shantytowns. "Of course," she writes, "shantytowns are not concentration or refugee camps; their inhabitants are not prevented from coming and going, or from working. But they live on the symbolic border of the nation, occupying an ambivalent 'inside/outside' citizenship status" (Grinberg 2012: 206). Shantytowns are distinguished from other regions of Buenos Aires not by their poverty, which abounds elsewhere in the city as well, but by the illegality of their occupancy. The land on which they sit is not owned by those who live there (or rented from legal owners), although many residents have paid previous occupants for their small pieces of it or pay regular rent to someone who claims it.[4] The city water contractor does not provide water except through one open pipe; there is no electrical power; in fact, there are no streets and the city does not include the region on its maps (Grinberg 2012: 205). Police do not routinely patrol through the shantytowns but remain at the border. When they do come in, they may injure or kill residents with impunity (Grinberg 2012: 218). While the state claims the right to impose any regulations it chooses in the shantytowns, it does not accept any responsibility for the well-being of the residents, many of whom have never even been issued the standard Argentine identity card that all citizens are supposed to receive; they are undocumented in their own country.

While life in a favela is a lot different from life in any US city or suburb, most Argentinians living in shantytowns—like most of the residents of Ferguson, Missouri—are marked as racially other to the larger, surrounding population. The ground upon which the shantytowns stand was once marsh and grassland where Native people hid from the invading Spaniards. Impassable on horseback, it was the borderland of the Spanish territorial conquest. Residents of shantytowns are descendants of those Indigenous people, but they are mostly of mixed race now to a great extent because of Spanish capture and rape of Native women.[5] Still, they are typically darker than other residents of Buenos Aires (Grinberg 2012: 210). Their status, as well as the status of the territory they inhabit, is marked not only by current practices but also by that colonial and racist history.

If Agamben's concept of the state of exception can apply to shantytowns and ghettos as well as camps (and he would no doubt accept such an application even if he would disagree with Grinberg that the shantytown is a *more* suitable paradigm than the concentration camp), we can also use the related concept of *homo sacer* to name the residents of such places. *Homo sacer* is a term Agamben takes from ancient Roman law. The status of *homo sacer*, conferred upon an individual by a sovereign power, placed that person outside the protection of the law, leaving him prey to anyone who might injure or even kill him with impunity. Yet he was not simply set free of the law; he remained subject to it—inside it and outside it simultaneously. Agamben asserts that this ancient violence of the ban is a founding gesture of sovereignty and as such has always existed and can never disappear. Sovereign establishment and continued existence requires the status of *homo sacer*. Such people are abandoned by the law, outside its protection, and vulnerable to the violence its supposed "enforcers" can launch against it with no repercussions for themselves. Insofar as these vulnerable residents are racialized—whether even apart from their localization in these areas or simply because of it—we may say that the paradigm of the camp/the shantytown is increasingly the blueprint that states use to govern raced populations. As the state of exception becomes the norm, it does so first of all and primarily for those raced other to the white European/American.

This last is a point that Agamben himself does not make. In fact, as Falguni Sheth has argued, Agamben's own analysis works against this idea, for he presumes that each subject stands in the same relation to sovereign authority as every other subject does, each in danger of abandonment, of becoming *homo sacer*. Regardless of one's race and regardless of the history of racial oppression in a given region, those who are members of the historically oppressed race and those who are members of the historically oppressing race are equally at risk in their relation to the sovereign power. Thus, as Sheth emphasizes, "there is no acknowledgement of a power differential between *different subject populations* in relation to each other or to the sovereign, that is, the unit of analysis is an individual subject" (Sheth 2009: 45). With no exploration of the origins and histories of states of exception, Agamben's analysis cannot explain why there are in fact pre-existing racial differences between populations under the same sovereign who are and are not abandoned by law. Agamben's individualization of *homo sacer* covers over other racial facts as well, as Mark Rifkin's work points out.

Rifkin agrees with Agamben that modern sovereignty constitutes itself by exercise of the ban. He contends that, as a settler state, the United States was only able to found its sovereignty by rendering Native peoples "peculiar," that is, by excepting them from (the protection of) the law (Rifkin 2009: 91). Reservations are a prime example, he contends, of Agamben's state of exception. His analysis thus agrees with Grinberg's that a "camp" need not be a sealed area; people may exit and enter. What is essential to the state of exception is that sovereign law does not apply within the territory of abandonment, so that people living within are outside the law's protection. Rifkin traces the juristic contortions required for courts to maintain US authority to regulate the reservations while at the same time recognizing sovereignty of tribal nations. He quotes Justice Clarence Thomas from a 2004 decision: "In my view, the tribes either are or are not separate sovereigns, and our federal Indian law cases untenably hold both positions simultaneously" (Rifkin 2009: 107). But what seems to Thomas to be anomalous is, according to Rifkin inspired by Agamben, foundational.

> The jurisdictional imaginary of the United States is made possible only by *localizing* Native peoples, in the sense of circumscribing their political power/ status and portraying Indian policy as an aberration divorced from the principles at play in the rest of US law, and that process of exception quite literally

opens the *space* for a legal geography predicated on the territorial coherence of the nation.

(Rifkin 2009: 97)

US territory *includes* the reservations—thus making it one continuous sovereign territory—while it *excludes* tribes from its officially recognized polity—thus simultaneously occluding and maintaining its status as conqueror and occupying force.

Like Sheth, however, Rifkin has serious criticisms of Agamben's concepts. The quotation in the previous paragraph emphasizes the spatial—literally, the geographic—dimension of the reservation as state of exception. Although for decades the United States made treaties with Indian nations, treating them as separate sovereignties, it makes laws that apply to people on Native lands and regulates political entities that pre-date its own existence. How is that legal? "The official answer . . . is that Native populations and lands are within the domain over which the United States is sovereign." This answer, Rifkin points out, is "tautological, self-serving, and resting on nothing more than outright assertion" (Rifkin 2009: 106), but it indicates the extreme importance of location in relation to the state of exception. Rifkin proposes to amend Agamben's analysis to address ways in which sovereign power produces not only *homo sacer*, bare life, but also what he calls "bare habitance" (Rifkin 2009: 90). Sovereign power regulates proper embodiment—relegating those who do not appear or comport themselves properly to zones of indistinction without protection—but it also regulates "legitimate modes of collectivity and occupancy" (Rifkin 2009: 90). Native peoples are not living in states of exception simply because they are, as individuals, Native Americans; they are living in states of exception because they are not merely individuals. They are tribes, nations, collectivities. As Sheth holds, Agamben's analysis does not easily encompass groups or populations with histories vis-à-vis other groups; his treatment is individualizing. Over against Agamben, Rifkin insists on the importance of groups as well as—and as in part constituted by—their historical modes of habitation. For it was Native peoples' anomalous—by European standards—modes of inhabiting land that "justified" European expropriation in the first place, at least in North America. Native people did not divide and fence off land for agricultural production; where agriculture was practiced in eastern North America prior to 1607, it was by girdling and burning trees in small areas of forests for a few seasons of planting and then moving on to a new spot, leaving the last to regenerate. Agriculture was a tribal effort, not the work of individuals and families. And living space was to some extent mobile and multiple, with encampments for seasonal hunting and fishing in addition to more permanent structures in villages or compounds. John Locke notoriously denigrates these practices in *The Second Treatise of Government*, insisting that European agricultural methods are the only practices that constitute a legitimate claim to ownership of land. He writes:

> God, when he gave the World in common to all Mankind, commanded Man also to labour, and the penury of his Condition required it of him. God and his Reason commanded him to subdue the Earth, *i.e.*, improve it for the benefit of Life, and therein lay out something upon it that was his own, his labour. He that in Obedience to this Command of God, subdued, tilled and sowed any

part of it, thereby annexed to it something that was his *Property*, which another had no Title to, nor could without injury take from him.

(Locke II.V.32 1960: 332–333)

Native peoples' collective habitation and use of resources and their seasonal mobility did not count, in Locke's view and those of many of his countrymen, as obedient occupation and improvement, which could only be individualized and stationary. Such collective, mobile techniques and modes of life were ungodly and unreasonable. Such populations were "peculiar," as Rifkin says, to put it mildly, and they posed a threat to US sovereignty that could only be contained if they were immobilized. As Rifkin points out, placing Native peoples on reservations was not a self-confident sovereign gesture, as Agamben's analysis would lead us to imagine. It was a gesture born of anxiety (Rifkin 2009: 90).

Rifkin's critique of Agamben on the basis of his study of Native peoples in the United States leads him to suggest that Agamben must be "indigenized" before his work can be useful. We must adjust

> the persistent inside/outside tropology he uses to address the exception, specifically the ways it serves as a metaphor divorced from territoriality; the notion of "bare life" as the basis of the exception, especially the individualizing ways that he uses that concept; and the implicit depiction of sovereignty as a self-confident exercise of authority free from anxiety over the legitimacy of state actions.
>
> (Rifkin 2009: 90)

Along with Grinberg's and Sheth's insistence that the states of exceptions in racialized ghettos and shantytowns must be understood against a historical background of shifting networks of power vis-à-vis multiple populations, it seems that Agamben's value for critical thought and analysis of race and racism has some significant limitations. In light of these criticisms, we may turn to the work of Michel Foucault.

Foucault addresses the issue of race at least twice in his *oeuvre*. The first comments to make a published appearance are in Part Five of *The History of Sexuality, Volume 1*, published in the fall of 1976. There Foucault introduces the concept of biopower, his name for the vast and complex network of power relations resulting from the "explosion of numerous and diverse techniques for achieving the subjugation of bodies and the control of populations" in the West through the late eighteenth and nineteenth centuries (Foucault 1980: 140). As networks of biopower assembled, the primary target of knowledge and power altered.

> Power would no longer be dealing simply with legal subjects over whom the ultimate dominion was death, but with living beings, and the mastery it would be able to exercise over them would have to be applied at the level of life itself.
>
> (Foucault 1980: 142–143)

Management of individual bodies took the form of normalizing disciplinary techniques designed to direct and channel developmental processes to bring living beings into conformity with statistical norms (or at least to identify them as abnormal in some measure and to husband that abnormal developmental trajectory). Management of populations took the form of techniques of security designed to influence population trends—birth and death rates, crime rates, and so forth. Living bodies and living populations were two separate types of target, but both were dynamic and developmental—that is, *living*— beings. Strategies that bring these differing targets and techniques close together promised and proved to be exceedingly effective. Sexualization (of both bodies and populations) is such a strategy, and racialization is an integral aspect of it (and vice versa, with emphasis falling on one or the other depending on analytic context).[6] By the twentieth century, bodies were sexualized, constrained, and cultivated in the name of racial hygiene, and populations were racialized in eugenic purification campaigns designed to ensure the continued vitality and development of the species.[7] This is the point, Foucault asserts, where racism emerges—"racism in its modern, 'biologizing,' statist form" (Foucault 1980: 149). Nazism was only the most obvious manifestation of this racism; similar, if somewhat less dramatic, manifestations can be found in all the biopolitical nation-states of twentieth-century Europe and America.

In the spring semester before the publication of *The History of Sexuality*, Foucault gave a course at the Collège de France (now published as *Society Must Be Defended*), in which we find a much longer discussion of race. He introduces race in Lecture 3, where he locates its emergence in seventeenth-century England. With an increasingly unpopular king on the throne, an underclass began to tell itself a story about the origins and mechanisms of its own felt oppression: once upon a time, before the Norman Conquest, the Saxons had lived under an ancient constitution that protected their liberty. But then, the Normans imposed their laws on the conquered Saxons, laws that were nothing more than another form of Norman weaponry. On the surface, England might seem to be a multitiered monarchy, but appearances are deceiving. In reality, there were two mass collectivities pitted against one another—an ongoing war between Normans and Saxons, a race war. Race war discourse began, Foucault argues, as a counter-discourse, a way of resisting the legitimacy of the state and the power of sovereignty.

Like almost all weapons, however, race war discourse can be put to contradictory uses. Boulainvilliers used it in eighteenth-century France to justify and reinstate the power of the nobility (see Foucault 1997: 128ff). Still, different as these deployments' purposes may be, neither is racist in any contemporary sense—that is, they do not posit a natural hierarchy of races or racial morphologies or characters, nor do they assert the existence of a superior or an inferior race. Race is a matter of lineage, language, religion, and law, not a matter of health, intelligence, or moral worth.

Only when race is absorbed into biopower do we begin to see racism of a familiar sort.[8] Foucault does not delve into the process by which lineal race became morphological race, which became a field of problematization in eighteenth-century anthropology, but this process set the stage for race to be absorbed into developmental discourses. Accounting for morphological races by way of migration and the effects of climate, anthropologists claimed that mild temperatures and abundant year-round sources of food resulted in biological, intellectual, and moral stagnation in southern races, while environmental adversity fostered foresight, diligence, and self-restraint in those of the north. Races then represented developmental stages along the way toward human perfection, which meant that some were superior and some inferior to others.[9] Superior races approached the human ideal, while inferior races moldered in developmental retardation or total arrest; some might even be regressing toward savagery and extinction. It was only rational that law and public policy should take account of these alleged scientific facts and discriminate on the basis of them. Public safety and well-being demanded it. Incivility, let alone savagery, poses a threat to life and property. Furthermore, there is no point in expending valuable resources on large numbers of people who cannot learn or contribute to the advancement of society (whatever race they may be members of); they are best relegated to the realm of menial labor to produce for the support of their superiors' endeavors. Should they prove useless for that purpose—for reasons of ill-health, mental deficiency, or simply numerical superfluity—or if they prove too costly to control, they will have to be forcefully subdued and perhaps eliminated.

Forceful elimination of human beings—whether through active killing or through deprivation and neglect—seems antithetical to the aims of a biopolitical state. Yet the protection and management of life also involves the judicious administration of death. Resources, sometimes scarce, must be allocated; some people may have to suffer for the preservation of the whole. For this very reason, race and the racism it underwrites are indispensable tools, Foucault asserts: "What is racism? It is primarily a way of introducing a break into the domain of life that is under power's control: the break between what must live and what must die" (Foucault 1997: 254–255). The field of life is continuous; all individual members of the state's population are living beings. But the invention of a hierarchy of races serves to fragment that biological field. All are living beings, yes, but these lives are not equally valuable—not equally worthy. In fact those who are inferior are threats to the lives and health of those who are superior—and therefore of the whole. Population managers can thus justify their life-supporting or life-depriving resource allocations even when it means some will suffer; it is legitimate to allocate and act in ways that will eliminate inferior individuals and tend toward the elimination of inferior races: the health of the living population requires their hastened deaths. Foucault writes,

> The fact that the other dies does not mean simply that I live in the sense that his death guarantees my safety; the death of the other, the death of the bad race, of the inferior race (or the degenerate, or the abnormal) is something that will make life in general healthier: healthier and purer.
>
> (Foucault 1997: 255)

How biopolitical racism will manifest or be deployed and play out differs across different political and cultural situations. Sometimes individuals will be more or less abandoned, as Agamben's analysis suggests, removed from the protection of the law and left vulnerable to abuse and death. This is clearly happening to many populations of color around the world today as well as to some poor and disabled white populations. But Foucault's analysis allows for other, very different scenarios. States can become intensely involved with some segments of populations of color, captivating them, micromanaging them, molding them. Loïc Wacquant has argued that, post-1996, "welfare" in the United States entails unprecedented levels of surveillance over impoverished populations, especially women of color. The purpose is not to "free" people from impoverished dependency but to normalize them, to discipline them to fit into a new type of mass workforce for the modern world—not the world of information technology that politicians so often reference but the neoliberal world of the chronically sub-employed, a world without full-time contracts, health and retirement benefits, union support, living wages, paid sick leave, or even regular shifts, a world where one's day-to-day livelihood is always precarious and one's life is, therefore, always at risk. Success (if it can be so called) in this work-world requires careful time management (juggling inconvenient and unreliable public transportation with employers' unpredictable part-time scheduling and make-do child care arrangements, for example), calculated budgeting and restrained purchasing, and foresight and resourcefulness far beyond that practiced by a typical middle-class householder. Although the reality is that neoliberal governments have not allocated the kind of money that would be necessary to make these normalized disciplinary regimes function effectively,[10] the ideal does exist in bureaucratic outline form and to some extent in the life experiences of those who struggle to survive in the system.

Foucault's analysis of biopower, contrary to Agamben's, does not privilege the state. The state is a set of institutional structures that function within large networks of power relations, and in some, but only some, strategic regimes those institutional structures are paramount. Increasingly, however, as Foucault noted in his lectures series in the late 1970s, biopower is deployed through largely non-state market mechanisms. Fragmentation of the biological continuum into races can serve market purposes very well. Races become niche markets. Pharmaceutical corporations advertise and sell diagnostics and drugs to raced consumers. Fashion and entertainment industries produce styles and content for raced audiences. Likewise racism: when raced populations are not themselves significant as markets because their ability to consume is constrained by their relative lack of disposable income, they can become the object of or ground for other kinds of markets—such as (predominantly white) markets for the consumption of security. The existence of impoverished populations of color sells guns, home surveillance and alarm systems, and—of course—prisons. Politicians found they could win campaign contributions and votes with calls for more prisons, but sitting legislators and executives were loath to increase public spending to staff and maintain them adequately. That confluence of events led to the rise of private prisons in the United States, first introduced in Kentucky in 1981.[11] By 2008, 8% of all prisoners in the United States were in private facilities. By 2010, Corrections Corporation of America, established in 1983, was one of the United States' largest employers and was traded on the New York Stock Exchange (Harcourt 2011: 235). The racialized poor might not be high-dollar consumers, but trafficking in racialized confinement could prove quite lucrative.

For Foucault, relations of power form networks of varying strengths and densities. Whereas for Agamben, at least as interpreted by Sheth, each individual stands first of all in relation to the sovereign power and all individuals' relations to the sovereign are initially the same, for Foucault relations of power may be not only hierarchical but lateral and even multidirectional. There is no paradigmatic power relation. Each situation must be examined, therefore, without the presumption of a center or a hierarchy. There are camps—Guantanamo for example—and there are reservations, ghettos, prisons, and any number of other sites in which race is reproduced or reiterated and mobilized. No one type of site serves as model for the others. Across them we find similarities and differences, and both are significant for anti-racist analysis and action.

Furthermore, all situations have a history—a history of prior power relations that may reverberate within them still, as Grinberg's analysis of Buenos Aires' shantytown illustrates. Eric Garner died at the hands of a police officer not just because of the racial situation on Staten Island in 2014 but because of decades and centuries and their millions and billions of interactions among black, white, and brown people in highly complex and differential relationships—variously gendered and raced relationships among citizens and subjects and between citizens and subjects and officials of the state.[12] What

Rifkin identifies as sovereign anxiety can also be read as a power network's awareness of its own radical contingency manifest in its drive to reproduce itself.

Foucault's approach, unlike Agamben's, can enable us to form plausible and useful answers to the question of why it is so often raced individuals and communities that are abandoned, impoverished, intensively managed, persecuted, or otherwise maltreated.[13] Useful answers lie in our development of the specific genealogies of situations. There are continuities across different racial situations because those different situations are historically entangled with one another at multiple points. But the fact that there are differences in how what we now identify as racism arises and operates means that there is also reason to believe that these situations can be brought to change. We are not doomed forever to repeat the scene of abandonment in the state of exception.

Foucault's genealogical analytics of biopower and race provide possibilities that Agamben's sovereign analysis does not, although it does not offer a definitive account of race or racism or even of power dynamics. Nevertheless, as stated at the beginning of this chapter, the value of either approach lies not in its approximation to some extra-theoretical truth but in what measure of assistance it affords us as we oppose racist oppression and create alternatives to racist practices and styles of life. As the anti-racist uses to which they have been put demonstrate, both bodies of work have something to offer, and both have limitations. Only when we examine the specifics of our own situations and possibilities for change will we be able to render an informed political and philosophical judgment adequate for our own geographical specificity and moment in history.

Notes

1. This is not to say that racial identities cannot also, at times, be sources of strength, solidarity, community, and enjoyment. I would argue, however, that when this is so, it occurs in the face of the kinds of suffering and oppression that the more general mechanisms of racial identification impose; it occurs as an effect of countermoves in resistance to prevalent oppression—or occasionally as a means of bolstering a failing sense of power, as in the "heritage not hate" displays of confederate battle flags in some parts of the United States.
2. The relation between sovereignty and *homo sacer* is complex and constitutes the heart of Agamben's 1998 book, but it is not necessary to analyze that relationship in this chapter. I refer interested readers to *Homo Sacer* itself and to the essays contained in Norris 2005.
3. For some discussion, see Parfitt 2009.
4. Hernando de Soto's take on shantytowns is quite different from Grinberg's. Rather than states of political and legal exception and zones of intense suffering, he sees them as areas of amazing, if undercapitalized, entrepreneurship. He does not examine Buenos Aires, but based on his analysis of Lima, Peru, and other shantytowns around the globe, I believe he would see Buenos Aires in a similar light. See de Soto, 2000, chapter 2.
5. Not all unions were involuntary on the part of the Native women, of course. But many were, and the Spaniards certainly had the upper hand in any case.
6. This is an historical, not a logical or ontological claim; these strategies, as they formed and developed in Anglo North America intimately informed one another, as I argued in my 1999 monograph.
7. This happened with more or less intensity throughout Europe and North America but also in Australia, Japan, and some parts of South America.
8. Foucault concedes that racisms existed long before this period, if by racism we mean simply treating people according to membership in a race (however defined) rather than as individuals. Modern racism is a much more complex phenomenon, however. See Foucault 1997, 254.
9. For an in-depth account of this process, see McWhorter 2009.

10 Wacquant notes that the US Congress never approved money to train and install the number of government workers and the data tracking systems necessary to enforce the five-year life cap. See Wacquant 2009, 104.
11 I have seen conflicting dates and locations for the establishment of the first in the latest wave of private prisons. Whereas Harcourt, as cited in the text, gives the location as Kentucky and the year as 1981, Wacquant gives the location as Chattanooga, Tennessee, and the year as 1983. He says this construction began at the behest of the Immigration and Naturalization Service. See Wacquant 2009, 168.
12 Garner was a 43-year-old African American resident of Staten Island, NY, who died as a result of a choke hold placed on him by a police officer on July 17, 2014. His death was ruled homicide by the medical examiner. A bystander's video of the event went viral. See the *New York Daily News*: www.nydailynews.com/new-york/nyc-crime/eric-garner-death-ruled-homicide-medical-examiner-article-1.1888808.
13 As an anonymous reviewer of this chapter pointed out, Foucault does not give us answers to the question of why the particular people who are raced have become raced in the ways that they are. I do think, however, that Foucault's genealogical method or approach can help us develop such answers. I offer my own work as an example; see McWhorter 2009, especially 2.

References

Agamben, Giorgio. (1998). *Homo Sacer: Sovereign Power and Bare Life*, trans. Daniel Heller-Roazen, Stanford, CA: Stanford University Press.
———. (2005). *State of Exception*, trans. Kevin Attell, Chicago: University of Chicago Press.
BBC. (2010). "Cameron Describes Blockaded Gaza as a 'Prison.'" (July 27) www.bbc.com/news/world-middle-east-10778110.
de Soto, Hernando. (2000) *The Mystery of Capital: Why Capitalism Triumphs in the West and Fails Everywhere Else*, New York: Basic Books.
Foucault, Michel. (1980) *The History of Sexuality, Volume 1: An Introduction*, trans. Robert Hurley, New York: Vintage Books.
———. (1997) *"Society Must Be Defended": Lectures at the Collège de France 1975–1976*, trans. David Macey, New York: Picador.
Grinberg, Silvia. (2012) "Colonial Histories: Biopolitics and Shantytowns in the Buenos Aires Metropolitan Area," in Marcelo Svirsky and Simone Bignall (eds.), *Critical Connections: Agamben and Colonialism*. Edinburgh: Edinburgh University Press, pp. 204–225.
Harcourt, Bernard E. (2011). *The Illusion of Free Markets: Punishment and the Myth of Natural Order*, Cambridge: Harvard University Press.
Law Enforcement Exchange Program. "Empowering Law Enforcement Protecting America." www.jinsa.org/files/LEEPbookletforweb.pdf.
Locke, John. (1960). *Two Treatises of Government*, ed. Peter Laslett, Cambridge: Cambridge University Press.
McWhorter, Ladelle. (2009). *Racism and Sexual Oppression in Anglo-America: A Genealogy*, Bloomington: Indiana University Press.
Norris, Andrew (ed.) (2005) *Politics, Metaphysics, and Death: Essays on Giorgio Agamben's* Homo Sacer. Durham: Duke University Press.
Parfitt, Trevor. (2009) "Are the Third World Poor *Homines Sacri*? Biopolitics, Sovereignty, and Development." *Alternatives* 34: 41–58.
Rifkin, Mark. (2009) "Indigenizing Agamben: Rethinking Sovereignty in Light of the 'Peculiar' Status of Native Peoples." *Cultural Critique*, no. 73 (Fall): 88–124.
Roos, Jerome. (2014) "What Happens in Ferguson Does Not Stay in Ferguson." *Telesurv* (August 24). www.telesurv.net/english/opinion/What-Happens-in-Ferguson-Does-Not-Stay-in-Ferguson-20140824-0027.html.
Sheth, Falguni. (2009). *Toward a Political Philosophy of Race*, Albany: State University of New York Press.
Wacquant, Loïc. (2009) *Punishing the Poor: The Neoliberal Government of Social Insecurity*, Durham: Duke University Press.

Part II
ALTERNATIVE TRADITIONS

10
RIGHTS, RACE, AND THE BEGINNINGS OF MODERN AFRICANA PHILOSOPHY

Chike Jeffers

Western race-thinking didn't just happen to emerge as Europe became modern. Modernity and Race helped bring each other into being, and they sustained and spurred each other through different stages of development . . . [P]erhaps the most successful racializing institution in history prepared the way for today's global economy: the transnational exchange markets and financial frameworks of global capitalism cut their teeth on the transatlantic slave trade.

(Taylor 2013: 23–24)

Paul Taylor's description of a symbiotic, foundational, and co-constitutive relationship between race and modernity provocatively challenges us to avoid studying either of these two things without giving thought to the other. This chapter will explore the race-modernity connection by examining key moments in the history of philosophical thought in Africa and the African diaspora. I will discuss four thinkers who can be viewed as founding figures of modern Africana philosophy, drawing attention to the ways in which the concept of rights can be seen as significant for each of them. Taylor's guidance on how to think about race and modernity helps us to see this pattern of interest in rights as unsurprising, for if modernity is partly constituted by the conceptualization and institutionalization of racial differences, with the latter processes prominently involving the dehumanization and subjugation of African peoples, it is not surprising that Africana thinkers in the modern era would be especially invested in a discourse revolving around notions of freedom and equality.

In the first section of this chapter, however, I will raise questions about how tightly we should tie modernity, rights, and race together in the story of Africana philosophy through a discussion of Zera Yacob, a seventeenth-century Ethiopian thinker. Zera Yacob criticizes the practice of slavery with an argument that appears to make him a theorist of natural rights similar to John Locke, but it is not clear that he thought about race at all. By contrast, the thinkers I discuss in the second, third, and fourth sections of the chapter (Anton Wilhelm Amo, Lemuel Haynes, and Quobna Ottobah Cugoano, respectively) undoubtedly thought about race and, indeed, developed theories of natural rights (in the cases of Haynes and Cugoano) or conventional rights (in Amo's case) with an eye toward addressing anti-black racial oppression. These three thinkers may thus be seen as founders of modern Africana philosophy in precisely the ways for which Taylor prepares us. I will conclude by explaining why Cugoano represents the most intriguing and instructive case of all.

Zera Yacob, Early Modern Ethiopia, and Natural Rights

Zera Yacob's *Hatäta*, or "inquiry," commonly called his *Treatise* (Sumner 1985), begins with an account of his birth in 1599 in the city of Axum and his education, which led him to become a teacher. After being falsely portrayed to the emperor as seditious, he fled Axum and lived for two years in a cave. The thoughts he had in this cave represent the bulk of his treatise. He reflects, most prominently, on religious disagreement: How does one know whether those who interpret things in accordance with the Ethiopian Orthodox version of Christianity are right, as opposed to those who believe in the Roman Catholicism brought to Ethiopia by Jesuits from the Iberian peninsula? How does one judge whether the Muslims or the Jews have it right? Zera Yacob's reasoning leads him to conclude that the way to truth is not through accepting any particular religious viewpoint but rather through relying upon one's own reason.

In light of this position, he subjects the claims of various religions to critical scrutiny, rejecting as of human rather than divine origin anything that he finds does not comport with reason. For example, all of the Abrahamic religions are criticized for encouraging fasting, as eating is how we survive and thus not eating for significant periods of time is irrational. Toward the end of the treatise, returning to autobiography, he tells of how he left the cave and settled in the town of Enfraz, where he worked as a scribe for a rich man and taught the man's two sons. One of those sons was Walda Heywat, who became a kind of disciple of Zera Yacob and at whose request Zera Yacob's *Hatäta* was written in 1667. Walda Heywat also wrote a treatise of his own, and its preface reports the peaceful death of Zera Yacob in 1692.

Claude Sumner has commented upon the significance of the *Hatäta* by saying that "MODERN PHILOSOPHY, in the sense of a personal rationalistic critical investigation, BEGAN IN ETHIOPIA with *Zär'a Ya'əqob* at the same time as in England and in France" (1985: 227). This is a bold yet plausible claim. There are at least two reasons that, jointly, make it illuminating to view Zera Yacob as a pioneering modern philosopher, the first in the Africana tradition. The first, evoked by Sumner, has to do with the fruitfulness of comparing his approach to philosophy to that of thinkers living at the same time, such as Descartes. Consider this representative passage on the importance of Descartes by Jeffrey Tlumak:

> Descartes' philosophy embodies the central, modern idea that each person can discover which beliefs are true, and what actions are right, without imposition of outside authority. But his individualism is especially radical. He pursues truth in the solitude of his own thinking, using extreme doubt as a vital tool.
> (2007: 1)

It is striking that we could substitute Zera Yacob's name for Descartes's own in this passage and it would remain a very appropriate description.

This reason for describing Zera Yacob's treatise as modern philosophy, however, seems insufficient to me, for if we were to discover a text from, say, fifth-century Ethiopia in which a similar combination of suspicion of religious authority and trust in reason were expressed, I might say that it surprisingly anticipates modern themes but I would not classify it as modern. A second, linked reason to classify Zera Yacob as modern, then, involves the usefulness of understanding his historical context as part of an evolving *early modern world*. As Jerry Bentley (2007) tells us, a number of historians have worked to extend the concept of early modernity from its initial application in European history to a global scope. To distinguish the period, Bentley writes: "by the term *early modern world* I mean the era about 1500 to 1800, when cross-cultural interactions increasingly linked the fates and fortunes of peoples throughout the world, but before national states, mechanized industry, and industrial-strength imperialism decisively changed the dynamics governing the development of world history" (2007: 22).

Zera Yacob's Ethiopia exemplifies the distinctiveness of this period as an era of global history. The presence of Jesuits in Ethiopia is an example of the kind of long-range cross-cultural interaction that Bentley identifies as newly common in early modernity. In 1543, Portugal aided Ethiopia in repelling an invasion by Somali Muslim forces, who were in turn backed by the Ottoman Empire. This military assistance helped lay the groundwork for Iberian Jesuit influence at Ethiopia's royal court, leading eventually to King Susenyos's conversion in 1622. The king then declared Catholicism the state religion, thus replacing the Ethiopian Orthodox faith that dated back to the fourth century. Zera Yacob's flight from Axum was caused by an enemy of his falsely claiming that he had been encouraging rebellion against the king in defense of the ancient faith. There was, indeed, much resistance and King Susenyos was forced to declare religious liberty in 1632. After he abdicated power in favor of his son, Fasiladas, the latter promptly re-established the Orthodox Church as state religion and soon expelled the Jesuits.

This context of religious conflict gave rise to Zera Yacob's reflections on truth and knowledge, just as religious conflict shaped early modern Europe in ways affecting the development of modern philosophy there. John Marshall (2006) clarifies what gave rise to Locke's *Letter Concerning Toleration*, for example, by describing in detail the forms and levels of religious intolerance in France, England, and the Netherlands. When the broad historical context of the early modern world is taken into account, the thematic connections we can draw between Zera Yacob and Locke's concerns with freedom of conscience appear less accidental. It is thus quite illuminating to count the *Hatäta* as a paradigmatic work of modern philosophy.

Let us turn now to the topic of rights. As far as I know, Zera Yacob does not use any word in Ge'ez (the traditional literary language of Ethiopia, in which his treatise is written) that can be said to correspond directly to our term "rights." In his fifth chapter, though, Zera Yacob criticizes Islam by arguing for the wrongness of slavery in a manner nicely illuminated by ascribing to him a belief in natural rights. He writes:

> Likewise the [Muslims] said that it is right to go and buy a man as if he were an animal. But with our intelligence we understand that this [Muslim] law cannot come from the creator of man who made us equal, like brothers, so that we call our creator our father. But Mohammed made the weaker man the possession of the stronger and equated a rational creature with irrational animals; can this depravity be attributed to God?
>
> (Sumner 1985: 238)

Compare this with Locke's explanation in his *Second Treatise of Government* of why, even in a state of nature, we are bound by reason to recognize each other as having rights to life, health, liberty, and our possessions:

> For Men being all the Workmanship of one Omnipotent and infinitely wise Maker; All the Servants of one Sovereign Master, sent into the World by his order and about his business, they are his Property, whose Workmanship they are, made to last during his, not one another's Pleasure. And being furnished with like Faculties, sharing all in one Community of Nature, there cannot be supposed any such *Subordination* among us, that may authorize us to destroy one another, as if we were made for one another's uses, as the inferior ranks of creatures are for ours.
>
> (1988 [1689]: 271)

Despite various differences, we find in both passages a description of a natural order in which God is superior to us while we are superior to nonhuman animals. Our place in the middle of this hierarchy secures our natural freedom and equality. None of us can claim superiority over each other as our Creator can over us and, while other creatures may be made to serve our purposes, we can recognize our special standing in the order of creation—and thus our right to be free from coercion—by recognizing our shared capacity for rational thought.

What should we make of this similarity? Note that it would be anachronistic to describe Zera Yacob's argument as "Lockean," for the *Second Treatise of Government* was published over two decades after Zera Yacob wrote his *Hatäta*. This points us toward the limits on the usefulness of viewing Zera Yacob and Locke as sharing an early modern world. Consider Richard Tuck's *Natural Rights Theories: Their Origin and Development* (1979), which explores categories of Roman law, locates the birth of natural rights discourse in the late medieval period, and examines figures like Hugo Grotius, John Selden, and Thomas Hobbes before giving Locke attention in the final chapter. Scholarship like this places Locke in a certain lineage of thought, which shaped him just as much as the political context of his times. Zera Yacob does not stand in that lineage. Indeed, when comparing Zera Yacob to Descartes and Locke, we should remember that Locke read and was influenced by Descartes, learning from his approach to philosophy even while rejecting central views of his. There is a sense in which Locke and Descartes share a modernity that Zera Yacob does not, a point that need not lead us to deny that Zera Yacob is a modern philosopher but rather to say that he inhabits a *different modernity*.

It is furthermore noteworthy that, when he criticizes slavery, Zera Yacob is not talking about the transatlantic slave trade and the treatment of Africans by Europeans but rather his understanding of the precepts of Islam. Bentley's point about the early modern world being before "industrial-strength imperialism" is apt here, as Zera Yacob's experience of Europeans was an experience of powerful outsiders but not of conquering or would-be conquering subjugators (as compared with Ethiopians of the nineteenth century, who experienced a punitive expedition by the British and an attempted invasion by the Italians, or Ethiopians of the twentieth century, who experienced Italian occupation). Rather than relations of domination between races, Zera Yacob's sense of what divides humanity involves, above all, religious differences.

In fact, it seems fair to say that it is not simply that religion matters more than race to Zera Yacob but rather that, for Zera Yacob, race as we know it does not exist. One might think there is a kind of racial distinction involved in the way that he refers to Jesuits as "*Frang̃*," a Ge'ez word that literally means "foreigner." But note that he uses that word in a way that is interchangeable with "Catholic" and in a way that contrasts not with a term for people from Ethiopia but rather with a term translated into English as "Copt." His use of this term is clearly rooted in the fact that the Ethiopian Orthodox Church was at that time administratively underneath the Coptic Church of Egypt. Consider now this passage from chapter 2:

> And while I was teaching and interpreting the Books, I used to say: "The *Frang̃* say this and this" or "The Copts say that and that," and I did not say: "This is good, that is bad," but I said: "All these things are good if we ourselves are good." Hence I was disliked by all: the Copts took me for a *Frang̃*, the *Frang̃* for a Copt.
>
> (Sumner 1985: 231)

Clearly the problem was not that some people viewed Zera Yacob as a European foreigner. The label "foreigner," rather, is being treated as interchangeable with a religious position that anyone can take up, demonstrating that the idea of a racial divide here is simply absent. Modern Africana philosophy as pioneered by Zera Yacob is thus, in important ways, *disconnected* from European modernity, both from its specific lineages of thought and from the sharp racial distinctions created by the transatlantic slave trade and slavery in the Americas.

Anton Wilhelm Amo, the Holy Roman Empire, and Conventional Rights

Anton Wilhelm Amo was born in 1703 in Axim (not to be confused with Axum) in what is today Ghana. Given that the country of Ghana only came into being in 1957, we may call the region in which he was born Nzemaland. The Nzema are one of the subgroups of the Akan people, who make up about half the population of Ghana today. Amo was no more than four years old when he was taken from his homeland to the Netherlands, probably by the Dutch West India Company. This corporation was a major player in the slave trade, but it has been argued that Amo may have been taken not as a slave but to be trained for missionary purposes. He was brought to what is now Germany and given to Duke Anton Ulrich, who reigned over the principality of Brunswick-Wolfenbüttel. He was baptized, received the name Anton Wilhelm, and an education good enough that, in 1727, he was able to enroll in the University of Halle, which had become a center of Enlightenment through the presence of luminaries such as Christian Wolff. He studied law and defended a dissertation that is now unfortunately lost, although it will, nevertheless, be the central focus of this section.

From Halle, Amo went to the University of Wittenberg, where he attained the degree of doctor of philosophy and, in 1734, defended a second dissertation titled *De Humanae Mentis Απάθεια* ("On the Apathy of the Human Mind"). One important feature of this work is its critique of Descartes on the precise relationship between mind and body. Note here the contrast with Zera Yacob: while Zera Yacob can be seen as similar to Descartes but must be recognized as outside the lineage leading to and branching out from him, Amo, like Locke, did philosophy in the wake of Descartes and critically responded to his work. Amo taught at Wittenberg, Halle, and also the University of Jena. Then, at some point before 1753, he left Europe and returned to his place of birth, possibly as a result of experienced hostility in Europe. It is in 1753 that a Dutch physician visiting Axim met with him, later reporting that he lived there "like a hermit" and had "acquired the reputation of a soothsayer" (Abraham 2004: 198). He was said to be in touch with his father and sister, but a brother of his had been sold into slavery in Suriname. We cannot be sure when Amo died.

Let us now reflect upon his first dissertation, which he defended in 1729. It is a shame we cannot read it, as I consider it the first known work of Africana political philosophy in a European language. Its title was *De Jure Maurorum in Europa* ("On the Rights of the Moors in Europe"). While we lack the text itself, we have this description of it from the university journal at Halle:

> In it, not only has he shown from law and history that the kings of the Moors were once enfeoffed by the Roman Emperor, and that every one of them had to obtain a royal patent, which Justinian also issued, but he also especially investigated how far the freedom or servitude of Moors purchased by Christians extends in Europe according to the commonly accepted laws.
> (Abraham 2004: 192; translation altered)

There is much in this description that makes one curious to see the work itself. For example, who are all these kings supposedly made vassal to the Roman emperor? The Roman Empire never covered more than North Africa, and while some usages of the term "Moor" would fit with a focus on North Africa, the topic of servitude to Europeans clearly suggests that Amo is concerned with "Moors" in the broader sense in which he counts as one (note that he is referred to in his baptismal record as "a little Moor" and, at the time of his confirmation in 1721, his last name was recorded not as "Amo" but "Mohre") (Abraham 1996: 427). If we assume that Amo did not make the blatantly false claim that all kingdoms throughout Africa were incorporated into the Roman Empire as a matter of historical fact, could it be that it is precisely the linguistic fact that we only speak of "Africa" and "Africans" because the name of the Roman province of Africa was extended to cover the continent in its entirety that justifies, in his view, treating the continent as a whole as heir to the legal legacy of ancient Rome?

Whatever the answer to this question, it is fascinating to note that Amo's dissertation addresses the question of slavery not by appealing, as Zera Yacob does, to an account of natural rights, but rather to an account of *conventional* rights. He relies solely on what has been accepted legally and historically to argue for a shift in the dominant viewpoint regarding the enslavement of Africans. But what exactly is this shift? William Abraham plausibly states that the "kernel of Amo's argument was that Africans were entitled to the same immunities and privileges to precisely the extent that the erstwhile European vassals of Rome enjoyed them, for the African kings had been likewise subject to Rome" (1996: 430). But which immunities and privileges? Abraham writes of Roman law providing for "the inviolability of the person" and claims that Amo relies on this to imply the illegality of slavery (1996: 430). But, as Amo certainly would have known, Roman law did not render slavery illegal. Justinian's *Institutes*, for example, although notably including the claim that slavery is "contrary to the law of nature," provides rules and regulations surrounding the practice in full acceptance of its role in civil society (Justinian 1987 [533]: 37). And, of course, as we have noted, Amo relies not on natural rights but legal convention to make his argument. Although I have seen no scholar admit this before, it is the case that, for all we know, Amo may have countenanced some compatibility between slavery and the law, for the description of his thesis does not clarify what he sees as the legal limitations on servitude.

Nevertheless, I think there is good reason to speculate that Amo's purpose was to argue for the abolition of slavery in Europe. The reason I have in mind requires that we once again pay attention to what portion of the early modern world provided the immediate context for and thus shaped the intellectual activity of the thinker in question. Amo was raised, educated, and worked as a philosopher within the Holy Roman Empire, that conglomeration of mainly Germanic territories that is often traced back to the rule of Charlemagne in the ninth century and which lasted until the Napoleonic Wars at the beginning of the nineteenth century. Unlike in ancient Rome, Europeans were not held as slaves in the Holy Roman Empire of Amo's time. My speculation, then, is that Amo aimed to rely not on the legal status of slavery in ancient Rome but on the practices surrounding slavery in his own milieu. The point of talking about the ancient Roman incorporation of Africa, in that case, would be to exploit the self-understanding of the Holy Roman Empire as the continuation of the ancient Roman Empire and specifically of the Christian Roman Empire inaugurated by Constantine and later ruled by Justinian, who actually recovered African territory previously lost to Vandals during his rule in the sixth century. The argument would thus be that the evolution toward freedom from slavery in Europe legally applies to Africans as well once we recognize Europe and Africa as parallel geopolitical spaces emerging from a shared history of Roman imperial rule, a political legacy that the Holy Roman Empire sought to embody and extend.

Having noticed the contrast between Zera Yacob's focus on natural rights and Amo's on conventional rights, we must now acknowledge the difference between them with regard to thinking about race. While race arguably does not exist for Zera Yacob, Amo's rights-based argument against slavery is race-conscious at least in its motivation, as it aims to address the system of anti-black oppression that so thoroughly shaped his world, even if he himself was never a slave. That being said, while we might describe Zera Yacob's argument against slavery as *non-racial*, Amo's argument can be described as *deracializing* in aspiration. Confronted by a divide between and a hierarchy of white and black on the basis of a booming trade in slaves, he responded by evoking the common subjugation of Europeans and Africans to Roman imperial power. The picture of Europe and Africa suggested by his thesis is characterized not by racial difference but rather by legal and political continuity.

There is a paradox here, though. Amo deracializes Europeans and Africans by adopting a particularly European point of view on the world. Africa is viewed from the perspective of the Roman Empire, understood as the foundation of modern Europe. Indeed, it is shocking to think that an African would treat the conquest of Africa by a European empire as the basis of African freedom! Lewis Gordon has noted that Amo chose to "emphasize the significance of his Africanness" given that he often included "Afer" when signing his name (2008: 38). But the use of "Afer" in one's name was a

Latin convention originally identifying the bearer as being from the Roman province of Africa, centered around Carthage in present-day Tunisia. Thus even Amo's expression of African pride involved identifying with ancient Rome. He represents the founding of modern Africana philosophy as thoroughly shaped by European modernity.

Lemuel Haynes, Revolutionary America, and Natural Rights

Lemuel Haynes is the first and only of the four philosophers I am discussing to have been born outside Africa. He was born in 1753 in West Hartford, Connecticut, to a white mother and a black father, who was said to be "of unmingled extraction" and possibly a slave (Roberts 1994: 576). He never knew his father and did not grow up with his mother, but rather as an indentured servant with a family in Granville, Massachusetts. Despite the lack of freedom inherent in this condition, he was treated as a valued member of this family, whose strongly religious character moulded him as he pursued his largely self-directed education. At 21, shortly after being freed from servitude, Haynes joined the American Revolution, enlisting first as a minuteman and participating in the Siege of Boston in 1775 and then, the next year, as a private in the Continental Army, reinforcing the troops at the captured Fort Ticonderoga. It is around this time that he produced his earliest writings, one of which will be the focus of this section. After the war, Haynes began to display a talent for delivering sermons. When he was ordained as a minister in 1785, he was likely the first black clergyman in the United States whose role was made official in this way. He began serving Congregationalist churches and, in 1788, accepted the call to pastor an all-white church in Rutland, Vermont. He served there for 30 years before being pushed out, partly on the basis of racism. Haynes continued to preach elsewhere until his death in 1833.

In parallel with Amo, Haynes is a figure of African background who managed to attain a position of recognized intellectual authority in an overwhelmingly European-dominated landscape during the era in which blackness in the West connoted, above all, slavery. One interesting thing about Haynes, though, is the way our memory of him has changed through discoveries made long after his death. Until the 1980s, it was reasonable for a historian who came across Haynes to be struck by his seeming avoidance of talk about race and slavery. He was, in his time, a respected minister with a Calvinist view of his faith, influenced in particular by a form of Calvinism known as the New Divinity, the roots of which lay in the thought of colonial America's famous philosopher-theologian, Jonathan Edwards. Haynes's most famous sermon, delivered in 1805, was a stinging rebuke of the Unitarian Universalism of his contemporary, Hosea Ballou. It is representative of most of his sermons in having no noticeable connection to his racial background.

In the early 1980s, however, Ruth Bogin discovered an unfinished, unpublished essay of his titled "Liberty Further Extended." While it is undated, it was very likely written in the second half of 1776, after the printing and circulation of the Declaration of Independence. Given that Amo's first dissertation is lost, it is the oldest philosophical text we possess arguing for an end to anti-black oppression that was written by a black thinker. It is also interesting to compare it to the other previously unknown writing of his that Bogin discovered: a poem called "The Battle of Lexington," likely written during his time as a minuteman in Boston. The poem, a "patriotic ballad," is an unadulterated celebration of the Patriot cause and indictment of the British (Bogin 1985). Haynes even participates in the practice of speaking of "slaves" as what the British would have the Americans be, a condition to which they prefer death (Bogin 1985: 504). "Liberty Further Extended," on the other hand, is a fiery critique of the hypocrisy of white Americans fighting for freedom while perpetuating slavery. Rita Roberts (1994) argues that the contrast between the poem and the essay show us the swift political evolution of a black soldier. As she puts it, "the victims of the ballad became the savage oppressors of the essay" (1994: 580).

Haynes's commitment to natural rights discourse is front and center in the essay, as he writes early on that "[l]iberty, & freedom, is an innate principle" and identifies the source of this principle as God:

> Liberty is a Jewel which was handed down to man from the cabinet of heaven, and is Coaeval with his Existance. And as it proceed[s] from the Supreme Legislature of the univers, so it is he which hath a sole right to take away; therefore, he that would take away a man's Liberty assumes a prerogative that Belongs to another, and acts out of his domain.
>
> (Bogin 1983: 94)

As with Zera Yacob and Locke, God's superiority over us is the basis of our natural freedom. With this established, the goal of the essay is to argue that nothing about this principle differs when black people are involved—natural freedom is natural freedom. Haynes highlights that this is unfortunately controversial in a way that demonstrates the significance of his immediate political context:

> To affirm, that an Englishman has a right to his Liberty, is a truth which has Been so clearly Evinced, Especially of Late, that to spend time in illustrating this, would be But Superfluous tautology. But I query, whether Liberty is so contracted a principle as to be Confin'd to any nation under Heaven; nay, I think it not hyperbolical to affirm, that Even an affrican, has Equally as good a right to his Liberty in common with Englishmen.
>
> (Bogin 1983: 94)

Bogin claims that Haynes's use of the term "Englishman" rather than "American" throughout the essay—even when he is clearly talking about people in the colonies or, rather, newly united states—is among the reasons to think that it was written in 1776, early in the Revolution (Bogin 1983: 90). While that may be true, the use of "Englishman" and "affrican" also helps to highlight ancestry in a way that makes the racial divide Haynes is confronting stand out, more than it would if he had used the term "American." The effect is the suggestion that the Revolution has involved Englishmen fighting other Englishmen to affirm the freedom that all Englishmen rightfully claim while the Africans, who are not Englishmen, are wrongfully excluded. Haynes, unlike Amo, does not seek to ignore but rather directly confronts the racial divide.

In this way, Haynes reframes the Revolution and tempers excitement about it, despite being a participant or, perhaps, precisely because, as a participant who was also black, he had a clear sense of its strengths and weaknesses. I think "Liberty Further Extended," despite being unfinished and unpublished, shows Haynes to be one of the great theorists of the American Revolution. Given that this is a quintessentially modern event,

Haynes as theorist of that event is as a paradigmatically modern thinker. But what does it mean to conceive of Haynes not just as modern but as a founding figure of modern *Africana* philosophy?

It occurs to me that a useful analogy can be drawn between "Liberty Further Extended" and a landmark feminist text like Mary Wollstonecraft's *A Vindication of the Rights of Woman*, written in 1792, shortly after the French Revolution. Cora Kaplan (1986) has described *Vindication* as an attempt to take advantage of the great excitement that the French Revolution caused among a certain segment of the British intelligentsia, herself included, in order to make progress on the status of women. Kaplan explains:

> Arguments initially directed at a corrupt ruling class on behalf of a virtuous bourgeoisie inevitably opened up questions of intra-class power relations. With *A Vindication* Wollstonecraft challenged her own political camp, insisting that women's rights be put higher on the radical agenda. Addressed to Talleyrand, taking issue with Rousseau, speaking the political jargon of her English contemporaries, *A Vindication* invited the enlightenment heritage, the dead and the living, to extend the new humanism to the other half of the race.
>
> (1986: 37)

In other words, Wollstonecraft sought to transcend the limitations of European modernity as she knew it, not in order to pursue something outside European modernity but rather precisely because of her desire to push European modernity in its radical Enlightenment phase toward the ultimate fulfillment of its potential. This is how I see "Liberty Further Extended": as an attempt to push the natural rights tradition further, given the contextually radical aim of attaining for people of African descent the freedom that this mode of thinking promised white people. Haynes cannot be seen as helping to inaugurate modern Africana philosophy by bringing a different intellectual heritage to the table. Rather, what Haynes brings to the table that is different is a missing concern, namely, concern for the group with which he was associated by means of his paternal ancestry. Modern Africana philosophy, as we see it in Haynes, is simply that outgrowth of modern European philosophy within which black people speak and black lives matter.

Quobna Ottobah Cugoano, Fanti Culture, and Natural Rights

Like Amo, Quobna Ottobah Cugoano was an Akan, specifically a Fanti, born in Ajumako in 1757. At the age of 13, he was kidnapped and sold for "a gun, a piece of cloth, and some lead" and then brought to Grenada as a slave (Cugoano 1999 [1787]: 14). After nine months there, he spent another year elsewhere in the West Indies before being brought to England in 1772. We do not know for certain how he gained his freedom, but his arrival in England took place after a significant ruling, known as the Mansfield decision, that was widely viewed as abolishing slavery within the nation. He eventually gained employment as a servant to painters Richard and Maria Cosway and, while employed by them, became active in the fight against the slave trade in 1780s London. In 1787, he published a book, the full title of which is *Thoughts and Sentiments on the Evil and Wicked Traffic of Slavery and Commerce of the Human Species, Humbly Submitted to the Inhabitants of Great-Britain, by Ottobah Cugoano, a Native of Africa*. He also published a shortened and revised version in 1791. Unfortunately, we do not know what became of him after this year.

Like Haynes, Cugoano is a natural rights theorist. Near the beginning of his book, Cugoano describes those who have come before him in writing against the slave trade and slavery as "[t]hose who have endeavoured to restore to their fellow-creatures the common rights of nature" (1999 [1787]: 9). Cugoano is even like Haynes in reflecting on the significance of the American Revolution, writing shortly thereafter: "since the last war, some mitigation of slavery has been obtained in some respective districts of America, though not in proportion to their own vaunted claims of freedom" (1999 [1787]: 10).

Note, however, a significant difference: while there is a powerful passage in "Liberty Further Extended" in which Haynes imagines the agony of a mother in Africa mourning the loss of a child to the slave trade, Cugoano did not need to use his imagination to reflect on life in Africa—only his memory. Unlike Amo, who was taken away as a small child, Cugoano had reached adolescence when snatched from his country. Until the age of 13, he lived immersed within Fanti culture. The short autobiographical portion of the book even includes interesting ethnographic information, such as when he says he lived somewhere for "about twenty moons" and then explains that this converts to two years (1999 [1787]: 12). Existing scholarship on Cugoano has, in my view, ignored what this immersion in Fanti culture means for thinking about Cugoano's intellectual formation. It is my suspicion that we misunderstand much about Cugoano—including his argument for recognizing natural rights—if we fail to pay attention to his persistent attachment to his Fanti cultural background.

Consider first this claim he makes while rebutting caricatures of Africans as carelessly selling one another, even family members: "Those people annually brought away from Guinea [i.e., the West African coast], are born as free, and are brought up with as great a predilection for their own country, freedom and liberty, as the sons and daughters of fair Britain" (Cugoano 1999 [1787]: 27). On the one hand, what he says here may seem obvious: no one wants their freedom taken away. On the other hand, Cugoano undercuts here the common idea of Western life and thought as involving an inclination toward freedom unlike what can be found anywhere else, offering testimony as someone from elsewhere.

It is not, the case, however, that he sees no difference between Africans and Europeans and it is also not the case that he views them as equal in every possible way. We see this in a key passage dealing with how one recognizes whether slavery is wrong if one does not believe in divine revelation. Cugoano writes:

> In that respect, all that they have to enquire into should be, whether it be right or wrong, that any part of the human species should enslave another; and when that is the case, the Africans, though not so learned, are just as wise as the Europeans; and when the matter is left to human wisdom, they are both liable to err. But what the light of nature, and the dictates of reason, when rightly considered, teach, is, that no man ought to enslave another; and some, who have been rightly guided thereby, have made noble defences for the universal natural rights and privileges of all men.
>
> (1999 [1787]: 28)

I take it that "learning" here refers to something like modern Western attainments in science, industry, the spread of literacy, and so on, while "wisdom" means something like rational capacity. Europeans may culturally exceed Africans with respect to "learning," but Cugoano argues that Africans must be recognized as possessing equal rational capacity. Furthermore, he holds that "learning" is neither necessary nor sufficient for recognizing the existence of natural rights, as of two people, one with learning and one without, both are liable to err in not recognizing the category and both are capable of succeeding in recognizing it. We can explain this last point by connecting it to the equal desire for freedom Cugoano ascribes to us all. If we notice this feeling within ourselves and acknowledge the signs that others feel it as well, we may rationally arrive at the conclusion that we should treat others how we wish to be treated, that is, as free beings. Selfishness, however, may block this chain of reasoning and we may privilege our own feeling for freedom while ignoring that of others.

What I think this means is that, for Cugoano, as for Zera Yacob, the idea of natural rights is not really embedded within a modern European intellectual tradition. Certain formulations of it may be paradigmatically European, but it is ultimately a concept that transcends cultural boundaries, which also means that one can come up with paradigmatically Fanti formulations of it. Cugoano thus does not fit neatly into the framework of modern Africana philosophy as a form of modern European philosophy into which Amo and Haynes fit. But, of course, neither is he disconnected from the European tradition in the way Zera Yacob is. Cugoano, I believe, represents modern Africana philosophy as a convergence of African and European intellectual trajectories, a hybrid case of radicalizing European thought from within, as with Haynes, while also modernizing African thought through comparing indigenous and foreign viewpoints and using reason to decide what makes the most sense, like Zera Yacob.

I take Cugoano to be, in this way, a model for Africana philosophy going forward. The riches of the Western philosophical tradition must be valued but also made sharper and more liberating through the use of a critical philosophy of race lens. At the same time, there must be constant efforts to transcend the Western framework by rooting Africana philosophy in oral and literary traditions from Africa and the diaspora. In many instances, we may come to a conclusion like Cugoano's about natural rights: that what we thought of as particularly Western is not and that the cross-cultural recognition of a shared concept may strengthen our sense of commitment to the value at stake.

References

Abraham, W. E. (1996) "The Life and Times of Anton Wilhelm Amo, the First African (Black) Philosopher in Europe," in M. K. Asante and A. S. Abarry (eds.), *African Intellectual Heritage: A Book of Sources*, Philadelphia: Temple University Press.

———. (2004) "Anton Wilhelm Amo," in K. Wiredu (ed.), *A Companion to African Philosophy*, Malden, MA: Blackwell.

Bentley, J. H. (2007) "Early Modern Europe and the Early Modern World," in C. H. Parker and J. H. Bentley (eds.), *Between the Middle Ages and Modernity: Individual and Community in the Early Modern World*, Lanham, MA: Rowman & Littlefield.

Bogin, R. (1983) "'Liberty Further Extended': A 1776 Antislavery Manuscript by Lemuel Haynes," *William & Mary Quarterly* 40 (January): 85–105.

———. (1985) "'The Battle of Lexington': A Patriotic Ballad by Lemuel Haynes," *William & Mary Quarterly* 42 (October): 499–506.

Cugoano, Q. O. (1999 [1787]) *Thoughts and Sentiments on the Evil of Slavery*, ed. Vincent Carretta, New York: Penguin Classics.

Gordon, L. R. (2008) *An Introduction to Africana Philosophy*, Cambridge: Cambridge University Press.
Justinian. (1987 [533]) *Justinian's Institutes*, trans. P. Birks and G. McLeod, Ithaca: Cornell University Press.
Kaplan, C. (1986) *Sea Changes: Culture and Feminism*, London: Verso.
Locke, J. (1988 [1689]) *Two Treatises of Government*, ed. P. Laslett, Cambridge: Cambridge University Press.
Marshall, J. (2006) *John Locke, Toleration and Early Enlightenment Culture*, Cambridge: Cambridge University Press.
Roberts, R. (1994) "Patriotism and Political Criticism: The Evolution of Political Consciousness in the Mind of a Black Revolutionary Soldier." *Eighteenth-Century Studies* 27 (Summer): 569–588.
Sumner, C. (1985) *Classical Ethiopian Philosophy*, Addis Ababa: Commercial Printing Press.
Taylor, P.C. (2013) *Race: A Philosophical Introduction*, 2nd edition, Cambridge: Polity Press.
Tlumak, J. (2007) *Classical Modern Philosophy: A Contemporary Introduction*, London: Routledge.
Tuck, R. (1979) *Natural Rights Theories: Their Origin and Development*, Cambridge: Cambridge University Press.

11
AFRICANA THOUGHT
Lewis R. Gordon

To place Africana thought in the category of "alternative traditions" suggests the normative position of this collection to be, perhaps, European and Euro-American thought. In effect, philosophy as Euro-normative philosophy already raises the metaphilosophical question of legitimate location. What follows does not build from the premise of "alternative," as part of the critique of Euromodern thought offered from Africana thought is that the former is an appeal to a false universal that in effect masks a de facto particularity. Africana thought, then, is an appeal to reality premised on taking seriously a point of departure often occluded in the reverie of Euromodern thought.

The context of this chapter is, as well, a volume on philosophy, which makes this section's designation of *thought* a form of bringing into question the legitimacy of its *philosophical* status. A critique of that position would take up too much space here. For now, let us simply accept that *thought* is a broader concept than *philosophy*, which is a species of the former. Thus, within Africana thought, there is Africana philosophy.

The term "Africana," however, is a more recent designation of African diasporic peoples. Its use dates back to at least W.E.B. Du Bois's call for an *Encyclopedia Africana* in 1909 (see Lewis 1993: 379; Outlaw 1996; L. Gordon 2000). Referring to African and African influences, it does not exclude the possible mixtures and convergences of things non-African with those African. Though African peoples preceded the events through which an African diaspora emerged, the beginnings of forced conditions, a hallmark of diaspora status, date back to the Arabic slave trade on the continent during the periods of the Caliphates leading up to the pivotal event of their expulsion from Christendom and the demise of Andalusia in the last decade of the fifteenth century. The defeat of the Moors in Grenada in January 1492 and the process of "Reconquest" continued under Queen Isabella and King Ferdinand in Spain took to the seas and landing in the Bahamas in October of that year were crucial moments in the birth of Christian globalism resulting in the transformation of that world into Europe and Euromodernity (Mignolo 2011; L. Gordon 2008; Dussel 1995).

I am using the word "modern" and the term "modernity" to mean the establishment of an order of power in which a particular group imposes itself as the future of humankind. Thus, when Columbus and his crew met the Caribs (or Kalinago) and Taínos in 1492, the events that unfolded affected, through conquest, which groups presumed their place in the future and which ones faced their extinction but for the sake of fighting for their continued existence. Wherever a group of people emerges as the course of humanity's future, they become the modern. The rest face the question of disappearance or joining them through some convergence, hybridization, or mimicry of the world imposed and that to come.

Though the pattern of imposition and modernization has occurred throughout history, there were differences in the one that emerged from the fifteenth century onward. Euromodernity introduced notions of "primitivism" and "Nativism," wherein some groups *belong to the past* because the future is for settlers and moderns. Euromodernism brought along and cultivated, in other words, an anthropology linked to a conception of time governed by notions of who was, who is to become, and simply who *must be*. As the initial conflict was theological and religious, a form of theonaturalism of who belonged inside the orbit of the Christian god and who did not accompanied it. During the period of the Caliphates, the term *raza* referred to two kinds of people who did not belong: Jews and Moors. This term became foundational for the subsequent anthropology as it was eventually transformed into the word *race* (L. Gordon 2014, 2008; Gordon and Gordon: 2009; Nirenberg 2007; Park 2013; Taylor 2013; Covarrubias Orozco 1611).

Race grew, then, out of the ongoing process of global colonization and enslavement for which it was at the core of the unfolding philosophical anthropology of Euromodernity. African peoples forced into that process experienced their transformation from the variety of ethnic groups to which they belonged into a singular category of racialization: blacks.

Though Africans were not the only people to become blacks in Euromodernity—think of Australian Aboriginals, darker Southwest Asians, and even at times some First Nation peoples of the Americas—the mark of blackness has been tagged onto dark-skinned Africans and their descendants more than many other groups. These reasons are historic. The ascendance of the British Empire and the subsequent impact of at least three of its former colonies—Australia, South Africa, and the United States—led to the prevalence of its racial terms. Earlier empires, such as the Danish, Dutch, French, Portuguese, and Spanish, forged their brands of racial anthropology with basically two constants: the black and the Native were basic terms in which varieties of mixture were interwoven in a schema leading to a purified hierarchy of dominant whiteness. In the transition of Africans into blacks was then also that of Europeans into whites, with Amerindians and East Asians functioning in gradations and movements to fit the basic opposition of black and white. In the end, these terms were relational despite the historical efforts to make them ontological and unconnected. Black, in other words, was simply the furthest distance from white, and white, in similar kind, was the greatest from black. In between were varieties whose movements were sometimes anomalous. For example, whereas "yellow" seemed on course to "white," "red" wasn't so clear, especially where it emerged from "yellow," as in North America (L. Gordon 2007). In all, however, the linking of blackness to Africanness made race a subfield of study in Africana thought and by extension Africana philosophy.

Africana Thought as an Intellectual Enterprise

Race and racism posed several difficulties for Africana thought. The first is the Euromodern tendency to conflate not only modernity with European but also thought, retroactively, with Europeans. Colonialism and enslavement consigned the status of property and subhumanity to the colonized and the enslaved, which left the logic of rationality and reason in the minds and souls of those who imposed such on them. Debates dating back to those between Bartolomé Las Casas and Juan Ginés de Sepúlveda explored challenges to the inner life and mind of such dominated peoples (Hanke 1975). Combatting such was at first defense of what such people *felt* and subsequently the meaning to such experience. Challenging the view that thought could only be brought to such from the outside—from, that is, European *thought*—the explanation of experience meant also taking responsibility for ideas. Contrary to the dominant model of white stewardship of thought, then, is the rejection of a basic fallacy—namely, that colonized, enslaved, and dominated peoples don't *think* (L. Gordon 2000; Henry 2000; Neocosmos 2016).

The challenge of thinking is similar to that of time. Where Euromodernity was imposed, a form of crisis emerged among those whom it affected. In thinking and struggling for a future in which they belong, such people in effect created intellectual practices and struggles the consequence of which are alternative Modernities. For Africana peoples, such endeavors could be called "Afromodern" (Kirkland 1992–1993; Comaroff and Comaroff 2011). Born of such a struggle for existence and legitimacy, Africana thought is, then, a modern endeavor, but it is so through a form of forced metatheoretical stance: thought indigenous to a world and time to which it is also rejected. It is a thought, in other words, marked by psychoanalytical melancholia, a subjectivity and consciousness born of loss. Paradoxically, this loss cannot be marked by a return, for "blacks" and "Africana" had no pre-colonial history. The "belonging" and "returning," then, are elsewhere—indeed, to a future without promise of being such in terms currently understood.

More concretely, these challenges of in effect legitimacy pertain to anti-intellectual tendencies of antiblackness. Similar to the not-out-of-Africa thesis, there is a not-from-blacks version with regard to ideas. Biography and experience, though an advance from the soulless and mindless presumptions of being pure property, lead to those of deferred thought and legitimate experience. If theory, and by extension philosophy, offers interpretation and meaning to experience, then the privileging of Europeans as sources of thought leave a trail to the experience on which such thought is based or the interpretation of which such thought emerged. The reduction of thought to whiteness means, then, the privileging of what whites experience. Thus, the effort *to explain* black experience in such terms erases the legitimacy of its subject. The problems of colonization and racism return, then, in the form of knowledge and thought—in short, epistemic colonization.

Africana thought responds to this phenomenon through taking responsibility for the production of theory, and again by extension philosophy, *from and through* Africana experience and the practices of its interpretation and meaning. Thus, the critique of Euromodern imposition is not only that it is a form of colonization of thought but also that it is a form of *de-intellectualization of Africana thought*. To advance such thought as an intellectual project requires examining the set of epistemic and theoretical problems emerging from the situation of such thought. That the situation is one of historical colonization, enslavement, exploitation, and oppression leads to questions not only regarding the meaning of such concepts but also their transformation and, more radically, the enterprise of their study. At least three philosophical questions follow: (1) What does it mean to be human? (2) What is freedom? (3) What must be said about the historic use of rationality and reason for the advancement of dehumanization and bondage at levels material and epistemic? Reformulated, such thought devotes attention to philosophical anthropology, philosophy of freedom and liberation, and metacritiques of reason and justificatory practices (L. Gordon 2008).

Philosophical anthropology addresses the core concern of a philosophy of race and racism, as the latter challenge who counts as human and who does not. As a dehumanizing practice, racism presumes particular modes of what it means to be human, and those usually are, in standpoint fashion, those making the challenge. Pointing to the circularity of racists presuming themselves as the legitimate standpoint of evaluation of all others, though correct, does not address the question of what is involved in being human beyond fallacious models. Delving further unveils the circularity at work with the selection of any group, as a form of bad faith emerges in which human beings have to be identified as human in order to be rejected as such. Racism is here revealed to be a form of human effort to dehumanize certain groups of human beings (L. Gordon 1999). How are human beings identified in the first place, however?

Pursuing human identification leads to various moves of evidentiality, definition, and argumentation in which the problem of the questioner and the questioned comes to the fore. Any human effort to define humanity places the human being in a metatheoretical relationship with the community to the human world. This metahuman relationship to the human being collapses into a classical incompleteness problem. The human being, in other words, is an open instead of closed subject, yet the openness is experientially linked through the social world of culture in which human beings live and, crucially, *appear* to each other as human beings. This intersubjective experience cannot be developed here. That it is a shared experience of meaning brings to the fore its phenomenological significance. It is, in other words, human consciousness of human reality made evident by its communicative richness. There are, in other words, certain meanings human beings can only communicate with other human beings, despite claims of radical, cultural relativism. The ability *to learn* such a rich array of signifiers and symbols alerts us to a human world the denial of which demands in effect our claiming not to see what is seen.

The discussion has already headed into the metacritique of reason and justifications. The concern with freedom should also be evident. The eradication of colonialism, enslavement, and oppression require an understanding of what it means to be free and liberated. Broken chains don't automatically entail freedom, however, as the quality of life that ensues may be such that enslavement in effect has taken a new form. African diasporic peoples have seen such in the network of legal and power relations that transform post-colonization and post-slavery into ongoing systemic dehumanization such as racism, sexism, and other forms of oppression. Racism and sexism are intertwined here because the initial philosophical anthropology of theonaturalism from Christian conquerors offered Aristotelian premises of gender differentiation that at first constructed whole groups of conquered peoples as effeminate or undeveloped men. The transition to racialization brought particular women into the fold of the fully human while in effect racializing other groups of women in a separation of gender, sex, and race. Abstract underdevelopment became a lack of form that sought material embodiment (unformed bodies) in the feminine and the dark (Butler 2011; Gordon 1997b). Many paradoxes and contradictions emerged such as males who are not men, females who are not women, and, added to all this, another dynamic of development and underdevelopment—namely, maturation and immaturity. What, then, are Africana women and men if not ultimately women and men?

LEWIS R. GORDON

Some Additional Theoretical Themes

Africana philosophy incorporates ideas from African American philosophy, Afro-Caribbean Philosophy, African philosophy, philosophy of race and racism, and those from philosophy of history, including the complicated question of how the connection to people of ancient Africa, who had no reason to think of themselves in Afromodern terms, are part of the project of reincorporation because of efforts to erase their Africanness when their intellectual contributions are appreciated or reject their achievements when their being African is accepted. The question of Africana *intellectual history* becomes an important theme in what is in effect a battle for historical membership. Eurocentric history makes history European. Demonstrating that position as fallacious, as with the human question, particularizes European history and raises a meditation on history and historiography.

The particularizing of European claims to universality is a form of argument recurring in Africana philosophy. It is in effect a critique of secularized theodicy as a form of idolatry (L. Gordon 2013). Theodicy defends the existence of a given god in the face of evil and injustice. If the god is omnipotent, omniscient, and good, why do infelicities occur? Classic responses are twofold. First, a god's knowledge and intentions are supposedly beyond human comprehension. The wrongs of the world simply *appear* to be such because of human inability to see the larger picture. Second, a good god produces a world of free will. What human beings do with that freedom is another matter. The sources of evil and injustice are human ill will, bad behavior, and mistakes. Crucial here is that the god is left pristine.

As colonialism, enslavement, and racism impose suffering on black and other people of color, how, many black people may be compelled to ask, could one defend the Euromodern world? Secular theodicean responses simply place a system, norm, or individual in the place of the god and issue the same classical responses: (1) the ultimate justice of the system will be revealed, and (2) present evil falls upon those who pose the question or suffer from injustice. Ottobah Cugoano addressed the fallacies here in his *Thoughts and Sentiments on the Evil of Slavery*. He argued that enslavers were committing an act of hubris through assuming the position of gods. To appeal to their intrinsic goodness is idolatry. In the nineteenth century, the Haitian anthropologist and philosopher Anténor Firmin (1885) argued a similar phenomenon emerged in arguments appealing to the supposed intrinsic scientific legitimacy of European man. Frederick Douglass made a similar observation at the moral level particularly in his second and third autobiographies, *My Bondage and My Freedom* and *The Life and Times of Frederick Douglass*. Idolatry saturates racist thought. A consequence of such is the presumption of intrinsic evil in those dominated. Thus, as Du Bois famously formulated, black people are addressed in American societies (across the Americas) as problems instead of people who face problems. What remains intact is the presumption of an intrinsically good society and system. Euromodernity, in other words, ultimately offers itself as a god if not, in absolute form, G-d.

Du Bois advanced this argument in dialectical fashion in his explorations of twoness and double consciousness. We saw earlier the problem of Afro-melancholia, wherein blacks are indigenous to a world that rejects them. Du Bois (1903) expanded that insight into his theory of double consciousness (J. Gordon 2007). Such blacks are simultaneously aware of their rejected status in such a world and the perspective from which that rejection takes place. They both experience being rejected and the point of view of their rejection, the latter of which is presumed "legitimate." In the historic antiblack societies of Euromodernity, another way of referring to this circumstance is "white normativity" (Westley 1997). White normativity advances the rejection of blackness as legitimate, which means the suffering occasioned from such, ultimately, right. The double bind of blacks, then, is not only the problem of rejection but also the notion of illegitimate rejection of black suffering. The logic leads to the conclusion of *deserved suffering*. Blacks thus become problems that are supposedly the source of their own suffering. As with idolatrous theodicy, the system or society is released from fault as infelicity is invested against those who suffer. As a phenomenon of which blacks are *conscious*, this experience is also phenomenological. This movement to the phenomenological raises two important sources of critique. The first is a suspension of the ontological status of such claims. Can human beings ever really *be*, intrinsically, problems? A phenomenological critique requires a movement of ontological suspension to examine the phenomenon. This places the conscious subject in a metacritical relationship to the self as an object of study. Put differently: the ability to experience suffering in a critical way brings to the fore the humanity of the sufferer. This realization of human suffering leads to a second, dialectical movement. If the suffering is legitimate only where the sufferer is not human, then the contradiction of being able to examine the suffering critically raises the question of the human being who suffers. A new awareness emerges, which we could call the dialectical movement into second stage or potentiated double consciousness: black people are not problems but are instead people—human beings—who face problems. This understanding leads both to systemic and systematic critique (L. Gordon 2000: chapter 4).

The systemic critique is of a system that *makes people into problems* instead of addressing problems of systemic origins. In short, as a human phenomenon, a social system isn't perfect; however, when it advances itself as perfect, it becomes idolatrous and treats itself as immune to critique. Potentiated double consciousness emerges as dialectical systemic critique in Africana thought, and by extension Africana philosophy (Henry 2016: 27–58). Africana philosophy, in other words, is the exposure of what Euromodern philosophy suppresses in order to appear as complete, perfect, and universal. This exposure is the particularizing subtext of this discussion. The argument is, however, more radical than it may at first appear. The less radical position is to point out that exposed particularities masked as universalities nevertheless depend on a greater universality. Africana philosophy, in other words, could be advancing itself as the *more universal* philosophy. This argument, however, would collapse into the form of idolatry through an appeal to the logic of reversed contraries instead of attunement to contradictions. The former is, in effect, an effort to demonstrate a larger, complete domain. The latter, however, admits human limitations and appeals, instead, to an expanding but not complete domain. In short, whereas the former re-appeals to *the* universal, the latter admits *universalizing* practices—those reaching for an expanded humanity and reality (L. Gordon 2016a, 2016b).

This expanding dialectic is at the core of much Africana philosophy. It often leads to a form of systemic critique in which the dominating system is turned against itself. Anténor Firmin, Anna Julia Cooper, W.E.B. Du Bois, C.L.R. James, Frantz Fanon, and many more have argued, for instance, that Euromodern science often failed to be scientific when it comes to the study of black people. Euromodern anthropology fails to be anthropological (Firmin); history and sociology fail to be historical and sociological (Cooper, Du Bois, James); psychiatry and psychology, and indeed, most of the human sciences fail to be rigorous because of presuppositions of non-humanness as the legitimate condition of studying human phenomena (Firmin and Fanon). These critical moves also predate the list of thinkers here, as similar arguments emerged in the writings of eighteenth-century philosophers such as Ottobah Cugoano and Wilhelm Amo, Lemuel Haynes, and even Benjamin Banneker. It is a critique also present in those ranging from twentieth-century luminaries thinkers of decolonization and revolution all the way to academic movements ranging from professional African (Wiredu 2004) and African American philosophy (Lott and Pittman 2002) to Afrocentricity/Africology (Asante and Ledbetter 2015), Black Feminist thought (J. James and Sharpley-Whiting 2000), Black Existentialism (Gordon 1997a, 2000), and Afropessimism (Sexton 2011; Wilderson 2008). The main thesis, with the exception of Afropessimism, is this: thought on black people is transformed when the *humanity* of black people, their *agency*, is included in the methods, research, and theory. Afropessimists are critical of appeals to the humanity of black people, as they argue that blackness is the negation of the human. There isn't room to develop that discussion and my critique of it here (see Gordon, forthcoming).

I have characterized the occlusion of black humanity in discussions of oppression and racism as forms of methodological bad faith. It is bad faith because it constructs a false reality (pleasing falsehoods) as truth and elides displeasing truths. Racism has a similar logic: the identification of human beings for the sake of denying their humanity. As much of racism involves the evasion of displeasing truths (reality), it draws upon methodological and disciplinary resources for support. Fanon identified this phenomenon well in his analysis of what could be called "unreasonable reason" (Fanon 1952; Gordon 2015). It is where reason exits whenever blacks enter the room. This metaphor pertains to epistemic, scientific, and other forms of intellectual production of racist reality. Its implications extend beyond racism, however, to a problem of theory, thinking, and disciplinary formation wherever there is sufficient ideological and idolatrous pressure to turn away from reality. Capitalist fundamentalism, for instance, offers many incentives for disciplines collapse into misrepresentations of reality through appeals to pleasing falsehoods instead of displeasing truth. I've described these phenomena as forms of *disciplinary decadence* (Gordon 2006, 2016a).

Practices of methodological fetishism and disciplinary idolizing are what I call disciplinary decadence. Similar to the racists' construction of themselves as standards (without justification) to which all others must be measured, disciplinarily decadent practitioners demand reality to bend to their discipline. We could expand this critique to ethnoscience. The reduction of Euromodernity and Europeans *into exemplars of science itself* is similarly decadent. It closes off science into the classic fallacy of appealing to a false authority.

Transcending such problems demands, I've argued, a teleological suspension of disciplinarity. Reaching for reality, in other words, demands being willing to go beyond the methodological limitations of one's discipline. To do such requires a form of communicative practice in which meaningful reality unfolds. This *communicative practice* is another way of arguing for interaction, of addressing contradictions (instead of the Manichean structure of contraries), and, therein, realizing universalizing instead of a presumed universal practice.

The call for interaction challenges anthropological, methodological, and political presumptions of legitimacy as "purity." Recent Africana philosophy offers critical discussions of such notions through explorations into conceptions of mixture beyond those of conglomeration—of different wholes put together—but living interaction in the form of *creolization* (J. Gordon 2014a, 2014b; Monahan 2011, 2017). Distinguished from *creolism* or *Creolité*, notions connected to kinds of people and their ideological preference, creolization is a process term referring to the impossibility of unilateral influence in the human world. Wherever human beings interact, wherever human phenomena interact, cross-influence occurs. Thinking back to the example of Columbus's landing in the Bahamas and his exploration of the Caribbean, admission of the humanity of the First Nations peoples there requires acknowledging the influence they also had on those who were conquering them. It also requires exploring their point of view, as best we can, as their world was changing into a conception of time premised on a struggle for their continued existence under hegemonic systems devoted to their extinction. Enslaved African peoples faced similar existential temporal and normative struggles as they fought not only for survival but also dignity and freedom under similar conditions. Though similar, the logic is not, however, the same. First Nations peoples of the Americas, for example face the temporal problem of absence despite their presence. They inhabit our times as "ghosts," which means their struggle for the future is one of impact and consequence. Antiblack racism tends to regard black people as too numerous; their suffering includes, then, a presumed exponentiality of being problems wherever they exist or appear. On the African continent, the logic shifts according to First Nations status in some places and bare antiblack racism in others (L. Gordon 2000: chapter 8). At the linguistic level, as Jane Anna Gordon has argued, these issues come to the fore in basilectal versus the supposedly pure, hegemonic speech. The human world cannot be maintained, however, without human interaction from its many manifestations. Thus, purity, as Michael Monahan argued, requires a form of insularity leading, ultimately, to nonrelations. The critique of nonrelationality is at the core of Africana existential thought, where the rejection of imposing nonrelationality on the human is rejected as a contradiction of terms. Worse, the imposition of the nonrelational (nonhuman) onto human reality also creates a peculiar form of suffering: oppression.

Africana philosophy thus leads to a variety of additional theoretical themes. One, as shown in the work of Michele Moody-Adams (1997), Kwasi Wiredu (1996), and this author (L. Gordon 2016b, 2012a, 2012b), is the importance of understanding the broad significance of culture. Instead of as a relativist term for how people do certain things differently in different places, the concept shifts when understood as the disclosure of human modes of living. Meaning, for instance, requires symbolic richness beyond signification, as Ernst Cassirer showed (Cassirer 1923–1929). Africana philosophy of culture thus also raises the metaphilosophical question of whether philosophy even makes sense outside of a cultural framework. Put differently, culture, as a condition of meaning, is also a transcendental condition for the emergence of philosophy. This is not a relativist argument. It is one similar to the critique of idolatry offered throughout this essay. To treat culture as a pollutant, as that which desecrates philosophy, leads to philosophy masking the particularity of its emergence. It also leads to the fallacy of confusing source with content. Culture as a condition for the emergence of philosophy does not entail philosophical content being cultural. That which refers and that to which something refers are not always identical.

Africana philosophy as a creolizing practice means, also, that its practitioners should reject its purification. This means that it should not be a practice *opposed to European philosophy* but instead one that particularizes ideas from European and other forms of philosophies with fidelity to relevance in the quest for establishing rigorous human relationships with reality. This means, then, that resources of evidence and evidentiality come to play in Africana philosophical practice as an expectation of what is to be done in all philosophical efforts attuned to reality and truth.

The creolization and teleological suspension of disciplinarity argument also raises questions about philosophical anthropology. Purification models attempt to study the human being through appeal to a single, essential feature. This often leads to the dissection or separation of an element of human reality as representation of the whole. It is an age-old fallacy, yet it is committed all the time across nearly every discipline. The recent celebration of intersectionality theory is a fine example of overcoming that fallacy. Though not new—as intersectional arguments permeate much of Africana thought—the importance of continued reflection on multiple convergence, multidimensionality, and ambiguity is key for any philosophical anthropology premised on fidelity to human relationality. Crucial here, however, is that intersectionality doesn't fall into the disciplinarily decadent model of Euclidean metaphors and ontological accumulations of identity. If so, there wouldn't be a living intersectionality, since one could simply map on intersections in advance and have an a priori theory of privileged location premised on whatever criterion one chooses—for example, suffering, economic deprivation, or other forms of opportunity. Understanding that no human being lives exclusively as a class, gender, race, or sexual orientation, or some other identity, and that it is impossible, without disaggregating relations or collapsing into bad faith, to see a human being who manifests only one of these, demand a conception of intersectionality that is communicatively rich and attuned to lived human reality.

The critical question of relationality opens the door to many other areas of philosophical reflection. Though colonialism, enslavement, and racism point directly to political philosophical concerns, considerations of relationality and freedom raise metaphysical questions as part of the legitimate purview of Africana philosophy. My own work draws upon resources not only from phenomenology, pragmatism, and analytical philosophy but also models drawn from East Indian transcendentalism, Japanese Zen Buddhism, Ethiopian, Akanian, ancient KMT/Egyptian, and other African models of relationality. The third element of the triumvirate I posed earlier—metacritiques of justification and reason—also draw upon philosophies of logic not only from the global North but also the South, as the question of the logicality of logic and, also, the reasonability of logic and its cogency isn't limited to the Euromodern concept of the west.

The political philosophical sphere is also rich with possibilities for creative developments. Concerns of social justice, sovereignty, and legitimate power aren't the only problems of political thought. The metacritical question of *political thought* is one posed in Africana philosophy, just as the question of idolatrous systemic thought is a concern. But more, the universal versus particular argument comes to the fore in critical work on justice, sovereignty, and legitimacy. If the guiding assumption of their universality is brought into question, for instance, then they may be *particular* aspects of normative political reality. Institutions may be such that an enriched or expanded philosophical anthropology and philosophy of culture may mean new norms to explore. Or, it could be such that previous norms have been transformed through their ongoing relationship with new challenges. For example, the presumed universality of Euromodernity meant the foci of philosophical reflections on injustice often collapsed into a formalism that erased the actual injustices at work in the worlds in which such theories were being formed. Some critics, such as Charles Mills (2005), examined this concern through the Rawlsian language of "ideal" and "non-ideal" theory. I think Mills was correct to point out the bad faith in the ideal theory approach, but his critique, given the arguments offered in this essay, is simply not radical enough. Doesn't *all* theory strive to go beyond the non-ideal? In other words, it's a false dilemma to presume the binary of ideal versus non-ideal. It is similar to universal versus particular. Advancing *universalizing practices* brings to the fore the work of theory itself. In short, the retreat to the ideal as a way of evading the dehumanizing practices of Euromodernity is a form of bad faith. The response, however, is to invoke the critical norms of evidence—in short, establish relations with the world of accountability, that is, rigorous theory.

Africana political philosophy raises the question, then, of normative possibilities beyond the stock of concepts offered in Euromodernity. Dominated peoples have concepts brought into crisis through the epoch of colonization. The critical work on those norms in the face of imposed ones suggests a form of ongoing, potentiated double consciousness of normative life. That means such traditions may actually be addressing the world humanity could cultivate as the presumed legitimacy of colonial practices falls.

"Where do we go from here?" is, then, a question of a wide-open terrain for Africana philosophy. As relational, it means not only working with the global resources available for creative ideas but also being open to that which has not yet been thought but whose future depends on the intellectual commitments and intellectual virtues of today.

References

Asante, Molefi K., and Ledbetter, Clyde, Jr. (eds.). (2015) *Contemporary Critical Thought in Africology and Africana Studies*, Lanham: Lexington Books.
Butler, Judith. (2011) *Bodies That Matter: On the Discursive Limits of Sex*, New York: Routledge.
Cassirer, Ernst. (1923–1929) *Philosophie der symbolischen Formen*, Berlin: Bruno Cassirer.
Comaroff, Jean, and Comaroff, John. (2011) *Theory From the South: Or, How Euro-America Is Evolving Toward Africa*, New York: Routledge.
Cooper, Anna Julia. (1998) *The Voice of Anna Julia Cooper, Including "A Voice From the South" and Other Important Essays, Papers and Letters*, eds. Charles Lemert and Esme Bhan, Lanham: Rowman & Littlefield.
Covarrubias Orozco, Sebastian de. (1611) *Tesoro de la lengua castellana, o española*, Madrid, Spain.
Cugoano, Quobna Ottobah. (1999) *"Thoughts and Sentiments on the Evil of Slavery" and Other Writings*, New York: Penguin Books.
Douglass, Frederick. (1950) *The Life and Writings of Frederick Douglass*, Vols. 1–5, ed. Philip Foner, New York: International.
Du Bois, W.E.B. (1903) *The Souls of Black Folk: Essays and Sketches*, Chicago: A.C. McClurg.
———. (1938) *Black Reconstruction in America, 1860–1880*, New York: Harcourt, Brace.
Dussel, Enrique. (1995) *The Invention of the Americas: Eclipse of "the Other" and the Myth of Modernity*, trans. Michael D. Barber. New York: Continuum.
Fanon, Frantz. (1952) *Peau noire, masques blancs*, Paris: Éditions du Seuil.
Firmin, Anténor. (1885) *De l'égalité des races humaines: anthropologie positive*, Paris: Librairie Cotillon.
Gordon, Jane Anna. (2007) "The Gift of Double Consciousness: Some Obstacles to Grasping the Contributions of the Colonized," in Nalini Persram (ed.), *Postcolonialism and Political Theory*, Lanham: Lexington Books, pp. 143–161.

———. (2014a) "Creolising Political Identity and Social Scientific Method: An Essay in Celebration of CODESRIA's 40th Year." *Africa Development* 39, no. 1: 65–80.

———. (2014b) *Creolizing Political Theory: Reading Rousseau Through Fanon*. New York: Fordham.

Gordon, Jane Anna, and Gordon, Lewis R. (2009) *Of Divine Warning: Reading Disaster in the Modern Age*. New York: Routledge.

Gordon, Lewis R. (ed.). (1997a) *Existence in Black: An Anthology of Black Existential Philosophy*, New York: Routledge.

———. (1997b) *Her Majesty's Other Children: Sketches of Racism from a Neocolonial Age*, Lanham: Rowman & Littlefield.

———. (1999) *Bad Faith and Antiblack Racism*, Amherst, NY: Humanity Books.

———. (2000) *Existentia Africana: Understanding Africana Existential Thought*, New York: Routledge.

———. (2006) *Disciplinary Decadence: Living Thought in Trying Times*, New York: Routledge.

———. (2007). "Thinking Through 'We' Other African Americans," in Yoku Shaw-Taylor and Steven A. Tuch (eds.), *The Other African Americans: Contemporary African and Caribbean Families in the United States*, Lanham: Rowman & Littlefield, pp. 69–92.

———. (2008) *An Introduction to Africana Philosophy*, Cambridge: Cambridge University Press.

———. (2012a) "Black Existence in Philosophy of Culture." *Diogenes* 59, nos. 3–4: 96–105.

———. (2012b) "Essentialist Anti-Essentialism, With Considerations From Other Sides of Modernity." *Quaderna: A Multilingual and Transdisciplinary Journal*, no. 1: http://quaderna.org/wp-content/uploads/2012/09/Gordon-essentialist-anti-essentialism.pdf

———. (2013) "Race, Theodicy, and the Normative Emancipatory Challenges of Blackness." *South Atlantic Quarterly* 112, no. 4 (Fall): 725–736.

———. (2014) "Justice Otherwise: Thoughts on *Ubuntu*," in Leonhard Praeg (ed.), *Ubuntu: Curating the Archive*, Scottsville, SA: University of KwaZulu Natal Press, pp. 10–26.

———. (2015) *What Fanon Said: A Philosophical Introduction to His Life and Thought*, New York: Fordham University Press.

———. (2016a) "Disciplining as a Human Science." *Quaderna: A Multilingual and Transdisciplinary Journal*, no. 3: http://quaderna.org/disciplining-as-a-human-science/

———. (2016b) *La sud prin nord-vest: Reflecții existențiale afrodiasporice*. Cluj, Romania: IDEA Design & Print.

———. (Forthcoming) "Thoughts on Afropessimism." *Contemporary Political Theory*.

Hanke, Lewis. (1974) *All Mankind Is One: A Study of the Disputation Between Bartolomé De Las Casas and Juan Gines De Sepulveda in 1550 on the Intellectual and Religious Capacity*, Chicago: Northern Illinois University Press.

Henry, Paget. (2000) *Caliban's Reason: Introducing Afro-Caribbean Philosophy*, New York: Routledge.

———. (2016) "Africana Phenomenology: Its Philosophical Implications," in Jane Anna Gordon, Lewis R. Gordon, Paget Henry, Aaron Kamugisha, and Neil Roberts (eds.), *Journeys in Caribbean Thought: The Paget Henry Reader*, London: Rowman & Littlefield, pp. 27–58.

James, C.L.R. (1989) *The Black Jacobins: Toussaint L'Ouverture and the San Domingo Revolution*, New York: Vintage.

James, Joy, and Sharpley-Whiting, T. Denean (eds.). (2000) *The Black Feminist Reader*, Malden, MA: Blackwell.

Kirkland, Frank Kirkland. (1992–1993). "Modernity and Intellectual Life in Black," *Philosophical Forum* 24, nos. 1–3: 136–165.

Lewis, David Levering. (1993) *W.E.B. Du Bois: A Biography of a Race (1868–1919)*, New York: Holt.

Lott, Tommy, and Pittman, John (eds.). (2002) *A Companion to African American Philosophy*, Oxford: Blackwell.

Mignolo, Walter. (2011) *The Darker Side of Western Modernity: Global Futures, Decolonial Options (Latin America Otherwise)*, Durham: Duke University Press.

Mills, Charles W. (2005) "'Ideal Theory' as Ideology." *Hypatia* 20, no. 3 (Summer): 165–184.

Monahan, Michael. (2011) *The Creolizing Subject*, New York: Fordham University Press.

———. (2017) "Introduction: What Is Rational Is Creolizing," in Michael Monahan (ed.), *Creolizing Hegel*, London: Rowman & Littlefield.

Moody-Adams, Michele. (1997) *Fieldwork in Familiar Places: Morality, Culture, & Philosophy*, Cambridge, MA: Harvard University Press.

Neocosmos, Michael. (2016) *Thinking Freedom in Africa*, Johannesburg, SA: Wits University Press.

Nirenberg, David. (2007) "Race and the Middle Ages: The Case of Spain and Its Jews," in Margaret R. Greer, Walter D. Mignolo, and Maureen Quilligan (eds.), *Rereading the Black Legend: The Discourses of Religious and Racial Difference in the Renaissance Empires*, Chicago: University of Chicago Press, pp. 71–87.

Outlaw, Lucius T. (1996) *On Race and Philosophy*, New York: Routledge.

Park, Peter K.J. (2013) *Africa, Asia, and the History of Philosophy: Racism in the Formation of the Philosophical Canon, 1780–1830*, Albany: State University of New York Press.

Sexton, Jared Sexton. (2011) "The Social Life of Social Death: On Afro-Pessimism and Black Optimism." *InTensions Journal* 5 (Fall/Winter): 1–47.

Taylor, Paul C. (2013) *Race: A Philosophical Introduction*, 2nd edition, Cambridge: Polity.

Westley, Robert St. Martin. (1997) "White Normativity and the Rhetoric of Equal Protection," in Lewis R. Gordon (ed.), *Existence in Black: An Anthology of Black Existential Philosophy*, New York: Routledge, pp. 91–98.

Wilderson, Frank. (2008) "Biko and the Problematic Presence," in Amanda Alexander, Nigel Gibson, and Andile Mngxitama (eds.), *Biko Lives! Contestations and Conversations*, New York: Palgrave, pp. 95–114.

Wiredu, Kwasi. (1996) *Cultural Universals and Particulars*, Bloomington: Indiana University Press.

——— (ed.). (2004) *A Companion to African Philosophy*, Malden, MA: Blackwell.

12

THEORIZING INDIGENEITY, GENDER, AND SETTLER COLONIALISM

Shelbi Nahwilet Meissner and Kyle Whyte

Introduction

In 1924, Virginia passed the Racial Integrity Act. The act enforced the one-drop rule, which made it so that someone was either white or colored, and one drop of non-white meant someone was colored. The only exception to the one-drop rule occurred in cases where white people claimed to be descendants of any Indigenous women, which included Pocahontas. While white people who claimed an often-fictional Indigenous great-grandmother were classified as white, actual Indigenous people were homogenized as "colored," their Indigenous ancestry omitted from public records (Tuck and Yang 2012: 10). In Canada until 1985, "section 12(1)(b) of the Indian Act discriminated against Indian women by stripping them and their descendants of their Indian status if they married a man without Indian status" (Lawrence 2003). In Aotearoa/New Zealand, though Māori women traditionally had the responsibility of serving as speakers for their *whanau*, *hapu*, and *iwi* (families and communities), British settlers negotiated the Treaty of Waitangi solely with Māori men. And later, the Native Land Act of 1909 was a deliberate attempt by settlers to destroy the *whanau* and *hapu* kinship structures and replace them with nuclear, patriarchal family and community structures (Mikaere 1994).

In these cases, a person's racial, social, cultural, and political identities as a member of an Indigenous people or community, that is, their Indigenous identities, are mediated by heterosexual and patriarchal gender oppression. For Indigenous peoples all over the world, racial identities such as "Indian blood" are woven into colonial fabrics that seek to impose oppressive versions of "Indigeneity" on Indigenous peoples. While philosophers often focus on some aspects of racial identities, it is also true that Indigeneity, as an *often* imposed social, cultural and political category, has an important place in the philosophy of race. Though Indigeneity does not always correspond to what is referred to as "race" in the philosophy of race, as such discussions tend towards interrogations of "biological" and/or "visual" conceptions of race. Indigeneity includes a particularly fluid notion of identity that, at times, biological and/or visual theories of race can mask.

Indigenous identity, or Indigeneity, then, refers to *a person's claims to be* or *a person's acceptance by others as* a member or descendent of one or more Indigenous peoples or communities as among the racial, social, cultural, or political groups to which someone belongs; Indigenous identity also refers to a person's status or responsibilities, self-perceived or delegated by others, as a member or descendent of one or more Indigenous peoples or communities. The cases above demonstrate situations in which a person's gender, for example, significantly determines what Indigenous identities that person can claim, what identities that person is accepted as, or what that person's status and responsibilities are within particular peoples and communities.

The fluidity one finds in Indigenous identity is composed, in part, by an always already present negotiation between Indigenous persons themselves and the imposed categories of Native, Sioux, Aboriginal, *Anishinaabe-kwe*, Indian, Indigenous, Māori, and many others. While some of the categories in this list are used by people to express liberatory identities, these categories are nonetheless complicated by the fact that they also, at the same time, have legacies of being created and imposed through colonial processes.

The entanglement of Indigeneity, heterosexuality, and patriarchy, for example, are imposed or heavily regulated by settler colonialism and can never be avoided or erased when one speaks of Indigenous identity. This erasure may be common in many discussions of "biological" and/or visual investigations into race. However, such erasures would be uncommon and, quite frankly, distortive in an account of Indigeneity. Indigeneity is a negotiation influenced by a confluence of factors impacting who we believe we are and who we are considered to be at any given point in time. So in talking about Indigeneity one cannot extract race and examine it absent of other forms of social, cultural, and political identification and how those imposed categories order colonial societies. And we will not do so here. Instead, our goal is to analyze Indigeneity and gender oppression, referencing race where it is relevant.

We will use "patriarchy," from now on, to refer to heterosexual patriarchy. Settler colonialism refers to a particular structure of colonial oppression in which the colonizing society seeks to dispossess Indigenous peoples of their territories through erasing the histories and presences of Indigenous peoples in these territories (Lefevre 2015). US settler colonialism, our focus here, imposes many different racial, cultural, and political identities on Indigenous peoples as specific tactics of erasure aimed at replacing Indigenous peoples with settlers on Indigenous territories, justifying violence against Indigenous persons, romanticizing histories of settlement, and bolstering perceptions of the moral superiority of settler populations.

As a woman of Luiseño and Cupeño descent (first author) and a Potawatomi man and member of the Citizen Potawatomi Nation (second author), the entanglement of Indigeneity and patriarchy is part of our experiences negotiating settler oppression in our work and personal lives in the context of the United States. We will try to give voice to the structures of erasure behind some of our experiences by bringing together a range of cases from academic literatures of how oppressive impositions of Indigenous identities are interwoven with patriarchy. An important pattern of oppression emerges when we reflect on these cases: patriarchy is a fundamental part of the structure of settler colonial erasure.

US settler patriarchy, as part of the structure of erasure, issues specific tactics that accomplish erasure by delegitimizing Indigenous political representation and diplomacy, breeding distrust and creating oppressive dilemmas within Indigenous communities, and justifying and obscuring violence against Indigenous women, girls, and Two-Spirit persons. We conclude by gesturing to the idea that the resurgence of Indigenous identities as part of decolonization movements must simultaneously be tied to the decolonization of Indigenous relationships to gender and land. In making this argument, we are seeking to distill rather briefly a few of the concepts and arguments advanced within complex literatures in Indigenous studies, including Indigenous feminisms (e.g., Barker 2015; Goeman and Denetdale 2009) and Indigenous gender studies (e.g., Calhoun et al. 2007; Anderson et al. 2012), for philosophers of race.

Indigeneity, Patriarchy, and US Settler Colonialism

Native American and Indigenous Studies literatures have explored the histories of North American Indigenous peoples prior to and during European and US colonization to understand Indigenous systems of identification and gender. There are two findings from these literatures that we wish to present in this section. First, historically, there was no such thing as "Indigeneity" that referred to some discrete racial, social, cultural, or political identity. Second, many Indigenous peoples never had dualistic gender systems that privileged men and the small nuclear family. We are highlighting these findings in order to set up the next section that explores how European colonialism and—especially—US settler colonialism imposed patriarchy on Indigenous peoples and communities through the imposition of settler forms of Indigeneity.

We will begin by first establishing as a premise that Indigenous peoples in many parts of what is now called North America lived in societies organized according to complex cultural, social, political, diplomatic, and ecological systems that sought to strike upon, through learning from and reflecting on experiences, the best approaches to living well within certain ecoregions and among different neighboring societies (see Trosper 2002 for example). What we refer to today as "Indigenous identities" or "Indigeneity"—or Indian, Native American, First Nations, Métis, Tribal member, and so on—would not have made much sense to many of our ancestors based on how they were accustomed to identifying and gendering themselves.

For example, in many societies, such as *Anishinaabe/Neshnabé* society, persons often identified themselves according to a mixture of clan identities, geographic locations of inhabitation, roles within political alliances, among many other aspects of their ways of life. Hence, introducing oneself to someone else involved more than one's name and some statement of membership in a racial, social, cultural, or political group. One could be crane clan, which communicated ancestry from sandhill cranes and certain leadership responsibilities (Bohaker 2010); *Bodwewadmi* (i.e., Potawatomi), which implied one is a fire keeper, which refers to a political role in relation to other *Anishinaabe* polities (faith keepers, trade keepers, etc.) (Clifton 1986); or from an ecoregion, like a particular river valley (Secunda 2006). In terms of leadership, there were not universal leaders all year round because the political organization of *Anishinaabe/Neshnabé* society changed according to the seasons (Benton-Banai 2008).

The complexity and fluidity of identity within Indigenous societies explains why today, even among urban and rural Indigenous communities that have changed greatly in the wake of settler colonialism, taking time to introduce oneself is a non-negotiable aspect of beginning a new relationship. People are expected to describe things such as what their names mean, what geographies they live in, who their families and ancestors are, and what goals they have for their lives and for protecting the well-being of their communities. Often people choose to perform songs, dances, spoken-word, and prayers as part of their expressions of who they are, even when people have known each other for many years or are related as family or of a common community.

Gender systems for many Indigenous peoples are also fluid, differing greatly from gender norms pervasive in US settler society. While "man/woman" distinctions do not necessarily accord with many Indigenous languages and cultures, we will invoke them for the sake of space in this chapter since we are writing in academic English language discourse. In some societies, women were responsible for managing and harvesting plants and engaging in agricultural activities, whereas men were responsible for hunting and/or fishing activities. But even these distinctions were not as clear-cut. For example, in some Ojibwe societies, women responsible for rice harvesting would also, during their stewardship activities throughout the year, engage in hunting activities (Norrgard 2014). This gender system positioned men and women differently as stewards of key environmental resources with gendered knowledge as well as gendered connections to the landscape—but also admitted of fluidities that are impermissible in some more rigid gender systems.

Indigenous societies often see men and women as moral equals and women feature in prominent leadership roles, from management to diplomacy (Allen 1992). Many Indigenous societies featured more than two genders and gender-based violence was not a part of society (Deer 2004; Roscoe 1987). The gendered responsibilities of people in different categories varied by community. Indigenous languages often feature specific names for these genders and responsibilities that go along with participation in that gender. Non-binary individuals are often respected for excelling at particular traditional activities and responsibilities, though it is important to note that non-binary individuals often participated in masculine or feminine roles and were not discriminated against for doing so (Roscoe 1987).

Returning to Anishinaabe peoples, *agokwa* and *okitciakwe*, respectively, are Ansishinabemowin terms that refer to "the biological male that performed the gender roles of a woman" and "a biological woman who performs the gender roles of a man" (McGeough 2008; Sayers 2014). According to McGeough, the *agokwa* and *okitciakwe* had important communal and spiritual responsibilities and Anishinaabe people traditionally see gender "being fluid and not fixed or determined by one's biological sex" (McGeough 2008; Sayers 2014; Noodin 2014).

Richard White, in *The Middle Ground*, describes Algonquian gender and kinship. "Depending on her tribal identity, an Algonquian woman often has a more durable and significant relationship with her mother, father, brothers, sisters, or grandparents, or with other, unrelated women than with her husband or husbands," and notes the governance value of an Algonquian woman's non-marital relationships had more influence than her relationships with her husband, including "her own membership in ritual organizations or, among some tribes such as the Shawnees, Huron-Petuns, and Miamis, her own political status in the offices confined to women" (White 1991: 50).

As with the previous discussion of identity, Indigenous persons today engage in and reconstruct traditional gender roles and responsibilities as part of their resurgence as self-determining peoples. Indigenous peoples are taking leadership on addressing issues ranging from sexual violence to environmental justice using gender-based leadership structures and responsibilities (Deer 2004; Whyte 2014). We can imagine then that Indigenous forms of identification and gendering were based on assumptions about the nature of culture, society, politics, diplomacy, and human-ecological relationships that are not reflected in the same assumptions of US or Canadian settler societies today.

The Entanglement of Settler Patriarchy and Indigeneity

European colonialism and US settler colonialism directly seek to impose their own definitions of Indigeneity to replace the identity and gender systems described in the previous section with settler patriarchy. We will describe categories of tactics of how this occurred. We divide this section into four distinct though intertwined topical areas: marriage and ancestry, language, sexual violence, and children.

Marriage and Ancestry

Richard White, in *The Middle Ground*, discusses how eighteenth-century colonial encounters with pre-US colonialists (e.g., the French) involved the colonists' attempted assimilation of Indigenous gendered identities. In Algonquian territories, White writes that French men sought Indigenous women for sex and marriage, often dispossessing Indigenous women of their land in the process (White 1991: 60). French Christian sexual mores discouraged Indigenous practices of polygamy, polyandry, and casual "adultery." The French enforced policies of monogamous, heterosexual, nuclear marriages between Indian women and French men (White 1991: 50–52).

The French were curious and revolted by "the berdaches of the Illinois and the acceptance of homosexual relations among many Algonquian peoples" (White 1991: 60).[1] While many scholars reject today the concept of "berdache," it is used to describe a number of nonbinary genders of different Indigenous peoples. White discusses how the French colonizers sought to dismantle Algonquian gender systems:

> In attempting to impose their own cultural categories on the actions of Algonquian women, the French tended to . . . define a woman in terms of . . . her actual or potential husband—who may not have been anywhere near being the most significant figure in the woman's life.
>
> (White 1991: 50)

Many Indigenous cosmologies feature conceptions of love and kinship that are non-monogamous and non-patriarchal. Kim TallBear refers to the invention of monogamous heterosexual marriage as a "white nationalist veneer over our lives" and details the role of marriage in the national agenda in Canada and in the United States prior to the nineteenth century (TallBear 2016). TallBear notes: "Part of saving Indians from their savagery meant pursuing the righteous monogamous couple-centric nuclear family co-produced with private property including the partitioning of the tribal land base into individually owned allotments held under men's names" (TallBear 2016: 13:43). TallBear explains that prior to colonization, the "fundamental social unit" of Dakota people was the "extended kin group, including plural marriage" (TallBear 2016: 14:42).

TallBear believes there is "a possibility for greater emotional, environmental, and economic sustainability in extended kin networks" (TallBear 2016: 19:54). However, European missionaries and their later American counterparts treated non-monogamy and mixed families as shameful, immoral concepts. Many mothers were encouraged by missionaries and later, Indian agents from the Department of the Interior, to abandon their non-heteropatriarchal conceptions of kinship and to document their children as descendants of men and, ideally, as descendants of white men if possible. Though great-great-grandmothers listed their children as descendants of white men to survive the Christianized colonial mores inflicted upon them, this well-intentioned white-washing resulted, in various cases, in the false ascription of non-Indigeneity to some persons who were documented as 'white.'

The US Dawes Act (1887) intended to usurp more Indigenous territories by partitioning land into parcels owned by individual Indians who were pushed to become farmers with male-run nuclear families (Allen 1990). Settlers took the leftover lands and preyed upon the Indian allotments. People identified as Indian for the purpose of allotment of private property were, then, expected to fit these gender expectations over time once they took responsibility over the individual property. The allotment process involved a way of transferring Indians from uncivilized matrilineal law to civilized patrilineal law (Dixon 2012).

Gender, marriage, and enrollment issues are very common in Indian country. In *Santa Clara Pueblo v. Martinez*, gender was closely tied to qualifications of enrollment. In this case, Julia Martinez, an enrolled member of Santa Clara Pueblo, brought a claim under the Indian Civil Rights Act (ICRA) that the Santa Clara Pueblo had violated her right to equal protection because under the Pueblo's law, her children cannot be tribal members, cannot legally reside within the Pueblo, and cannot possess land within the Pueblo because Martinez married a non-member. Yet in 1978, the Supreme Court ruled that judicial review would undermine the Tribe's right to rule themselves (Getches, Rosenfelt, and Wilkinson 2011: chapter 6). As Valencia-Webber notes, *Santa Clara Pueblo v. Martinez* "has long attracted attention from feminists and human rights advocates, because they see a woman's claim of gender discrimination pitted against a Pueblo's claim of tribal sovereignty" (Valencia-Weber 2011: 451).

In at least eleven federally recognized Tribes, the history of acceptance of different genders and different kinship structures is completely erased by laws that prohibit same-sex marriage. In 2005, the Navajo Nation enacted the Diné Marriage Act, which states that "Marriage between persons of the same sex is void and prohibited." Jennifer Nez Denetdale attributes the passage of the Diné Marriage Act to a "reinscription of patriarchy" and argues that "for Navajos, the prevailing Navajo national mood is connected to the resurgence of American imperialism and, in particular, manifests a hatred and intolerance of difference within Navajo society" (Denetdale 2009: 134). The 2015 U.S. Supreme Court ruling that guarantees marriage rights to same-sex couples has no bearing on tribal laws. Two Spirit, LGBTQ, and gender non-binary community members create safe spaces at Two Spirit gatherings and powwows by excluding elders who are non-allies.[2]

So far, some of the examples we discussed involve the disappearance of Indigenous women as ancestors. Yet settlers have appropriated the idea of themselves having Indigenous women as ancestors as a tactic of erasure that contributes to settlers' goal to indigenize themselves. Eve Tuck, following Vine Deloria Jr., describes this as the Indian-grandmother complex, which serves as a defense mechanism of white US settlers to disassociate themselves from the moral and causal responsibilities of being descendants of violent colonizers. Tuck writes, "In this move to innocence [the Indian-grandmother complex], settlers locate or invent a long-lost ancestor who is rumored to have had 'Indian blood,' and they use this claim to mark themselves as blameless in the attempted eradications of Indigenous peoples" (Tuck and Yang 2012: 10).

Deloria speculates that the Indian-grandmother complex allows for settlers to claim ownership, albeit usually through imaginary means, of the stolen land upon which they reside: "Do they need some blood tie with the frontier and its dangers in order to experience what it means to be an American? Or is it an attempt to avoid facing the guilt they bear for the treatment of the Indians?" (Deloria 1969: 2–4). Tuck points out that sometimes those afflicted with Indian-grandmother complex actually use their mythical Indian ancestor to further stake their claim to American-ness and their membership in the white racial category. "In the racialization of whiteness . . . white people can stay white, yet claim descendance from an Indian grandmother" (Tuck and Yang 2012: 10). Sufferers of the Indian-grandmother complex get to have their stolen cake and remain white.

Language

Many Indigenous languages of Turtle Island contain within them a set of gendered roles and relationships that differ significantly from those present in Western languages (âpihtawikosisân 2012; Briner, forthcoming; Noodin 2014). Gender is not binarized in some Indigenous languages. These grammars are either non-gendered, or make space for third, fourth, and fifth gender states (âpihtawikosisân 2012; Briner, forthcoming). When Indigenous languages are forced into hibernation by violent assimilative forces like missionizing, boarding schools, legal kidnapping, and the like, speakers and would-be speakers are deprived not only of opportunities and abilities to communicate, they are robbed of grammars rooted in non-binarized conceptions of gender.

One's grammar can certainly be said to affect one's perspective on their world in various ways, including one's approach to knowledge (epistemology), cultures, and reciprocal moral relationships to other humans and nonhumans (âpihtawikosisân 2012; Briner, forthcoming). While we do not seek to make a case here for linguistic determinism, it is nonetheless important to recognize that the significance of how linguistic colonization replaces the ancestral languages with languages that do not afford spaces for non-patriarchal gender roles, or for non-male/female gender states. When the language is forced into hibernation, the capacity to use language that expresses liberatory and egalitarian ancestral gender systems is also forced into hibernation. While Indigenous peoples find other ways to express themselves creatively through languages such as English, create empowering art, performance and media, and continue to develop and practice decolonizing and anti-colonial epistemologies, cultures, and interspecies relationships, the significance of linguistic colonization must certainly be noted.

Language, in terms of designations or names for particular identities, can also be problematic within the English language in the US or Canadian settler contexts. Terms such as "Two-Spirit" or "LGBTQ" have to be used, for practical purposes, as identifiers for persons. However, these terms do not come close to connoting the multiple Two-Spirit identities that are diverse both according to Tribe but also to what features are important as part of that identity, such as sexual orientation, self-presentation, and so on. On the latter point, we mean that "Two-Spirit" itself does not map onto "gay" or "lesbian" directly. Though many Two-Spirit persons may also seek to identify as LGBTQ, there is a complexity of Indigenous persons' identities that may be threatened, intentionally or otherwise, by more dominant gender discourses in the US settler state.

Sexual Violence

Sexual violence occurs closely with impositions of settler definitions of Indigeneity. Before describing some examples, some introductory points are necessary. Indigenous women are leaders, integral components of extended kin networks, life-givers, and cultural keepers. As part of the settler project to successfully indigenize settlers and their descendants as rightful owners and occupants of stolen land, settlers destroy and redefine the identities of Indigenous women. As a deeply troubling example of this, Indigenous women's identities become marked by features that render their rape as excusable and acceptable. Colonial logic codes Indigenous lands and bodies as objects for the taking. The sovereignty and self-governing abilities of a Tribe are affected by the lack of avenues for justice for Indigenous women survivors of sexual violence.

Sexual violence against Indigenous women, girls and Two-Spirit persons is a pervasive dimension of Indigenous experiences of settler colonialism. On the issue of rape, Sarah Deer argues that "rape is a fundamental result of colonialism, a history of violence reaching back centuries" (Deer 2015: x). Deer explains that rape within tribal communities is "inextricably linked to the way in which the US developed and sustained a legal system that has usurped the sovereign authority of tribal nations" (Deer 2015: xiv). Andrea Smith also argues that colonialism itself is "structured by the logic of sexual violence." She argues that because Indian bodies are "dirty," they are considered sexually violable and "rapable," making Indian people not respected in their "bodily integrity" (Smith 2005: 73).

Indigenous women, girls and Two-Spirit persons are raped more often than members of other groups. According to Amnesty International, Indigenous women are "2.5 times more likely to be raped or assaulted than other women in the U.S." and "at least 86 per cent of the reported cases of rape or sexual assault against American Indian and Alaska Native women, survivors report that the perpetrators are non-Native men" (Amnesty International 2007). Yet rapists, especially white ones who are not in a public, established relationship with a member of a tribal community, rarely run the risk of being caught. In 2013, the Violence Against Women Act (VAWA) authorized criminal jurisdiction of Tribes over non-Indian perpetrators of rape that are nonetheless severely limited, only relevant in cases of sexual violence committed by white husbands, boyfriends, and domestic partners. Deer writes, "consequently, women who are raped by persons within other relationships (e.g., acquaintances, relatives, or strangers) are not covered by the recent legislative change, and authority over such crimes will require Congress to enact additional reforms to federal law" (Deer 2015: xviii).

Deer writes that because the American legal system is imposed upon Indigenous lands and Indigenous bodies, and because there are limited avenues for recourse legal or otherwise in Indian country against sexual predators, the abilities for self-determination of Tribes are compromised. She writes, "It is impossible to have a truly self-determining nation when its members have been denied self-determination over their own bodies" (Deer 2015: xvi). Here, Deer depicts sexual violence as a serious threat to tribal sovereignty, highlighting the inextricably intertwined nature of gender oppression and Indigenous identity.

A further identity aspect involves the solutions to sexual violence. In cases where Indian men are the perpetrators, both punitive solutions and some reconciliatory solutions are not effective. In "Decolonizing Rape Law," Sarah Deer argues that Anglo-American courts, in virtue of their roots in colonial violence, are inadequate spaces for justice-seeking on behalf of Indigenous women survivors of sexual violence (Deer 2009). She also argues that the peacekeeping model of justice, in virtue of the tendency for Indigenous men to internalize settler heteropatriarchal values, is inadequate as well. She explains that the individualism of settler patriarchy allows Indigenous men the distance they need to avoid having a sense of accountability to their communities to truly cease desiring to enact sexual violence again.

Sexual violence against Indigenous women has endured because it is part and parcel of the desire to seize Indigenous lands. Historically and contemporarily, the trafficking of Indigenous women, girls, and Two-Spirit persons is one of the means by which sexual violence against them is perpetrated. Deer explains that "contemporary efforts to stop sex trafficking in the United States are disingenuous because they fail to account for the widespread sexual slavery of Native women throughout the past five hundred years" (Deer 2015: xxi). Reports of "man camps," in which Indigenous women are trafficked and prostituted at contemporary fracking sites, cannot be separated from "earlier histories of the rape of Native women during the Gold Rush and other moments in American economic booms" (Deer 2015: xxi). Without interrogation of the fact that the sexual violence against Indigenous people today is enacted in the same colonial spirit as it was in the past, solutions to widespread sexual violence against Indigenous people are destined for failure.

Children

Indigenous communities have been subject to the systematic kidnapping and relocation of their children. Boarding schools and adoption have been ideal tools for settler society to infiltrate and dismantle Indigenous communities, and racialized gender discrimination against Indigenous women has been integral to these processes. Settler colonial practices of forced adoption and compulsory education not only systematically stripped Indigenous communities of future generations, they also work in tandem with practices of compulsory heterosexuality, which have a vast impact on Indigenous identities in the US.

Many boarding schools, in an attempt to assimilate Indigenous children into white American culture, banned the speaking of Indigenous languages and participation in Indigenous life stage ceremonies, and instead, enforced strict gendered protocols for students. Boys and young men were required to cut their long "feminine" hair, and devote themselves to learning industrial farming, mechanics, wartime assembly-line production, and Bible verses (Bahr 2014). Girls and young women were required to dress as "good ladies" and learn sewing, housekeeping, and cosmetology (Bahr 2014: 22–26; Jacobs 2008: 203).

The Sherman Institute in Riverside, California, distributed Indigenous students to the surrounding community as a (largely unpaid) labor force. Young Indigenous women, highly coveted by whites, were groomed to serve "their ladies" and to attract a husband (Bahr 2014: 22–26). Testimonies from young Indigenous women in the "outing" program at Sherman insinuate that some of the men they worked for harassed them, assaulted them, and in some cases, coerced the girls into marriage (Bahr 2014: 22–26).

In "The Great White Mother," Margaret Jacobs argues that "white women were integrally involved in the removal of American Indian children to boarding schools and that their involvement implicated them in one of the most cruel, yet largely unexamined, policies of colonialism within the American West" (Jacobs 2008: 192). White women reformers deemed Indigenous women unfit as mothers, their children hence having "to be removed from their homes and communities to be raised properly by white women within institutions" (Jacobs 2008: 192). White women's "[construction of] indigenous mothers as degraded and sexually immoral, misguided and negligent, and even cruel and unloving" as a "key practice of colonialism" because "such representations contributed to justifying state policies of indigenous child removal" (Jacobs 2008: 202).

Indigenous children are removed from their homes today more than any other demographic (Woolman and Deer 2014: 944). Joanna Woolman and Deer argue that the perspectives of Indigenous women must be taken into account in the methodologies of child protection because of the dominance of colonial logics. Woolman and Deer chronicle the more contemporary abuses of the child protection system. After compulsory boarding-school era had come to a close, "social workers became the new saviors of Native children and interfered with families for the 'crimes' of poverty and isolation . . . child welfare workers often explicitly argued that Native babies and children would be better off if they were living with non-Native, affluent families" (Woolman and Deer 2014: 955).

By the end of the 1960s, "between twenty-five and thirty-five percent of Native children had been separated from their families" (Woolman and Deer 2014: 957). The epidemic of what amounts to legal kidnapping justified by racism and colonial logic became so overwhelming that Congress was forced to enact the Indian Child Welfare Act (ICWA) in 1978. ICWA "signaled an acknowledgment that the American legal system had been used as a tool to destroy Native families" and was designed to prioritize that Indigenous children remain within their communities (Woolman and Deer 2014: 957). Though ICWA has made significant strides, Indigenous children still remain among the most likely to be taken from their homes.

As boarding schools and adoption practices were used to define Indigenous identities on settler terms, we see in these examples how settler tactics entangled imposed identity formation and imposed hetero-patriarchal gendering. The cases illustrated above—the attempted destruction of traditional Indigenous kinship networks, the assimilative practices of the compulsory education era, and the continued forced removal of Indigenous children from their communities—function to deprive Indigenous communities of future generations. The deprivation of a continuing generation is a genocidal attempt to destroy the possibility of the community having a future. Because Indigenous women were and are systematically deemed "unfit mothers" by settler society, racialized gender discrimination within the adoption system plays a key role in the erasing of Indigenous identities.

Implications of Gender/Identity and Oppression

Settler colonial erasure involves the imposition of oppressive Indigenous identities as an approach for establishing the hegemony of settler patriarchy within Indigenous communities and nations. We see the above examples as establishing a pattern of oppression. To us, settler patriarchy is a fundamental part of the structure of erasure. Again, we subscribe to the philosophical view that settler colonialism is a particular form, or structure, of oppression that is characterized by one society's goal to erase another society. The settler colonial structure of oppression advances through "on the ground" tactics that enable and enact erasure. The examples above are the "on the ground" tactics.

The entanglement of imposed Indigeneity and patriarchy are integral components of settler erasure for at least three reasons: (1) the delegitimization of Indigenous political representation and diplomacy, (2) the breeding of distrust and creation of oppressive dilemmas within Indigenous peoples and communities, and (3) the justification and obscuring of violence against Indigenous women, girls and Two-Spirit persons. We begin with some further descriptions of (1), (2), and (3), and continue on to review how the tactics discussed in the previous section express (1), (2), and (3), including as many examples as is feasible given the space we have to write.

The first reason, delegitimization of Indigenous political representation and diplomacy, refers to the deliberate attempt to erase two ideas in particular: Indigenous peoples' sovereignty pre-exists the formation of the US and European invasion; Indigenous forms of governance operate very differently than that of the US settler state and settler society—organizationally, culturally, and linguistically.

In the second reason, breeding distrust refers to deliberate attempts to divide members of Indigenous people and communities against one another by making each member feel as if the others do not have their best interests at heart. Settler patriarchy breeds distrust in that arbitrary male privilege creates circumstances in which men are more likely to assume their privilege is natural or traditional and are more concerned with protecting their privilege than in working to dismantle patriarchy. Oppressive dilemmas refer to the imposition of choice-situations on Indigenous persons in which each choice option carries a bad consequence and no choice option can be seen as somehow better than the others (Frye 1983). In settler contexts, dilemmatic choice-situations produce erasure over time. For example, Tribes who adopt US forms of government as a choice over time can come to believe that that form of government is their original and *only* legitimate form of governing authority.

Finally, the third reason, obscuring of violence, refers to deliberate settler tactics that seek to disappear systems and cases of violence as ways to assuage settler guilt, alleviate individual or collective senses of responsibility, and justify settlers' beliefs in the morality of their aspirations to legitimately occupy Indigenous territories.

In terms of the first reason, settler patriarchy is informed fundamentally by a man/woman gender binary and racialized notions of identity, such as blood quantum. It functions to delegitimize Indigenous political representation and diplomacy. In the settler systems, men are superior to women and men are seen as a better fit for significant, visible leadership and diplomatic positions in society. The settler gender system is a catch-all system in which it is not possible for individuals to fall outside of the categories "man" and "woman" without having to somehow define themselves as pathological or "in between." Settler patriarchy destabilizes Indigenous political systems by subverting the traditional leadership of Indigenous women and non-binary people. Treaties between Indigenous peoples and settlers were largely negotiated by men. Over time, some Indigenous men embrace these roles in morally troubling ways—in some cases arguing problematically that they are indeed traditional.

Recall from the first section that Indigenous political systems are often based on extended kinship networks and seasonally adaptive forms of political authority and responsibilities that work to adjust to the dynamics of ecosystems. Marriage in tandem with allotment has been used as a tool for infiltrating and disassembling Indigenous communities for assimilation, the destruction of extended kinship systems, and settler acquisition of Indigenous land. By promoting the subservient white woman as an ideal mother, settler heteropatriarchal policies systematically stole Indigenous children from their families, classifying Indigenous mothers as unfit and stripping Tribes of future generations. Stripping Indigenous communities of their children systematically compromises sovereignty and Tribes' abilities to self-govern.

Through linguistic colonization, settler society actively dispossesses Indigenous peoples of their languages, subverting non-binarized conceptions of gender, and disconnecting Indigenous people from integral components of traditional governance. By disrupting language and alternative conceptions of gender, colonizers attempted to take control of Indigenous lands and people, delegitimizing traditional systems of governance and diplomacy. For example, diplomatic relationships between Indigenous peoples and the US all take place in English. Given there is no respect for Indigenous languages, there is no need on the part of the US to consider how it would communicate through Indigenous languages or what protocols would be required with particular Indigenous peoples that would feature engagement with women and Two-Spirit persons more prominently.

All of these cases divest Indigenous political sovereignty of its linguistic, gender, and cultural difference. Without these differences, Indigenous political sovereignty over time comes to mirror both US forms of government and the United States' desired status for Indigenous peoples as dependent on the US and subject to plenary power. Destruction of women's leadership, for example, erases women's voices and leverage from political engagement. Destruction of Indigenous languages requires Indigenous persons to engage diplomatically only in the English language.

The second reason, breeding distrust and dilemmas for Indigenous persons, is also a key part of the entanglement of imposed identities and genders. The integration of patriarchy within Indigenous peoples and communities and the federal punitive system create and maintain distrust between men and women, girls, and Two-Spirit persons, those most vulnerable to sexual violence from Indigenous men. Indigenous men often fall prey to the internalization of heterocolonial patriarchal values. Men's adoption of patriarchy also comes out in statements such that re-seizing land takes priority over the protection of women and girls—which assumes that prioritization is even needed in the first place.

The predominance of men in Indigenous governments, such as those of federally recognized Tribes, divides men and women because the former share in settler structures of power privileging men. When men are associated with leadership in practices such as cultural and linguistic revitalization, women who have similar aspirations—aspirations that often more accurately correspond to historic leadership in certain cases—cannot trust men to unsettle their own male privileges.

One oppressive dilemma Indigenous women, girls, and Two-Spirit folks are forced into concerns the intersection of sovereignty and voicing concerns about violence. There are two approaches to addressing violence within an Indigenous community. As Deer argues, Anglo-American courts, in virtue of their roots in colonial violence, are inadequate spaces for justice-seeking on behalf of Indigenous women survivors of sexual violence. She also argues that the peacekeeping model of justice, in virtue of the tendency for Indigenous men to internalize settler heteropatriarchal values, is inadequate as well. Though both of these avenues for justice-seeking are inadequate, Indigenous women survivors of violence are forced to choose one bad option over the other.

Indigenous children who are being abused, and their advocates, are also forced into a dilemma. Alerting authorities to an abusive situation is met with shame and a sense of communal betrayal because the racist, colonial project of child protective services has aided the removal of children from communities (Woolman and Deer 2014: 957–958). Because this option is not adequate, survivors of abuse can remain silent, which may result in the isolation and pain of suffering alone without resources and can even run the risk of possible escalation of violence.

Settler patriarchy also forces Two-Spirit, LGBTQ, and non-binary persons who are subject to violence or discrimination into environments of distrust as well as dilemmas. The internalization of settler heteropatriarchal values has caused many Indigenous nations to adopt laws banning same sex marriages and tribal community members to voice hatred for non-heterosexual and/or non-binary identities. Because of this, Two-Spirit, LGBTQ, and non-binary persons are not always afforded safe spaces within their own communities. Two-Spirit, LGBTQ, and non-binary persons who are subject to violence and discrimination are also presented with dilemmas because alerting authorities or raising public awareness of their own oppression can be seen as an invitation to the colonizer to intervene and trample tribal sovereignty.

Finally, settler patriarchy justifies and obscures violence against Indigenous women, girls, and Two-Spirit persons. Many of the examples referenced earlier in this section can also be categorized accordingly. The Indian grandmother complex, as mentioned earlier, is a common invocation that both normalizes and disappears sexual violence. Sexual relations with Indigenous women, regardless of whether the details of a particular claimant's ancestry actually occurred, are transformed into "interesting tidbits" about a settler's ancestry. Gender violence is bound up in this rhetoric in that the Indigeneity of the woman ancestor in question can be conquered, vanquished, and disappeared by white male ancestors.

Even in cases where someone casually references the fact that their alleged ancestor was raped or denied the right to choose not to identify as Indigenous, the tone of the referencing often renders these actions as profoundly historic and unrelated to the issues that Indigenous women face today with being unable to pass on their Indigeneity to their children, their widespread disappearances and murders, and the heightened risks of sexual violence. The Indian grandmother or princess complex trivializes and decontextualizes settler violence. Imposed settler identities deny Indigenous women the capacity to pass on Indigeneity to their descendants. Indigenous identity is defined by settler society as dwindling and inevitably destined for assimilation and disappearance.

Settler patriarchy also obscures the violence against Indigenous women in rape law. While the 2013 Violence Against Women Act provides some legal recourse for Indigenous women who are raped by non-Indian husbands and non-Indian boyfriends, the Act does not protect Indigenous women who are raped by non-Indian acquaintances or strangers (Deer 2015: xviii). The American legal system is imposed onto Indigenous lands and bodies via colonial violence, but provides little to no protection for Indigenous women against the sexual violence that continues to fortify and justify colonialism. Heterocolonial patriarchy fundamentally consists in dualisms like man/woman, humanity/land, the civilized/the uncivilized, with the former of each dualism being normatively empowered. As many of the Indigenous feminists cited above have noted, colonial logic requires that the world be shaped along these dualisms, that nothing fall outside of these categories, and that the former of each dualism (man, humanity, the civilized) are able to conquer, control, and tame the latter of each dualism (woman, land, the uncivilized). Because settler society is organized from such logic, violence is obscured and justified.

Conclusion

Given the previous analysis, we seek to gesture to an argument we cannot fully make here about the resurgence of Indigeneity as a liberatory identity. TallBear, among others, have shown how more people are embracing Indigenous identities as powerful ways of reconnecting with social, cultural, and familial relations and resisting colonialism (TallBear 2013). Resurgent and liberatory approaches to Indigenous identity often focus on concepts that, in the English language, do not immediately carry with them any gendered meaning. These concepts include spirituality, political sovereignty, Red Power, stewardship/guardianship (of plants/animals/ecosystems), Wellbriety, kinship, militant decolonization, language and culture revitalization, among others. Since, as we have attempted to show, oppressive impositions of Indigenous identities are forms of erasure that are closely connected to patriarchy, it is no small issue that these concepts do not treat gender liberation as fundamental to resurgence and liberatory projects.

Many of the authors we have cited look at how the disruption of settler colonialism entails the dismantling of settler patriarchy. Deer, for example, argues that because sexual violence is integral to colonization, tribal nations ought to "develop and strengthen their response as part of broader political work toward achieving sovereignty" (Deer 2015: xvi). Woolman and Deer argue that because gender oppression is central to the genocidal project of removing Indigenous children from their communities, the perspectives of Indigenous women must be central in attempts to reform child protective services. Deer maintains that settler colonialism demands "a response that centers a contemporary Native woman in her unique place and time, empowering her to access the collective strength and insight that have helped her people survive" (Deer 2015: xiv).

Settler colonialism seeks to dispossess Indigenous peoples of land and supplant them as rightful occupiers. To achieve these ends, settler colonial logic has decentered and disempowered women, girls, and Two-Spirit persons through sexual violence and the systematic attempted destruction of extended kin networks, matrilineal governance, non-binary gender systems, and languages. Resurgence and liberatory projects that fail to take seriously the connections between oppressive identity impositions and gender oppression will fall prey to the underlying imposed patriarchy that exists within Indigenous peoples and communities. The resurgence of Indigenous identities as part of the decolonization movements must simultaneously be tied to the decolonization of Indigenous relationships to gender and land.

Notes

1. "Berdache" is a term, used by largely American anthropologists in the twentieth century, to characterize Indigenous research subjects who anthropologists believed were men, but presented wearing women's clothes, working women's traditional labor, and often serving important and unique ceremonial and governance roles. For more, see (Roscoe 1987).
2. See, for example, www.outsaskatoon.ca/elders_supports (accessed September 10, 2016) and www.baaits.org/about (accessed February 22, 2017), and on file with authors.

References

Allen, P. G. (1990). *Spider Woman's Granddaughters: Traditional Tales and Contemporary Writing by Native American Women*, Boston: Beacon Press.

———. (1992) *The Sacred Hoop: Recovering the Feminine in American Indian Traditions*. Boston, MA: Beacon Press.

Amnesty International. (2007) *Maze of Injustice: The Failure to Protect Native American Women From Sexual Violence in the USA*, New York: Amnesty International.

Anderson, K., Innes, I., and Swift, J. (2012). "Indigenous Masculinities: Carrying the Bones of the Ancestors," *Canadian Men and Masculinities: Historical and Contemporary Perspectives*, 266–284.

âpihtawikosisân. (2012). Language, Culture, and Two-Spirit Identity from http://apihtawikosisan.com/2012/03/language-culture-and-two-spirit-identity/.

Bahr, D. M. (2014) *The Students of Sherman Indian School: Education and Native Identity Since 1892*, Norman: University of Oklahoma Press.

Barker, J. (2015) "Indigenous Feminisms," in José Antonio Lucero, Dale Turner, and Donna Lee VanCott (eds.), *The Oxford Handbook of Indigenous People's Politics*, Oxford: Oxford University Press.

Benton-Banai, E. (2008). *Anishinaabe Almanac: Living Through the Seasons*, M'chigeeg, Ontario: Kenjgewin Teg Educational Institute.

Bohaker, H. (2010) "Reading Anishinaabe Identities: Meaning and Metaphor in Nindoodem Pictographs." *Ethnohistory* 57(1): 11–33.

Briner, K. (2017 forthcoming). "Hina tanu hani?hutui? What Are We Going to Do?" *Great Plains Journal*, no. 51/52 (citing with author's permission).

Calhoun, A., Goeman, M., and Tsethlikai, M. (2007) "Achieving Gender Equity for American Indians," in S. Klein, B. Richardson, D. A. Grayson, et al. (eds.), *Handbook for Achieving Gender Equity Through Education*, New York: Routledge, pp. 525–552.

Clifton, J. A. (1986). *People of the Three Fires: The Ottawa, Potawatomi, and Ojibway of Michigan*, Grand Rapids: Michigan Indian Press, Grand Rapids Inter-Tribal Council.

Deer, S. (2004). "Sovereignty of the Soul: Exploring the Intersection of Rape Law Reform and Federal Indian Law," *Suffolk University Law Review* 38: 455.

———. (2009) "Decolonizing Rape Law." *Wicazo Sa Review* 24, no. 2: 149–167.

———. (2015) *The Beginning and End of Rape*, Minneapolis: University of Minnesota Press.

Deloria, V. (1969) *Custer Died for Your Sins*, Norman: University of Oklahoma Press.

Denetdale, J. N. (2009) "Securing Navajo National Boundaries: War, Patriotism, Tradition, and the Diné Marriage Act of 2005." *Wicazo Sa Review* 24, no. 2: 131–148.

Dixon, S. L. K. (2012) "The Dynamics of Native American Women and Their Experiences: Identifying Ideologies and Theories That Help Explain Oppression," in S. T. Gregory (ed.), *Voices of Native American Educators*. Boulder: Lexington Books, pp. 15–38.

Frye, M. (1983) *The Politics of Reality: Essays in Feminist Theory*. Crossing Press Feminist Series, Trumansburg, NY: Crossing Press.

Getches, D. H., Rosenfelt, D. M., and Wilkinson, C. F. (2011) *Cases and Materials on Federal Indian Law*, Vol. 6. Eugene: School of Law, University of Oregon.

Goeman, M. R. and Denetdale, J. (2009) "Special Issue: Native Feminisms: Legacies, Interventions, and Indigenous Sovereignties." *Wicazo Sa Review* 24: 9–13.

Jacobs, M. (2008) "The Great White Mother: Maternalism and American Indian Child Removal in the American West, 1880–1940," in *One Step Over the Line: Toward a History of Women in the North American Wests*, Edmonton: University of Alberta Press.

Lawrence, B. (2003) "Gender, Race, and the Regulation of Native Identity in Canada and the United States: An Overview." *Hypatia* 18, no. 2: 3–31.

Lefevre, T. A. (2015) "Settler Colonialism," in J. Jackson (ed.), *Oxford Bibliographies in Anthropology*. Oxford: Oxford University Press, pp. 1–26.

McGeough, M. (2008) "Norval Morrisseau and the Erotic," in *Me Sexy: An Exploration of Native Sex and Sexuality*, Vancouver: Douglas & McIntyre, pp. 59–86.

Mikaere, A. (1994). "Māori Women: Caught in the Contradictions of a Colonised Reality," *Waikato Law Review* 2: 125.

Noodin, M. (2014) *Bawaajimo*, East Lansing: Michigan State University Press.

Norrgard, C. (2014) *Seasons of Change: Labor, Treaty Rights, and Ojibwe Nationhood*, Chapel Hill: University of North Carolina Press Books.

Roscoe, W. (1987) "Bibliography of Berdache and Alternative Gender Roles Among North American Indians." *Journal of Homosexuality* 14, nos. 3–4: 81–172.

Sayers, Naomi. (2014). "Indigenous Peoples: Language Revitalization & Gender Identity," https://kwetoday.com/2014/05/03/indigenous-peoples-language-revitalization-gender-identity/

Secunda, B.W. (2006) "To Cede or Seed? Risk and Identity Among the Woodland Potawatomi During the Removal Period." *Midcontinental Journal of Archaeology* 31, no. 1: 57–88.

Smith, A. (2005). *Conquest: Sexual Violence and American Indian Genocide*, Cambridge: South End Press.

TallBear, K. (2013). *Native American DNA: Tribal Belonging and the False Promise of Genetic Science*, Minneapolis: University of Minnesota Press.

———. (2016) "Making Love and Relations Beyond Settler Sexualities," *Social Justice Institute*. www.youtube.com/watch?v=zfdo2ujRUv8: University of British Columbia.

Trosper, R.L. (2002) "Northwest Coast Indigenous Institutions That Supported Resilience and Sustainability." *Ecological Economics* 41: 329–344.

Tuck, E., and Yang, K.W. (2012). "Decolonization Is Not a Metaphor." *Decolonization: Indigeneity, Education & Society* 1, no. 1: 1–40.

Valencia-Weber, G. (2011) "Three Stories in One: The Story of Santa Clara Pueblo v. Martinez," in C. Goldberg, K.K. Washburn and P.P. Frickey (eds.), *Indian Law Stories*. Albuquerque: University of New Mexico School of Law, p. 451.

White, R. (1991) *The Middle Ground: Indians, Empires, and Republics in the Great Lakes Region, 1650–1815*, Cambridge: Cambridge University Press.

Whyte, K.P. (2014) "Indigenous Women, Climate Change Impacts and Collective Action." *Hypatia: A Journal of Feminist Philosophy* 29, no. 2: 599–616.

Woolman, J. and Deer, S. (2014). "Protecting Native Mothers and Their Children: A Feminist Lawyering Approach." *William Mitchell Law Review* 40, no. 3: 943–989.

13

THE HISTORY OF RACIAL THEORIES IN CHINA

Frank Dikötter

Human beings display endless ingenuity in devising ways of discriminating and abasing each other, whether this is done in the name of religion, culture, gender, class, or nation. Until recently, the notion of 'race' was one of the most effective barriers against equality, as human beings were classified into discrete clusters claimed to correspond to biological units, distributed hierarchically on a scale of evolution with winners at the top and losers at the bottom. Eye color, skin tone, cranial shape, or hair texture were seen as markers of profound biological differences between humans, justifying such diverse institutions as the transatlantic slave trade, apartheid, and the Holocaust.[1]

The idea that people could be classified on the basis of some real or imagined physical signifier took on global dimensions in the nineteenth century. The reason for this explosion of interest in racial theories seems simple enough: they were exported alongside guns and germs by Europeans as they conquered the rest of the world. But Europeans had also used religion to convert, exploit, or exterminate the heathens around them, although Christianity failed to reap much of a harvest, notably among Hindus and Muslims. Unlike religion, 'race' presented something new. It was part of a modern way of thinking and understanding the world. The term given to this new worldview was 'science,' and it invoked reason rather than faith. Science underpinned the astonishing innovations in transportation, communication, and manufacturing that were made in the nineteenth century. If science could produce machine guns and predict the movement of celestial objects, surely it was just as credible when it divided human beings into distinct biological groups?

Racial theories offered another advantage. Not only did they harness the authority of science, invoking seemingly objective facts grounded in nature, but they were also very versatile. Like the ever-evolving idiom of science, the language of race was rich, flexible, complex, and always changing. And like the guns used by colonisers, they could be turned against their carriers and made to serve very different purposes.

Racial theories first made an appearance in China at the end of the nineteenth century. The reason they were taken up was due, in part, to pre-existing cultural and social traditions. While there was no such thing as a notion of 'race' in ancient or imperial China, the very term for the color 'yellow' had many positive connotations. In Europe the idea of a 'yellow race' probably only appeared at the end of the seventeenth century as a reaction to Jesuit reports from China on the symbolic value of the color yellow.

The concept did not exist in the ancient world, and was not used by travelers of the Middle Ages such as Marco Polo, Pian del Carpini, Bento de Goes, or any of the Arab traders. In 1655, the first European mission to the Qing described local people as having a white complexion, 'equal to the Europeans,' except for some in the south who were 'slightly brown.' The first scientific work in which the notion of a 'yellow race' appeared was François Bernier's 'Etrennes adressées à Madame de la Sablière pour l'année 1688.'[2]

Yellow, on the other hand, was one of the five 'pure' colors in imperial China and symbolized the Center. It was the color of the emperor of the Middle Kingdom, ancestral home of the 'descendants of the Yellow Emperor' who were thought to have originated in the valley of the Yellow River. After the country was invaded by the Manchus, a frontier people who established the Qing in 1644, some scholars who remained loyal to the Ming gave a new twist to the symbolic significance of the color 'yellow.' One of the most virulent critics of Manchu rule was Wang Fuzhi (1619–1692). Like many other scholars who refused to serve the new dynasty, he viewed the invaders as morally inferior barbarians. Wang titled one of his more important works, published in 1656, the *Yellow Book*: the last chapter contrasted the imperial color yellow to 'mixed' colors and named the empire as the 'yellow center.'[3]

Equally important was a long-standing tradition of favoring fair skin, referred to as 'white' from ancient times. A light complexion was highly valued, and poetry often compared the fairness of female paragons to white jade. Men were no exception, and at court some nobles even used powder to whiten their faces. In contrast, the darkness of peasants who tilled the fields under the burning sun was viewed with disdain. The polarity between fair and dark, based on a feudal hierarchy which distinguished landlords from peasants, was projected onto outsiders as the empire discovered other parts of the world. By the Ming dynasty, a profuse vocabulary focused on the darker skin tones of people in Southeast Asia, South Asia, the Middle East and Africa. Europeans, on the other hand, were described as hairy creatures who were 'ash white' or reddish. As one nineteenth-century poem on the British and Indian troops fighting the first Opium War put it: 'The white ones are cold and dull as the ashes of frogs, the black ones are ugly and dirty as coal.'[4]

***

While the symbolic importance given to the color yellow and a negative view of dark skin may have been prevalent, the notion of 'race' did not appear until the end of the nineteenth century. A key moment was the country's devastating defeat in 1894–1895 against Japan, a country usually described as a mere vassal. The enemy's triumph was unexpected, even by those who had been aware of the empire's shortcomings, and led a number of scholar officials to question traditional modes of governance. For the first time, leading reformers like Yan Fu, Liang Qichao, and Kang Youwei turned away from Confucianism to seek enlightenment abroad, hoping to find the keys to wealth and power on the distant shores of Europe instead. They searched the writings of such foreign luminaries as Charles Darwin and Herbert Spencer for a unifying concept that could bind all the emperor's subjects together, hoping to forge a modern, powerful nation capable of resisting foreign encroachments. They discovered the notion of 'race' and used new evolutionary theories from England to present the world as a battlefield in which different breeds struggled for survival, as 'yellows' competed with 'whites' over inferior 'browns,' 'blacks,' and 'reds.' Their message of racial unity in a universe red in tooth and claw was enormously popular, mainly because it resonated so much with more traditional ideas about the lineage (*zu*).

The lineage was a social organization claiming common descent which came into being in its modern form under the Song (960–1279). A patrilineage was transmitted through the production of sons, and was generally confined to a cluster of villages where it owned land, schools, and an ancestral hall. Some of them dominated entire regions. Descent lines were recorded in genealogies (*zupu*), a task that might require the labour of many lineage members. The last edition of the genealogy of the Zeng in Hunan, which traced its descent from a prince of the Xia dynasty whose father had reigned from 2218 to 2168 BCE, involved 106 participants. Attempts to establish a blood link with a mythical ancestor were based on the need for social prestige. Genealogies also proved that the lineage was pure and that there had not been intermarriage with any of the peoples that had invaded and ruled the empire.[5]

Considerable friction could arise between lineages, and feuds prevailed throughout the Qing, although they were more common in the southeast, where the institution had grown more powerful than in the north. Armed battles could involve many thousands of combatants: a major conflict between the Hakka and Punti in 1856–1867 took a toll of 100,000 victims.[6]

The reformers portrayed 'race' as the extension of a massive, ancient lineage, tracing the origins of every inhabitant back to the Yellow Emperor, a mythical figure thought to have reigned from 2697 to 2597 BCE. In order to bolster their message of change in the face of imperialist aggression, the reformers invoked the threat of racial extinction (*miezhong*), basing their vision of doom on more popular anxieties about the disappearance of the lineage (*miezu*): 'They will enslave us and hinder the development of our spirit and body . . . The brown and black races constantly waver between life and death, why not the 400 million of yellows?'[7]

Hierarchy underpinned the reformers' view of a world divided into 'races,' as superior 'white' and 'yellow races' were opposed to the 'darker races,' doomed to extinction through evolutionary inadequacy. Their racial theories resonated with social distinctions specific to the empire, where 'common people' (*liangmin*) were legally separated from 'mean people' (*jianmin*) until the early eighteenth century. Tang Caichang (1867–1900) phrased it in evenly balanced clauses reminiscent of his classical education: 'Yellow and white are wise, red and black are stupid; yellow and white are rulers, red and black are slaves; yellow and white are united, red and black are scattered.'[8] Others wrote about 'noble races' (*guizhong*) and 'low races' (*jianzhong*), 'superior races' (*youzhong*) and 'inferior races' (*liezhong*), 'historical races' and 'ahistorical races' (*youlishi de zhongzu*).

The reformers used evolutionary theories very selectively, claiming that racial survival (*baozhong*) in a context of international competition was the inescapable consequence of profound evolutionary forces. Instead of appealing to Charles Darwin's emphasis on competition between individuals of the same species, they were inspired by Herbert Spencer's focus on group selection. For reformers like Yan Fu, Liang Qichao, and Kang Youwei, evolutionary forces were underpinned by the principle of racial grouping, as individuals of a race should unite in order to survive in the struggle for existence much as each cell contributed to the overall health of a living organism. They also ignored the neo-Darwinian explanation of evolution as a branching process, adopting instead a Neo-Lamarckian theory of unilinear evolution which viewed human development as a single line of ascent from the apes: the embryo developed in a purposeful way towards maturity in a process that could be guided by human intervention into the social and political environment. Neo-Lamarckism offered a flexible vision of evolution which closely suited the political agenda of the reformers, as human progress in the realm of politics was seen to be conducive to the racial improvement of the species.

The reformers were no revolutionaries, and they proposed a form of constitutional monarchy that included the Manchu emperor. Their understanding of the 'yellow race' (*huangzhong*) was broad enough to include all the people living within the imperial realm. But their political ascendancy came to an abrupt end in 1898, as the empress dowager rescinded all their decrees and executed several court officials sympathetic to their message of political reform.

Soon a number of more radical intellectuals started advocating the overthrow of the Qing dynasty. Not without resonance to the 1789 and 1848 political revolutions in Europe, the revolutionaries represented the ruling Manchus as an inferior 'race' which was responsible for the disastrous policies which had led to the decline of the country. In contrast, they viewed the majority of people in China as a homogeneous 'Han race.' Whereas the reformers had envisaged 'race' (*zhongzu*) as an extension of the lineage (*zu*), encompassing all people dwelling on the soil of the Yellow Emperor, the revolutionaries excluded the Mongols, Manchus, Tibetans, and other peoples from their definition, which was narrowed down to the Han, an ancient term that referred to a dynasty but was now given a new twist. To describe the Han, they used the term of *minzu*, combining the idea of a people (*min*) with the fiction of patrilineal descent (*zu*). The term first appeared in 1903 in an attempt to find a political rationale for the modern nation-state. *Minzu*, often translated as 'nation' or even 'nationality,' designated a lineage that shared a territory and an ancestor: it was both a racial and a corporate unit and is more accurately translated as *Volk*. This vision of blood and soil was eloquently illustrated by Zou Rong, one of the more influential revolutionaries. He proudly proclaimed that:

> When men love their race, solidarity will arise internally, and what is outside will be repelled. Hence, to begin with, lineages were united and other lineages repelled; next, lineages of villages were united and lineages of other villages repelled; next, tribes were united and other tribes were repelled; finally, the people of a country became united, and people of other countries were repelled. This is the general principle of the races of the world, and also a major reason why races engender history. I will demonstrate to my countrymen, to allow them to form their own impression, how our yellow race, the yellow race of which the Han race is part, is able to unite itself and repel intruders.[9]

The Manchus were overthrown in a revolution in 1911, as a millenarian empire gave way to a modern republic. Racial theories proliferated in the following decades, as nationalists portrayed the Chinese as a people with shared physical attributes and a line of blood which could be traced back to the most ancient period. As Sun Yatsen, the founder of the Nationalist Party, put it in his famous *Three Principles of the People*,

> The greatest force is common blood. The Chinese belong to the yellow race because they come from the blood stock of the yellow race. The blood of ancestors is transmitted by heredity down through the race, making blood kinship a powerful force.[10]

With the rise of a modern print culture, driven by many private publishing houses and by the general growth in literacy after the fall of the empire, similar ideas appeared in travel literature, scientific publications, and even school textbooks. The opening sentence of a chapter on 'human races' in a 1920 textbook for middle schools declared that

> among the world's races, there are strong and weak constitutions, there are black and white skins, there is hard and soft hair, there are superior and inferior cultures. A rapid overview shows that they are not of the same level.[11]

Even in primary schools, readings on racial politics became part of the curriculum:

> Mankind is divided into five races. The yellow and white races are relatively strong and intelligent. Because the other races are feeble and stupid, they are being exterminated by the white race. Only the yellow race competes with the white race. This is so-called evolution... Among the contemporary races that could be called superior, there are only the yellow and the white races. China is the yellow race.[12]

There were endless studies disseminating racial theories in the name of science. Chen Yucang (1889–1947), director of the Medical College of Tongji University and a secretary to the Legislative Yuan, boldly postulated that the degree of civilization was the only indicator of cranial weight: 'If we compare the cranial weights of different people, the civilised are somewhat heavier than the savages, and the Chinese brain is a bit heavier than the European brain.'[13] Liang Boqiang, in an oft-quoted study on the 'Chinese race' published in 1926, took the blood's 'index of agglutination' as an indicator of purity, while the absence of body hair came to symbolize a biological boundary of the 'Chinese race' for a popular writer like Lin Yutang (1895–1976), who even proclaimed that 'on good authority from medical doctors, and from references in writing, one knows that a perfectly bare mons veneris is not uncommon in Chinese women.'[14]

Tens of thousands of students used the openness of the republican era to pursue a higher education abroad. By 1930, Chinese students outnumbered any other foreign nationality at American universities, as knowledge in all areas was hotly pursued. Many became experts in their own fields, which ran the full gamut from avionics to zoology. Some of them wrote entire volumes on racial matters, in particular those working in medicine, genetics, geography, anthropology, and criminology. Li Chi published *The Formation of the Chinese People: An Anthropological Inquiry* in English with Harvard University Press in 1928, having gathered thousands of measurements of skulls and noses to determine that a group of Tungus were responsible for diluting the divine race of the Yellow Emperor through intermarriage. Zhang Junjun, who studied psychology at Columbia University but read voraciously on anthropology and eugenics in his spare time, authored two books suggesting that the ancestors of the Han race had type O blood flowing through their veins, a purity subsequently vitiated by racial admixture with barbarian tribes.[15]

Quite a few of these scholars, like many biologists everywhere at the time, interpreted lack of national strength as a sign of racial decline. They latched on to the burgeoning field of eugenics, which was widely popular in the academic community in Europe and the United States, hoping to improve their country's heredity through the strict control of human reproduction. One such was Pan Guangdan (1898–1967), a graduate in zoology from Dartmouth College who went on to read for a higher degree at Columbia University in 1922 and founded the Chinese Eugenics Institute together with the Chinese Committee for Racial Hygiene. Through his numerous publications, which often combined modern science with a more traditional focus on the genealogies of patrilineal families, he turned eugenics into a household word in China.[16]

Pan Guangdan, like other scholars at the time, was deeply conversant with the international eugenics movement, but he did not simply replicate what he had learned in the United States. Thus in August 1930 he reviewed *The American Negro*, a book edited by Donald Young, noting how some of the contributors to the volume were idealists who were unwilling to speak in terms of racial inequality. This was particularly true of 'many scholars of Jewish origin,' Pan noted, posing as an outside observer who benefited from a more objective perspective:

> But to be true to observable facts, in any given period of time sufficiently long for selection to take effect, races *as groups are* different, unequal, and there is no reason except one based upon sentiment why we cannot refer to them in terms of inferiority and superiority, when facts warrant us. It is to be suspected that the Jewish scholars, themselves belonging to a racial group which has long been unjustly discriminated against, have unwittingly developed among themselves a defensive mechanism which is influencing their judgments on racial questions. The reviewer recalls with regret that during his student days [in the United States] he had estranged some of his best Jewish friends for his candid views on the point of racial inequality.[17]

By the 1930s many educated people had come to identify themselves and others in terms of 'race,' even if they varied enormously in the meanings they attributed to real or imagined physical markers of difference. In fact, only a few isolated voices in republican China openly refuted the existence of a racial taxonomy in the human species. Zhang Junmai, for instance, wisely excluded 'common blood' from his definition of the nation. Qi Sihe, a noted historian, also criticized the use of racial categories of analysis by some of his colleagues and pointed out how 'race' was a declining notion in parts of Europe.[18] But in general, racial ideas were so versatile that they cut across most political positions.

Racial theories became taboo following the communist takeover of China in 1949. Anthropology departments were suspended by the end of 1949, and social sciences like anthropology and sociology were condemned as 'bourgeois' a few years later in 1952. Pan Guangdan was singled out for severe criticism, while Mendelian laws of inheritance and T. H. Morgan's chromosome theory were rejected for ideological reasons. As in the Soviet Union, the idea that humans were determined by their genetic makeup was seen to be politically incorrect, and supporters of the Russian biologist Trofimo Lysenko argued instead that acquired characteristics could be inherited while environmental influences could be manipulated so as to alter an organism's features.

But 'race' was too resilient a notion simply to be abolished by decree. And while the Chinese Communist Party appealed to 'class' as a unifying concept, it did not abandon the politically vital distinction between a 'majority' on the one hand and a range of 'minorities' on the other. The communists perpetuated the idea that linguistically and culturally diverse people in China actually belonged to a single, homogeneous group united by ties of blood called the 'Han.' As the political boundaries of the country claimed by the communists corresponded largely to those of the Qing empire, people in the strategically and economically vital border regions of Xinjiang and Tibet were portrayed as 'minorities' in their own homelands. The communists swiftly proceeded to classify 41 so-called minority nationalities (*shaoshu minzu*), a number which increased to 56 by the time of the 1982 census.[19]

Although the idea of equality between different *minzu* was promoted by the regime in order to combat 'Han chauvinism' (*Da Han minzuzhuyi*), the representation of the Han as an absolute majority endowed with superior political and cultural attributes and hence destined to be the vanguard of the revolution and the forefront of economic development dominated official discourse during the Maoist period. In a manner recalling the racial taxonomies used by the revolutionaries at the beginning of the twentieth century, 'minority nationalities' were represented as less evolved branches of people who needed the moral and political guidance of the Han to ascend the scales of civilization. The idea of the Han as a politically more advanced and better endowed *minzu* pervaded the early decades of the communist regime, when assimilationist policies were eagerly pursued. Immediately after 1949, hundreds of thousands of demobilized soldiers, petty thieves, beggars, vagrants, and prostitutes were sent to help develop and colonise the Muslim belt which ran through Gansu, Ningxia, Qinghai, and Xinjiang. Colonists were also sent to Tibet and other border regions dominated by people who were once in the majority, but were now referrred to as 'minorities'.

The emphasis on class struggle and doctrinaire insistence on ideology at the expense of economics was reversed after the death of Mao Zedong in 1976. After the ascent to power of Deng Xiaoping in 1979 and the gradual opening of the country, scientific research started to develop in a number of politically sensitive domains. One of the effects of the revival of physical anthropology and genetics was massive research on the 'minority nationalities.' Instead of portraying them as culturally or 'racially' distinct groups of people, a whole range of studies started claiming that they were organically linked to the majority of Han people. This was not an innovation, but harked back to the republican era, when the Nationalist Party, founded by Sun Yatsen, had already proposed a vision which emphasized both the organic unity of all the peoples living within the political boundaries of China and the inevitable fusion of non-Han groups into a broader Chinese nation dominated by the Han. Chiang Kaishek (1887–1975), the effective head of the country from 1927 to 1949 and leader of the Nationalist Party, clearly expressed this vision of the nation as a culturally diverse but racially unified entity in his important work titled *China's Destiny*, written during the fight against Japan in the Second World War:

> Our various clans actually belong to the same nation, as well as to the same racial stock. Therefore, there is an inner factor closely linking the historical destiny of common existence and common sorrow and joy of the whole Chinese nation. That there are five peoples designated in China is not due to differences in race or blood, but to religion and geographical environment. In short, the differentiation among China's five peoples is due to regional and religious factors, and not to race or blood. This fact must be thoroughly understood by all our fellow countrymen.[20]

Chiang Kaishek had referred to this line of descent as a 'Chinese nationality' (*Zhonghua minzu*). Although this approach remained marginal in the republican era, it became mainstream in the People's Republic after 1979. The notion of a 'Chinese nationality' became the basis for arguing that the political boundaries of the country were based on biological markers. Tibetans and Uighurs, for instance, were depicted as people who were merging biologically into a larger 'Chinese nationality' of which the Han formed the core.

Serological studies were carried out in the 1980s to highlight the biological proximity of all minority people to the Han.[21] Mainly initiated by Professor Zhao Tongmao, estimations of genetic distance based on gene frequency claimed that the racial differences between population groups living within China—including Tibetans, Mongols and Uighurs—were comparatively small. Serologists also observed that the 'Negroid race' and the 'Caucasian race' were more closely related to each other than to the 'Mongoloid race.' Zhao Tongmao put the Han at the very center of his chart, which branched out gradually to include other minority groups from China in a tree highlighting the genetic distance between 'yellows' on the one hand and 'whites' and 'blacks' on the other. His conclusion underlined that the Han were the main branch of the 'yellow race' in China to which all the minority groups could be traced: the political boundaries of the People's Republic, in other words, appeared to be founded on clear biological markers of genetic distance.[22]

In similar vein, skulls, hair, eyes, noses, ears, entire bodies, and even the penises of thousands of subjects were routinely measured, weighed, and assessed by anthropometrists in the 1980s and '90s in attempts to identify the 'special characteristics' (*tezheng*) of minority people. To take but one example, Zhang Zhenbiao, a senior anthropometrist writing in the prestigious *Acta Anthropologica Sinica*, reached the following conclusion after measuring 145 Tibetans:

> As demonstrated by the results of an investigation into the special characteristics of the heads and faces of contemporary Tibetans, their heads and faces are fundamentally similar to those of various other nationalities of our country, in particular to those of our country's north and northwest (including the Han and national minorities). It is beyond doubt that the Tibetans and the other nationalities of our country descend from a common origin and belong, from the point of view of physical characteristics, to the same East-Asian type of yellow race (*huangzhongren de Dongya leixing*).[23]

The political implications of such research for minorities was apparent in the government's promotion of China as the 'homeland of the modern yellow race,' of which even Outer Mongolia was described as an organic and integral part.[24]

To this day, within both scientific institutions and government circles, different peoples in China are represented as one relatively homogeneous 'Chinese nationality' (*Zhonghua minzu*) of which all minorities are organic parts. As W.J.F. Jenner puts it rather appropriately, the idea of a 'Chinese nationality' means, in effect, that 'all the nationalities are, beneath their apparent diversity, one.'[25]

Belief in the idea that humans have different origins was also revived in the 1980s, and served to reinforce this nationalist vision of racial unity. Prominent researchers represented Beijing Man at Zhoukoudian as the 'ancestor' of the 'Mongoloid race' (*Menggu renzhong*). A great number of hominid teeth, skull fragments, and fossil apes, discovered at different sites scattered over China since 1949, were used to support the view that the 'yellow race' (*huangzhong*) was in a direct line of descent from its hominid ancestor in China. Although palaeoanthropologists in China acknowledged that the fossil evidence pointed to Africa as the birthplace of all humans, highly regarded researchers like Jia Lanpo repeatedly emphasized that humanity's real place of origin should be located in East Asia. Wu Rukang, also one of the most eminent palaeoanthropologists in China, came very close to upholding a polygenesist thesis in mapping different geographical spaces for the 'yellow race' (China), the 'black race' (Africa) and the 'white race' (Europe): 'The fossils of homo sapiens discovered in China all prominently display the characteristics of the yellow race . . . pointing at the continuous nature between them, the yellow race and contemporary Chinese people.'[26]

Early hominids present in China since the early Middle Pleistocene (one million years ago) were believed to be the origin to which all the population groups in the People's Republic could be traced back. Physical anthropologists also invoked detailed craniological examinations to provide 'irrefutable evidence' about a continuity in development between early hominids and the 'modern Mongoloid race.'[27] Scientific research on fossil bones was carried out to represent the nation's racial past as characterized by the gradual emergence of a Han 'majority' into which different 'minorities' would have merged.[28] As one close observer has noted,

> In the West, scientists treat the Chinese fossil evidence as part of the broad picture of human evolution worldwide; in China, it is part of national history—an ancient and fragmentary part, it is true, but none the less one that is called upon to promote a unifying concept of unique origin and continuity within the Chinese nation.[29]

These theories have not changed substantially with new DNA evidence. Every new discovery in China, it seems, is jumped upon to question the 'Out of Africa' thesis. When an ancient skull was dug up in Henan in 2008, it was widely interpreted as evidence that most of the people living in China were descendants of a native lineage whose uninterrupted evolution could be traced back millions of years. As the *China Daily* put it, 'The discovery at Xuchang supports the theory that modern Chinese man originated in what is present-day Chinese territory rather than Africa.'[30]

These were not the isolated musings of a few excentric intellectuals. The *Acta Anthropologica Sinica*, China's flagship journal in human anthropology quoted above, was systematically investigated by a team of researchers. They discovered that between 1982 and 2001, all of the 779 articles directly related to the study of human variation used the notion of 'race' and none of them questioned its value. The authors of the survey contrasted their findings to those obtained in Poland and the United States, the two other countries they surveyed, and concluded that in China, 'race seems to be accepted as "natural" by all generations of anthropologists.'[31]

Racial theories have underpinned nationalism in China since 1895. Precisely because of the extreme diversity of religious practices, family structures, spoken languages and regional cultures of population groups that have been defined as 'Chinese,' the notion of race has become a very powerful and cohesive form of identity. While heavily dependent on the ever-changing language of science, the flexibility of racial theories are part of their appeal, as different groups, from the late Qing reformers, the anti-Manchu revolutionaries and members of the Nationalist Party to the Chinese Communist Party, have adapted them to very different political and social contexts.

But there is a constant. From the moment the Qing crumbled, the notion of race has been used to portray all parts of the imperial realm, from Taiwan to Xinjiang and Tibet, as organically constitutive of the modern nation-state. This has become particularly obvious since 1949, as the Chinese Communist Party has established the borders of the People's Republic along the territory reached by the Qing at the height of its expansion in the nineteenth century. Just as the Bolsheviks inherited a realm conquered by the tsars, so the communists claimed an empire won by the Manchus. Unlike the Bolsheviks, who set up a union of socialist republics, the leadership in Beijing was soon committed to turning the many peoples inside its borders into a single, homogeneous nationality, referred to as a *Zhonghua minzu*. Racial theories, in other words, are used to represent the political boundaries of the People's Republic as clear biological markers, encompassing an organically unified 'Chinese nationality.'

Notes

1 This article is based on Frank Dikötter, *The Discourse of Race in Modern China*, 2nd ed. (New York: Oxford University Press, 2015), to which readers interested in fuller arguments should turn.
2 The key work on this issue is Pierre Huard, "Depuis quand avons-nous la notion d'une race jaune?" *Institut Indochinois pour l'Etude de l'Homme* 4 (1942): 40–41; besides the pioneering article of Huard, one can also read Walter Demel, "Wie die Chinesen gelb wurden. Ein Beitrag zur Frühgeschichte der Rassentheorie," *Historische Zeitschrift* 255 (1992): 625–666; and Michael Keevak, *Becoming Yellow: A Short History of Racial Thinking* (Princeton: Princeton University Press, 2011).
3 Ian McMorran, "Wang Fu-chih and the Neo-Confucian Tradition," in *The Unfolding of Neo-Confucianism*, ed. William T. De Bary (New York: Columbia University Press, 1975), 438; Ernstjoachim Vierheller, *Nation und Elite im Denken von Wang Fu-chih (1619–1692)* (Hamburg: Gesellschaft für Natur- und Völkerkunde Ostasiens, 1968), 30.
4 Jin He, "Shuo gui" (About ghosts) in *Yapian zhanzheng wenxue ji* (*Collection of Literary Writings on the Opium War*), comp. A Ying (Beijing: Guji chubanshe, 1957), 44.
5 The following is mainly based on Hu Hsien Chin, *The Common Descent Group in China and Its Functions* (New York: Viking Fund Publications in Anthropology, 1948).
6 Harry J. Lamley, "Hsieh-tou: The pathology of violence in south-eastern China," *Ch'ing-shih Wen-t'i*, 3, no. 7 (1977): 1–39; see also Mark C. Elliott, *The Manchu Way: The Eight Banners and Ethnic Identity in Late Imperial China* (Stanford: Stanford University Press, 2001).
7 Yan Fu, *Yan Fu shiwen xuan* (*Selected Poems and Writings of Yan Fu*) (Beijing: Renmin wenxue chubanshe, 1959), 22.
8 Tang Caichang, *Juedianmingzhai neiyan* (*Essays on Political and Historical Matters*) (Taipei: Wenhai chubanshe, 1968), 468.
9 Tsou Jung, *The Revolutionary Army: A Chinese Nationalist Tract of 1903*, intro. and transl. by John Lust (Paris: Mouton, 1968), 106.
10 Sun Wen (Sun Yatsen), *Sanminzhuyi* (*The Three Principles*) (Shanghai: Shangwu yinshuguan, 1927), 4–5; this translation follows Frank W. Price, *San min chu i: The Three Principles of the People* (Shanghai: China Committee, Institute of Pacific Relations, 1927), 8–9.
11 Fu Yunsen, *Renwen dili* (*Human Geography*) (Shanghai: Shangwu yinshuguan, 1914), 9–15.
12 Léon Wieger, *Moralisme officiel des écoles, en 1920* (Hien-hien, 1921), 180, original Chinese text.
13 Chen Yucang, *Renti de yanjiu* (*Research on the Human Body*) (Shanghai: Zhengzhong shuju, 1937), 180.
14 Lin Yutang, *My Country and My People* (New York: John Ray, 1935), 26.

15 Li Chi, *The Formation of the Chinese People: An Anthropological Inquiry* (Cambridge, MA: Harvard University Press, 1928); Zhang Junjun, *Zhongguo minzu zhi gaizao* (*The Reform of the Chinese Race*) (Shanghai: Zhonghua shuju, 1935).
16 Dikötter, *The Discourse of Race in Modern China*, 117–119.
17 Pan Guangdan, review of Donald Young, ed., *The American Negro*, in *The China Critic*, Aug. 28, 1930. 838.
18 Dikötter, *The Discourse of Race in Modern China*, 101.
19 An essential book for understanding ethnic nationalism in China is Dru C. Gladney, *Muslim Chinese: Ethnic Nationalism in the People's Republic* (Cambridge, MA: Harvard University Press, 1991); on the project of "ethnic" classification one should read Thomas Mullaney, *Coming to Terms With the Nation: Ethnic Classification in Modern China* (Berkeley: University of California Press, 2010).
20 Chiang Kaishek, *China's Destiny* (New York: Roy, 1947), 39–40.
21 Material in the next four paragraphs comes from Frank Dikötter, "Reading the body: Genetic knowledge and social marginalisation in the PRC," *China Information* 13, no. 2–3 (1998): 1–13.
22 Zhao Tongmao, *Renlei xuexing yichuanxue* (*Genetics of Human Blood Groups*) (Beijing: Kexue chubanshe, 1987), 351–371; see also Yuan Yida and Du Ruofu, "Zhongguo shiqige minzu jian de yichuan juli de chubu yanjiu" ("Preliminary investigation of the genetic distance between seventeen ethnic groups in China"), *Yichuan xuebao* 10, no. 5 (1983): 398–405.
23 Zhang Zhenbiao, "Zangzu de tizhi tezheng" ("The physical characteristics of the Tibetan nationality"), *Renleixue xuebao* 4, no. 3 (1985): 250–257; the only reference to a European study in Zhang Zhenbiao's research was an article published in 1954 in the *Annals of Eugenics*.
24 W.J.F. Jenner, "Race and history in China," *New Left Review* 11 (2001): 74.
25 Ibid., 57.
26 Wu Rukang, *Guren leixue* (*Paleoanthropology*) (Beijing: Wenwu chubanshe, 1989), 205–206; see also Wu Rukang, *Renlei de qiyuan he fazhan* (*The Origin and Evolution of Ancient Man*) (Beijing: Kexue chubanshe, 1980); on Peking Man, one should also read Barry Sautman, "Myths of descent, racial nationalism and ethnic minorities in the People's Republic of China," in *The Construction of Racial Identities in China and Japan: Historical and Contemporary Perspectives*, ed. Frank Dikötter (London: Hurst; Honolulu: University of Hawaii Press, 1997), 75–95; Barry Sautman, "Peking Man and the politics of paleoanthropological nationalism in China," *Journal of Asian Studies* 60, no. 1 (2001): 95–124.
27 For instance, Yang Qun, "Kaoguxue yu renleixue" (Archaeology and anthropology) in *Renleixue yanjiu* (Studies in Anthropology), ed. Zhongguo renlei xuehui (Beijing: Zhongguo shehui kexue chubanshe, 1987), 288–302.
28 See, for instance, Han Kangxin and Pan Qifeng, "Gudai Zhongguo renzhong chengfen yanjiu" (Research into the racial composition of ancient China), *Kaogu xuebao* 2 (1984): n.p.
29 John Reader, *Missing Links: The Hunt for Earliest Man* (London: Penguin Books, 1990), 111.
30 "Stirring find in Xuchang," *China Daily*, Jan. 28, 2008.
31 Qian Wang, Goran Štrkalj and Li Sun, "On the concept of race in Chinese biological anthropology: Alive and well (Discussion)," *Current Anthropology* 44, no. 3 (2003): 403.

References

Chen Yucang. (1937) *Renti de yanjiu* (*Research on the Human Body*), Shanghai: Zhengzhong shuju.
Demel, Walter. (1992) "Wie die Chinesen gelb wurden: Ein Beitrag zur Frühgeschichte der Rassentheorie." *Historische Zeitschrift* 255: 625–666.
Dikötter, Frank. (1998) "Reading the Body: Genetic Knowledge and Social Marginalisation in the PRC." *China Information* 13, nos. 2–3: 1–13.
———. (2015) *The Discourse of Race in Modern China*, 2nd edition, New York: Oxford University Press.
Elliott, Mark C. (2001) *The Manchu Way: The Eight Banners and Ethnic Identity in Late Imperial China*, Stanford: Stanford University Press.
Fu Yan. (1959) *Yan Fu shiwen xuan* (*Selected Poems and Writings of Yan Fu*), Beijing: Renmin wenxue chubanshe.

Gladney, Dru C. (1991) *Muslim Chinese: Ethnic Nationalism in the People's Republic*, Cambridge, MA: Harvard University Press.

Han Kangxin and Pan Qifeng. (1984) "Gudai Zhongguo renzhong chengfen yanjiu" ("Research into the Racial Composition of Ancient China"). *Kaogu xuebao* 2: n.p.

Huard, Pierre. (1942) "Depuis quand avons-nous la notion d'une race jaune?" *Institut Indochinois pour l'Etude de l'Homme* 4: 40–41.

Hu Hsien Chin (1948) *The Common Descent Group in China and Its Functions*. New York: Viking Fund Publications in Anthropology.

Jenner, W.J.F. (2001) "Race and history in China," *New Left Review* 11: 74.

Jin He. (1957) "Shuo gui" ("About Ghosts"), in A. Ying (comp.), *Yapian zhanzheng wenxue ji (Collection of Literary Writings on the Opium War)*, Beijing: Guji chubanshe, p. 44.

Kaishek, Chiang. (1947) *China's Destiny*, New York: Roy.

Keevak, Michael. (2011) *Becoming Yellow: A Short History of Racial Thinking*, Princeton: Princeton University Press.

Lamley, Harry J. (1977) "Hsieh-tou: The Pathology of Violence in South-Eastern China." *Ch'ing-shih Went'i* 3, no. 2: 1–39.

Li Chi (1928) *The Formation of the Chinese People: An Anthropological Inquiry*, Cambridge: Harvard University Press.

Lin Yutang. (1935) *My Country and My People*, New York: John Ray.

McMorran, Ian. (1975) "Wang Fu-chih and the Neo-Confucian Tradition," in William T. De Bary (ed.), *The Unfolding of Neo-Confucianism*, New York: Columbia University Press.

Mullaney, Thomas. (2010) *Coming to Terms With the Nation: Ethnic Classification in Modern China*, Berkeley: University of California Press.

Pan Guangdan. (1930) "Review of *The American Negro*, edited by Donald Young." *China Critic* (August 28): 838.

Price, Frank W. (1927) *San min chu i: The Three Principles of the People*, Shanghai: China Committee, Institute of Pacific Relations.

Reader, John. (1990) *Missing Links: The Hunt for Earliest Man*, London: Penguin Books.

Sautman, Barry. (1997) "Myths of Descent, Racial Nationalism and Ethnic Minorities in the People's Republic of China," in Frank Dikötter (ed.), *The Construction of Racial Identities in China and Japan: Historical and Contemporary Perspectives*, London: Hurst, pp. 75–95.

———. (2001) "Peking Man and the Politics of Paleoanthropological Nationalism in China." *Journal of Asian Studies* 60, no. 1: 95–124.

"Stirring find in Xuchang." (2008) *China Daily* (January 28).

Sun Wen (Sun Yatsen). (1927) *Sanminzhuyi (The Three Principles)*, Shanghai: Shangwu yinshuguan.

Tang Caichang. (1968) *Juedianmingzhai neiyan (Essays on Political and Historical Matters)*, Taipei: Wenhai chubanshe.

Tsou Jung. (1968) *The Revolutionary Army: A Chinese Nationalist Tract of 1903*, introduced and trans. John Lust. Paris: Mouton, p. 106.

Vierheller, Ernstjoachim. (1968) *Nation und Elite im Denken von Wang Fu-chih (1619–1692)*, Hamburg: Gesellschaft für Natur- und Völkerkunde Ostasiens.

Wang, Qian, Goran Štrkalj, and Li Sun. (2003) "On the Concept of Race in Chinese Biological Anthropology: Alive and Well (Discussion)." *Current Anthropology* 44, no. 3: 403.

Wieger, Léon. *Moralisme offciel des écoles*, en 1920 . Hien-hien, 1921 (original Chinese text).

Wu Rukang. (1980) *Renlei de qiyuan he fazhan (The Origin and Evolution of Ancient Man)*, Beijing: Kexue chubanshe.

———. (1989) *Guren leixue (Paleoanthropology)*, Beijing: Wenwu chubanshe.

Yang Qun. (1987) "Kaoguxue yu renleixue" ("Archaeology and anthropology"), in Zhongguo Renlei Xuehui (ed.), *Renleixue yanjiu (Studies in Anthropology)*, Beijing: Zhongguo shehui kexue chubanshe, pp. 288–302.

Yuan Yida and Du Ruofu. (1983) "Zhongguo shiqige minzu jian de yichuan juli de chubu yanjiu" ("Preliminary Investigation of the Genetic Distance Between Seventeen Ethnic Groups in China"). *Yichuan xuebao* 10, no. 5: 398–405.

Yunsen, Fu. (1914) *Renwen dili (Human Geography)*, Shanghai: Shangwu yinshuguan.

Zhang Junjun. (1935) *Zhongguo minzu zhi gaizao (The Reform of the Chinese Race)*, Shanghai: Zhonghua shuju.

Zhao Tongmao. (1987) *Renlei xuexing yichuanxue (Genetics of Human Blood Groups)*, Beijing: Kexue chubanshe.

Zhang Zhenbio."Zangzu de tizhi tezheng" ("The Physical Characteristics of the Tibetan Nationality"). *Renleixue xuebao* 4, no. 3: 250–257.

14
RACISM IN INDIA[1]
Ania Loomba

Race, to adapt Stuart Hall's words about blackness, is "a narrative, a story, a history. Something constructed, told, spoken, not simply found."[2] Upon such narration depends its visibility, its centrality to the way we understand history, philosophy, and literature, and how we conceive our present political commitments. Although recent scholarship has investigated the multiple lineages and histories of racial difference, and the different philosophies in which racial thinking was embedded, the dominant narrative about it still conceives of it as a post-Enlightenment ideology forged on the twin anvils of colonialism and Atlantic slavery, and one that hinges on pseudo-biological notions of human differentiation, especially somatic color.[3] Many histories of racial differentiation that do not fit into this narrative are neglected. In South Asia, for instance, while ideologies of difference are not exactly neglected, there is a strenuous effort made to deny that they are racial. In my understanding, ideologies are racial in effect when somatic color or other physiognomic traits, religion, ritual status, or geographic origin are perceived to be inherited, innate, or indicate some essential truth about a group of people, *and* when these perceptions justify the treatment of this group as intellectually or morally inferior, its systematic oppression, and the policing of the boundaries between it and the more privileged members of society. This is the understanding that will guide my discussion of key philosophies that have shaped the racial landscape of India, with occasional references to other parts of South Asia.[4] As I do so, I will also trace what has been at stake in the effort to align them with, or to exclude them from, the established narrative about race.

***

On September 30, 2014, the *New York Times* carried a story with the heading "Beating of African Students by Mob in India Prompts Soul-Searching on Race."[5] It described a horrific incident in which three men from Gabon and Burkina Faso were practically lynched in a New Delhi metro station by men who shouted "Bharat Mata Ki Jai," or "Victory for Mother India." It was not clear what prompted this attack, but explanations included an allegation that they had misbehaved with women, and made "anti-India" comments. In January that year, another mob, led by a minister of the newly elected Delhi government, had dragged four young African women out of their beds at midnight, shouted racist slurs at them, held them captive, and forced them to urinate publically in order to undergo drug tests. The incident prompted widespread acknowledgment, rare in Indian media, that racism against Africans and other blacks is rampant in India. Since then many other such incidents have been publicized and discussed in India.[6]

Such antipathy should not come as a surprise in a country where dark skin is widely reviled. Diepiriye Kuku, an American student in India, wrote in an English-language newsmagazine:

> Racism in India is systematic and independent of the presence of foreigners of any hue. This climate permits and promotes this lawlessness and disdain for dark skin. Most Indian pop icons have light-damn-near-white skin. Several stars even promote skin-bleaching creams that promise to improve one's popularity and career success. Matrimonial ads boast of fair, v. fair and v. very fair skin alongside foreign visas and advanced university degrees. Moreover, each time I visit one of Delhi's clubhouses, I notice that I am the darkest person not wearing a work uniform. It's unfair and ugly.[7]

These hostile attitudes to black Africans are not new, even though Africans have lived in India for many centuries not just as slaves but also as artisans, military commanders, traders, and even rulers.[8] This complex history was reshaped during British rule in India. Even as the British characterized South Asians as inferior to Europeans, they suggested that the former were—intellectually and culturally—superior to blacks, who were, however, considered physically stronger.[9]

European racial hierarchies were reproduced at every level by South Asians, even by anti-colonial nationalists fighting British racism, as is evident from Mahatma Gandhi's opinions about "kaffirs" in South Africa, from whom he sought to distance himself even as he protested white discrimination against Indians:

> Ours is one continual struggle against a degradation sought to be inflicted upon us by the Europeans, who desire to degrade us to the level of the raw Kaffir whose occupation is hunting, and whose sole ambition is to collect a certain number of cattle to buy a wife with and, then, pass his life in indolence and nakedness.[10]

Efforts to build Afro-Asian solidarities in the postcolonial era were similarly complicated by negative attitudes to Africans. African students came in large numbers to study under new government of India schemes, but they found it hard to find social acceptance. Paternalism as well as racism marked the official relations between India and African countries.[11] Similar attitudes have also shaped the mentalities of Indians in the United States, at least from the early twentieth century onwards. According to the 2000 US Census, 25% of second-generation South Asian Americans identified themselves as white.[12]

Was color prejudice simply introduced by centuries of British colonial rule in India? Did Indians internalize and reproduce Victorian racial hierarchies, which entrenched a division between all whites and all people of color, but at the same time also posited distinctions and gradations between the latter? Before the British, the Portuguese and Dutch had brought European ideas of difference and color to the Indian subcontinent. But it is important to remember that such ideas were not imposed upon a blank slate, as it were, but interacted with pre-existing ideologies and hierarchies. The crucial question is this: "were Victorian notions of race accepted so eagerly because they resonated with earlier ideas of social difference, or did they instead represent a qualitatively new way of distinguishing groups of people?"[13] In this chapter, I will indicate some key points of resonance, as well as disjuncture, between colonial and pre-colonial ideologies that are necessary to understand contemporary ideas about race in South Asia.

Let me start by briefly invoking the seventeenth-century history of Portuguese Goa. Here the Europeans were struck by the divisions within Indians, and used the word "caste" to describe them. They used the word to describe social rank, religious groupings (for example, "caste of Moors" or "caste of Christians"), and also the hierarchies within Hindu society. In 1567, the Portuguese *Sacred Council of Goa* noted that

> In some parts of this Province (of Goa) the Gentoos [Hindus] divide themselves into distinct races or castes (*castas*) of greater or less dignity, holding the Christians as of lower degree, and keep these so superstitiously that no one of a higher caste can eat or drink with those of a lower.[14]

Note that "race" and "caste" are here used interchangeably, and also that upper-caste Hindus are described as regarding Christians as equivalent to their own lower castes.

The situation was to change dramatically over time. As the Portuguese entrenched their rule, their own hierarchies of difference reversed this situation. The inter-mixing between the Portuguese and Indians resulted in stratifications that mirrored the hierarchies in colonial America:

> Firstly, the European-born Portuguese, or *Reinol*. Secondly Portuguese born in India of pure European parentage, who were very few and far between. Thirdly, those born of a European father and a Eurasian mother, who were termed *castiço*. Fourthly, the half-breeds, or *Mestiços*. Fifth and last, the indigenous pure-bred Indians and those with hardly a drop of European blood in their veins.[15]

As in the Americas, in India too the Europeans drew a distinction between European settlers in the colonies and those who remained at home. But if in colonial Mexico or Peru, they saw European inter-breeding as a way of improving the racial identity of the local people, in Asia fears of the racial degeneration of Europeans were rampant. Here, for example, is the Dutch traveler John Huighen van Linschoten's description of Portuguese settlers in India in 1598:

> The Portugals in India are many of them married with the natural born women of the country, and the children proceeding of them are called mestiços, that is, half-countrymen. These mestiços are commonly of yellowish colour, notwithstanding there are many women among them that are fair and well formed. The children of the Portugals, both boys and girls, which are born in India, are called Castiços, and are in all things like unto the Portugals, only somewhat differing in colour, for they draw toward a yellow colour: the children of those Castiços are yellow, and altogether like the Mestiços, and the children of Mestiços are of colour and fashion like the natural born countrymen or Decanijns of the country, *so that the posterity of the Portugals, both men and women being in the third degree, do seem to be natural Indians, both in colour and fashion.*[16]

These fine color lines generated within Eurasians of different hues were to leave a lasting mark within Asia.

In Dutch Sri Lanka, similar caste-race groups emerged:

> 1. The Europeesch, those born in Europe. 2. The Casties, who were born on the island but whose parents were born in Europe, 3) the Mixties, who were of mixed European and Asian origin. And 4) the Psuties, who were descendants of the Casties. The distinction between the Casties and Psusties points to the notion that a prolonged stay in Asia on the part of Europeans inevitably led to degeneration.[17]

There, too, classification was shaped by clothing, occupation, caste, and ethnicity. These definitions were malleable, since both the Portuguese and the Dutch asked individuals to perform duties not ritually prescribed by their caste.[18] One fascinating example of their intervention is when the Dutch, seeking to increase the number of cinnamon peelers who belonged to the Salagama group, decreed that all children fathered by a Salagama man should take on his caste identity, no matter what the mother's caste. This reversed the existing convention that the children of a higher-caste man and a lower-caste woman would take on the mother's caste status.[19]

These histories remind us that European and South Asian ideologies of difference have collided and intermeshed for many hundred of years. If black Africans face hostility in India, if darker skinned people are looked down upon by Indians at home and elsewhere, it is not simply because Indians have internalized foreign, colonial ideologies, but also because these ideologies worked through, and reworked, pre-colonial and indigenous notions of identity and difference. Caste was the most important of these, but as I will show, caste ideologies cannot be separated from those that turn on religious identity, regional belonging, and somatic difference.

***

Caste has been described as India's "hidden apartheid," but as a matter of fact, the violence of the caste order is hardly concealed.[20] As I write this, there are reports of a village council decreeing that two young sisters, aged 23 and 25, be raped by all the men in the village. They are to be punished for a "crime" committed by their brother—he eloped with a woman of a higher caste.[21] The siblings are all Dalits or "Untouchables," among the more than 160 million outcastes who are situated outside the pale of caste society, stigmatized even more than the lowliest within it. It is impossible to summarize the complex and regionally variable hierarchies of caste, but basically they pivot around four large groups or "varnas"—Brahmins (priests and teachers), Kshatriyas (rulers and warriors), Vaishya (merchants), and sudras (workers and peasants). This bio-moral and occupational fourfold division was proposed by writers of classical law manuals who wished to promote order in a society they saw as disintergrating. The categories took hold in the popular imagination, so that thousands of existing endogamous groups or "jatis" sought to identify themselves, or were identified by rulers, along this notional scale.[22] While large sections of sudras are stigmatized, "outcastes" or Untouchables are even more so. Indeed, it is the difference of outcastes from the rest that is of fundamental importance to the material and ideological basis of caste. Gandhi called outcastes "Harijan" (Children of God); the paternalism of that name is contested by the term "Dalit" (broken or crushed people), which was adopted by anti-caste activists in the

1970s. This term includes those outcastes who converted to other religions, whereas the governmental nomenclature "Scheduled Castes" does not.[23]

Stories such as that of the two young sisters are routine. Inter-caste marriages or love affairs, especially those between lower-caste men and women of higher castes, regularly result in murders, kidnapping, and the public punishment of the individuals and their families. As with black women during slavery, Dalit women remain subject to constant sexual assault by upper caste men. Not unlike blacks during the days of Jim Crow, Dalits are subject to different forms of discrimination—they are denied access to places of worship, clean water, housing and land; their children are still kept out of schools or ill-treated within them; and they are forced into menial and degrading occupations, notably manual scavenging. Despite governmental policies of affirmative action, they remain largely excluded from the country's businesses, educational establishments, judicial services, and bureaucracy.[24] Caste segregation shapes India's rural landscape, as well as large parts of its urbanity.

The violent effects of this apartheid have been obscured by its very longevity and because it is woven into the fabric of everyday life. Martin Macwan writes:

> The systematic elimination of six million Jews by Nazis hit us hard on the face because it took place in such a short span of time. In the case of Dalits, though the "genocide" has been systemic, it has taken place at a slow pace. The current government statistics of murder, rape and assault that Dalits are subjected to paint a horrible picture if extended to a history of 3000 years. We have reason to believe that approximately 21,90,000 Dalits have been murdered, 32,85,000 raped and over 7,50,00,000 assaulted.[25]

If caste violence does not provoke the outrage the Holocaust or South African apartheid did, it is because of the widespread notion that it is a unique ideology, embedded in Hinduism's ritual order, and incomparable with any other idea of difference. But the caste order is patently a class order. The lowest castes and the Dalits constitute the bulk of the laboring populations (although of course some upper castes may be impoverished, and some lower castes well off). It is important to emphasize that endogamy is itself a means of conserving the connection between caste and class. But like race, caste is also more than class—economic advancement does not result in caste mobility, or inoculate anyone from caste discrimination. Indeed, as with racialized populations, it is precisely an attempt at upward mobility, both economic betterment and aspiration to education, or marriage with someone of a higher caste, that results in violence. In an early essay, Stuart Hall pointed out that "Race is, in short, the modality in which class is 'lived,' the medium through which class relations are experienced, the form in which it is appropriated and 'fought through.'"[26] This is exactly true of caste as well.

It was because he understood this material basis of caste that American sociologist Gerald D. Berreman suggested in 1960 that it was productive to compare caste with race in the southern United States:

> In both the United States and India, high castes maintain their superior position by exercising powerful sanctions, and they rationalize their status with elaborate philosophical, religious, psychological, or genetic explanations. The latter are not sufficient in themselves to maintain the systems, largely because they are incompletely accepted among those whose depressed position they are thought to justify.

In both places castes are economically interdependent. In both there are great differences in power and privilege among, as well as class differences within, castes and elaborate barriers to free social intercourse among them.[27]

Berreman's view challenged the supposition, enshrined in Eurocentric scholarship, that caste was a unique social hierarchy, one that was accepted by all rungs of Hindu society, and therefore could not be compared with race. Berreman was harshly dismissed by Chicago sociologist Oliver Cromwell Cox, whose book *Caste, Class, and Race* argued for the dissimilarity of the two concepts, because he felt that thinking about race as caste obscured the deep connections between American racial hierarchies and capitalism. But Cox's contrast between these concepts depended upon ignoring the material and economic aspects of *caste*, and thus echoing the Eurocentric view of it as unique and incomparable to any other kind of hierarchical society.

It is the absence of any tendencies toward radical social change in the caste system which is of consequence. There has been no progressive social movement for betterment among outcaste castes in Brahmanic India. . . . The caste system is not a simple societal trait which may be universalized by "cross-cultural comparison." Rather, it constitutes the social and institutional structure of a distinct pattern of culture. To identify it with race relations in the South seems to be no less an operation than to identify the social structures of capitalism and Hinduism.[28]

This conclusion is remarkable on many counts: not only does it ignore the entire volatile history of anti-caste movements of the twentieth century, but in suggesting that race is an outcome of capitalism and caste of Hinduism, it places caste firmly outside any mode of production. In contrast to Cox, Berreman's pioneering scholarship highlighted that both systems of discrimination are anchored in economic oppression, but it also suggested that both exceed simple economic determinism. In this respect he was outlining the logic of caste as it had been articulated by anti-caste activists such as Jyotirao Phule and B. R. Ambedkar, who I will discuss at greater length shortly. Forcing one group of people to be landless, work for others, live apart, be reviled and raped, and face constant collective violence, makes India undeniably a slave society as much as the United States. And indeed, the comparison between caste and race, and its intersections with class, is most valid when it comes to the Dalit/non-Dalit divide, which is of a different order than the differences between other castes. The difference between Dalit and non-Dalit is the most policed, the most rigidly enforced divide, and the most marked forms of racial distinction are drawn at that line.[29]

Dominant Indian scholarship also tended to regard caste as "unique," and until recently, there was, as Chris Fuller notes, "an inclination towards Indianist intellectual parochialism."[30] Such parochialism was on full display when Dalit activists wanted to have caste discrimination discussed at the 2001 United Nations Conference Against Racism in Durban. They found that it was still hard to dislodge theories of caste exceptionalism. In their efforts to deny the validity and implications of the Dalit stance, the government of India as well as some of the country's most pre-eminent sociologists argued that caste and race are very different concepts. Resorting to the colonial and pseudoscientific definition of race as a concept based on the idea of biological difference, they argued that caste was, on the other hand, based on a socially ordained hierarchy.[31] Indeed, one such sociologist protested that to compare caste to race would be to view India through Western and Eurocentric eyes, and thus to deny its irreducible uniqueness. But Dalit activists were not arguing for the *identity* of the two concepts but for the *comparability of their effects*. They were arguing that casteism is a form of racism, fully as virulent in its effects, and equally condemnable. Earlier anti-caste activists had made the same point, although they were divided on the issue of the congruence of race and caste. Writing when the pseudo-scientific understanding of race was still prevalent, they wanted to deny that caste has any biological basis, but they could not argue the same for race. As far back as 1873, Jotirao Phule compared the "thraldom" of caste to the experience of slavery in the United States.[32] Others coming after him tried to connect with black activists and thinkers, and in 1973, the militant Dalit Panther group explicitly claimed an affinity with the Black Panthers.[33]

As I have already indicated, the history of European governance in South Asia makes it hard to think of caste as an entirely isolated ideology untouched by Western attitudes. Ironically, it was British colonialists who firmly defined caste as the essential feature of Hinduism, and therefore of Indian society, even as they tried to bring it into alignment with theories of race as they were evolving in Europe. The historian Nicholas Dirks argued that they systemized Indian ideologies of caste and tried to use these as the basis for understanding and controlling the heterogeneous population of the region. In contrast with the eighteenth century and early nineteenth century, where very little was written about caste, in the late nineteenth century caste became "the locus of all important information about Indian society" as well as "the basis for all governmental interventions." In particular, the 1901 Census of India played a crucial role "in installing caste as the fundamental unit of India's social structure."[34] Sir Herbert Risley, the Census Commissioner of India, is a key figure in this history. His sprawling text, *The People of India*, used anthropometry to align caste with European racial categories and hierarchies. Risley claimed that his research—involving cranial measurement and other latest "techniques" of race assessment—proved that caste divisions corresponded to the racial hierarchies of European science. The upper castes were closer to Europeans than were the lower so that "community of race, and not, as has frequently been argued, community of function, is the real determining principle, the true *causa causans*, of the caste system."[35]

Risley's ideas dovetailed with the theory of an Aryan conquest of India as propounded by the German orientalist Max Müller. According to this theory, the Aryans came to India via Central Asia, and over time, became the upper castes, conquering indigenous people who were forced to toil for them, and who came to constitute the bulk of the lower castes. Included in the latter category were the darker-skinned inhabitants of South India, or Dravidians. Linguistic discoveries of the time suggesting that North Indian languages were related to an Indo-Aryan group, and those of the South to a different "Dravidian" group appeared to bolster such a theory of Aryan conquest. The "Aryan myth" as it is now widely termed, aligned caste, region, and indigeneity with European notions of race. The Aryan myth was enthusiastically supported by European intellectuals and Orientalists, as well as by the Indian upper castes.[36] It was both questioned and appropriated by anti-caste movements and thinkers. For example, anti-Brahmin movements in South India deduced from the Aryan myth that no Brahmin could be a true Dravidian. Thus Dravidian identity and dignity could only be safeguarded by expelling Brahmins. The anti-caste philosopher and activist E. V. Ramasamy, popular as Periyar, who started the Self-Respect Movement, used this strategy, but he also questioned the equation of Dravidians with the lower castes and Aryans with the higher castes: "I am not a believer in the race theory as propounded by the late Nazi leader of Germany. None can divide the South Indian people into two races by means of any blood test. It is not only suicidal but most reactionary."[37] In his view, there had indeed been a historic clash between Aryans and Dravidians, but the division between these two groups of peoples did not correspond to caste identities as the Aryan myth suggested. In other words, he turned the self-identification of Tamil Brahmins as Aryans against them, while also ridiculing the theory they held to.

Previously, in the nineteenth century, Jotirao Phule had compared the Aryan conquest to the colonization of the New World:

> The cruelties which the European settlers practiced on the American Indians on their first settlement in the new world had certainly their parallel in India in the advent of the Aryans and their subjugation of the aborigines [that is, Dravidians] ... This, in short, is the history of Brahman domination in India. ... In order, however, to keep a better hold on the people they devised that weird system of mythology, the ordination of caste.[38]

Later, B. R. Ambedkar, the most important modern leader of Dalits, was to question the idea that the Aryans were a race:

> to hold that distinctions of caste are really distinctions of race ... is a gross perversion of facts. ... The caste system does not demarcate racial division. The caste system is the social division of people of the same race.[39]

Ambedkar's refusal to think about caste as race marks his opposition to theories that suggested there were real genetic differences between the castes, and his acceptance of the dominant theories of race at the time. At the same time, as I will discuss later, Ambedkar's work makes it possible for us to see, once we have discarded such a pseudobiological view of race, the parallels between racism and casteism.

***

Such appropriations and refutations notwithstanding, the Aryan myth became part of South Asia's racial landscape. It informed, for example, the 1923 application of Bhagat Singh Thind for US citizenship on the grounds that he was "a high caste Hindu, of full Indian blood," and thus should be considered on par with white immigrants who at the time were the only immigrants eligible for naturalization. The Aryan myth also informed the judgment that rejected Thind's application; the judge concluded that despite the strictures of caste, there had been too much "intermixture of the 'Aryan' invader with the dark-skinned Dravidian" in India. Therefore Thind couldn't be pure Aryan, and there was distinct racial difference between someone like him and the "great body of our people."[40] The Thind case reveals the racial assumptions of both the US state and many Indian immigrants to the United States, a majority of whom are upper caste. Till today, they understand themselves to be racially superior to African Americans, and caste ideologies are a crucial component of this self-perception.[41]

In India, even left-wing intellectuals and activists bought into the idea that "Aryans ... possessed a superior civilization and culture" and compared the lower castes and other "backward races" in India with "Negroes."[42] In 2001, precisely at the time when Dalit groups were lobbying to take their case to Durban, the Aryan myth was upheld by a study published in the journal *Genome Research* which argued that "the upper castes [in India] have a higher affinity to Europeans than to Asians, and the upper castes are significantly more similar to Europeans than are the lower castes."[43] Even though such conclusions have been rebutted not just by historians but also by geneticists, they continue to be part of the "common sense" of South Asian societies.[44] Today, the Aryan myth underlies the prejudice on the part of North Indians who are generally fairer towards those of the South, who are darker.[45]

But there is equal, if not greater prejudice, accompanied by racist practices, on the part of *both* North Indians and South Indians towards people from the seven states that lie in the North-East of India, a region which borders China, and whose people are understood as "Mongoloid" and hence racially different. Following India's war with China in 1962, thousands of Chinese-Indians were incarcerated in internment camps, and held for years without trial. Today, people from the North-East are routinely asked whether they are from China. In recent years, students from this region have suffered discrimination and violence in both the North and the South of the country. Here it is not dark skin but particular facial and bodily features, as well as cultural habits, that are targeted. Typecast as "chinkies," eaters of strange foods, sexually promiscuous, and Westernized, North-Easterners face harassment in public places, discrimination in their workplace, and indifference or hostility from the police.[46]

Even more vulnerable are India's Adivasis or First People, a large and diverse population that makes up around 8% of India's population. Largely forest or hill dwellers, Adivasis have, since colonial times, faced encroachment of their mineral- and produce-rich lands as well as violence and prejudice from both the state and mainstream India. Although not regarded as ritually impure by caste Hindus, they are nevertheless viewed as primitive and devoid of culture. Colonial anthropology and law advanced the idea that Adivasis were criminals—the Criminal Tribes Act of 1871 had ruled that all the people belonging to about 200 tribes (largely nomadic, pastoralist, hill and forest dwelling, and Adivasi) were criminals by profession. But since the British understood that occupation in India was linked to caste, and since they increasingly viewed caste as race, colonial administrators suggested that criminality was part of the very nature of particular groups of people: as one administrator explained:

> When we speak of professional criminals, we ... (mean) a tribe whose ancestors were criminals from time immemorial, who are themselves destined by the usage of caste to commit crime, and whose descendants will be offenders against the law, until the whole tribe is exterminated.[47]

Colonial law thus suggested that particular kinds of labor and ways of living indicated not just social but quasi-biological differences between groups of people. These differences marked and defined the mental and moral make-up of people, more than their bodies. These mentalities, moreover, would be transmitted through generations, and were unchangeable. Criminality resulted from forms of labor decreed by caste; in other words, occupation shaped an internal and unchanging nature. A criminal gene had been located without the use of genetic vocabularies. Colonial ideologies became widespread common sense, but the point I am making is also that these ideologies appropriated and transformed existing categories of difference, notably those of caste. This was the case even though color and other somatic differences were unevenly or even not attached to these categories. Certainly not all lower castes or tribal peoples are darker skinned, and today, scholars who want to differentiate caste from race always point to this fact. However, fairness is understood to be an attribute of the high-born, and darkness—both literal and metaphoric—that of the low.

In contemporary India, the racist stereotypes of Adivasis as criminally inclined and violent, or else childlike and primitive, continue to be evoked to justify violence against them. Today, they are the among the most marginalized people, but they have also organized to become the most militant. Drawing upon a long history of challenging the colonial state, they are the backbone of an armed resistance to the Indian State which seeks to facilitate the entry of Indian and foreign big businesses into the forests and hills of the Adivasi homelands. This is a violent process—huge numbers of tribal people are displaced as Indian and foreign companies seek to build large dams, or extract minerals in massive quantities from indigenous lands. The resistance movement, now led by groups who call themselves Maoist, faces the military might of the Indian state, which has labeled this movement as the greatest internal security threat in the country.[48]

***

I have been delineating the intricate braiding of region, caste, and indigeneity that shapes racial philosophies in India. Such layering is further complicated by the question of religious difference. Most people today, in India and abroad, tend to understand caste as an essential and unique feature of Hinduism, and Hinduism alone. But caste differentiation also structures Muslim, Christian, and Sikh communities in South Asia. Each of these communities is divided by caste, so that those who converted from Hinduism in order to escape the stigma of caste find themselves still trapped in its grip. Thus, many upper-caste Christians, especially in South India, still observe rituals of purity and pollution and caste rules of marriage vis-à-vis lower-caste Christians.[49] In North India, and in Pakistan, Dalit Christians are condemned to occupations such as scavenging. That these attachments to "tradition" have very real material benefits for the upper castes is dramatically illustrated by the fact that after the Partition of British India in 1947, the newly formed state of Pakistan, ostensibly formed as an Islamic Republic and haven for Muslims, refused to allow Dalits, including those who identified as Hindus and Christians, to migrate to India. To do so would be to lose a huge population of menial workers, condemned to occupations reviled by others.[50] All over South Asia, Muslims also remain divided by caste hierarchies that have a huge overlap with class stratification. According to a report submitted by various non-governmental organizations (NGOs) to the UN Committee on the Elimination of Racial Discrimination (CERD) in 2009, "Pakistan is one of the few countries of the world where slavery still exists in the form of bonded labour." Most bonded workers in Pakistan come from Dalit and lower-caste Muslim and Christian families.[51]

It is widely supposed that caste practices continue to structure Muslim or Christian communities because converts to these religions from Hinduism carry their ideologies with them. Although this cannot be denied, caste groups emerged not only from Hindu society, but more messily out of diverse occupational and power groups across regional and religious affiliations. Extending and complicating Nicholas Dirks's argument that it was British rule that calcified caste, a recent book by historian Sumit Guha argues that not just the British, but Hindu, Muslim, Buddhist, Dutch, and Portuguese rulers all endorsed or even created particular groupings and castes for administrative and particularly taxation purposes.[52] The historically variable and shifting groupings included, at one time, Portuguese Christians as a caste, as well as Parsis, who came to India from Iran, as another. If caste was shaped by these diverse sets of rulers and their interventions into a wide range of subjects, then it cannot be seen as emerging neatly from Hindu religious texts and practices.

To emphasize only the ritual implications of the caste order is to erase its political, economic, and social functions, and also to occlude the violence that accompanies the enforcement of this order. Colonial and Eurocentric scholarship achieved precisely such erasure, and the pinnacle of such scholarship was Louis Dumont's influential book *Homo Hierarchicus*. Dumont identified ancient religious Hindu texts as the basis of caste, and argued that despite the bewildering variation in caste practices, there was a common underlying core to them. This was a belief in hierarchy, to which *all* participants, including those at the bottom, subscribed. The Indian was "homo hierarchicus," to be contrasted with his Western antithesis, "homo aequalis." *Homo Hierarchicus* did not regard the caste order as exploitative, because according to it, Indians did not view caste as an economic order at all: "an economic phenomenon presupposes an individual subject; here on the contrary everything is directed to the whole, to the 'village community,' if one likes, but then as part and parcel of a necessary order."[53] Couched though it is in a modern, and very particular, sociological vocabulary, Dumont's thesis harks back to a long tradition of racial philosophy in Europe which divided human beings into people who were by nature slaves, and others who were naturally liberty-loving.[54]

What Dumont's thesis denies, and anti-caste thinkers were at pains to show, was that caste ensures systematic exploitation of a group of people by deeming them inferior through birth. That is why it is a racial ideology. In 1936, B.R. Ambedkar offered a brilliant exposition of the intermeshing of the ritual, social, political, and economic elements of the system. Ambedkar describes how in his part of the country,

> the Untouchable was required to carry, strung from his waist, a broom to sweep away from behind himself the dust he trod on, lest a Hindu walking on the same dust should be polluted. In Poona, the Untouchable was required to carry an earthen pot hung around his neck wherever he went—for holding his spit, less his spit falling on the earth should pollute a Hindu who might unknowingly happen to tread on it.[55]

Ambedkar pointed out that the ritualistic aspect of caste only rendered its economic work more pernicious, and more permanent; as he famously put it, "the caste system is not merely a division of labour. *It is also a division of labourers.*"[56] Caste hierarchies enable not only cheap and dispensable labor but forced labor. Caste ideology is what sanctions particularly oppressive forms of labor, perpetuates them, and indeed, disguises its everyday violence. Historically, as some recent revisionary scholarship has argued, most Dalits have been unfree laborers, not simply actors in a ritual drama. As Nathaniel Roberts succinctly puts it:

> Quintessential outsiders, Dalits were paradoxically indispensable to the very existence, symbolic and material, of caste society: Compelled to remove polluting substances, their labor guaranteed that others remained pure; hereditarily tied to producing for others, they underwrote other castes' material privilege.

Were "untouchables" consigned to a life of hard agricultural labor on account of their impurity, or was being coded impure and assigned polluting tasks simply part of what it meant to be under the total domination of others?[57]

Rupa Viswanath has demonstrated that the colonial state, while pushing some kinds of caste divisions as categories of governance, sought to deny Dalit difference precisely because it brought to the fore the existence of slavery, which they were not supposed to officially condone. Christian missionaries too defined caste as primarily a religious matter. When caste is understood as a matter of ritual precedence, the most important erasure is that of the tight link between slavery and Dalitness.[58]

Like the history of Atlantic slavery, the history of caste is a story of labor, land, and property, through which other social and religious ideologies were refracted and shaped. Like that history, caste entrenches the exploitation, by a minority, of a large part of the populace. As with slavery, however, caste violence also exceeds a simply economic logic, so much so that it appears irrational, excessive, and "backward."

***

The uneven attachments of caste to all religious groups in South Asia notwithstanding, the differences *between* religious groups are also central to racial ideologies in South Asia. Recall that British colonial scholarship and administrative practices had also folded caste into a Hindu and pan-Indian order. Dumont's theory of caste too identified India with Hinduism. The equation of Hinduism with India lies at the heart of right-wing Hindu ideologies, but it was also enabled by a supposedly liberal Hindu like Gandhi, who despite his ostensibly multifaith vocabulary, articulated his vision of a free India in terms of a return to "Ram Rajya" or the idyllic rule of the Hindu God Rama, which is celebrated by religious texts for its perfectly functioning caste system. Ambedkar exposed Gandhi's devotion to the caste system and to a Hindu vision of India, quoting him as saying that

> The seeds of Swaraj (self-rule) are to be found in the caste system. Different castes are like different sections of the military division. Each division is working for the good of the whole. . . . To destroy the caste system and adopt the Western European social system means that Hindus must give up on the principle of hereditary occupation which is the soul of the caste system.[59]

Gandhi preached against beef-eating, indulged in by lower castes, Muslims and Christians in India, and today the fulcrum of a violent campaign against them by the Hindu Right. As Nathaniel Roberts has elaborated, although Gandhi spoke of a multifaith nation, his rhetoric and his practice identified the "interests of his favored community, the Hindus, with that of the nation as a whole."[60] Gandhi was central to a historical shift whereby Dalits, not recognized as Hindus by caste Hindus until the early twentieth century, began to be—strenuously and even forcibly—included within the fold. Gandhi worked to ensure that Ambedkar's demand for a separate electorate for Dalits in independent India came to naught. The legal inclusion of Dalits as Hindus as did not mean that their *status* changed within Hindusim, but it did mean that Hindus became a majority in India. In this way, the histories of caste difference and those of religious difference are deeply interconnected.[61]

The equation of India with Hindus is a central tenet of faith for the Hindu Right. In their view, Muslims, India's largest minority group today, are foreigners who belong to

Pakistan, or to some other Muslim homeland. The idea that Muslims are a race apart from all Hindus was honed during the widespread carnage that accompanied the 1947 Partition of India, and is articulated with ever-greater stridency and violence by the Hindu Right. The overlap between their views of Muslims with European Islamophobia is striking: according to both, Muslims are inherently violent, and are culturally so different that they can never assimilate into Hindu India. In recent years, with the aggressive expansion of Hindu fundamentalism, this idea has spread wider and deeper into the Indian mainstream, and has been manifested in recent pogroms against them. It was evident during the large-scale attack upon Muslims in 2002 in the Western state of Gujarat.[62] While particularly horrific, this was not an isolated incident, but one outcome of the systematic growth of a neo-fascist Hinduism since the 1947 Partition of the country. The perpetrators proclaimed that such "punishments" were necessary to teach Muslims their place; prominent leaders of the Hindu Right asserted that this "successful experiment" would be repeated elsewhere in the country.[63] It was also consequential for India as a whole; Narendra Modi, who in his role as chief minister of Gujarat presided over the pogrom in which officers of the state were implicated, was later elected as prime minister of India.[64]

***

I have suggested that the histories of caste and religious difference are interconnected, and also that Dalits as well as Muslims are viewed in racialized terms. Dilip Menon observes, however, that casteism and communalism (a word that is used in India to indicate conflict between religious communities) are treated quite differently. Hindu majoritarian violence against Muslims has been taken far more seriously by Indian intellectuals than has caste violence, he argues, and "in a curious way, caste violence becomes the object of *reportage* and communal violence the object of *theorizing*."[65] Right-wing Hindu organizations have been able to enlist Dalits and lower-caste Hindus against Muslims by inviting them to be part of "a Hinduism open to questioning and change, while at the same time projecting the menace of a resurgent and competitive Islam" (14). Recent scholarship offers more detailed insights into the wooing of lower-castes, Dalits, and tribal populations by the Hindu Right, which works not only by invoking the specter of Islam but also by providing "social services" such as education and health care to these populations, especially where the Indian state has failed to do so.[66] But at the same time, Hindu right-wing ideologies also position these two groups in similar ways—both Muslim and Dalit men are seen as potential violators of the chastity of Hindu/upper-caste women and both are considered inherently violent. Recent reports confirm that Dalits and Muslims both find it difficult to rent houses from caste Hindus. Most importantly, anti-Muslim and anti-Dalit violence are often carried out by the same organizations. Very recently, there are signs that Muslims and Dalits may come together to fight right-wing Hindu nationalism, which is a very significant development that could alter the political landscape of India.

In an essay written some years ago, Etienne Balibar suggested that modern "neo-racism" (or "racism without race," which "does not have the pseudo-biological concept of race as its main driving force") illustrates that today "culture can also function like a nature," becoming an uncrossable barrier between "us" and "them." It is significant that Balibar compared new forms of racism, directed at largely Muslim immigrants in Europe, to the anti-Semitism of Reconquista Spain. Scholars of the early modern period in Europe, including myself, have made the point that these "new" forms of racism drew upon long and continuing histories.[67] In other words, it is not the case that religious discrimination is the "latest" form of racism; in fact, it was always central to European and trans-Atlantic ideologies of race. Scholars have drawn attention to the ways in which Muslim and Jewish identities were pathologized in Iberia, even as, at the same time, Europeans simultaneously marshaled their observations of other peoples in Asia and Africa to construct new ideologies of difference.[68] But to call Islamophobia and anti-Semitism "racisms *without race*" is to leave intact a theory of race which depends upon its pseudo-biological definition, and ultimately, therefore, to reassert a boundary between those theories of difference which marshal "nature" and those which invoke "culture." In practice, both nature and culture can be and have been invoked to justify racist categories of identity and the oppressive practices that such categories seek to legitimize; which is the case, as I have argued here, with racist thought in South Asia.[69]

In a powerful lecture on incarceration in the United States as the latest avatar of the institutions of racial apartheid, Michelle Alexander repeatedly referred to the formation of a "caste hierarchy" or a "racist casteism," by which she meant a system which defines people by birth, identifies them by color, and finds ingenious ways of renewing itself.[70] Alexander is hardly the first to use the word "caste" in the context of race in the United States—not just scholars and activists, including W.E.B. Du Bois, but many literary writers had done so.[71] An African American woman, Julia Collins, wrote a novel called *The Curse of Caste, or the Slave-Bride* which was serialized in 1865. In 1903 N.J.W. Le Cato also published a novel by the same name; both books highlight the slippery nature of racial identity. But Alexander's use of the word caste has a very particular purpose because, as she pointed out, she is speaking in, and to, a society which likes to call itself color-blind. The word "caste" underlines precisely the ways in which the system of discrimination she addresses is based on birth, and segregates people into particular professions and particular neighborhoods, and, most importantly, suggests that they inhabit a particular, intractable culture. Alexander's pointed usage of "caste," the flip side of the coin to Dalit activists' use of "race," reminds us that by forging conceptual connections between the different racisms across the globe, we are often able to more precisely pinpoint—and resist—those we encounter at home.

Notes

1. Rupa Viswanath's careful reading and astute comments on this essay have been invaluable. Nathaniel Roberts has long helped me think about caste. I also thank Auritro Majumdar and Suvir Kaul for their engagements with this essay.
2. Hall, "Minimal Selves," 45.
3. Jonathan Burton and I have traced how this bias has resulted in a neglect of early modern racial histories, as well as in an outmoded theorization of race as a catgeory. See the introduction to our *Race in Early Modern England: A Documentary Companion*, 1–36.
4. "South Asia" is a construct that emerged in the US academy during the Cold War. It supposedly encompasses the region in and around the Indian subcontinent, but demographic and cultural variations within it are enormous, making generalizations unsustainable.
5. Mackey, "Beating of African Students by Mob."
6. See, for example, Bhuyan, "Black's Not a Darker Brown."
7. Kuku, "India is Racist and Happy About It."
8. See, for example, Diouf, "Africans in India" and "South Asia."

9 Here is what Sir Harry Johnson, the first commissioner of British Central Africa visualized in 1894:

> On the whole, I think the admixture of yellow that the Negro requires should come from India, and that eastern Africa and British central Africa should become the America of the Hindu. The mixture of the two races would give the Indian the physical development which he lacks, and he in turn would transmit to his half-Negro offspring the industry, ambition, and aspiration towards civilized life which the Negro so markedly lacks. (Quoted by Cedric Robinson, *Black Marxism*, 131)

10 *The Collected Works of Mahatma Gandhi*, Vol. I, 409–410.
11 See, for example, Gupta, "A Note on Indian Attitudes to Africa," 170–178, and Burton, *Brown Over Black: Race and the Politics of Postcolonial Citation*.
12 Morning, "The Racial Self-Identification of South Asians in the United States," 76. For a superb analysis of South Asian racial politics in the United States, see Prashad, *The Karma of Brown Folk*, ix.
13 Rogers, "Racial Identities and Politics in Early Modern Sri Lanka."
14 Decree 2nd of the *Sacred Council of Goa*, 1567. Camoes also uses it in this sense.
15 Boxer, *Race Relations in the Portuguese Colonial Empire, 1415–1825*, 62.
16 Burnell, ed., *John Huighen van Linschoten His Voyage to Goa, and Observations of the East Indies*, 183 (emphasis added).
17 Rogers, "Racial Identities and Politics," 155.
18 It is important to note here that, in practice, caste and occupation were never an exact fit, and such prescriptions were usually designed to enforce hierarchy. Thus, only a small percentage of Brahmins are priests, but virtually all "paraiyars" or untouchables were slaves.
19 Rogers, "Racial Identities and Politics," 156.
20 Barbour et al., "Hidden Apartheid: Caste Discrimination Against India's 'Untouchables.'"
21 Rail, "Khap Orders Dalit Women Raped After Brother Elopes."
22 I thank Rupa Viswanath for suggesting the importance of this point.
23 The best short overview of caste is Roberts, "Anthropology of Caste," 461–463.
24 See Thorat and Newman, ed., *Blocked By Caste: Economic Discrimination in Modern India*.
25 Macwan, "(Un)Touchable in Durban."
26 Hall, "Race, Articulation and Societies Structured in Dominance," 341.
27 Berreman, "Caste in India and the United States," 120–127. Berreman was scoffed at by his better-known opponent, Oliver Cromwell Cox, the pre-eminent Marxist sociologist whose 1948 book *Race, Caste and Class* is a classic in the field. See Oliver Cromwell Cox, "Berreman's 'Caste in India and the United States.'"
28 Ibid.
29 I thank Rupa Vishwanath for pointing this out to me.
30 Fuller, "Caste, Race, and Hierarchy in the American South," 604–621.
31 See Thorat and Umakant, ed., *Caste, Race and Discrimination: Discourses in an International Context*.
32 Phule, *Slavery* (in the Civilised British Government Under the Cloak of Brahmanism). As Arundhati Roy notes, Phule dedicated his book to "the good people of the United States as a token of admiration for their sublime disinterested and self-sacrificing devotion in the cause of Negro slavery"; Roy, "The Doctor and the Saint," 76.
33 See the Dalit Panthers' manifesto, *Untouchable! Voices of the Dalit Liberation Movement*, 141–147.
34 Dirks, "Castes of Mind," 67–68. For a different understanding, see Bayly, "Caste and 'Race' in Colonial Ethnography of India."
35 Risley, "The Study of Ethnology in India," 260. Some recent scholarship suggests that Risley's anthropology of caste did not have much effect on colonial policy as such. See Fuller, "Anthropologists and Viceroys: Colonial Knowledge and Policy Making in India 1871-1911."
36 See Figueira, *Aryans, Jews, Brahmins: Theorizing Authority Through Myths of Identity*.
37 Ramasami, *Words of Freedom: Ideas of a Nation*, 72.

38 Quoted by Omvedt, *Dalit Visions: The Anti-Caste Movement and the Construction of an Indian Identity*, 17.
39 Ambedkar, *The Annihilation of Caste*, 237–238.
40 See *United States v. Bhagat Singh Thind*. See also López, *White by Law: The Legal Construction of Race*.
41 See also Prashad, *The Karma of Brown Folk*, for an analysis of the politics of South Asian communities in the United States and US immigration policies.
42 E.M.S. Namboodiripad, a prominent leader of the Communist Party, is quoted and analyzed by Menon, *The Blindness of Insight: Essays on Caste in Modern India*, 47.
43 Bamshad et al., "Genetic Evidence on the Origins of Indian Caste Populations," 991.
44 A 2011 study published in the *American Journal of Human Genetics* by a team from the prestigious Centre for the Cellular and Molecular Biology in Hyderbad concluded, as the Centre's director put it, that "There is no genetic evidence that Indo-Aryans invaded or migrated to India or even something such as Aryans existed." See Sharma, "Indians Are Not Descendants" and Tharoor, "The Aryan Race." For the report, see Metspalu et al., *Shared and Unique Components of Human Population Structure*.
45 Thapar, "The Ugly Indian: How We Are Racist to Our People."
46 See Press Trust of India, "Bangalore to Gurgaon," in *FirstPost*; "Discrimination Against North-East People a Reality," in *Economic Times*; and "India's Northeast Speaks Out About Racism," in *Al-Jazeera*.
47 Major Nemhard is quoted in the Criminal Tribes Bill, *Proceedings of the Council of the Governor-General of India Assembled for the Purpose of Making Laws and Regulations*, 420.
48 See Roy, *Walking With the Comrades*.
49 See, for example, this news report: Mondal, "Dalit Catholics Continue to Battle Upper-Class Oppression." Arundhati Roy's novel, *The God of Small Things*, traces the deep-seated racism of Syrian Christians and Roman Catholics in Kerala. The writer Bama Faustina Soosairaj, known as Bama, herself a nun for seven years, chronicles the lives of Dalit Christian women in Tamil. Nadu. She was ostracized for her autobiographical novel *Karukku* (1992).
50 Bhavnani, *The Making of Exile: Sindhi Hindus and the Making of India*, 89. The book also discusses the discrimination faced by those who did happen to migrate to India.
51 Thardeep Rural Development Programme et al., *The Choice of Reforms*.
52 Guha, *Beyond Caste: Identity and Power in South Asia, Past and Present*. I am indebted to Nathaniel Roberts for drawing my attention to this book, and for sharing his review of it. See Roberts, "Setting Caste Back on its Feet."
53 Dumont, *Homo Hierarchicus: The Caste System and Its Implications*, 107.
54 See Loomba and Burton, *Race in Early Modern England: A Documentary Companion*.
55 Ambedkar, *Annihilation*, 214.
56 Ambedkar, *Annihilation*, 232; emphasis in original.
57 Roberts, "Anthropology of Caste," 462.
58 Viswanath, *The Pariah Problem: Cast, Religion and the Social in Modern India*. See also Guha, *Beyond Caste*, and Roberts "Anthropology."
59 Ambedkar, "Gandhism," 151.
60 Roberts, *To Be Cared For: The Power of Conversion and Foreignness of Belonging in an Indian Slum*, 144.
61 See also Viswanath, "'Silent Minority: Celebrated Difference, Caste Difference and the Hinduization of Independent India," 140–150.
62 Over three days, more than a thousand Muslims were slaughtered, over twenty thousand Muslims evicted from homes and business, at least 250 women raped, scores of children butchered, fetuses brutally ripped from wombs, and Hindu symbols carved into women's bodies. See the report by Human Rights Watch, "India: Gujarat Officials Took Part in Anti-Muslim Violence," and Kannabiran, *Tools of Justice: Non-discrimination and the Indian Constitution*.
63 Haynes, *Religious Transnational Actors and Soft Power*, 107. A detailed and moving documentation and analysis of the events is Rakesh Sharma's 2004 film, *Final Solution*. While particularly horrific and consequential for the country, given that Narendra Modi, the chief minister of Gujarat at that time, was then elected as the prime minister of the country, this was not an isolated incident, but one outcome of the systematic growth of a neo-fascist Hinduism since the 1947 partition of the country.

64 A detailed report by investigative journalist Ashish Khetan shows that the state itself was involved in the planning and execution of the pogrom. See Khetan, "The Truth."
65 Menon, *The Blindness of Insight: Essays on Caste in Modern India*, viii.
66 Thachil, *Elite Parties, Poor Voters*.
67 See Loomba and Burton, "Introduction," *Race in Early Modern England: A Documentary Companion*, 1–36.
68 See, for example, Mariscal, "The Role of Spain in Contemporary Race Theory"; Root, "Speaking Christian: Orthodoxy and Difference in Sixteenth-Century Spain"; Friedman, "Jewish Conversion, the Spanish Pure Blood Laws and Reformation: A Revisionist View of Racial and Religious Anti-semitism"; and Sweet, "The Iberian Roots of American Racist Thought."
69 See also Loomba, "Race and the Possibilities of Comparative Critique."
70 Alexander, "Mass Incarceration in the Age of Colorblindness." The point is made at greater length in Alexander's celebrated book, *The New Jim Crow: Mass Incarceration in the Age of Colorblindness*.
71 For the use of caste by scholars of race, see Fuller, "Caste, Race, and Hierarchy in the American South," 615.

References

Alexander, Michelle. (2012) *The New Jim Crow: Mass Incarceration in the Age of Colorblindness*, New York: New Press.

———. (2013) "Mass Incarceration in the Age of Colorblindness." Lecture delivered at Penn Humanities Forum, University of Pennsylvania, September 5.

Ambedkar, B.R. (2002) "Gandhism," in Valerian Rodrigues (ed.), *The Essential Writings of B.R. Ambedkar*, New Delhi: Oxford University Press, pp. 149–172.

———. (2014) *The Annihilation of Caste*, New Delhi: Navayana.

Bamshad, Michael, et al. (2001) "Genetic Evidence on the Origins of Indian Caste Populations." *Genome Research* 11, no. 6: 994–1004.

Barbour, Stephanie, et al. (2007) "Hidden Apartheid: Caste Discrimination Against India's 'Untouchables.'" *Human Rights Watch*, February 12.

Bayly, Susan. (1995) "Caste and 'Race' in Colonial Ethnography of India," in Peter Robb (ed.), *The Concept of Race in South Asia*, Oxford: Oxford University Press, pp. 165–218.

Berreman, Gerald D. (1960) "Caste in India and the United States." *The American Journal of Sociology* 66, no. 2: 120–127.

Bhavnani, Nandita. (2014) *The Making of Exile: Sindhi Hindus and the Making of India*, Chennai: Tranquebar Press.

Bhuyan, Anoo. (2015) "Black's Not a Darker Brown," *Outlook Magazine* (June 13).

Boxer, C.R. (1963) *Race Relations in the Portuguese Colonial Empire, 1415–1825*, Oxford: Clarendon Press.

Burnell, Arthur Coke (ed.). (1988) *John Huighen van Linschoten His Voyage to Goa, and Observations of the East Indies*, New Delhi and Madras: Asian Educational Services.

Burton, Antoinette. (2012) *Brown Over Black: Race and the Politics of Postcolonial Citation*, New Delhi: Three Essays Collective.

The Collected Works of Mahatma Gandhi, Vol. I, pp. 409–410.

Cox, Oliver Cromwell. (1961) "Berreman's 'Caste in India and the United States.'" *American Journal of Sociology* 66, no. 5: 511.

Criminal Tribes Bill. (1906) *Proceedings of the Council of the Governor-General of India Assembled for the Purpose of Making Laws and Regulations*, Vol. 9: 419–427.

Dalit Panthers. (1986) "Manifesto," in Barbara R. Joshi (ed.), *Untouchable! Voices of the Dalit Liberation Movement*, London: Zed Books, pp. 141–147.

Decree 2nd of the *Sacred Council of Goa*, 1567. Archivo Portuguez Oriental. Nova Goa, 1857, fasc. 4.

Diouf, Sylviane. (2013) "Africans in India: From Slaves to Generals and Rulers." *Africa and the African Diaspora*, New York Public Library, March 11. www.nypl.org/blog/2013/01/31/africans-india-slaves-generals-and-rulers.

Dirks, Nicholas B. (1992) "Castes of Mind." *Representations* 37: 56–78.
"Discrimination Against North-East People a Reality: Survey." (2014) *Economic Times*, December 6.
Dumont, Louis. (1980) *Homo Hierarchicus: The Caste System and Its Implications*, Chicago: University of Chicago Press.
Figueira, Dorothy M. (2015) *Aryans, Jews, Brahmins: Theorizing Authority Through Myths of Identity*, New Delhi: Navayana.
Friedman, Jerome. (1987) "Jewish Conversion, the Spanish Pure Blood Laws and Reformation: A Revisionist View of Racial and Religious Anti-Semitism." *Sixteenth-Century Journal* 18: 3–29.
Fuller, C. J. (2011) "Caste, Race, and Hierarchy in the American South." *Journal of the Royal Anthropological Institute* 17, no. 3: 604–621.
———. (2016) "Anthropologists and Viceroys: Colonial Knowledge and Policy Making in India, 1871–1911." *Modern Asian Studies* 50, no. 1: 217–258.
Guha, Sumit. (2013) *Beyond Caste: Identity and Power in South Asia, Past and Present*, Leiden: Brill Indological Library.
Gupta, Aniruddha. (1970) "A Note on Indian Attitudes to Africa." *African Affairs* 69, no. 275: 170–178.
Hall, Stuart. (1980) "Race, Articulation and Societies Structured in Dominance," in *Sociological Theories: Race and Colonialism*. Paris: UNESCO, p. 381.
———. (1988) "Minimal Selves," in Lisa Appignanesi (ed.), *Identity—the Real Me: Postmodernism and the Question of Identity*, London: ICA Documents.
Haynes, Jeffrey. (2012) *Religious Transnational Actors and Soft Power*, New York: Ashgate.
"India: Gujarat Officials Took Part in Anti-Muslim Violence." (2002) *Human Rights Watch*, April 30.
"India's Northeast Speaks Out Against Racism." (2014) *Al-Jazeera*, February 19.
Kannabiran, Kalpana. (2012) *Tools of Justice: Non-Discrimination and the Indian Constitution*, New York: Routledge.
Khetan, Ashish. (2007) "The Truth." *Tehelka*, November 3.
Kuku, Diepiriye. (2009) "India Is Racist and Happy About It." *Outlook Magazine* (June 29).
Loomba, Ania. "Race and the Possibilities of Comparative Critique." *New Literary History* 40, no. 3 (2009): 501–522.
Loomba, Ania, and Jonathan Burton. (2007) "Introduction," in Ania Loomba and Jonathan Burton (eds.), *Race in Early Modern England: A Documentary Companion*, New York: Palgrave Macmillan, pp. 1–36.
López, I. F. Haney. (1996) *White by Law: The Legal Construction of Race*, New York: New York University Press.
Mackey, Robert. (2014) "Beating of African Students by Mob in India Prompts Soul-Searching on Race." *New York Times*, September 30.
Macwan, Martin. (2001) "(Un)Touchable in Durban." *Seminar* 508: n.p.
Mariscal, George. (1998) "The Role of Spain in Contemporary Race Theory." *Arizona Journal of Hispanic Cultural Studies* 2: 7–23.
Menon, Dilip. (2006) *The Blindness of Insight: Essays on Caste in Modern India*. New Delhi: Navayana.
Metspalu, Mait, et al. (2011) "Shared and Unique Components of Human Population Structure and Genome-Wide Signals of Positive Selection in South Asia." *AJHG* 89, no. 6: 731–744.
Mondal, Sudipto. (2015) "Dalit Catholics Continue to Battle Upper Caste Aggression," *Hindustan Times*, August 2.
Morning, Ann. (2001) "The Racial Self-Identification of South Asians in the United States." *Journal of Ethnic and Migration Studies* 27, no. 1: 61–79.
Omvedt, Gail. (1995) *Dalit Visions: The Anti-Caste Movement and the Construction of an Indian Identity*, New Delhi: Orient Longman.
Phule, Jotirao. (2002) "*Slavery* (in the Civilised British Government Under the Cloak of Brahmanism), 2nd ed., translated by Maya Pandit," in G. P. Deshpande (ed.), *Selected Writings of Jotirao Phule*, New Delhi: Left Word Books.
Prashad, Vijay. (2001) *The Karma of Brown Folk*, Minneapolis: University of Minnesota Press.
Press Trust of India. (2014) "Bangalore to Gurgaon: Here's Why Racism in India Should Be Dealt With an Iron Hand." *FirstPost*, October 16.

Rail, Sandeep. (2015) "Khap Orders Dalit Women Raped After Brother Elopes, SC Seeks Police Reply." *Times of India*, August 19.

Ramasami, Periyar E. V. (2010) *Words of Freedom: Ideas of a Nation*, New Delhi: Penguin Books.

Risley, H. H. (1891) "The Study of Ethnology in India." *Journal of the Anthropological Institute of Great Britain and Ireland* 20: 235–263.

Roberts, Nathaniel. (2008) "Anthropology of Caste," in William S. Darity (ed.), *International Encyclopedia of the Social Sciences*, 461–463. New York: Macmillan Reference.

———. (2015) "Setting Caste Back on Its Feet," *Anthropology of This Century* 13: n.p.

———. *To Be Cared For: The Power of Conversion and Foreignness of Belonging in an Indian Slum*, Berkeley: University of California Press.

Robinson, Cedric. (1983) *Black Marxism: The Making of a Black Radical Tradition*, London: Zed Books.

Rogers, John D. (1995) "Racial Identities and Politics in Early Modern Sri Lanka," in Peter Robb (ed.), *The Concept of Race in South Asia*, New Delhi: Oxford University Press, pp. 146–164.

Root, Deborah. (1998) "Speaking Christian: Orthodoxy and Difference in Sixteenth-Century Spain." *Representations* 23: 118–134.

Roy, Arundhati. (2012) *Walking With the Comrades*, New York: Penguin Books.

———. (2014) "The Doctor and the Saint," in B.R. Ambedkar and S. Anand (ed.), *The Annihilation of Caste*, New Delhi: Navayana, p. 76.

Sharma, Dinesh C. (2011) "Indians Are Not Descendants of Aryans, Says New Study," *India Today*, December 10.

"South Asia." (2011) *The African Diaspora in the Indian Ocean World*, Schomburg Center for Research in Black Culture, New York Public Library, http://exhibitions.nypl.org/africansindianocean/essay-south-asia.php

Sweet, James H. (1997) "The Iberian Roots of American Racist Thought." *William and Mary Quarterly* 54, no. 1: 143–166.

Thachil, Tariq. (2014) *Elite Parties, Poor Voters*, Cambridge: Cambridge University Press.

Thapar, Karan. (2014) "The Ugly Indian: How We Are Racist to Our People." *Hindustan Times*, February 10.

Thardeep Rural Development Programme, et al. (2009) "The Choice of Reforms: The Human Rights Situation of Ethnic, Linguistic, Religious Minorities, Scheduled Castes Hindus and Indigenous People in Pakistan." Presented at the 74th Session of the United Nations Committee on the Elimination of Racial Discrimination.

Tharoor, Ishaan. (2011) "The Aryan Race: Time to Forget About It?" *Time*, December 15.

Thorat, Sukhdeo, and Newman, Katherine S. (ed.). (2010) *Blocked by Caste: Economic Discrimination in Modern India*, New Delhi: Oxford University Press.

Thorat, Sukhdeo, and Umakant (ed.). (2004) *Caste, Race and Discrimination: Discourses in an International Context*, New Delhi: Indian Institute of Dalit Studies.

United States v. Bhagat Singh Thind, 261 US 204 (1923).

Viswanath, Rupa. (2010) *The Pariah Problem: Cast, Religion and the Social in Modern India*, New York: Columbia University Press.

———. (2015) "Silent Minority: Celebrated Difference, Caste Difference, and the Hinuduization of Independent India," in Steven Vertovec (ed.), *Routledge International Handbook of Diversity Studies*, New York: Routledge, pp. 140–150.

Part III
METAPHYSICS AND ONTOLOGY

15
ANALYTIC METAPHYSICS
Race and Racial Identity
Jorge J. E. Gracia and Susan L. Smith

Introduction

Although the philosophy of race has been the center of attention for many philosophers, particularly in the second half of the twentieth century and the beginning of the twenty-first, the metaphysics of race has lagged behind. Also lagging has been the attention paid by analytic philosophers to race in general and the metaphysics of race in particular. Most analytic philosophers have tended to address what they consider to be more pressing practical problems having to do with the ethics and politics of race. This contrasts with the greater emphasis that Continental philosophers, for example, have given race, although they, even more than analytic philosophers, have neglected the metaphysics of race. The purpose of this article is to bring attention to some samples of the work from philosophers who work roughly within the analytic tradition in the metaphysics of race, including Robin O. Andreasen, Kwame Anthony Appiah, J. Angelo Corlett, J.L.A. García, Joshua Glasgow, Jorge J. E. Gracia, and Naomi Zack. Many others deserve attention, such as Ian Hacking, Michael Hardimon, Sally Haslanger, and Michael Root, but space limitations make it impossible to do proper justice to their views.

The article is divided into ten sections, dealing with the following topics: analytic metaphysics, race and racial identity, Appiah's reduction of race to racial identity, Zack's radical elimination of race, Corlett's reduction of race to ethnicity, García's opposition to racial and ethnic identities, Glasgow's reconstructionist account of race, Gracia's Constructionism in race and ethnicity, Andreasen's Cladism, and a conclusion.

Analytic Metaphysics

Analytic philosophy was born at the beginning of the twentieth century as a reaction against what were perceived to be the speculative excesses, unclear exposition, and muddled thinking of nineteenth century idealism and its disregard for empirical science and the rigor of logic. Among its most influential early proponents were G. E. Moore, Bertrand Russell, Ludwig Wittgenstein, and the members of the Vienna Circle, such as

Rudolph Carnap, Herbert Feigl, Kurt Gödel, and Moritz Schlick. No set of characteristics is common to all members of the initial group of analytic philosophers and those who subsequently joined it. Indeed, perhaps the best way to describe analysis is in the words of Max Black, who states that "the label of 'analysis' . . . serves well enough to identify philosophers who share a common intellectual heritage and are committed to the clarification of basic philosophical concepts" (Black 1963: v).

Still, some general tendencies found in analysis can be added to the aim mentioned by Black, such as a method characterized by breaking wholes into parts, a concern with language, an interest in logic and its use in philosophical discourse, a positive attitude toward science, and the conviction that non-empirical claims of a non-syntactical sort, such as those frequently made by metaphysicians, are suspect and should be subjected to careful scrutiny (see Carnap 1959). This and other tendencies make analysis appear as a turn toward the development of a more scientific and rigorous way of doing philosophy. The anti-metaphysical bias of analysts was particularly evident among its founding members and persisted for a good part of the twentieth century. More recently, however, analysts have reversed this course, embracing metaphysics with considerable enthusiasm.

Metaphysics is often described as the part of philosophy that studies being, reality, or fundamental principles. But how is this claim to be cashed out in order to include the wide range of views and approaches found among metaphysicians? One way of doing it is by conceiving the discipline as the study of most general categories and the relation of less general categories to the most general ones (Gracia 2014). If understood thus, one task of metaphysics is to establish a list of most general categories, as Aristotle did, for example, with substance, quantity, quality, relation, action, passion, and so on. Another task of the discipline is to determine how less general categories, such as "color," are related to the most general categories such as, for Aristotle, "quality."

Understood in this way, it should be clear that metaphysics not only is different from other disciplines, but also plays a prominent role in philosophy for two reasons. The first, because none of the other disciplines is concerned with the establishment of a list of most general categories. The second, because no other discipline tries to determine how less general categories are related to the most general ones. Scientists are also concerned with the establishment of categories, and their interrelations, but they are not concerned with coming up with a list of most general categories. A physicist, for example, will develop a list of categories that will include "matter" and "atom," but will not be concerned with how these categories fit into the most general categories, such as "substance" or "quality," using an Aristotelian scheme as an example.

But how does analytic metaphysics differ from non-analytic metaphysics? If we keep in mind the methodological principles that seem to be favored by analysts, we can see that the search for the list of most general categories and the way in which less general categories fit into them, is not essentially different for analysts and non-analysts. Rather, the difference consists in the way analysts go about doing metaphysics, for the emphasis on analysis, conceptual clarity, language, science, logical rigor, and empirical evidence does significantly alter the approach followed.

The task of an analytic metaphysics of race and racial identity, then, involves the identification of more general categories in which race and racial identity fit (e.g., being, reality, social construct, set, property, clade, nation, and so on) and how they differ from other categories with which they might be confused (e.g., family, species, nationality, class, and so on). This is in fact the task pursued by the authors discussed in the rest of this article. Keep in mind, however, that the discussion of race and racial identity is not the province of analytic metaphysicians alone. Nor is it the case that those analytic philosophers who discuss race and racial identity have restricted their discussion to the views of analytic philosophers.

Race and Racial Identity

The discussion of race in the United States goes back to the late nineteenth and early twentieth centuries and the work of pioneers such as W.E.B. Du Bois, Alain L. Locke, and Alexander Crummell among others, who first tried to understand race. The roots of analytic philosophy were being developed at the time in Europe, but analytic philosophers were not interested in race, let alone a metaphysics of race and racial identity. Their focus, generally in line with that of logical positivism, was science, logic, and related disciplines, so that the investigation of race for them was confined to that of specialized sciences such as biology. This disinterest continued well into the second half of the twentieth century. Although there were some early discussions of race by analytic philosophers, they tended to concern ethical and social issues rather than metaphysics. The turn toward a more metaphysical approach arose from the discoveries in genetics in the seventies that indicated, contrary to widely accepted views, that the biological grounds for race were either very limited or non-existent.

The argument against race was based on several facts: (1) genetic differences between races are minuscule if compared with what members of different races have in common (Lewontin 1972; Nei and Roychoudhury 1982); (2) no single gene can be used to classify populations into races (Cavalli-Sforza et al. 1994: 19); (3) no strict correlation exists between the directly observable traits of a person, known as phenotypes, and genetic specifications inherited from parents, known as genotypes (Cavalli-Sforza et al. 1994: 6–7); (4) particular phenotypes result from different gene combinations and do not adhere to stable racial boundaries (King 1981: 50–51; Zack 2002: 43); and (5) there are no strict boundaries between what are regarded as racial groups, rather these groups gradate from one to another (Cavalli-Sforza et al. 1994: 17–19).

These discoveries gave rise to the controversy concerning the reality of race: If (1)–(5) are true, can race be still considered real or is it a mere social construction? Three basic responses were given to this question at the outset. *Eliminativism* argues that race should be eliminated from discourse, because all racial discourse is biological and race has no biological bases. *Reductionism* rejects the notion of race, but substitutes it with such other notions as racial identity or ethnicity. And *Constructionism* preserves the notion of race, but understands it not as a biological fact, but as a social construction. Many varieties of these three basic positions have been proposed, but we shall concentrate on a handful of examples.

Not everyone was convinced of the unreality of race. Some have continued to hold that race has some biological basis. For example, several versions of *Cladism*, which looks to ancestral lineage for an understanding of racial groupings, have been proposed. This in turn has generated a strong reaction among those who oppose any biological basis for race for fear that it might reify race and, in turn, promote racism. Supporters of Cladism respond to this by pointing out that their conception of race does not imply racism and must be evaluated on its merits alone rather than by its social repercussions.

To the question of the reality of race must be added that of the relation of race to social identity. Does it make sense to speak of racial identity, and how is that different from speaking about race? The term "identity" comes from the Latin *idem* which means "the same." A thing is identical to itself, and two or more things are identical with respect to some property they have, such as humans with respect to having the capacity to laugh or certain hair color. Moreover, being identical to something else in some sense implies that the things in question are different from other things. That humans are identical with respect to the capacity to laugh makes them different to those beings that do not have such capacity, such as lions and rocks.

From this comes the talk about persons and social groups as having identities. Identity in this sense involves having something that is particular to a person (i.e., personal identity) or group of persons (i.e., social identity) and is different from other persons or groups of persons. Because particular races are composed of people that are supposed to share some features with other members of their racial groups and not with members of other racial groups, it has become common to talk about racial identities. Thus we speak of black and white identities. But does it make sense to talk in this way? Philosophers disagree on this point.

Appiah's Reduction of Race to Racial Identity

A pioneer and still major figure in the discussion of race is Kwame Anthony Appiah. His position can be classified as a form of Reductionism. It is articulated in his influential essay, "Race, Culture, and Identity: Misunderstood Connections," published in *Color Conscious*, a book that has made history in race studies. Appiah not only rejects any biological conception of race claimed to be based on factual evidence or conceptual analysis, but also a cultural understanding of it. Rather than race, he proposes that we should use the concept of racial identity. As he puts it: "First, ... American social distinctions cannot be understood in terms of the concept of race.... Second, replacing the notion of race with the notion of culture is not helpful ... And third, ... we should use instead the notion of racial identity" (Appiah 1996: 32).

Appiah's criticism of the notion of race is developed in terms of two theories of meaning, the ideational and the referential, since credible claims about race must be based on a clear meaning for the term "race." The ideational account, strictly speaking, requires a coherent set of beliefs associated with the use of the term (Appiah 1996: 35, 36). The referential account requires something in the world that provides an effective causal explanation of the use of that term.

Appiah argues, however, that the history of the concept of race in the United States reveals no identifiable objective phenomenon to which people respond when they talk about race that can effectively function causally (Appiah, 1996: 40, 72). Nor is there a uniform set of coherent beliefs about race (Appiah 1996: 72). This indicates that we do not have either a proper referent of the word "race" or a proper idea of race. In short, Appiah points out,

> you can't get much out of a race concept, ideationally speaking, from any of these [American] traditions; you can get various possible candidates from the

referential notion of meaning, but none of them will be much good for explaining social or psychological life, and none of them corresponds to the social groups we call "races" in America.

(Appiah 1996: 74)

Instead of race or the concept of race, Appiah proposes, we should adopt the concept of racial identity. This, in his view, adheres much better to what we do when we speak about races, racial phenomena, and racial groups. He defines racial identity as:

a label R, associated with [1] *ascriptions* by most people (where ascription involves descriptive criteria for applying the label); and [2] *identifications* by those who fall under it (where identification implies a shaping role for the label in the intentional acts of the possessor, so that they sometimes act *as an R*), where there is a history of associating possessors of the label with an inherited racial essence (even if some who use the label no longer believe in racial essences).

(Appiah 1996: 81–82)

The conditions of racial identity, then, are ascription by others, self-identification by the labeled, and a set of descriptions, used for both ascriptions and as norms for action, that has a historical association to a label involving a racial essence. It does not matter for racial identity that race has any reality, or even that we have a consistent concept of race. What matters is that people label some other people and themselves in certain ways and that the labels include a notion of inherited racial essence. A racial essence consists of a set of conditions regarded as necessary and sufficient for a particular race, whether in fact such conditions exist or not. The key, for Appiah, is the labeling, which he regards as crucial. The label comes first, and it is only afterwards that other features, such as cultural traits, are associated with it and used for action (Appiah 1996: 89). In his own words: "Collective identities . . . provide what we might call scripts: narratives that people can use in shaping their life plans and in telling their life stories" (Appiah 1996: 97).

Appiah's view involves both the elimination of race as a reality and of a cogent concept of race. In place of these he proposes certain procedures of labeling, varying descriptions, and attempts by those described to tailor action to those descriptions. Unlike radical eliminativists, he finds a substitute for race and its concept in the concept of racial identity. This, he argues, reflects accurately the way humans function with respect to racial phenomena.

Zack's Radical Eliminativism

A supporter of a radical form of Eliminativism is Naomi Zack. Although she is not an analytic philosopher in the historical sense mentioned earlier, she shares with analytic philosophers an interest in science. Echoing the conclusions of biologists, she holds that race is not a biological reality, that is, a fact that exists independently of human thought, and this makes race a social construction and not a characteristic of anything in the world (Zack 2002: 106ff.). From this she concludes that the concept of race is in fact meaningless and groundless, a remnant of archaic science (Zack 2001). "Black" and "white" do not exist, except as terms that refer to fictional concepts invented by humans; they belong with such concepts as unicorn and centaur.

The main problem with racial taxonomies, as Zack sees it, is that they lack an objective basis, which is a reason why they have proven extraordinarily unstable in the hands of taxonomists and often reflect personal preferences rather than facts. In her own words: "'Race' means a biological taxonomy or set of physical categories that can be used consistently and informatively to describe, explain, and make predictions about groups of human beings an individual members of these groups" (Zack 2002: 1).

According to Zack, "there have been four bases for ideas of physical race in common sense: geographical origins of ancestors; phenotypes or physical appearance of individuals; hereditary traits of individuals; [and] genealogy" (Zack 2002: 26). But all four fail the scientific test. And, since science does not support the reality or concept of race, we must do away with it completely. Further, we commit the fallacy of ontological obligation when we continue to use the term "race" as if we are referring to something real.

In spite of the support in science that eliminativists have found, their position has been attacked by reductionists and constructivists whether working in the analytic tradition or not. One early, and prominent, example outside the analytic tradition is that of Lucius T. Outlaw Jr., who works in the American Pragmatic tradition. He has argued that, even if not a biological reality, race is real and has affected and still affects society in significant ways, a reason why it cannot be eliminated from our discourse or consideration (Outlaw 1996). This sentiment is echoed by most of the authors discussed here.

Corlett's Reduction of Race to Ethnicity

In *Race, Racism, and Reparations*, Corlett articulates a version of Reductionism that responds to strong versions of Eliminativism and differs from Appiah's view of racial identity. His position rejects race but develops a genetic view of ethnicity that takes the place of race, and in some ways looks very much like it.

Corlett presents his view as a solution to the practical problems posed by public policy. He begins by distinguishing between two analyses, one in terms of "public policy" and another "metaphysical," which in his opinion do not have to coincide (Corlett 2003: 51). His main concern is with the first, but he also offers a concrete proposal for the second. Sally Haslanger also advocates something quite similar to a "public policy" account of race. Though she largely eschews a metaphysical approach to race, she does see the utility of acknowledging race as a social category in order to eliminate racial injustices (Haslanger 2005).

According to Corlett, the primary purpose of a public-policy analysis of ethnicity is "to accurately classify people into categories of ethnicity for purposes of justice under the law" (Corlett 2003: 46). The focus of his book is reparations for members of ethnic and racial groups that have suffered discrimination and other social ills as a result of their ethnicity or race. Now, these sorts of reparations require an accurate identification of people along ethnic and racial lines, although the need to come up with accurate classificatory criteria for ethnic and racial groups is not just a requirement of reparations; it is also required for the implementation of other social policies, such as affirmative action. After Corlett presents his position in the context of the Latino ethnic group, he claims that it "serves more than any other philosophical conception of who and what we are as Latinos to assist governments in enacting and administering positive public policies aimed at Latinos" (Corlett 2003: 60). His conclusions have a broader application and are not meant to apply only to Latinos. They are intended for all ethnic groups, although Corlett uses Latinos because he considers them to be a clear and effective illustration. Moreover, since ethnicity takes the place of race, his conclusions should also be applicable to what others refer to as races.

In Corlett's own words, his view is that, "for public policy considerations, genealogy ought to be construed as both a necessary and sufficient condition of award or benefit" (2003: 51 et passim). If reparations are to be justified for Latinos, a genetic tie is both necessary and sufficient to implement them, and the government in charge of the implementation needs to pay attention to it. Still, Corlett agrees, there is more to belonging to an ethnic group than genealogy. To be a Latino is more than just having Latino ancestry. Here is where the metaphysical analysis comes in, giving rise to a graded conception in which to be Latino is a matter of degree and involves a number of factors. As Corlett puts it:

Aside from public policy consideration, however, factors that would go toward making one more or less a Latino may include the degree to which one knows and respects a Latino language or dialect thereof; possesses and respects a traditional Latino name; engages in and respects Latino culture or parts thereof; accepts and respects himself or herself as a Latino; is accepted and respected as a Latino by other Latinos; and is construed as a Latino by outgroup members.... each of these conditions admits of degrees.... [but] neither (sic)... is either necessary or sufficient to make one a Latino."

(2003: 51)

In sum, the metaphysical view of an ethnic group consists of a list of conditions (Corlett does not tell us whether the list is exhaustive), each of which is subject to degree, resulting on one being more or less a member of the group. Consistently with this, the public policy view also is subject to degree, although in contrast with the metaphysical view, it is presented as a necessary and sufficient condition for the implementation of public policy.

García's Opposition to Racial and Ethnic Identities

García has been a constant critic of talk of identity, whether racial or ethnic. Indeed, he has objected to the most salient philosophical views on such identities, including those of Appiah, Zack, Corlett, Gracia, and Alcoff. He criticizes the inconsistency of the eliminativist views of Appiah and Zack with their preservation of the notions of racial and ethnic identities (García 2007: 46–49); Gracia's attempt to reconcile anti-essentialist views of race and ethnicity with his commitment to a historical familial view of ethnic identity (2007: 53–54; 2014); Corlett's comparative and scalar conception of group identity (2007: 54–62); and Alcoff's masquerading normative and ideological politics as epistemology and ontology (2000: 68).

García's position is not entirely negative. Instead of the concept of identity and its use in various contexts, he suggests "that we should strive toward what might be called ethno-racial skepticism and a deflationary conception of race and ethnicity" (2007: 69). He aims for simplicity and clarity, pointing out that the very notions of race and ethnicity are complex and difficult, posing problems for determining their extension and content. Indeed, according to García, we are very unclear about the extension and content of ethnic and racial affiliations. The understanding of this complexity and difficulty in these notions is made worse, rather than easier, by the introduction of the notion of identity, which is itself complex and difficult. Instead of introducing this notion in discussions of race and ethnicity, we might do much better in our investigation, for example, "to replace as much as possible such putative, ascribed affiliations with more restrained talk of ethnic (and, more problematically, racial) *background*, especially ancestry" (2007: 73).

One of the benefits of staying away from identity talk in the context of racial and ethnic groups, he argues, is that it dispenses with a number of confusions. One example is the misguided understanding of anyone's self-image as having to do with the group rather than with what it should be, namely, the self (2007: 76). Another is the view that race or ethnicity "can give 'meaning' to its participants' (members') lives," which is entirely too vague to be of any use (2007: 77). Rather than putting emphasis on racial or ethnic affiliations, García proposes that we adopt "a new interpersonalist personalism" that emphasizes our status as human beings, as rational animals, or even as creatures of God.

Glasgow's Reconstructionist Account of Race

Although Glasgow's account of race could be considered to be constructionist in that it conceives of race as a social kind, he instead labels it "reconstructionist" and distinguishes it from other constructionist approaches by utilizing, at least in part, experimental philosophy. Focusing on ordinary use, he argues that race terms should be understood to refer only to "wholly social categories," because retaining these terms "may even operate as a source of meaning in life and of perspectives from which we come to know the world and ourselves" (Glasgow 2009a, 139). Glasgow's reconstruction comes into play when he acknowledges that the contemporary use of the term "race" is mistakenly, but inextricably linked to biology. Still, he argues, we should continue to use the term and allow it to refer to the racial groupings we currently accept, although these groupings, after proper reconstruction, should be regarded as social kinds, not biological realities.

The first step in articulating the meaning of "race," which Glasgow considers to be a conceptual question, is to ask what people mean when they use it. The answer is to be found in empirical studies that reveal our common sense understanding of race. Once we find out the characteristics of race embedded within the concept of it, we can then, as a subsequent step, investigate the reality of those characteristics. If they do not exist, then the concept refers to a non-existent entity and must be reconstructed.

The conclusion that Glasgow draws from his research into the common sense notion of race is that "race-thinking seems to involve both biological *and* social elements" (2009b: 78). While he does allow that there are some correlations between race and certain physical characteristics, he holds that these correlations do not justify a biological component to race. The fact that there is a disproportionate occurrence of a medical condition, even a genetic one, in a particular racial group just means "that it is common among people whom *we have categorized* as a race, rather than one that is demarcated in nature" (109). Such differences can be the result of environmental pressures based on social categorization constructed by society. As an example he cites the disproportionate occurrence of hypertension in black males resulting from social pressures where we have a social cause that results in a biological effect.

In conclusion, then, if our common sense understanding of race includes biological elements and no such elements are warranted because they do not exist, then we are using "race" mistakenly to refer to a non-existent entity. Glasgow may be considered an anti-realist in the sense that he believes there is no biological basis for race. In spite of this conclusion, however, he favors the preservation of racial discourse to the extent that, properly understood, it can be beneficial for addressing some social issues. We should neither completely eliminate nor "wholeheartedly conserve it, but we should *replace* racial discourse with a nearby discourse" that uses racial terms only to refer to social categories (2). As he puts it:

> the word "race" in ordinary discourse purports to refer to something biological. Since no such biological thing exists, we have reason to get rid of that discourse. However, if we simultaneously replace it with the language of race, then we will implement a discourse that refers to a wholly social object, which turns out to be real
>
> (1)

Thus reconstructed, racial discourse is useful in that, for example, it allows us to preserve racial identity and race-conscious policies. Racial identity is important for people to maintain proper conceptions of themselves and race-conscious policies, such as affirmative action, can promote equal opportunity (133). In short, we should continue to speak of race, but we should understand it as not having a biological import.

Gracia's Constructionism in Race and Ethnicity

Gracia rejects radical Eliminativism, such as that of Zack, and the Reductionism of Appiah and Corlett. In agreement with Outlaw, he keeps the notion of race, but rejects its identification with racial identity or ethnicity. His position preserves a distinction between race and ethnicity and allows for the notion of racial and ethnic identities. He calls his view of race the Genetic Common-Bundle View and his view of ethnicity the Historical-Familial View (Gracia 2005: 82 and 24; 2000: 27–33). Both incorporate a familial dimension.

Gracia begins by making a distinction between "a race" considered as a group of people, "race" considered as a property of members of a group, and "racial identity" which is the possession of the racial property. These correspond with, but are different from, "an ethnos" (or ethnic group), "ethnicity" (a property of members of the ethnic group), and "ethnic identity." A race as a group of people consists of a sub-group of individual human beings who satisfy the following two conditions:

> (1) each member of the group is linked by descent to another member of the group who is in turn also linked by descent to at least some third member of the group; and (2) each member of the group has one or more physical features that are (i) genetically transmittable, (ii) generally associated with the group, and (iii) perceptually perspicuous.
>
> (2005: 85)

Race as a property consists in the set of characteristics that satisfy these conditions. And racial identity is the higher order relational property of having such a property.

Gracia argues that neither one of the two conditions required by a race, taken by itself, is sufficient for racial membership, unless one were to adopt the infamous One-Drop Rule, which is inconsistent and hence unacceptable (see Malcomson 2000). The One-Drop Rule is inconsistent as a racial marker because it can function effectively only if applied discriminately to some races and not others. This means that being related by descent to a member of some race, who is in turn related by descent to at least some third member of that race, is not sufficient for someone to be a member of the race, since the person in question may not share in any of the features generally associated with members of it (Gracia 2005: 85–86). This, Gracia claims, is the reason why we say that people can change races whereas in fact, and strictly speaking, there is no such racial change. The presumed change amounts to the recognition that the persons in question do not satisfy the conditions sufficient for belonging to a particular race while they meet the conditions of belonging to another race. The change is one of labeling, that is, of what we call the persons, rather than of being, that is, of what the persons are.

In the same way, according to Gracia, having physical features associated with a particular race does not automatically make a person a member of the race or serve effectively to identify the person as such (2005: 86). Some Indians, Italians, and blacks have many phenotypes in common, but the first two are not considered to be members of the black race because they do not satisfy the descent condition.

Although Gracia uses the notion of family to understand both race and ethnicity, he distinguishes ethnicity from race in that it is conceived in terms of history and does not require the two stated racial conditions. This means that ethnicity is a more flexible notion and contingent on historical events, even if such historical events may include descent and certain phenotypes as required in race. It is for this reason that race and ethnicity are often confused with each other as happens with Hispanics/Latinos (Gracia 2000).

Gracia's position with respect to race and ethnicity may be considered constructionist insofar as, apart from descent and the inherited and physical character of the phenotypes that make up the distinguishing racial property of a racial group, the choice of the particular features is the result of social construction and thus may vary from society to society. Ethnicity is also a construct but, unlike race, it is not constrained by descent or inheritable physical phenotypes, although these may in fact be part of the distinguishing ethnic property of particular ethnic groups. Still, both races and ethne are familial groups when this metaphor is used broadly.

Andreasen's Cladism

Most, if not all, accounts of race as a biological entity have come under heavy criticism. Some have been accused of being motivated by a racist agenda, whereas others have been criticized because of their theoretical flaws. Among recent authors who reject such charges is Andreasen. She proposes that races be understood using a cladistic method. She defines races as "sets of lineages that share a common origin" (Andreasen 2000: S655). Cladism as used in biology refers to the grouping of organisms by ancestry. This contrasts with evolutionary taxonomy, in which the groupings are based on ancestry and adaptation, or a phenetic approach in which the groupings are based on perceived similarities (see also Kitcher's similar approach in 1999).

One of the strengths of Cladism, for Andreasen, is its inherent objectivity insofar as the construction of an ancestral lineage is not subject to cultural biases or social preferences as may be the case in the phenetic approach. Additionally, Cladism does not rely on "kind-specific essences" as some previous biological approaches did. In her view, such essentialist approaches were not compatible with evolutionary theory, whereas phylogenetic approaches, such as Cladism, "are historical, since they define taxa in terms of evolutionary history . . . [and] aim to represent the evolutionary branching process" (Andreasen 2000: S656).

Different methods of constructing ancestral lineages have been proposed, but Andreasen relies on the research of Luigi Cavalli-Sforza, Masatoshi Nei and Arun Roychoudhury, and Allan Wilson and Rebecca Cann for her construction. Accordingly, gene frequencies are used to construct groupings, of which Andreasen proposes nine (New Guinean & Australian, Pacific Islander, SE Asian, NE Asian, Arctic NE Asian, Amerindian, European, Non-European Caucasoid and African). She acknowledges that these groupings rely on some controversial data, but this does not preclude the possibility of their representational accuracy.

Andreasen's version of Cladism is unique among biological accounts of race in that it neither looks at racial groups as subspecies, nor does it propose that such groups have any significance in terms of complex social characteristics. Indeed, for Andreasen a cladist approach is compatible with social Constructionism and the claim "that most CS [common sense] beliefs about the biological reality of race are empirically unjustified" (Andreasen 2000: S662). There is nothing biologically meaningful with respect to common sense notions of race, but this does not mean there is no biologically meaningful way of creating racial groupings. Cladist racial groupings, rather than relying on subjective criteria, such as skin tone similarity or hair type, provide an objective and biological basis for racial groups. Cladist groups can change or become extinct and new races can emerge. Andreasen also claims that races are disappearing because geographic reproductive isolation is not occurring to the extent it did before technological advances allowed humans to travel the globe.

Conclusion

Although recent analytic philosophers have explored many aspects of race, in metaphysics they have often focused on the questions of the reality of race, the distinction between race and other social categories such as ethnicity, and the viability and nature of racial identities. All the authors discussed here have something to say about the first two topics and most of them also about the third. Their discussions can be characterized as metaphysical both because they have raised questions dealing with the reality of race and they have provided categorizations of race in terms of more general categories that distinguish it from other phenomena.

Appiah disputes the reality of race and the cogency of the corresponding concept providing a linguistic analysis based on the notion of racial identity. Zack rejects any uses of the language or concept of race because they imply a biological reality that does not exist. Corlett rejects the reality and concept of race, but unlike Appiah argues in favor of substituting race by ethnicity. Gracia proposes distinctions between "a race," "race," and "racial identity" on the one hand and "an ethnos," "ethnicity," and "ethnic identity" on the other. A race is a group of people and thus real, but race is a property of members of a group that is the result of social construction, although some of its components are real first-order properties. García's effort focuses on arguing against the concept of racial and ethnic identity. Identity for him should be restricted to personal identity, although this does not entail that people may not be appropriately classified as belonging to a race or an ethnic group. Glasgow offers a view of race that, similar to eliminativist positions, acknowledges a disconnect between common sense ideas of race and the reality of race. His approach differs from eliminativist approaches in that he argues for retaining the term "race" while reconstructing its meaning so that it exclusively refers to a social construction. Andreasen argues for a biological understnding of race that relies on a phylogenetic account of racial groupings in terms of clades that is potentially compatible with constructionist theories.

Although not all the authors discussed address the same problems and, when they do, they seldom agree with each other, some common elements distinguish them from other philosophers of race belonging to non-analytic traditions. In terms of topics, they focus on race, ethnicity, identity, and their interrelations, introducing distinctions between them that are often ignored in non-analytic accounts. Unlike philosophers who tend to shun metaphysical analyses, they often explicitly take these up and argue for their fundamental role in any account of race. Likewise, they tend to include Constructionist elements even when their overall positions rely on non-constructionist bases. In line with the scientific origins of analysis, analytic philosophers generally pay particular attention to scientific discoveries, integrating them into their views as much as possible. For the most part, they seek to make original contributions to race theory backed up by carefully crafted arguments in accordance with the method of analysis. And although analysts often discuss political, social, and moral issues, their accounts do not include as many witnessing narratives, contrasting with other traditions that often give such narratives a predominant place in their discussions. Particularly infrequent in analytic accounts are autobiographical narratives, insofar as analysts prefer to deal with conceptual matters rather than personal ones. Finally, in accordance with the method of analysis, members of this tradition approach race and racial questions through the analysis of language.

These differences with other philosophical traditions give analytic discussions of race a character quite different from those of other philosophical traditions. Indeed, the originality and value of analytical treatments of race owe much to these differences; it is precisely because of them that analysts have been able to pinpoint subtle, but significant and different nuances in the conceptions of race, ethnicity, and identity that had been ignored by other philosophers. And it is thanks to those differences that analytic accounts constitute real alternatives to other accounts, and challenge the assumptions that guide them.

References

Andreasen, Robin O. (2000) "Race: Biological Reality or Social Construct?" *Philosophy of Science* (Supplement) 67: S653–S66.

Appiah, K. Anthony. (1996) "Race, Culture, Identity: Misunderstood Connections," in K. Anthony Appiah and Amy Gutmann (eds.), *Color Conscious: The Political Morality of Race*. Princeton: Princeton University Press, pp. 30–105.

Black, Max. (1963) *Philosophical Analysis: A Collection of Essays*, Englewood Cliffs: Prentice Hall.

Carnap, Rudolf. (1959) "The Elimination of Metaphysics Through the Logical Analysis of Language." Trans. Arthur Pap, in A. J. Ayer (ed.), *Logical Positivism*, Glencoe, IL: Free Press.

Cavalli-Sforza, Luigi, et al. (1994) *The History and Geography of Human Genes*, Princeton: Princeton University Press.

Corlett, J. Angelo. (2003) *Race, Racism, and Reparations*, Ithaca: Cornell University Press.

García, J.L.A. (2007) "Racial and Ethnic Identity?" in Jorge J. E. Gracia (ed.) *Race or Ethnicity? On Black and Latino Identity*. Ithaca: Cornell University Press, pp. 45–77.

———. (2014) "Is Being Hispanic an Identity?" in Iván Jaksić (ed.), *Debating Race, Ethnicity, and Latino Identity: Jorge J. E. Gracia and His Critics*. New York: Columbia University Press, pp. 91–105.

Glasgow, Joshua. (2009a) "In Defense of a Four-Part Theory: Replies to Hardimon, Haslanger, Malloon, and Zack." *Symposia on Gender, Race, and Philosophy* 5, no. 2: 1–18.

———. (2009b) *A Theory of Race*, New York: Routledge.

Gracia, Jorge J. E. (2000) *Hispanic/Latino Identity: A Philosophical Perspective*, Oxford: Blackwell.

———. (2005) *Surviving Race, Ethnicity and Nationality*, Lanham: Rowman & Littlefield.

———. (2014) "The Fundamental Character of Metaphysics." *American Philosophical Quarterly* 51, no. 4: 305–317.

———. (2015) "Race, Ethnicity, Nationality, and Philosophy: A Response," in Iván Jaksić (ed.), *Debating Race, Ethnicity, and Latino Identity: Jorge J. E. Gracia and His Critics*, New York: Columbia University Press, pp. 65–87.

Haslanger, Sally. (2005) "What Are We Talking About? The Semantics and Politics of Social Kinds." *Hypatia* 20, no. 4: 10–26.

King, James C. (1981) *The Biology of Race*, Berkeley: University of California Press.

Kitcher, Philip. (1999) "Race, Ethnicity, Biology, Culture," in Leonard Harris (ed.), *Racism*, New York: Humanity Books, pp. 87–119.

Lewontin, Richard C. (1972) "The Apportionment of Human Diversity." In T. Dobzhansky, M. K. Hecht, and W. C. Steere (eds.), *Evolutionary Biology*, Vol. 6. New York: Appleton-Century-Crofts, pp. 381–398.

Malcomson, Scott, L. (2000) *One Drop of Blood: The American Misadventure of Race*, New York: Farrar, Straus and Giroux.

Nei, Masatoshi, and Roychoudhury, A. K. (1982) "Genetic Relationship and Evolution of Human Races." *Evolutionary Biology* 14: 1–59.

Outlaw, Lucius, T., Jr. (1996) *On Race and Philosophy*, New York: Routledge.

Zack, Naomi. (2001) "Race and Philosophic Meaning," in Bernard Boxill (ed.), *Race and Racism*, Oxford: Oxford University Press, pp. 43–57.

Zack, Naomi. (2002) *Philosophy of Science and Race*, New York: Routledge.

16
AMERICAN EXPERIMENTALISM
Harvey Cormier

The nineteenth was the first century of human sympathy,—the age when half wonderingly we began to descry in others that transfigured spark of divinity which we call Myself; when clodhoppers and peasants, and tramps and thieves, and millionaires and—sometimes—Negroes, became throbbing souls whose warm pulsing life touched us so nearly that we half gasped with surprise, crying, "Thou too! Hast Thou seen Sorrow and the dull waters of Hopelessness? Hast Thou known Life?" And then all helplessly we peered into those Other-worlds, and wailed, "O World of Worlds, how shall man make you one?"

W.E.B. Du Bois, *The Souls of Black Folk*

It is not widely appreciated that William James put the experimentalist understanding of thinking called pragmatism to work in connection with the idea of race. He did, though, and he was not alone. James thought about human races not in mechanical scientific terms, or as inevitable causal products of their physical geographical environment, but in terms of choice and creation. In his picture, we human beings invented, and continue to invent and develop, our races or peoples in pursuit of a better future. In what follows, I try to explain this philosophical picture of race and compare it with that of James's student W.E.B. Du Bois. James's and Du Bois's two pictures may seem very different; James's view is so naturalistic that we can think of his "races" as biological phenomena like species, while Du Bois made a point of describing race as a kind of social construction that is apart from biology. Still, I think it is useful to see these figures as sharing a picture of human races as willed and hopeful social experiments. Moreover, I think that there is still something to be said today for this picture.

I

James described his pragmatism as "the empiricist temper regnant" (James 1978: 31). Not because it featured an epistemology with sensory data as its positive foundations, and not because its metaphysics identified feelings and perceptions as the atomic particles of the universe; instead, pragmatism was empiricist in "temper" because it explained how we human believers pick, retain, and discard beliefs using our manifold *experiences* of life. The good or "true" beliefs and principles were the ones that provided us with satisfactory experiences, while the bad or false ones did the opposite. This understanding of truth turned experiences into a "corridor" among our ideas, including not only our scientific, moral, and philosophical theories but even our religious outlooks. It was how we entered those ways of thinking and how we left them when the time was right. It was above all an *experimentalist* story of thought, speech, and belief; we were to create hypotheses, principles, and faiths, then try them on for size. In the end, even pragmatism itself was to get this treatment. (See Cormier 2000, especially chapter 1, for a comparison of James's pragmatism with traditional empiricism.)

This practical approach to thinking and belief was, and is still, inspired by science, especially the Darwinian variety. Darwin and Wallace had seen that in natural selection, nature designs successful forms of life by experimenting, creating organisms randomly and then winnowing out the losers unsuited to their diverse environments. Pragmatic philosophers observe a similar process at work as human thinkers more or less randomly create ideas and then winnow out the bad ones. Nature performs its experiments blindly while we human thinkers sometimes work self-consciously, especially in the *hypothesize-test-hypothesize* process known as science; but despite that large difference, these natural and human processes are alike enough to illuminate each other. Both involve using materials of uncertain reliability to cope, better and better over time, with an uncertain world.

Still, despite being inspired by Darwinian science in two ways, pragmatism is not a "scientism." It does not claim that scientifically skeptical, self-conscious hypothesizing followed by sensory observations is the only rational way to think. William James is of course famous for his idea, compatible with his pragmatism, that we should sometimes exercise the "will to believe," our capacity to adopt certain beliefs not because scientific evidence supports them but because we want to have beliefs (James 1979: 18–20 esp.). Sometimes moral and religious beliefs, especially, get neither support nor disproof from scientific observations, and we rightly adopt them because they satisfy us and we expect them to make our lives of experience still more satisfactory in the future. We thus use our experiences of life as a way into—and, who knows, maybe we will someday use them as a way out of—our particular religious and moral beliefs. Moreover, James holds that "[F]aith in a fact can help create the fact." A belief like "I can get to know God" resembles a belief like "I can make this person like me" in that if people believe either thing preemptively, that belief can sometimes help *make itself true* (James 1979: 28–29). These are beliefs in the possibility of successful *action*, and succeeding at actions sometimes requires some Little-Engine-That-Could, *I-think-I-can* faith, not the kind of skeptical thinking we usually associate with science.

This story of experimental thinking, believing, and faith-having is centered around individual thinkers, persons who have unique experiences and are forced to invent novel ideas to help them make sense of things. Many of these new ideas will turn out in the end not to help much, but the ones that do work out for a while—and for more people than the individual thinkers alone—will be identified as "truths" for as long as they keep working out. Indeed all truths are ideas or beliefs that depend for their origin and continued existence on this human struggle to make do; there is no truth out there in the world just sitting and waiting to be found. Thus James notoriously claims that human beings make the truth. But this is not the absurd and self-refuting claim that we individual thinkers make our own realities as we produce thoughts that satisfy us and us alone. Instead this means that truth, the stuff that fills our libraries, our conversations, and the head of anybody with common sense, is no more than the aggregate of all our useful beliefs, those singular products of struggle. Truth ends up a social phenomenon, but it depends for its origin on individual thinkers and their unique experiences. By making these contributions, individual human beings play a role in their societies like the one individual organisms play in their biological races and species.

II

One of James's best-known remarks, found emblazoned over the elevators in the lobby of William James Hall on the Harvard campus, is "The community stagnates without the impulse of the individual. The impulse dies away without the support of the community." This is a passage from the lecture "Great Men and their Environment" (James 1979: 163–189). There James argues that human communities, which he alternately describes as "nations" and "races," depend for their development on particular individuals much as plant and animal species do.

This offers Darwinian opposition to the views of Herbert Spencer and his followers. Though Spencer was actually both a follower of and an influence on Darwin—his description of evolution by natural selection as "survival of the fittest" was adopted by Darwin and featured in later editions of *The Origin of Species*—James argued that Spencer's evolutionary view was not Darwinian enough. It underestimated the importance of individual organisms and overestimated the importance of physical environments in the development of biological species, and it went on to overestimate the importance of both physical and social environments in the development of human races. In Darwin's and Wallace's own theories, particular individual plants, animals, and human beings in specific, one-off circumstances were indispensable to the development of all the races and species that actually did develop over natural history. The forms of life we find here on earth might have been entirely different, even in the same environments and with the same physical laws, had certain individual organisms not happened to come along and make their distinctive genetic and behavioral contributions. And James thinks that human "races," peoples, or populations are like plant and animal species in this regard. They have been decisively shaped by the impulses of specific individuals, even if those individuals could never have done their shaping without some social cooperation.

Spencer, by contrast, offered the view that became "social Darwinism." Individuals are not real causal forces in that story, and the idea that individual human beings are free to change the big natural world-system is a lot of superstition. As Spencer says in his *Study of Sociology*, great human leaders and creators are not "deputy gods," and so

> the origin of the great man is natural; and immediately this is recognized, he must be classed with all other phenomena in the society that gave him birth as a product of his antecedents. . . . [T]he genesis of the great man depends on the long series of complex influences which has produced the race in which he appears, and the social state into which that race has slowly grown. . . . Before he can remake his society, his society must remake him. . . . If there is to be anything like a real explanation of [the social changes he makes], it must be sought in that aggregate of conditions out of which both he and they have arisen.
> (Spencer 1961: 30–31; cited at James 1979: 233)

And we cannot really intentionally improve the social circumstances that nature has created for us:

> [W]ith mankind as with lower kinds, the ill-nurtured offspring of the inferior fail in the struggle for existence with the well-nurtured offspring of the superior; and in a generation or two die out, to the benefit of the species. A harsh discipline this, most will say. True; but nature has much discipline which is harsh, and which must, in the long run, be submitted to. The necessities which she imposes on us are not to be evaded, even by the joint efforts of university graduates and workingmen delegates; and the endeavor to escape her harsh discipline results in a discipline still harsher. Measures which prevent the dwindling away of inferior individuals and families, must, in the course of generations, cause the nation at large to dwindle away.
> (Spencer 1978: 204)

This is a rugged individualism that denies the individual any power to do anything, or at least anything that will improve the social world.

Spencer's followers were sometimes—and sometimes still are today—even more explicitly deterministic and more clearly concerned with what we would recognize today as human races. Grant Allen argued that

> If the people who went to Hamburg had gone to Timbuctoo, they would now be indistinguishable from the semi-barbarian negroes who inhabit that central African metropolis; and if the people who went to Timbuctoo had gone to Hamburg, they would now have been white-skinned merchants driving a roaring trade in imitation sherry and indigestible port. . . . The differentiating agency must be sought in the great permanent geographical features of land and sea; . . . these have necessarily and inevitably moulded the characters and histories of every nation upon the earth.
> (Allen 1878: 121, 123; cited at James 1979: 235–236)

But in criticism of Spencer and Allen, James cited Alfred Russell Wallace's book *Malay Archipelago*:

> Borneo and New Guinea, as alike physically as two distinct countries can be, are zoölogically wide as the poles asunder; while Australia, with its dry winds, its open plains, its stony deserts, and its temperate climate, yet produces birds and quadrupeds which are closely related to those inhabiting the hot, damp, luxuriant forests which everywhere clothe the plains and mountains of New Guinea.
> (Wallace 1883: 13; cited at James 1979: 240)

Geography is not destiny for either the animals or for us. The peculiarities of mutating animals can, if they are adaptive, propagate and change an entire population of animals over generations into another "race" or even another species, and those initial peculiarities are not determined by the "great permanent geographical features of land and sea." They are instead tiny random insertions into those large physical environments. They are not completely independent of physical causation—maybe nothing is, and thus maybe nothing is random in that sense—but no general law determines their appearance. The same peculiarities can appear and spread in very different environments and fail to appear or spread in all similar environments. Moreover, individual human beings make analogous random insertions of peculiar motivations and ideas into their physical and social environments, and those "impulses" can spread and change human communities as dramatically as mutations anthropogenic change species. They can even go on to change the large physical environment. Think "climate change."

James notes that

> the social surroundings of the past and present hour exclude the possibility of accepting certain contributions from individuals; but they do not positively define what contributions shall be accepted, for in themselves they are powerless to fix what the nature of the individual offerings shall be.
> (James 1979: 231)

Hence individual persons are a *force* in social development in much the same way individual organisms are in species development. It goes without saying that particular persons are not gods and do not create their and their societies' futures by solitary fiat, but they can, do, and should *make a difference* in how their societies turn out. And, of course, just as individual organisms and their contingent "offerings" have often been a force in *successful* adaptations to the physical environment, likewise individual persons' contingent contributions have played a role in the development of the most successful human populations. Thus "university graduates and workingmen delegates" may well have something positive to contribute to the development of society as they try to make life better for the worst-off citizens. No guarantees, of course; we will have to look to the future and see. But at least Darwin's theory of evolution does not argue the contrary in advance.

Again, there are present-day Spencerians who have not got this message. There are still evolutionary psychologists who argue that human beings have, thanks to their original physical environment, inevitably developed certain behavioral tendencies that are incompatible with certain forms of social life. E. O. Wilson is credited with a terse summing-up and endorsement of one such argument concerning Marxism, for competitive human beings if not for altruistic bees and ants: "Wonderful theory. Wrong species" (McKie 2006). Such scientific thinkers answer the question "Nature or nurture?" with "Nature," or at least with "Both." Moreover, some contemporary social Darwinists are committed, like Spencer himself, to the idea that different human populations have been shaped by different original natural environments and thus have different tendencies and abilities. They argue that nature has produced not only really distinct human races but hierarchies among them, making some races naturally more intelligent and suited to civilization than others and setting limits to what can be done with some racial groups whatever attempts at socialization might be made. Nurture cannot trump nature, after all. (These researchers, including figures like J. Philippe Rushton, call themselves "racial realists"; Ian Hacking and Philip Kitcher call them "ogre naturalists." See Rushton 1995, Hacking 2005, and Kitcher 2012.)

However, a Jamesian answer to the nature-nurture question is, basically, "Neither." Neither physical geography, socialization, nor their combination has determined what our human populations are now or are becoming. Existence precedes essence, in a way, both for human beings and for populations of them. Persons are still parts of the natural world, of course, and the process by which they create themselves and their groups is a natural process much like the one by which plant and animal species create themselves. (Sometimes the human process is equally unselfconscious and non-forward-looking.) But both of these processes are, as Charles S. Peirce might have said, tychistic (see Peirce 2009: 135–157). *Chance* is operating in them, providing needed raw material—genetic material in the case of the animals and plants, intellectual material in the human case.

The individuals who provide that raw material are turning-places in natural history, human history, and the histories of their different races. For the Spencerian who discounts them and their contributions, the world is basically a big, rational, four-dimensional block whose events are entirely predictable because nothing ever really happens there. But James says that by appealing in this way to the Eternal and Unchanging Rational Whole in his explanation of how people and peoples got to be the way they are, Spencer in effect answers every question: "God is great." Genuine and successful scientific thinking looks at least sometimes to the particular and the proximate in explanation of events. In James's example, if we want to account for the death of a sparrow after we see a little kid throw a rock, asking what must have happened after the Big Bang or in the history of the Celts is a waste of mental energy. We might as well check the zodiac; in the block universe, a *really* full horoscope would answer all questions about sparrow deaths, too. But even if the world is in fact a block, this is obviously not how science works. Instead in a case like this we will look to the particular and contingent case of rock-throwing that we actually observed, and we will thus not only halt the development of an adolescent psychopath but also display what James calls "an efficient as distinguished from an inefficient intellect," or scientific rather than superstitious thinking (James 1979: 163–164, 176).

Thus, James will say, social Darwinism is not really the scientific outlook it pretends to be. We can have a biological understanding of races even as we take them to be shaped and steered by the individuals inside them, so long as we understand biological science to describe a world of change and contingent developments that depend on discrete individual actors and events—which is the way Darwin himself understood it.

III

W.E.B. Du Bois also fought Spencer's kind of scientism and mechanism regarding race in his own way. In his well-known historical and sociological studies of African American communities and in his literary essays and fiction examining black life and culture, the black race was not a biological taxon that could be discerned by means of inherited physical characteristics. Instead it was "a vast family of human beings, generally of common blood and language, always of common history, traditions and impulses, who are both voluntarily and involuntarily striving together for the accomplishment of certain more or less vividly conceived ideals of life." While these "ideals" are "subtle forces" that

> have generally followed the natural cleavage of common blood, descent and physical peculiarities, they have at other times swept across and ignored these. At all times, however, they have divided human beings into races, which, while

they perhaps transcend scientific definition, nevertheless, are clearly defined to the eye of the historian and sociologist.

(Du Bois 1970: 75–76)

Thus although different human races have contingently been associated with differing physical and physiological traits, they are essentially historical and social phenomena that cannot be accounted for by science—or at least not by the natural sciences, the sciences that someone like Spencer would have taken as the model of human knowledge.

Du Bois developed his distinctive picture of race under the influence of both American and German teachers. He studied philosophy under James and Josiah Royce at Harvard University, went on to earn an M.A. at Harvard in history, and then went overseas for postgraduate study in economics in Berlin. He returned to the United States to complete his dissertation and become the first black scholar to earn a Harvard Ph.D., and he then began his historical and sociological research, aiming ultimately to help solve "the problem of the color-line," or to use scientific understanding of his own "race" to guide policy makers and fight bigotry and oppression.

To do this, he needed a concept of race in order to know what to investigate and how. In fact, he subtitled *Dusk of Dawn*, his story of his own work, "the autobiography of a race-concept." That concept evolved as his program for "the Negro" did, but it was always the concept of a social construction rather than a physical or biological essence. Race was not a matter of "grosser physical differences of color, hair and bone" passed down by "blood" (Du Bois 1970: 75). His famous definition was succinct: "The black man is a person who must ride 'Jim Crow' in Georgia" (Du Bois 2007: 77). And his studies of black communities were not accounts of mechanical, inevitable social processes but instead stories of choices based on experiences. He set out to describe the factual effects of discrimination, education levels, and economic conditions on black community life, but he also wanted to answer the question: "How does it feel to be a problem?" (1996: 101). If he could do both of these things, he was confident that he would be able to provide a genuine, action-guiding understanding of the history and the present life of the people categorized as "black."

Du Bois had studied in Berlin with such figures as the sociologist and political philosopher Max Weber, the historian Heinrich von Treitschke, the economist Gustav von Schmoller, and the psychologist, historian, sociologist, and philosopher Wilhelm Dilthey. As Kwame Anthony Appiah tells the story (Appiah 2014), these figures had a formative influence on Du Bois and his approach to social science. Dilthey, who distinguished the fact-finding of the *Naturwissenschaften* or natural sciences from the imaginative and sympathetic law-seeking of the *Geisteswissenschaften* or social sciences, held that "Nature we explain [*erklären*], but psychic life we understand [*verstehen*]" (Dilthey 1990: 144; Dilthey 2010: 119; cited at Appiah 2014: 78). To provide this understanding, the social scientist has to show the world as it looks through the eyes of the subject of study. Du Bois tried to do this not only in his literary work but also in his socio-historical research.

Schmoller was known as a member of the "younger historical school" of economists, who preferred societies to isolated individuals as the methodological starting point for their research. They argued that economics could only be genuinely scientific by using statistics and empirical generalizations based on observations of specific social and historical circumstances. They challenged classical economic theory, and, when they in turn were challenged by neo-classicists of the "Austrian school," they fought in a famous *Methodenstreit* or method-conflict that anticipated debates persisting in economics today. They argued that human social phenomena should be studied differently from the phenomena of natural science, especially since in the end social science should result in policy prescriptions and even assessments of justice; but they still held that those social phenomena should be studied by means of careful empirical observation. Social scientists should not be positivists, but they should "leave the *sollen* [or what should be] for a later stage and study the *geschehen* [the facts, what actually happened] as other sciences have done." (Du Bois recorded this aphorism of Schmoller's in his notebook; cited at Broderick 1958: 369 and Appiah 2014: 31.)

In his meticulous studies of such phenomena as black life in the Reconstruction-era South and the 1917 East St. Louis race riot, Du Bois displayed both respect for the facts and Schmoller's kind of effort to understand sympathetically. An example from *Black Reconstruction*:

> "Fifty Dollar reward.—Ran away from the subscriber, his Negro man Pauladore, commonly called Paul. I understand Gen. R. Y. Hayne has purchased his wife and children from H. L. Pinckney, Esq., and has them on his plantation at Goosecreek, where, no doubt, the fellow is frequently lurking. T. Davis." One can see Pauladore "lurking" about his wife and children.
>
> The system of slavery demanded a special police force and such a force was made possible and unusually effective by the presence of the poor whites. This explains the difference between the slave revolts in the West Indies, and the lack of effective revolt in the Southern United States. In the West Indies, the power over the slave was held by the whites and carried out by them and such Negroes as they could trust. In the South, on the other hand, the great planters formed proportionately quite as small a class but they had singularly enough at their command some five million poor whites; that is, there were actually more white people to police the slaves than there were slaves. Considering the economic rivalry of the black and white worker in the North, it would have seemed natural that the poor white would have refused to police the slaves. But two considerations led him in the opposite direction. First of all, it gave him work and some authority as overseer, slave driver, and member of the patrol system. But above and beyond this, it fed his vanity because it associated him with the masters. Slavery bred in the poor white a dislike of Negro toil of all sorts. He never regarded himself as a laborer, or as part of any labor movement. If he had any ambition at all it was to become a planter and to own "niggers." To these Negroes he transferred all the dislike and hatred which he had for the whole slave system. The result was that the system was held stable and intact by the poor white.
>
> (Du Bois 1998: 12)

This historical work conveys facts, but it also deploys irony, drama, and keenly observed accounts of how things seemed to the actors on the scene. *Black Reconstruction* goes on to live up to its somewhat florid subtitle, *An Essay Toward a History of the Part Which Black Folk Played in the Attempt to Reconstruct Democracy in America, 1860–1880*.

But though Du Bois's approach to history and sociology reflects the influence of his German mentors, he found early in his career that even the softer, *geistige* law-seeking the Germans prescribed would not provide the understanding of black life in America that he sought. He asked himself, as he tried to make sense of racial conflict,

> [F]or what Law was I searching? In accord with what unchangeable scientific law of action was the world of interracial discord about me working? I fell back upon my Royce and James and deserted Schmoller and Weber. I saw the action of physical law in the actions of men; but I saw more than that: I saw rhythms and tendencies; coincidences and probabilities; and I saw that, which for want of any other word, I must in accord with the strict tenets of Science, call Chance. I went forward to build a sociology, which I conceived of as the attempt to measure the element of Chance in human conduct. This was the Jamesian pragmatism, applied not simply to ethics, but to all human action, beyond what seemed to me, increasingly, the distinct limits of physical law.
> (2007: 38)

Thus he adopted James's pragmatism and gave up what he understood to be the Germans' search for "Law" in social science. He did not give up trying to be scientific; instead, he adopted a different, more Darwinian account of scientific understanding. He would thus go on to account for black history and life in a new way. He would lay out lots of empirically observed facts, but he would still acknowledge the utter contingencies of human life in society. He would take pains to illustrate something that preceding historical and sociological works had missed or suppressed—namely, the ways black Americans used their particular experiences and shaped, or strived to shape, their lives and communities with their ensuing contingent choices.

Du Bois appreciated what many present-day interpreters of James's pragmatism have not—namely, the whole point of it. James's theory of truth and meaning is above all a way of showing how and why we individual thinkers introduce chance effects into our world. Like nature, we strive to produce novelties that survive, endure, and shape the world so that it contains more fitness. (We strive, as Du Bois says, both voluntarily and involuntarily, though nature always lacks real volitions.) Unless we appreciate the way human thinkers introduce their new, contingent ideas in the hope of finding satisfactory guides to action, we will not really understand what people, and peoples, have done or can do in the world. But we can appreciate this human characteristic, and even in a scientific way, if we take the Darwinian natural-history approach found in James's version of pragmatism. Du Bois went on to do just this in his different kinds of writing.

However, Du Bois did not acknowledge the extent to which this approach to the development of human races was continuous with any kind of biological one. Some of his best-known comments disparage the whole idea of biological race, and he explicitly rejected the mechanistic biology that saw life-processes as inevitable and socio-historical investigation as unnecessary. Did Du Bois perhaps see this kind of mechanism in the law-seeking scientific work of his German teachers? Is this what he was dissenting from when he "fell back upon . . . Royce and James and deserted Schmoller and Weber"?

While Schmoller seems to have persisted in a kind of colonialist social Darwinism, always holding that natural racial characteristics were significantly responsible for the behavior and social plight of the "lowest races" such as blacks (see Zimmerman 2010: 109–110), he still saw cultural, *geistige* phenomena at work in human life generally, and he would have abhorred Spencer's totally mechanistic thinking. And Max Weber and

Dilthey were founders of modern hermeneuticist thought about interpretation. (The essays in Weber 1949 are widely taken to develop the idea of the hermeneutic circle for modern social science; see Dilthey and Jameson 1972 for Dilthey's appropriation of classical and Biblical hermeneutics.) Through their different uses of the concept *Verstehen* or understanding, they marked off human activity as an area of investigation separate from the study of physical necessity. They were thus as opposed as Schmoller to dehumanizing Spencer-like views. What advantage was there, then, in following James instead of Weber? There was one feature of James's approach to scientific thinking that was important to Du Bois and that the German outlook lacked: that was room to draw non-physical, non-physiological *racial* distinctions and discern distinct "spirits," "messages," and "ideals" among the different *races*.

Weber had started out in his early work as a social Darwinist, attributing many of the political and social difficulties of Africans to both the nature and the culture of the Negro. But over time he left his scientific racism behind, and indeed, by the time of his *Economy and Society*, he held that "The whole conception of ethnic groups is so complex and so vague that it might be good to abandon it altogether" (Weber 1978: 385). He did not in fact abandon that concept, and he instead went on to define it explicitly, but his definition was in terms of subjective belief in an imagined origin. An ethnicity was only an identity; it did not constitute "a group with concrete social action" like a kinship group (Weber 1978: 389). Dilthey explicitly depreciated sub- and trans-national groups like families, tribes, and races as factors in the development of nations or peoples, which were the real subjects of historical processes. Thanks to economic, political, and cultural forces, members of the same race might be physically similar while differing profoundly in *Geist*. "[W]hile [genealogically] related peoples show a kinship of somatic types which maintains itself with marvelous constancy, their historical and spiritual physiognomy creates ever more refined differences in all the various spheres of the life of a people" (Dilthey 1991: 92). And, again, Schmoller held on to a scientific racism even as he added cultural factors to his story of human development.

Thus the tendency of the Germans was against the idea of non-physical, socially constructed race as sociologically significant. But Du Bois was determined to describe what the people known as "Negroes" had contributed, and still had to contribute as a family-like group, to the larger human story. He held that "For the development of Negro genius, of Negro literature and art, of Negro spirit, only Negroes bound and welded together, Negroes inspired by one vast ideal, can work out in its fullness the great message we have for humanity" (Du Bois 1970: 79).

The black race was, and should be, bound together by a *history* of which hereditary physical and physiological similarities were merely a "badge." That badge symbolized the "social heritage of slavery; the discrimination and insult" (Du Bois 2007: 59). The English "race" over its history had come to stand for "constitutional liberty and commercial freedom," the Germans for "science and philosophy," the Romance race for "literature and art," and by holding on to and charting their own long-neglected history, the black race would enable itself to make a similar contribution, one involving a unique sensitivity to widely unappreciated injustice. That message would be, in the end, of value to all the races, all the motifs in the human symphony.

Du Bois allowed that the "Negro" categorization, like all similar racial ones, was "inaccurate" (1928: 96–97; cited at Appiah 2014: 158); perhaps no such "black race" existed in extra-conceptual reality, and maybe there was not even a coherent concept of such a group—yet. Du Bois was struggling to create that concept by means of his intellectual life. But somehow, despite this, it seemed clear that all humanity had something important to learn from the black experience of captivity and striving for justice; and the way the world looked through the eyes of "black" people could be lost if that label was.

If we could hold on to that label, we still would not be able to *explain* blackness, but we could hope to *understand* it. We might not be able to account for it even in terms of the psychological laws or universal cultural structures the Germans sometimes aspired to find, but we would begin to see ourselves in the people who found themselves together on a unique journey from slavery to second-class citizenship. (Of course even black people can fail to see this story as their own, so some of them may need to develop this understanding.) And, after developing this sympathy, we will be in a better position to make policy and value judgments concerning the people who have made this journey and who are still on the road.

IV

This last issue is the most important for Du Bois, who wants to learn, for himself and his fellow leaders in the Talented Tenth, how the experiences and choices of blacks have figured in their past survival and might figure in their future. This explains what Kwame Anthony Appiah identifies as Du Bois's internal Methodenstreit, his whiplash between individualism and collectivism. Du Bois is as clear as he can be in rejecting the idea, attributable to "the individualistic philosophy of the Declaration of Independence and the laisser-faire philosophy of Adam Smith," that individuals are at the bottom of historical events; he says that "the Pharaohs, Caesars, Toussaints and Napoleons of history . . . were but epitomized expressions" of their "vast races" (Du Bois 1996: 40). But he nevertheless believes that, thanks to "Chance," no race has a future that is preordained or guaranteed by sociologically discernible laws; thus unless certain talented, educated individuals in the black race choose to take their special leadership role, black ideals are in jeopardy. Moreover, the job of those would-be-great individual leaders will not be that of spreading ideals that all black people, or even the majority, share. Instead, Du Bois's Negro Academy

> seeks to comprise something of the *best* thought, the most unselfish striving and the highest ideals. There are scattered in forgotten nooks and corners throughout the land, Negroes of some considerable training, of high minds, and high motives, who are unknown to their fellows, who exert far too little influence. These the Negro Academy should strive to bring into touch with each other and to give them a common mouthpiece.
>
> (Du Bois 1996: 45)

That is, it should help the leaders develop and promulgate *their* ideas and ideals, at first among other blacks and then among the other races. Maybe those ideals would not have been forged and adopted even by the leaders except in circumstances unique to Africans or their descendants, and maybe they will resonate with other black persons' emotional lives especially or uniquely once word gets out; even so, many of the most important black ideas and ideals have originated, and will originate in the future, in the thoughts of "scattered," neglected individuals.

Of course the Toussaints and Tutankhamens of the world could not have become what they were or done what they did had they either been born to or stayed in total isolation. Neither could the Napoleons, Catherine the Greats, Newtons, or Leonardos. They were special persons, but they could have had all their personal uniqueness and no socio-historical greatness whatever had the societies around them not given them education and assistance—and even resistance, which stopped them from taking the wrong path or toughened them up on the right one. But a community will have needed the contributions of earlier individuals to have those concepts ready to share, and in the future the community will need more new "impulses" of individuals, as James would have put it, to improve or even merely to remain stable in changing circumstances. Thus the relationship between individuals and society is a reciprocal relationship of mutual support, and even mutual creation and re-creation over time. Neither the individual nor society is at the bottom or foundation here; there is no foundational position in this ongoing process.

Individuals in this pragmatic story do not play the role of atomic constituents of society. They are not Schmoller's bugbears, the individual rational actors of classical or neoclassical economics. (Richter 2015: 148–149 distinguishes Schmoller's more sociological understanding of economic actors from that of the "neoinstitutionalists.") Individuals make and remake their societies not by being cog-parts in a machine-whole but by engaging in a *conversation* with that society. They soak up its ideas and share its experiences, they have their own peculiar experiences and distinctive emotional and intellectual reactions, and then they generate and offer new ideas from their eccentric perspectives. Those ideas either meet sympathetic ears and spread through the society or meet scorn and die away. And Du Bois's Talented Tenth is the scattered group of individuals poised to enter this push-and-pull relationship with their society and then perhaps to be acclaimed as great persons of history.

Still, even if great individuals have needed social relationships, did they need relationships to their "races," or their sub- or trans-national ethnic groups? That sounds doubtful if we question whether any such groups are really to be found out there in the world beyond our concepts, and even more so if we question whether there is a clear concept of race to begin with. However, Du Bois's argument for the usefulness of race talk is striking because it is just that—an argument that race labels are useful, strategic, pragmatically necessary. Du Bois says not that those labels carve preexisting human nature at its joints but rather that "the race idea, the race spirit, the race ideal" is the "vastest and most ingenious invention of human progress," or a tool for making lives better in the future.

Whose lives? At first, the label "black" will better the lives of the people who have to ride Jim Crow in Georgia. By accepting this label and resisting motivations to "lose our race identity in the commingled blood of the nation," people now categorized as black will enable themselves to contribute to the "development of Negro genius, of Negro literature and art, of Negro spirit." After that they will live in a better black culture with better leaders. If talented black people refuse to band together under that label, they may go on to be great Mississippians, Americans, or human beings, but there will be no great intellectual or political leaders moving the "black race" forward. Some people will, as a matter of fact, still have to live under that label whether they accept it or not, and they will not progress politically or socially, or at least not as efficiently as they would if they strived together as a "vast family." And in the end that will be too bad not only for black people but also for everyone else. "[T]hat black to-morrow which is yet destined to soften the whiteness of the Teutonic to-day" will not come to pass. If the black "banner" is someday hung on the "broad ramparts of civilizations" "and hallowed by the travail of 200,000,000 black hearts beating in one glad song of jubilee" (Du Bois 1996: 42), then the black wisdom of centuries will be spread among all human beings, providing lessons we can all learn as we create and re-create all the races—including, perhaps, finally, the human race. But if that banner is never hung, that uniquely black wisdom may be lost. Certainly it will not be preserved and spread as determinedly as it would be by people who saw that wisdom and that banner as their own.

V

That is Du Bois's story, anyway, or at least it was in the early and middle periods of his thinking. His later years, as he grew closer to and finally joined the Communist Party, involved different thoughts about race and its relations to economic class. But it is this earlier story, in which the black American "would not bleach his Negro soul in a flood of white Americanism" (1996: 102), that still resonates strongly today. When the much-lauded journalist and commentator Ta-Nehesi Coates says that the American goal now is not to become post-racial but rather post-racist (Coates 2015b), and when Coates insists on the idea that race is a social construction based on historical and present-day sociopolitical realities (Coates 2013), he is seizing racial ideas and using them in something like Du Bois's pragmatic way. Coates's goal has ultimately been the annihilation of racial distinctions rather than the proud hoisting of the black banner, but Du Bois also looked past the culmination of the black cultural story to a social result that benefits all of humanity. (Interestingly, Coates in his latest work has evidently come to regard racial distinctions and white supremacy as indefeasible natural realities. He says of the police who killed a young black friend: "The earthquake cannot be subpoenaed. The typhoon will not bend under indictment." See Coates 2015a: 83; and see Rogers 2015 for a critique in response.)

Du Bois's kind of socio-historical attempt to understand race has faced some ingenious criticism from Kwame Anthony Appiah. He once argued that we cannot define a race in terms of its history any more than we could do the same with a person. We would have to know who a person was before we could identify any bit of history as part of *her* history; analogously, we would have to know which people counted as "white" or "black" before we could identify any historical events as part of white or black history and then use those events in categorizing the white or black race. Of course we would then fall back on biology and physiology in figuring out who is who, and so all attempts to use a historical concept of race for purposes of group solidarity and development will involve reinstituting the scientifically discredited biological conception of race. (Appiah 1985: 26–29). In the end, looking for "black people," even with the best political intentions, is like looking for "witches"—another scientifically discredited concept (Appiah 1989: 40).

But as an undergraduate student once asked me, does this mean we can never identify a group of people using a historical criterion? Do we need an independent criterion to identify groups like "the people who were onboard in the bus crash and their heirs"? So much for class-action lawsuits, if so. And surely something like chattel slavery in the Americas might work just as well to pick out a group of human beings and their kin, ancestors, and descendants. Moreover, we obviously might need to pick out such a group if we want to understand, for example, why some people who share a lot of kinship relations did so much worse materially and politically than others in the post–Civil War South. That kind of investigation is nothing like a witch hunt.

Du Bois does pick out such a group, and he describes this group as wearing, by and large, a "badge" of color that has brought insults and injuries over history. But is he really falling back on laws of biological inheritance, here? He does not make this clear, but he might merely be augmenting his historical criterion with a *typical* visible feature, rather than an essential one, of that historically defined group. Such a feature, created in many but not all group members by hereditary physiology, might be a matter of racial *tendency* rather than essence or definition. (Appiah considers racial characteristics as a matter of tendencies in his discussion of Matthew Arnold at 1998: 55.) Spotting a black person by color might be like spotting an American man by his inability to speak a foreign language and his inclination to tour European cathedrals wearing shorts. Those criteria would be imperfect but reliable and connected with socio-historical causes and consequences.

Of course not all "blacks" have had a visible "badge." Du Bois certainly knew that some have had no trouble "passing" for white. And there have even been the odd cases in which some people, because of the cultural roles they played, have, either intentionally or by accident, wound up candidates for the designation "black" though they had no (recent) African ancestors at all. (Wayne Joseph and doubtless others came before Rachel Dolezal. See Kaplan 2003 and Holloway 2015 for stories of these two crossers of racial boundaries.) Hence the boundaries of the socio-historical category "black," very imperfectly indicated by the hereditary badge of color, will be fuzzy and constested. Still, the vexedness of this category is not exactly news, and an account of it that is not itself somewhat vexed should cause even more suspicion than the category.

In any case, Appiah has, over the years, reconsidered the idea that a socio-historical understanding of race requires reinstituting a biological account. He has allowed more recently that it is possible to think of race-labels as categories something like "Irish-American," "Yankees fan" and "member of my bowling league," which band people together benignly by shared social interests alone. The problem, he notes, is that while race-labels can have this kind of "recreational" use, they also have a bad tendency to "go imperial" and demand recognition whether they are doing us good or not (Appiah 1998: 101–104). We should therefore be ready to throw them overboard when they become more trouble than they are worth.

Since race is the issue, however, and we are therefore talking about questions of human dignity and political and economic justice over centuries, "recreational" will not really be the best term for these labels and their use. If Du Bois is right, black folks' "glad song of jubilee" will commemorate matters of life and death, unlike "Here Come the Yankees." Fortunately there is a better term waiting, a better way of describing the use to which we can put the concept of blackness even though it picks out nothing pre-classified by nature. Thinking in James's terms, we can think of race-talk not merely as "recreational" but as "practical" or "pragmatic."

Perhaps this was what Du Bois was doing when he embraced "the Jamesian pragmatism" and set out to leave his German teachers behind. He had come to believe that racial concepts were valuable because they were tools we human beings could use with the goal, conscious or unconscious, of changing the world and bettering our lives. But how could a categorizing term make life better without reflecting pre-existing realities? Maybe, indeed, in something like the way "Yankees fan" does it: by creating and then increasing local human solidarity, then contributing to a more complex solidarity with fans of the other teams. Thus Appiah is right to see a parallel here; "recreational" value is in the end one kind of "pragmatic" value. But there are other kinds, and thus there are still more helpful analogies to draw.

"American," is, I think, one such analogous label, even if "Irish-American" is not. "American," like "black," has often been a matter of life and death, so it seems inapt to think of it as a merely recreational identity. But it should still not be allowed to "go imperial," since it marks no real, intrinsic, essential quality in its wearers and since other identifying qualities can be just as important, or even more important, to their possessors. Some people are stuck with that label at birth as a matter of whom they are born to, but they can renounce it. (Other people will still use it to categorize them whether they like it or not, though, just as people will still find themselves being labeled "black" whether they like it or not.) Alternatively people can choose to embrace that label and wear it with other "Americans" in a large, scattered locality. Bound together under that label they may devise and achieve a unique set of American ideals, even if some Americans belong to subgroups and transnational groups that have their own distinct ideals to work on at the same time. After all, subgroups working in harmony for the greater good is what the big experiment known as the United States of America is all about. *E pluribus unum*, and all that; this is a country designed around the project of sharing multiple identities. And if Americans who do not share all their identities in common someday find a way to work together and also to live peacefully among other nations, contributing as a group to worldwide happiness—don't laugh, it could happen—then that label will also have been of value to humanity at large.

When Du Bois compared blacks to the German and English "races," perhaps he was showing that he would have drawn an analogy like this one. If so, we might describe him as a kind of black nationalist as well as a social constructionist. Without advocating the development of a black homeland with borders, an army, and a bicameral legislature, he did want to encourage black people to think of themselves as a distinct nation in a looser sense, maybe the same sense James had in mind when he used the terms "race," "community," and "nation" more or less interchangeably. If so, then we might reasonably say that James and Du Bois shared a pragmatic picture of "races" as phenomena that make a kind of Darwinian scientific sense.

However, considering the damage to humanity that the idea of race has done over the centuries, we may wonder whether scientific credibility is enough of an excuse to keep lugging this super-explosive device around in our conceptual toolkit. Racial thinking can not only go imperial, it can go nuclear. Why, then, risk making things still worse than they are? Du Bois will respond that his kind of scientific-yet-sympathetic racial sociology can be useful in a large project not only of recreation but of re-creation, of taking a despised group and remodeling it into even more of a political, social, and cultural force than it has been so far. It will do this partly by making that group aware of its own power and partly by helping members of other groups understand the people they despise.

Of course we do not get to know with certainty and in advance whether this kind of thinking will, on balance, pay off. Certainly we have seen plenty of deadly conflicts among the "families," "peoples," and "nations" to which Du Bois compares races, and a conflict among nations once *literally* went nuclear. Nevertheless, we are disinclined to get rid of nation-talk or family-talk, since many if not all of the greatest and most beneficial accomplishments in human history have been made by individuals operating, and cooperating, in groups like these. A pragmatist about race may therefore recommend that we run some risk and try a hopeful experiment, keeping the black community, family, people, nation, or race together long enough so that, thanks in part to the remarkable individual leaders it contains, it can make its contribution to the human conversation, or rather carry on contributing. Especially under new conditions of sympathetic understanding, despite the evil that has been done in the name of race, and despite the evident fact that races are made as much as found, this experiment—like the American experiment—remains a reasonable thing to try.

References

Allen, Grant. (1878) "Nation Making." *Popular Science Monthly Supplement* 13–20: 121–127.
Appiah, Kwame Anthony. (1985) "The Uncompleted Argument: Du Bois and the Illusion of Race," in Henry Louis Gates (ed.), *Race, Writing, and Difference*, Chicago: University of Chicago Press.
———. (1989) "The Conservation of 'Race.'" *Black American Literature Forum* 23, no. 1: 37–60.
———. (1998) *Color Conscious: The Political Morality of Race*, Princeton: Princeton University Press.
———. (2014) *Lines of Descent: The W.E.B. Du Bois Lectures*. Cambridge, MA: Harvard University Press.
Broderick, Francis L. (1958) "German Influence on the Scholarship of W.E.B. Du Bois." *Phylon* 19, no. 4: 367–371.
Coates, Ta-Nehesi. (2013) "What We Mean When We Say 'Race Is a Social Construct.'" *Atlantic*. Accessed July 30, 2015. www.theatlantic.com/national/archive/2013/05/what-we-mean-when-we-say-race-is-a-social-construct/275872/
———. (2015a) *Between the World and Me*, New York: Spiegel & Grau.
———. (2015b) "There Is No Post-Racial America." *Atlantic*. Accessed July 30, 2015. www.theatlantic.com/magazine/archive/2015/07/post-racial-society-distant-dream/395255/
Cormier, Harvey. (2000) *The Truth Is What Works: William James, Pragmatism, and the Seed of Death*, Lanham: Rowman & Littlefield.
Dilthey, Wilhelm, and Jameson, Frederic. (1972 [1900]). "The Rise of Hermeneutics." *New Literary History* 3, no. 2: 229–244.
———. (1990 [1894]) *Die geistige Welt: Einleitung in die Philosophie des Lebens: Gesammelte Schriften V*, ed. G. Misch, Göttingen: Vandenhoeck & Ruprecht.
———. (1991 [1883]) *Introduction to the Human Sciences: Selected Works*, Vol. 1, ed. Rudolf A. Makkreel and Frithjof Rodi, Princeton: Princeton University Press.
———. (2010 [1887–1911]). *Understanding the Human World: Selected Works*, Vol. 2, ed. Rudolph A. Makreel and Frithjof Rodi, Princeton: Princeton University Press.
Du Bois, W.E.B. (1928) "The Name 'Negro.'" *Crisis* (March): 96–97.
———. (1944) "My Evolving Program for Negro Freedom," in Rayford W. Logan (ed.), *What the Negro Wants*, Chapel Hill: University of North Carolina Press.
———. (1970 [1897]) *W.E.B. Du Bois Speaks: Speeches and Addresses, 1890–1919*, ed. Philip S. Foner. New York: Pathfinder.
———. (1996) *The Oxford W.E.B. Du Bois Reader*, ed. Eric J. Sundquist. Oxford: Oxford University Press.
———. (1998 [1935]) *Black Reconstruction: An Essay Toward a History of the Part Which Black Folk Played in the Attempt to Reconstruct Democracy in America, 1860–1880*, New York: Free Press.
———. (2007 [1940]) *Dusk of Dawn: An Essay Toward an Autobiography of a Race Concept*, Oxford: Oxford University Press.

Hacking, Ian. (2005) "Why Race Still Matters." *Daedalus* 134: 102–116.

Holloway, Kali. (2015) "Why It Was So Easy for Rachel Dolezal to Slip Into Black Skin." *Alternet*. Accessed July 30, 2015. www.alternet.org/why-it-was-so-easy-rachel-dolezal-slip-black-skin.

James, William. (1978 [1907]) *Pragmatism and the Meaning of Truth*. Cambridge, MA: Harvard University Press.

———. (1979 [1897]) *The Will to Believe and Other Essays in Popular Philosophy*, Cambridge, MA: Harvard University Press.

Kaplan, Erin Aubry. (2003) "Black Like I Thought I Was." *Alternet*. Accessed July 30, 2015. www.alternet.org/story/16917/black_like_i_thought_i_was.

Kitcher, Philip. (2012) *Preludes to Pragmatism: Toward a Reconstruction of Philosophy*, Oxford: Oxford University Press.

McKie, Robin. (2006) "The Ant King's Latest Mission." Accessed July 28, 2015. www.theguardian.com/world/2006/oct/01/usa.science.

Peirce, C. S. (2009 [1890–1892]) *Writings of Charles S. Peirce: A Chronological Edition*, Vol. 8. Bloomington: Indiana University Press.

Rogers, Melvin L. (2015) "Between Pain and Despair: What Ta-Nehisi Coates Is Missing." *Dissent*. Accessed August 1, 2015. www.dissentmagazine.org/online_articles/between-world-me-ta-nehisi-coates-review-despair-hope.

Richter, Rudolf. (2015) *Essays on New Institutional Economics*, Cham: Springer.

Rushton, J. Philippe. (1995) *Race, Evolution, and Behavior*, New Brunswick: Transaction Press.

Spencer, Herbert. (1961 [1874]) *The Study of Sociology*, Ann Arbor: University of Michigan Press.

———. (1978 [1897]) *The Principles of Ethics*, Vol. I. Indianapolis: Liberty Classics.

Wallace, Alfred Russel. (1883). *The Malay Archipelago: The Land of the Orang-utan and the Birds of Paradise: A Narrative of Travel, With Studies of Man and Nature*. New York: Palgrave Macmillan.

Weber, Max. (1949 [1903–1917]) *The Methodology of the Social Sciences*, New York: Free Press.

———. (1978 [1922]) *Economy and Society: An Outline of Interpretive Sociology*, Berkeley: University of California Press.

Zimmerman, Andrew. (2010) *Alabama in Africa: Booker T. Washington, the German Empire, and the Globalization of the New South*, Princeton: Princeton University Press.

17
PHENOMENOLOGY AND RACE (OR RACIALIZING PHENOMENOLOGY)
Gail Weiss

Fanon's Phenomenological Challenge

The major influence that the phenomenological concepts introduced in the early twentieth century by Edmund Husserl had upon many of the most famous philosophers of the twentieth century, including Martin Heidegger, Jean-Paul Sartre, Simone de Beauvoir, and Maurice Merleau-Ponty, has been well documented. Although each of these thinkers took up and transformed Husserlian phenomenology in remarkably innovative and productive ways, the publication in 1952 of Frantz Fanon's *Peau noire, masques blancs* (*Black Skin, White Masks*) broke new ground in its revolutionary application and critique of Husserl's phenomenological method. Indeed, the philosophical upheaval produced by this amazing text continues unabated today, over a half century after its original publication. More specifically, Fanon's work has played a central role in inaugurating what Lisa Guenther calls a "critical phenomenology," a rigorous philosophical mode of inquiry that abandons the meta-level of "pure" subjective description advocated by Husserl, and directly addresses the constitutive social, political, psychological, economic, historical, and cultural dimensions of the phenomena under investigation. As Guenther observes, "[b]y critical phenomenology I mean a method that is rooted in first-person accounts of experience but also critical of classical phenomenology's claim that the first-person singular is absolutely prior to intersubjectivity and the complex textures of social life" (Guenther 2013: xiii)." Subjectivity, critical phenomenologists emphasize, develops *in and through* our intersubjective experiences, not apart from them. Thus, there is no way to inoculate one's own first-person perspective from the influences of others since the former is always already mediated by the social world(s) in which one lives. This core insight regarding the essential intersubjective dimensions of subjectivity, while implicit in Husserl's own work, has played a central role in phenomenological accounts such as Fanon's that seek to address the first-person experience of racial oppression.

Fanon's emphasis upon the formative role others play in an individual's psychic development can be traced not only to his formal psychoanalytic training but also to his distinctive experience growing up as a colonized subject in the French Antilles. While some of his philosophical contemporaries, including Beauvoir and Merleau-Ponty, also insist upon the interdependency of self and other, there are at least two reasons why Fanon's work constitutes such a radical phenomenological intervention with profound implications for critical race theory. The first is his definitive rejection of a central tenet of Husserlian phenomenology, namely, the possibility of providing "neutral" or universal descriptions of the phenomena one is examining that would hold true for all possible subjects. Indeed, through his searing descriptions of the systematic, daily dehumanization he and other native Martinicians suffer at the hands of their French colonizers, Fanon powerfully undermines Husserl's overly confident claim that

> All that which holds for me myself holds, as I know, for all other human beings whom I find present in my surrounding world. Experiencing them as human beings, I understand and accept each of them as an Ego-subject just as I myself am one and as related to this natural surrounding world.
> (Husserl 1982: 55)

Rather than simply rejecting Husserl's uncritical presumption that each human being we encounter is understood and accepted by us "as an Ego-subject just as I myself am one," Fanon presents this affirmation of our equal humanity as a regulative ideal that unfortunately is often belied by the dehumanizing treatment many human beings have suffered (and continue to suffer) at the hands (and in the minds) of others. Thus, what is for Husserl a fairly straightforward factual statement that grounds his universal claims regarding the essential features of human consciousness, is problematized by Fanon as a hasty assertion that has more frequently been deployed to justify the exclusion of some people from the domain of the human as opposed to placing all human beings on an equal footing. For, as Fanon poignantly observes: "if equality among men is proclaimed in the name of intelligence and philosophy, it is also true that those concepts have been used to justify the extermination of men" (Fanon 2008: 12).

Beauvoir's groundbreaking, interdisciplinary analysis of women's oppression under patriarchy in *The Second Sex*, which appeared three years prior to *Black Skin, White Masks*, also provides a serious departure from and challenge to the (allegedly) universal phenomenological descriptions of consciousness, being-in-the-world, freedom, and perception offered by Husserl, Heidegger, Sartre, and Merleau-Ponty, and in so doing, it provides an important precedent for Fanon's own account (Beauvoir 2010). While this text includes both fictional and non-fictional accounts of women's distinctive experiences within a male-dominated society, Beauvoir does not offer the reader personal anecdotes of her own sexist treatment as a (white) woman in a (white) man's world; instead, she utilizes the same dispassionate language employed by classical phenomenologists to describe women's experience as "the second sex." Rather than indicting Beauvoir for not being radical enough, however, it is crucial to recognize that one of the reasons that *The Second Sex* was and remains such an important text is precisely *because* she deploys classical phenomenological tools to address a decidedly non-traditional subject, namely women's second-class status under patriarchy. Thus, while her controversial topic, like Fanon's, marks a definitive departure from the "typical" phenomenological analysis provided by her peers, and, in so doing, helps pave the way for the latter's work since she also focuses directly on the internalization of oppression and the resultant damage done to one's self-understanding, relations with others, and life aspirations, her philosophical style, or manner of writing about these important issues, adheres more closely to established philosophical conventions.

Rejecting Beauvoir's strategy of pairing an unconventional topic with a more impersonal style, Fanon offers his readers a visceral, autobiographical account of the irreversible psychic, linguistic, familial, cultural, educational, and economic damage wrought by the legally sanctioned domination of one set of human beings, who are deemed to be irredeemably inferior, by another. This is a second reason why his work has played such a crucial role in the development of a new, critical phenomenology of race. Fanon's brutally honest, first-person descriptions of the evils of anti-black racism, like those more recently offered by American critical race phenomenologist George Yancy and others, make ethical demands upon their readers, calling upon them to recognize their own ignorance of and responsibility for the perpetuation of racism. By rejecting altogether the separation of "pure" phenomenological descriptions from the urgent social, political, and profoundly ethical issues that are inevitably raised by them, Fanon's work charts a new course for phenomenology, namely as an indispensable ally in the struggle for social justice.

Denaturalizing the Natural Attitude

To do full justice to the influence that Husserlian phenomenology, which seeks to provide comprehensive, unbiased, first-person descriptions of lived experience, has had upon critical race theory, as well as the profound impact that critical race theory, with its powerful revelations concerning the lived experience of racism, has had upon phenomenology, it is helpful to turn to two of the most problematic, yet most important phenomenological concepts introduced by Edmund Husserl to describe the aim and method of his new philosophy in his classic 1913 text, *Ideas Pertaining to a Pure Phenomenology and to a Phenomenological Philosophy*, namely, "the natural attitude" and the "phenomenological reduction [epoché]." "The natural attitude" is a paradoxical expression in its own right, for in a crucial sense it is not natural at all. Rather, it consists of tacitly accepted and thoroughly *naturalized* beliefs, behaviors, value judgments, and affective responses that an individual gradually acquires through her daily intersubjective experiences from her earliest childhood. Though it is critical race and feminist theorists rather than Husserl who develop the rich implications of this point, his own descriptions of the "givenness" of the natural attitude make it clear that it is not innate, "hardwired," or pre-determined in any way, but instead is a thoroughly historical, culturally variable, socially constructed, and extremely complex phenomenon that becomes sedimented over time into a typical or habitual orientation toward the world. As such, it is relatively stable, functioning in the background of our experience to establish the parameters for what is viewed as normal, natural, and desirable. And yet, as history has shown us, in the face of unfamiliar or extraordinary experiences that defy or even rupture the complacency of the natural attitude, it also has the potential to undergo radical transformation, an alteration that, depending on the severity, duration, and public attention associated with the atypical event, is capable of affecting it permanently, for better or worse.

The possibility of fundamentally changing the natural attitude by expanding the horizons of what counts as "normal" or "familiar" is not taken up by Husserl. It is this latter possibility, however, that critical race, feminist, and disabilities studies scholars have seized upon, leaving traditional, Husserlian phenomenology, with its goal of pure description, and its failure to acknowledge sufficiently the determining role that social and material conditions play in establishing natural attitudes in the first place, definitively behind. And yet, at the same time, Husserl's insistence upon the crucial importance of providing comprehensive, unbiased descriptions of lived experience that take us beyond the limits of our natural attitudes to the truths revealed by "the things themselves" remains, I would argue, the indispensable first step in recognizing and ultimately eliminating racism, sexism, ableism, and other unjustifiable prejudices from our own natural attitudes.

As critical race theorists, feminist theorists, and Marxist theorists have forcefully demonstrated, an individual's natural attitude reflects her racial, sexual, gender, class, and other social identities. Whether these identities are embraced, contested, or unacknowledged, whether they are sites of privilege or marginalization, if they play a central role in a person's life then they will undoubtedly shape her natural attitude, although the respective influences of an individual's multiple and disparate identities upon her natural attitude will inevitably vary from person to person and context to context. What *can* be considered natural about the natural attitude from a Husserlian perspective, despite its contingency, relativity, and conventionality, is that it enables us to take the existence of the world, ourselves, and others for granted, without explicit reflection, as we go about our daily lives. Another important reason why the natural attitude is understood by Husserl to be natural is that it emerges organically over time and across space in and through an individual's mundane interactions with others, eventually providing a (more or less) reliable framework that establishes a person's "normal" expectations for herself, others, and the more general world of her concern. Insofar as it provides the basic presuppositions or "default" perspective that each of us brings to bear on our respective situations, it largely functions in the background, shaping the meaning we give to our experiences on an ongoing basis, most often without our explicit notice. Indeed, if we do reflect upon the natural attitude and the way it tacitly establishes our sense of the familiar, we are no longer operating within it, but, in fact, performing what Husserl calls the phenomenological reduction, which involves re-examining the familiar world from a fresh perspective, or as if we were experiencing it for the first time.

Though we all leave the perspective of the natural attitude from time to time, whether voluntarily or involuntarily, especially when we confront situations that defy our pre-established expectations, it is the philosopher who seeks to systematically examine the presuppositions that underpin the natural attitude from this altered perspective. More specifically, it is only by willfully detaching oneself from the comfort provided by the natural attitude, Husserl suggests, that the phenomenologist can provide a comprehensive and essential description of one or more aspects of our lived experience without relying on taken-for-granted assumptions about it. In order to accomplish this goal, he asserts, a person must undertake the phenomenological reduction, a systematic, reflective activity which involves "bracketing" or "suspending" the familiar, everyday world presented through the natural attitude, a world, he tells us, that "is there for me not only as a world of mere things, but also *with the same immediacy* as a world of objects with values, a world of goods, a practical world" (Husserl 1982: 53; emphasis added). Comparing this method to that of Descartes, who claims over 200 years earlier at the outset of *The Meditations* to have freed himself from the cultural, historical, scientific, and personal values, biases, and predilections that had previously guided his understanding of himself, others, and the world, Husserl maintains that the phenomenologist can, with a similar effort, describe "the things themselves" without presuppositions, thereby arriving at an essential understanding of them that can in turn be verified by any other person employing the same method.

Both Husserl's and Descartes's very optimistic conviction that a person can (albeit only after serious mental exertion), set aside her familiar or "taken-for-granted" perspective on some aspect of her lived experience in order to provide an essential description of it that would hold true for any other individual has been challenged not only by phenomenologists, critical race theorists, feminist theorists, queer theorists, and disability studies scholars, but also by a wealth of empirical evidence, including the conflicting testimonies of witnesses to a given event who are asked to provide an unbiased, detailed description of exactly what happened. While witness testimonies are often requested or even demanded by others in the immediate aftermath of unanticipated, extremely traumatic incidents such as violent crimes, contexts that differ quite radically from Descartes's voluntary choice to dispassionately examine his former beliefs in his comfortable armchair by the fire or Husserl's own investigation of the essential structure of human consciousness in his home study, the goal in each of these cases remains basically the same, namely, to provide an in-depth, first-person account of an episode or phenomenon that is, at least in principle, intersubjectively verifiable.

Even though several extremely persuasive criticisms have been and continue to be made regarding Husserl's presumption that it is possible to bracket and "put out of play" the habitual presuppositions and value judgments that underpin one's own natural attitude, the aim of providing just such an unbiased description of the familiar world by attending to features of it that typically escape one's notice precisely *because* they are so familiar, has remained a persistent and powerful regulative ideal in phenomenology as well as in critical race theory, feminist theory, disability studies, queer theory, decolonial studies, and other fields that, in contrast to traditional Husserlian phenomenology, do not restrict themselves to the admittedly important labor of description, but rather seek to *improve* the basic social, political, historical, and material conditions that have such a major impact on what an individual accepts as natural in the first place. In fact, I would argue, the goal of providing an unbiased description of a person's, group's or community's lived experiences could not be more pressing if one is seeking to identify and ultimately combat the familiar and painful experiences of marginalization and oppression that so forcefully impact the natural attitudes of underprivileged people but that are often invisible to those who enjoy racial, sexual, class, able-bodied, and/or other cultural advantages.

While many of Husserl's critics have remained skeptical of his claim that phenomenology can be practiced as rigorously as any of the natural sciences because the former relies so heavily upon the subjective experience of a given individual who must make a personal effort to suspend customary or habitual ways of understanding her experience in order to re-examine it from a new, unfamiliar perspective, Husserl frequently reminds his readers that every "objective" scientific investigation also depends upon the subjectivity of the observer to carry it out and verify it, and thus there is no way to bypass our subjective experience in order to arrive at objective truths about the world in which we live; indeed, the former is the only means of accessing and identifying the latter. Husserl thus affirms the primacy of the first-person, subjective perspective as the foundation of all knowledge claims whatsoever, a core claim that is also embraced by critical race as well as feminist activists and theorists. And yet to say that we can't transcend or escape our subjective perspective whether we are doing science or phenomenology is not to say that the first-person perspective is itself infallible, nor does it imply that it is solipsistic or formed in isolation from others. On the contrary, Husserl emphasizes that each person's subjective experience is itself undergirded by a "zone of indeterminacy," namely, historical, cultural, temporal, spatial, and thoroughly intersubjective "horizons" that we continuously draw upon to make sense of ourselves, others, and the world that we share. The goal of the phenomenological reduction, Husserl suggests, is to render these multiple horizons and the constitutive role they play in framing our expectations for a particular experience visible, in all of their indeterminacy. And, it is the impossibility of achieving this goal due to the essential indeterminacy of these horizons that leads Maurice Merleau-Ponty to famously declare in the preface to his 1945 *Phenomenology of Perception*, that "the most important lesson of the reduction is the impossibility of a complete reduction" (Merleau-Ponty 2012: lxxvii). For Merleau-Ponty, however, this is not intended to be a fatal critique of Husserl or of phenomenology, but rather a guarantee that the phenomenologist's work is never done, since new perspectives can always be taken up with respect to a given phenomenon, yielding in turn new insights on the subject in question.

What, we might ask, do these Husserlian claims about the method and goals of phenomenology have to do with race? Nothing and everything, it would seem. Nothing, because Husserl never discusses race, much less acknowledges that an individual's racial identity (whether actively embraced or contested), as well as her gender, sexuality, class, and bodily abilities, can profoundly affect her life experiences, and in turn, her subjective perspective, thereby seeming to threaten the possibility of arriving at universal descriptions of the phenomena we encounter that would hold true for all of us regardless of where, when, and how we live. Everything, because Husserl's account of the "natural attitude" or the "default," familiar perspective that most of us adopt most of the time in our lives is, as previously noted, itself profoundly influenced by an individual's racial as well as sexual, class, religious, national, and other identities, identities that are largely determined for us by others even as we each embody and modify (or, as Judith Butler notes in *Gender Trouble* and *Bodies That Matter*, fail to embody or modify) them in our own idiosyncratic ways. While it seems evident on Husserl's own account that even two family members' natural attitudes will not be identical insofar as each possesses her own subjective perspective and has had unique experiences, it is also the case that one's natural attitude is never constructed *ex nihilo* by a single individual operating independently of others. Moreover, the crucial question of whether we can indeed bracket our (not so natural) natural attitudes and the prejudices that form them, putting them "out of play" in order to provide neutral, intersubjectively valid descriptions of "the things themselves" as Husserl himself sought to do, is itself an extremely controversial issue with profound implications for *both* contemporary phenomenology and critical race theory. Indeed, it is this very Husserlian project of suspending the natural attitude, with all of its attendant difficulties, that marks not only the limits but also the promise of phenomenology for contemporary critical race theory.

Racist Legacies: Constrained Horizons and Compromised Bodily Agency

In his 1945 *Phenomenology of Perception*, Merleau-Ponty emphasizes the central role our bodies play in all aspects of our lived experience. Not only are our bodies mobile perceptual agents (or "body-subjects") in their own right but we also communicate with others and the world *through* our bodies via both non-verbal and verbal gestures. Our bodies, Merleau-Ponty repeatedly suggests, are what anchor us within the world, establishing our unique place in it and our perceptual orientation toward it. Furthermore, our concrete bodily presence within the world is precisely what enables us to be perceived and responded to by others, which in turn affects not only how we perceive and respond to them but also how we view and understand ourselves. Moreover, as Adrienne Rich, Luce Irigaray, Julia Kristeva, and other feminist theorists have pointed out, our bodily interactions with others precede our explicit awareness of them since they are already taking place in utero. Indeed, as numerous empirical studies have amply illustrated, we can be harmed or benefitted by the actions of others and our material environments before we are even born.

Despite his welcome insistence upon the central role others, our social class, and our larger cultures play in shaping the gestures we use, the attitudes we adopt, and the perspectives we develop in our lives, Merleau-Ponty, like Husserl (and unlike Sartre, whose character Garcin famously declares in *No Exit* that "hell is other people"), offers far too rosy a picture of our relations with others, presenting them most often in an enabling light that encourages bodily agency rather than a disabling one that inhibits it. For instance, in the chapter, "The Body as Expression, and Speech," Merleau-Ponty declares:

> Communication or the understanding of gestures is achieved through the reciprocity between my intentions and the other person's gestures, and between my gestures and the intentions which can be read in the other person's behavior. Everything happens as if the other person's intention inhabited my body, or as if my intentions inhabited his body. The gesture I witness sketches out the first signs of an intentional object. This object becomes present and is fully understood when the powers of my body adjust to it and fit over it. The gesture is in front of me like a question, it indicates to me specific sensible points in the world and invites me to join it there. Communication is accomplished when my behavior finds in this pathway its own pathway. I confirm the other person and the other person confirms me.
>
> (Merleau-Ponty 2012: 190–191)

In contrast to the rich possibilities for individual and community development that would presumably flow from this mutually beneficial, embodied exchange between self and other is the undeniable fact that, as Fanon, Beauvoir, Iris Marion Young, Robert Murphy, and so many other critical race, feminist, and disability theorists have demonstrated, it is incompatible with the actual conditions of domination that have defined the parameters of "normal" existence for the majority of human beings in the past, the present, and the foreseeable future. Indeed, this reciprocal, embodied affirmation of oneself by another has historically not been a universal human birthright which we all enjoy equally throughout our lives, but a *privilege* that is extended to some bodies (e.g., white, male, heterosexual bodies) more than others. And, it is precisely this recognition of the unequal and unjust treatment suffered by so many people because of their presumed racial, gender, sexual, and other "deficiencies," that continues to provide the strongest possible ethical motivation for critical phenomenology today.

To contest Merleau-Ponty's very positive phenomenological description of intersubjective communication, as critical race, feminist, and disability theorists have done, however, is not to dispute that this would indeed be a very desirable state of affairs if it actually obtained; rather, the critique concerns the fact that Merleau-Ponty's vision of an interpersonal harmony of intentions in which "I confirm the other person and the other person confirms me" is not an accurate description of reality. Instead, it is a white, male philosopher's fantasy that is erroneously (wishfully?) presented as a fait accompli. And even if this is a *good* fantasy that might be held up as an ethical ideal we should all be striving for in our embodied exchanges with others, by failing to acknowledge how often such a mutual affirmation of self and other is belied by the inhuman treatment people inflict upon one another every day, as well as by the structural inequalities that actively constrain our horizons of possibility and compromise bodily agency, the phenomenologist fails to do justice to the very phenomena she seeks to describe.

Fanon concludes *Black Skin, White Masks* with a dream of a new social order defined by relations of discovery and desire rather than subjugation. The bright future he envisions clearly resonates with the mutually affirming forms of human communication proffered by Merleau-Ponty, yet, unlike Merleau-Ponty, Fanon never presents this currently unachievable reality as a description of our everyday relations with others. "I, a man of color," he tells us, "want but one thing":

> May man never be instrumentalized. May the subjugation of man by man— that is to say, of me by another—cease. May I be allowed to discover and desire man wherever he may be.
>
> (Fanon 2008: 206)

As Fanon and critical race phenomenologists well realize, obtaining this wish requires that it must also become the wish of the colonizers who have profited for centuries from the economic, social, political, cultural, psychological, and material oppression of other human beings. For, as history teaches us, the collective refusal of colonized peoples to accept their inferior status, though crucial, is almost never sufficient to bring about fundamental changes in the prevailing natural attitude that normalizes relationships of domination between colonizer and colonized. To convince those people who have benefited from existing social and political structures because they are members of the dominant race, gender, religion, and so forth, to acknowledge and make amends for their unearned privileges through a de-naturalization of their natural attitudes, is a tall order. Indeed, as critical race, feminist, and disabilities activists and scholars have shown us, it requires a variety of overlapping strategies that work best in conjunction with one another, not alone.

The multiple methods critical race theorists have employed both to draw attention to, and to help end our long sordid history of racial subjugation include (but are by no means restricted to) identifying and combating controlling images of black people and other racial minorities (Fanon, Collins, Gordon); exposing the racist horizons that tacitly structure our perceptions from earliest infancy (Butler, Ahmed); encouraging the cultivation of anti-racist habits of perception (Al-Saji, Fielding); deconstructing the reductive effects of a hegemonic black-white binary that fails to do justice to the complexity of racial identities (Alcoff, Cho); embracing the unique, non-normative perspectives that flow from mixed and/or multiple identities (Lorde, Anzaldua, Ortega);

interrogating how racist institutional structures, such as the prison-industrial complex, disproportionately target black people and other racial minorities, consigning many prisoners to a "social death" that simultaneously stigmatizes (and often impoverishes) their families (Davis, Alexander, Guenther, Sheth, Coates); advocating the expansion of our racial, cultural, temporal, spatial, and class-bound horizons through boundary-crossing experiences such as "world"-travelling (Lugones); and illuminating how taken-for-granted assumptions such as ontological expansiveness, or the idea that white people are entitled to enter any space they choose, actively, yet often invisibly, advantages white people (especially educated white men) and simultaneously threatens countless other people, many of whom have paid with their lives, for either deliberately or inadvertently presuming to share the spatial trappings of white privilege (Sullivan, Young, Yancy).

To end racist, sexist, ableist, and other forms of discriminatory treatment, whether by people, communities, and nations, and/or by educational, social, and political, institutions, critical phenomenologists suggest, we must examine not only specific racist structures and incidents, but also the familiar, taken-for-granted assumptions that are tacitly operative in our lived experience, influencing how, when, why, where, and with whom people interact as well as the significance both individuals and societies attribute to these encounters. Although several of the authors I have cited above are not ordinarily regarded as phenomenologists or directly associated with the phenomenological tradition, their work, I am suggesting, directly advances a critical phenomenology of race insofar as they seek to describe, accurately, comprehensively, and in as unbiased a manner as possible, the racial identities, racial prejudices, racist perceptions, racist institutions, and the subtle as well as unsubtle varieties of racist oppression that are operative in our everyday lived experience. Controlling images of racial groups, sedimented habits of racial privilege, racist perceptual horizons, denigrated racial identities, and internalized racial inferiority, these critical race scholars show us, are not esoteric or ephemeral phenomena but pervasive, structural components of our natural attitudes, despite the fact that they have historically escaped the radar of the white, male phenomenologists who are credited with establishing this dynamic field of inquiry.

The task of phenomenology, as Husserl first articulates it, is to provide essential descriptions of "the things themselves," which in turn requires an examination of the spatial, temporal, perceptual, linguistic, cultural, and social horizons that serve to contextualize and normalize them. Clearly, the largely unarticulated and unquestioned presuppositions that underpin our racialized natural attitudes, our racial identities, our racial interactions, and the racial worlds we inhabit are urgently in need of this type of phenomenological attention, even as we recognize that these phenomena are never uniform in their appearance or effects but are experienced differently by each of us, in varied times and spaces, depending on our own relative positioning in the prevailing social hierarchy.

The detailed, moving, and often painful accounts of the lived experience of racial oppression offered by critical race phenomenologists not only provide corrective descriptions of social reality that present it as it truly is, and not as we might wish it could be, but also help to fulfill a pressing ethical and political imperative, namely, to provide a full accounting of the deleterious effects of racial injustice so that we can deploy more productive strategies for its eradication in the future. It is noteworthy that many (though not all) of the strategies critical race phenomenologists offer appear to be negative, that is, they involve things we need to *stop* doing in order to de-naturalize oppressive natural attitudes as well as oppressive behaviors and institutions. And, while the list of behaviors, perceptions, identities, stereotypes, and social, legal, and educational institutions that need to be fundamentally altered to combat racial ignorance, unearned racial privileges, racial hierarchies, and the ubiquity of racial oppression seems to get longer by the day, it is also important to remember, as Alcoff argues in *The Future of Whiteness*, that:

> because racial concepts are social, ideas about particular races can change pretty radically in different social contexts, across time and space, both in terms of the *content* of the ideas and in terms of how this particular content is *valued*. Nothing about our social identities is absolutely fixed.
> (Alcoff 2015: 39)

Lest we are tempted, however, to appeal too hastily to the concrete ways in which people's racial identities have changed over time, to the fact that these are dynamic, not static phenomena, in an attempt to minimize the guilt and shame we may feel concerning our own racial ignorance and racial responsibilities, the active persecution of an ever-growing number of racial minorities in the twenty-first century serves as a palpable reminder that not every change is for the better. Moreover, we must continue to contend with one of the major barriers to eliminating racist oppression once and for all, namely, as Mills, Sullivan, and many other critical race theorists have pointed out, the fact that it so frequently operates tacitly and pre-reflectively, rather than overtly. As Mills astutely observes, we are:

> Socialized from birth to discern race, the marker of full and diminished personhood, we learn to apprehend this world through a sensory grid whose architecture has been shaped by blueprints still functioning independent of our will and conscious intent, and resistant to our self-conscious redrawing.
> (Mills 2014: 37)

While it seems undeniable that the racist blueprints that structure our perceptions "independent of our will and conscious intent" are indeed "resistant to our self-conscious redrawing," as Mills asserts, and while this may seem to be a cause for extreme pessimism regarding the possibility of identifying and overcoming racist perceptual habits, it is precisely the clear-sighted diagnoses provided by critical phenomenologists of race that challenge us to work collectively, in strategic alliances with others across racial, gender, class, cultural, sexual, and other socially constructed barriers, to eliminate naturalized racist attitudes. Such a project does not, it should be noted, call upon us to jettison our racial identities altogether, even if we were in a position to do so (which we certainly are not). Indeed, as Alcoff insists, "identity terms are not mere historical holdovers of oppression, or ideological claims, but explanatory terms that help us to make sense of what we experience as well as to comprehend larger historical events" (Alcoff 2015: 46–47). Racial identities, Alcoff maintains, need not be racist despite the racist histories in which they are embedded. The challenge posed by critical race phenomenology, then, is not to deny or minimize the importance of our racial identities but rather, to identify and thereby disrupt the racist natural attitudes that so often accompany them, and that represent one of the greatest obstacles to the realization of an anti-racist future.

References

Ahmed, Sara. (2007) "A Phenomenology of Whiteness." *Feminist Theory* 8, no. 2: 149–168.
Alcoff, Linda Martín. (2006) *Visible Identities: Race, Gender, and the Self*, Oxford: Oxford University Press.
———. (2015) *The Future of Whiteness*. Cambridge: Polity Press.
Alexander, Michele. (2011) *The New Jim Crow: Mass Incarceration in the Age of Colobrlindness*, New York: New Press.
Al-Saji, Alia. (2009) "A Phenomenology of Critical-Ethical Vision: Merleau-Ponty, Bergson, and the Question of Seeing Differently." *Chiasmi International* 11: 375–398.
Anzaldua, Gloria. (2012) *Borderlands/La Frontera: The New Mestiza*, 4th edition, San Francisco: Aunt Lute Books.
Beauvoir, Simone de. (2010) *The Second Sex*, trans. Constance Borde and Sheila Malovany-Chevallier, New York: Alfred A. Knopf.
Butler, Judith. (1990) *Gender Trouble: Feminism and the Subversion of Identity*, New York: Routledge.
———. (1993a) *Bodies That Matter: On the Discursive Limits of "Sex,"* New York: Routledge.
———. (1993b) "Endangered/Endangering: Schematic Racism and White Paranoia," in Robert Gooding-Williams (ed.), *Reading Rodney King Reading Urban Uprising*, New York: Routledge, pp. 15–22.
Cho, Sumi K. (1993) "Korean Americans vs. African Americans: Conflict and Construction," in Robert Gooding-Williams (ed.), *Reading Rodney King Reading Urban Uprising*, New York: Routledge, pp. 196–211.
Coates, Ta-Nehisi. (2015) "The Black Family in the Age of Mass Incarceration." *Atlantic* (October 2015). Accessed April 3, 2016. www.theatlantic.com/magazine/archive/2015/10/the-black-family-in-the-age-of-mass-incarceration/403246/.
Collins, Patricia Hill. (2000) *Black Feminist Thought: Knowledge, Consciousness, and the Politics of Empowerment*, 2nd edition, New York: Routledge.
Davis, Angela Y. (2003) *Are Prisons Obsolete?* New York: Seven Stories Press.
Descartes, René. (1979) *Meditations on First Philosophy*, trans. Donald A. Cress, Indianapolis: Hackett.
Fanon, Frantz. (2008) *Black Skin White Masks*, trans. Richard Philcox, New York: Grove Press.
Fielding, Helen A. (2015) "Cultivating Perception: Phenomenological Encounters With Artworks." *Signs: Journal of Women in Culture and Society* 40, no. 2: 280–289.
Gordon, Lewis R. (1995) *Bad Faith and Antiblack Racism*, Atlantic Highlands: Humanities Press.
Guenther, Lisa. (2013) *Solitary Confinement: Social Death and Its Afterlives*, Minneapolis: University of Minnesota Press.
Husserl, Edmund. (1982). *Ideas Pertaining to a Pure Phenomenology and to a Phenomenological Philosophy*, trans. F. Kersten, Dordrecht: Kluwer Academic Publishers.
Irigaray, Luce. (1985) *Speculum of the Other Woman*, trans. Gillian C. Gill, Ithaca: Cornell University Press.
Kristeva, Julia. (1986) "Stabat Mater," in Toril Moi (ed.) and Leon S. Roudiez (trans.), *The Kristeva Reader*, New York: Columbia University Press, pp. 160–186.
Lorde, Audre. (1992) "Age, Race, Class, and Sex: Women Redefining Difference," in Russell Ferguson, et al. (eds.), *Out There: Marginalization and Contemporary Culture*, Cambridge, MA: MIT Press, pp. 281–287.
Lugones, María. (1987) "Playfulness, 'World'-Travelling, and Loving Perception." *Hypatia* 2, no. 2: 3–19.
Merleau-Ponty, Maurice. (2012) *Phenomenology of Perception*, trans. Donald A. Landes, New York: Routledge Press.
Mills, Charles. (2014) "Materializing Race," in Emily S. Lee (ed.), *Living Alterities: Phenomenology, Embodiment, and Race*, Albany: State University of New York Press, pp. 19–41.
Murphy, Robert. (2001) *The Body Silent: The Different World of the Disabled*, New York: W. W. Norton.
Ortega, Mariana. (2016) *In Between: Latina Feminist Phenomenology, Multiplicity, and the Self*, Albany: State University of New York Press.

Rich, Adrienne. (1995) *Of Woman Born: Motherhood as Experience and Institution*, New York: W. W. Norton.
Sartre. (1989) "No Exit," in Stuart Gilbert (trans.), *No Exit and Three Other Plays*, New York: Vintage Books.
Sheth, Falguni A. (2009) *Toward a Political Philosophy of Race*, Albany: State University of New York Press.
Sullivan, Shannon. (2006) *Revealing Whiteness: The Unconscious Habits of Racial Privilege*, Bloomington: Indiana University Press.
———. (2014) *Good White People: The Problem With Middle-Class White Anti-Racism*, Albany: State University of New York Press.
Yancy, George. (2014) "White Gazes: What It Feels Like to Be an Essence," in Emily S. Lee (ed.), *Living Alterities: Phenomenology, Embodiment, and Race*, Albany: State University of New York Press, pp. 43–64.
Young, Iris. (2000) *Inclusion and Democracy*, Oxford: Oxford University Press.
———. (2005) *On Female Body Experience: "Throwing Like a Girl" and Other Essays*, Oxford: Oxford University Press.

Part IV

EPISTEMOLOGY, COGNITION, AND LANGUAGE

18
EPISTEMIC INJUSTICE AND EPISTEMOLOGIES OF IGNORANCE

José Medina

Miranda Fricker has defined epistemic injustice "as a kind of injustice in which someone is *wronged specifically in her capacity as a knower*" (2007: 20). Although the topic of epistemic injustice has recently received a lot of attention, it had been systematically ignored in idealized discussions in epistemology that assumed the equal status and participation of all subjects in the epistemic practices in which understanding, belief, and knowledge are formed, communicated, and used. Idealized theories of understanding, belief, and knowledge disregard the differential epistemic agency of different subject positions and social locations, and they also neglect the internal relations and dialectics between understanding and misunderstanding, believing and disbelieving, knowing and ignoring. Taking seriously the power dynamics within epistemic practices involves unmasking "epistemologies of ignorance" that protect the voices, meaning, and perspectives of some by silencing the voices, meanings, and perspectives of others. Marxist theory, critical race theory, feminist theory, and queer theory have all produced powerful diagnoses of these "epistemologies of ignorance" by analyzing the impact of different forms of oppression (linked to class, race, gender, and sexuality) on our epistemic practices, and the different forms of epistemic injustice that relations of oppression produce. Although *epistemologies of ignorance* have been discussed by that name only recently (Mills 1997; Sullivan and Tuana 2007), they have always been a key theme of race theory, and they have figured prominently in the philosophies of race of classic authors such as Sojourner Truth, Anna J. Cooper, W.E.B. Du Bois, Alain Locke, and Frantz Fanon, to name a few. Philosophers of race have developed robust discussions of social facts, experiences, and meanings that, as a result of racial oppression, become invisible, inaudible, or simply unintelligible in certain social locations and for certain perspectives that protect themselves from facing their involvement in racial oppression with a shield of *active* ignorance. The sections that follow elucidate the accounts of racial *active* ignorance and racial epistemic injustices developed in classic philosophies of race and in contemporary reflections on "epistemologies of ignorance."

The first section of this chapter will examine the relationship between racial ignorance and different kinds of dysfunctions and epistemic injustices such as unequal access to and participation in knowledge practices, silencing, vitiated testimonial dynamics, patterns of misinterpretation and distortion, and so forth. The second section will elucidate what counts as *epistemic resistance*, exploring how individuals and groups living under conditions of racial oppression can use their epistemic resources and abilities to undermine and change oppressive structures and the complacent cognitive-affective functioning that sustains those structures. This section will sketch, in broad strokes, the key elements of an *insurrectionist epistemology*. Finally, in the last section I will discuss how epistemic violence can be fought on the grounds, in our daily activities, through *micro-practices of resistance*.

The Will *Not* to Believe: Invisibility, Inaudibility, Insensitivity

When Sojourner Truth poignantly asked "And ain't I a woman?," she was unmasking and denouncing bodies of racial ignorance that sustained and protected mainstream conceptions of gender—heterosexist and invisibly whited conceptions of femininity that marginalized black women. When W.E.B. Du Bois wrote about piercing "the veil of ignorance" and eloquently described what it meant to lead one's life "behind the veil," he was identifying the cognitive dysfunctions that resulted from the social invisibilization of the experiences and perspectives of racially oppressed groups. When Ralph Ellison (1952) described the invisibility of the black man as produced by white people's insistence to see only the black man's "surroundings, themselves, or figments of their imagination," he was dissecting a cognitive pathology, that of the *white gaze*: a racialized way of seeing that proceeds through the carefully cultivated refusal to see and acknowledge certain things and the suppression of other ways of seeing and experiencing the world. The racial ignorance these authors described is a very *active* and *contentful* form of ignorance: it is something more than a gap or an emptiness that can simply be filled when the opportunity arises; it is an ignorance that creates epistemic privileges and epistemic harms by protecting the epistemic agency of some and by blocking the epistemic agency of others.

Racial ignorance interferes with the meaning-making and knowledge-producing capacities and activities of individuals and groups in unfair ways, and therefore it produces epistemic injustices of two kinds. In the first place, when the unfair epistemic treatment of a subject concerns her *credibility* in testimonial dynamics, we have an instance of what Fricker has termed *testimonial injustice*: the subject is judged as less credible than other subjects in the same epistemic predicament would be; she doesn't receive the trust that she deserves, her capacity for ascertaining truth is called into question, and her inclusion and participation in knowledge-producing practices are compromised (if allowed at all). So, for example, when police officers racially stereotype a black bystander in a crime scene as a suspect involved in the crime rather than as a witness, he is not treated as a reliable observer and his account of the events are not taken as prima facie believable or displaying positive epistemic qualities (accuracy, reliability, veridicality, etc.). In the second place, when the unfair epistemic treatment of a subject concerns her *intelligibility* in communicative dynamics, we have an instance of what Fricker has termed *hermeneutical injustice*: the subject is judged as unintelligible or less intelligible than other subjects; her words and meanings are not taken in their own terms, her capacity for meaning and understanding is undermined, and her agency in meaning-making and meaning-expressing practices is compromised (if not eliminated altogether). So, for example, when a subject's racialized language or accent is perceived as ignorant, less articulate or clear, less reliable or accurate, she is less likely to be asked questions that require cognitive sophistication, her interpretations and perspectives are less likely to be understood in their own terms, and she is more likely to be taken as unable to make full sense of certain areas of experience or to contribute to certain semantic domains.

Both kinds of racial epistemic injustices—testimonial and hermeneutical—are created and perpetuated by epistemic dysfunctions that are constitutive of racial ignorance. These dysfunctions produce the phenomenon of *epistemic hiding*, that is, of making subjects and their experiences and perspectives invisible and inaudible, or visible and audible only precariously and in a distorted way—"through a glass darkly," as it were. In racial testimonial injustices, the epistemic dysfunctions involve an *active* tendency to *mis*hear certain voices and perspectives and to *dis*believe their contributions. In racial hermeneutical injustices, the dysfunctions involved foster not simply the inability to interpret or make sense (the formation of interpretative gaps or semantic lacunas), but also and more importantly, the *active* tendency to *mis*interpret the experiences of racial others. When pockets of this *active* racial ignorance are formed, what is rendered invisible and inaudible (or precariously visible and audible) are not only things that are entirely outside the reach of the racially ignorant person's life, but also things that reside in the most intimate corners of her cognitive and affective life. In critical race theory we find these two different notions of what has been rendered experientially alien: the *simply alien* and the *alienated familiar*.

As Charles Mills explains in "Alternative Epistemologies," the *simply alien* comprises "experiences that are outside the hegemonic framework in the sense of involving an external geography" (1998: 28). It is an exhibition of "the simply alien," for example, when "a muckraking Frederick Engels brings details of British slum conditions to the shocked attention of a middle-class audience" (1998: 28). But even more interesting for the analysis of *active* racial ignorance is the *alienated familiar*, which comprises "experiences that are outside because they redraw the map of what was thought to be already explored territory" (1998: 28). Confronting interpretations that make you radically rethink your most familiar experiences is not easy. It can be quite shocking to hear that something you thought you knew well what it was—well-meant acts of charity toward worse-off others, for example—can be experienced by the other subjectivities involved quite differently—as a subtle form of racism, or as passive-aggressive acts that keep people in subordinate positions and demand their gratitude and conformity. Indeed, confronting the alienated familiar is more disruptive than being exposed to the simply alien; and more resistances are mobilized to block that confrontation or to stage it so that the alienated familiar appears as pathological or unintelligible experience that can simply be dismissed. It is here, in the resistance to confront the alienated familiar, that we find what I have termed "the will *not* to believe" (Medina 2015), the cognitive-affective investment in not knowing, in protecting one's beliefs and meanings through a resistant insensitivity to meanings and perspectives that can create *friction* in one's epistemic life.

Although traditionally depicted as a form of *blindness*, the active racial ignorance I am describing is no regular kind of blindness, but a very generalized form of *insensitivity* or *numbness*. The metaphor of *blindness* misleadingly disguises important features of active racial ignorance and the distinctive kind of insensitivity it involves. In the first place, the terms "insensitivity" and "numbness" are more appropriate than "blindness" because, although clearly related to our embodied sentience, they are not restricted to one sensory modality and can be easily extended to the non-perceptual—and indeed the epistemic deficiencies in question go beyond our perceptual organs and concern our interpretative and conceptual capacities. In the second place, the terms "numbness" and "insensitivity" can avoid the ableism of the metaphor of blindness. Indeed, the equation of blindness with ignorance is offensive and contributes to the "otherness" of people with disabilities. Finally, in the third place, the metaphor of blindness is conceptually inept because it hides a key feature of active racial ignorance: namely, its *self-effacing* nature, its self-hiding and self-denying mode of operation. Whereas the blind person is acutely aware that there are things that escape her and she leads her life adjusting to this perceptual deficit, the actively insensitive person is quite oblivious of there being anything at all she is missing and she arrogantly assumes that she is attuned to everything there is to know about the social world. This is what I have called the *meta*-level of racial insensitivity. Active racial ignorance involves *meta-ignorance*: the insensitive person is ignorant of her own ignorance, unable to recognize that there is anything she is missing concerning racial experiences and meanings. This is a key element of the contrast between *active* racial ignorance and other (less recalcitrant, less harmful, and easier to eradicate) forms of ignorance.

When our ignorance is nothing more than the absence of true belief and/or the presence of false belief, learning should be easy: we just unmask false beliefs and inculcate true ones. However, in the case of active ignorance, learning is resisted and blocked in a number of different ways: because of a lack of interest in knowing or understanding better, because of a vested interest in not knowing or understanding, because of distortions and preconceptions that get in the way of seeing things in a different way, and so forth. Adapted from my essay "Ignorance and Racial Insensitivity," (2016) here is a schematic contrast between the key features of *passive versus active ignorance*:

Passive ignorance: (1) absence of true belief
　　　　　　　　　 (2) presence of false belief
Active ignorance: (3) cognitive resistances (e.g., prejudices, conceptual lacunas)
　　　　　　　　　 (4) affective resistances (e.g., apathy, interest in not knowing—"the will *not* to believe")
　　　　　　　　　 (5) bodily resistances (e.g., feeling anxious, agitated, red in the face)
　　　　　　　　　 (6) defense mechanisms and strategies (e.g., deflecting challenges, shifting burden of proof)

As I understand it, active racial ignorance involves being cognitively and affectively numbed to the lives of racial others: being inattentive to and unconcerned by their experiences, problems, and aspirations; and being unable to connect with them and to understand their speech and action. How can this racial insensitivity be displaced? Resisting racial insensitivity is a particularly challenging task for two reasons. On the one hand, there is what I have termed *the problem of meta-ignorance*: racial insensitivity protects itself from being recognized and resisted; there are individual and collective mechanisms of epistemic hiding that are so insidious that individuals and groups (even entire cultures) often are in a recalcitrant state of self-denial that disarms any critical intervention and neutralizes any attempt to wake them up from their racist slumbers.

On the other hand, resisting racial insensitivity also encounters *the problem of the individual and the collective*: racial insensitivity resides simultaneously both in individuals and in entire groups (in social, cultural, and institutional attitudes and relations). Since racial insensitivity operates both at the interpersonal level and at the level of sociocultural and institutional practices, any attempt to diagnose and treat the problem *only* at one level will be partial and deficient: individuals cannot by themselves overcome the well-entrenched forms of racial insensitivity they have inherited; but, on the other hand, institutions and social structures cannot overcome patterns of racial ignorance through purified procedures and protocols without remaking the attitudes, habits, and communicative dynamics of the individuals who inhabit those institutional and structural spaces. In the next two sections I will highlight some resources and arguments available in the epistemology of race to address these problems, developing an argument for the need to cultivate sustainable insurrectionary acts and practices of resistance both in interpersonal relations and in structural and institutional settings.

Epistemic Resistance and Insurrection of Subjugated Knowledges

How can we resist racial insensitivity? The available forms of resistance against it and the feasible processes of sensitizing the racially ignorant subject will vary widely depending on the identity, environment, and trajectory of the subject in question. How does the subject partake in patterns of racial knowledge and ignorance? How does racism and dysfunctional racial relations affect her cognitive and affective life and shape her sensibility? It all depends on the set of social locations, positions, and relations that one sees oneself enmeshed in as one navigates the social world and finds oneself enjoying and suffering (sometimes simultaneously!) racial privileges and racial harms.

Disregarding racial harms and privileges and desensitizing oneself to racialized aspects of social life are well-entrenched defense mechanisms of racial insensitivity, but they are not always available to all the agents who co-inhabit the social world from different locations and perspectives. Racial ignorance is a luxury that oppressed subjects typically cannot have. As many race theorists have emphasized, racially oppressed subjects have no option but to master the dominant perspectives of privileged groups that shape the social world. In this way oppressed subjects accomplish the epistemic feat of maintaining active in their minds (at least) two cognitive perspectives simultaneously, the dominant perspective of the privileged and the non-dominant perspective(s). Following Du Bois, this has been described as having *a double consciousness*. The epistemic perspectives of oppressed subjects often exhibit a characteristic kind of split or hybridity, whereas the cognitive functioning of privileged elites tends to be more monolithic and one-sided, often operating in complete disregard of other perspectives. In his discussion of double consciousness Du Bois states that the American Negro is "born with a veil and gifted with second sight in this American world" (1903/1994: 2). The Negro is painfully aware of his veiled existence and he looks at himself as veiled, as white Americans do. This split consciousness can produce anxiety, paralysis, and epistemic dysfunctions. As Robert Gooding-Williams (2011) has argued, it is a misunderstanding (and a misinterpretation of Du Bois) to think of double consciousness as being, in and of itself, an enlightened condition; it is the Du Boisian notion of "second-sight" that has that role. Not just by virtue of having a double consciousness, but by virtue of inhabiting it critically, the Negro can pierce the veil of ignorance of the white world and develop an alternative way of seeing, a "second-sight", a *resistant perception* alongside the dominant perception he has internalized.

Patricia Hill Collins (1990/2000) has called attention to the resistant perceptions and interpretations of women of color in her black feminist epistemology. Thanks to a bifurcated consciousness, she argues, black women can generate self-representations that enable them to resist the demeaning racist and sexist images of black femininity in the white world. Hill Collins finds the critical payoff and subversive potential of double consciousness in allowing the subject to take critical distance from the dominant perspective. Double consciousness brings with it the *opportunity* to develop the ability to shift back and forth between two ways of seeing and, hence, the ability to make comparisons and contrasts between perspectives. But notice that this is only a *possibility*; there is no guarantee that every double consciousness will have this flexibility and dynamic inner structure and will lead to the development of a "second-sight" and it remains possible for subjects with double consciousness to live in cognitive dissonance.

Concurring with Hill Collins and other race theorists, the *epistemology of resistance* I have developed (Medina 2012) identifies the ability to shift back and forth between epistemic perspectives and to establish instructive comparisons and contrasts between them as the special source of critical power and lucidity available to oppressed subjects. The mere coexistence of epistemic perspectives is not sufficient for lucidity and epistemic virtues to emerge; there must be beneficial *epistemic friction* between the alternative standpoints available. On my view, epistemically virtuous double consciousness is the consciousness that has *epistemic counterpoints inside it* that produce beneficial *epistemic friction*. As Andrea Pitts (2016) has pointed out, an excellent account of (both beneficial and detrimental) *internal epistemic friction* can be found in Gloria Anzaldúa's description of the process of confronting one's "shadow self," which includes one's epistemic gaps and complicity with patterns of ignorance and insensitivity (Anzaldúa 2009: 551). As Pitts (2016) shows, the kind of confrontation with one's own forms of racial ignorance that Anzaldúa describes operates at two levels: at the first-order level of ignoring specific things about racial subjectivities and racial groups (including one's own), and at the meta-level of ignoring (being confused about, or simply being inattentive to) what one knows and does not know about racial positionality and relationality and one's capacities for racial learning. As Pitts puts it:

> the kind of confrontation with one's own forms of ignorance and ways of self-knowing that Anzaldúa describes is an important point of convergence with what Medina calls epistemic resistance. Epistemic resistance, in Medina's work, echoes Anzaldúa's distinction between "inner works" and "public acts," and her distinction between the "inner/spiritual/personal" and the "social/collective/material" .... Medina argues that epistemic resistance appears in two forms: internal and external, with two potential valences: positive and negative [i.e. beneficial or detrimental].
>
> (Pitts 2016: 362)

Beneficial internal epistemic friction exerts resistance against racial insensitivity by forcing oneself to be self-critical, to confront one's limitations and to become attentive to internalized patterns of ignorance. But there is also *detrimental* internal epistemic friction that is complicit with racial insensitivity and protects racial ignorance by blocking learning and resisting alternative ways of knowing. This connects with what Mariana Ortega (2006) has termed "being lovingly, knowingly ignorant." Ortega describes this form of ignorance taking place among white feminists who appropriate the work of women of color for their own aims, but nonetheless they resist the interrogation of their own racialized positions (Ortega 2006: 61–62).

But how does the epistemic friction of conflicting racial perspectives operate externally as they confront each other? And how can social practices and communicative dynamics be arranged so that the interaction of perspectives result in beneficial epistemic friction that fosters the resistance against racial insensitivity? In other words, how can we cultivate practices of epistemic resistance so as to stage an "insurrection of subjugated knowledges," to borrow Foucault's phrase? (see McWhorter 2009 and Medina 2011, 2012). In the reminder of this essay, I want to highlight some resources and suggestions from the recent literature in the epistemology of race.

In *The Racial Contract*, Charles Mills (1997) put *white ignorance* in the agenda of critical race theory. Arguing that privileged white subjects have become unable to understand the world that they themselves have created, Mills called attention to the cognitive dysfunctions and pathologies inscribed in the white world and its epistemic economy, which revolves not only around the epistemic exclusions and stigmatizations of peoples of color, but also around a carefully orchestrated self-hiding of the white gaze. As Mills suggests, white ignorance is a form of self-ignorance: the inability to recognize one's own racial identity and the presuppositions and consequences of one's racial positionality. Not having developed expressive practices and interpretative devices to understand their experiences of racialization, white subjects have been lost in a racialized world. A lot has been written on the invisibility of whiteness and the hypervisibility of blackness in the racialized world of American culture (see Hill Collins 1990/2000 and 2005). But of course whiteness has been invisible only for the white gaze but not for racially oppressed subjects, who—as Mills emphasizes—have formed a powerful counter-public, with their alternative experiences and interpretations, and their counter-memory.

Along with other epistemologists of race, Mills (1998) argues that oppressed groups have a distinctive set of experiences and they are well positioned to bring about an "inversion of perspectives." Mills's proposals for correcting racial ignorance are twofold: a "cognitive therapy" that treats the dysfunctions and pathologies of white ignorance; and an epistemic "inversion" that makes learning possible and promotes healthy epistemic dynamics. Both correctives require privileging the epistemic perspective of oppressed subjects. Although oppressed subjects can indeed fall victim to socially generated illusions, they often have more resources to undo these illusions, they have a richer (or more heterogeneous) experiential life that they can use to dismantle the accepted description of reality that rules the day. Members of subordinate groups typically have experiences that from the point of view of the dominant ideology or hegemonic perspective are considered *alien* and are swept under the rug of the *alienated familiar* in the world of the privileged. Alien experiences of this sort call a radical questioning of assumptions and taken-for-granted interpretations. People (including the experiencing subject) may not be ready to accept these alien experiences as genuine experiences and they may not answer the call for a radical rearticulation or *inversion* of perspectives; instead, their reaction may be to dismiss the experience and block any alternative descriptions of social realities that may result from it. This is to be expected since it is difficult to accept descriptions that challenge our world as we understand it; and the more invested people are in their understanding of social realities, the more reluctant they will be to accept alternative ones. But all the more reason to be attentive to alien experiences and receptive to their critical and transformative potential.

Mills has been criticized for a naïve cognitivism that forgets that the process of undoing racial insensitivity involves much more than "cognitive therapy" (see Bailey 2007). The fight against racial oppression indeed involves things that go beyond the merely cognitive: it involves the restructuring of habits and affective structures; and it also involves political action and deep cultural transformations. The liberation of the meanings, experiences and perspectives of the oppressed call for something more complicated than a mere "inversion of perspectives" that replaces the dominant memory with a counter-memory, the dominant imagination with a counter-imagination, and so forth. The more complicated business of redrawing conceptual boundaries and rearticulating epistemic norms through critical engagements and subversive communicative moves is what my notions of *epistemic resistance* and *epistemic insurrection* try to capture. Resisting epistemic oppression requires exerting epistemic friction on the grounds, that is, through practices that exert pressure and create trouble so as to halt and disrupt oppressive dynamics. In this sense I have argued for the importance of epistemic disobedience and insurrection for combatting epistemic oppression, especially when such oppression takes an extreme form and makes cooperation extremely difficult and painful if not impossible.

To conceptualize extreme epistemic oppression I propose the notion of *epistemic death*. Just like Orlando Patterson (1982) has identified the phenomenon of *social death* as occurring when people are deprived of rights and liberties and not given full status of subjects under the law, we also need to identify the phenomenon of *epistemic death*, which occurs when a subject's epistemic capacities are not recognized and she is given no standing or a diminished standing in existing epistemic activities and communities. As I understand it, the concept of epistemic death has been foreshadowed in many accounts of the epistemic injuries produced by racism such as those developed by Maria Stewart, James Baldwin, and Gloria Anzaldúa. Stewart developed an understanding of epistemic oppression as a form of "deadening" and "numbing" of mental capacities that can kill oneself as a subject of knowledge, for "there are no chains so galling as the chains of ignorance—no fetters so binding as those that bind the soul, and exclude it from the vast field of useful and scientific knowledge" (1932/1987: 45). Baldwin described the predicament of the black man in the United States as an "endless struggle to achieve . . . human identity, human authority" after internalizing

> fear as deep as the marrow of the bone; doubt that he was worthy of life, since everyone around him denied it; . . . rage, hatred, and murder, hatred for white men so deep that it often turned against him and his own, and made all love, all trust, all joy [all life] impossible.
>
> (Baldwin 1998: 98)

And Anzaldúa forcefully described Anglo White privilege as killing her voice and her capacity to be heard and understood in her own terms, as using "linguistic terrorism" to annihilate her self: "*El Anglo con cara de inocente nos arranco la lengua.* Wild tongues cannot be tamed, they can only be cut out" (1987: 76). "Repeated attacks on our native tongue diminish our sense of self" (1987: 80).

The *epistemic death* that can result from racial oppression includes phenomena such as *testimonial death*, occurring when subjects are not given even minimal amounts of credibility and are prevented from participating in testimonial dynamics; and *hermeneutical death*, occurring when subjects are not treated as intelligible communicators and are prevented from participating in meaning-making and meaning-sharing practices. Under conditions of epistemic death, subjects owe nothing to those practices and communities that contribute to their annihilation; epistemic obligations (such as answering questions, telling the truth, sharing information, etc.) are suspended because one should not be expected to cooperate with practices that undermine one's own status and agency or that of one's fellows. Moreover, besides relaxing and suspending obligations, epistemic death also creates a right (if not a duty) to fight epistemically by any means necessary (including the right to lie, to hide, to sabotage, to silence others, etc.), demonstrating loyalty and solidarity only with alternatives epistemic communities (communities of resistance). But notice that while suspending cooperation with oppressive epistemic practices and institutions, epistemic insurrection aims at facilitating cooperation under fair conditions when non-oppressive epistemic dynamics and norms are established.

We can identify epistemic insurrectionary practices of all sorts that interrupt and disrupt the established epistemic economy of a society and its practices and institutions. There are insurrectionary practices that target oppressive epistemic presumptions and dynamics in public and private life, in education, in the media, in film and art, in public policy, in linguistic habits, in communicative dynamics, in the protocols and procedures of our institutions, and so forth. There are insurrectionary practices that are not only cognitive, but also affective; and there are insurrectionary practices that are not confined to the individual, but they involve entire publics and social movements and concern structures and institutions. Indeed dismantling epistemic norms and dynamics is not simply a cognitive and individualistic enterprise. Epistemic insurrectionary practices must include aesthetic, ethical, pedagogical, political, religious, and other forms of activities that create beneficial epistemic friction and contain subversive interventions that have the potential to open people's hearts and souls to marginalized racial perspectives and to expand their racial sensibilities. We can think of African American literary figures such as Maya Angelou, Audre Lorde, or Toni Morrison as involved in such epistemic insurrectionary practices against racial insensitivity. This kind of epistemic insurrection can also be seen in the innovative works of African American filmmakers who have revolutionize film-viewing and film-interpretation by turning the interpretative resources and scripts of genres such as *film noir* against themselves, using this subversion for uprooting racist assumptions and unmasking racial ignorance. For example, Dan Flory (2008) has argued that black *noir*—that is, the new film *noir* produced by black filmmakers in recent decades—has the potential to disrupt and disable racial insensitivity: "By urging viewers to think and reflect on their presumptions about race, many of these films [mobilize] alternative systems of social cognition that challenge dominant systems of moral knowledge"; and they "demonstrate how racist oppression deforms African-American life even as the majority of white Americans perceive it as nothing out of the ordinary" (2008: 4). And of course this critical and subversive potential can be generalized to other cinematic genres such as comedy (think, for example, of *Dear White People*). In fact, since Aristotle, comedy has been considered a particularly apt form of social commentary that can accommodate radical critique. In that sense, we can understand provocative stand-up comics of color such as Dave Chapelle and Margaret

Cho (or even more mainstream ones such as George Lopez, Richard Pryor, or Chris Rock) as radical social critics and epistemic insurrectionists against whiteness.

Just as Leonard Harris (2002) challenges moral theories to meet the challenge of rendering insurrectionist acts not only permissible, but also dutiful, under conditions of oppression, I have developed a similar argument with respect to epistemic oppression: when there are well-entrenched patterns of epistemic violence, epistemic insurrectionary acts should be considered *individually* permissible for victims of such violence and their allies, and *collectively* required by society and by the publics and organizations that can do something to disrupt oppressive dynamics and discontinue patterns of epistemic violence. In the next and final section, following Kristie Dotson's account of "epistemic violence," I will elucidate the kinds of epistemic insurrectionary acts that are required for resisting such violence, sketching and defending the move toward an insurrectionist epistemology that emerges from the recent literature on epistemic injustice.

No Justice, No Peace: Epistemic Violence and Epistemic Resistance

The demonstrators protesting against the killing of Michael Brown in the summer of 2014 were often accused by the authorities and the media of disturbing the peace. But what *peace*? One of their slogans was "No Justice, No Peace," which, far from being a threat, was a way of denouncing that there was no peace to be disturbed to begin with, that such peace was the dangerous and harmful illusion of a privileged class sheltered from the structural violence under which the black majority of Ferguson, Missouri, lives: systematic police brutality, extreme poverty, high unemployment rates, lack of representation in public institutions (from law enforcement to municipal, state, and federal offices), and so forth. Disregarding or denying these realities, indulging in the fiction of a social *peace* that most members of society do not enjoy, *that itself* is a form of epistemic violence: the affirmation of this illusory peace involves a *harmful* performative contradiction, for it performatively reenacts and reinscribes the very violence that it purports to deny, pretending that those whose experiences are being silenced have an equal voice, equal representation, equal access to institutions, and so forth. *Epistemic violence* of this sort, which silences and unfairly constrains the voices of some, is intimately connected with other forms of violence that helps to facilitate, such as psychological and emotional violence, symbolic and cultural violence, institutional (social, political, legal) violence, and even physical and material violence (from being beaten or killed to being denied access to health care and social services).

We need to distinguish the different kinds of violence (physical-material, institutional, structural, epistemic, etc.) that are part of racism, but we also need to elucidate their interrelations and examine how the many faces of racial violence work together in insidious ways. If racial *peace* remains a fiction today because of the many kinds of racial violence that are still pervasive, even if invisible to some segments of the population, the work toward racial justice will require fighting against *all* those patterns of violence, and prior to that another thing is required: making those different forms of violence visible, and calling attention to the fact that their very invisibility is a form of violence, *epistemic violence*. In what follows, following Kristie Dotson, I will elucidate some forms of epistemic violence and some forms of epistemic resistance. Far from being exhaustive, this elucidation is only a small step towards the kind of insurrectionist epistemology needed to fight against epistemic violence.

Building on Gayatri Spivak's (1998) use of the expression "epistemic violence" as a way of marking the silencing of marginalized groups, Kristie Dotson (2011) has developed an account of epistemic violence by analyzing different ways in which the "on-the-ground practices of silencing" operate. As Dotson puts it, "epistemic violence in testimony is a refusal, intentional or unintentional, of an audience to communicatively reciprocate a linguistic exchange owing to pernicious ignorance" (2011: 238). Dotson identifies two different kinds of silencing that epistemic violence can produce in testimonial exchanges: *testimonial quieting* and *testimonial smothering*. As Dotson explains, "testimonial quieting occurs when an audience fails to identify a speaker as a knower" (2011: 242) because of negative stereotyping, or the operation of what Hill Collins has termed "controlling images," which heavily influence how black women are socially perceived. Specific to my discussion here, controlling images may stigmatize black women as a group and preclude their being fairly appraised as credible, mature, and capable epistemic agents (see Hill Collins's analysis of "controlling images" that heavily influence how black women are socially perceived as "mammies," "jezebels," or "welfare queens" in Hill Collins 2000: 72–81, and also Hill Collins 2005).

The second kind of silencing produced by epistemic violence that Dotson identifies is *testimonial smothering*, which is a form of self-silencing that occurs when the speaker perceives her audience as unwilling or unable to provide appropriate uptake. As Dotson puts it, "testimonial smothering . . . is the truncating of one's own testimony in order to insure that the testimony contains only content for which one's audience demonstrates testimonial competence" (2011: 244). Dotson identifies three circumstances that routinely provokes this kind of self-silencing: (1) when the content of the testimony is unsafe and risky; (2) when the audience demonstrates incompetence with respect to the content of the testimony to the speaker; and (3) when there are patterns of pernicious ignorance that make it unlikely (if not impossible) to be understood and appropriately taken up in that testimonial climate (even if the signals of distrust or inability to understand or believe are implicit or hidden). As Dotson points out, the first case can be illustrated by Kimberlé Crenshaw's discussions of what has been historically unsafe, risky testimony in "non-white" communities, as for example women-of-colors' silence around occurrences of domestic violence (Crenshaw 1991). The other two cases can be illustrated by paying attention to the silencing effects of *racial micro-aggressions* (Sue, Capodilupo, and Holder 2008: 329).

Racial micro-aggressions typically function as subtle forms of intimidation and epistemic violence which, if they are not explicitly called out, resisted, and neutralized, can have silencing effects. Sarcastic tones, disapproving glances, skeptical stares, looking confused, puzzled, or unable to follow, and constantly interrupting or questioning one's meaning are some of the communicative intimidations that can silence people or implicitly encourage them to limit their speech or take a discursive detour. This is well illustrated by one of the examples that Dotson examines. In "Conversations I Can't Have" (1996), Cassandra Byers Harvin describes an encounter in a public library with a white woman who asked her what she was working on, and when Harvin answered that she was researching raising black sons in the United States, the white woman promptly replied, "How is that any different from raising white sons?" Harvin explains that the question as well as the tone gave her the distinct impression that her interlocutor thought that she was "making something out of nothing" (1996: 16). This clearly had a silencing effect on Harvin, who tells us that she politely pretended that she was running out of time and exited the conversation. As Dotson explains, this racial micro-aggression demonstrated testimonial incompetence on the audience's part, but it also performed a *micro-invalidation*, which is "characterized by communications that exclude, negate, or nullify the psychological thoughts, feelings, or experiential reality of a person of color" (Dotson 2011: 247). In other cases, micro-aggressions can contain micro-insults, micro-intimidations, micro-harassment, and other forms of micro-behaviors that exert epistemic violence. Micro-aggressions are ways of performatively enacting racial insensitivity, often in subtle and insidious ways so that they go almost unrecognized by the people involved (more often by the perpetrators and by the bystanders than by their victims), but not without having consequences and producing epistemic harms that even if they seem negligible can amount to the systematic undermining of the epistemic capacities of subjects and groups. Empirical studies in the social sciences are only now gathering a wealth of evidence of the multiple and far-reaching harms that micro-aggressions can cause to individual subjects and even entire groups.

I want to conclude with the suggestion that, although seemingly small and negligible, a crucial part of an insurrectionist epistemology is *micro-resistance*. Precisely because micro-aggressions occupy such a central part in unfair communicative practices, the eradication of epistemic injustices will require micro-practices that disarm and subvert micro-aggressive moves at the same level at which they occur. Micro-aggressions call for *micro-resistance*, for micro-practices of resistance in which the insidious aggressive moves with disabling effects are neutralized, halted, or at least weakened. Micro-practices of resistance are heavily situated and contextualized moves that often require a lot of inventiveness and cunning as well as other epistemic virtues such as courage. Their effectiveness will never be guaranteed since the resisting act may need many things to succeed (cooperation of others, vulnerability of the targeted aggressor, etc.). But no matter how fragile, precarious, and minimally efficacious, micro-practices of resistance are worth pursuing in a sustained and concerted way because, just as any single act of micro-aggression may not do a lot of harm but collectively micro-aggressions help to maintain a culture of intimidation and epistemic violence, micro-activities of resistance taken collectively can help to undermine, weaken, and ultimately destroy such culture and to create one of support and mutual protection instead, even if no single act of micro-resistance will achieve that by itself.

Examples of micro-resistance can be: answering a question with another question that sends the disabling skeptical exercise back to the questioner; responding to a puzzling look with another puzzling look; to a claim such as "I am not sure I understand you" with a claim that casts similar doubts on the interlocutor; to a stare, gesture, or insinuation that calls into question one's competence with a stare, gesture, or insinuation that calls into question the aggressor's authority or ability to call into question other people's competence, and so forth. And note that acts of micro-resistance do not need to be issued necessarily by the person suffering the epistemic violence of the micro-aggression, but it can be produced effectively (sometimes even more effectively) by others involved in the interaction even though they were not targeted, and in some cases even by bystanders and eavesdroppers. In some cases, micro-invalidations can be countered with a who-are-you-to-invalidate response, or with a way of deflecting or shifting the unfair argumentative burden being posed; but in other cases micro-invalidations may call for resistant micro-validations, or alternative ways of validating and supporting subjects who, in the given context, are not likely to be given full or equal epistemic standing and agency. Micro-practices of resistance can also work preventively, for example by proactively offering gestures of validation to members of a group that has been stigmatized or is likely to encounter micro-invalidations in a particular context.

If nothing else, acts of micro-resistance can help alleviate or share the energy expended "rebounding" from micro-aggressions. But if effectively deployed and sustained sufficiently over time and across contexts, ideally with institutional backing and a support structure, they can also neutralize or at least counter the denigrating messages that micro-aggressions convey; they can minimize (if not eliminate) the negative consequences micro-aggressions can have; and they can prevent the harms epistemic violence produces or at least protect as much as possible the vulnerabilities of those exposed to it. Note that, although micro-practices of resistance will be performed by particular individuals in particular contexts, they also concern institutional settings, structural conditions, and collective attitudes and collective—or *chained*—actions; and in some cases they can even involve explicit institutional policies and legal frameworks. By supporting micro-practices of resistance, communities, publics, institutions, and their policies and structures can help the prevention of racial micro-aggressions and offer mechanisms of protection for when they happen; they can help to improve climates and facilitate the formation of a counter-culture of support. What Jennifer Saul (2014) has said about sexually harassing and counter-harassing micro-behaviors can also be said about racial micro-aggressions and micro-acts of resistance: we shouldn't underestimate "the power of small things—microbehaviours or microinequities—to create an unwelcoming environment" (p. 20); but we should not underestimate "the power of small things" to help bring about big changes either. As Saul argues, just as there are microbehaviors that make up harassing environments, there are also microbehaviors that counter them and can prevent the formation of such environments. People are often unaware of the power of microbehaviors. Communities, organizations, and institutions should promote discussions of microbehaviors in their daily activities so that people become more aware of how they can disable harassing attitudes and micro-aggressions, and help to meliorate climates and environments.

Of course epistemic violence goes beyond micro-aggressions and dysfunctional interpersonal dynamics, and an insurrectionist epistemology will need to include many other things besides micro-practices of resistance for fighting epistemic injustices. We need to be attentive to the many faces of racial violence and the complex and multilayered harms that racism produces. We need to pay attention to the complex relations between the interpersonal level and the structural and institutional level at which epistemic injustices operate, and to the agential involvement and complicity with racial epistemic harms of individuals, groups, and institutions, so that we can fully appreciate the diverse ways in which we can encourage solidarity against epistemic violence, instigate insurrectionary attitudes and actions, and mobilize and sustain social movements of resistance striving toward epistemic justice. Micro-practices of resistance are simply some among the many subversive practices we need to cultivate to empower oppressed voices and to facilitate "insurrection of subjugated knowledges" in order to produce a more equitable distribution of epistemic resources and more fair access to and participation in meaning-making and knowledge-producing practices. The multifaceted and heterogeneous fight against the epistemic injustices produced by racial insensitivity will not have an end, but it has no shortage of beginnings, of strategies of resistance and subversive moves which oppressed subjects and their allies have produced. Indeed the fight is well underway: No Justice, No Peace.

References

Anzaldúa, G. (1987) *Borderlands/La Frontera: The New Mestiza*, New York: Aunt Lute Books.

———. (2009) "Let Us Be the Healing of the Wound: The Coyolxauhqui Imperative—la sombra y el sueño," in Gloria Anzaldúa and AnaLouise Keating (eds.), *This Bridge We Call Home*, New York: Routledge.

Bailey, A. (2007) "Strategic Ignorance", in S. Sullivan and N. Tuana (eds.), pp. 77–94.

Baldwin, J. (1998) "The Fire Next Time," in *Collected Essays*, New York: Penguin Random House.

Crenshaw, K. (1991) "Mapping the Margins: Intersectionality, Identity Politics, and Violence Against Women of Color." *Stanford Law Review* 43: 1241–1299.

Dotson, K. (2011) "Tracking Epistemic Violence, Tracking Practices of Silencing." *Hypatia: A Journal of Feminist Philosophy* 26, no. 2: 236–257.

Du Bois, W.E.B. (1903/1994) *The Souls of Black Folks*, New York: Dover.

Ellison, R. (1952) *Invisible Man*, New York: Vintage Books.

Flory, D. (2008) *Philosophy, Black Film, Film Noir*, University Park: Penn State University Press.

Fricker, M. (2007) *Epistemic Injustice: Power and the Ethics of Knowing*, Oxford: Oxford University Press.

Gooding-Williams, R. (2011) *In the Shadow of Du Bois: Afro-Modern Political Thought in America*, Cambridge, MA: Harvard University Press.

Harris, L. (2002) "Insurrectionist Ethics: Advocacy, Moral Psychology, and Pragmatism," in J. Howie (ed.), *Ethical Issues for a New Millenium*, Carbondale: Southern Illinois University Press.

Harvin, C.B. (1996) "Conversations I Can't Have." *Progressive Woman's Quarterly* 5, no. 2: 15–16.

Hill Collins, P. (1990/2000) *Black Feminist Thought: Knowledge, Consciousness, and the Politics of Empowerment*, Boston: Unwin Hyman.

———. (2005) *Black Sexual Politics: African Americans, Gender, and the New Racism*, New York: Routledge.

McWhorter, L. (2009) *Racism and Sexual Oppression in Anglo-America: A Genealogy*, Bloomington: Indiana University Press.

Medina, J. (2011) "Toward a Foucaultian Epistemology of Resistance: Counter-Memory, Epistemic Friction, and *Guerrilla* Pluralism." *Foucault Studies* no. 12 (October): 9–35.

———. (2012) *The Epistemology of Resistance: Gender and Racial Oppression, Epistemic Injustice, and Resistant Imaginations*, New York: Oxford University Press.

———. (2015) "The Will *Not* to Believe: Pragmatism, Oppression, and Standpoint Theory," in S. Sullivan and E. Tarver (eds.), *Feminist Interpretations of William James*, University Park: Penn State University Press, pp. 256–289.

———. (2016) "Ignorance and Racial Insensitivity," in Rik Peels and Martijn Blaauw (eds.), *The Epistemic Dimensions of Ignorance*, Cambridge: Cambridge University Press, pp. 178–201.

Mills, C. (1997) *The Racial Contract*, Ithaca: Cornell University Press.

———. (1998) "Alternative Epistemologies," in C. Mills (ed.), *Blackness Visible: Essays on Philosophy and Race*, Ithaca, Cornell University Press, pp. 21–39.

Ortega, M. (2006) "Being Lovingly, Knowingly Ignorant: White Feminism and Women of Color." *Hypatia: A Journal of Feminist Philosophy* 21, no. 3: 56–74.

Patterson, O. (1982) *Slavery and Social Death: A Comparative Study*, Cambridge, MA: Harvard University Press.

Pitts, A. (2016) "Gloria E. Anzaldúa's *Autohistoria-teoría* as an Epistemology of Self-Knowledge/Ignorance." *Hypatia: A Journal of Feminist Philosophy* 31, no. 2: 352–369.

Saul, J. (2014) "Stop Thinking So Much About 'Sexual Harassment'." *Journal of Applied Philosophy* 31, no. 1: 307–321.

Spivak, G. (1998) "Can the Subaltern Speak?" in Cary Nelson and Lawrence Grossberg (eds.), *Marxism and the Interpretation of Culture*, Urbana: University of Illinois Press.

Stewart, M.W. (1932/1987) "Why Sit Ye Here and Die?" in Marilyn Richardson (ed.), *Maria W. Stewart: America's First Black Woman Political Writer*, Bloomington: Indiana University Press, pp. 45–49.

Sue, D.W., C.M. Capodilupo, and A.M.B. Holder. (2008) "Racial Micro-Aggressions in the Life Experience of Black Americans." *Professional Psychology: Research and Practice* 39, no. 3: 329–336.

Sullivan, S., and Tuana, N. (eds.) (2007) *Race and Epistemologies of Ignorance*, Albany: State University of New York Press.

19
IMPLICIT BIAS AND RACE
Michael Brownstein

Introduction

In 1928 L. L. Thurstone asked 239 white male students at the University of Chicago to report their preferences between pairs of "races" and "nationalities," such as "Greek vs. Mexican," "American vs. Hindu," and "Negro vs. Turk." Unsurprisingly, one of the most discrepant responses between pairs was in the "American vs. Negro" comparison, with almost all participants strongly preferring "Americans" to "Negros." (The very fact that Thurstone distinguished between "American" and "Negro" or "Hindu" is perhaps also unsurprising, and unsettling. See Devos and Banaji (2005) on associating "white" with "American.") Compare this to Brian Nosek and colleagues' finding in 2007 that in a pool of 700,000 subjects the most frequent answer to the question, "who do you prefer, black people or white people?" was "I have no preference." The disparities between these findings underscores how dramatically explicit (i.e., verbally reported) black-white racism—white people's prejudices and racial attitudes toward black people—has declined over the past 75 years in the United States (see also Judd et al. 1995 and Schuman et al. 1997; for discussion of implicit bias directed toward non-black members of socially stigmatized groups, such as Asians and Latinxs, see Dasgupta (2004)). Despite this, it's clear that racial discrimination persists systematically, pervasively, and brutally in the United States. This presents a puzzle that philosophers, sociologists, political scientists, economists, psychologists, and others have considered. Why do stark racial disparities in housing and hiring, police violence and incarceration, medical treatment and health outcomes, and on and on, persist in places like the United States today, if most people's beliefs about race have changed so much?

One part of the answer is that what people say explicitly—on a questionnaire like Thurstone's or one of its contemporary analogues, such as the Modern Racism Scale (MRS; McConahay 1986)—does not represent the whole of what people feel or think. This is news to almost nobody, of course. What is news to many is that some element of people's thoughts and feelings can be measured without having to ask them directly what they think or feel, using a host of "indirect" measurement techniques, most prominently the "Implicit Association Test" (IAT; Greenwald et al. 1998). The IAT is one of many reaction time measures that asks participants to sort words or pictures into categories as quickly as possible while making as few errors as possible. A person taking the most well-known IAT—the black-white IAT—will be presented with variations of the images in Figures 19.1–19.4.

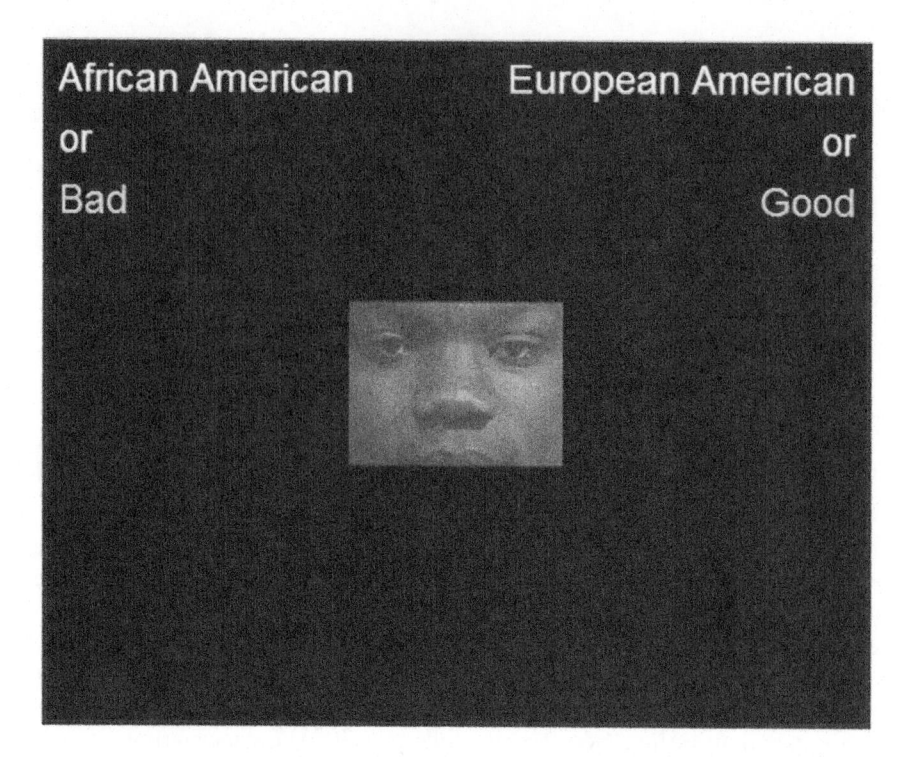

Figure 19.1 Implicit Association Test
Screenshots from the Project Implicit website, accessed on May 24, 2017, https://implicit.harvard.edu/implicit/. Reprinted with permission.

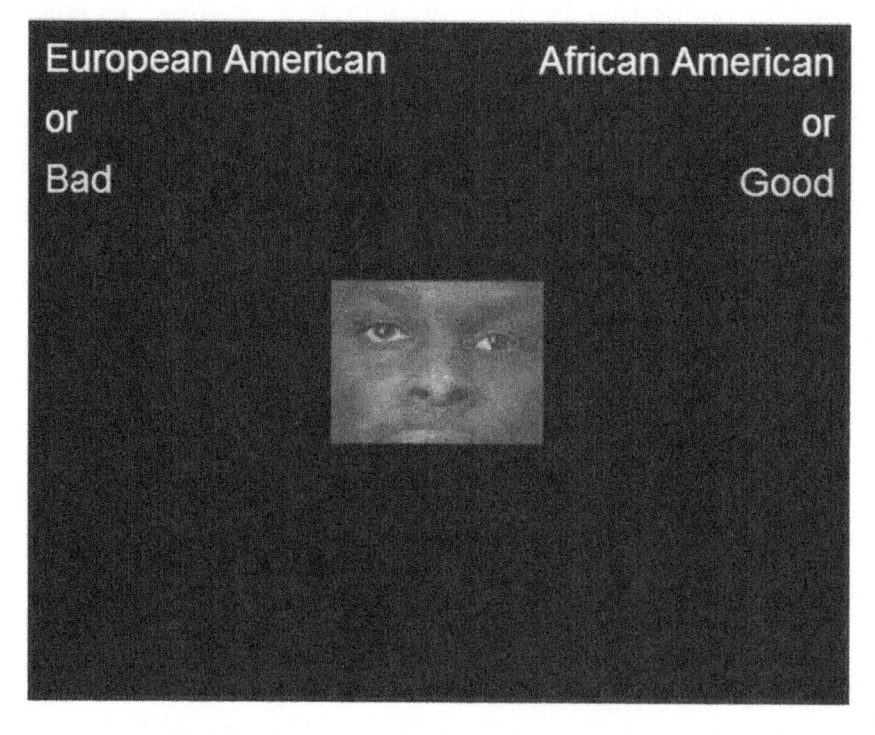

Figure 19.2 Implicit Association Test
Screenshots from the Project Implicit website, accessed on May 24, 2017, https://implicit.harvard.edu/implicit/. Reprinted with permission.

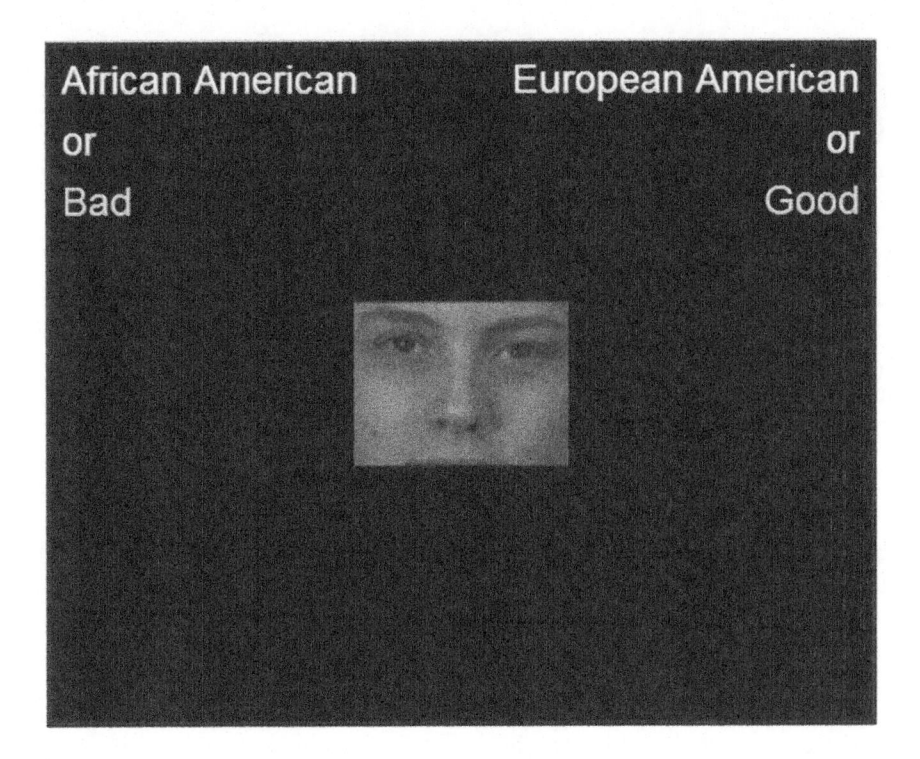

Figure 19.3 Implicit Association Test
Screenshots from the Project Implicit website, accessed on May 24, 2017, https://implicit.harvard.edu/implicit/. Reprinted with permission.

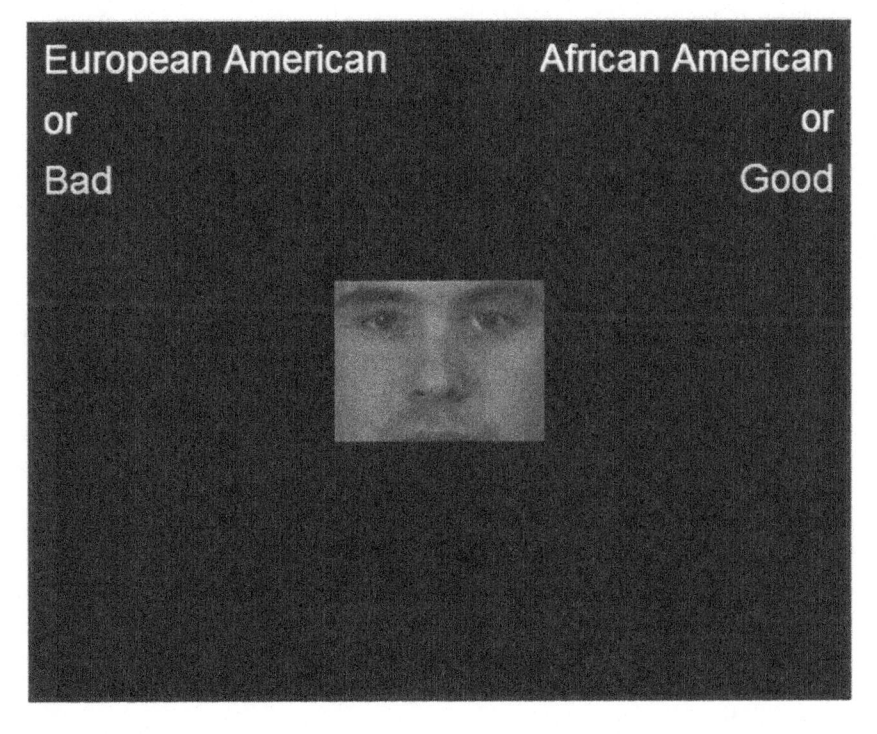

Figure 19.4 Implicit Association Test
Screenshots from the Project Implicit website, accessed on May 24, 2017, https://implicit.harvard.edu/implicit/. Reprinted with permission.

The goal is to sort the pictures to the left or right. Notice that the categories on the left and right pair a social group label with a positive or negative word. In Figures 19.1 and 19.3, the pairing is "compatible" with widespread negative attitudes toward black people, while in Figures 19.2 and 19.4 the pairing is "incompatible." Most white subjects (over 70%) will be faster and make fewer mistakes on compatible than on incompatible trials (Nosek et al. 2007). Researchers consider this to represent an "implicit preference" for white faces over black faces. Remarkably, while roughly 40% of black participants demonstrate an implicit in-group preference for black faces over white faces, and 20% show no preference, roughly 40% of black participants demonstrate an implicit out-group preference for white faces over black faces (Nosek et al. 2002; Ashburn-Nardo et al. 2003; Dasgupta 2004). This finding has upended the view that in-group favoritism is the primary driver of implicit bias. Rather, it appears that implicit bias is driven by a combination of in-group favoritism and sensitivity to the value society places on particular groups.

The significance of computerized reaction time measures like the IAT could seem small if it weren't for an extensive body of literature showing that IAT scores sometimes predict discriminatory behavior. The stronger one's associations of good with white faces and bad with black faces on the black-white IAT, the more likely one is, for example, to judge otherwise equivalent curricula vitae (CV) better if they have white-sounding names on them than black-sounding names (Bertrand et al. 2005). Doctors who demonstrate more implicit bias on the IAT are more likely to attribute equivalent symptoms to coronary artery disease and recommend thrombolysis for white patients compared to black patients (Green et al. 2007). And perhaps most ominously, in light of continued shootings of unarmed black men by police officers, the stronger one's implicit biases as measured by the IAT, the more likely one is to "shoot" unarmed black men in a computer simulation than unarmed white men (Correll et al. 2002; Glaser and Knowles 2008), a pattern that remains when study participants are black as well as when they are police officers (Plant and Peruche 2005). These are just a flavor of the disturbing findings. Overall, the IAT is particularly useful for predicting negative non-verbal and "micro-behaviors" (Valian 1998, 2005; Dovidio et al. 2002; Cortina 2008; Cortina et al. 2011; Brennan 2013) and action undertaken when information is incomplete, decisions need to be made quickly, or agents are stressed or under cognitive load.

The IAT (and other indirect measures) is thought to quantify "implicit biases." Implicit bias is a term of art referring to prejudiced implicit attitudes, and implicit attitudes are, of course, contrasted with explicit attitudes. By and large, explicit attitudes can be thought of as what people report on questionnaires or other "direct" measures. But what is an implicit attitude? There are two questions here. First, what is an attitude? In psychology, attitudes are understood as likings or dislikings; or, more formally, as associations between a concept and an evaluation (Nosek and Banaji 2009). This conceptualization of attitudes is importantly different from the typical usage in philosophy, which is much more expansive (including beliefs, desires, intentions, etc.). Unless otherwise indicated, hereafter I'll discuss attitudes in the psychological sense. The structure of attitudes, in particular implicit attitudes, is a matter of theoretical contention (Gendler 2008a, 2008b; Levy 2012, 2015; Madva 2012, 2016b; Mandelbaum 2013, 2016; Beeghly 2014; Brownstein 2016; Brownstein and Saul 2016a, 2016b), but I won't address this topic directly.

The second question is what makes an attitude implicit. Following the general characterization of implicit attitudes found in the empirical literature, most philosophers have focused on two qualities: lack of awareness of one's implicit attitudes and lack of control over them. For example, here is Daniel Kelly and Erica Roedder's characterization in their influential 2008 paper:

> the IAT requires subjects to make snap judgments that must be made quickly, and thus without moderating influence of introspection and deliberation and often without conscious intention. Biases revealed by an IAT are often thought to implicate relatively automatic processes.
>
> (525)

Similarly, Jennifer Saul (2012: 244) describes implicit biases as "unconscious tendencies to automatically associate concepts with one another," and in a similar vein elsewhere I call implicit biases "relatively unconscious and relatively automatic features of prejudiced judgment and social behavior" (Brownstein 2015: 1).

The qualifiers found in these definitions—"relatively" automatic, "relatively" unconscious, "tendencies" to. . . —reflect the fact that research increasingly suggests that there are senses in which people *are* conscious of their implicit attitudes and *can* control them. Implicit attitudes are unlike features of our minds to which we have no direct introspective access, like the fact that visual stimuli from the retina are processed upside-down. We can learn this fact, but we can't know it introspectively. Similarly, implicit attitudes *can* be reshaped and even possibly eliminated using certain "self-regulation" techniques. That is, implicit biases are unlike untrainable reflexes, such as pupillary dilation.

Recent research on awareness of and control over implicit biases calls for further consideration of what makes an attitude implicit. Such consideration has many philosophical ramifications, in addition to simply clarifying the construct called implicit bias. For example, whether we are morally responsible for having implicit biases or for acting in ways influenced by implicit bias depends on what it means for those biases to be implicit (Kelly and Roedder 2008; Smith 2008, 2012; Levy 2012, 2015; Holroyd 2012; Saul 2013; Levy and Mandelbaum 2014; Brownstein 2015; Madva 2017; and the chapters by Faucher, Glasgow, Sie and Voorst Vader-Bours, Washington and Kelly, and Zheng in Brownstein and Saul 2016a, 2016b). Moreover, whether the pervasiveness of implicit bias is cause for skepticism about our ability to make unbiased assessments of CVs, resumes, student papers, and more will also depend on what implicitness entails. A third philosophical question—which has received less attention than these—focuses on what, in broad terms, the empirical literature on implicit bias tells us about contemporary attitudes toward race. This is the question on which I will focus here.

To be clear, my aim is *not* to give an argument about the nature of racism in the modern world or in the United States. Rather, my aim is to give an argument about what the research on implicit bias tells us about attitudes toward race in a broad sense. An important caveat is that the participants in most research to date have been white undergraduates in the US and UK, so in reality my argument will be about what the research on implicit bias tells us about this population. (See Dunham et al. (2006) for an example of research on implicit intergroup attitudes in non-US or UK populations.) Is the dramatic decline in explicit racial prejudice within this population due to actual changes in people's racial attitudes? Or is it rather due to changes in what is socially acceptable to say and do? Or perhaps attitudes have changed, but largely only in respect of subjects' awareness of them. Here, then, are three possible faces of contemporary black-white racial cognition, as represented by the literature on implicit bias: (1) racial attitudes have changed wholesale over the past century; (2) racial attitudes as such haven't changed, but social norms have; (3) racial attitudes have "split" into conscious and unconscious attitudes.

While each of these is possible, I will not give the first option—that racial attitudes have changed wholesale—any further consideration. There is no doubt that *specific* racial attitudes, or specific components of racial attitudes, have changed. But it is beyond question that racial prejudice persists today.

Research on implicit bias can only reveal an incomplete picture of racial prejudice and discrimination, of course. Psychological research on racial cognition cannot capture many crucial political, economic, and institutional causes of discrimination and prejudice (Anderson 2010; see Madva 2016a, forthcoming for discussion). Nevertheless, it can tell us much, and understanding what it tells us is important. I will begin in the next section by describing the two most prominent ways that researchers in the empirical literature have characterized implicit racial attitudes. Different theories of implicit social cognition, I shall try to show, align with different philosophical interpretations of contemporary racial cognition. One theory stems from research on automaticity and considers implicit biases to reflect people's "true" attitudes in the absence of "contamination" by strategic self-presentation considerations (i.e., considerations of how one wants to be received by others). On the interpretation I will call "True Attitudes," which follows from this theory, most people's ownmost attitudes toward socially stigmatized groups (e.g., blacks, women, Latinos, the elderly, members of the LGBTQ community) really are prejudiced, yet in some circumstances people are able to control these prejudiced thoughts and feelings in order to act in accord with social norms. A second theory stems from research on memory and considers implicit biases to be unconscious counterparts to people's conscious attitudes. On the interpretation I call "Driven Underground," people often have conflicting thoughts and feelings about others based on their perceived social group membership, and some of those thoughts and feelings are unavailable to introspection. These two interpretations of implicit bias— "True Attitudes" and "Driven Underground"—have different ramifications for questions about moral responsibility, epistemology, and ethics. However, both conceptions are somewhat flawed, I will argue in the third section. After that I will then argue that what makes attitudes implicit is not a difference in their *content*, but rather a difference in the *processes* that cause implicit attitudes to form and change. A leading process-focused theory of implicit attitudes is Bertram Gawronski and Galen Bodenhausen's Associative-Propositional model of evaluation (APE; 2006, 2011). APE suggests that an attitude is implicit when it is "validity-inapt." I conclude by considering what the research on implicit bias tells us about contemporary racial attitudes if APE's conceptualization of implicitness is correct.

True Attitudes and Driven Underground

Research on implicit social cognition has two distinct roots, one focusing on automaticity and the other focusing on unconsciousness. These manifested in two related streams of research, the first, focusing on automaticity and led by Russ Fazio, and the second, focusing on unconsciousness and led by Anthony Greenwald and Mazarin Banaji. Fazio and Greenwald/Banaji's research led to two different interpretations of modern racial cognition: "True Attitudes" and "Driven Underground."

(What follows in the next two paragraphs is derived from Brownstein (2016), which is in turn indebted to the cogent history of research on implicit social cognition found in Payne and Gawronski (2010) and Amodio and Devine (2009). Note that the two streams of research I discuss below are not the only significant influences on implicit social cognition research. John McConahay's "Modern Racism Theory" (McConahay et al. 1981; McConahay 1982) argues that explicit prejudice has been funneled into more socially acceptable beliefs about public policy, such as affirmative action and desegregation programs. This is probably true, but does not account for well-documented effects of implicit attitudes on socially unacceptable behavior, such as biased review of résumés and CVs. Similarly, Jack Dovidio's and Samuel Gaertner's work on "aversive racism" (Gaertner and Dovidio 1986; Dovidio and Gaertner 2004) has been very influential but does not account for the full scope of contemporary research. Aversive racism is characterized by unconscious negative feelings, but it is clear that implicit black-white racial bias is equally, or perhaps even primarily, driven by *preferences* for whites compared to aversions to blacks (Brewer 1999; Dixon et al. 2012; Greenwald and Pettigrew 2014).)

Fazio's work was influenced by the cognitive psychology of the 1970s, which distinguished between "controlled" and "automatic" information processing in memory (e.g., Shiffrin and Schneider 1977). What Fazio showed was that attitudes can also be understood as activated by controlled or automatic processes. The "sequential priming" technique (Fazio 1995) measures social attitudes by timing people's reactions (or "response latencies") to stereotypic words (e.g., "lazy" or "nurturing") after exposing them to social group labels ("black," "women," etc.). Most people are significantly faster to identify a word like "lazy" in a word-scramble after being exposed to the word "black" (compared with "white"). A faster reaction of this kind is thought to indicate a relatively automatic association between "lazy" and "black." According to Fazio's MODE model of attitudes ("Motivation and Opportunity as Determinants"; Fazio 1990; Fazio and Towles-Schwen 1999; Olson and Fazio 2009), these associations are activated in the presence of relevant cues and facilitate an automatic attitude-to-behavior process. In some cases, though, people have control over their automatic associations. The difference between direct and indirect measures (e.g., a questionnaire like the MRS and reaction time tests like sequential priming and the IAT), on this view, reflects a difference in the control subjects have over their responses. MODE understands control in terms of motivation and opportunity to exert effortful, deliberative control over one's behavior. When someone has low motivation or opportunity to rein in her automatic associations, those associations will guide her behavior and judgment. For example, MODE explains lower correlations between implicit and explicit racial attitudes, compared with higher correlations between implicit and explicit attitudes toward food and consumer preferences, in terms of race being a socially sensitive topic compared with the latter preferences. On socially sensitive topics like race, that is, people are more motivated to control their automatic reactions. Indirect measures like sequential priming and the IAT manufacture this situation (of low control due to low motivation and/or opportunity to deliberate).

The broader notion embedded in this research was that indirect measures offer a window onto people's attitudes themselves, independent of other factors that affect behavior, such as higher-order goals, self-presentation concerns, or cognitive depletion. Indeed, Fazio and colleagues (1995) characterized sequential priming as a "bona fide pipeline" to people's attitudes. In fact, MODE technically denies the distinction between implicit and explicit attitudes. Rather, it is a "one-process" model. Attitudes as such are captured by techniques like sequential priming; it is the degree of control people have over their attitudes, in conjunction with the strength of their attitudes, which determines their responses. This leads to the interpretation I call "True Attitudes," as it conceptualizes indirect measures as capturing our prejudices before they are "contaminated" by controlled processes, such as a desire to present oneself as unprejudiced. Such desires and motives occur *downstream* from racial attitudes, according to MODE.

In contrast to MODE, Greenwald, Banaji, and colleagues' research focused on unawareness of implicit attitudes. This stream of research interprets scores on direct measures of racial attitudes to represent the attitudes people know they have, while scores on indirect measures are thought to represent the introspectively unidentified "traces" of past experiences on one's feelings, thoughts, and behaviors. This research was influenced by theories of implicit memory, which was understood generally as the influence of past experience on later behavior without conscious memory of the past experience (e.g., Jacoby and Dallas 1981; Schacter 1987). One can see the role of theories of implicit memory in Greenwald and Banaji's seminal definition of implicit attitudes as "introspectively unidentified (or inaccurately identified) traces of past experience that mediate favorable or unfavorable feeling, thought, or action toward social objects" (1995: 8). Here the emphasis is not on automaticity but on the introspective unavailability of implicit attitudes, or, alternately, the introspective unavailability of the past experiences that formed those attitudes. Borrowing a concept from Dovidio and Gaertner (1986), I call the interpretation this view leads to "Driven Underground." The guiding idea is that in the modern world people persist in holding both prejudiced and unprejudiced racial attitudes, but don't themselves know about the former. What precisely "knowing about" one's implicit attitudes means can be interpreted in different ways (see discussion below).

Awareness and Control Over Implicit Attitudes

In addition to emphasizing different features of implicitness—"True Attitudes" emphasizing automaticity and "Driven Underground" emphasizing unconsciousness—these two approaches also deny what the other claims. On the one hand, Fazio and colleagues deny that direct and indirect measures capture two different kinds of mental states, one conscious and the other unconscious. Olson and Fazio (2009: 49), for example, write, "[MODE] maintains that people tend to generally be aware of their attitudes and that it is motivational forces, not some consciousness-impervious shield, that prevents their verbal expression." On the other hand, Greenwald and Banaji emphasize that implicit attitudes are not reflections of automatic processing alone. Rather, much of their research focuses on the combined contributions of automatic and controlled processes to the formation and change of implicit attitudes themselves.

Both of these denials helpfully illuminate components of what is clearly a complex phenomenon. Implicit attitudes are neither outside of conscious awareness as such nor are they completely automatic states. For example, despite uncorrelated scores on direct and indirect tests (i.e., what people report on a questionnaire vs. how they score on a test like the IAT), people are fairly good at predicting their own implicit attitudes (Hahn et al. 2013). And when people are told that the IAT is "as close to a lie detector test as is possible," most people's scores move significantly closer to their scores on direct measures (Nier 2005). The literature on awareness of implicit attitudes is growing too. At present, it appears that people are comparatively more aware of what their implicit attitudes are (their "content") than they are aware of the causal origins of their implicit attitudes or of the many ways that their implicit attitudes influence their behavior. This point is underscored by Nosek and Hansen (2008) who examined a wide range of implicit attitudes (toward race, gender, food, sports teams, brand names, political figures, etc.) in over 100,000 participants and found that the best way to predict a person's implicit attitudes toward ψ is to ask them explicitly how warmly they feel about ψ.

That people tend to lack source and impact awareness of their implicit attitudes may provide succor for "Driven Underground," depending on whether "Driven Underground" is a view about awareness of one's mental states as such or, rather, a view about awareness of the origins and effects of one's mental states. If "Driven Underground" defines implicit attitudes as introspectively unavailable mental *states*, then data demonstrating that people lack source and impact awareness of their implicit attitudes does not vindicate it. Wilson and colleagues (2000) and Banaji (2001) define implicit attitudes as mental states in this way. Greenwald and Banaji's definition of implicit attitudes as "traces of past experience" suggests a less mentalistic interpretation of "Driven Underground," according to which what people are unaware of is the origins of their implicit attitudes. This less mentalistic interpretation may be a better representation of the data, but it is unclear how much it can clarify what makes an attitude implicit, since we are often unaware of the origins and effects of our explicit attitudes (cf. the large literature on confabulation in consumer preferences, for example Nisbett and Wilson (1977); see Payne and Gawronski (2010) for discussion).

The literature on control over implicit attitudes is extensive and complex, but it makes clear that implicit biases are not automatic in the sense of being inescapable (akin to motor reflexes or automatisms like sleepwalking), as proponents of "True Attitudes" have suggested (e.g., Fazio et al. 1986; Bargh 1999). For example, when people adopt specific "if-then" plans (known as "implementation intentions") to behave in unbiased ways, the effects can be significant. In the context of a "shooter bias" simulation (see the first section of this chapter), in which one's goal is to shoot all and only those individuals shown holding guns (rather than other objects such as cell phones), biased responding decreases significantly if one says to oneself beforehand, "if I see a person with a gun, then I will shoot!" (Mendoza et al. 2010). Other effective strategies for shifting implicit biases involve increasing one's exposure to images, film clips, or even mental imagery depicting members of stigmatized groups acting in stereotype-discordant ways (Blair et al. 2001; Dasgupta and Greenwald 2001) and engaging in meaningful intergroup contact (Dasgupta and Rivera 2008). Of course, care must be taken in considering which data on control over implicit attitudes do and do not cut against "True Attitudes." MODE predicts that implicit attitudes can be controlled downstream from their activation, but it pointedly denies that implicit attitudes themselves involve controlled processes. To get a handle on this distinction, imagine the difference between Ulysses having his men bind him to the mast of his ship in order to resist the allure of the Sirens—which is a form of self-control downstream from the activation of desire—and someone else who has managed to change or eliminate the desire itself.

What Is Implicit About Implicit Attitudes?

The discussion thus far may leave readers understandably confused. If implicit attitudes are neither unconscious nor automatic, then why consider them to be distinct from explicit attitudes? One way to move forward is to recognize that automaticity and (un)consciousness are kinds of operating *conditions*. That is, they are descriptions of when—the conditions under which—implicit attitudes are operating. Indirect tests like the IAT manufacture these conditions; they do not require people to know that their social attitudes are being measured, nor do they provide people sufficient time to control their responses deliberatively. But one must exercise care in making an inference from these characteristics of tests to the nature of the mental states illuminated by these tests. Moreover, explicit attitudes sometimes operate under these conditions as well. Personality inventories are explicit measures, but it is not clear that people know what is being measured when taking them (e.g., people might not know they are being asked about their degree of neuroticism when they are asked whether they get stressed out easily).

Instead of defining implicit attitudes in terms of the conditions under which they are manifested, an alternative is to define them in terms of the *principles* according to which they operate. Several groups of researchers have taken this route. Here I will focus on Gawronski and Bodenhausen's "Associative-Propositional" model of evaluation (APE; Gawronski and Bodenhausen 2006, 2011), which treats implicit and explicit attitudes as behavioral manifestations of two distinct kinds of mental process.

According to APE, all information is stored in the mind in the form of associations. For example, the statement, "black people are a disadvantaged group" represents the association between "black people" and "disadvantaged group" (Gawronski and Bodenhausen 2011). As we move through the world, the associations stored in our memories are constantly activated. Hearing the name "Malcolm X," for example, might activate the thought that black people are a disadvantaged group. Of course, a person will have many associations with the name Malcolm X, just as with virtually any cue. Nevertheless, APE offers a complex account of which associations will be activated in a given context. APE refers to this process of the activation of associations as *associative processing*. Sometimes, however, we are concerned to validate the information supplied by associative processing. That is, sometimes we are concerned with whether a given association is true or false. APE refers to this process of validation as *propositional processing*. The result of propositional processing might be the thought that "it is true (false) that black people are a disadvantaged group." The differences between associative and propositional processes comprise the heart of APE. And the fundamental difference between them are the "laws" according to which they operate. While associative processes are driven by the spatiotemporal contiguity of stimuli with associations stored in memory, propositional processes are driven by subjective assessments of truth.

APE is put to work to distinguish implicit and explicit attitudes in the following way. When a person reads through a pile of résumés (for example), she may notice (consciously or unconsciously) the names of the job candidates. These names will trigger associations with particular social groups (e.g., Jamal may trigger associations with black men; Emily may trigger associations with white women). In addition, people often associate positive and negative stereotypes with particular social groups. For example, many white Americans associate negative stereotypes such as "lazy" and seemingly positive stereotypes such as "athletic" with black men. (I say "seemingly" because stereotypes such as "athletic" can be positive in some contexts but negative in others; see Madva and Brownstein (2016).) Upon registering the name "Jamal," these stereotypes may become activated. Because this is an associative process, the name Jamal may activate the concept lazy in independence of whether the person believes it to be true or false that people with the name Jamal tend to be lazy. Such activated associations may manifest in the consciousness of the résumé reader as a vague negative gut feeling, although this emergence into consciousness is not a defining feature. What *is* crucial, according to APE, are the ways in which an activated association gives rise to behavior. One possibility is that associative processing "guides" the résumé reader's response. This is the situation manufactured by the IAT and other indirect measures. A second possibility is that the reader transforms her association into a proposition (e.g., "black people are lazy"), which she then endorses or rejects. This is the situation manufactured by questionnaires and other direct measures of attitudes.

APE offers a complex account of the interaction of associative and propositional processes, as well as the relations between associative and propositional processing and consciousness and automaticity, the result of which are predictions about the conditions under which one or the other process will guide a person's behavior. APE is surely not accepted by all theorists, although there is widespread support for process-focused accounts of implicit attitudes. If APE represents a plausible model of the empirical data, what does it tell us about modern racism?

Two Faces of Prejudice

APE suggests that the implicit/explicit divide does not track automaticity/controlled processes, nor does it track non-conscious/conscious mental states per se, although control over and consciousness of one's mental states act as important moderators of the activation of implicit attitudes. Rather, the implicit/explicit divide tracks the difference between mental processes that are and are not "validity-apt." One face of prejudice—represented by explicit, "old-fashioned" racism—reflects what people take to be true. On some interpretations, a natural way to express this is that propositional processing issues in beliefs. This stems from the notion that beliefs "track truth" or have the "aim" of being true (Velleman 2000; Gendler 2008a, 2008b). Related interpretations of prejudiced propositional attitudes might instead stress concepts like "endorsement" or "identification" (e.g., Frankfurt 1971) or "judgment-sensitivity" (Scanlon 1998; Smith 2005, 2008, 2012). What holds all of these notions together is the idea that the person *takes a stand* toward the content of her attitudes, regarding them as true or false, mine or not mine, valid or invalid.

The other face of prejudice—represented by implicit bias—reflects the information one has encoded from one's social environment, media, and so on. But this reflection of information is complex. First, it is *not* a reflection of "material" reality alone. The black-violent implicit stereotype is not just a reflection of crime statistics, but also cultural messaging, such as depictions of black men in film, television, and other forms of culture. (See Jussim et al. (2009) and Hardin and Banaji (2013) for discussion.) Second, associative processes are *not* merely a reflection of "cultural knowledge," that is, they are not a reflection of stereotypes "in the air" or what a person thinks other people think (Nosek and Hansen 2008). Rather, associative processes reflect one's own enculturation and social learning, in independence of whether one regards one's associations as one's own or as what others think. Third, many factors, including personality, age, socioeconomic status, and so on, mediate and moderate the ways in which one encodes information. For example, APE claims that the activation of associations depends largely on the "fit" between the stimuli a person encounters and her preexisting associations. Thus the activation of associations in response to one and the same stimulus may be quite different for two people who have different preexisting associations.

There is no obvious go-to category to represent what these associative processes issue in. Tamar Gendler (2008a, 2008b) has recommended the *sui generis* state that she calls an "alief," which, roughly can be understood as a mental state with relatively fixed and tightly bound representational, affective, and behavioral components. For Gendler, aliefs are automatic and (largely) unconscious, and are meant to represent the psychological underpinnings of implicit bias. Of course, the name we give to these states is far less important than the properties we ascribe to them. The key property, I have suggested, is that they reflect complex yet validity-inapt processes of enculturation. Implicit attitudes are normatively deviant because they are largely insensitive to the rules that we ourselves set down, this is, our beliefs, values, and ideals. Call this view "arationality": research on implicit bias shows that different kinds of racial attitudes operate according to different kinds of rules. Tests of implicit bias reveal neither our true attitudes nor our sublimated, underground attitudes. Rather, they reveal our arational attitudes.

Broadly, what this tells us is that contemporary racial attitudes reflect the ways in which we are imperfectly rational creatures. Human beings are, perhaps, distinct in the animal kingdom in our ability to set normative standards for ourselves, and to treat those standards not only as conventions but as sources of morality. Explicit racism plays this game. It takes a (grossly perverted) stand on what is right and wrong. Implicit bias, however, does not play this game. It shows us to be imperfectly rational in a different sense, namely, that much of what we think, feel, and do does not stem from the setting of normative standards, from a concern for morality, or for a concern for "who we are" or "who we want to be." In this sense, the empirical literature on implicit social cognition simply throws more fuel on the fire—the fire of bounded rationality—that cognitive and social psychologists, behavioral economists, and others have been burning for the past 40 or so years (Banaji 2003; Hardin and Banaji 2013). No doubt, automaticity and unconsciousness are central elements of what makes us boundedly rational creatures. But automaticity and unconsciousness are themselves not the processes that render an attitude implicit, and indeed, many of our beliefs, values, and other explicit attitudes can be automatic and unconscious (Railton 2009, 2014; Arpaly and Shroeder 2012). Rather, it is a relative immunity to those features of our minds that enable our distinct rationality that marks implicitness.

In the broadest sense, research on implicit bias calls us to rethink the relationship between morality and rationality. It is increasingly and abundantly clear that having good intentions and respectable beliefs is insufficient for being the kind of moral creatures we wish to be, and, that having bad intentions and unrespectable beliefs is not necessary for being an immoral creature. Research on implicit bias calls us to reject any conception of rational agency on which this is mysterious.

References

Amodio, D., and Devine, P. (2009) "On the Interpersonal Functions of Implicit Stereotyping and Evaluative Race Bias: Insights From Social Neuroscience," in R. Petty, R. Fazio, and P. Briñol (eds.), *Attitudes: Insights From the New Wave of Implicit Measures*, Hillsdale, NJ: Erlbaum, pp. 193–226.

Anderson, E. (2010) *The Imperative of Integration*, Princeton: Princeton University Press.

Arpaly, N., and Shroeder, T. (2012) "Deliberation and Acting for Reasons." *Philosophical Review* 121, no. 2: 209–239.

Ashburn-Nardo, L., Knowles, M. L., and Monteith, M. J. (2003) "Black Americans' Implicit Racial Associations and Their Implications for Intergroup Judgment." *Social Cognition* 21, no. 1: 61–87.

Banaji, M. (2001) "Implicit Attitudes Can Be Measured," in H. L. Roediger, J. S. Nairne, I. Neath, and A. Surprenant (eds.), *The Nature of Remembering: Essays in Remembering Robert G. Crowder*. Washington, DC: American Psychological Association, pp. 117–150.

Bargh, J. (1999) "The Cognitive Monster: The Case Against the Controllability of Automatic Stereotype Effects," in S. Chaiken and Y. Trope (eds.), *Dual-Process Theories in Social Psychology*, New York: Guilford Press, pp. 361–382.

Beeghly, E. (2014) *Seeing Difference: The Epistemology and Ethics of Stereotyping*, Ph.D. diss., University of California, Berkeley.

Blair, I., Ma, J., and Lenton, A. (2001) "Imagining Stereotypes Away: The Moderation of Implicit Stereotypes Through Mental Imagery." *Journal of Personality and Social Psychology* 81, no. 5: 828–841.

Bertrand, M., Chugh, D., and Mullainathan, S. (2005) "Implicit Discrimination." *American Economic Review*: 94–98.

Brennan, S. (2013) "Rethinking the Moral Significance of Micro-Inequities: The Case of Women in Philosophy," in F. Jenkins and K. Hutchinson (eds.), *Women in Philosophy: What Needs to Change?* Oxford: Oxford University Press.

Brewer, M. (1999) "The Psychology of Prejudice: Ingroup Love and Outgroup Hate?" *Journal of Social Issues* 55, no. 3: 429–444.

Brownstein, M. (2015) "Attributionism and Moral Responsibility for Implicit Bias." *Review of Philosophy and Psychology* 7, no. 4: 765–786.

———. (2016) "Implicit Bias, Context, and Character," in M. Brownstein and J. Saul (eds.), *Implicit Bias and Philosophy: Volume 2, Moral Responsibility, Structural Injustice, and Ethics*, Oxford: Oxford University Press.

Brownstein, M., and Saul, J. (eds.). (2016a) *Implicit Bias & Philosophy: Volume 1, Metaphysics and Epistemology*, Oxford: Oxford University Press.

———. (eds.). (2016b) *Implicit Bias and Philosophy: Volume 2, Moral Responsibility, Structural Injustice, and Ethics*, Oxford: Oxford University Press.

Correll, J., Park, B., Judd, C., and Wittenbrink, B. (2002) "The Police Officer's Dilemma: Using Race to Disambiguate Potentially Threatening Individuals." *Journal of Personality and Social Psychology* 83: 1314–1329.

Cortina, L. (2008) "Unseen Injustice: Incivility as Modern Discrimination in Organizations." *Academy of Management Review* 33: 55–75.

Cortina, L., Kabat Farr, D., Leskinen, E., Huerta, M. and V. Magley. (2011) "Selective Incivility as Modern Discrimination in Organizations: Evidence and Impact." *Journal of Management* 39, no. 6: 1579–1605.

Dasgupta, N. (2004). "Implicit Ingroup Favoritism, Outgroup Favoritism, and Their Behavioral Manifestations." *Social Justice Research* 17, no. 2: 143–168.

Dasgupta, N., and Greenwald, A. (2001) "On the Malleability of Automatic Attitudes: Combating Automatic Prejudice With Images of Admired and Disliked Individuals." *Journal of Personality and Social Psychology* 81: 800–814.

Dasgupta, N. and L. Rivera (2008) "When Social Context Matters: The Influence of Long-Term Contact and Short-Term Exposure to Admired Group Members on Implicit Attitudes and Behavioral Intentions." *Social Cognition* 26: 112–123.

Devos, T., and Banaji, M.R. (2005) American = white? *Journal of Personality and Social Psychology* 88, no. 3: 447.

Dixon, J., Levine, M., Reicher, S., and Durrheim, K. (2012) "Beyond Prejudice: Are Negative Evaluations the Problem and Is Getting Us to Like One Another More the Solution?" *Behavioral and Brain Sciences* 35(6): 411–425.

Dovidio, J., and Gaertner, S. (2004) "Aversive Racism." *Advances in Experimental Social Psychology* 36: 1–51.

Dovidio, J., Kawakami, K., and Gaertner, S. (2002) "Implicit and Explicit Prejudice and Interracial Interaction." *Journal of Personality and Social Psychology* 82: 62–68.

Dunham, Y., Baron, A.S., and Banaji, M.R. (2006) "From American City to Japanese Village: A Cross-Cultural Investigation of Implicit Race Attitudes." *Child Development* 77, no. 5: 1268–1281.

Fazio, R. (1990) "Multiple Processes by Which Attitudes Guide Behavior: The MODE Model as an Integrative Framework." *Advances in Experimental Social Psychology* 23: 75–109.

———. (1995) "Attitudes as Object-Evaluation Associations: Determinants, Consequences, and Correlates of Attitude Accessibility," in R. Petty and J. Krosnick (eds.), *Attitude Strength: Antecedents and Consequences*. Ohio State University Series on Attitudes and Persuasion, Vol. 4, Hillsdale, NJ: Lawrence Erlbaum, pp. 247–282.

Fazio, R.H., Jackson, J.R., Dunton, B.C., and Williams, C.J. (1995) "Variability in Automatic Activation as an Unobtrusive Measure of Racial Attitudes: A Bona Fide Pipeline?" *Journal of Personality and Social Psychology* 69, no. 6: 1013.

Fazio, R.H., Sanbonmatsu, D.M., Powell, M.C., and Kardes, F.R. (1986) "On the Automatic Activation of Attitudes." *Journal of Personality and Social Psychology* 50: 229–238.

Fazio, R., and Towles-Schwen, T. (1999) "The MODE Model of Attitude-Behavior Processes," in S. Chaiken and Y. Trope (eds.), *Dual-Process Theories in Social Psychology*, New York: Guilford Press, pp. 97–116.

Frankfurt, H. (1971) "Freedom of the Will and the Concept of a Person." *Journal of Philosophy* 68, no. 1: 5–20.

Gaertner, S.L., and Dovidio, J.F. (1986) *The Aversive Form of Racism*, San Diego: Academic Press.

Gawronski, B., and Bodenhausen, G. (2006). "Associative and Propositional Processes in Evaluation: An Integrative Review of Implicit and Explicit Attitude Change." *Psychological Bulletin* 132, no. 5: 692–731.

———. (2011) "The Associative-Propositional Evaluation Model: Theory, Evidence, and Open Questions." *Advances in Experimental Social Psychology* 44: 59–127.

Gendler, T. (2008a) "Alief and Belief." *Journal of Philosophy* 105, no. 10: 634–663.

———. (2008b) "Alief in Action (and Reaction)," *Mind and Language* 23, no. 5: 552–585.

Glaser, J. and Knowles, E. (2008) "Implicit Motivation to Control Prejudice." *Journal of Experimental Social Psychology* 44: 164–172.

Green, A., Carney, D., Pallin, D., Ngo, L., Raymond, K., Lezzoni, L., and Banaji, M. (2007) "Implicit Bias Among Physicians and Its Prediction of Thrombolysis Decisions for Black and White Patients." *Journal of General Internal Medicine* 22: 1231–1238.

Greenwald, A., and Banaji, M. (1995) "Implicit Social Cognition: Attitudes, Self-Esteem, and Stereotypes." *Psychological Review* 102, no. 1: 4.

Greenwald, A., McGhee, D., and Schwartz, J. (1998) "Measuring Individual Differences in Implicit Cognition: The Implicit Association Test." *Journal of Personality and Social Psychology* 74: 1464–1480.

Greenwald, A., and Pettigrew, T. (2014) "With Malice Toward None and Charity for Some: Ingroup Favoritism Enables Discrimination." *American Psychologist* 69, no: 7: 669–684. http://dx.doi.org/10.1037/a0036056

Hahn, A., Judd, C., Hirsh, H., and Blair, I. (2013) "Awareness of Implicit Attitudes." *Journal of Experimental Psychology-General* 143, no. 3: 1369–1392.

Hardin, C., and Banaji, M. (2013) "The Nature of Implicit Prejudice: Implications for Personal and Public Policy." *Behavioral Foundations of Public Policy*: 13–30.

Holroyd, J. (2012) "Responsibility for Implicit Bias." *Journal of Social Philosophy* 43, no. 3: 274–306.

Jacoby, L., and Dallas, M. (1981) "On the Relationship Between Autobiographical Memory and Perceptual Learning." *Journal of Experimental Psychology: General* 110, no. 3: 306.

Judd, C. M., Park, B., Ryan, C. S., Brauer, M., and Kraus, S. (1995). "Stereotypes and Ethnocentrism: Diverging Interethnic Perceptions of African American and White American Youth." *Journal of Personality and Social Psychology* 69, no. 3: 460.

Jussim, L., Cain, T. R., Crawford, J. T., Harber, K., and Cohen, F. (2009). "The Unbearable Accuracy of Stereotypes," in T. Nelson (ed.), *Handbook of Prejudice, Stereotyping, and Discrimination*, New York: Psychology Press, pp. 199–227.

Kelly, D., and Roedder, E. (2008) "Racial Cognition and the Ethics of Implicit Bias." *Philosophy Compass* 3, no. 3: 522–540.

Levy, N. (2012) "Consciousness, Implicit Attitudes, and Moral Responsibility." *Noûs* 48: 21–40.

———. (2015) "Neither Fish Nor Fowl: Implicit Attitudes as Patchy Endorsements." *Noûs* 49, no. 4: 800–823.

Levy, N., and Mandelbaum, E. (2014) "The Powers That Bind: Doxastic Voluntarism and Epistemic Obligation," in J. Matheson and R. Vitz (eds.), *The Ethics of Belief*, Oxford: Oxford University Press, pp. 15–32.

Madva, A. (2012) *The Hidden Mechanisms of Prejudice: Implicit Bias and Interpersonal Fluency*, Ph.D. diss., Columbia University.

———. (2016a) "A Plea for Anti-Anti-Individualism: How Oversimple Psychology Misleads Social Policy." *Ergo* 3, no. 27: doi: http://dx.doi.org/10.3998/ergo.12405314.0003.027.

———. (2016b) "Why Implicit Attitudes Are (Probably) Not Beliefs." *Synthese* 193: 2659–2684.

———. (2017) "Implicit Bias, Moods, and Moral Responsibility." *Pacific Philosophical Quarterly*. doi: 10.1111/papq.12212

Madva, A., and Brownstein, M. (2016) "Stereotypes, Prejudice, and the Taxonomy of the Implicit Social Mind." *Noûs*. doi:10.1111/nous.12182.

Mandelbaum, E. (2013) "Against Alief." *Philosophical Studies* 165: 197–211.

———. (2016) "Attitude, Association, and Inference: On the Propositional Structure of Implicit Bias." *Noûs* 50, no. 3: 629–658.

McConahay, J. (1982) "Self-Interest Versus Racial Attitudes as Correlates of Anti-Busing Attitudes in Louisville: Is It the Buses or the Blacks?" *Journal of Politics* 44, no. 3: 692–720.

———. (1986) "Modern Racism, Ambivalence, and the Modern Racism Scale," in J. Dovidio and S. Gaertner (eds.), *Prejudice, Discrimination, and Racism*, San Diego: Academic Press, pp. 91–125.

McConahay, J., Hardee, B., and Batts, V. (1981) "Has Racism Declined in America? It Depends on Who Is Asking and What Is Asked." *Journal of Conflict Resolution* 25, no. 4: 563–579.

Mendoza, S., Gollwitzer, P., and Amodio, D. (2010) "Reducing the Expression of Implicit Stereotypes: Reflexive Control Through Implementation Intentions," *Personality and Social Psychology Bulletin* 36, no. 4: 512–523.

Nier, J. (2005) "How Dissociated Are Implicit and Explicit Racial Attitudes? A Bogus Pipeline Approach." *Group Processes & Intergroup Relations* 8: 39–52.

Nisbett, R. E., and Wilson, T. D. (1977) "Telling More Than We Can Know: Verbal Reports on Mental Processes." *Psychological Review* 84, no. 3: 231.

Nosek, B. A., and Banaji, M. R. (2009) "Implicit Attitude," in T. Bayne, A. Cleeremans, and P. Wilken (eds.), *The Oxford Companion to Consciousness*, Oxford: Oxford University Press, pp. 84–85.

Nosek, B. A., Banaji, M. R., and Greenwald, A. G. (2002) "Harvesting Intergroup Implicit Attitudes and Beliefs From a Demonstration Website." *Group Dynamics* 6: 101–115.

Nosek, B., Greenwald, A., and Banaji, M. (2007) "The Implicit Association Test at Age 7: A Methodological and Conceptual Review," in J. A. Bargh (ed.), *Automatic Processes in Social Thinking and Behavior*, Philadelphia: Psychology Press.

Nosek, B. A., and Hansen, J. J. (2008) "The Associations in Our Heads Belong to Us: Searching for Attitudes and Knowledge in Implicit Evaluation." *Cognition and Emotion* 22, no. 4: 553–594.

Olson, M., and Fazio, R. (2009) "Implicit and Explicit Measures of Attitudes: The Perspective of the MODE Model." *Attitudes: Insights From the New Implicit Measures*: 19–63.

Payne, B., and Gawronski, B. (2010) "A History of Implicit Social Cognition: Where Is It Coming From? Where Is It Now? Where Is It Going?" in B. Gawronski, and B. Payne (eds.), *Handbook of Implicit Social Cognition: Measurement, Theory, and Applications*, New York: Guilford Press, pp. 1–17.

Plant, E. A., and Peruche, B. M. (2005) "The Consequences of Race for Police Officers' Responses to Criminal Suspects." *Psychological Science* 16, no. 3: 180–183.

Railton, P. (2009) "Practical Competence and Fluent Agency," in D. Sobel and S. Wall (eds.), *Reasons for Action*, Cambridge: Cambridge University Press, pp. 81–115.

———. (2014) "The Affective Dog and Its Rational Tale: Intuition and Attunement." *Ethics* 124, no. 4: 813–859.

Saul, J. (2012) "Skepticism and Implicit Bias." *Disputatio Lecture* 5, no. 37: 243–263.

———. (2013) "Unconscious Influences and Women in Philosophy," in F. Jenkins and K. Hutchison (eds.), *Women in Philosophy: What Needs to Change?* Oxford: Oxford University Press.

Scanlon, T. (1998) *What We Owe Each Other*, Cambridge: Harvard University Press.

Schacter, D. (1987) "Implicit Memory: History and Current Status." *Journal of Experimental Psychology: Learning, Memory, and Cognition* 13: 501–518.

Schuman, H., Steeh, C., and Bobo, L. (1997) *Racial Attitudes in America: Trends and Interpretations*, 2nd edition, Cambridge, MA: Harvard University Press.

Shiffrin, R., and Schneider, W. (1977) "Controlled and Automatic Human Information Processing: Perceptual Learning, Automatic Attending, and a General Theory." *Psychological Review* 84: 127–190.

Smith, A. (2005) "Responsibility for Attitudes: Activity and Passivity in Mental Life." *Ethics* 115, no. 2: 236–271.

———. (2008) "Control, Responsibility, and Moral Assessment." *Philosophical Studies* 138: 367–392.

———. (2012) "Attributability, Answerability, and Accountability: In Defense of a Unified Account." *Ethics* 122, no. 3: 575–589.

Thurstone, L. L. (1928) "Attitudes Can Be Measured." *American Journal of Sociology* 33, no. 4: 529–554.

Valian, V. (1998) *Why So Slow? The Advancement of Women*, Cambridge, MA: MIT Press.

———. (2005) "Beyond Gender Schemas: Improving the Advancement of Women in Academia." *Hypatia* 20: 198–213.

Velleman, D. (2000) "On the Aim of Belief," in *The Possibility of Practical Reason*, Oxford: Oxford University Press.

Wilson, T. D., Lindsey, S., and Schooler, T. Y. (2000) "A Model of Dual Attitudes." *Psychological Review* 107: 101–126.

20

THE MARK OF THE PLURAL

Generic Generalizations and Race

Daniel Wodak and Sarah-Jane Leslie

Albert Memmi once wrote that "the mark of the plural" signals the depersonalization of the colonized:

> The colonized is never characterized in an individual manner; he is entitled only to drown in an anonymous collectivity ("They are this." "They are all the same."). If a colonized servant does not come in one morning, the colonizer will not say that she is ill, or that she is cheating, or that she is tempted not to abide by an oppressive contract. . . . He will say, "You can't count on them." It is not just a grammatical expression. He refuses to consider personal, private occurrences in his maid's life; that life in a specific sense does not interest him, and his maid does not exist as an individual.
> (Memmi 1957/1991: 129)

Memmi's observations about the mark of the plural may strike some as obscure or hyperbolic. But we believe they are prescient. Drawing on recent work in linguistics, psychology, and philosophy, we will argue that the mark of the plural plays an even more important, and more damaging, role in race relations than Memmi suggests.

Let's clearly imagine the circumstance that Memmi describes. A white family's black maid does not come to work one morning. The children ask why. The father answers:

(1) Blacks are unreliable. You can't count on them.

Using (1) as our central case, we will ask five questions about the nature and effects of this speech act, and the wider phenomenon that it represents.

First, what is the grammatical expression employed, and what makes it distinctive? In section one, we explain that it is a *generic generalization* about a racial group, and it shares the distinctive features of generic generalizations about animal groups, such as "Tigers have stripes," "Ducks lay eggs," and "Mosquitos carry the West Nile virus."

Second, what does the use of generic generalizations communicate to "us" about "them"? What does the father's use of (1) communicate to his children? In section two, we argue that it communicates that one racial group (blacks) is essentially different from another (whites), and that this explains why members of that group possess a negative property ("being unreliable"), which in turn explains why those individuals behave as they do (why the maid has not come to work that morning). Despite its surface simplicity, (1) communicates complex, false, and pernicious information that most likely could not be imparted to children in any other way. We offer an explanation of how this works.

Third, how does the use of generics about "us" affect "us"? In section three we argue that generics about racial groups expose members of those groups to two types of pernicious psychological pressures ("stereotype threat" and "ideal realization"). These pressures can bring it about that individuals who are members of the relevant group conform to harmful stereotypes about that group.

Fourth, how does the use of generic generalizations contribute to the very construction of the racial categories that divide "us" from "them"? In section four, we argue that generic generalizations are central to the construction of social categories like racial groups, and to masking the fact that those categories describe a constructed rather than natural world.

Finally, how should we change or challenge the use of generics about race? So much of the information that is communicated by (1) is not explicitly stated or consciously thought by the speaker or the audience. We argue that it is both difficult and insufficient for someone who is appropriately socially situated to negate the harmful falsehoods that are communicated by (1). We will end by noting that the Socratic method may be an efficacious, albeit limited, way to engage with those who make claims like (1).

Before proceeding further, it is worth noting that while we will use (1) as our central example of a generic generalization about a racial group, this is a very broad phenomenon (consider, for instance, *Asians are good at math*, *Latinos are passionate*, and the title of the popular 1992 film *White Men Can't Jump*). Since these generics presuppose and reinforce a division between an in-group ("us") and an out-group ("them"), we will we continue to mention these categories throughout, though their referents are fluid: the in-group and out-group shift between generics. Obviously we do not endorse these categorization schemes; it would simply be remiss to ignore their salience in social cognition about race.

What Are Generic Generalizations?

Generic generalizations like (1) differ from quantified generalizations such as:

(2) All blacks are unreliable.
(3) Most blacks are unreliable.
(4) Some blacks are unreliable.

In many ways, (2)–(4) are similar to (1): they are all generalizations, after all. What distinctive features set (1) apart from (2)–(4), and why do they warrant our focus on generic rather than quantified expressions?

The most obvious and immediate feature that sets generic generalizations apart is the absence of a quantifier—"all", "most," or "some"—in (1). But this is only the way into a complex set of issues. The distinctive features of generics are best understood by considering examples of generics about animal groups like "Tigers have stripes," "Ducks lay eggs," and "Mosquitos carry the West Nile virus."

It is comparatively easy to understand what is communicated by quantified generalizations like "All tigers have stripes," "Most ducks lay eggs," and "Some mosquitos carry the West Nile virus." But it is more difficult to capture what is communicated by the generic versions of these generalizations. Why is "Tigers have stripes" true even though there are albino tigers? Why is it true that *Ducks lay eggs*, but false that *Ducks are female*, even though there are more female ducks than egg-laying ducks? And why is it true to say "Mosquitos carry the West Nile virus" even though fewer than 1% do so, yet false to say "Mosquitos don't carry the West Nile virus" even though some (in fact, over 99%) don't do so?

To answer these questions, we must reflect on how we think about both the groups and the properties involved in these generic generalizations. We frequently make generic generalizations about kinds—like tigers, ducks, and mosquitos—that are highly *essentialized* in the psychologists' sense: we implicitly take members of these kinds to share some distinctive, non-obvious, and persistent property or underlying intrinsic nature that causally grounds their common properties and dispositions (see Gelman (2003), and for discussion of the relationship between the philosophical and psychological notion of essence, see Leslie (2013)).

Leslie (2007, 2008, 2012) argues that it is useful to distinguish three types of (descriptive) bare plural generics, which correspond to different ways in which the property that is attributed is related to the relevant kind. First, there are *majority generics*, where the property just happens to be possessed by *most* members of the relevant kind (e.g., "Barns are red," "Cars have radios"). Second, there are *characteristic generics*, where the property is widely possessed by members of the kind in virtue of their common intrinsic natures (e.g., "Tigers are striped"). Third, there are *striking property generics*. Here the property that is attributed is taken to be dangerous or harmful (such as the property of carrying the West Nile virus); this licenses the generic even when the property has a very low prevalence among members of the group, provided that the group is believed to have a shared intrinsic nature. Of these three types of bare plural generics, only majority generics are free of any implicit reference to the notion of a shared nature or essence. However, evidence suggests that majority generics are by default understood as characteristic generics (see Cimpian and Markman 2009, 2011; Haslanger 2011; and Leslie 2014).

We propose that we should understand what is communicated by racial group generics along these same lines. That is, we should understand (1) as by default communicating that members of the kind *blacks* share some distinctive, non-obvious and persistent property or underlying nature that causally grounds their common properties and dispositions, and that the property *being unreliable* is characteristic of that kind (i.e., widely possessed by individuals who are black in virtue of their shared intrinsic nature). Other racial generics may involve striking properties (e.g., "blacks are violent"), and so get to be asserted independently of any controlling considerations of actual prevalence.

Our account of what is communicated by (1) is based on Leslie's account of generics (see Leslie 2007, 2008, 2012). But it is not dependent on that view. For instance, we have said nothing about what information is communicated by (1) as part of its semantic meaning rather than pragmatic implicature (as Haslanger 2014 proposes). Of course, for each semantic proposal there are objections and alternatives (such as a set-theoretic approach, Barwise and Cooper 1981; see also Liebesman 2011, but cf. Leslie 2015). For the sake of brevity, we will not consider them here. Our working account is fairly ecumenical, but not entirely uncontroversial.

Why focus on generic rather than quantified generalizations? First, several researchers have proposed that generic sentences may be language's way of letting us give voice to our cognitive systems' most basic forms of generalization (e.g., Gelman, Sanchez and Leslie, 2016; Leslie 2008, 2012; Meyer, Gelman and Stillwell 2011; Sutherland, Cimpian, Leslie and Gelman 2015). Second, it is now well established that generic generalizations play a particularly important role in our cognition of social categories like "blacks" (see Wodak et al. 2015, and references therein). Third, experimental evidence suggests that qualified statements like (2) are recalled as generic generalizations like (1) (Gelman, Sanchez and Leslie, forthcoming; Leslie and Gelman 2012). So any attempt to understand the role played by quantified statements like (2) would be incomplete without an understanding of the role played by generics like (1). Finally, specific forms of prejudice are passed on to children by adults—children do not inherit their prejudicial schemes of classification through their genes—and by far and away the most dominant form of child-directed generalizations are generic in form (Gelman 2003).

This is why we take the concerns raised by Memmi's observations about the mark of the plural to be best understood in relation to the category of generic generalizations. Superficially there is some initial awkwardness about this, since not all generics involve bare plurals. There are generally taken to be three distinct syntactic types of generic reference: first, indefinite (aka "bare") plural generics, like "Tigers hunt at night" and "Italians are fond of pasta"; second, indefinite singular generics like "A tiger hunts at night" and "An Italian is fond of pasta"; and finally, definite singular generics like "The tiger hunts at night" and "The Italian is fond of pasta" (Krifka et al. 1995). In the case of social categories, the definite plural construction can take on a generic meaning, e.g., "The Italians are fond of pasta," though outside the social realm this construction tends not to have a clear generic interpretation (Krifka et al. 1995). There are important conceptual and linguistic differences between these types of generics (see, e.g., Greenberg 2003; Leslie et al. 2009; Prasada, Khemlani, Leslie and Glucksberg 2013). But all that we wish to note here is that, setting these complications aside, the father could have had have a similar effect by answering his children with any of the following:

(5) The black is unreliable. You can't count on them.
(6) A black is unreliable. You can't count on them.
(7) The blacks are unreliable. You can't count on them.

Understanding that there are singular and plural generics is important to any estimation of the frequency of generics about race. Zaidi (2010) lists examples of stereotypes about Hispanics from textbooks published between 1961 and 1993; many involve definite singular generics, like "The Latin American considers his home his sanctuary" and "The Central American citizen is no more fit for a republican form of government than he is for an arctic expedition." As Zaidi writes, these generalizations "portray Hispanics as one-dimensional characters that are defined by their essences" (2010: 157).

We have already seen enough to suggest that it is unfortunate that generics about racial, ethnic and national groups continue to be printed in academic works. Occasionally, but only occasionally, this attracts criticism. Consider the following passage from Richard J. Evans's review of Alon Confino's *A World Without Jews* in the *London Review of Books*:

> One of the book's most obvious flaws is its constant reference to "Germans" as if all Germans were Nazis and Anti-Semites. Confino is careful not to include the definite article, but time and again a statement about "some Germans" expands within a few pages to become simply "Germans." Thus it was "Germans" who, "via the raw emotions of hatred, anger, mockery, fear, transgression and guilt" expressed in the burning of the Torah scrolls, "conveyed a sentiment, perhaps even an understanding, that a Germany without Jews was becoming a reality."
>
> (2015: 19)

These are uses of generics by an eminent professor of history in a book published by Yale University Press. Even the well-educated still use and accept generics about groups that give voice to cognitively primitive generalizations, and communicate essentialist beliefs.

Generics About *Them*

In light of this, we can now clarify how generics like (1) about racial groups work to communicate complex, false, and pernicious information to non-members of the groups, including children. The relevant information comes in three stages.

The first stage concerns the nature of *them*. In saying (1), the father implicitly communicates that "they" (blacks) are essentially different from "us" (whites). It communicates that blacks as a group share a distinctive essence, making them fundamentally different from "us". This accords with the general tendency to view racial groups in essentialist terms: claims about "[t]he 'soul of the Oriental,' 'Negro Blood,' . . . 'the passionate Latin,'" Allport wrote, "all represent a belief in essence. A mysterious mana (for good or evil) [that] resides in a group, all of its members partaking thereof" (1954: 173–174).

This claim that generics transmit essentialist beliefs to children is supported by experimental evidence from Rhodes, Leslie and Tworek (2012). In their experiments, four-year-old children and adults were shown an imaginary social group—"Zarpies"— who could not be mapped on to any familiar essentialized group. The use of generics in describing Zarpies resulted in a marked increase in the tendency of children and adults to essentialize Zarpies. And the inculcation of essentialist beliefs about Zarpies in a separate group of adults resulted in a marked increase in their use of generics in describing Zarpies to children. This suggests an intimate connection between generics and essentialism: hearing generics results in the essentialization of social groups; and the essentialization of social groups increases the use of generics in describing those groups.

Hence, uses of generics like (1), particularly if repeated over time, are likely to impart to children the notion that blacks share a distinctive, fundamental inherent nature—a dangerous falsehood. Members of highly essentialized social groups are more likely to have diminished social status and be subjected to prejudice (Haslam et al. 2000; Haslam and Levy 2002). When "the civilized" essentialize others, Patterson writes, they "impoverish their own understanding of these other groups and obscure their own affinity with them. Ultimately, this fuels their fear of these groups" (Patterson 1997: 87–88).

The second stage concerns the properties attributed via the generic. If *being unreliable* is attributed as a characteristic property of blacks, this communicates not only that the children can expect individual members of that racial group to share this negative trait, but that little can be done to change this—it is grounded in their inherent nature, not explained by extrinsic circumstances. When striking properties—like *being violent*—are attributed to racial groups, the audience will not even need much evidence of their prevalence to accept the generic. This would not be quite such bad news if the acceptance of generics did not result in poor probabilistic inferences about the likelihood of arbitrary members of the kind to have the striking property in question (Khemlani, Leslie and Glucksburg 2012). Once accepted, striking property generics "appear to be commonly taken in a rather strong sense, as though the quantifier *always* had implicitly crept into their interpretation" (Abelson and Kanouse 1966: 172). In other words, the cognitive mechanism which generics give voice to lets us rapidly move from "Some Germans were Anti-Semites" to "Germans were Anti-Semites," which is then taken to have an inferential power akin to "All Germans were Anti-Semites"—this is the basis of Evans's complaint against Corfino.

The third stage of the information communicated by generics is that they *explain* salient phenomena. Generics like (1) are used to explain one individual's conduct in terms of the properties of a group. Recall Memmi's observation that the father explains the absence of the family's maid by claiming that *they* are unreliable. He does not consider alternative explanations, such as that *she* is ill, or "tempted not to abide by an oppressive contract": "He refuses to consider personal, private occurrences in his maid's life; that life in a specific sense does not interest him, and his maid does not exist as an individual."

Even when a group-level explanation is apt, generics still communicate something mistaken: that the *intrinsic* nature of the group, rather than their extrinsic circumstances, is the relevant explanatory factor. As Haslanger writes, the common features of conduct of members of a group often "obtain by virtue of [a] broad system of social relations within which the subjects are situated, and are not grounded in intrinsic or dispositional features of the subjects themselves"; yet this is "obscured" by the "systematically misleading" use of generics as explanations (2011: 179–180).

Zaidi's examples of generics about Hispanics illustrate this point well. In *Spanish for Secondary Schools* (1961), the authors wrote: "The Spaniard is primarily a man of feeling, rather than of action, foresight or method. His overvaluation of the individual diminishes his sense of solidarity with the larger community." Zaidi notes that here the authors "fail to consider that if the people of Spain seemed somewhat lacking in expressions of solidarity in 1961, then perhaps the repressive Franco dictatorship, which by then had already ruled Spain for three decades, might have been at least partly to blame" (2010: 159). Similar observations are made about the fifth edition of *Civilización y Cultura*, from 1991: "to read *Civilización y Cultura*, one would think that underdevelopment, poverty, and crime result from congenital defects in Puerto Ricans rather than from colonization and globalization" (2010: 166). These are instances of what Andrei Cimpian (2015) calls the "inherence heuristic": an intuitive tendency to explain patterns (Puerto Rican poverty and crime) in terms of the inherent (i.e., "essential") properties of their constituents (Puerto Ricans' "congenital defects"), while overlooking extrinsic, environmental factors.

As we move further into the political sphere, it becomes more apparent that the use of such generics as explanations is intimately connected to tacit *justifications*. Consider the opinion of Lord Cromer, the English representative in Egypt from 1882 to 1902:

> Want of accuracy, which easily degenerates into untruthfulness, is in fact the main characteristic of the Oriental mind. The European is a close reasoner; his

statements of fact are devoid of any ambiguity; he is a natural logician, albeit he may not have studied logic; he is by nature skeptical and requires proof before he can accept the truth of any proposition; his trained intelligence works like a piece of mechanism. The mind of the Oriental, on the other hand, like his picturesque streets, is eminently wanting in symmetry. His reasoning is of the most slipshod description.

(as cited by Said 1994: 38)

This stream of generics about "the European" and "the Oriental" is a tacit justification for the power of the former over the latter. That "they" are fundamentally different from "us" not only explains why they are powerless and we are powerful; it justifies the right of "the European" to "not only to manage the nonwhite world but also to own it" (Said 1994: 108).

So, by saying (1) the father communicates to his children that *they* (blacks) are essentially different from *us* (whites), and that these differences explains why *they* possess a negative property (unreliability), which in turn explains why those individuals behave as they do (why the maid has not come to work that morning); and moreover, it tacitly justifies why *we* have *them* as servants, rather than vice versa. It is hard to imagine a better way of communicating such complicated, misleading, and harmful information to any audience, let alone to young children, in so few words.

Generics About *Us*

Generics about racial groups not only shape how we see others, but how we see ourselves. Generics about *us* communicate that we are essentially different from *them*. One non-obvious reason why this is harmful is that essentialist beliefs undergird a *fixed* conception of abilities, with the resultant conception of certain demanding tasks as requiring inherent, natural talents, rather than hard work and incrementally acquired traits. When individuals adopt a fixed conception of abilities they are more likely to underperform in, or just avoid, challenging activities; failures are taken to be evidence of immutable shortcomings (Dweck 1999, 2006). (One possible explanation for the dearth of African Americans, as well as women, in academic fields like philosophy is that members of that marginalized group are falsely led to believe that they lack the inherent talents required for success in the field *and* to believe that others regard them lacking those inherent talents (Leslie et al. 2015).)

Relatedly, if an individual's membership in a social kind is made salient, this can impair that individual's performance in certain activities. This robustly documented phenomenon is known as "stereotype threat," the effects of which are amplified if either the group is viewed in essentialist terms or the performance is thought to be grounded in a fixed ability (for an excellent overview, see Steele 2010). A highly pertinent illustration of stereotype threat comes from an experiment where black and white students were engaged in the same activity: playing golf (Stone et al. 1999). When students were told that the activity was testing their "sports intelligence," black students underperformed. When students were told that the activity was testing their "natural athletic ability," white students underperformed. Black and white students know that the generics "blacks are unintelligent" and "whites are not naturally athletic" are commonly believed. Repeated experiences of stereotype threat not only impair performance, but result in diminished confidence in one's abilities and interest in the relevant activity (Gilovich et al. 2006: 467–468); en masse, this can seem to confirm the stereotype.

There is a clear connection—which is supported by further research (Cimpian et al. 2012)—between stereotype threat and generics. The problem that the students in the preceding experiment face is that once a negative stereotype about their group is made salient, they no longer appear to themselves just as individuals: they show awareness that their individual performance as golfers will be judged as representative of their group, in accordance with stereotypes about that group. Even highlighting an individual's membership in a positively stereotyped group can impair her performance, provided that the stereotype is activated in a blatant manner (Cheryan and Bodenhausen 2000). When the stereotype is activated subtly, individuals' performance may improve: this is the phenomenon of "stereotype lift" (Walton and Cohen 2003).

While stereotype threat affects both dominant and marginalized groups (as in the golfing experiment), the effects on the latter are more pernicious. In the United States there are far more negative stereotypes about blacks than whites. And there are far more activities that white individuals can engage in without being conscious of their race, which is often regarded as naturally diverse, and so not as susceptible to specific stereotypes. Other racial groups do not have this privilege.

Stereotype threat is a well-documented pernicious psychological pressure affecting individuals' behavior (see meta-analyses by Nguyen and Ryan (2008) and Walton and Cohen (2003)). But it is not the only psychological pressure connected to the use of generics about racial groups. Another is what we will call "ideal realization."

This pressure is connected to normative, as opposed to descriptive, generics. To illustrate the distinction, consider "Boys cry" and "Boys don't cry." Both could be accepted, without incoherence, when the former *describes* how crying is characteristic of boys while the latter *proscribes* crying by boys. "Boys don't cry" communicates that there are distinct *ideals* for boys and girls, and that not crying is part of the ideal of boy-ness, such that individual boys who cry are admonished for failing to instantiate or realize this ideal. (For different ways of understanding this ideal and its connection to the semantics or pragmatics of generics, see Leslie 2015, and Haslanger 2014). Normative generics exert a significant psychological pressure: they create a sense of obligation among members of a group to possess features which otherwise few would feel either an obligation or a desire to possess (Leslie 2015).

Descriptive and normative generics can be hard to disentangle, given that they have the same surface form. One way to distinguish the two is to consider the use of graded comparisons. In a society where normative generics like "Women are submissive" and "Men are assertive" are widely accepted, an assertive woman might be declared "more of a man" than a submissive man. Consider Linda Grant's comment in 2012 that Margaret Thatcher "is twice the man and twice the woman of any other MP [Member of Parliament]". Similarly, we encounter seemingly paradoxical threshold claims such as "Hillary Clinton is the only man in the Obama administration." These claims are best understood as assessments of the degrees to which individuals realize distinct gender ideals: Hillary Clinton was taken to instantiate ideals of masculinity to a greater degree than her male colleagues (for more discussion, see Leslie 2015).

Similar graded and threshold claims are made with regard to racial groups. Biracial children in the United States are frequently taken to be, in the words of Earl Sweatshirt, "too white for the black kids, and too black for the whites." Barack Obama has frequently been accused of "acting white," most notably by Jesse Jackson in 2007. In October 2014, (black) Seattle Seahawks players reportedly declared that their (black) quarterback Russell Wilson was "not black enough." Ex-NBA star Charles Barkley responded:

> With young black kids [who] do well in school, the loser kids tell them, oh, you are acting white . . . [F]or some reason, we are brainwashed to think if you are not a thug or an idiot, you are not black enough. If you go to school, make good grades, speak intelligent, and don't break the law, you are not a good black person.

Both the initial report about the Seahawks, and Barkley's response, remain controversial, as is the empirical literature on the phenomenon of "acting white" (see Fryer and Torelli 2010). But the general point stands: in-group generics can work to (1) essentialize features of the group and (2) insinuate tendentious group-wide ideals.

In summary, the use of generics about *us* communicates that *we* are an essentialized kind (exposing individuals to stereotype threats) and that *we* ought to instantiate the ideals of *our* kind (exposing individuals to a further pressure to conform to harmful stereotypes).

The Construction of *Us* and *Them*

Barkley's response helps to illustrate the complex relationship between descriptive and normative generics. One way to understand this connection is in terms of Haslanger's claim that two assumptions form part of the common ground in conversations that employ generics (2014: 379): a descriptive assumption that robust regularities are due to the essential natures of things, and a normative assumption that things should express their essential natures. Now consider the generic "blacks are thugs." This claim might be accepted by those who take thuggishness to be a *striking* property of blacks: it is a dangerous, though not prevalent, attribute of some members of this racial group. Once accepted, striking property generics are often employed as though the property they involve was in fact prevalent—as though, as Abelson and Kanouse frame it, the quantifier "always" had implicitly crept into their interpretation. So some might come to accept that thuggishness among blacks is a robust regularity, and hence assume that it is a *characteristic* property of blacks. Here Haslanger's suggestion would be that it is assumed that blacks *should* express their (falsely) essentialized natures; thus "blacks are thugs" comes to be accepted as a *normative* generic. This leaves individual blacks in the fraught position wherein behaving in ways that can be deemed "thuggish" is taken to confirm an offensive descriptive generic, yet abstaining from such behaviors can lead to their being admonished for "acting white" or "not being black enough."

This relationship between descriptive and normative generics produces looping effects. Once a group is highly essentialized, unusual, aberrant actions on behalf of the few may be taken to characterize the group as a whole (for discussion, see

Leslie, forthcoming), and uncommon traits may be taken to be statistically normal. As Haslanger writes, "what's statistically normal is taken to be evidence of how things are by nature," and hence an inevitability to be accommodated; and how things are by nature is taken to be how things "ought to be," and thereby legitimated and socially enforced (Haslanger 2014: 389). The use of descriptive and normative generics in determining what is normal, natural, and good helps explain how stereotypes of particular racial groups are socially constructed: that is, it helps explain how traits like thuggishness have become associated with groups like blacks.

Generics may play a further role in the social construction of race. As Appiah (1996: 54) famously argued, there are no actual racial groups whose members share an essence (or, in his words, share "certain fundamental, heritable, physical, moral, intellectual, and cultural characteristics with one another that they [do] not share with members of any other race"). But on many plausible views (see Ritchie 2015), false essentialist beliefs are causally or constitutively involved in the social construction of racial groups. We know that hearing racial generics results in the essentialization of social groups, and conversely the essentialization of social groups increases the use of generics in describing those groups. Moreover, such generics *mask* the fact that these racial categories are socially constructed: once groups are essentialized, categories that are artificial come to seem natural, and a social order that is historically contingent and changeable seems inevitable and immutable—or at the very least, simply responsive to the "natural" social order.

Changing and Challenging Generics

If racial generics play a role in the persistent social construction of race, then successfully changing or challenging the use of generics about racial groups may be a particularly efficacious means of changing the social construction of race. But *how* can we successfully change or challenge the use of generics about race?

Langton, Haslanger and Anderson (2012) argue that we should "insist on explicitly quantified statements." If you were to restrict yourself to quantified generalizations about racial groups, this would be a commendable change in your own conduct. But it would not be enough. The information communicated by your quantified generalizations may be recalled by others in generic form (Leslie and Gelman 2012; Sanchez, Gelman and Leslie, 2016). And your abstaining from generics about race does not redress the harms caused by others' uses of generics like (1), if they are simply left unchallenged.

Effectively challenging generics like (1), however, turns out to be quite difficult. In part, this is because generics are difficult to negate by appealing to counterexamples. "Tigers are striped" is true even if there are some stripeless albino tigers, and "Mosquitos carry the West Nile virus" is true even if 99% of mosquitos don't carry the West Nile virus. Likewise, many will accept "blacks are unreliable" even when they are aware that some, many or most blacks are highly reliable. Even if one were aware that *no* blacks are thugs, one may continue to assert that "blacks are thugs" as a normative generic: one would simply take all actual blacks to fall short of this ideal, just as one can take all actual women to fall short of the ideals (e.g., "submissiveness") associated with that gender category. "There are no real women any more" is a not-unheard-of old-school social conservative lament.

This difficulty in challenging generics like (1) is compounded by *slippage* between different interpretations of the same generic. Langton, Haslanger and Anderson (2012) discuss this with regard to a speaker's use of the generic "Latinos are lazy." You could respond by presenting an onslaught of counterexamples, but then the speaker can accept that "although many Latinos aren't lazy, they tend to be—thus embracing the characteristic generic"; or, alternatively, you could respond by arguing that Latinos show no greater tendency towards laziness than any other group, but the "speaker can then suggest that, although it is not part of the nature or essence of Latinos to be lazy, most are." The fact that majority, characteristic, striking, and normative generics all take the same surface form allows for a "slide back and forth between different interpretations of the utterance," which in turn "allows speakers to avoid taking responsibility for the implications of their claims" (Langton, Haslanger and Anderson 2012).

A final difficulty with challenging generics like (1) is that much of the harmful information it communicates is not explicitly stated or consciously thought by the speaker or the audience. Responding with "blacks aren't unreliable" or "blacks aren't thugs" does not negate the *presupposition* that there are distinct essences and/or ideals for whites and blacks. This presupposition is especially hard to negate when it is transmitted to young children who can understand generics, but cannot explicitly understand notions like "essence" and "ideal."

Where does this leave us? We agree with Langton, Haslanger and Anderson (2012) that generics about racial groups should be rejected because they *either* contain, presuppose, and implicate harmful falsehoods *or* can easily be interpreted to do so. But we suggest that a more successful means of challenging such generics may be to engage in Socratic inquiry. If a speaker makes claims like (1), ask what he or she means. Ask probing questions that make slippery claims precise and implicit assumptions explicit. "Do you think all blacks are unreliable? If not, what percentage of blacks do you think are unreliable? What percentage of whites do you think are reliable? What explains the difference? Is it in the nature of blacks to be unreliable, or is this just a historical accident?" Instead of assuming the difficult burden of showing that the utterance was false, force the speaker to take responsibility for and either defend or disavow whatever falsehood they had in mind.

Of course, the Socratic method only addresses *linguistic* obstacles (slippage, presupposition) to challenging generics. So it has serious limitations: it does nothing to resolve other obstacles, like the entrenched power dynamics that make it all but impossible for, say, a black servant to challenge a white father's use of generics like (1).

Conclusion

Memmi's remarks about the mark of the plural may strike many as obscure or hyperbolic, but we believe that they can be made precise by homing in on a particular class of grammatical expressions—generics—that make individual members of marginalized racial groups "drown in anonymous collectivity." Indeed, we have argued that generics are involved in the construction and transmission of the racial categories that divide *us* from *them*, and in doing so communicate false beliefs about distinct essences, ideals, and properties. These beliefs shape how we see others, how we see ourselves, and how we see our social world, in ways that are deeply morally objectionable yet difficult to challenge.

References

Abelson, R. P. and Kanouse, D. E. (1966) "Subjective Acceptance of Verbal Generalizations," in S. Feldman (ed.), *Cognitive Consistency: Motivational Antecedents and Behavioral Consequents*, New York: Academic Press, pp. 171–197.

Allport, G. (1954) *The Nature of Prejudice*, New York: Addison Wesley.

Appiah, K. A. (1996) "Race, Culture, Identity: Misunderstood Connections," in K. A. Appiah and A. Gutmann (eds.), *Color Conscious: The Political Morality of Race*, Princeton, NJ: Princeton University Press, pp. 30–105.

Barwise, J. and Cooper, R. (1981) "Generalized Quantifiers and Natural Language." *Linguistics and Philosophy* 4, no. 2: 159–219.

Cheryan, S. and Bodenhausen, G. V. (2000) "When Positive Stereotypes Threaten Intellectual Performance: The Psychological Hazards of Model Minority Status." *Psychological Science* 11: 399–402.

Cimpian, A. (2015) "The Inherence Heuristic: Generating Everyday Explanations," in R. Scott and S. Kosslyn (Eds.), *Emerging Trends in the Social and Behavioral Sciences*, Hoboken, NJ: Wiley and Sons, pp. 1–15.

Cimpian, A., and Markman, E. M. (2009) "Information Learned From Generic Language Becomes Central to Children's Biological Concepts: Evidence From Their Open-Ended Explanations." *Cognition* 113, no. 1: 14–25.

———. (2011) "The Generic/Nongeneric Distinction Influences How Children Interpret New Information About Social Others." *Child Development* 82, no. 2: 471–492.

Cimpian, A., Mu, Y., and Erickson, L. C. (2012) "Who Is Good at This Game? Linking an Activity to a Social Category Undermines Children's Achievement." *Psychological Science* 23, no. 5: 533–541.

Dweck, C. S. (1999) *Self-Theories: Their Role in Motivation, Personality and Development*, Philadelphia: Psychology Press.

———. (2006) *Mindset: The New Psychology of Success*, New York: Random House.

Evans, R. J. (2015) "Written Into History." *London Review of Books* 37, no. 2: 17–19.

Fryer, R. G. and Torelli, P. (2010) "An empirical analysis of acting white," *Journal of Public Economics* 94, nos. 5–6: 380–396.

Gelman, S. A. (2003) *The Essential Child: Origins of Essentialism in Everyday Thought*, Oxford: Oxford University Press.

Gelman, S. A., Sanchez Tapia I., and Leslie S. J. (2016). "Memory for Generic and Qualified Sentences in Spanish Speaking Children and Adults" *Journal of Child Language* Nov 43, no. 6: 1231–1244.

Gilovich, T., Keltner, D., and Nisbett, R. E. (2006) *Social Psychology*, W. W. Norton, pp. 467–468.

Greenberg, Y. (2003) *Manifestations of Genericity*, London: Routledge.

Haslam, N. and Levy, S. (2006) "Essentialist Beliefs About Homosexuality: Structure and Implications for Prejudice." *Personality and Social Psychology Bulletin* 32: 471–485.

Haslam, N. Rothschild L., and Ernst, D. (2000) "Essentialist Beliefs About Social Categories." *British Journal of Social Psychology* 39: 113–127.

Haslanger, S. (2011) "Ideology, Generics, and Common Ground," in *Feminist Metaphysics: Explorations in the Ontology of Sex, Gender, and the Self*, Dordrecht: Springer, pp. 179–208.

———. (2014) "The Normal, the Natural and the Good: Generics and Ideology." *Poetica and Societa* 3: 365–392.

Khemlani, S., Leslie, S. J., and Glucksberg, S. (2012) "Inferences About Members of Kinds: The Generics Hypothesis." *Language and Cognitive Processes* 27: 887–900.

Krifka, M., Pelletier, F. J., Carlson, G. N., ter Meulen, A., Chierchia, G., and Link, G. (1995). "Genericity: An Introduction," in G. N. Carlson and F. J. Pelletier (eds.), *The Generic Book*, Chicago: University of Chicago Press.

Langton, R., Anderson, L., and Haslanger, S. (2012) "Language and Race," in G. Russell and D. G. Fara (eds.), *Routledge Companion to Philosophy of Language*, London: Routledge, pp. 753–767.

Leslie, S. J. (2008) "Generics: Cognition and Acquisition." *Philosophical Review* 117, no. 1: 1–49.

———. (2012) "Generics," in G. Russell and D.G. Fara (eds.), *Routledge Companion to Philosophy of Language Routledge*, pp. 355–367.
———. (2013) "Essence and Natural Kinds: When Science Meets Preschooler Intuition." *Oxford Studies in Epistemology* 4: 108–165.
———. (2014) "Carving Up the Social World With Generics," in *Oxford Studies in Experimental Philosophy*, Vol. 1, Oxford: Oxford University Press, pp. 208–232.
———. (2015) "Generics Oversimplified." *Noûs* 49, no. 1: 28–54.
———. (2015) "Hillary Clinton Is the Only Man in the Obama Administration': Dual Character Concepts, Generics, and Gender." *Analytic Philosophy* 56, no. 2: 111–141.
———. (Forthcoming) "The Original Sin of Cognition: Fear, Prejudice, and Generalization." *Journal of Philosophy*.
Leslie, S.J., and Gelman, S.A. (2012) "Quantified Statements Are Recalled as Generics." *Cognitive Psychology* 64: 186–214.
Leslie, S.J., Cimpian, A., Meyer, M., and Freeland, E. (2015) "Expectations of Brilliance Underlie Gender Distributions Across Academic Disciplines." *Science* 347, no. 6219: 262–265.
Leslie, S.J., Khemlani, S., Prasada S., and Glucksberg, S. (2009) "Conceptual and Linguistic Distinctions Between Singular and Plural Generics." Proceedings of the 31st Annual Cognitive Science Society.
Liebesman, D. (2011) 'Simple Generics.' *Noûs* 45, no. 3: 409–442.
Memmi, A. (1991 [1957]) *The Colonizer and the Colonized*, Boston: Beacon Press.
Meyer, M., Gelman, S.A., and Stilwell, S.M. (2011) "Generics Are a Cognitive Default: Evidence From Sentence Processing," in L. Carlson, C. Hölscher, and T. Shipley (eds.), *Proceedings of the 33rd Annual Conference of the Cognitive Science Society*, pp. 913–918.
Nguyen, H.H.D. and Ryan, A.M. (2008) "Does Stereotype Threat Affect Test Performance of Minorities and Women? A Meta-analysis of Experimental Evidence." *Journal of Applied Psychology* 93, no. 6: 1314–1334.
Patterson, T.C. (1997) *Inventing Western Civilization*, New York: Monthly Review Press.
Prasada, S., Khemlani, S., Leslie, S.J., and Glucksberg, S. (2013). "Conceptual Distinctions Amongst Generics." *Cognition* 126: 405–422.
Rhodes, M., Leslie, S.J., and Tworek, C. (2012) "Cultural Transmission of Social Essentialism." *Proceedings of the National Academy of Sciences* 109, no. 34: 13526–13531.
Ritchie, K. (2015) "The Metaphysics of Social Groups." *Philosophy Compass* 10, no. 5: 310–321.
Said, E. (1978/1994) *Orientalism*, New York: Vintage.
Steele, C.M. (2010) *Whistling Vivaldi: And Other Clues to How Stereotypes Affect Us*, New York: W.W. Norton.
Stone, J., Lynch, C.I., Sjomeling, M., and Darley, J.M. (1999). "Stereotype Threat Effects on Black and White Athletic Performance." *Journal of Personality and Social Psychology* 77, no. 6: 1213–1227.
Sutherland, S.L., Cimpian, A., Leslie, S.J., and Gelman, S.A. (2015). "Memory Errors Reveal a Bias to Spontaneously Generalize to Categories." *Cognitive Science* 39, no. (5): 1021–1046.
Walton, G.M. and Cohen, G.L. (2003) "Stereotype Lift." *Journal of Experimental Social Psychology* 39: 456–467.
Wodak, D., Leslie, S.J., and Rhodes, M. (2015) "What a Loaded Generalization: Generics and Social Cognition." *Philosophy Compass* 10, no. 9: 625–635.
Zaidi, A.S. (2010) "Essentialist Stereotypes in Textbooks on Hispanic Studies." *Humanity and Society* 34: 157–168.

21
PSYCHOANALYSIS AND RACE
Kelly Oliver

While the founder of psychoanalysis, Sigmund Freud, discusses civilization and the infant's move into the social, he rarely addresses social problems, particularly oppression and its psychic consequences. Although Freud acknowledges the effect of social conditions on the psyche, he and his followers seldom consider how those social conditions become the conditions of possibility for an individual's psychic life and subject formation. While Freudian psychoanalytic theory has addressed itself to questions of subjectivity and subject formation, traditionally it has done so without considering the subject's social position, or more significantly the impact of that subject position or social conditions on the formation of the psyche.

We need more than an application of psychoanalytic concepts to social institutions or psychic formations in order to explain the effects of oppression and racism on the psyche. To explain why so many people suffer at the core of their subjectivity and its concomitant sense of agency when they are abjected, excluded, or oppressed by mainstream culture, we need a psychoanalytic social theory that reformulates psychoanalytic concepts as social. Psychoanalytic social theory should be based on social concepts of subject formation that consider how the psyche is formed and deformed within particular types of social contexts.

Theories that do not consider subject position, social context, and the role of social conditions in subjectivity and psychic formation not only cover over the differential power relations addressed by some contemporary theorists using psychoanalysis, but they also cover over the differential subjectivities produced within those relations. Without considering subject position, we assume that all subjects are alike and thereby level differences; or like traditional psychoanalysis, we end up developing a normative notion of subject-formation based on a particular group, traditionally white European men.

Freudian Psychoanalysis and Social Conditions

If Freud normalizes a white male European subject, and we risk perpetuating this normalization by using his concepts without transforming them, then why turn to psychoanalytic theory at all to discuss race and the effects of racism on the psyche? Even if we could do away with the prejudice of Freud's nineteenth-century theories and their twentieth-century versions, psychoanalysis still deals with individuals at odds with the social, so what can we gain from turning psychoanalytic concepts based on individuals into social concepts? How can we balance the social and the psyche in order to develop concepts that articulate their relationality and the link between them?

There are two primary facets of psychoanalysis that make it crucial for social theory in general, and race theory in particular: the centrality of the notion of the unconscious and the importance of sublimation as an alternative to repression. Both of these facets come to bear in important ways on the fact that all of our relationships are mediated by meaning, that we are beings who mean. As beings who mean, our experiences are both bodily and mental. Unconscious drive force or energy operates between soma and psyche. We could say that our being is brought into the realm of meaning through unconscious drive energy and their affective representations.

The psychoanalytic concept most appropriate to a discussion of unconscious drive energy making its way into the realm of meaning is sublimation. Although this notion remains underdeveloped in Freud's writings (Freud supposedly burned his only paper on sublimation, thus subjecting it to literal sublimation by fire), and it has been used without much further development since, it is central to social theory, especially to a social theory of oppression and racism. We need a theory that explains how we articulate or otherwise express our bodies, experiences, and affects, all of which are fluid and energetic, in some form of meaningful signification so that we can communicate with others. Oppression and racism undermine the ability to sublimate by withholding or foreclosing the possibility of articulating and thereby discharging bodily drives and affects. The bodies and affects of those othered have already been excluded as abject from the realm of proper society.

As Frantz Fanon argued, drives are much more fluid than those of traditional psychoanalytic theory. Fanon rejects Freud's notion that sublimation is the result of redirecting sexual drives in particular and his notion that the drives originate within one body. Rather, all forms of signification presuppose the sublimation of drives and their affective representations into the realm of meaning. If it is true, as Freud suggests, that affects are representations of drives, then it also true that our greatest access to drives should be through the affective realm. In fact, if drives remain unconscious until brought to analysis and subjected to interpretation, it makes sense to focus on affects in order to begin to understand our bodily impulses and experiences.

Drives and affects do not originate in one body or one psyche but rather are relational and transitory—they can move from one body to another. Following Fanon, we could say that the negative affects of the oppressors are "deposited into the bones" of the oppressed ([1961] 1968, 52). Affects move between bodies; colonization and oppression operate through depositing the unwanted affects of the dominant group onto those othered by that group in order to sustain their privileged position. Diagnosing the colonization of psychic space demands a close analysis of the affects of oppression and how those affects are produced within particular social situations.

Sublimation is necessary for beings to enter the realm of meaning. The first acts of meaning are available through the sublimation of bodily impulses into forms of communication. Moreover, sublimation allows us to connect and communicate with others by making our bodies and experiences meaningful; we become beings who mean by sublimating our bodily drives and affects. Sublimation, then, is necessary for both subjectivity or individuality and community or sociality. Sublimation is the lynchpin of a psychoanalytic social theory, for it is sublimation that makes idealization possible. And without idealization we can neither conceptualize our experience nor set goals or ideals for ourselves; without the ability to idealize, we cannot imagine our situation otherwise, which is to say that without idealization we cannot resist domination. Sublimation and idealization are necessary not only for psychic life but also for transformative and restorative resistance to racist oppression. Sublimation and idealization are the cornerstones of our mental life, yet they have their source in bodies, bodies interacting with each other. It is through the social relationality of bodies that sublimation is possible. But, in an oppressive culture that abjects, excludes, or marginalizes certain groups or types of people by racializing them, sublimation and idealization can become the privilege of dominant groups. The psychoanalytic notions of sublimation and idealization become fundamentally social concepts that are necessary to subjectivity and its concomitant sense of agency.

Fanon and "Negrophobia"

Engaging with notions of sublimation and idealization, Frantz Fanon transforms Freudian psychoanalytic theory by considering the ways in which the colonial situation with its racialization of the colonized leads to pathologies on both sides. Fanon's diagnosis of colonial obsessions and phobias not only complicates Freud's focus, which is more often than not on individual traumatic experiences rather than on social institutions, but also interrogates what Freud considered "common" phobic objects, such as animals, for example, horses, chickens, or rats. In contrast, Fanon develops what he calls "Negrophobia," which is social rather than individual in nature.

In traditional Freudian psychoanalytic theory both obsession and phobia are considered affective disorders insofar as they operate on the affective level. Freud distinguishes obsession from phobia according to their affective operations:

> Two constituents are found in every obsession: 1) an idea that forces itself upon the patient; 2) an associated emotional state. Now, in the group of phobias this emotional state is always one of "anxiety," while in true obsessions other emotional states, such as doubt, remorse, or anger, may occur just as well as anxiety.
> ([1895] 1962: 74–75)

For Freud, whereas in obsession the extreme affect associated with an original troubling idea—an idea that can have its source in a traumatic experience—moves to a substitute idea, in phobia the anxiety or fear remains attached to the original idea, which can either be what he calls a "common" phobia or an individual one (see 1895, 1894). He says of obsession that

> any idea can be made use of which is either able, from its nature, to be united with an affect of the quality in question, or which has certain relations to the incompatible idea which make it seems as though it could serve as a surrogate for it.
> (Freud [1894] 1962: 54)

Furthermore, obsessional neurosis is associated with the "internalization of a sadomasochistic relation in the shape of tension between the ego and a particularly cruel super-ego" (Laplanche and Pontilas 1973: 281). Freud, at least in his early writings, is more interested in obsessions that do not originate in traumatic experience and phobias that are not "common."

Colonization, however, produces obsessional relations in the colonized through social trauma that is repeated daily on almost all levels of social life. On Fanon's analysis, the idea that forces itself on the colonized is the idea of his own inferiority and the white man's superiority. The affects that are associated with these ideas are a complex of anger and shame. The self-reproach typical of obsessional neurosis is the result of the internalization of—or more accurately, the infection with—the particularly cruel super-ego of the colonized, a super-ego that abjects the colonized as racialized others. Fanon suggests that the strong affects engaged by the inferiority complex of colonization become associated with gaining the recognition and love of the colonizer. Anger directed towards the colonizer turns inward and becomes anger and shame directed towards the self, which in turn flips over into the desire for recognition and love from those very same people who have rejected the colonized as barbaric in the first place. In this regard, the need for recognition from the colonizer is a symptom of the pathology of colonization (Oliver 2001). The colonizer's violent and cruel super-ego is forced onto the colonized to produce an inferiority complex, which in turn leads to the obsessive need for recognition from the "superior" white colonizer. The colonized's anger at the violence and degradation leveled against him by the colonizer is transferred to the idea of his own inferiority. The colonized suffer from an obsession with gaining love and recognition from their harsh dominators.

Insofar as the super-ego of racist imperialist ideology takes over culture, the phobia or fear of racialized others becomes what Freud calls a common phobia, a phobia accepted by dominant society. Fanon insists on investigating for whom the black body, especially the body of the black man, is a phobic object and why. Within the colonial ideology, the black body is abjected, which affects not only the treatment of black "natives" by white colonizers but also the psyche of the colonized who are forced to negotiate their own abjection within the dominant culture. The phobia is "common" and is a socially prescribed phobia.

Phobia and Abjection

Here, Julia Kristeva's theory of abjection may be more useful than Freud's theory of phobia precisely because it emphasizes the social aspects of phobia, particularly what Freud calls common phobias. With her theory of the abject and abjection, Kristeva develops Klein's thesis that ambivalence is a defense against ambiguity. Kristeva defines a notion of abjection with which she diagnoses separation and identification in both individuals and nations or societies. She suggests that the abject is not, as we might ordinarily think, what is grotesque or unclean; rather it is what calls into question borders and threatens identity. The abject is on the borderline, and as such it is both fascinating and terrifying.

In *Powers of Horror*, Kristeva says "to each ego its object to each super-ego its abject" ([1980] 1982: 2). For Kristeva, the abject is not yet an object but rather that which calls into question boundaries. The abject is the in-between that challenges all categorization. She maintains that on the social level the abject and abjection are ways of negotiating our relationship to, or separation from, other animals and animality; while on the personal individual level abjection is a way of negotiating separation from the maternal body (Kristeva [1980] 1982: 4). Phobias always take us back to the abject with its questionable borders. In other words, it is ambiguity itself that is the phobic "not-yet-object." Phobia is a type of defense against this ambiguity. What we exclude as abject recalls our own ambiguous borders in relation to animality and maternal origins. Phobia, then, is the result of the subject's own fear and aggressivity that come back to him from outside: "I am not the one that devours, I am being devoured by him" (Kristeva [1980] 1982: 39). This is precisely what Fanon describes when he discusses what he calls the white man's "Negrophobia."

Although Fanon's analysis of "Negrophobia" is provocative (for example when he suggests that negrophobic white women fantasize about being raped by black men in what turns out to be their desire for sexual fulfillment), it points to the threat of ambiguity associated with the abject. Fanon proposes that Negrophobia is the affect at the root of the white man's world ([1952] 1967: 155); and all evil and malefic powers are associated with the abjected black body. This abjected black body determines white man's bodily schema (Fanon [1952] 1967: 160). In this sense, the white man's sense of himself as good and civilized is defined against the black body, which he abjects as evil and animal. This abjection follows the logic of shoring up borders as a defense against ambiguity. Fanon's text suggests that there is a fear of ambiguous borders—borders of animality and racial borders—behind Negrophobia, which is primarily a fear of the black man's imagined sexual powers. He says, parodying phobic stereotypes of Negro animality and miscegenation,

> As for the Negroes, they have tremendous sexual powers. What do you expect, with all the freedom they have in their jungles! They copulate at all times and in all places. They are really genital. They have so many children that they cannot even count them. Be careful, or they will flood us with little mulattoes.
> (Fanon [1952] 1967: 157)

This passage suggests that the real fear is not of the black body or of the animal, but rather of the breakdown of borders between civilized and barbaric, human and animal, white and black.

Fanon describes the white man's phobia as the correlate, even cause, of the black man's obsession and inferiority complex. He also diagnoses a "sensitizing" and "collapse of the ego" as a result of the interiorization of the white man's phobia that leads to the black man's obsession with gaining recognition from his oppressors (Fanon [1952] 1967: 154). Moving away from Freud, he insists that the neurosis of the colonized is the result of the cultural or social situation rather than individual psychology (Fanon [1952] 1967: 152). Phobia and obsession make up the pathology of the colonial situation rather than a few neurotic individuals.

Colonization attempts to force the colonized to take on the white man's anxiety over his uncertain and ambiguous borders (both physical and psychological). This anxiety is manifest in the white man's phobia, which acts as a defense against unwanted affects that are projected onto racialized others. The success of the colonization of psychic space can be measured by the extent to which the colonized internalize—or should we say become infected by—the cruel super-ego that abjects them and substitutes anger against their oppressors with an obsessive need to gain their approval. In other words, the colonization of psychic space is dependent upon the colonized internalizing the inferiority/superiority dichotomy that sustains the colonizer's self-identity. This logic is full of self-contradictions that insure its failure. Indeed, the logic of colonization is paradoxical because it requires the colonized to internalize the lack of an interior, soul, or mind (Oliver 2001).

Lacan and Race Theory

Literary critics Kalpana Seshadri-Crooks and Juliet Flower MacCannell in different ways address the relationship between race, affect, and colonization, using the vocabulary of Lacanian theory, through which we can extend our analysis of the colonization of psychic space. Following Fanon, both theorists describe the racialization of colonization as the result of phobia and a cruel superego. Seshadri-Crooks argues that "the paradox is that Whiteness attempts to signify the unsignifiable, i.e. humanness, in order to preserve our subjective investment in race" (2000: 45). Following this Lacanian train of thought, we could say that whiteness attempts to signify the unsignifiable intersection of being and meaning in human beings. For Lacan there is always a fundamental split between being and meaning. How can we signify our being as beings who mean? On Lacan's analysis either we signify and—to use Sartre's phrase—make ourselves a lack of being, or we simply are (being) in which case we do not mean. As Seshadri-Crooks explains, "Whiteness is merely a signifier that masquerades as being and thereby blocks access to lack" (2000: 45). On Seshadri-Crooks's analysis, whiteness operates as a transcendental signifier, itself outside of the realm of signification. Whiteness poses as Nature or Being, or more precisely as the Essence of Human Being. The paradox is that whiteness both signifies Nature or Being (the lack of lack), and the lack of being that makes meaning—that is to say human existence—possible. As Seshadri-Crooks describes it, this encounter with the lack of lack or Being produces anxiety in the raced subject and this anxiety in turn produces a phobic object, namely the surface of the body, the skin and other surface traits (2000: 45–46). On her analysis, all of us are raced subjects trying to live up to the impossible ideal of whiteness. Within the colonial logic, whiteness becomes an ethical good that is impossible to attain; and the phobic object must be excluded in order to sustain the good or clean and proper body image (Seshadri-Crooks 2000: 37).

For Juliet Flower MacCannell, like Seshadri-Crooks, whiteness is related to the Real beyond signification (2000). But, whereas for Seshadri-Crooks, whiteness or race is not in the Real but poses as Nature as a defense against the anxiety of confronting the contingency, even arbitrariness, of our own nature, for Flower MacCannell race is the result of the White Man's Real, which infects the colonized. Like Fanon, Flower MacCannell is concerned to diagnose how it is that colonization affects the psyches as well as the material conditions of those colonized.

Reading *Fanon's Black Skin, White Masks*, Flower MacCannell maintains that colonization is effective because it infects the colonized with she calls the "White Man's Thing":

> the colonized body is one that has been exposed or invaded by drives other than its own. The colonization of the subject arrives through the White Man's Thing. The signifier that had granted one person his humanity is displaced by a

dehumanizing Thing not his own. The signifier *white* carried its own traumatic Thing in its wake and invaded the colonized with it.

(2000: 65)

Flower MacCannell argues that the dehumanization of colonization takes place through a kind of advertising campaign of sorts that infects the colonized with the White Man's desire ultimately fueled by the death drive, a death drive that does not properly belong to the colonized. Resonant with our analysis so far, Flower MacCannell maintains that the colonized are infected with the colonizer's sadistic superego, a superego that protects its own humanity by dehumanizing the other as foreclosed phobic "object."

Flower MacCannell says, "the proper name of the White Man's Thing is 'the Good'" (2000: 66). The White Man's fantasy of the Good displaces the colonized's own fantasies; and the White Man's unconscious invades the unconscious of the colonized. Colonization is not just an invasion of physical space but also an invasion of psychic space. The ideology of colonization centers on the notion that the civilizing mission is driven by an ethical imperative to bring the Good to the "barbarians." As Flower MacCannell describes this operation, it turns on the contradictory function of the Good in the psyche of the White Man. The White Man is caught between the social pressure to sacrifice pleasure for the common good and the perverse demand of the superego to enjoy without regard for others. She argues, "colonialism provided the perfect outlet for both the guilt of enjoyment and the imperative to enjoy the colonizer's own superego imposed" (2000: 72). The bad good—enjoyment, bodily pleasure, affect—is projected onto the colonized who are seen to laugh and dance without regard for the common good, while the Good—civilized restraint over pleasure and affect—is reserved for the White Man.

Resonant with Seshadri-Crooks's notion that the surface of the body is the most immediate place where the anxiety produced by the transcendental signifier whiteness attaches its phobia, Flower MaCannell claims that "race was the weak point or lesion where the alien's Good was inserted" (2000: 73). Because the body seems to inhabit the realm of Nature or the Real, it is supremely susceptible to a Good that divides the world into Nature versus Culture, Barbaric versus Civilized, Animal versus Human. Within the logic of this civilized Good, the body always falls to the other side. And insofar as this Good must insist that it is Universal, all differences, including different notions of good, become nothing more than justification for the civilizing mission and evidence of the need for colonization; all other goods become lesser goods in need of the lesson of the Universal Good. Nothing short of an alternative Universal Good can compete; anything "less" is at a disadvantage when faced with the White Man's claim to *The Truth* and *The Good*. The construction and maintenance of this Universal Good is further complicated by the operations of the Western civilizing mission to cover over its abjection and exclusion of the black body as bad or evil. As Lewis Gordon points out,

> Fanon realized that the more he asserted his membership in Western civilization the more he was pathologized, for the system's affirmation depends on its denial of ever having illegitimately excluded him; he is, as in theodicy, a reminder of injustice in a system that is supposed to have been wholly good.
>
> (2000: 4)

Fanon demonstrates that the effectiveness of colonization and its inherent racism are not merely epistemological but also psychological. Taking her lead from Fanon, Flower MacCannell argues that the psychic consequence of colonialism is that the White Man's desire becomes the only desire; it displaces the colonized's own desires and takes root as a perverse desire for the White Man's Thing. This desire is not only the desire for the White Man's goods (material goods and moral Goods) but also for the Thing that lies behind them.

The colonized, then, are "infected" with the cruel superego that sets up an impossible desire by both demanding and prohibiting it at the same time. Whereas this perverse superego constructs and protects the White Man's subjectivity and defines the place of his ego, Fanon maintains that in the colonized it becomes a mass attack against the ego ([1961] 1968: 252; [1952] 1967: 143). As Fanon points out, the effects on the colonized are the opposite of the effects on the colonizer. Most simply this is because while the perverse operations of the cruel super-ego make the White Man, they can never make the black man over (fully) into the White Man. The black man is denied both the desired (eroticized phobic) object—The Good and/or the white maternal breast (good and bad)—as well as the place of the subject, the White Man.

The pathology of colonialism takes place on the level of deepest desire and affect, the very construction of the psyche with its unconscious and conscious desires. The colonizer infects the colonies with his perverse and paradoxical desires and affects, which attach to the surface of the bodies of the colonized, in whom they often appear as somatic and psychic symptoms or what, as we have seen, Fanon calls "the emotional sensitivity" that is "kept on the surface of the skin like an open sore" ([1952] 1967: 52).

Given this analysis of the colonization of psychic space and the transmission of affect, Fanon's insistence on the healing power of violence in his later works can be seen in a new light. Fanon prescribes violent resistance to colonialism not just in order to regain territory and physical freedoms but also in order to regain a sense of agency, which is undermined through the colonization of psychic space. As Fanon says in *The Wretched of the Earth*,

> From the moment that you and your like are liquidated like so many dogs, you have no other resource but to use all and every means to regain your importance as a man. You must therefore weigh as heavily as you can upon the body of your torturer in order that his soul, lost in some byway, may finally find once more its universal dimension.
>
> ([1961] 1968: 295)

(Note too that Fanon insists that you must pressure the body to get to the soul.) Violent resistance restores the sense of agency or action lost through racist oppression. Fanon says, "At the level of individuals, violence is a cleansing force. It frees the native from his inferiority complex and from his despair and inaction; it makes him fearless and restores his self-respect" ([1961] 1968: 94, cf. 293; cf. 1964 [1994], 121). For Fanon, violence plays an important function for nation building and collective history; collective violence creates a sense of collectivity and collective history and restores the sense of agency that is undermined by colonialism. If the colonizer attempts to render the colonized a subhuman object incapable of rational thought and subjective agency, then active resistance serves to restore a sense of agency to the oppressed. For Fanon, violence is one effective means (along with love and understanding) to address what he calls the "mass attack against the ego" leveled against the colonized by the colonialism (1961 [1968], 252).

In addition, we can imagine that violence is necessary to redirect the colonizer's affects—particularly anger—back where they belong. Violence directed inward by colonialism is now redirected outward. Fanon suggests that the colonizer "deposits" anger into the "bones" of the colonized. This anger becomes directed inward and leads to colonized violence against themselves. The struggle against colonialism must include a struggle to free psychic space from this domination by the cruel superego of the colonizer (see Zahar 1974). If the White Man's anger has been deposited in the bones of the colonized, then that anger must be excised; it must be redirected outward. If colonial affects are deposited in the bodies of the colonized at the same time that colonial prohibitions against affect infect them, then those affects must be sent back to their proper place.

Sketching the Terrain of Psychoanalytic Race Theory

Fanon's use of psychoanalysis has been central to contemporary race theorists who employ psychoanalytic theory. Following Fanon, there are three approaches to psychoanalysis and race: taking psychoanalytic concepts and applying them to race; using analysis of race to challenge psychoanalytic concepts; and transforming psychoanalytic concepts through an engagement with race. Most critical race theorists who turn to psychoanalysis employ various combinations of all three. For example, most of the essays in Christopher Lane's collection *The Psychoanalysis of Race* are good examples of insightful applications of psychoanalytic concepts (1998). They take psychoanalytic concepts like melancholy, desire, or abjection, and extrapolate from the individual to social and political institutions. They use psychoanalytic concepts to diagnose particular social situations, cultural productions, or the psychic formations of group identities. Some theorists, however, like many mentioned here, not only apply psychoanalysis to oppression and racism, but also transform psychoanalytic concepts (alienation, misrecognition, paranoia, identification, unconscious, ambivalence, melancholy, among others) into social concepts by developing a psychoanalytic theory based on a notion of the psyche that is thoroughly social.

Insofar as the psyche does not exist apart from social relationships and cultural influences, psychoanalytic theory must take into account social circumstances. And, vice versa, if there are always unconscious dynamics that affect our investments in, and reactions to, social phenomena, then social theory must engage psychoanalysis. If the psyche is thoroughly social, we need a social psychoanalytic theory not only to diagnose social phenomena, but also to explain individual and group subject formation. We cannot explain the development of individual or group identity apart from its social context. But neither can we formulate a social theory that can explain the dynamics of oppression and racism without considering the psychic dimension. We need a theory that operates between the psyche and the social. In order to analyze racial identity and racist prejudice, we need a psychoanalytic social theory through which the very terms of psychoanalysis are transformed into social concepts (cf. Oliver 2004).

Perhaps inspired by Judith Butler's use of Freud's theory of melancholy to explain heterosexual desire as the foreclosure of homosexual desire, many race theorists have used melancholy to describe the ambivalence of racial identification. For example, in *The Melancholy of Race*, Anne Anlin Cheng uses Freud's theory of melancholy to diagnose Asian Americans' relation to American culture by interpreting and applying the concept of melancholy to various literary and artistic productions (2000). She argues the racism not only leads to a sense of loss and grief for its victims, but also loss and grief are formative of racial identities. The dynamic of loss and compensation described by Freud as melancholy becomes pivotal for thinking about racial identification. Similarly, David Eng and Shinhee Han combine Freud's theory of melancholia with Klein's theory of good and bad objects in order to diagnose the depressive position of Asian Americans within American culture; they argue, "processes of immigration, assimilation, and racialization are neither pathological or permanent, but involve the fluid negotiation between mourning and melancholia" (2000). Like Cheng, Eng and Han argue that racial identification is melancholic. These theorists use the Freudian notion of melancholy to discuss the elements of fantasy in dominant discourses about immigration, citizenship, and disease and health, among others.

Some theorists such as Mikko Tukhanen, Kalpana Seshadri-Crooks, Rey Chow, and Homi Bhabha turn from Freud to Jacques Lacan to analyze race and racism. For example, Homi Bhabha uses Lacanian concepts of mimicry and ambivalence to analyze race and desire (cf. Lacan 1977). He develops notions of hybridity, ambivalence, and stereotype, all of which have as their basis the psychoanalytic notion of the ambivalence and fluidity of desire combined with the fantastic aspect of identity. In other words, our desires are always ambivalent and our identities are always, at least in part, fantasies. Race and racism, then, are the products of ambivalent desires and fantastic identities rather than fixed, transcendent, or natural (1994). For Bhabha, the "double vision" or ambivalence of all desire and identity opens up the possibility of resistance to domination: "*double* vision which in disclosing the ambivalence of colonial discourse also disrupts its authority" (1994: 126). Psychoanalysis is central to Bhabha's analysis of the fluidity and ambivalence of both identity and desire.

Following Bhanha, Tukhanen uses Lacan's theory of mimicry in the mirror stage, and the misrecognition and paranoid identification essential to it, to investigate the ambivalence inherent in redeploying racial stereotypes in emancipatory ways. Examining reactions to the history of both white and black Blackface, Tukhanen argues that Lacanian psychoanalysis can help us make sense of the seemingly contradictory ways in which Blackface both perpetuated racist stereotypes and challenged them through parody (2010). Like Bhabha, Tukhanen finds psychoanalysis useful in diagnosing what otherwise might seem like simple contradictions rather than ambivalence inherent in psychic connections to both identity and desire (2010).

Seshadri-Crooks also analyzes racialized images in popular culture and film using Lacanian psychoanalysis. She brilliantly argues that whiteness operates like the Lacanian phallus as an ideal against which we all fall short (2000). Substituting the concept of whiteness for the Lacanian phallus, she extends these transformed Lacanian concepts to literature and film. She shows how the concept of race is tied to a notion of whiteness such that all human beings are divided into groups in relationship to the category of whiteness. She thereby shows how race continues to affect every facet of our lives even while it operates through a fantasy of transcendental whiteness.

Like Seshadri-Crooks and others, Rey Chow provocatively uses Lacanian concepts to analyze various kinds of cultural productions including film and literature. She argues that psychoanalysis is necessary to understand the motivations for identity politics. In other words, she insists that we must diagnose the psychic dimensions of identity formation, which are effaced in many discussions of identity politics. Relying on Lacanian notions of misrecognition, the real, and trauma, Chow diagnoses the double consciousness of post-colonial and racialized experience (e.g., 1998: 2014).

For all of these theorists, Freud's notion of the unconscious, especially as it entails ambivalence and melancholy, along with Lacan's elaborations of these notions, especially the notion of misrecognition in the mirror stage, play a central role in analyzing race and racism. Psychoanalysis provides a theoretical framework for diagnosing ambivalence inherent in both identity and desire. The psychoanalytic subject is always a fluid subject whose identities and desires are thoroughly permeated by fantasy and ambivalence. Thus, psychoanalytic theory complicates simple notions of black and white or oppressed and oppressor and helps to explain why and how race and racialization affect everyone. Finally, psychoanalysis demands that we endlessly investigate and question our own unconscious desires as they affect our beliefs and actions. Psychoanalysis, then, has profound ethical implications. Although, insofar as they remain unconscious, we never completely know our desires, they always affect us. Our unconscious desires and phobias govern, if not determine, our beliefs and actions. Thus, the ethics of psychoanalysis demands that we explore our own unconscious desires and phobias, and our own investments in violence, in order to vigilantly and continuously attempt to bring the unconscious motives of our actions to consciousness. Not to do so is to risk repeating racism rather than understanding and overcoming it.

References

Bhabha, Homi. (1994) *The Location of Culture*, New York: Routledge.
Cheng, Anne Anlin. (2000) *The Melancholy of Race*, Oxford: Oxford University Press.
Chow, Rey. (1998) *Ethics After Idealism*, Bloomington: Indiana University Press.
———. (2014) *Not Like a Native Speaker*, New York: Colombia University Press.
Eng, David L., and Han, Shinhee. (2000) "A Dialogue on Racial Melancholia." *Psychoanalytic Dialogues* 10, no. 4): 667–700.
Fanon, Frantz. (1967 [1952]). *Black Skin, White Masks*, New York: Grove Press.
———. (1968 [1961]). *Wretched of the Earth*, New York: Grove Press.
———. (1994 [1964]) *Toward the African Revolution*, trans. Haakon Chevalier, New York: Grove Press.
Freud, Sigmund. (1895 [1962]). "Obsessions and Phobias: Their Mechanism and Their Etiology," in James Strachey (ed. and trans.), in collaboration with Anna Freud, *The Standard Edition of the Complete Psychological Works of Sigmund Freud, Volume 3*, London: Hogarth, pp. 69–82.
———. (1989 [1962]) "The Neuro-Psychoses of Defense," in James Strachey (ed. and trans.), in collaboration with Anna Freud, *The Standard Edition of the Complete Psychological Works of Sigmund Freud, Volume 3*, London: Hogarth, pp. 45–61.
Gordon, Lewis. (2000) *Existentia Africana: Understanding Africana Existential Thought*, New York: Routledge.
Kristeva, Julia. (1982 [1980]) *The Powers of Horror*, trans. Leon S. Roudiez, New York: Columbia University Press.
Lacan, Jacques. (1977) *Écrits*, trans. A. Sheridan, New York: Norton.
Lane, Christopher (ed.). (1998) *The Psychoanalysis of Race*, New York: Columbia University Press.

Laplanche, Jean, and Pontalis, Jean-Bertrand. (1973) *The Language of Psycho-Analysis*, trans. Donald Nicholson-Smith, New York: W. W. Norton.

MacCannell, Juliet Flower. (2000) *The Hysteric's Guide to the Future Female Subject*, Minneapolis: University of Minnesota Press.

Oliver, Kelly. (2001) *Witnessing: Beyond Recognition*, Minneapolis: University of Minnesota Press.

———. (2004) *The Colonization of Psychic Space*, Minneapolis: University of Minnesota Press.

Seshadri-Crooks, Kalpana. (2000) *Desiring Whiteness*, New York: Routledge.

Tuhkanen, Mikko. (2010) *The American Optic: Psychoanalysis, Critical Race Theory, and Richard Wright*, Albany: State University of New York Press.

Zahar, Renate. (1974) *Frantz Fanon: Colonialism and Alienation*, trans. W. F. Feuser, New York: Monthly Review Press.

Part V

NATURAL SCIENCE AND SOCIAL THEORY

22
RACE AND BIOLOGY
Rasmus Grønfeldt Winther

Introduction

Imagine landing in the largest city, the capital, of an alien planet. You are stunned to see that every humanoid is within a few centimeters of the same height, everyone has a nearly identical muscular body, and everyone's facial features are quite similar—high cheekbones, small noses, and black eyes. Perhaps most surprising to you, everyone has purple skin. The ambassador accompanying you tells you the purple skin is a consequence of interacting skin pigment proteins, the double sun of that planetary system, and generation upon generation of voluntary random breeding. As you walk to your important meeting, the ambassador also informs you that every adult humanoid on the planet looks the same. She is no exception. Call this planet "Unity."

Now recall Darwin's natural experimental laboratory of evolution you learned about in high school biology, the Galápagos Islands, and the variety of finch and tortoise species found there. But let us now populate them, in our minds, with identical small populations of early humans. Add a few more dozen islands that are larger, have distinct environments, and are distant and mutually unreachable. Throw in a few million years of evolution. Humans on the islands of this thought experiment will come to be quite different indeed, in body, behavior, and culture. Call this scenario "Galápagos-Writ-Large."

Is *Homo sapiens* anno 2020 more like the inhabitants of Unity or Galápagos-writ-large? Modern genetics and genomics teach that our species is much closer to Unity.

Although less reductionist approaches to the biological sciences exist (Maturana and Varela 1980; Levins and Lewontin 1985; Maynard-Smith and Szathmáry 1995; Oyama 2000; Noble 2006; Winther 2008; Pigliucci and Müller 2010), most scientific practice on race and biology today is performed at the genetic and genomic level. The thrust here is to explore this level. In particular, seven theses on human genetic variation establish a crisp evolutionary picture of our species as relatively young, quickly expanded, and fairly continuous in genetic variation across our entire geography. It seems crucial to cover such facts so that the reader may form her or his own judgments about statements such as the following ones made by philosophers in prestigious venues:

> The lack of fixed traits for each so-called race means that race cannot be inherited as is popularly thought. Rather, the specific physical characteristics variably associated with races in cultural contexts are inherited through family

descent as is the rest of human biology. Race, therefore, supervenes on human genealogy or family inheritance.

(Zack 1999: 84)

There are no racial genes responsible for the complex morphologies and cultural patterns we associate with different races.

(Haslanger 2000: 43)

The concept of race is the concept of a group of human beings . . . (1) distinguished from other groups of human beings by visible physical features of the relevant kind, . . . (2) whose members are linked by a common ancestry, [and] (3) who originate from a distinctive geographic location.

(Hardimon 2003: 451–452)

After laying out the empirical facts, I consider their biological and philosophical implications. I survey proposals about the metaphysics of racial "kinds of people" (Hacking 2007a, 2007b), organized around *biogenomic*, *biological*, and *social* levels (Kaplan and Winther 2014). Theories of race require distinguishing at least four questions:

1. The "biogenomic race" question: is there genetic structure in human populations and what is it?
2. The "semantic" question: does the genetic structure correspond to extant designations of populations or kinds, in different languages?
3. The "biological race" question: does the genetic structure correspond to significant genetically based differences for socially valued phenotypes?
4. The "social race" question: are there racialized social kinds?

The Galápagos-writ-large scenario is an extreme version of the existence of biogenomic race. Biogenomic race exists when a species is subdivided into populations corresponding to standard uses of, for example, racial, national, or ethnic designations (see Winther and Kaplan 2013; Kaplan and Winther 2014). Most practitioners do not take their genomic work on human populations to be about race (Coop et al. 2014; Philosophy in a Multicultural Context Research Cluster: http://ihr.ucsc.edu/portfolio/philosophy-in-a-multicultural-context/).

Worrying about the semantics of race involves reflecting on appropriate conditions of application of racial terms, kinds, concepts, and names; on the nature of the reference relations of such terms (etc.) to the world; and on the processes of baptism and justification, whether in ordinary discourse, behaviors, and norms, or in biology, of these terms (etc.) in the first place (see Sarah-Jane Leslie, this volume; Mallon 2006; Spencer 2014; Ludwig 2015). As one example of addressing semantic concerns, the very baptism of "biogenomic race" is justified because slippage between the terms "populations" and "races" is common but can be avoided when we recognize complex and subtle differences between the two terms (Reardon 2005; Morning 2011; Kaplan and Winther 2014; Winther, Giordano, Edge and Nielsen 2015).

Biological races exist when a stable correlational or, better yet, causal mapping can be drawn between group genetic differences and socially significant or valued phenotypic characters such as cognitive abilities and perhaps also disease proclivities. It is especially in the domain of the biological race question (i.e., in the metaphysics of biological race) that fraught political and moral questions and challenges emerge. Indeed, exploring human genetic variation and the existence (or not) of biogenomic race would be a wholly abstract and intellectual endeavor except for its politically and morally relevant consequences (Lewontin 1970; Hacking 2005; Kitcher 2007; Winther and Kaplan 2013).

Finally, social races exist when there are psychologically and communally perceived stable kinds of racialized people, often leading to systematic discrimination and oppression (Mills 1998; Haslanger 2000; Hacking 2005).

Importantly, a normative question lurks: what are the beneficial and what are the pernicious effects of employing racial categories, and of perceiving the existence (or not) of various sorts of race, and who is affected and how? Whether this should be made a distinct question, thereby making ontological and semantic questions logically distinct and perhaps even prior to the normative question, as a standard analytical metaphysical approach would prefer, or whether such a normative question should not be separated out since it suffuses all the others, as pragmatic, conventionalist, or more sociological approaches would argue, is a difficult matter also bracketed in this entry (Spencer 2012; Ludwig 2015; Winther, Millstein and Nielsen 2015).

Fact Sheet: Seven Theses About Human Genetic Variation

A few basic definitions are necessary. The *genome* is the entire DNA sequence in an individual of a species; the genome is made up of long strings of DNA *nucleotides*, which take four forms represented by the letters A, C, G, T. A *locus* is a specific part of a genome, a "chunk" of the nucleotide sequence (though it can be composed of non-continuous nucleotide sequences), often used in our language coextensively with *gene*, and often but not necessarily functional, in the sense that the locus (or gene) is causally or mechanistically associated with some (part of a) phenotype. An *allele* is one of various versions of a locus (or gene), differing with another allele at one nucleotide or more, and existing in a population of a species. Our genome is divided into 23 pairs of *chromosomes*, 22 of which are standard autosomes and one of which is the sex chromosomes, our mitochondria also have unique genes. The facts below focus on autosomes, unless otherwise specified. Given this conceptual background, population genetics is the attempt to make evolutionary theory mathematically explicit by viewing evolution as the change of allele frequencies across generations, within and across populations and species. Population geneticists develop mathematical models. Furthermore, they subject the explanatory and predictive population-genetic theory to empirical tests (Lewontin 1974; Hartl and Clark 1989; Nielsen and Slatkin 2013). Complex facts about human genetic variation revealed by our best contemporary population genetics can be summarized in the following seven theses:

1. Low average nucleotide diversity
2. Small inter-species differences
3. Widely distributed alleles
4. Non-African variation is basically a subset of African variation
5. Most genetic variation is among individuals within populations
6. Even so, clustering populations and classifying individuals is reliable
7. The further apart on human migration routes that two populations are, the less genetically similar they are.

These basic quantitative features of human genetic variation can be understood without reference to population genetic theory. Or they can be the targets of population genetic models deploying important theoretical parameters such as mutation rate (μ), selection coefficient (s), and effective population size (N_e) (Hartl and Clark 1989; Nielsen and Slatkin 2013; Winther, Giordano, Edge, Nielsen 2015). Let us explore the seven theses.

1. *Low average nucleotide diversity.* Of species whose genomes have been extensively mapped, *Homo sapiens* has unusually low average nucleotide diversity. All members of *Homo sapiens* are basically identical at, on average and approximately, 999 base pairs out of 1,000 (Li and Sadler 1991; Yu et al. 2002). Given a total genome size of 3 billion nucleotides, and an average difference of about 0.1% between any two humans, two individuals will typically differ at approximately 3 million nucleotides. For comparison: *Drosophila* fruit flies, the standard workhorse for genetic studies, differ from each other on average by 1%, which is 10 times our diversity (Li and Sadler 1991); bonobos differ by 0.077%, chimpanzees by 0.134%, and gorillas by 0.158% (Yu et al. 2004). Maize has even more nucleotide diversity than *Drosophila*, and soybeans have slightly more than humans (Brown et al. 2004). Admittedly, *Homo sapiens* has more diversity than most big cats—roughly twice that of lions and leopards (unfortunately for their future prospects, cheetahs have near 0% diversity) (O'Brien et al. 1985). Wherever you may be from, you and I are genetically quite similar. Unity indeed.

2. *Small inter-species differences.* Average across-genome nucleotide identity between humans and chimpanzees is 98.77% (i.e., 1.23% nucleotide divergence), 98.69% between humans and bonobos, and 98.36% between humans and gorillas (Yu et al. 2004). Even human and mice genomes are roughly 85% identical (Batzoglou et al. 2000). Actual similarity is less than immediately apparent since genes (or parts of genes) are rarely linearly and continuously arranged on the genome, and genes change order and structure across species. Meaningful species-to-species comparisons of gene structure and gene number can therefore not be straightforwardly made only by comparing average nucleotide sequence similarities. Further evolutionary inferences about, for example, which nucleotide sequences can be traced back to common ancestors and which converged independently need to be made, and gene functionality must be assessed (Dicks and Savva 2007; Gerstein et al. 2007; Hahn et al. 2007).

3. *Widely distributed alleles.* Most human populations contain most of the common alleles present in our species. Approximately 92% of common alleles (i.e., alleles not present in just one person or a few people) are found in two or more of the following regions: Africa, America, Central/South Asia, East Asia, Europe, Middle East, and Oceania). That is, only about 8% of all common alleles are geographically private (i.e., the allele is unique to a single region). Over 82% of alleles are found in three or more regions, and approximately 47% of alleles are found in *all* regions (Rosenberg 2011).

4. *Non-African variation is basically a subset of African variation.* Africa is much more genetically variable than the rest of the world, and much of the rest of the world's variation is a subset of African genetic variation. African populations have approximately twice the nucleotide diversity of non-African populations. That is, two people whose recent ancestors are of African origin differ on average by about 1:900

nucleotides (0.11%), whereas two people whose recent ancestors are of European origin differ on average only by approximately 1:1600 (0.063%) (Yu et al. 2002; Campbell and Tishkoff 2008; Wall et al. 2008). Second, Africa also has approximately half of the total number of private alleles (Rosenberg 2011). As a third measure of variation, consider the distribution of all the approximately 8,000 alleles surveyed in Rosenberg (2011). Of these, roughly 82% were found in Africa, much more than any other single continent. Furthermore, most alleles (87%–90%) found in one non-African continent were also found in Africa, but not the converse. For example, only 74% of alleles observed in Africa are also found in Europe, and only 63% of alleles identified in Africa are also located in the Americas (Rosenberg 2011; Figure 22.1). Indeed, the number of total alleles per region diminishes, unsurprisingly, as we move farther away from Africa (along human migration routes), in the following ranked order: Middle East, Europe, Central/South Asia, East Asia, Oceania, and America (Figure 22.1). A final measure of genetic variation relevant here is heterozygosity, which is a measure of how evenly distributed alleles at

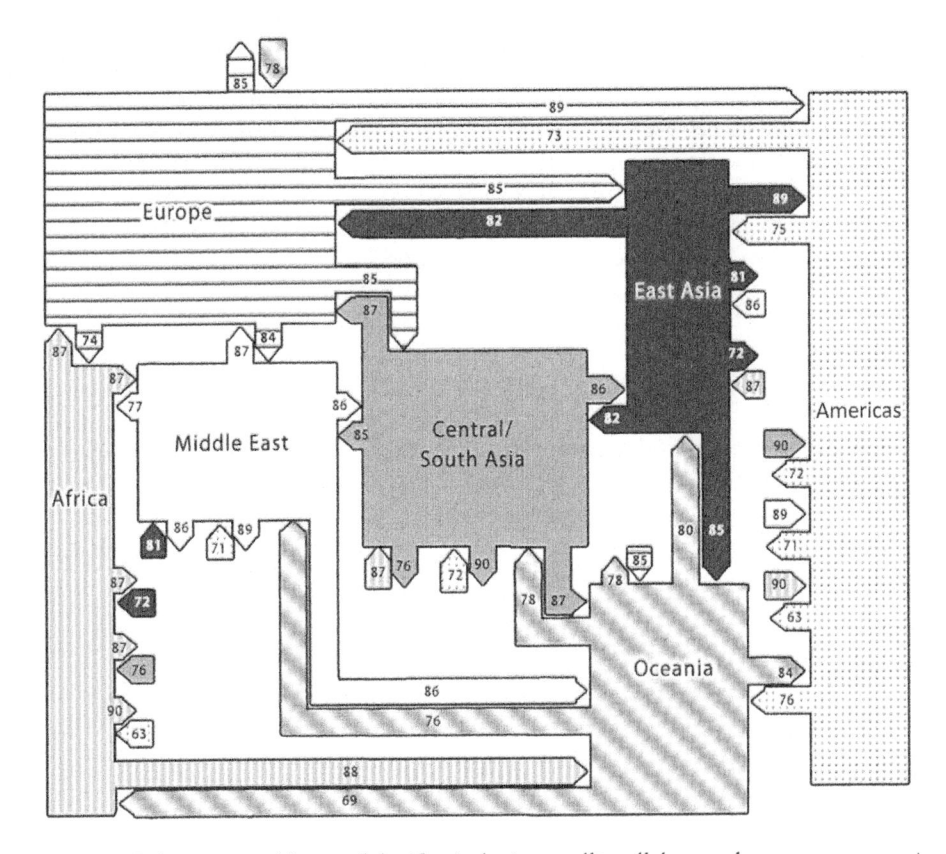

Figure 22.1 "Schematic world map of the 'flow' of microsatellite alleles. . . . boxes represent regions of the world, positioned geographically. Links entering into a geographic region indicate the percentages of distinct alleles from the geographic region found in other regions. . . . For example, averaging across loci, 87% of alleles observed in Europe are also observed in Africa, whereas 74% of alleles observed in Africa are also observed in Europe."

Source: Figure 9, Rosenberg 2011, 680; redrawn by Michelle Dick, UC Santa Cruz. Reprinted with kind permission.

each locus are in a given population, averaged across loci. Low heterozygosity for a locus means that most genotypes in that population are homozygous (e.g., AA or aa) rather than heterozygous (Aa) (Hartl and Clark 1989). Interestingly, within-population heterozygosity diminishes as a tight linear function of geographic distance from Addis Ababa, Ethiopia (Figure 22.2).

The loss of (i) nucleotide diversity, (ii) private alleles, (iii) total alleles, and (iv) genetic heterozygosity as we move away from Africa can be explained in terms of a *serial founder effect* model (see #7). As *Homo sapiens* migrated out of Africa, we went through a series of genetic bottlenecks in which relatively smaller groups colonized new areas (Ramachandran et al. 2005; Lawson Handley et al. 2007). These groups represented only some of the genetic variation of the parental population, as measured by (i)–(iv) (these are all theoretically correlated measures; Kaplan and Winther 2013). People reaching America via the Bering Strait went through this bottleneck process the highest number of times (though indigenous Oceanian populations also experienced almost as many, some of them non-overlapping with the Americans). Is Africa like the capital of the Unity world?

5. *Most genetic variation is among individuals within populations, and not across populations.* How much more genetically similar (on average) are two randomly chosen individuals from the same population as compared (on average) to a randomly chosen individual from that population and an individual from *another* population, either from anywhere within the same continental region or from anywhere within another continental region? Lewontin (1972) was the first to address this question explicitly, proposing an information-theoretic measure of genetic variation and applying it to genetic data on 17 blood proteins from worldwide blood samples of people. To the surprise of many at the time, his measure of genetic variation was, on average, 85% as large when calculated for a single population as it was when calculated for the world as a whole. (The earliest published data explicitly giving just this statistical result can be found in Table 12, "World Variation of Gene Frequencies," Cavalli-Sforza 1966: 367.) More completely, Lewontin found that the total global heterozygosity could, on average, be (approximately) divided or partitioned thus: 5% at the continental region level (African, European, and Asian); 10% at the across-population level, within continental regions (e.g., Ghanaian, Kikuyu, Tutsi, Zulu), and 85% within populations (e.g., Zulu). For instance, Table 22.1 shows a

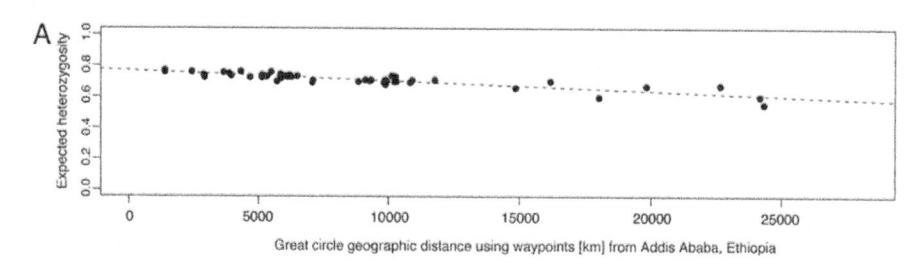

Figure 22.2 The amount of heterozygosity of each of approximately 40 worldwide populations diminishes as a function of their respective distance, along (approximate) migration routes, from Addis Ababa

Source: Figure 4A, Ramachandran et al. 2005, 15946. Reprinted with kind permission.

Table 22.1 Allele frequencies of three distinct genes across continental regions, as presented in Cavalli-Sforza and Bodmer (1971), and used in Lewontin (1972) and (1974). Frequencies are rounded from four to two significant figures. Empty cells indicate lack of data. The data gathering methodology involved "selecting whenever possible populations from Northern Europe . . . Central or South Africa . . . and China" (Cavalli-Sforza and Bodmer 1971: 724). See especially data tables in Cavalli-Sforza and Bodmer (1971), 724–733; Lewontin (1974), 152–157.

Gene	Alleles	Africans	Europeans	Asians
Duffy	Fy	0.94	0.03	0.1
	Fya	0.06	0.42	0.9
	Fyb	0	0.55	0
Auberger	Aua	0.64	0.62	
	Au	0.36	0.38	
Xg	Xg^a	.55	.67	.54
	Xg	.45	.33	.46

range of kinds of loci, using data from Cavalli-Sforza and Bodmer (1971). Lewontin's results imply that at most variable loci, different human groups tend to have relatively similar allele frequencies. Thus, the *Duffy* gene is an atypical example, as it is more extremely diverged than average (e.g., 0.94%: 0.03%: 0.1% for one of three alleles), and *Auberger* indicates less variation across populations than the average human locus. The *Xg* gene is typical of the human genome, showing some small variation across continental regions (see #6 for a simple statistical toy case). More technically, Lewontin's measure shares important theoretical properties with the standard inter-population heterozygosity F_{ST} measure developed by Wright (1931), which is a measure comparing expected and actual heterozygosities of populations, or (equivalently) a measure assessing the amount of inter-population genetic difference (Hartl and Clark 1989; Holsinger and Weir 2009; Nielsen and Slatkin 2013; Winther 2014). Interestingly, Lewontin's partitioning numbers have withstood the test of time, although the percentages vary slightly, often with a higher within-population percentage partition (Barbujani et al. 1997; Rosenberg et al. 2002; Rosenberg 2011; Li et al. 2008). Remind you of Unity?

6. *Even so, clustering populations and classifying individuals is reliable.* Even if most variation is within populations, if we accumulate information across loci, then reliable inferences can be made both about existent populations (clustering) and the population membership(s) of any particular individual (classifying) (Rosenberg et al. 2002; Edwards 2003; Tal 2012; Edge and Rosenberg 2015; Rosenberg 2017; Winther 2017). A computer program, Structure, was designed to do this (Pritchard et al. 2000). Consider a simple case of 100 loci spread across a haploid genome (i.e., single, not paired, chromosomes). Each locus can have a G or an H allele. The frequency of G alleles is 2/5 in population A and 3/5 in population B—very much in line with the expected allele-frequency differences in #5, and analogous to tossing a biased coin (in statistical jargon: binomial sampling). Now imagine that we genotype a person of unknown origin and find that she has a total of 40 G alleles across these 100 sites. Around 8% of people from population A will have this many G alleles, but only about one in 40,000 people from population B will

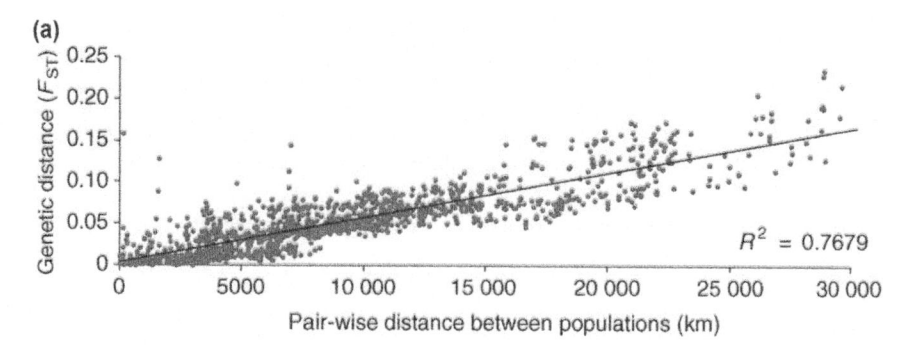

Figure 22.3 High correlation between pairwise F_{ST} and pairwise geographic distance of worldwide populations
Source: Figure 1a, Lawson Handley et al. 2007, 435. Reprinted with kind permission.

have this many G alleles. We can thus infer with high confidence that the person is from population A, and our confidence will only increase as we sample more loci. After all, each new locus is analogous to another coin toss—the more times we toss a biased coin, the closer we get to the actual bias frequency (e.g., 0.4 in population A). Thus, with even small differences in allele frequencies at each locus for distinct populations, by examining enough loci, we can use this procedure to become as confident about population membership as we like (Edwards 2003, Fig. 1, 799). Might subtle genetic differences between humanoids from distinct regions exist even on Unity?

7. *The further apart on human migration routes that two populations are, the less genetically similar they are.* If we plot F_{ST} between pairs of worldwide populations against the geographic distance between population pairs, a clear linear inverse correlation is found (Figure 22.3; R^2 = 0.77; Serre and Pääbo 2004; Ramachandran et al. 2005; Lawson Handley et al. 2007). To simplify, the further apart two populations are from one another, the higher their F_{ST}—namely, the more dissimilar their allele frequencies are. Indeed, changes in allele frequency differences across increasingly different populations will tend to occur smoothly. That is, the differences are clinal, under the *isolation by distance* model (Wright 1943; Malécot 1955). In addition to clinal variation, there are small discontinuous jumps in genetic distance associated with geographic barriers including the oceans, the Himalayas, and the Sahara. A serial founder effect model, based on, but slightly more nuanced than, the isolation by distance model, thus seems the appropriate theoretical model of human migrations (Ramachandran et al. 2005; Rosenberg et al. 2005; Rosenberg 2011).

In combination, these seven theses suggest that we are a relatively young species that has expanded in geography and numbers fairly quickly. Our genetic variation still very much overlaps across even continental regions.

Biological Implications

These basic patterns of human genetic diversity can be used for further biological inferences. Trees can be drawn representing our evolutionary history. Since a variety of phylogenetic tree-building methods are available (Felsenstein 2004; Winther 2017) and because our species has on occasion mated across large distances, such trees are useful primarily at low levels of resolution. Human trees tend to be consonant with a map of migrations (e.g., Cavalli-Sforza and Feldman 2003: 270; Sommer 2015; for the first population genetic map of human genealogy, see Edwards and Cavalli-Sforza 1964: 75, presented and discussed in Winther 2017). At higher levels of detail, a *trellis*, *network*, or *reticulate* rather than a *tree* model of human evolution seems more plausible (Templeton 1999, 2002; Winther and Kaplan 2013: 63–66; consult Andreasen 2007 for a *cladistic* race concept, and Kitcher 1999 for a *reproductive isolation* race concept; but see Kitcher 2007; Millstein 2015).

Using significant population genetic theory, we can also build trees that represent the history of individual genome segments (Nielsen and Slatkin 2013). Using coalescent methods, the *mitochondrial Eve*—copies of whose mitochondrial DNA, which is transmitted maternally, exist (with variations) in every person today—has been estimated to have lived 99,000 to 148,000 years ago. Similarly, the *Y-chromosomal Adam*, copies of whose Y-chromosome exist in every man today, lived anywhere from 120,000 to 338,000 years ago (Mendez et al. 2013; Poznick et al. 2013). The Most Recent Common Ancestor for European populations can also be estimated (Ralph and Coop 2013).

Notably, some loci are almost certainly experiencing natural selection. Some are targets of local selection, in which different alleles are favored in distinct parts of the globe. Consider the gene *SLC24A5*, which influences skin color variation. The ancestral allele, strongly associated with dark skin in African populations, is practically fixed—that is, present in every individual genome—in most African populations (as well as in most global populations outside of Europe or the Middle East). The derived allele, highly correlated with light skin in European populations, is effectively fixed in most European and Middle East populations (Sabeti et al. 2007). The explanation for selection on skin color is not yet completely clear, but there are several plausible explanations (Wilde et al. 2014).

Clear signatures of local selection are rare. Indeed, *SLC24A5* was one of only "twenty-two strongest candidates for natural selection" out of more than 300 candidate regions (Sabeti et al. 2007: 913–914). It was studied for its unusually divergent geographic distribution (Clark et al. 2003) and its link to known molecular mechanisms of melanin production (Lamason et al. 2005). Though there almost certainly are other loci like this (e.g., altitude adaptation in Tibetans, itself perhaps caused by gene mixing with archaic hominids; Huerta-Sánchez et al. 2014; Sabeti et al. 2006), their frequency and phenotypic consequences are unknown. Despite journalistic yarn-spinning by some (Wade 2014; effectively reviewed by Orr 2014), and despite a few other genes such as *FOXP2*, the so-called language gene (Enard et al. 2002), our knowledge about causal links between genes and behavior remains scant. And this is precisely the fraught epicenter of interest. Might some of the genes for cognitive abilities or certain diseases lie in the relatively small fraction of geographically private alleles (8%) or across-continental heterozygosity (5%–10%)?

Philosophical Implications

Philosophers interested in biological aspects of race tend to focus on two issues: (1) concepts of race and (2) the metaphysics of race. The metaphysics of race involves debates among three kinds of attitudes towards the reality of race, at three possible operational levels: realism, anti-realism, and conventionalism, about biogenomic, biological, and social race, respectively.

The biogenomic racial realist (e.g., Dobzhansky and Edwards; consult Winther and Kaplan 2013; Kaplan and Winther 2014) concedes that human sub-populations should be admitted as legitimate biological entities (i.e., the biogenomic question above). This realist believes that biogenomic races correspond, at least sometimes, to socially entrenched categories of, for example, racial, national, or ethnic designation (i.e., the semantic question above).

In contemporary literature, Sesardić (2013) accepts the existence of biogenomic races, which he takes to be foundational for biological racial realism. Spencer's tempered defense of biological race in *Homo sapiens* explicitly appeals to biogenomic race, and he distances himself from both standard conceptions of race and from social concerns (Spencer 2012, 2014). Spencer should probably be read as a biogenomic racial realist, arguing that we are more like Galápagos-writ-large than most everyone else admits. When Hochman (2013) denies the reality of human races by noting that human F_{ST}'s would hardly force the identification of similar populations in non-human populations, he critiques biogenomic race. A Unity scenario is accepted. Long and Kittles (2003) attempt to destroy biogenomic race in a manner analogous to Hochman.

In addition to realist and antirealist positions, there are at least two other live options on the metaphysics of biogenomic race. Conventionalism about biogenomic race is defended by Winther (2011, 2014), Kaplan and Winther (2013, 2014), Winther and Kaplan (2013), and Ludwig (2015). According to a conventionalist perspective, interpreting the reality (or not) of biogenomic races depends on the variety of "explanatory interests" deployed (Ludwig 2015: 245–247), and the measures and models used, in particular analyses. Strictly speaking, a fourth option is the ontological *reification* of race (Gannett 2004; Kaplan and Winther 2013; Winther 2014; critique in Spencer 2013), in which "what is cultural or social is represented as natural or biological, and what is dynamic, relative, and continuous is represented as static, absolute, and discrete" (Gannett 2004: 340), or, alternatively, mathematical models are "conflated and confused with the world" (Winther 2014: 204; Winther 2018). Both conventionalism and reification can be interpreted as lying either between realism and antirealism, or perhaps outside of any spectrum defined by realism and antirealism as the two extremes. The reader may wish to draw her or his own conclusions on the metaphysics of biogenomic race based, among other considerations, on section two of this chapter.

The sticking point here is the reality (or not) of *biological* race. The entire issue of biogenomic groups, populations, or races would not be so politically, socially or morally challenging if nothing rode on it (Helen Longino, pers. comm.). If putative group membership only determined socially insignificant characters such as toenail width, normative concerns would be much less salient. The open possibility of finding genes correlated with, for instance, cognitive abilities, makes the study of human genetic variation consequential. For instance, Lewontin (1972) concludes thus: "since . . . racial classification is now seen to be of virtually no genetic or taxonomic significance . . . no justification can be offered for its continuance" (397). Elsewhere he makes his position more explicit:

> The taxonomic division of the human species into races places a completely disproportionate emphasis on a very small fraction of the total of human diversity.

That scientists as well as nonscientists nevertheless continue to emphasize these genetically minor differences and find new "scientific" justifications for doing so is an indication of the power of socioeconomically based ideology over the supposed objectivity of knowledge.

(Lewontin 1974: 156)

Lewontin's statement does not imply that he denies #6 (Feldman and Lewontin 2008). His intelligent ire has been aimed less at biologists studying human genetic variation (Lewontin 1978 is a brief response to Mitton 1977) and more at hereditarians including Jensen (1969), Herrnstein and Murray (1995), Lynn and Vanhanen (2002), Wade (2014) and others. Hereditarians argue that many contemporary social, political, and economic inequalities are partly due to hereditary differences in the (average) innate capacities of different continental region "races." They endorse a Galápagos-writ-large picture of biological race, and are less concerned with the details of biogenomic race. In addition to Lewontin, many commentators, such as Coop et al. (2014) and Kaplan and Winther (2014) also deny the existence of biological race. Another option is to withhold judgment until individual genes for socially and morally significant traits such as cognitive or behavioral abilities are identified and clear and explicit selective scenarios and mechanistic penetrance established (consult Longino 2013). The discourse around biological race highlights the *pragmatics* of race, namely, the ways scientific practices intertwine with social concerns and context, and with normativity (Winther, Millstein, and Nielsen 2015).

Characterizations of social race are explored in detail elsewhere in this volume. Kendig (2011) baptizes a hybrid "physiosocial" form of realism: "race can be best understood in terms of one's experience of his or her body, one's interactions with other individuals, and one's experiences within particular cultures and societies" (191). The only philosophical point I shall make here is that, broadly speaking, most realists about social race are making a descriptive point: social race is real in most societies—it is measurable and is experienced within a system teeming with discrimination and oppression. However, some of these same social racial realists imply a prescriptive point of wishing to resist current power structures in order to attain a *post-racial* society, which remains an elusive social vision to characterize (e.g., Mills 1998; Taylor 2015).

Conclusion

As a species, we are closer to Unity than to Galápagos-writ-large. Moreover, there are multiple views on offer regarding the metaphysics and pragmatics of race. Should we stop racializing ourselves and abandon our conceptualizations and uses of biogenomic or biological race?

Perhaps not. First, a number of ongoing areas of biomedicine and forensics lean heavily on population genetics deploying biogenomic and biological race categories. For instance, health outcome disparities between racial groups in the United States are dramatic (Murray et al. 2006). Some researchers explain such disparities by hypothesizing factors in the average genome, so to speak, of distinct groups (Collins et al. 2003; Risch et al. 2002). Others argue that such systematic differences result from shared social circumstances, especially various consequences of racism. That is, "race becomes biology" via mechanisms of "embodiment of social inequality," such as "allostatic load" (see Gravlee 2009; Kaplan 2010; see also Lorusso and Bacchini 2015). Less controversially, some kinds of racialized categories are critical for matching potential donors in stem cell/bone marrow transplants (Hacking 2005; Bergstrom et al. 2009). Second, DNA forensics via genetic profile matching on related individuals is used increasingly throughout the world. Lest misidentifications occur, DNA forensics requires knowledge of the background population from which individuals are sampled, or statistical methods for correcting the lack of such knowledge (Rohlfs et al. 2012).

Many biological researchers of good will are astutely aware of the potential discriminatory and oppressive social effects of biomedicine and forensics. Even so, there are clearly many legitimate and historical reasons to worry that at least some forms of research on biogenomic and biological race could perniciously exacerbate social problems, as we saw in the critiques of the hereditarians by Lewontin and others. Vigilance, dialogue, and mutual co-teaching are crucial in the complex area of race and biology.

Acknowledgments

Paul Taylor kindly invited me to contribute to this volume. Quentin Coudray, Michael D. Edge, Joseph Hendry, David Ludwig, Lucas McGranahan, and Mette Smølz Skau critiqued earlier versions of this chapter. Exchanges on these topics with Anthony Edwards, Ian Hacking, Jonathan Kaplan, Richard Lewontin, Helen Longino, Carlos López Beltrán, Amir Najmi, Rasmus Nielsen, Noah Rosenberg, Bøllemis Skau, Omri Tal, and Michael J. Wade are very much appreciated.

References

Andreasen, R.O. (2007) "Biological Conceptions of Race," in M. Matthen and C. Stephens (eds.), *Philosophy of Biology*, Amsterdam: Elsevier, pp. 455–481.

Barbujani, G., Magagni, A., Minch, E., and Cavalli-Sforza, L.L. (1997) "An Apportionment of Human DNA Diversity." *Proceedings of the National Academy of Sciences (USA)* 94: 4516–4519.

Batzoglou, S., Pachter, L., Mesirov, J.P., Berger, B., and Lander, E.S. (2000) "Human and Mouse Gene Structure: Comparative Analysis and Application to Exon Prediction." *Genome Research* 10: 950–958.

Bergstrom, T.C., Garratt, R.J., and Sheehan-Connor, D. (2009) "One Chance in a Million: Altruism and the Bone Marrow Registry." *American Economic Review* 99: 1309–1334.

Brown, G.R., Gill, G.P., Kuntz, R.J., Langley, C.H., and Neale, D.B. (2004) "Nucleotide Diversity and Linkage Disequilibrium in Loblolly Pine." *Proceedings of the National Academy of Sciences (USA)* 101: 15255–15260.

Campbell, M.C., and Tishkoff, S.A. (2008) "African Genetic Diversity: Implications for Human Demographic History, Modern Human Origins, and Complex Disease Mapping." *Annual Review of Genomics and Human Genetics* 9: 403–433.

Cavalli-Sforza, L.L. (1966) "Population Structure and Human Evolution." *Proceedings of the Royal Society of London B* 164: 362–379.

Cavalli-Sforza, L.L., and Bodmer, W.F. (1971) *The Genetics of Human Populations*, San Francisco: Freeman.

Cavalli-Sforza, L.L., and Feldman, M.W. (2003) "The Application of Molecular Genetic Approaches to the Study of Human Evolution." *Nature Genetics* 33: 266–275.

Clark, A.G., Nielsen, R., Signorovitch, J., Matise, T.C., Glanowski, S., Heil, J., Winn-Deen, E.S., Holden, A.L. and Lai, E. (2003) "Linkage Disequilibrium and Inference of Ancestral Recombination in 538 Single-Nucleotide Polymorphism Clusters Across the Human Genome." *American Journal of Human Genetics* 73: 285–300.

Collins, F. S., Green, E. D., Guttmacher, A. E., and Guyer, M. S. (2003) "A Vision for the Future of Genomics Research." *Nature* 422: 835–847.

Coop, G., Eisen, M. B., Nielsen, R., Przeworski, M., and Rosenberg, N. A. (with many more signatories online) (2014) "A Troublesome Inheritance," Letter, *New York Times Book Review*. www.nytimes.com/2014/08/10/books/review/letters-a-troublesome-inheritance.html.

Dicks, J., and Savva, G. (2007) "Comparative Genomics," in D. J. Balding, M. Bishop, and C. Cannings (eds.), *Handbook of Statistical Genetics*, 3rd edition, Chichester: John Wiley & Sons, pp. 160–199.

Edge, M. D., and Rosenberg, N. A. (2015) "Implications of the Apportionment of Human Genetic Diversity for the Apportionment of Human Phenotypic Diversity." *Studies in History and Philosophy of Biological and Biomedical Sciences* 52: 32–45.

Edwards, A.W.F. (2003) "Human Genetic Diversity: Lewontin's Fallacy." *BioEssays* 25: 798–801.

Edwards, A.W.F., and Cavalli-Sforza, L. L. (1964) "Reconstruction of Evolutionary Trees." *Systematics Association Publication No. 6, Phenetic and Phylogenetic Classification*, 67–76.

Enard, W., Przeworski, M., Fisher, S. E., Lai, C. S., Wiebe, V., Kitano, T., Monaco, A. P., and Pääbo, S. (2002) "Molecular Evolution of *FOXP2*, a Gene Involved in Speech and Language." *Nature* 418: 869–872.

Feldman, M. W., and Lewontin, R. C. (2008) "Race, Ancestry, and Medicine," in B. A. Koenig, S. S-J. Lee and S. S. Richardson (eds.), *Revisiting Race in a Genomic Age*, New Brunswick, NJ: Rutgers University Press, pp. 89–101.

Felsenstein, J. (2004) *Inferring Phylogenies*, Sunderland, MA: Sinauer Associates.

Gannett, L. (2004) "The Biological Reification of Race." *British Journal for the Philosophy of Science* 55: 323–345.

Gerstein, M. B., Bruce, C., Rozowsky, J. S., et al. (2007) "What Is a Gene, Post-ENCODE? History and Updated Definition." *Genome Research* 17: 669–681.

Gravlee, C. C. (2009) "How Race Becomes Biology: Embodiment of Social Inequality." *American Journal of Physical Anthropology* 139: 47–57.

Hacking, I. (2005) "Why Race Still Matters." *Daedalus* (Winter): 102–116.

———. (2007a) "Kinds of People: Moving Targets." *Proceedings of the British Academy* 151: 285–318.

———. (2007b) "Natural Kinds: Rosy Dawn, Scholastic Twilight." *Royal Institute of Philosophy Supplements* 61: 203–240.

Hahn, M. W., Demuth, J. P. and Han, S-G. (2007) "Accelerated Rate of Gene Gain and Loss in Primates." *Genetics* 177: 1941–1949.

Hardimon, M. O. (2003) "The Ordinary Concept of Race." *Journal of Philosophy* 100: 437–455.

Hartl, D., and Clark, A. (1989) *Principles of Population Genetics*, Sunderland, MA: Sinauer Associates.

Haslanger, S. (2000) "Gender and Race: (What) Are They? (What) Do We Want Them to Be." *Noûs* 34: 31–55.

Herrnstein, R. J. and Murray, C. (1995) *The Bell Curve: Intelligence and Class Structure in American Life*, New York: Free Press.

Hochman, A. (2013) "Against the New Racial Naturalism." *Journal of Philosophy* 110: 331–351.

Holsinger, K. E. and Weir, B. S. (2009) "Genetics in Geographically Structured Populations: Defining, Estimating and Interpreting F_{ST}." *Nature Reviews Genetics* 10: 639–650.

Huerta-Sánchez, E., Jin, X., Asan, Bianba, Z., Peter, B. M., et al. (2014) "Altitude Adaptation in Tibetans Caused by Introgression of Denisovan-Like DNA." *Nature* 512: 194–197.

Jensen, A. (1969) "How Much Can We Boost IQ and Scholastic Achievement?" *Harvard Educational Review* 39: 1–123.

Kaplan, J. M. (2010) "When Socially Determined Categories Make Biological Realities: Understanding Black/White Health Disparities in the U.S." *Monist* 93: 281–297.

Kaplan, J. M., and Winther, R. G. (2013) "Prisoners of Abstraction? The Theory and Measure of Genetic Variation, and the Very Concept of 'Race.'" *Biological Theory* 7: 401–412.

———. (2014) "Realism, Antirealism, and Conventionalism About Race." *Philosophy of Science* 81: 1039–1052.

Kendig, C. (2011) "Race as a Physiosocial Phenomenon." *History and Philosophy of the Life Sciences* 33: 191–222.

Kitcher, P. (1999) "Race, Ethnicity, Biology, Culture," in L. Harris (ed.), *Racism*, Amherst, NY: Prometheus Books, pp. 87–117.

———. (2007) "Does 'Race' Have a Future?" *Philosophy and Public Affairs* 35: 293–317.

Lamason, R. L., Mohideen, M-A.P.K., Mest, J. R., Wong, A. C., Norton, H. K., et al. (2005) "SLC24A5, a Putative Cation Exchanger, Affects Pigmentation in Zebrafish and Humans." *Science* 310: 1782–1786.

Lawson Handley, L. J., Manica, A., Goudet, J., and Balloux, F. (2007) "Going the Distance: Human Population Genetics in a Clinal World." *Trends in Genetics* 23: 432–439.

Levins, R., and Lewontin, R. C. (1985) *The Dialectical Biologist*, Cambridge, MA: Harvard University Press.

Lewontin, R. C. (1970) "Race and Intelligence." *Bulletin of Atomic Scientists* 26: 2–8.

———. (1972) "The Apportionment of Human Diversity." *Evolutionary Biology* 6: 381–398.

———. (1974) *The Genetic Basis of Evolutionary Change*, New York: Columbia University Press.

———. (1978) "Single- and Multiple-Locus Measures of Genetic Distance Between Groups." *American Naturalist* 112: 1138–1139.

Li, J. Z., Absher, D. M., Tang, H., Southwick, A. M., Casto, A. M., Ramachandran, S., Cann, H. M., Barsh, G. S., Feldman, M., Cavalli-Sforza, L. L., and Myers, R. M. (2008) "Worldwide Human Relationships Inferred From Genome-Wide Patterns of Variation." *Science* 319: 1100–1104.

Li, W-H., and Sadler, L. A. (1991) "Low Nucleotide Diversity in Man." *Genetics* 129: 513–523.

Long, J., and Kittles, R. A. (2003) "Human Genetic Diversity and the Nonexistence of Biological Races." *Human Biology* 75: 449–471.

Longino, H. (2013) *Studying Human Behavior: How Scientists Investigate Aggression & Sexuality*, Chicago: University of Chicago Press.

Lorusso, L. and Bacchini, F. (2015) "A Reconsideration of the Role of Self-Identified Races in Epidemiology and Biomedical Research." *Studies in History and Philosophy of Science, Part C: Studies in History and Philosophy of Biological and Biomedical Sciences* 52: 56–64.

Ludwig, D. (2015) "Against the New Metaphysics of Race." *Philosophy of Science* 82: 244–265.

Lynn, R. and Vanhanen, T. (2002) *IQ and the Wealth of Nations*, Westport, CT: Praeger.

Malécot, G. (1955) "Remarks on the Decrease of Relationship With Distance." *Cold Spring Harbor Symposia on Quantitative Biology* 20: 52–53.

Mallon, R. (2006) "'Race': Normative, Not Metaphysical or Semantic." *Ethics* 116: 525–551.

Maturana, H., and Varela, F. (1980) *Autopoiesis and Cognition: The Realization of the Living*, Dordrecht, Netherlands: D. Reidel.

Maynard Smith, J., and Szathmáry, E. (1995) *The Major Transitions in Evolution*, New York: W. H. Freeman.

Mendez, F. L., Krahn, T., Schrack, B., Krahn, A-M., Veeramah, K. R. et al. (2013) "An African American Paternal Lineage Adds an Extremely Ancient Root to the Human Y Chromosome Phylogenetic Tree." *American Journal of Human Genetics* 92: 454–459.

Mills, C. W. (1998) "'But What Are You Really?' The Metaphysics of Race," in C. W. Mills (ed.), *Blackness Visible: Essays on Philosophy and Race*, Ithaca: Cornell University Press, pp. 41–66.

Millstein, R. L. (2015) "Thinking About Populations and Races in Time." *Studies in History and Philosophy of Science, Part C: Studies in History and Philosophy of Biological and Biomedical Sciences* 52: 5–11.

Mitton, J. B. (1977) "Genetic Differentiation of Races of Man as Judged by Single-Locus and Multilocus Analyses." *American Naturalist* 111: 203–212.

Morning, A. (2011) *The Nature of Race: How Scientists Think and Teach About Human Differences*, Berkeley: University of California Press.

Murray, C.J.L., Kulkarni, S. C., Michaud, C., Tomijima, N., Bulzacchelli, M. T., Iandiorio, T. J. and Ezzati, M. (2006) "Eight Americas: Investigating Mortality Disparities Across Races, Counties, and Race-Counties in the United States." *PLoS Medicine* 3(9), e260: 1513–1524.

Nielsen, R., and Slatkin, M. (2013) *An Introduction to Population Genetics: Theory and Applications*, Sunderland, MA: Sinauer Associates.

Noble, D. (2006) *The Music of Life: Biology Beyond Genes*, New York: Oxford University Press.

O'Brien, S. J., Roelke, M. E., Marker, L., Newman, A., Winkler, C. A., Meltzer, D., Colly, L., Evermann, J. F., Bush, M., and Wildt, D. E. (1985) "Genetic Basis for Species Vulnerability in the Cheetah." *Science* 227: 1428–1434.

Orr, H. A. (2014) "Stretch Genes: Review of Wade 2014." *New York Review of Books*, June 5. www.nybooks.com/articles/archives/2014/jun/05/stretch-genes/

Oyama, S. (2000) *The Ontogeny of Information: Developmental Systems and Evolution*, 2nd edition, Durham: Duke University Press.

Philosophy in a Multicultural Context Research Cluster. Various event discussions. Santa Cruz, CA, and New Haven, CT, October 20, 2012–March 5, 2015. http://ihr.ucsc.edu/portfolio/philosophy-in-a-multicultural-context/

Pigliucci, M., and Müller, G. B. (2010) *Evolution: The Extended Synthesis*, Cambridge, MA: MIT Press.

Poznick, G. D., Henn, B. M., Yee, M-C., Sliwerska, E., Eukirchen, G. M. et al. (2013) "Sequencing Y Chromosomes Resolves Discrepancy in Time to Common Ancestor of Males Versus Females." *Science* 341: 562–565.

Pritchard, J. K., Stephens, M., and Donnelly, P. (2000) "Inference of Population Structure Using Multilocus Genotype Data." *Genetics* 155: 945–959.

Ralph, P., and Coop, G. (2013) "The Geography of Recent Genetic Ancestry Across Europe." *PLoS Biology* 11, no. 5: e1001555, 1–20.

Ramachandran, S., Deshpande, O., Roseman, C. C., Rosenberg, N. A., Feldman, M. W., and Cavalli-Sforza, L. L. (2005) "Support From the Relationship of Genetic and Geographic Distance in Human Populations for a Serial Founder Effect Originating in Africa." *Proceedings of the National Academy of Sciences (USA)* 102: 15942–15947.

Reardon, J. (2005) *Race to the Finish. Identity and Governance in an Age of Genomics*, Princeton: Princeton University Press.

Risch, N., Burchard, E., Ziv, E., and Tang, H. (2002) "Categorization of Humans in Biomedical Research: Genes, Race and Disease." *Genome Biology* 3: 2007.1–2007.12.

Rohlfs, R. V., Fullerton, S. M., and Weir, B. S. (2012) "Familial Identification: Population Structure and Relationship Distinguishability." *PLoS Genetics* 8, no. 2: e1002469, 1–13.

Rosenberg, N. A. (2011) "A Population-Genetic Perspective on the Similarities and Differences Among Worldwide Populations." *Human Biology* 83: 659–684.

———. (2017) "Variance-Partitioning and Classification in Human Population Genetics," in R. G. Winther (ed.), *Phylogenetic Inference, Selection Theory, and History of Science: Selected Papers of AWF Edwards With Commentaries*, Cambridge: Cambridge University Press.

Rosenberg, N. A., Mahajan, S., Ramachandran, S., Zhao, C., Pritchard, J. K., and Feldman, M. W. (2005) "Clines, Clusters, and the Effect of Study Design on the Inference of Human Population Structure." *PLoS Genetics* 1, no. 6, e70, 660–671.

Rosenberg, N. A., Pritchard, J. K, Weber, J. L., Cann, H. M., Kidd, K. K., Zhivotovsky, L. A., and Feldman, M. W. (2002) "Genetic Structure of Human Populations." *Science* 298: 2381–2385.

Sabeti, P. C., Schaffner, S. F., Fry, B., Lohmueller, J., Varilly, P., Shamovsky, O., Palma, A., Mikkelsen, T. S., Altshuler, D., and Lander, E. S. (2006) "Positive Natural Selection in the Human Lineage." *Science* 312: 1614–1620.

Sabeti, P. C., Varilly, P., Fry, B., Lohmueller, J., Hostetter, E., Cotsapas, C., Xie, X., Byrne, E. H., McCarroll, S. A., Gaudet, R., Schaffner, S. F., Lander, E. S., and the International HapMap Consortium. (2007) "Genome-Wide Detection and Characterization of Positive Selection in Human Populations." *Nature* 449: 913–918.

Serre, D., and Pääbo, S. (2004) "Evidence for Gradients of Human Genetic Diversity Within and Among Continents." *Genome Research* 14: 1679–1685.

Sesardić, Neven. (2013). "Confusions About Race: A New Installment." *Studies in History and Philosophy of Biological and Biomedical Sciences* 44: 287–293.

Sommer, M. (2015) "Population-Genetic Trees, Maps, and Narratives of the Great Human Diasporas." *History of the Human Sciences* 28, no. 5: 108–145.

Spencer, Q. (2012) "What 'Biological Racial Realism' Should Mean." *Philosophical Studies* 159: 181–204.

———. (2013) "Biological Theory and the Metaphysics of Race: A Reply to Kaplan and Winther." *Biological Theory* 8: 114–120.

———. (2014) "A Radical Solution to the Race Problem." *Philosophy of Science* 81: 1025–1038.
Tal, O. (2012) "The Cumulative Effect of Genetic Markers on Classification Performance: Insights From Simple Models." *Journal of Theoretical Biology* 293: 206–218.
Taylor, P.C. (2015) "Taking Postracialism Seriously: From Movement Mythology to Racial Formation." *Du Bois Review* 11: 9–25.
Templeton, A.R. (1999) "Human Races: A Genetic and Evolutionary Perspective." *American Anthropologist* 100: 632–650.
———. (2002) "Out of Africa Again and Again." *Nature* 416: 45–51.
Wade, N. (2014) *A Troublesome Inheritance: Genes, Race And Human History*, New York: Penguin.
Wall, J.D., Cox, M.P., Mendez, F.L., Woerner, A., Severson, T., and Hammer, M.F. (2008) "A Novel DNA Sequence Database for Analyzing Human Demographic History." *Genome Research* 18: 1354–1361.
Wilde, S., Timpson, A., Kirsanow, K., Kaiser, E., Kayser, M., Unterländer, M., Hollfelder, N., Potekhina, I.D., Schier, W., Thomas, M.G., and Burger, J. (2014) "Direct Evidence for Positive Selection of Skin, Hair, and Eye Pigmentation in Europeans During the Last 5,000 y." *Proceedings of the National Academy of Sciences (USA)* 111: 4832–4837.
Winther, R.G. (2008) "Systemic Darwinism." *Proceedings of the National Academy of Sciences (USA)* 105: 11833–11838.
———. (2011) "¿La cosificación genética de la "raza"? Un análisis crítico," in C. López Beltrán (ed.), *Genes & mestizos: genómica y raza en la biomedicina Mexicana*, Mexico City: UNAM, pp. 237–258.
———. (2014) "The Genetic Reification of 'Race'? A Story of Two Mathematical Methods." *Critical Philosophy of Race* 2: 204–223.
———. (ed.). (2017) *Phylogenetic Inference, Selection Theory, and History of Science: Selected Papers of AWF Edwards With Commentaries*, Cambridge: Cambridge University Press.
———. (2018) *When Maps Become the World*, Chicago: University of Chicago Press, http://ihr.ucsc.edu/when-maps-become-the-world/
Winther, R.G., Giordano, R., Edge, M.D., and Nielsen, R. (2015) "The Mind, the Lab, and the Field: Three Kinds of Populations in Scientific Practice." *Studies in History and Philosophy of Biological and Biomedical Sciences* 52: 12–21.
Winther, R.G., and Kaplan, J.M. (2013) "Ontologies and Politics of Bio-Genomic 'Race'." *Theoria: A Journal of Social and Political Theory (South Africa)* 60: 54–80.
Winther, R.G., Millstein, R.L., and Nielsen, R. (2015) "Introduction: Genomics and Philosophy of Race." *Studies in History and Philosophy of Biological and Biomedical Sciences* 52: 1–4.
Wright, S. (1931) "Evolution in Mendelian Populations." *Genetics* 16: 97–159.
———. (1943) "Isolation by Distance." *Genetics* 28: 114–138.
Yu, N., Chen, F-C., Ota, S., Jorde, L.B., Pamilo, P., Patthy, L., Ramsay, M., Jenkins, T., Shyue, S-K., and Li, W-H. (2002) "Larger Genetic Differences Within Africans Than Between Africans and Eurasians." *Genetics* 161: 269–274.
Yu, N., Jensen-Seaman, M.I., Chemnick, L., Ryder, O., and Li, W-H. (2004) "Nucleotide Diversity in Gorillas." *Genetics* 166: 1375–1383.
Zack, N. (1999) "White Ideas," in C.J. Cuomo and K.Q. Hall (eds.), *Whiteness: Feminist Philosophical Reflections*, Lanham, MD: Rowman & Littlefield, pp. 77–84.

23
EUGENICS
Camisha Russell

Our race is overweighted, and appears likely to be drudged into degeneracy by demands that exceed its powers. . . . We can, in some degree, raise the nature of man to a level with the new conditions imposed upon his existence, and we can also, in some degree, modify the conditions to suit his nature. It is clearly right that both these powers should be exerted, with the view of bringing his nature and the conditions of his existence into as close harmony as possible.
—Francis Galton, Hereditary Genius: An Inquiry into
Its Laws and Consequences (1869)

It is significant that we have reached a point in human history at which further attempts to make the world a better place will have to include not only changes to the world, but also changes to humanity, perhaps with the consequence that we, or our descendants, will cease to be human in the sense in which we now understand that idea.
—John Harris, Enhancing Evolution: The Ethical Case
for Making Better People (2007)

As we probably are only beginning to realize today, in times when genetic screening, testing, and patenting pervade all sectors of social and economic life, and with the synthetic powers of genomics on the horizon, the epistemic space that heredity came to constitute has reconfigured life in its entirety.
—Staffan Müller-Wille and Hans-Jörg Rheinberger, Heredity Produced:
At the Crossroads of Biology, Politics, and Culture (2007)

This chapter is perhaps overweighted by epigraphs, yet I include all three because they represent the wider discourses that I am attempting to read together here under the heading of "Eugenics." The first epigraph from Francis Galton—the man who coined the now infamous term in 1883—represents the discourses of the original, Modern-era eugenics movements. Though diverse, these eugenics discourses of the late nineteenth and early twentieth centuries were permeated by the language of race. They were also deeply nationalist discourses, concerned with maintaining or recovering not only biological, but cultural vigor. The cures they offered for the perceived malaises of Modern (Western) civilization were based on an emerging understanding of the scientific principles of heredity.

The second epigraph represents the discourses of contemporary, so-called *liberal* eugenics. The language of race has no place in these discourses, except as part of a disavowal of the racism of the "bad old" eugenics. They are deeply (neo)liberal, concerned with our personal responsibility for broader societal or global well being as exercised through our free personal choice. They propose solutions to the perceived threats of global environmental disaster or human extinction based in the contemporary science and technologies of genetics. In other words, liberal eugenicists wish to reclaim the word "eugenics," protecting its practices from past injustices by ensuring that all eugenic technologies are freely chosen by individuals only for use on themselves and/or their children.

Finally, the third epigraph suggests that, despite the effort of new eugenicists to distance themselves and their aims from the bad reputation of earlier, involuntary eugenic (and genocidal) practices, the two sets of discourses exist in a shared (and dominant) epistemic space centered around the idea of (and obsession with) heredity. An epistemic space is a broadly shared way of knowing and making sense of the world that is so pervasive as to often go unnoticed and/or uninterrogated. As Troy Duster (2003) puts it, we have come to see the world through a "prism of heritability." This epistemic space, I would argue, is also the home of the race idea and of scientific racism.

Prompted by recent work in liberal eugenics, and in keeping with skeptics of such work, in what follows, I engage in a necessarily brief exploration of the shared epistemic space of heredity, race, and eugenics with the aim of addressing the question: can we have a eugenic project free from or purged of racism? To answer "yes," I claim, would require definitions of *race* and *racism* that are both narrow and ahistorical. By contrast, a broader understanding of the terms and of their historical contexts makes a non-racist and truly just eugenics appear much more elusive. First, I will describe the chief characteristics of eugenic ideologies and programs. I will also show how some proponents of a new, liberal eugenics defend their aims. Next, I will offer a critical account of the relationship between science and technology in the Modern era, focusing on the role that technological advances and ambitions played in the development of race science. I will then point to some of the ways in which power and coercion operate in (neo)liberal reprogenetic contexts. Finally, I will address a few of the ways in which racism, broadly conceived, still haunts (or manifests in new forms within) new eugenic programs.

What Do Eugenicists Have in Common?

The historical manifestation of eugenics that casts the greatest shadow over proponents of a liberal eugenics is not that laid out by Francis Galton (which was primarily concerned with the vitality of the English race). Rather, it is that of Nazi Germany, with its euthanasia and forced sterilizations (first practiced against unfit "Aryans"), medical experimentation, and mass exterminations. However, we ought not let this single most shocking and oft-discussed case prevent us either from recognizing that eugenics was truly "trans-national modernist philosophy" (Turda 2010: 4), or from taking into account the existence of diverse eugenics movements around the globe, often with different goals, beliefs, and proposed policies (Buchanan et al. 2000: 28–29). Far from being a unified movement with a single objective, eugenics before the First World War must be understood as a broad coalition of persons or groups promoting overlapping yet diverse scientific, social, or political agendas, including—in America alone—scientists, socialists, sexual reformers, immigrant radicals, physicians, agriculturalists, and popularizers (Zenderland 1998: 7).

Among the differences to be found between various proponents of eugenics were: (1) whether a eugenicist favored *positive eugenics* (encouraging the most fit marry among themselves and have larger families) or *negative eugenics* (curbing the fertility of those judged least fit); (2) the extent to which eugenic interests were combined with a focus on race; (3) the specific policies that were recommended; and (4) political orientation (Buchanan et al. 2000: 32–37). Of course, the fact of this diversity also points to the ubiquity of eugenic thinking at the time. Moreover, even where eugenics language appears racially neutral or simply to be referring to the *human* race, the reality is that most eugenicists had in mind the improvement of the white race (or races), working on the assumption that other, inferior races were likely to degenerate and die off on their own (McWhorter 2009: 202).

In their ambitious, jointly written work on questions of ethics and justice in the application of new genetic technologies to human beings, bioethicists Buchanan, Brock, Daniels and Wikler (2000) identify three core tenets shared by most eugenicists of the early twentieth century. The first was a concern about degeneration, understood either as a consequence of modern social processes interfering with natural selection by rescuing and nurturing the unfit, or as the result of race mixing, the products of which were thought to be inferior to either "pure" race from which they came. The second was a belief in the heritability of a variety of not merely physical, but *behavioral* traits, like talents, temperaments, proclivities, and dispositions. Therefore, third, was the belief "that social problems had both a biological basis and, to some degree, a potential biological remedy" such that "reproduction was seen by all eugenicists as an act with social consequences rather than a private matter" (Buchanan et al. 2000: 41–42).

Buchanan et al. (2000: 42–43) go on to argue that "concern for human betterment through selection—that is, by taking measures to ensure that the humans who do come into existence will be capable of enjoying better lives and of contributing to the betterment of lives of others" is an "unexceptionable" aim, concluding that "much of the bad reputation of eugenics is traceable to attributes that, at least in theory, might be avoidable in a future eugenic program." They begin their defense of a future eugenic program by pointing to the "pseudoscience" on which the old eugenics was based and to the bigotry, racism, and class prejudices with which it was infused. On their account, the eugenics movement was, in this respect, simply "a creature of its time" (Buchanan et al. 2000: 45).

They then consider and reject a number of theses about the wrong of eugenics. They defend the right—and indeed the duty—of parents to avoid bringing into the world children with severe disabilities. They argue that most of the values pursued by eugenicists, like intelligence and self-control, are widely shared by the population. They find—making no reference to the rather recent use of welfare policies to discourage or penalize reproduction among poor black women or to disability studies critiques of the ways in which prenatal genetic testing and genetic counseling are performed (Roberts 1999; Shakespeare 2005)—that "reproductive freedoms are sufficiently well-established that we need not entertain serious fears about the return of coercive eugenics in the wake of the Human Genome Project" (Buchanan et al. 2000: 50).

Having thus addressed major critiques of eugenics that might be thought necessarily to persist in any genetic program, Buchanan et al. are left with only the problems of poor science and unjust applications. With respect to the first, they argue that we should probably be glad that the earlier eugenicists didn't have the genetic knowledge to actually change the human gene pool. By contrast, they claim: "Our powers are much more impressive, and humankind's future abilities to rewrite our genetic code are apparently limitless" (Buchanan et al. 2000: 56).

Working from the assumption that we now have the scientific and technological means to make a real difference in people's genetic lives, their question becomes how to do so justly. Likening the "central moral problem of eugenics" to the "perennial ethical quandary of public health," they suggest that we seek a just balance between public welfare and private freedoms (Buchanan et al. 2000: 52). Such a balance is to be struck through careful attention to the effects of the new genetics on reproductive freedoms, by ensuring the "distribution" of self-respect to all members of the population despite differences in ability and performance that may arise from genetic intervention, and by ensuring that genetic difference does not result in a ghettoizing of those seen to carry higher genetic health risks. If we can do this work and remain vigilant with respect to the return of past abuses of eugenics, their argument goes, then there is no need to avoid pursuing its benefits.

In other words, Buchanan et al. argue for a conceptual and ethical distinction between racist ideology and the idea of improving the health of a population through eugenic measures. They believe there are ways to develop genetic science and deploy genetic technologies to pursue both private and public goods without bringing about the coercion and abuse that the term "eugenics" now connotes. Such arguments can be very compelling and seem to be based in solid reasoning; they operate, however, only on the surface of the issue, failing to utilize key insights from the philosophy of technology or science and technology studies. They seem to see science as a neutral form of knowledge that is merely more or less accurate, and technologies as tools emerging from that knowledge that are also neutral prior to their use by human agents. Thus, science must be improved and technologies mastered and put to good and just use.

Beyond "Poor Science" and "Unjust Applications"

When we seek to understand and evaluate the broader epistemic space of heredity rather than specific eugenic practices, however, we find that the notion of mastering technology is as much a part of the problem as it is a solution. In his philosophical exploration of the essence of technology, Martin Heidegger points out that prior to both the actual manufacture of technological artifacts *and* the science that enables them is the identification of the things around us in nature as materials for the production of those artifacts. "Modern science's way of representing pursues and entraps nature as a calculable coherence of forces," he writes, and, as such, it "will never be able to renounce this one thing: that nature report itself in some way or other that is identifiable through calculation and that it remain orderable as a system of information" (Heidegger 1993: 326–328). Furthermore, for Heidegger, one of the fundamental characteristics of modern technology (as opposed to prior technology) is the belief that the energy concealed in nature is something to be unlocked, transformed, stored, distributed, and switched about, ultimately ordered into interlocking systems to be regulated and secured. Heredity is such a system of information—one which pursues and entraps humanity as a calculable coherence of biogenetic forces, asking those forces to explain more and more about our lives. Modern technology thus seeks to improve our human situation by regulating and securing these biogenetic forces.

Heidegger's description of the relation between technology and science in the modern era helps us to think critically about the relation between race science and the technological practices of eugenics because it suggests that the two are more fundamentally related than some scholars would like to believe. Rather than seeing eugenics as the political misapplication of a conceptually prior and flawed racial science, Heidegger's view invites us see an essential human drive to master nature as that which underlies the epistemic space of heredity, which includes not only eugenics, but both the concept of race and the subsequent attempts to justify race scientifically. Eric Voegelin (1997: 177n14) makes a similar point about this conceptual relationship between (race) science and modern technology when he writes that: "Modern race theories give the impression of an aggressive optimism because, like technology, they are eager to put to use the lawful course of nature in order to arrive at a specific objective they consider desirable." In Heideggerian terms, when race came to be seen as a *force* or *cause* in nature, it became part of nature's concealed energy and thus something to be unlocked and transformed—something to be mastered for optimal societal efficiency and yield.

What is particularly important here in thinking about the relationship between race (as science) and eugenics (as technology) is Heidegger's assertion that technology does not simply follow after science, but rather offers the conceptual framework within which science is produced in the first place. In other words, human goals (and research biases) are to be found in the science itself, not merely its technological applications. This relationship can be seen in the way that animal breeding as a technology provided the conceptual framework within which the scientific race concept emerged and developed, a fact which shows that eugenic thinking was much more essential to the race concept itself than is typically recognized.

In Kant's essay on race, arguably the first articulation of a scientific race concept, we find definitions of species, race and variety that all rest on rules of reproduction. Two animals belong to the same species if they can meet "Buffon's rule" by mating and producing fertile offspring. Racial deviations between two animals of the same species are those deviations that are consistently preserved in reproduction through many generations. Two animals of the same species belong to different races if, when they mate, they produce half-breed offspring (that is, the enduring racial deviations belonging to the two parents are mixed in the offspring). Deviations belonging to mere varieties are those that may or may not be preserved in reproduction. These rules of reproduction, which shape the first scientific concept of race, and which remain important in accounts of race-mixing as driving history (as in Klemm and Gobineau), have clear origins in the study of mating and breeding possibilities in non-human animals, which study, I would argue, is based in the *technology* of animal breeding (Voegelin 1997: 167–168; Gobineau 1970: 175).

Indeed, one account of the origin of the term "race" (in its current use as a way of describing human groups or lineages) traces its first emergence to the Spanish language, where *raza* was extended to human beings from a more primary definition referring to the "caste or quality of authentic horses" (Smedley 1993: 38). In the French context, Buffon, of whom Kant made use in his attempts to divide animals according to laws, claimed "one of the most salient distinctions between human tribes was that between civilization and the savage state." Comparing this directly to the difference between domesticated and wild animals, Buffon concluded, "all the insights of professional livestock breeders could be exploited to explain mankind." Buffon's theories, then, heavily relied on presumed parallels between human and non-human animal physiology—what was called the "analogical method" (Augstein 1996: xv). The analogical method was useful because the practice or technology of animal (and plant) breeding operated successfully well in advance of any scientific theories that could effectively explain breeders' results, with breeders establishing practice-based axioms and breeding rules that yielded significant power to mold organisms for specific features from the mid-eighteenth century on (Müller-Wille and Rheinberger 2007: 12). Indeed, Müller-Wille and Rheinberger point to the erosion in the early nineteenth century of institutional barriers like those between naturalists and breeders as paving the way for the discourse of heredity. In some cases, like that of Pierre-Louis Moreau de Maupertuis (writing before Buffon in the first half of the eighteenth century), no erosion of barriers was necessary. Maupertuis both bred his own pets looking for hereditary patterns and recorded the genealogy of a human family in Berlin, some members of which were born with extra fingers and toes (polydactyly) (Terral 2007: 255). This is clearly visible in the work of Charles Darwin, and even earlier in that of his grandfather, physician Erasmus Darwin (who was also the grandfather of Francis Galton). For the elder Darwin, analogies to animal breeding served not only to generate theories about the heredity nature of human disease, but also suggested that human progress could be pursued biologically by learning the laws of nature and then exerting power over them. Indeed, for a number of physicians in the mid- to late-eighteenth century, comparisons to animal breeding pointed not only to the *possibility* of human improvement through control of reproductive practices, but also to its *desirability* and *wisdom* (Gregory 1774: 29–30; Vandermonde 1756: 91–92).

These views suggesting the possible benefits of technological control of human reproduction using analogies to animal breeding practices (which though effective in improving livestock could not yet be explained scientifically) form the background against which Kant attempted to elaborate a scientific race concept using rules of reproduction. And, indeed, Kant felt the need to address (and reject) this technological possibility in his essay on race. Though Kant does not adopt a policy of human intervention in reproduction, the fact that he is aware of such proposals and addresses them in his essay is significant. It not only challenges a view of eugenics as the (immoral) technological application of an *already* developed racial science, but also suggests that thoughts on human reproductive control understood by analogy to animal breeding framed Kant's purposive view of nature in terms of races. In other words, it offers further evidence in favor of Heidegger's claim that human projects (technology) shape the human view of nature (science), even where explicit pursuit of technological control of nature is rejected.

As animal breeding became increasingly elaborate and fashionable in eighteenth-century England, it came to represent and perpetuate a particular Modern view of the world. The English gentlemen-farmers who sought systemically to improve breeds of cattle and sheep during this period also established new institutions for the comparison and improvement of animal types, such as the country fair. According to Da Cal (1992), while fairs for selling animals were nothing new, "the cult of types" was. Stud services for "improving" types and "bettering" stocks not only made money, but were viewed as "a patriotic service to the 'National Herd.'" Similarly, a new world of thoroughbred horses sprung up, with a more simple admiration for fine animals being overlain by systematization and officialized codes concerning the horses' genealogical "blood" and "temperament." From about 1791 on, "thoroughbreds" were listed by parentage in an official stud-book, "an equine equivalent of the human 'blue-blood's' family tree." By the 1850s, the obsession with animal pedigree even led to a domestic "poultry craze." "Scarcely surprising, then," writes Da Cal (1992: 718–719), "that this same period would see the highpoint of scientific and literary fascination with human types, from the physiognomic treatises of Lavater or F. X. Messerschmidt or the comparative anatomy of Negroes and apes, to the extensive Romantic literature describing 'customs' by national or social 'character.'" Charles Darwin's interest in and analogical use of animal breeding is also well documented in the Transmutation Notebooks he kept while constructing his theory of natural selection between 1837 and 1839. By the time of Darwin's major publications on natural selection (1859–1871), breeding was very much present in the public imagination. In this context (as compared to earlier animal husbandry), *moral character* has taken on greater significance. As Paul White (2007: 376) notes: "In Victorian discourses of breeding, natural historical and moral character were considerably intertwined."

Innovations in the management of animal populations can also be seen as paving the conceptual way for similar interventions on the human level. Many sanitation, hygiene, and vaccination practices in human populations (whether seen now as progressive or repressive) have animal analogs. For example, the Pasteur anti-rabies vaccine (1885) as "*the* image of effective social prophylaxis"; the dog pound as a way to gather and contain *potential* hazards (Da Cal 1992: 722); or the "lethal chamber" patented in the UK in the 1880s and first used on stray dogs (McWhorter 2009: 220). Though Da Cal (1992: 724) recognizes a number of other social factors and institutional backgrounds that contributed to the events of the Holocaust, he concludes, in what I see as a largely technological argument, that "the handling of animals is the only real social model, i.e. existing in industrial society, for the kind of segregation and elimination that the Nazis tried to carry out."

Without attempting to make any extreme, simplifying or totalizing claims, Da Cal (1992: 724–725) simply suggests that "the animal breeding sub-culture [was] a sort of 'lower common denominator' of biological information in the late XIXth and XXth century European societies," which was "key to transmitting 'highbrow' racist ideas to 'lowbrow' audiences" in that it "created a visual vocabulary and a living representation of race theory that was equally powerful on peasant farms or urban settings." So, too, in early twentieth-century American society, especially during the interwar period. There, county and state fairs included not only exhibitions on animals and farming, but also those designed to popularize the ideas of the American Eugenics Society. Such exhibitions also featured the highly popular "Fitter Families for Future Firesides" contests. Eventually, eugenics exhibitions in the United States found their way into national museums and larger *world* fairs as well (Bruinius 2006; Rydell 1993; Schneider 2009).

When we consider these ways in which the technologies of animal (and plant) breeding carved out and continued to shape the epistemic space of heredity, it becomes much more difficult to see the scientific thinking and discoveries that emerged within that space as merely neutral knowledge, whether that knowledge continues to be understood as true or (as in race science) has since been rejected as false. Beliefs in the power of human heredity to shape society and to be shaped in service of society (engendered by success in animal husbandry) are essential both to the race idea and to the support of any eugenic project.

Power and Coercion in Liberal Society

As discussed, it is important for proponents of a new, liberal eugenics that such a project has been understood as non-racial or non-racist. For them, this seems to mean that racial categorizations as currently understood ought not to be used in eugenic decisions. Thus far, I have used the notion of an epistemic space shared by race, heredity, and eugenics to trouble that understanding of racism. Yet it is also important for such proponents that their project be understood as non-coercive and respectful of individual liberty. It is to this concern that I now turn.

In his body of work, Michel Foucault uses notions of technologies, techniques, and practices to carry out genealogies and critiques of power, of subject formation, and of the variety of ideas and institutions through which power can be exercised. When uncovering and critiquing a particular regime of truth, he points not only to the ideas and assumptions that characterize the regime, but also the concrete means, instruments, rules, and practices through which that regime of truth emerges, is instantiated, and is maintained. Crucial to the instantiation and maintenance of neoliberalism in general—and of liberal eugenics in particular—are what Foucault calls *technologies of the self*, which

> permit individuals to effect by their own means or with the help of others a certain number of operations on their own bodies and souls, thoughts, conduct, and way of being, so as to transform themselves in order to attain a certain state of happiness, purity, wisdom, perfection and immortality.
>
> (Foucault 1988: 18)

(Note that such practices of *self* are "nevertheless not something that the individual invents by himself" but rather "patterns that he finds in his culture and which are proposed, suggested and imposed on him by his culture, his society and his social group" (Fornet-Betancourt et al. 1987: 122).)

As Nikolas Rose describes, in "advanced" liberal democracies, the governing of individuals and the population is in large part achieved through means and in arenas that are deliberately designated as non-political. Strategies of rule must seek to govern not "through 'society,' but through the regulated choices and aspirations to self-actualization and self-fulfillment" (Rose 1996: 41). Sites of reproductive and reprogenetic intervention are thus part of "a complex apparatus of health and therapeutics" that consists of "techniques of advice and guidance, medics, clinics, guides and counselors," which have as their focus "the management of the individual and social body as a vital national resource" (Rose 1996: 37). Insofar as national or social prosperity is thought to be achieved through individual prosperity, and insofar as individual prosperity is thought to require personal freedom, the State is believed to be taking a backseat while individuals are not simply *left*, but rather *exhorted* to govern themselves.

Thus, in (most defenses of) liberal eugenics, reproductive and reprogenetic technologies must be chosen and used without State intervention so as to appear free from obvious forms of power and domination. Yet these "private" interactions involve the exercise of great deals of power. To offer just three examples, I will consider Rose's discussion of the intrinsic relation of liberal rule to the authority of expertise, Sandel's discussion of compliance and hyper-responsibility in human enhancement, and Roberts' discussion of the link between privatization and punishment in reprogenetics.

As Rose points out, public distaste for State intervention does not necessarily lead to the banishment of authorities from our "private" lives. Rather, "authority is accorded to formally autonomous expert authorities" (Rose 1996: 46). For example, the parent who seeks to employ reprogenetic technologies as an investment in his/her child (or, increasingly, any parent at all), finds him/herself very much dependent on the expertise of doctors or other fertility experts to carry out his/her project. Indeed, most parents rely on medical experts even to understand what it is *possible* to desire and pursue in the field of reproduction through reprogenetics.

Practices around prenatal genetic testing demonstrate the major role of authority in one technology of the self. As disabilities theorists point out, many doctors simply expect women to undergo prenatal genetic testing and do not take time to discuss what it is, why it is being done, or what the potential consequences of an "abnormal" result would be. It is only after an "abnormal" result has already appeared that women or couples speak to a physician or genetic counselor about their "options." Studies indicate, however, that the presentation of these options favors therapeutic abortion of fetuses who will be born with disabilities and that these experts do not provide prospective parents with important forms of information that might make continuing the pregnancy feel more viable—for example, information about the wide range of severity in certain conditions or information from parents currently raising children with disabilities about their experiences (Parens and Asch 2000; Shakespeare 2005).

In his discussion about the ethics of all forms of human enhancement, including so-called designer children, Michael Sandel argues that the language of autonomy, fairness, and individual rights that permeates discussion of the issue fails to capture much of our deep uneasiness about the "pursuit of perfection." Where some opponents fear that genetic enhancements will "undermine our humanity by threatening our capacity to act freely, to succeed by our own efforts, and to consider ourselves responsible—worthy of praise or blame—for the things we do and for the way we are" (as in athletes who succeed via biotechnological enhancement of their skill), Sandel (2009: 78) argues that the "deeper danger" enhancements represent is a kind of *hyperagency*. Far from simply allowing people to do as they like or to freely pursue their individual projects, the availability of enhancements and biotechnological fixes appears as "a bid for compliance—a way of answering a competitive society's demand to improve our performance and perfect our nature" (Sandel 2009: 82).

Where we believe we fully control our or our children's traits and abilities, we lack an appreciation for the role of luck in our lives, in the fact that we may succeed where others fail. Rather than acknowledging what Sartre called our *facticity* even as we recognize that we have freedom in how we take up those givens in life, the availability of genetic enhancement suggests that there are no givens with which one must contend. This leads to an over-heightened sense of responsibility according to which, though we may also be praised for our skills and successes, we must be blamed for any lacks or failures. Socio-historical factors shaping one's life possibilities and outcomes fade into the background, and in the face of this dogmatic belief in individual responsibility, social solidarity is diminished. After all, if everyone is personally responsible for his or her own lot, there is little reason to respond with sympathy to those who are suffering or in need.

In a similar vein, Dorothy Roberts argues that there are crucial similarities between the reprogenetic technologies aimed at middle- and upper-class women whose reproduction is generally encouraged and those contraceptive technologies aimed at poor and non-white women, which she understands as *privatization* and *punishment*, respectively. "Both population control programs and genetic selection technologies," she suggests, "reinforce biological explanations for social problems and place reproductive duties on women that shift responsibility for improving social conditions away from the state" (Roberts 2005: 1344). Ultimately, insofar as they retain control over their own reproductive decisions, women become "gatekeepers of new social order" (Roberts 2005: 1357).

The many real problems plaguing poor and minority communities have long been blamed on "irresponsible" reproductive decisions within those communities, rather than on an extensive and continuing history of marginalization, exploitation, and discriminatory social policy. The contemporary focus on genetic correction and enhancement seems to exacerbate rather than reverse this trend. A focus on individually accessed technological solutions renders social and political solutions aimed at structural inequalities misguided or unnecessary. A privatization of the sources of inequality thus depoliticizes them.

What Do Eugenicists Have in Common? (Revisited)

My suggestion, then, is that eugenicists past and present share with each other (and with race scientists and animal breeders) a particular modern sensibility—a sensibility which Heidegger has described as technological in the way that it presents the natural world to human beings as something that challenges them to intervene in "natural" processes in the name of industry, efficiency, productivity, and ultimately perfectibility. With the modern period, we find science developing precisely *as* the interpretation of the natural world through technological metaphors. Nature is expected to exhibit a form of rationality and to reveal to man its essential laws. Following the discovery of such laws in the physical sciences, natural or biological scientists are tasked with uncovering the *laws*, *mechanisms*, and *final causes* of biological life (and indeed human history and culture).

In this context (and today), eugenicists emerge as those believers in the power of science and technology who perceive clear and present dangers to humanity on the horizon, and are thus driven to convince others that taking control of human nature (mental and physical) is an invaluable social good necessary to ensure human survival. Unfortunately, with a great deal of scientific knowledge and technological resources concentrated in the hands of authorities and expert practitioners, even to the extent that eugenicists convince the general public of the truth of their convictions, various forms (and degrees) of coercion (like those described above) will be inevitable.

But what of one major difference? What of the fact that (most) old eugenicists believed in biological race, while (most) new ones do not? Even if we continue to debate the merits and dangers of eugenics, ought we cease to debate them *as racial issues*? By way of conclusion, I will offer three reasons to continue to consider race and racism when evaluating contemporary eugenics.

First, we must recognize that the racist projects of the old eugenics did not simply disappear when the term fell out of favor after World War II. In fact, by 1940, *family planning/population control* had become "the banner or umbrella framework for an amalgam of birth control, eugenics, neo-Malthusian, and population/demographic interests" in the United States, developing into a fully articulated ideology by 1950. This term helped give the projects a veneer of scientific objectivity and "allowed racism to be expressed apparently neutrally concerning whole populations" (Clarke 1998: 184).

Subsequently, in the 1960s, this racism, framed as the threat of a "population explosion" in the Third World, was leveraged to obtain federal government involvement in contraceptive development and distribution (Clarke 1998: 202).

Compromises between the various groups united under this banner also shifted focus away from *birth control* as "a means of enhancing reproductive and sexual autonomy for women" and toward *contraception*, understood within "an economic ethic of childbearing—economic planning, eugenics, and population control, often with racialized agendas." This led to the development of contraception methods that were considered more "scientific" and that could remain under expert control while being "*done to* the people" (rather than being offered as resources to people in pursuit of their own life goals) (Clarke 1998: 201, my emphasis). The continuing racialized effects of this eugenic influence were clearly visible in the 1990s when proposals were made to distribute Norplant in black communities as a means of addressing poverty, while welfare reform measures penalized welfare mothers for having additional children, suggesting that the "key to solving America's social problems [was] to curtail Black women's birth rates" (Roberts 1999: 7). These ideas persist today in state-funded programs where women with low incomes can qualify for a free or low-cost annual gynecological exams *on the condition* that they also be seeking some form of birth control.

Second, it would be idealistic to the point of naïveté to imagine that current racialized inequalities will have no effect on access to eugenic technologies or the benefits of eugenic projects. If the aim is to use biotechnology to help human beings forestall or survive global environmental disaster, then particular attention ought to be paid to two specific forms of racialized inequality: race-based health disparities and environmental racism. Currently, there are well-documented, significant, and ongoing racial and ethnic disparities in American health, healthcare, and health outcomes. As compared to white Americans, African Americans in particular experience poorer health, earlier death, reduced access to health care, inferior treatment when accessing health care, and a decreased likelihood of recovery from various illnesses (LaVeist 2005). This gives us good reason to wonder whether racial and ethnic minorities (or populations of the global South) will have access to medical facilities offering biotechnologies. Even if some basic level of eugenics is made universally available, current capitalist structures suggest that certain forms of "designer" genetics may be set apart and made available for purchase by the economic elite. Moreover, a lower baseline level of health could mean that, even if racial and ethnic minorities enjoy equal access to biotechnology, they may not experience equal outcomes.

Current research in epigenetics supports this concern over equal outcomes since it suggests that environmental factors (both inside and outside of the human body) have significant and ongoing impacts on gene expression (Watters 2006). This means that the proven disparities between racial/ethnic groups both in mental and physical health *and* in exposure to environmental hazards and toxins could translate directly into biogenetic disparities, even where everyone had access to the "best" genetic makeup biotechnology could achieve. Indeed, *environmental racism*—the idea that non-whites are disproportionately exposed to environmental hazards, whether as a result of malicious, individual acts or larger processes of urban development, including white flight (Pulido 2000)—cuts more than one way as far as the dream of a just eugenics is concerned. Non-white and socioeconomically disadvantaged people in the United States and around the world are most likely to populate those areas and regions under greatest threat from the environmental risks that eugenicists seek to combat; yet their very inhabitation of high-risk areas means that the solutions eugenicists offer will be least effective for them. Not incidentally, those same non-white and socioeconomically disadvantaged people will be among the least likely to be involved with or empowered by biotechnological research, development, implementation, and distribution, meaning that even if biotechnologies are made available to their communities, those biotechnologies may not address the local problems as defined by those communities or solve those problems in ways that the communities find acceptable. In short, long histories of injustice and current inequalities give us every reason to expect that—even if eugenicists have the best of intentions for preserving the human race—poor, non-white humans will be the first endangered and the last saved.

Finally, even if all eugenic technologies were fully accessible and their use fully voluntary, the creation of two (or more) groups of human beings understood to have distinct biogenetic characteristics, capacities, and incapacities runs the risk creating all new races and accompanying racisms. That is, assuming that some people will choose to avail themselves of eugenic technologies and that some people will strictly avoid such measures, a perceived division may develop between the genetically modified and the genetically "natural." Such a division, especially if it is understood in terms of personal choice/responsibility, could serve as an instrument of social exclusion, oppression, and exploitation—just as with traditional racial divisions. For example, given the current lack of social solidarity already represented by resistance to government provision of universal healthcare in the United States, one can well imagine the creation of policies that would force the genetically "natural" to pay more for health care as a consequence of their "refusal" to pursue biogenetic perfection.

There will always be serious dangers to eugenic programs, especially where a reliance on biogenetic solutions to human or environmental problems leaves social solutions to those same problems untried, unappreciated, underfunded, or underdeveloped. If, however, such dangers truly pale in comparison to the global dangers eugenicists believe they can combat, they will need to pursue justice in their eugenic programs, not by *denying* issues of race and racism, but by confronting them head-on, acknowledging both the complex racialized history of their drive to human mastery and its significant present-day legacy.

References

Augstein, Hannah Franziska (ed.). (1996) *Race*, Bristol: Thoemmes Press.
Bruinius, Harry. (2006) *Better for All the World: The Secret History of Forced Sterilization and America's Quest for Racial Purity*, New York: Knopf.
Buchanan, Allen, Dan W. Brock, Norman Daniels, and Daniel Wikler. (2000) *From Chance to Choice: Genetics and Justice*, Cambridge: Cambridge University Press.
Clarke, Adele. (1998) *Disciplining Reproduction: Modernity, American Life Sciences, and "The Problems of Sex,"* Berkeley: University of California Press.
Da Cal, Enrique Ucelay. (1992) "The Influence of Animal Breeding on Political Racism." *History of European Ideas* 15, nos. 4–6: 717–725.
Darwin, Charles. (1999) *Origin of Species*, New York: Bantam Books.
———. (2004) *The Descent of Man, and Selection in Relation to Sex*, eds. Adrian J. Desmond and James R. Moore, London: Penguin.
Darwin, Erasmus. (1800) *Zoonomia; Or, The Laws of Organic Life*, Vol. 1, Dublin: P. Byrne.

———. (1803) *The Temple of Nature, Or, the Origin of Society: A Poem, With Philosophical Notes*, London: J. Johnson.
Duster, Troy. (2003) *Backdoor to Eugenics*, New York: Routledge.
Fornet-Betancourt, R., Becker, H., Gomez-muller, A., and Gauthier, J. D. (1987) "The Ethic of Care for the Self as a Practice of Freedom: An Interview With Michel Foucault on January 20, 1984." *Philosophy & Social Criticism* 12, nos. 2–3: 112–131.
Foucault, Michel. (1988) *Technologies of the Self: A Seminar With Michel Foucault*, eds. Luther H. Martin, Huck Gutman, and Patrick H. Hutton, Amherst: University of Massachusetts Press.
———. (2008) *The Birth of Biopolitics: Lectures at the Collège De France, 1978–1979*, ed. Michel Senellart and trans. Graham Burchell, Basingstoke: Palgrave Macmillan.
Galton, Francis. (1883) *Inquiries Into Human Faculty and Its Development*, London: Palgrave Macmillan.
———. ([1869] 2006) *Hereditary Genius: An Inquiry Into Its Laws and Consequences*, Amherst, NY: Prometheus Books.
Gobineau, Arthur. (1970) "Racial Inequality," in *Gobineau: Selected Political Writings*, trans. Michael D. Biddiss. London: Cape, pp. 18–176.
Gregory, John. (1774) *A Comparative View of the State and Faculties of Man With Those of the Animal World by John Gregory, . . . in Two Volumes*. London: Printed for J. Dodsley.
Harris, John. (2007) *Enhancing Evolution: The Ethical Case for Making Better People*. Princeton: Princeton University Press.
Heidegger, Martin. (1993) "The Question Concerning Technology," in David Farrell Krell (ed.), *Basic Writings: From Being and Time (1927) to The Task of Thinking (1964)*, San Francisco: Harper, pp. 307–341.
LaVeist, Thomas A. (2005) *Minority Populations and Health: An Introduction to Health Disparities in the United States*, San Francisco: Jossey-Bass.
McWhorter, Ladelle. (2009) *Racism and Sexual Oppression in Anglo-America: A Genealogy*, Bloomington: Indiana University Press.
Müller-Wille, Staffan, and Hans-Jörg Rheinberger (eds.). (2007) *Heredity Produced: At the Crossroads of Biology, Politics, and Culture, 1500–1870*, Cambridge, MA: MIT Press.
Parens, Erik, and Adrienne Asch (eds.). (2000) *Prenatal Testing and Disability Rights*, Washington, DC: Georgetown University Press.
Pulido, Laura. (2000) "Rethinking Environmental Racism: White Privilege and Urban Development in Southern California." *Annals of the Association of American Geographers* 90, no. 1: 12–40.
Roberts, Dorothy E. (1999) *Killing the Black Body: Race, Reproduction, and the Meaning of Liberty*, New York: Vintage Books.
———. (2005) "Privitization and Punishment the New Age of Reprogenetics." *Emory Law Journal* 54, no. 3: 1343–1360.
Rose, Nikolas S. (1996) "Governing 'Advanced' Liberal Democracies," in Andrew Barry, Thomas Osborne, and Nikolas Rose (eds.), *Foucault and Political Reason: Liberalism, Neo-Liberalism, and Rationalities of Government*, Chicago: University of Chicago Press, pp. 37–64.
Rydell, Robert W. (1993) *World of Fairs: The Century-of-Progress Expositions*, Chicago: University of Chicago Press.
Sandel, Michael J. (2009) "The Case Against Perfection: What's Wrong With Designer Children, Bionic Athletes, and Genetic Engineering," in Julian Savulescu and Nick Bostrom (eds.), *Human Enhancement*, Oxford: Oxford University Press, pp. 71–89.
Schneider, Amber N. (2009) *More Than Meets the Eye: The Use of Exhibitions as Agents of Propaganda During the Inter-War Period*, Master's thesis, Baylor University. Accessed February 10, 2015. https://beardocs.baylor.edu/xmlui/bitstream/handle/2104/5309/Amber_Schneider_masters%5B1%5D.pdf?sequence=2.
Shakespeare, Tom. (2005) "The Social Context of Individual Choice," in David T. Wasserman, Robert Samuel. Wachbroit, and Jerome Edmund Bickenbach (eds.), *Quality of Life and Human Difference: Genetic Testing, Health Care, and Disability*, Cambridge: Cambridge University Press, pp. 217–236.
Smedley, Audrey. (1993) *Race in North America: Origin and Evolution of a Worldview*, Boulder: Westview Press.

Terral, Mary. (2007) "Speculation and Experiment in Enlightenment Life Sciences," in Staffan Müller-Wille and Hans-Jörg Rheinberger (eds.), *Heredity Produced: At the Crossroads of Biology, Politics, and Culture, 1500–1870*, Cambridge, MA: MIT Press, pp. 253–276.

Turda, Marius. (2010) *Modernism and Eugenics*, New York: Palgrave Macmillan.

Vandermonde, Charles A. (1756) *Essai Sur La Manière De Perfectionner L'espèce Humaine*, Paris: Vincent.

Voegelin, Eric. (1997) *Race and State*, ed. Klaus Vondung and trans. Ruth Hein, Baton Rouge: Louisiana State University Press.

Watters, Ethan. (2006) "DNA Is Not Destiny: The New Science of Epigenetics." *Discover*, November 22. Accessed February 18, 2015. http://discovermagazine.com/2006/nov/cover.

White, Paul. (2007) "Acquired Character: The Hereditary Material of the 'Self-Made Man'," in Staffan Müller-Wille and Hans-Jörg Rheinberger (eds.), Heredity Produced: At the Crossroads of Biology, Politics, and Culture, 1500–1870, Cambridge, MA: MIT Press, pp. 375–398.

Zenderland, Leila. (1998) *Measuring Minds: Henry Herbert Goddard and the Origins of American Intelligence Testing*, Cambridge: Cambridge University Press.

24
FRAMING INTERSECTIONALITY
Elena Ruíz

Intersectionality is a term that arose within the black feminist intellectual tradition for the purposes of identifying interlocking systems of oppression. As a descriptive term, it refers to the ways human identity is shaped by multiple social vectors and overlapping identity categories (such as sex, race, class) that may not be readily visible in single-axis formulations of identity, but which are taken to be integral to robustly capture the multifaceted nature of human experience. As a diagnostic term, it captures the confluence of power and domination on the social construction of identity in order to remedy concrete harms that result from this convergence. It is not a prescriptive methodology or closed system of analysis, but rather an open-ended hermeneutic lens through which interconnected systems of oppression can come into focus in the fight for social justice.

For decades intersectionality has taken pride of place in feminist theories that focus on power and social inequality, as it points to the ways the relative invisibility of a social location or speaking position can produce real-world harms and further stratify (even redouble) inequities for historically marginalized populations like women of color. It has also become the dominant metaphor for talking about complex identities and conceptualizing alternatives to monistic models of selfhood. In time, intersectionality even gained enough citational force to be lauded as "the most important contribution that women's studies has made so far" (McCall 2005: 1771). This chapter explores the strengths and limitations of the intersectionality paradigm by surveying the academic history of the concept. I argue intersectional social theory is an important analytic tool for disassembling the systematicity of oppression faced by women and girls in the global South, but not in its current academic coinage.

The academization of intersectionality, like that of many advocacy strategies for historically marginalized communities, has been largely based on Anglo-normative interpretive concerns and disciplinary projects rather than the discursive lifeworld and historical realities of people of color. This suggests that the limitations of the intersectionality paradigm come, in large part, from the disciplinary appropriations of intersectionality, as academization created a much weaker version of the concept that operates under the purview of theoretical goals and projects that are altogether different from those built into its design. I call this latter version "operative intersectionality" to distinguish it from the strain black feminists devised as an advocacy strategy to diagnose and combat interlocking systems of oppression. Because operative intersectionality is primarily responsive to questions based on metaphysical concerns and identity-based philosophical models of selfhood, it needs to be decolonized to better meet the advocacy needs of today's global feminisms. This entails a genealogical return to the socio-political features of early intersectional thought, as conceived by black feminists. I conclude by noting that criticisms of intersectionality are largely criticisms of operative intersectionality and tend to be based on forms of methodological racism that function by erasing the work of women of color under the guise of argumentative neutrality and philosophical rigor. While I make no attempt to centralize the intersectional perspective across philosophical projects, I argue that making room for it in the discipline means coming to terms with the uncritical assumptions and racialized biases responsible for its marginalization.

Tracing Intersectionality

Intersectionality is not a new concept. It can be seen in black feminist writings since the nineteenth century and includes the works of Maria Stewart, Sojourner Truth, Anna Julia Cooper, Ida B. Wells, Elise McDougald, Sadie Alexander, and Francis Beale, to name only a few. Their work is based on critical examinations of lived experience in light of the systematic racism, sexism, and classism that permeated all aspects of their lives. As such, their writings disclose the existence of compound structural oppressions in society, since black women were at the crossroads of gendered bias in patriarchal society, racial bias in racialist republics, and class bias in stratified public life. Their analyses helped explain the constant sliding or erasure of their visibility in the political projects of white feminism, the constitutional and anti-racist projects of male abolitionists, and the economic and industrial advancements of the nation state. But they also helped explain the confluence of all these forces in the course of everyday life, how a simple encounter at the doctor or a public utilities office could yield discriminatory and materially harmful experiences, all under the guise of democratic neutrality and egalitarian social discourses. Their work thus constitutes a significant, systematic approach to combating oppressions based on critical examinations of lived experience—not only as women, but as socially situated black women at the intersections of multiple social forces and asymmetrical power relations. The focus was not on identifying primary features of social identity subject to power variances in culture, but on diagnosing the specific, historically situated forces of social life that worked together as causal determinants of black women's oppression. Classism, racism, and sexism along with heterosexism and ableism worked together to perpetuate harms against black women—sometimes visibly in outward public aggressions and sometimes invisibly, in the discursive exclusions of social policies, legal protections and social benefits of citizenship. But they were not the only identifiable features of how oppression functioned; Afro-Latinas, for instance, faced social exclusions along identity categories that included ethnic origin and linguistic difference. The genealogical roots of intersectionality thus homed in on the *operation of power* associated with features of identity, but identity as a fluid determinant of cultural attitudes and values in a given time and place. While it would be a mistake to downplay the primacy of race and gender in black feminist's analysis of oppression, it would be equally problematic to read early intersectional works as reducible to additive accounts of oppressed identities (leading to a reading of black women as "hyper-oppressed"). Early intersectional accounts of black women's identities was a way of giving voice to the outcome of the operations of power in their lives, which included structural and large-scale analyses of the determinants of oppression.

And yet, with the academic rise of the intersectional model of identity—which centers on a critique of monistic, unitary models of identity applicable to *any* social agent—the roots of intersectionality in black feminism and historically situated asymmetries of power have been expunged from intersectionality's history. Instead, intersectionality became a way to conceptualize the relation between multiple axes of oppression for any social agent, and was slowly reabsorbed by the discursive priorities and guiding norms of inclusivity in Anglophone feminist practice. The problem this raises is not a direct consequence of these norms, but the conceptual disarmament and dulling of a critical tool's important edge, one fashioned to be especially adept at combating the specificity of oppressions black women faced. The specificity of these oppressions rides on the "historical reality of Afro-American women's continuous life-and-death struggle for survival and liberation," which is a historical difference that makes a theoretical difference (Combahee River Collective 1978: 362).

Philosopher Katherine Gines (2011) has proposed a corrective to the erasure of this intellectual tradition by aptly noting its existence as a distinct, "proto-intersectional" intellectual tradition that preceded its academic articulation in the late twentieth century (275). Thematically, proto-intersectional thought is concerned with the articulation of multiple oppressions in the lives of black women. Francis Beale's "Double Jeopardy: To Be Female and Black" (1970) is thus a conceptually linked account of the double bind Sojourner Truth was also describing in her critiques of abolitionists who excluded women and feminists who effaced black women in their struggles. While thinking beyond binary or reductive accounts of women's lives became critical to giving voice to the phenomenologically complex realities black women faced—especially because so many of the existing social discourses worked to efface the cultural visibility of that complexity—it was by no means a theoretical exercise. Before the intersectionality paradigm was abstracted into many of its current apolitical formulations it was rooted in a critical examination of black women's lived experience *for the purposes of liberation from oppression*. Analyzing and making sense of the ways one is being harmed in order to produce coping and resistance strategies is thus the organizing fulcrum for many proto-intersectional narratives.

Over time, five key features emerged from black feminist intellectual traditions and their various articulations of the intersectionality paradigm: (1) an emphasis on lived experience as the starting point of critical inquiry; (2) an emphasis on the multidimensionality of experience; (3) a diagnostic acumen for the role of *power*; (4) a focus on the systematic, multivalent, and interlocking nature of oppressions; and (5) an emphasis on the emancipatory aims of critical analyses of structural oppressions. All five features come together in what is arguably the first methodological account of intersectionality, the Combahee River Collective's founding statement:

> The most general statement of our politics at the present time would be that we are actively committed to struggling against racial, sexual, heterosexual, and class oppression, and see as our particular task the development of integrated analysis and practice based upon the fact that the major systems of oppression are interlocking. The synthesis of these oppressions creates the conditions of our lives.
> (1978: 363)

ELENA RUÍZ

Despite the existence of the proto-intersectional tradition, academically, intersectionality is most often traced back to the 1980s, when black feminist legal scholar Kimberlé Crenshaw used the term heuristically to critique "the tendency to treat race and gender as mutually exclusive categories of experience and analysis" in doctrinal interpretations of US antidiscrimination law (1989: 140). Race and gender intersect, she argued. They are linked together and overlap in their various manifestations of power, privilege, subordination, and disadvantage. When a black woman experiences discrimination US law disambiguates which features of experience map on to being discriminated against on the basis of being a woman (sexism), and which on the basis of being black (racism). When it's both, they're "additive," but where identity is reduced to single-axis categories of "woman" and/or "black" that must operate independently of each other to fall under the right legal umbrella that protects them (e.g., Title VII vs. Title IX). Black women plaintiffs claiming compound discrimination have had to *sieve their experiences* through a categorical colander that separated out experiences of racism and those of sexism, only to try and put them back together into legal arguments and lexicons that were not equipped to capture the intersectional experience of black women in the first place. This is in itself a type of harm being done to black women plaintiffs: an intersectional oppression that results from the inability of legal frameworks to recognize the ways multiply-positioned subjects are precariously positioned in culturally asymmetrical ways.

According to Crenshaw, although it is possible to be discriminated against along a single axis of identity, her claim is that at minimum, minority women can't simply switch off their gender when experiencing racism, nor can they un-race their bodies while suffering sexism. And this is a critical facet of experience to understand if one is to seek legal remedy for an injurious experience, as one cannot grieve what is not acknowledged as existing. Discrimination, though it may appear to follow a single-axis trajectory, may in fact be operating along two or more axes, but with recourse to only one track of social visibility (and therefore legal audibility). As a case in point, Crenshaw cites *DeGraffenreid v. General Motors*, where five black women plaintiffs sued General Motors after the company's seniority and promotion system ensured no black woman could survive the recession-based layoffs, since the company had only recently begun hiring black women. The court pointed out that General Motors had a documented history of hiring women (albeit white women), therefore their claim of sex discrimination was dismissed. They had also hired black men, partially mitigating the claim to racism. The court, however, acknowledged the existence of broad allegations of racial discrimination in pending litigation against General Motors, suggesting during oral arguments that that the plaintiffs consolidate their claims with the black plaintiffs in that case. When counsel for the plaintiffs in *DeGraffenreid* declined, insisting that they were suing on behalf of *black women*—as they, specifically, were "the last to be hired and the first to be fired," making such discrimination against black women a perpetuation of past discrimination (thereby violating Title VII of the Civil Rights Act of 1964)—the court ruled that there was no legal precedent for establishing that "Black women are a special class to be protected from discrimination" (Crenshaw 1989: 141). The court worried that by adding the statutory protections given to women *and* those given to blacks, black women might establish special access to a "super-remedy" that protects them more than, for instance, a black man experiencing discrimination.

REFRAMING INTERSECTIONALITY

Crenshaw identifies several problems with this type of legal reasoning, four of which are key to the development of intersectional social theory. First, human experience is not additive but temporally thick with the simultaneous and dynamic intersections of socio-historical identity categories. One experiences a compound harm as a black woman, not as the sum of being a woman *and* black. Again, this is not to say that black women don't experience discrimination or mobilize politically along a single axis, only that it's never that simple for any subject who is multiply positioned across a number of historically asymmetrical social categories:

> I am suggesting that Black women can experience discrimination in ways that are both similar to and different from those experienced by white women and Black men . . . often they experience double-discrimination—the *combined effects* of practices which discriminate on the basis of race, and on the basis of sex. And sometimes, they experience discrimination *as* Black women—not the sum of race and sex discrimination, but as Black women.
>
> (Crenshaw 1989: 149, emphasis added)

Identity, on this account, is intersectional for multiply-positioned subjects like black women. It is approached as a social feature of identity based on historical contingencies, not an essence or immutable property of human identity, as Crenshaw is clear in not aspiring to propose "some new, totalizing theory of identity" (1991: 1244). Neither is it an essentialist construction of identity as "always multiple" or plural; the suggestion is simply that one cannot bracket out different dimensions of human identity in piecemeal fashion or cauterize the subject along intersections that happen to be especially ripe with power differentials *when trying to seek relief for injuries that operate through those very channels*. It will place the plaintiff in an experiential contradiction and a legal no-man's land.

The second problem this type of legal reasoning poses is the reliance on privileged interpretive frameworks that cannot robustly capture black women's experience of compound harms. For instance, in separating out race and gender, black women's experiences remain subordinated to the centrality of white women's and black men's experiences in the conceptualization of gender and race discrimination respectively. Single-axis thinking thereby "erases Black women in the conceptualization, identification, and remediation of race and sex discrimination by limiting inquiry to the experiences of otherwise-privileged members of the group" (Crenshaw 1989: 140). When we think of women, we centralize the experience of white women, and when we think of blacks, we centralize the experience of men. In the eyes of the court, black women were thus too much like the white women hired by General Motors and not different enough from black men suing General Motors to constitute an independent legal claim as black women. A third harm is extended to the public realm, where the intersectional experience is erased for black women who must navigate between the systematic exclusions of white feminism and male anti-racists in political projects. Crenshaw calls this double-bind facet of intersectionality "political intersectionality" to distinguish it from "structural intersectionality," which highlights the inadequacy of single-axis social remedies like anti-racism to address harms caused by intersectional oppressions, such as sexist racism. Yet a fourth problem, alluded to earlier, is the creation of a meta-legal harm that results when legal systems fail to provide relief as a result of the tacit operations of power in the conceptual frameworks employed in legal reasoning. Despite claims to procedural objectivity and ideological neutrality, *DeGraffenreid v. General Motors* demonstrates the ways the law is unable to capture (and thus remedy) the harms to black women plaintiffs on account of the "established analytical structure" for understanding the compound harms of racism and sexism: a more intersectional approach is thus needed in doctrinal interpretations of US anti-discrimination law.

We can further extend Crenshaw's analysis through a hermeneutical lens. On this account, one way of understanding the myopic nature of "the established analytical structure" legal reasoning employs is to look at the deeper, pre-predicative cultural interpretive lenses that guide the contours of legal reasoning, to the detriment of experiences unaccounted for by those ways of seeing and interpreting the world. Cultural interpretive lenses are a type of backdrop, a blueprint or social alphabet for turning bare experiences into articulable social phenomena—phenomena that derive their significance dialogically from their very intelligibility and communicability to others (usually understood through a shared language and communal share in the resources of expression). Every judgement thereby requires a prior *tacit* silhouette of meaning one grows into as a social being, a blueprint-shaped prejudgment or *prejudice* that the hermeneutic philosophical tradition typically sees as normatively neutral, since values are relative to the contingencies of cultural differences across time and place. On this view, prejudices are the epistemic *preconditions* to valuations,[1] and only valuations carry normative charge. (Paradoxically, this is also what makes it possible to critique racism with anti-racism, or slavery with emancipation, since the narrative contours of anti-racism and liberation take shape dialogically, in relation to and within the same hermeneutic tradition.) However, a more critical hermeneutic lens inclusive of power dynamics reveals just the opposite. That in fact, owing to the culturally asymmetrical operations of power in European colonial and Settler Imperial history, hermeneutical prejudices underlying attitudes towards race, gender, and personal identity can yield complex yet non-visible harms like the ones Crenshaw identifies. This is because these prejudices are not normatively neutral but stem from the conceptual orthodoxies, metaphysical assumptions and epistemic valuations of the historical lifeworld that emerged in Asia Minor in the fifth century BCE and formed the foundations of Western intellectual history—a tradition that historically occludes the lives and realities of people of color as part of that interpretive scaffolding.

In examining the court's ruling in *DeGraffenreid v. General Motors* we find deep conceptual biases towards occidental principles of uniformity, separability, and "the mathematical principles of permutation and combination" for understanding identity as a divisible substance (not to mention a discursive reliance on Greco-Roman myths as harbingers of truth) that form the basis of the court's intersectionally blind legal reasoning:

> The prospect of the creation of new classes of protected minorities, governed only by the mathematical principles of permutation and combination, clearly raises the prospect of opening up the hackneyed Pandora's box . . . [the plaintiffs have] cause for action for *race* discrimination, *sex* discrimination, *or alternatively either, but not a combination of both.*
>
> (413 F. Supp. 144)

The court ruled that black women were not a class of protected minorities and had no standing *as* "black women" using Aristotelian laws of identity, atomistic frameworks for conceptualizing the divisibility of the body, and additive logics based on binary models of divisibility. The claim is not that these ways of making sense of the world are incapable of capturing the realities of intersectional lived experience, or that they can't be strategically deployed to do so in light of postcolonial realities. The issue is that they often function on stealth mode through a simultaneous *erasure* of parallel cultural narratives and a devaluation of the interpretive resources of non-dominant historical communities.[2] If, as Nietzsche noted, the social history of millennia is encoded in language—in ways of seeing, naming, and formulating contexts of significance in culture—it matters that the resources of expression and interpretation behind legal reasoning are acknowledged as being tied to particular cultural traditions, their projects, values and historical assumptions. Leibnitzian notions of identity as uniformity, for instance, arose largely through liturgical and scriptural concerns that were themselves part of a longer conversation within the Western metaphysical and Judeo-Christian hermeneutical tradition. When conceptual orthodoxies are turned into interpretive resources in culture, power enters the equation, as these are very often resources that communities of color and women have historically had asymmetrical access to and participation in shaping. The court's summary judgment shows how the established analytical structure for understanding compound harms in legal claims is thus based on more primordial epistemic and metaphysical assumptions that historically disclose the visibility of white, normative identities. The law is biased, all the way down. And it is against this bias that the critical juridical and doctrinal work of interpreting antidiscrimination law—of "bending" it, as Crenshaw calls it—begins. Intersectionality can play a powerful role in this by showing the blind spots in single-axis thinking behind legal reasoning, but it is ultimately a practical confrontation with oppressive social relations rather than a theoretical confrontation of identity models in philosophy. For Crenshaw, failure to see the multifaceted web-like nature of gendered and racist oppression can result in social, institutional, and juridical systems that are structurally unresponsive to the needs, situations, and concerns of historically oppressed communities, and in fact may be the source of harm. Likewise, an institution or system (and discursive access thereto) may be incorrectly seen as inclusive of marginalized identities and communities at the same time that it works to oppress those communities, even with life-and-death consequences (see Crenshaw 2012).

Intersectionality, even as an academic concept, begins in a specific context of oppression where a court could speak about women of color, render legal verdicts about them, without the ability to legally acknowledge the embodied existence of the very women of color seeking justice in the courtroom. It is an analytic tool to help diagnose a problem (like the ability of a court to declare black women are not a special class to be protected from discrimination) and chart possible ways forward: if we lose sight of the problem, we erase part of the design. Feminist legal scholar Catharine MacKinnon thus aptly notes that "intersectionality begins in the concrete experience of race and sex together in the lives of real people, with Black women as the starting point" (2013: 1020).

Historical Reception and Criticisms

With its accelerated uptake in gender studies and the social sciences in the 1990s, the academic framing of intersectionality changed rapidly to prioritize the discursive projects of Anglo-American feminisms and the need for more generalizable, universalizable social theories compatible across a wider spectrum of specialized disciplinary jargons. As it disseminated across disciplines and popular culture, intersectionality broadened

ELENA RUÍZ

exponentially to address questions regarding the essential features of human identity, the social construction of subjective experience, and the role of single-axis thinking in disciplinary methods. In women's, gender and disabilities studies it became particularly relied on to discuss widening social identity axes and matrices of sexuality, non-gender conforming identities and ableist attitudes in culture. But it also suffered from centripetal dispersion across a vast disciplinary range, making the term a minimal stand-in for one's awareness that identity is not monotopic, or as a lexical trigger to escape charges of sexism or racism. It became possible to engage in debates using the term "intersectional" without reference to racialized women or the dynamics of power that affect specific historical communities.

Without critical attunement to the long history of black feminist's proto-intersectional intellectual projects, intersectionality fell prey to processes of academic mainstreaming, abstraction and ideological reticulation. Through ritualized iterations in academic programming, university curricula, and insular conference programming (which often obfuscated the intellectual presence of black women and minorities), intersectionality lost its gravitational pull in material contexts of oppression and became associated with more general, systems-level accounts of oppression as interlocking, ideas about complex personhood, and a battleground for academic debates over identity politics. At its broadest level, intersectionality came to be seen as a critical social theory whose main insight was a feminist account of identity. At the center of this account is the intersectional model of identity.

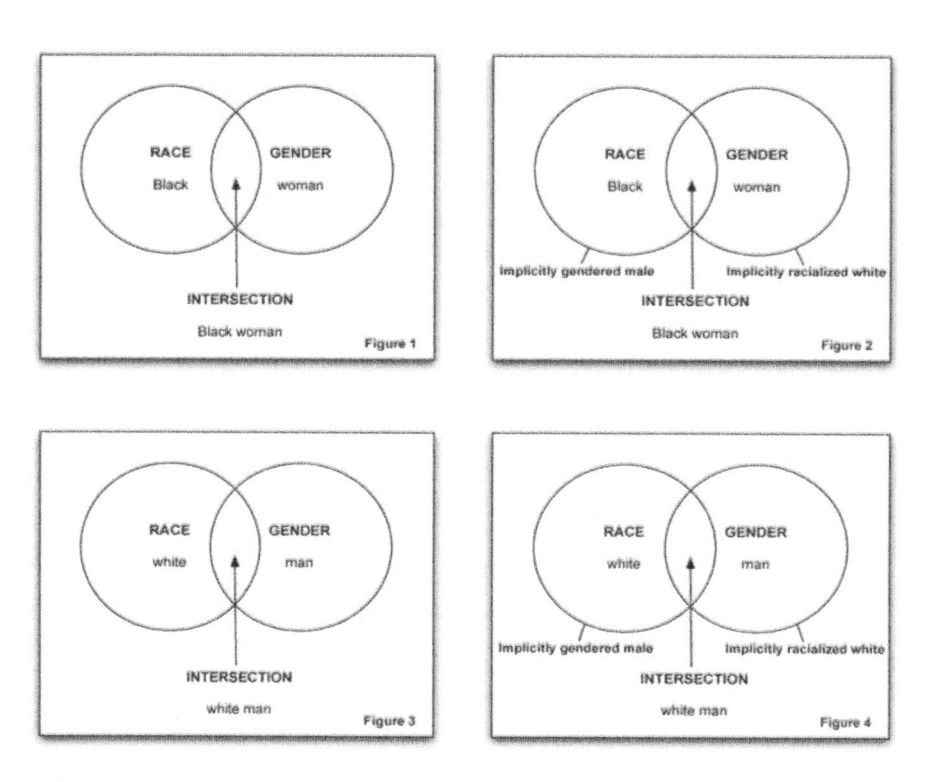

Figure 24.1 The intersectional model of identity[3].

The intersectional model of identity seeks to describe the social location of *any* individual in relation to the systems of oppression that shape the social construction of their identity. Race, class, and gender are constitutive of these systems insofar as they are often used implicitly to differentiate between social agents and mete out social goods unevenly, leading to structural inequities organized around social identities. By focusing on complex identity, the intersectional model of identity is said to help pluralize analyses of oppression that rely on simple hierarchical binaries, such as the patriarchal oppression of women by men, the domination of States over non-state actors, and the racialized oppression of blacks by whites. Oppressions are multiple, latticed, and interlocking in ways that symbiotically co-constitute structures of domination. Under this framework, intersectionality can be applied to any subject oppressed along "multiple" axes. Today, this identic model of intersectionality *operates* under the banner of intersectional feminisms, having unframed the concept from proto-intersectional framings of lived concerns. *Operative intersectionality*, as I call it, thus slowly supplanted black feminist's account of intersectionality. This was partly achieved by producing methodological questions and internal critiques that triangulated with classical concerns in Anglo-American feminisms (traditionally dominated by white, middle-class women), such as the need to produce politically inclusive models of solidarity to unify and focus struggles against patriarchal domination. Historically, these critiques are clustered along five main lines of argument. They charge that intersectionality:

1. Essentializes the experiences and identities of black women
2. Sidetracks the emancipatory projects of political feminism by dismantling the categorical force of "women" as a group and focusing on "difference"
3. Fails to address the processes that underlie, create and maintain the categories of race, sex, and gender
4. Privileges race and gender in the social construction of identity and is monotopic along only a handful of social identity axes
5. Perpetuates rather than overcomes the unitary model of identity by relying on analytically pure identity categories (as the precondition for their intersection).

When intersectionality is abstracted as an identitarian theory of "difference" rather than a situated advocacy strategy against oppression, critiques of essentialism, experiential overdeterminism, and identic underdeterminism arise. But these are criticisms of operational intersectionality, not feminist intersectionality. For Crenshaw, black women are not a monolithic category or *the* paradigm intersectional subjects of a theory of identity; the need to talk about black women and women of color comes from the situated realties of the ways some societies asymmetrically harm historical communities, especially through mechanisms that are seldom fully transparent to all social agents. Doctrinal definitions of discrimination were inadequate, not because they could not account for black women's identities, but because the lived materiality of black women's *experiences of* compound discrimination—*that* they were experiencing multiple oppressions—were being covered over by a framework that happened to prioritize specific understandings of identity (based on the intersectional exclusion of race and gender). But this is due to the historical provenance of sexist racism in occidental legal systems and the covering-over of that history as part of the neocolonial operation of power. Against the charge that intersectionality does not address the forces behind the categories of sex and gender, Crenshaw points out that intersectionality "addressed the larger ideological structures" behind how problems and solutions are framed for historically marginalized communities, since identity is a feature of the operations of power and not the other way around.

One way to understand this is to differentiate between analytical and hermeneutic accounts of identity production in intersectional thinking. The former holds that a subject is the product of schematized identic terms (or the confluence of analytical categories) symbolized in the intersectional model of identity. While these categories are not fixed, irreducibly stable, or uninflected by one another, the analytic model accounts for diachronic elements in identity production by sublating them as features of synchronic categories. Hermeneutic accounts, on the other hand, extend explanatory priority to the diachronicity of subject formation. They conceptualize human selfhood dialogically through the broader background of interpretive frameworks in which identities come to have meaning or get taken up, as in the products of the historical operations of power. On this account "intersectionality fills out the Venn diagrams at points of overlap where convergence has been *neglected*, training its sights where vectors of inequality intersect at crossroads that have previously been at best sped through" by virtue of historical prejudices (MacKinnon 2013: 1020). So the first model sees what appears, the latter what does not. Or better yet, what cannot appear, what resists its telling on account of the social forces and biases that work to occlude such visibility. Diachronicity is therefore key to intersectional feminisms because only against a backdrop of historical oppressions does the "neglect" become a salient feature of analysis. It is also important methodologically, as the synchronic schematization of the intersectional model of identity is based on Western metaphysical conceptual orthodoxies that re-inscribe substance ontology, which privileges the identification of what appears over what does not. (This is especially pernicious for diagnosing the tacit harms of multiple oppressions.) It also helps illuminate how intersectionality, as a hermeneutic lens that is diagnostic of power relations, is not an exhaustive compendium of social harms, a totalizing account of how oppression courses though one's life, nor how identity comes to be shaped by it on all accounts. Intersectional feminists like Patricia Hill Collins have aptly noted that all subjects are intersectional in stratified societies, yet if this is understood outside the diachronic and diagnostic feature of proto-intersectional thought, it leads to misdirected critiques of intersectionality's failures to pluralize the unified character of white men's identities.[4]

By way of academic mainstreaming, Anglo-American feminists have reframed the genealogy of intersectionality through a citational politics and disambiguation of terms internal to their own intellectual traditions. This does not mean they are uncritical, uncommitted to intersectional social justice—indeed most position themselves as advocates of it—or that intellectual traditions are monolithic or mutually exclusive. It does not suggest that all Anglo-American feminists are white women or assign political projects along racialized and gendered identity axes. But it does suggest that, at minimum, intellectual mainstreaming is not apolitical. It is not a value-free natural process organized around a forward-scoping developmental continuum that randomly selects or adapts concepts to fit the academic attitudes of a given time. Mainstreaming can and often does function within a micropolitics of power, chains of mystification and discursive regimes that disclose the lifeworld of some interpretive communities over others. The unstated goal of mainstreaming processes is thus to delink a concept from situated aspects of its origins to weaken its force outside a given domain of discourse—to change what is unrecognizably foreign in a concept to the more familiar stabilized forms one is accustomed to handling, interpreting, and critiquing. This is how an advocacy strategy forged in life-and-death circumstances became a loose academic term to denote that a person is not reducible to a single identity category. It has also made it more difficult to advance internal critiques and conceptual modifications within women of color intersectional feminisms that are attuned to the tectonic geopolitical shifts that affect our current struggles for liberation.

New Directions in Intersectional Feminisms

According to MacKinnon, "Intersectionality is meant to be applied to real-world problems, to unsettle oppressive logics, to plumb gaps or silences for suppressed meanings and implications, and to rethink how we approach liberation politics" (2015: vii–viii). Given its strengths for conceptualizing simultaneity, systematicity, asymmetry, and context-dependent strategies against oppression, decolonized of its reduction to identitarian theories Intersectionality is an important analytic tool for disassembling the systematicity of oppression faced by women and girls in the global South. This is not only in keeping with the conceptual (re)armament of proto-intersectional thought as a diagnostic of oppression, but also reflects intersectionality's history of deep engagements with third world and decolonial feminisms. Because cultural processes of decolonization in the global South often involved the need to account for the synchronicity of the various social systems through which oppression flowed—to demystify the inner workings of interlocking networks that together, worked to produce colonial domination—strong conceptual resonance between black and third world feminisms arose in the mid- to late twentieth century, often with cross pollination and theoretical inflection (Spivak, Mohanty, Lugones, Anzaldúa, Schutte).

In recent years a handful of scholars mindful of what it means to theorize identity out of specific geopolitical contexts have launched important challenges to the identic-based, operational model of intersectionality, focusing instead on the multidimensionality of experience and the multistable character or oppression in the fight for social justice. Among them, Kristie Dotson argues that intersecitonality "is a valuable mechanism for the construction of social facts concerning oppression, where oppression is understood as a multi-stable phenomenon" that allows (or opens up the possibility) for greater perceptibility of the jeopardizations covered over by monolithic cultural readings of oppression (2014). Her work moves us towards a liberational epistemology grounded in decolonial and intersectional theory, as intersectionality unsettles oppressive logics with attunement to the diachronic materiality of being.

Through its conceptual decolonization, intersectional social theory can be said to denote the complex ways in which the simultaneity of oppression functions through the localized, situated character of a speaker's social location in culture, where that location is like a nodal point on a web crisscrossed by multiple vectors of social forces that are multidimensional (but may appear one-dimensional from a given vantage point). From the perspective of legal narratives or institutional discourses, for instance, the speaker may appear as a single, monadic point along a two-dimensional line; a tightrope walker balancing the weight of seemingly discreet, enumerable forces on each end. From the tightrope walker's perspective, the multidimensionality of the experience expands to include wind direction, speed, psychic life, bodily motility, and exhaustion, and which she may feel to be essential to robustly describe her experience or enumerate her needs. Because social institutions often extend causal and explanatory priority to categories that exclude some identities as a tool of domination, the concept works to expand the capacity to bear witness to experiences of marginality and harm, especially for the purposes of vivifying and remedying oppressions. But it also works to diagnose system-level operations of power that function on stealth mode, thus helping sustain the systematic character of structural oppression alongside the appearance of democratic institutions and egalitarian ideals. It points to the ways oppressions do not act independently of one another in neat, cauterized ways, yet places the theoretical accent on the phenomenological gravity sustained by the lived experience of oppression. Lastly, while intersectional analyses call for a diachronic understanding of asymmetrical power relations in culture, it is not a closed system of analysis but an open-ended hermeneutic lens that helps disclose barriers in the fight for social justice.

In light of Dotson's work, we can also see that given the powerful analytic lens Intersectionality offers for thinking about oppression, power differentials, and social inequalities, its relative invisibility in contemporary philosophy—which cannot survive without disciplinary attunement to the material and epistemic struggles of oppressed peoples and communities of the global South—is unwarranted. While some critical race and feminist philosophers have long embraced intersectional analyses in their work, many continue to lag behind in defense of more mainstream, depoliticized, and universalizable frameworks for thinking through the relation between social identity and human experience. One problem this raises is the continuous re-centering of normative theories and perspectives that are not maximally equipped to address concerns that emanate from intersectional lived experience and the lives of people of color. Conceptually, intersectionality can do what philosophers must often look to multiple frameworks in combination to do, but whose admixture still elides the specific attunement to intersectional oppressions. It is this feature of academic practice that warrants criticism in light of the systematic presence of sexist racism in philosophy.

Conclusion

In this chapter I argued that the framing of intersectionality fell prey to processes of academic mainstreaming that weakened its diagnostic power and displaced its most important liberational features. In section one, "Tracing Intersectionality," I outlined the history of the concept by situating it in the long tradition of black feminist thought and critical legal studies, as illustrated in twentieth-century US antidiscrimination law. I discussed Kimberlé Crenshaw's seminal account of intersectionality and the proto-intersectional tradition that preceded it in nineteenth-century black feminist thought. In section two, "Historical Reception and Criticisms," I discussed the historical receptions and disciplinary critiques of intersectionality by drawing a distinction between scholars who emphasize questions surrounding the nature of human identity and those mindful of what it means to theorize identity out of specific geopolitical contexts. I argued the former result in a unique academized strain of intersectionality I termed "operative intersectionality" and identified its source to an uncritical triangulation with philosophical projects disconnected from the original impetus and critical design of intersectionality. In section three, "New Directions in Intersectional Feminisms,"

I highlighted the analytic power of conceptualizing the simultaneity of oppressions as key to a new wave of feminist liberation epistemologies. I concluded by calling for a reframing of the (co-opted) concept through processes of academic decolonization and pointed to recent thinkers, such as Dotson, as examples of liberational, decolonial uses of intersectional feminisms.

Notes

1. Understood as irreducible to mind-dependent states. It is better understood through a social epistemological lens that is productive of a kind of basic attitude towards things, a bodily comportment or way of pre-reflectively taking in the things we encounter in everyday life, from daily use of objects to our understanding of who we are in relation to our jobs, relationships, and values.
2. For example, the occidental privileging of knowledge through written documents (i.e., as logographic recording methods based on Romanized alphabetic literacy) undergirds the devaluation and limitations placed on third-person oral testimonies as hearsay, suggesting cultural power is more deeply embedded in legal reasoning than legal reasoning itself can disclose. This erasure is especially difficult to spot because the explanting of one interpretive framework is covered over by the implanting of another—in this case by the assumptive logic behind principles of scientific objectivity and sound LEGAL reasoning based on "precedent"—thus giving the appearance of procedural neutrality. This is followed by an internal cultural narrative of historical mystification that erases traces of this process in favor of developmental accounts of legal reason; racist and sexist myopias in the law can be explained away by a story about the law's nascence and necessary social evolution (while retaining its appearance of neutrality) rather than the cultural prejudices built into its design, its forms of analysis, and ways of adjudicating the alleged harms before it. The history of the legality of slavery and rape can thereby be neatly disassociated of from modern-day doctrinal interpretations of black women plaintiff's claims, or their systematic expurgation from court dockets.
3. Carastathis, 2008, 31.
4. See, for instance, Carastathis's claim that "intersectionality contributes nothing novel to our conception of the 'white man'—except, ironically, further confirmation of the 'unified' character of that identity" (2008, 28).

References

Beale, Frances. (1995 [1970]). "Double Jeopardy: To Be Black and Female," in Beverly Guy-Sheftall (ed.), *Words of Fire: An Anthology of African American Feminist Thought*, New York: New Press, pp. 146–155.

Carastathis, Anna. (2008) "The Invisibility of Privilege: A Critique of Intersectional Models of Identity." *Les Ateliers de L'éthique* 3, no. 2: 23–38.

Combahee River Collective. (1978) *Capitalist Patriarchy and the Case for Socialist Feminism*, ed. Zillah Einstein, New York: Monthly Review Press, pp. 362–373.

Cooper, Anna Julia. (1988) *A Voice From the South by a Black Woman of the South*, New York: Oxford University Press.

Crenshaw, Kimberlé Williams. (1989) "Demarginalizing the Intersection of Race and Sex: A Black Feminist Critique of Antidiscrimination Doctrine, Feminist Theory, and Antiracist Politics." *University of Chicago Legal Forum*: 139–167.

———. (1991) "Mapping the Margins: Intersectionality, Identity Politics, and Violence Against Women of Color." *Stanford Law Review* 43, no. 6: 1241–1299.

———. (2012) "From Private Violence to Mass Incarceration: Thinking Intersectionally About Women, Race, and Social Control." *UCLA Law Review* 59: 1419–1472.

Crenshaw Kimberlé Williams, Leslie McCall, and Sumi Cho. (2013) "Toward a Field of Intersectionality Studies: Theory, Applications, and Praxis." *Signs* 38, no. 4: 785–810.

DeGraffenreid v. General Motors Assembly Div., Etc., 413 F. Supp. 142 (E.D. Mo. 1976).

Dotson, Kristie. (2014) "Making Sense: The Multistability of Oppression and the Importance of Intersectionality," in Namita Goswami (ed.), *Why Race and Gender Still Matter: An Intersectional Approach*, London: Pickering & Chatto, pp. 43–58.

Gines, Katherine. (2011) "Black Feminism and Intersectional Analyses: A Defense of Intersectionality." *Philosophy Today* 55: 275–284, SPEP Supplement.

MacKinnon, Catharine. (2013) "Intersectionality as Method: A Note." *Signs: Journal of Women in Culture and Society* 38, no. 4: 1019–1030.

McCall, Leslie. (2005) "The Complexity of Intersectionality." *Signs: Journal of Women in Culture and Society* 30, no. 3: 1771–1800.

25
CANONIZING THE CRITICAL RACE ARTIFICE
An Analysis of Philosophy's Gentrification of Critical Race Theory

Tommy J. Curry

Introduction

As a discipline, philosophy has established its character through an obdurateness dedicated to preserving the truth of its authors, the efficacy of its logic, and the legacy of its theoretical schools. However, when engaging black theory little effort is made to maintain the heritage of black schools of thought. To the contrary, black theory is canonized by the extent to which its founding authors are displaced, and the particularity of its methods and concepts assimilated within the disciplinary narratives of the larger canon (Curry, 2011a; Curry, 2011b; Curry 2010). Critical Race Theory (CRT) is perhaps the clearest example of this anti-black dynamic within the academic discipline of philosophy. Richard Delgado's "Crossroads and Blind Alleys: A Critical Examination of Recent Writing About Race" argues that the popularization of CRT and its adoption by predominately white institutions and academic departments have hastened the deradicalization of the material analyses formulated by the original race-critics across multiple disciplines (Delgado 2004). The adoption of Continental philosophy and post-structuralism as the methods of analyzing problems of racism and other social inequalities has allowed many disciplines to embrace CRT as a general label designating any number of inquiries into questions concerning race generally without any attention to the methodological and theoretical commitments of Critical Race Theory in its original formulation. The initial formulation of CRT was racial realist, meaning it focused on the empirical and historically defined differences in economic status and political power, and made its concern the social stratifications which had emerged throughout America as the foundation of its analysis into not only the law but the routine function of white supremacist ideology more generally. The present-day interpretation and popular understanding of CRT however, is quite different, and imagined only to exist as a conceptual and discursive engagement with issues of identity, or privilege.

This chapter aims to articulate two major deficiencies in the adoption of Critical Race Theory within the discipline of philosophy—specifically how philosophers understand Bell's thinking about racism and CRT's methodological assumptions. The first section will discuss the idealist shift in Critical Race Theory as well as the thinking that came to replace its initial racial realist orientation. The second section will address the lack of engagement with the foundational works of Derrick Bell. Because many scholars associate Derrick Bell's work with one statement, "racism is permanent," there is not an exploration of his analyses of economics, history, and institutional power which are common themes throughout his corpus. In an attempt to correct the reductionism of Bell, which caricaturizes black radicals, I will analyze some of his lesser known works and contextualize them to his larger project and method. Finally, I will end with a brief reflection on the recent creation of Critical Philosophies of Race within the discipline of philosophy and its relationship to the misrepresentation of CRT. This comparative approach will highlight what I take to be a reinvention/rearticulating of arguments made over 30 years ago within a disciplinary tradition which altogether erases and ignores the substantive contributions of black, brown, and Indigenous authors for a disciplinary invention aimed at incorporating white voices and white authorship over black theory.

The Idealist Shift of Critical Race Theory

This shift in the focus of CRT towards more conceptual ventures was not altogether natural. There was nothing intuitively drawing CRT from its previous questions concerning the functioning of history, economics, politics, and law towards more contemporaneous constructs like discourse and identity. The popularization of CRT allowed a dispersion of its core ideas. The conceptualization and literatures philosophers are given and told are representative of CRT emerges from a mid-1990s institutionalization of CRT by elite institutions; ultimately the product of a mediation between younger scholars in the 1990s seeking entrance into the highest ranks of the academy by abandoning nationalist, Pan-African, and economic explanations of racism for works interpreting racism symbolically—an approach that "placed texts, narratives, scripts, stereotypes, and Freudian entities at the center of analysis" (Delgado 2004: 145). This viewing of race was not based on an amelioration of racism in American society such that a dissolving of the material, economic, and political differences between blacks, Indigenous, Latin peoples, and whites made it necessary to explain racial conflicts in terms of the attitudinal prejudice and discursive representations of non-white *others*; rather this was a paradigmatic shift within the academy as to how scholars studying American racism would be rewarded for understanding and interpreting racism. In philosophy, scholars with little to no actual course work concerning the origins of CRT, or a working knowledge of Derrick Bell's development of the theory, are embraced precisely because they seek to ameliorate racism, discrimination, and social inequality through dialogue, appeals to love, and calls to acknowledge one's (racial) privilege.

Fabio Rojas's *From Black Power to Black Studies: How a Radical Social Movement Became an Academic Discipline* (2007) explains how race conscious programs in Black Studies that echoed any form of cultural or politically oriented Black Nationalist thought were targeted and systematically de-radicalized. Ford Foundation grants were used to engineer the direction and scholarship of these departments toward political ideologies of desegregation and multiculturalism because "foundation officers were in strong disagreement with those activists and scholars who saw black studies as an institution primarily for the African American community . . . and discouraged black militancy within the academy" (Rojas 2007: 141). CRT sought institutionalization within an academic climate incentivized to censor and remain hostile to systemic nationalist paradigms and race conscious analyses of American racism. This attack on race conscious analyses coincided with idealism's proliferation across disciplines, and explains how the aims of deans, tenure committees, and elite institutions' ability to co-opt CRT was hastened within more traditional disciplines because of the threat a radical race-conscious paradigm represented. According to Delgado,

> Around the time that Critical Race Theory took the turn I mentioned, it was also gaining a degree of legitimacy in academic circles. Deans were bankrolling workshops and conferences and subsidizing new specialized law reviews to publish their proceedings . . . from the dean's perspective, is it not safer to fund scholarship that examines literary tropes than that which has the effrontery to propose that America's proudest moment—*Brown v. Board of Education*—came about because white folks decided to do themselves a favor? . . . From the perspective of the young scholar seeking tenure, it is certainly safer to attack a word or media image than law school hiring, the Supreme Court, or the Pioneer Fund. A media image cannot fight back or send a letter to one's dean.
> (Delgado 2004: 145–146)

Delgado's analysis should not be interpreted without the context of Fabio Rojas's aforementioned text—conversations and studies of American racism must be decidedly integrationist, multicultural, and non-militant. For racial realists, inspired by the works of black revolutionaries like Robert F. Williams, W.E.B. Du Bois, Paul Robeson, Huey P. Newton, and the militant resistance movements of the 1960s and 1970s which rejected desegregation as little more than a Cold War strategy to further US imperial interests abroad (Dudziak 1988, 2002, 2004), the predetermined and institutionalized consensus of universities in the United States meant their incorporation into disciplines would require a dire reformulation.

Racial realists begin their analysis with a historicization of *Brown v. Board of Education* and subsequent attempts to achieve racial integration which find these events to be primarily driven by white economic and political interests (Bell 2004). Following the pessimism of W.E.B. Du Bois, found throughout his work in the 1960s like "American Negroes and Africa's Rise to Freedom," and "[W]hites in Africa after Negro Autonomy," early realists like Derrick Bell, Richard Delgado (1992), Delgado and Stefancic (1995), Linda Greene (1998), and Kenneth Nunn (1997) found integration to be a superficial and politically expedient way to usurp the domestic power of black radicals while expanding their cultural allure abroad (Du Bois 1965). The racial realist demands a relevant historical and political analysis to ground their interpretation of racial events, while "Liberal integrationist ideology" as Gary Peller (2012) notes in *Critical Race Consciousness: Reconsidering American Ideologies of Racial Justice*, "is structured so that some social practices are taken out of the economy of race relations and understood to be undistorted by racial power" (14). This abstraction of racism away from the material is the calculus through which Critical Race Theory is interpreted as conforming-confirming established disciplinary theory and highlights the attractiveness of idealist theorizations over realist analysis. The idealist perspective

> holds that race and discrimination are largely functions of attitude and social formation. For these thinkers, race is a social construction created out of words, symbols, stereotypes, and categories. As such, we may purge discrimination by ridding ourselves of the texts, narratives, ideas, and meanings that give rise to it and that convey the message that people of other racial groups are unworthy, lazy, and dangerous.

Formulating racism as largely semiotic, a misrepresentation of the actual relationships race has to malicious meanings of the language structuring our thinking, idealism allows a post-1970s university to accept a paradigmatic approach to American racism which focuses on racial identity, mutual dialogue, and cross-racial understanding.

Throughout the academy, scholarship on racism is treated as theory or political ideology (a term used to mark its non-academic or anti-intellectual status) based on its underlying formulation of American racism. If a work on racism engages race and whiteness through an integrationist lens—as capable of transformation—which concedes the possibilities of American democracy as shown during the Civil Rights era, then it is considered suitable as race or political theory. If a work does not hold to the multiculturist and integrationist trajectory of American democracy, it is largely excluded from disciplinary knowledge and condemned as overly political and ideological. In "Race Consciousness," Gary Peller (1990) argues that integrationist ideology has determined the precepts through which race and racism are understood in mainstream American political culture as well as its institutions of higher learning. Because "integrationist ideology locates racial oppression in the social structure of prejudice and stereotype based on skin color, and . . . identifies progress with the transcendence of a racial consciousness" (Peller 1990: 760), race conscious orientations, like Black Nationalism, which critique the underlying assumptions of objectivity and racial neutrality to colonialism and the power to control cultural meanings, "became marginalized as an extremist and backward worldview, as the irrational correlate in the black community to the never-say-die segregationists of the white community" (Peller 1990: 790). This very rudimentary division of knowledge operates to censor and designate those works and scholars worthy of consideration, and those who are not, within disciplines. Scholars who articulate positions where racism and white supremacy are at the core of all other societal stratifications are routinely referred to as "radical," "ideological," or accused of being intellectually immature and backwards. These works are usually deemed non-philosophical, and more appropriate in more marginal fields like Black or Ethnic Studies.

Philosophy relies on the consensus of its audience towards integration. In the mind of many white liberals, segregation was the basis of racism, thus integration appears to be anti-racist a priori. In this way, racist theories and practices are absolved of their evil if done under the guise of integration, plurality, and inclusion. Consequently, philosophy remains unshakably racist (both in theory and practice) since no amount of empirical or historical evidence is ever considered a refutation of the failures or ineffectiveness of its cherished racial ideations. What white scholars believe to be anti-racism inevitably becomes the parameter of the conversations, theories, and authors allowed to comment on the problem at large. In short, the discipline of philosophy remains racist because one cannot test out of racism, no amount of evidence can challenge its a priori formulations. As such, the impressions of the white majority in philosophy, even when demonstrated to be empirically denied or historically untrue, remain the guiding ethos of black engagements with racism and oppression, as well as the barometer determining the value of Critical Race scholarship within the discipline.

Understanding Derrick Bell's Corpus: The Themes of Bell's Racial Realism

Derrick Bell is perhaps the most ignored black political theorist of the twentieth century. While Critical Race Theory is routinely mentioned in practically every philosophical text on race over the last two decades, the political theories, phenomenological investigations, and critical interventions by Bell have remained ignored (Curry 2008; 2011a; 2015). By and large, Derrick Bell's work is understood in the discipline of philosophy through his 1992 book *Face at the Bottom of the Well: The Permanence of Racism* (1992a) and his provocation of racial realism which argues that:

> Black people will never gain full equality in this country. Even those Herculean efforts we hail as successful will produce no more than temporary "peaks of progress," short-lived victories that slide into irrelevance as racial patterns adapt in ways that maintain white dominance. This is a hard-to-accept fact that all history verifies. We must acknowledge it and move on to adopt policies based on what I call: "Racial Realism." This mind-set or philosophy requires us to acknowledge the permanence of our subordinate status.
> (Bell 1992b, 373–374)

Many scholars simply stop here in their engagement(s) with Bell's thought. Since many scholars, black and white, in the academy identify as liberal or progressive, Bell's indictment of the Civil Rights movement is not only challenging, but offensive. The aversion many scholars and disciplines have to Bell's challenge leads not only to misunderstanding Bell's system and reducing racial realism to an ideological claim, but devalues Bell as a thinker and resource for race theorists. Bell envisioned racial realism as a paradigm aiming to understand how racism persists, and black conditions subtly worsen, while symbols of racial progress proliferate throughout American society and are celebrated as concrete racial advances. While the *racism is permanent thesis* is a position formulated by a marriage of sociology and jurisprudence that suggests racism is structural and immutable, a position bolstered by Bell's use of internal colonization analysis to understand the racial organization of American society, it is not synonymous to racial realism. Bell only reaches this conclusion at the end of his racial realist analysis which evaluates history, law, and the political economics behind the Civil Rights era (Bell 1993).

According to Bell, racial realism has four major themes. The first theme is historical and argues that "there has been no linear progress in civil rights. American racial history has demonstrated both steady subordination of blacks in one way or another, and if examined closely, a pattern of cyclical progress and cyclical regression" (1992a: 98). The second theme of Bell's theory is economic and argues for economic analysis to be utilized over ethical appeals to equality. Bell is adamant that "in our battles with racism, we need less discussion of ethics and more discussion of economics . . . Ideals must not be allowed to obscure the blacks' real position in the socioeconomic realm, which happens to be the real indicator of power in this country" (1992a: 98). The third theme of "salvation through struggle," or the rejection of "any philosophy that insists on measuring life's success on the achieving of specific goals—overlooking the process of living" (1992a: 98) is heavily related to Bell's fourth theme of the racial realist imperative which argues that "those who presently battle oppression must at least consider looking at racism in this realistic way, however unfamiliar and defeatist it may sound" (1992a: 99). For Bell, racial realism holds the possibility of truth and justice, but these values can only be had by honesty with ourselves that does not allow our intellect and imaginations for struggle to be captured by the lullabies of our oppressors. Because our abstract normative values (freedom, justice, etc.) are rooted in the consensus of whites, rather than the guarantee of rights enforced by law, the enjoyment blacks have of their hard-fought civil rights fluctuate based on the agendas and interests of the white populace and the state.

The more popular readings of Bell which that interpret him almost solely through some of his more provocative claims may be expedient, but such approaches do not allow for a careful or scholarly engagement with the founder of CRT—such an approach is simply reactive and lends to serious inaccuracies and misinterpretations of Bell's overall corpus. Bell's thinking did not simply emerge as a theoretical intuition about the world, rather it was the conclusion of a systematic analysis of the law, politics, civil rights cases, and economics. In fact, Bell's thinking about segregation, the ineffectiveness of civil rights policy, and racism was inspired by Judge Robert L. Carter—a pioneer civil rights lawyer and colleague of Thurgood Marshall. The parallel between Derrick Bell's work and that of Judge Robert L. Carter is uncanny. It was not until March of 2009 that Derrick Bell told me "Judge Carter is my major mentor and I could do a book about his influence on my outlook" (Bell, email, 2009). Carter's work is an interesting account of the jurisprudential issues at stake for blacks and the fickle constitutional doctrine of racial equality. If one reads Carter's work from his proclamations from the 1950s to the late 1960s, we see a transforming account of racism as being located within segregation to an account of racism that saw the institutional, cultural, and societal milieu of white superiority the foundation of American white supremacy (Carter 1953, 1955; Carter and Marshall 1955). Carter was well aware that "in dealing with the question of segregation, it must be recognized that these effects do not the place in a vacuum, but in a social context" (Carter 1953: 68). Because the "segregation of Negroes and other groups in the United States takes place in a social milieu in which race prejudice and discrimination exist" (Carter 1953: 68), Carter maintained that social cultural analyses (by this meaning the sociological, anthropological, psychological, and psychiatric) must be a fundamental component of understanding American race relations. In all reality, it is Carter's work that set the stage for Bell's future account of racism as white supremacy and his theory of interest convergence. As Robert L. Carter remarked in "The Warren Court and Desegregation,"

> *Brown*'s indirect consequences, therefore, have been awesome. It has completely altered the style, the spirit, and the stance of race relations. Yet the pre-existing pattern of white superiority and black subordination remains unchanged; indeed, it is now revealed as a national rather than a regional

> phenomenon. Thus, Brown has promised more than it could give, and therefore has contributed to black alienation and bitterness, to a loss of confidence in white institutions, and to the growing racial polarization of our society . . . Few in the country, black or white, understood in 1954 that racial segregation was merely a symptom, not the disease; that the real sickness is that our society in all of its manifestations is geared to the maintenance of white superiority.
> (Carter 1968: 243)

Exposing the shortcomings of Brown v. Board was a monumental criticism in the 1970s. Black and white scholars and activists alike were celebrating the recent achievements of the 1960s and 1970s, so a criticism of desegregation by black lawyers who worked to dismantle segregation was seen as heresy.

In 1977, Derrick Bell published "Racial Remediation: An Historical Perspective on Current Conditions," an article heavily influenced by Carter's "The Warren Court and Desegregation," which sought to explain how the racist-economic dimension of America's political organization determined the landmark racial achievements from the abolition of slavery to desegregation that were driving many of the ideas that American racism have improved, progressed, and in some cases dissipated. This essay introduced the economic premise behind what would later become Racial Realism. In the late 1970s, Bell argued that white interest determined black rights. Bell understood that the economic and political forces of white America awarded or took away black rights as it saw necessary for its own advancement. Bell was adamant that the

> measurable improvement in the status of some blacks, and predictions of further progress have not substantially altered the maxim: white self-interest will prevail over black rights. This unstated, but firmly followed principle has characterized racial policy decisions in this society for three centuries. Racial policies are still based on the sense-no less deeply held when it is unconscious-that America is a white nation, and that white dominance over blacks is natural, right and necessary as well as profitable and satisfying. This pervasive belief, the very essence of racism, remains a viable and valuable national resource.
> (Bell 1977: 6)

In the late 1970s, Bell conceptualized Civil Rights as a contingent rather than epochal change in American racism. Attention to Bell's intellectual genealogy shows that his arguments against liberal constitutionalism and political liberalism precedes the arguments Critical Legal Studies (CLS) launched against legal indeterminacy in the 1980s, and is at least contemporaneous with the founding of the CLS movement in 1977 (Unger 1983). Contrary to the characterization of Bell as simply addressing race, Bell's work is seeking to establish a paradigm to understand the complexities and historical duration of American racism. In his first book, *And We Are Not Saved: The Elusive Quest for Racial Justice* (1987), Bell constructs his argument against the alleged success of the Civil Rights movement as an empirical study of the socio-economic condition of the newly integrated black population in the United States. Unsurprisingly, Bell finds that after three decades of desegregation, and two decades after the passing of civil rights legislation, black Americans remain impoverished, jobless, and by effect politically impotent.

Throughout this text Bell asserts that the failure of the normative political and racial values to deliver economic ends to Black America doom actual black progress because black people become dependent on the political economy of white society for sustenance. A serious reading of Bell shows his analysis of American racism, even his pessimism in a political economic account of America's structural organization and cultural predilection against black progress, is based in the cumulative disadvantage that persists despite the promises of liberalism. Bell argues that the

> pattern of racial oppression in the past created the huge black underclass, as the accumulation of disadvantages were passed on from generation to generation, and the technological and economic revolution of advanced industrial society combined to insure it a permanent status.
>
> (124)

Similarly, in a conversation with the fictional character Geneva Crenshaw who argued that it was the fear America has of inter-racial sexual relations between black men and white women behind anti-miscegenation laws instead of the economic justifications proposed by Bell, Bell answers that

> one need not deny [these sanctions were motivated by whites' basic fear and abhorrence of interracial sex], to agree with Frantz Fanon that it is reasonable to assume that attitudes about sex are embedded in a given cultural and historical context; and that even if sexuality is basically biological, its form of expression is influenced by variables including economics, status, and access to power.
>
> (207–208)

Racism is enforced by the perambulation of everyday whites who are able to extend or retract the law based solely on their will. It is precisely this mirroring function of the law to white racial interests, be it bourgeois or not, that defines and constrains blackness. It is this economic dynamic and the power of racism (white racial interest) that directs and regulates black political progress; it is this process that Bell names as interest-convergence in "*Brown v. Board of Education* and the Interest Convergence Dilemma" (Bell 1980).

His most popularly known work, *Faces at the Bottom of the Well*, is at its core the product of his more empirically dense and historical work from years prior. In *Faces at the Bottom of the Well*, Bell attempts to convince the reader of the viability of a racial realist perspective through multiple case studies and hypotheticals. The chapters titled "Space Traders" and "Afrolantica" push black people to see the reality of the Civil Rights movement; this text is written as a play on the fears of black citizens after their celebration of racial equality. Bell asks the black citizenry, "Are your rights permanent?" "Can they be taken away?" "What and who allows you to enjoy equality temporarily?" These questions are sociological and historical, and as Bell shows central to the interpretation the group in power operationalizes through the law. "Space Traders" is an illustration of a new American slavery that shows black people do not in fact have to power to maintain their rights to American citizenship without the consent of the white population. Bell convincingly argues that if black equality is only maintained by white compassion, and whites are fickle creatures, then law and civil rights are contingent and not assured. If white interests and power award black rights, then blacks actually live in a constant state of fear, since both the white violence used against blacks, and white sympathy with blacks are dependent on white racial interests. This proposition has been called nihilist and fatalistic, because it suggests that the incremental progress black people have made in the United States is illusory. These criticisms however miss the point of Bell's normative thought. Bell argues that struggle against racism creates the value and existential worth for the oppressed, not the temporary rewards within a racist structure. Bell imagines black struggle as creating a world that is possible. "Afrolantica" is Bell's narrative of black cultural potency; it demonstrates that there is a conceptual geography, a reason, a material cultural reality that black Americans have access to that can create a different world. Bell believes that struggle against racism is culturally renewing and powerful, even though he remains pessimistic about the viability of racism's end (Curry 2012). Bell's alternative to the structural solidification of American racism is the marking out of a possible world for black people and new black realities.

The Critical Race Artifice

As demonstrated above, philosophy has not yet adequately understood or explored the works of the first generation of race-crits and the debates they had within the literature to justify moving beyond the primary authors or texts of the field. Critical Race Theory has not only exceeded the limitations of the law, but achieved a transdisciplinary reach whose conceptualizations and configurations of American racism influence scholarship in sociology, history, and education. Despite the widespread utilization of CRT, it is philosophy that finds this tradition wanting, in need of new thinkers—white thinkers—and more critical (Frankfurt School) tools. Given the new work in history concerning the Black Panthers and their views of black masculinity and black femininity, and the motivations behind Civil Rights organizations and armed resistance, it would seem that the exploration of the ideas and political theories behind the work of Bell and other first generation race-crits remain a rich and untapped intellectual resource for explorations of racism, economics, and sexuality (Joseph 2001, 2003; Cobb 2014). There is no need to turn to Europe simply because philosophy lacks the attention span or interest to dig into black America. The idealist tradition opened the door for various Continental theories to comment on the realities of anti-black racism. Today, it is believed that racism is merely an object of theory, a problem that can be analyzed most effectively through already canonized European thought and figures.

Critical philosophies of race (CPR) maintains a loose association with the currency utilized by many disciplines around the country for doing CRT, but differs from disciplines like sociology and education in that no black theorists are centralized at the historical helm and theoretical foundation of the movement. There is no mention of Derrick Bell, Mari Matsuda, or even Charles Lawrence III—the theorist credited by Richard Delgado for ushering in the idealist wave (bringing Continental philosophy) to CRT, or the problems encountered by race-crit scholars in their attempts to deal with anti-essentialist identities through post-intersectionality, the multiple histories of settlerism and genocide by Robert A. Williams Jr., the Eurocentrism and colonialism by Kenneth Nunn, and immigration. In the first reference piece on CPR, Robert Bernasconi argues:

> Critical Philosophy of Race calls itself "critical" not only because it investigations and attacks racisms wherever they may be found, but also in recognition of the pioneering work done both by critical race theory within legal studies, which is a forerunner of work in this area, and by critical theory (the Frankfurt

school). Although there is some overlap between [CRT] and [CPR] the former at least as developed initially tended to offer only a partial picture. It provided clear evidence for the view of race as socially constructed, for example, by documenting not only the differences between the laws defining someone's racial status from one state to the other, but also the various ways in which courts would apply these laws. This showed the extent to which the concept of race was not primarily a scientific concept, but critical race theorists might still be criticized for not giving sufficient weight to the role played by science in legitimating racial thinking. Critical race theory also tended to focus excessively on the legal framework established in the North American context, whereas critical philosophies of race is committed to a global perspective.

(Bernasconi 2012: 551)

But this explanation is as vague as it is puzzling. Bernasconi suggests that the advantage of a CPR perspective over a CRT perspective is that the philosophical variant exceeds the confines of American jurisprudence and as well as the geographical borders of the United States. Yet an investigation of the first three volumes of the *Critical Philosophy of Race* journal show that its focus is overwhelmingly Americanist. For example, the first volume of the *Critical Philosophy of Race* journal announcing the field of CPR focused on the black-white binary in race theory. The essays in the first volume of CPR primarily deal with American race relations and identity, as does the second issue of the volume, with the exception of an article about Afro-Mexicans by Mariana Ortega. The later volumes in 2014 and 2015 largely represent the same Americanist context with little to no internationalist or global perspective.

CPR's approach to race theory is consistent with Critical Race Theory literature in general and mimics the themes anthologized over a decade earlier in *Crossroads, Directions, and a New Critical Race Theory*.[1] This anthology specifically claimed that Critical Race Theory had to consider and develop towards more global and multidimensional considerations. In the introduction, the editors state:

> Despite the doubts, sneers, and attacks, CRT has not only survived but is also flourishing as it enters its second decade. Critical race feminists, critical race queers, and Latino/a critical theorists (LatCrits) have added sexual oppression, transnationality, culture, language, immigration, and social status to our original understanding of racism and class stratification to racial injustice.
>
> (Valdes, Culp, and Harris 2002)

The first volume, both issues 1 and 2, of the *Critical Philosophy of Race* journal actually dedicates its attention to specifically American understandings of race and racism (Otto 2017; Floya and Yuval Davis 1992). While there are discussions of racial identity beyond Blackness and whiteness, the writings in the first volume of CPR simply echo the work of LatCrits like Elizabeth Iglesias, Kevin R. Johnson, and Franscisco Valdes from the 1990s who called for a transatlantic and global account of citizenship, state power, and immigration (Valdes 1997a, 1997b; Martinez 1998; Iglesias 2001). If CPR simply reiterates work previously done by CRT that philosophers are not familiar with, then it would seem the perspective is not methodologically or conceptually distinct approach, but rather a disciplinary iteration of previously written theories and themes said not to exist.

From a materialist account, one must consider the conditions, cultural conditions, and institutions responsible for creating a new field of studying race within a racist discipline like philosophy. Who were the actors? What are the historical foundation and literatures that differentiate the perspective? What are the theoretical assumptions and how do these resist or empower certain political ideologies and actors? Whereas black intellectual traditions have rarely been recognized immediately, or acknowledged historically for their analysis and theoretical clarification of racism and colonialism, the creation of a field of study dedicated to racism should be a case study and object for investigation for some time into the future. This chapter is an attempt to better situate and historicize some of the debates and scholarship surrounding the mythology of Derrick Bell's work and the growing utilization of intersectionality. While it is beyond the scope of this chapter to fully account for the recent adoption of Critical Philosophies of Race as a perspective from which race can be studied, it is necessary for a comparative analysis and study of the concepts, precepts, and apparati utilized and assumed by the CPR and CRT. Further study and investigation into the normative ideas and historical literature of CPR is necessary for such study to occur. It is my intent that this chapter at least clarify some of the central ideas and debates within CRT literature and the misperceptions of the racial realist tradition. Without a delineation between the debates, concepts, and literatures of CPR and CRT, intersectionality and post-intersectionality, and racial realism and idealism, philosophy will be able to occupy the intellectual traditions of black and brown thinkers, their schools of thought and methods, while demanding these original texts and authors belong only to Black or Ethnics Studies or law. In other words, philosophy's gentrification of these territories of theory must be arrested and challenged.

Note

[1] The first volume of the CPR journal includes a session dedicated to the black-white binary. The essays primarily deal with American race relations and identity. The volume begins with Charles W. Mills, "Retrieving Rawls for Racial Justice? A Critique of Tommie Shelby," *Critical Philosophy of Race* 1.1 (2013): 1–27. The second essay is José Medina's "Colorblindness, Meta-Ignorance, and the Racial Imagination," 38–67, which is followed by Kyoo Lee's "Why Asian Female Stereotypes Matter to All: Beyond the Black and White, East and West, 86–103. Arguably the only transnational consideration is Namita Goswami's "The (M)other of all Posts: Post-Colonial Melancholia in the Age of Global Warming, 104–120. The second issue of volume 1 starts with a reply to Mills by Tommie Shelby titled "Racial Realities and Corrective Justice: A Reply to Mills," *Critical Philosophy of Race* 1.2 (2013): 145–162.

References

Bell, Derrick. (1977) "Racial Remediation: A Historical Perspective on Current Conditions." *Notre Dame Law Review* 52: 5–29.

———. (1980) "*Brown v. Board of Education* and the Interest Convergence Dilemma." *Harvard Law Review* 93, no. 3: 518–533.

———. (1992a) *Faces at the Bottom of the Well: The Permanence of Racism*, New York: Basic Books.

———. (1992b) "Racial Realism." *Connecticut Law Review* 24: 363–379.

———. (1993) "The Racism Is Permanent Thesis: Courageous Revelation or Unconscious Denial of Genocide." *Capital University Law Review* 22: 571–588.

———. (2004) *Silent Convenants: Brown v. Board of Education and the Unfulfilled Hopes for Racial Reform*, Oxford: Oxford University Press.
Bernasconi, Robert. (2012) "Critical Race Philosophies," in Sebastian Luft and Soren Overgaard (eds.), *Routledge Companion to Phenomenology*, New York: Routledge, pp. 551–562.
Carter, Robert L. (1953) "The Effects of Segregation and the Consequences of Desegregaton: A Social Science Statement." *Journal of Negro Education* 22, no. 1: 68–76.
———. (1968) "The Warren Court and Desegregation." *Michigan Law Review* 67: 237–248.
Carter, Robert L., and Thurgood Marshall. (1955) "The Meaning and Significance of the Supreme Court Decree." *Journal of Negro Education* 24, no. 3: 397–404.Cobb, Charles E., Jr. (2014) *This Non-Violent Stuff Will Get You Killed: How Guns Made the Civil Rights Movement Possible*, New York: Basic Books.
Curry, Tommy J. (2008) "Saved by the Bell: Derrick Bell's Racial Realism as Pedagogy." *Philosophical Studies in Education* 39: 35–46.
———. (2010) "Concerning the Underspecialization of Race Theory in American Philosophy: An Essay Outlining Ignored Bibliographic Sources Addressing the Aforementioned Problem." *Pluralist* 5, no. 1: 44–64.
———. (2011a) "The Derelictical Crisis of African American Philosophy: How African American Philosophy Fails to Contribute to the Study of African Descended People." *Journal of Black Studies* 42, no. 3: 314–333.
———. (2011b) "On Derelict and Method: The Methodological Crisis of Africana Philosophy's Study of African Descended People Under an Integrationist Milieu." *Radical Philosophy Review* 14, no. 2: 139–164.
———. (2012) "Shut Your Mouth When You're Talking to Me: Silencing the Idealist School of Critical Race Theory Through a Culturalogic Turn in Jurisprudence." *Georgetown Law Journal of Modern Critical Race Studies* 3, no. 1: 1–38.
———. (2015) "Back to the Woodshop: Black Education, Imperial Pedagogy, and Post-Racial Mythology under the Reign of Obama." *Teachers College Record* 117, no. 114: 27–52.
Delgado, Richard. (1992) "Derrick Bell's Racial Realism: A Comment on White Optimism and Black Despair." *Connecticut Law Review* 24: 527–532.
———. (2004) "Crossroads and Blind Alleys: A Critical Examination of Recent Writings about Race." *Texas Law Review* 82: 121–152.
Delgado, Richard, and Stefancic, Jean. (1995) "The Social Construction of Brown v. Board of Education: Law Reform and the Reconstructive Paradox." *William and Mary Law Review* 36, no. 2: 547–570.
Du Bois, W.E.B. (1965) "American Negroes and Africa's Rise to Freedom," in *The World and Africa: An Inquiry Into the Part Which Africa Has Played in World History*, New York: International, pp. 334–338.
———. (1986) *A Soliloquy on Viewing My Life From the Last Decade of Its First Century: The Autobiography of W.E.B. Du Bois*, New York: International.
———. (1996) "Whites in Africa After Negro Autonomy," in Eric J. Sudquist (ed.), *The Oxford W.E.B. Du Bois Reader*, New York: Oxford University Press, pp. 667–675.
Dudziak, Mary. (1988) "Desegregation as a Cold War Imperative." *Stanford Law Review* 41, no. 1: 61–120.
———. (2004) "Brown as a Cold War Case." *Journal of American History* 1: 32–42.
Floya, Anthias, and Yuval-Davis, Nira. (1992) *Racialized Boundaries: Race, Nation, Gender, Colour, and Class and the Anti-Racist Struggle*, London: Routledge.
Greene, Linda. (1998) "Jim Crowism in the 21st Century." *Capital University Law Review* 27: 43–60.
Hill, Lance. (2004) *Deacons for Defense: Armed Resistance and the Civil Rights Movement*, Chapel Hill: University of North Carolina Press.
Iglesias, Elizabeth. (2001) "LatCrit Theory: Some Preliminary Notes Towards a Transatlantic Dialogue." *University of Miami International and Comparative Law Review* 9: 1–32.
Johnson, Kevin R., and Martinez, George A. (1998) "Crossover Dreams: The Roots of LatCrit Theory in Chicana/o Studies, Activism and Scholarship." *University of Miami Law Review* 53: 1143–1175.
Joseph, Peniel E. (2001) "Black Liberation Without Apology: Reconceptualizing the Black Power Movement." *Black Scholar* 31, nos. 3-4: 2–19.
———. (2003) "Dashikis and Democracy: Black Studies, Student Activism, and the Black Power Movement." *Journal of African American History* 88, no. 2: 182–203.

Lawson, Bill. (2012) "The Aporia of Hope: King and Bell on the Ending of Racism," in Robert Birt (ed.), *The Liberatory Thought of Martin Luther King: Critical Essays of the Philosopher King*, Lanham: Lexington Books, pp. 321–340.

Nunn, Kenneth. (1997) "Law as Eurocentric Enterprise." *Law and Inequality Journal* 15: 323–372.

Otto, Jessica. (2017) "Derrick Bell's Paradigm of Racial Realism: An Overlooked and Unappreciated Theorist." *Radical Philosophy Review* 20.2: 243–264.

Peller, Gary. (1990) "Race Consciousness." *Duke Law Journal* 4: 758–847.

———. (2012) *Critical Race Consciousness: Reconsidering American Ideologies of Racial Justice*, Boulder: Paradigm.

Rojas, Fabio. (2007), *From Black Power to Black Studies: How a Radical Social Movement Became an Academic Discipline*, Baltimore: Johns Hopkins University Press.

Scott, Jacqueline. (2004) "Racial Nihilism as Racial Courage: The Potential for Healthier Racial Identities." *Graduate Faculty Philosophy Journal* 35, nos. 1–2: 297–330.

Unger, Roberto. (1983) *The Critical Legal Studies Movement*, Cambridge, MA: Harvard University Press.

Valdes, Francisco. (1997a) "Poised at the Cusp: Lat Crit Theory, Outsider Jurisprudence and Latina/o Self-Empowerment." *Harvard Latino Law Review* 2: 1–59.

———. (1997b) "Under Construction: LatCrit Consciousness, Community and Theory." *California Law Review* 85: 1087–1142.

Valdes, Francisco, Culp, Jerome McCristal, and Harris, Angela P. (2002) "Battles Waged, Won, and Lost: Critical Race Theory at the Turn of the Millennium," in Francisco Valdes, Jerome McCristal Culp and Angela P. Harris (eds.), *Crossroads, Directions, and a New Critical Race Theory*, Philadelphia: Temple University Press, pp. 1–6.

Part VI
AESTHETICS

26
RACE-ING AESTHETIC THEORY

Monique Roelofs

Introduction

Aesthetics has long been embroiled in problematic racial theories and activities. Contemporary scholars and artists push back against this tradition of thought and practice. The racial heritage in aesthetics calls for revisions of key concepts in aesthetics, such as notions of experience, the body, normativity, value, culture, and the nation. Post- and decolonial theorists along with philosophers of race and critical race feminists have commenced this work, as have artists and other makers of cultural productions. First offering a quick glimpse of the troubled theoretical history these critical voices challenge, this chapter goes on to describe the new philosophical outlooks they open up. I will continue with a sample of the many other themes and approaches that surface in the sharply contested area where aesthetics and race are mutually determinative of each other. We will examine, in particular, the topics of aesthetic sustenance and pleasure, appropriation, everyday aesthetics, and the categories philosophers call aesthetic concepts.

Aesthetic Histories and Canons

Racial conceptions historically permeate aesthetic theory. Readers of Immanuel Kant will recall his view that black persons are incapable of fine feeling, an important condition for aesthetic perception, and they will also remember his comments about the relatively deficient apprehensive propensities of Native Americans, Caribbeans, and other non-Europeans (Kant 1951; Eze 1997). Before Kant voiced these ideas, David Hume had already notified his readers of his denial of original thought to black people (Eze 1997). Edmund Burke (1990) had advanced as a legitimate instance of aesthetic perception the case of a young, white boy's horror at the sight of a black woman. Georg Wilhelm Friedrich Hegel, for his part, added the persuasion that Africa is located outside of world history (Eze 1997). These are examples of a broader racial heritage in aesthetics. Ideas about the racial grounds for aesthetic practices are far from new, as are observations on the aesthetic dimensions of racial constellations. In point of fact, for several centuries, philosophers have embedded suppositions about hierarchically conceived white, black, Amerindian, African, Arab, Jewish, and Asian identities—among many others—in their accounts of aesthetic qualities and experience. They have structurally given aesthetic meanings to racial differences, associating racialized attributes with disparate capacities to realize aesthetic value in the spheres of art, bodily appearance and comportment, and cultural practice generally. This line of thought is not confined to a small corner of the Western philosophical canon or an incidental site of inattention, but reaches into the core of European aesthetic visions.

Indeed, major eighteenth- and nineteenth-century figures in Western aesthetics have built pernicious racial tenets into their understandings of fundamental mechanisms of art and culture, assumptions that continue to reverberate in contemporary conceptual frameworks (West 1982; Wynter 1992; Eze 1994, 1997; Armstrong 1996; Bernasconi 1998; Korsmeyer 1998; Gooding-Williams 2006; James 2010; Roelofs 2014). These philosophers endorse problematic, aesthetically supported and aesthetically productive segments of institutionally embedded racialization as well as racially supported and racially productive strata of structurally emplaced aesthetic activity. Trajectories of what I call *aesthetic racialization*, a term that refers to the ways in which aesthetic elements support racializing processes, thereby, go in tandem with itineraries of what I dub *racialized aestheticization*, a term that denotes the contributions that racial constellations make to aesthetic phenomena (Roelofs 2014). Patterns of aesthetic racialization and racialized aestheticization are complicit in aesthetically legitimated and aesthetically generative forms of violence and injustice. Both at the level of aesthetic practice and scholarship, much work has happened to transform these structures.

Critical Frameworks

Challenging formations of aesthetic racialization and racialized aestheticization, theorists and artists have begun to develop alternative cultural and conceptual itineraries. I will sketch four avenues of reflection on and engagement with these formations. These include post- and decolonial perspectives, the approaches of canonical philosophers of race W.E.B. Du Bois and Frantz Fanon, the agenda of what I call critical race feminist aesthetics, and a painting and installation by Kara Walker, whose work puts pressure on racial positions and understandings.

Post- and Decolonial Theory: Alternative Traditions, Critiques of Modernity, and Counternarratives of Cultural Difference

Along with artists, art critics, curators, and activists, theorists are critically rethinking elements of the vexed Anglo-European heritage in philosophical aesthetics. This agenda encompasses the two-tiered, interconnected project of revising our understanding of the aesthetic and rhetorical underpinnings of modernity and the modern subject, phenomena that have racism and racialization at their basis (Gilroy 1993; Mignolo 2007), and of uncovering alternative philosophical and artistic traditions, ones that take a distance from problematic collaborations between aesthetics and race, as intersecting with factors such as coloniality.

Meanwhile central categories of analysis undergo shifts in meaning. Moving away from perspectives that reify notions of tradition and modernity, nation and empire, the global North and South, postcolonial theorists Stuart Hall, Gayatri Spivak, and Homi

Bhabha complicate received inside-outside oppositions informing these concepts, such as the distinctions between the subject of Western civilization and its disavowed Other, or between the contemporary nation and its alleged historical origins. Race, in these approaches, acquires an unstable place in encounters between historical pedagogies of culture and current symbolic iterations. Cultural difference thereby remains under production. Forms of critical agency are found in subjects' negotiations of heterogeneous conditions of enunciation, of ambivalent, disjunctive sites of cultural translation, and of double binds (Hall 1994; Bhabha 1994; Spivak 1999, 2012). Contemporary artworks both inform and resonate with these kinds of destabilization and navigation. A second line of critical approach to the intersection of aesthetic and race surfaces within the philosophy of race.

Du Bois's and Fanon's Views of Aesthetic Experience: Methodological, Conceptual, and Practical Implications

Major philosophers of race have explored aesthetic meaning and agency. W.E.B. Du Bois's and Frantz Fanon's views have implications for crucial concepts in aesthetics, namely, for notions of the body, experience, culture, value, and normativity that lie at the center of accounts of the aesthetic.

Discussing various types of art and craft, such as ironwork, dress, and poetry, Du Bois (1971a, 1971b, 1971c, 1986a, 1986c) and Fanon (1963, 1967) situate aesthetic objects in dynamic cultural processes. Both theorists indicate how the work of white culture makers generally benefits from forms of sponsorship, training, and approbation that are withheld from that of black cultural producers, which meets with prevailing patterns of devalorization and neglect. This view contains three important philosophical insights about aesthetic experience. First, in recognizing discrepancies between the modes of apprehension subjects direct at objects created by black and white cultural agents, Du Bois and Fanon understand aesthetic experience as a markedly racial phenomenon: racial conditions affect the ways in which we apprehend or engage art and artifacts, the possibilities for creation we enjoy, the meanings and significance we ascribe to cultural productions, and the level of excellence these entities can attain in our eyes.

Second, given that aesthetic experience, according to Du Bois and Fanon, derives its contents substantially from the racialized social matrix in which we enjoy it, it amounts to a moral, political and economic phenomenon as does race. Indeed, in their views, the political economy of race is incontrovertibly at work in the plane of the aesthetic. Both philosophers, at the same time, emphatically valorize aesthetic phenomena for the aesthetic productions they are. Thus, we find in both theorists' writings a principled recognition of the moral, political, and economic facets of aesthetic life and of the aesthetic dimensions of morality, politics, and economics. Meanwhile, neither side of these equations exhaustively constitutes or encompasses the other side. Du Bois and Fanon, in other words, acknowledge the workings of the aesthetic as a component of political economy and of our ethical comportment, and attest to the role of morality and political economy as determinants of aesthetic existence, without, however, reducing either of these two domains to the other.

A third and practical consequence of Du Bois's and Fanon's approaches is that ethical, political, economic, and aesthetic concerns, in their accounts, prescribe rigorous changes in our aesthetic conduct. Both theorists work to counter racial subjugation at the level of aesthetic norms and forms. We must thoroughly reorganize the conditions for the production and reception of cultural artifacts so as to permit aesthetic experience to flourish on new terms. This, then, promises to result in positive transformations in the existential circumstances of black people. Du Bois writes,

> until the art of the black folk compells recognition they will not be rated as human. And when through art they compell recognition then let the world discover if it will that their art is as new as it is old and as old as new.
> (1986a: 1002)

The practical shift Du Bois envisages reverberates in the theoretical field in which we ruminate on aesthetic normativity, value, and criteria of evaluation. According to Du Bois, we must *acquire* the norms and values that we should bring to our experience and interpretation of black art, in the course of a historical process of cultural amelioration. Blacks as well as whites, in Du Bois's view, need to enlarge their judgment of black work, albeit for different reasons: he tells the former to prepare themselves to measure their creations by their own standards, and urges the latter to bring themselves to a place where they can adequately appreciate the artistic values and qualities realized in black art.

Du Bois's consistent praise of beauty and of the aesthetic merits of productions by black artists, artisans, and laborers goes in tandem with observations on cultural, material, and artistic possibilities that fall short of ideals of civilization and remain yet to be realized. Like Du Bois, Fanon offers an ambivalent picture of the value of aesthetic experience. Fanon regards aesthetic elements such as stories and anecdotes as participants in the formation of a racialized corporeal image shaping bodily experience (1963: 111). Media productions including film, radio, and magazines, in his view, can support black and white lifeworlds. Poetry and music, as interpreted within actual racial conditions of apprehension and circulation, supply the terms in which established patterns of relationships among blacks and whites play out and run into blockages (1963). Fanon gives aesthetic experiences (e.g., those of singing, dancing, games, dinner parties, myths, clothing, housing, buildings, cars, bouquets) a role in the workings of colonization, processes of anticolonial resistance, and the institution of neocolonial hierarchies (1967). On simultaneously social, moral, political, epistemic, and aesthetic grounds, aesthetic experience, thus, is an ambivalent good for Fanon. On behalf of desirable traditions of art and craft, and with the aim of forging suitable grounds for social justice and the production of knowledge, we must channel aesthetic experience into liberatory directions. Indeed, according to Fanon, we must fashion it in ways that help us to engender adequately human forms of aesthetically modulated cultural life.

The notion of culture holds center stage in Du Bois's and Fanon's aesthetics. Both philosophers comprehend culture and cultures as racialized forms of collectivity. Approaching aesthetic elements as ingredients of more encompassing cultural flows, they forge a framework for critically appraising and reshaping our investments in these elements and flows. They indicate how procedures of cultural transmission and engagement, as a matter of empirical fact, rally institutional arrangements and organizations of labor, such as empire, coloniality, slavery, white supremacy, the nation-state, and schooling (Du Bois 1904, 1971a, 1971b, 1971c, 1986a, 1986c, 1986d; Fanon 1963, 1967). Culture and cultures, for Du Bois and Fanon, thus, are not stagnant or completed realities, but comprise malleable material productions.

Prominent aspects of Du Bois's and Fanon's accounts, such as their views of gender, sexual desire, communalism, and cultural politics, have come under critique (see, e.g., Chow 1998; Gooding-Williams 2009; Alston 2011; Roelofs 2014). The contemporary viability of Du Bois's and Fanon's analyses runs into drastic limits in these areas. It is not necessary to be on the whole in accord with their stances, however, to see that their conceptions of experience, normativity, value, the body, and culture yield vital insights into points of aesthetic method and into the grounds for aesthetic meaning that we actually and potentially have available to us. In both philosophers' cases, astute analyses of racial existence are of a piece with perspicacious views of aesthetic life. What these philosophers say about race is germane, in part, because of what it tells us about aesthetics. Likewise, their remarks on aesthetics are illuminating, in part, by virtue of the racial perspectives they thereby elaborate. Pressing problems with their accounts reverberate widely in their aesthetics and race theory. Nonetheless, the basic constituents of Du Bois's and Fanon's positions distilled here remain pertinent to critical work in both areas (see, e.g., Gooding-Williams 2006, 2009).

The themes Du Bois and Fanon foreground have also been broached by others, including Anna Julia Cooper (1998). She brings to the topics of culture building and aesthetic experience and standards an intersectional outlook, a stance that has been further developed by contemporary theorists of intersectionality in aesthetics.

Critical Race Feminist Aesthetics

Writers such as Cooper, Audre Lorde (1984), Gloria Anzaldúa (1987), and Angela Davis (1998) approach the entwinements of aesthetics and race from an intersectional perspective, that is, from a standpoint that takes note of the ways in which categories of race are inflected by other categories of difference, such as gender, class, sexuality, coloniality, ethnicity, nation, and ability, categories that they also qualify in turn. Twenty-first-century philosophers who understand the aesthetic functioning of race and the racial operations of aesthetics as fundamentally entangled with other categories of difference include Gooding-Williams (2006), James (2010), Roelofs (2014), and Taylor (2016). Given the pervasive operations of racialized aestheticization and aesthetic racialization, which also involve gendered, and class- and nation- modulated and modulating aestheticization and racialization (Roelofs 2014), a major theoretical program arises here. Highlighting a specific area of the broad field called critical race feminism, I want to signal explicitly the possibilities of and need for a critical race feminist aesthetics. By this I mean a line of investigation, at once practical and theoretical, that not only recognizes the troubled workings of the aesthetic in the areas of race, gender, and attendant orbits of social functioning, but also affirms the central role that aesthetic activities can and do play as elements of a simultaneously inventive and critical, collective engagement with modalities of race and gender, and with the registers of difference that intersect with these modalities, such as class and sexuality. This description offers a necessary, even if clearly not sufficient, condition for a critical race feminist aesthetics, a stance committed to thinking through the ties between aesthetics and race in their potential implications for a wide range of topics in the fields of culture and the arts, the humanities, and the sciences. As any practical and theoretical project of critique, the scope of this program is not circumscribable in the abstract, or apart from concrete historical moments and cultural or aesthetic locations, although, as my description

MONIQUE ROELOFS

suggests, we can identify a variety of themes and perspectives that arise, as I will do in the following.

Kara Walker: Aesthetic "Subtleties" as Racial "Subtleties"; Racial "Subtleties" as Aesthetic "Subtleties"

The complexity of our positioning in historical structures of racialized aestheticization and aesthetic racialization stands out clearly in the art of Kara Walker. Walker's work typically probes the ambivalences attendant on our racialized and racializing aesthetic positioning within historical matrices of culture, sexuality, and race (see Tang 2010) and, given the dual, practical, and theoretical aspirations of critical race feminist aesthetics, is fruitfully seen under this rubric. A recent example is the sculptural installation *A Subtlety, or the Marvelous Sugar Baby, an Homage to the unpaid and overworked Artisans who have refined our Sweet tastes from the cane fields to the Kitchens of the New World on the Occasion of the demolition of the Domino Sugar Refining Plant*, which Walker exhibited in the decommissioned Domino Sugar Refinery in Brooklyn, New York, in the summer of 2014 (Figures 26.1 and 26.2).

Figure 26.1 Kara Walker, Installation view: *At the behest of Creative Time Kara E. Walker has confected: A Subtlety, or the Marvelous Sugar Baby, an Homage to the unpaid and overworked Artisans who have refined our Sweet tastes from the cane fields to the Kitchens of the New World on the Occasion of the demolition of the Domino Sugar Refining Plant*, 2014. A project of Creative Time, Domino Sugar Refinery, Brooklyn, NY, May 10–July 6, 2014. © Kara Walker, courtesy of Sikkema Jenkins & Co., New York.

Photo: Jason Wyche.

Figure 26.2 Kara Walker, Installation view: *At the behest of Creative Time Kara E. Walker has confected: A Subtlety, or the Marvelous Sugar Baby, an Homage to the unpaid and overworked Artisans who have refined our Sweet tastes from the cane fields to the Kitchens of the New World on the Occasion of the demolition of the Domino Sugar Refining Plant,* 2014. A project of Creative Time, Domino Sugar Refinery, Brooklyn, NY, May 10–July 6, 2014. © Kara Walker, courtesy of Sikkema Jenkins & Co., New York.

Photo: Jason Wyche.

The piece consisted of a gigantic sugar-covered sphinx along with several far smaller, young, male attendants, made of dark-brown candy and resin. Donned with a kerchief, the statue prominently exposed her breasts and vulva for the viewer. The work played with the tensions and proximities between the cultivated and the uncultivated, white and brown, sexuality and work.

Walker's installation situated the viewer in an involved temporal web, marking the presence of historical labor routines in contemporary configurations of racialized and sexualized consumer taste. Not surprisingly, frictions arose as spectators' desires for mourning and protest came into conflict with their wish to craft their own forms of closeness to the spectacle and join the sculpture in a live performance partially of their own making, memorialized in selfies. Invoking an awareness of the violation and pain attendant on histories of economic commodification and sexual exploitation, and surrounding these feelings with elements of playfulness, satire, and humor, Walker's work underscores the intricate, or "subtle," spirals of meaning that we enact in the plane where aesthetics and race are mutually determinative of each other. Her art probes the images, emotional scenarios, and paths of identification informing sensuous economies of aesthetic racialization (gendering and class construction) and racialized (gendered and colonially inflected) aestheticization. She squarely situates the contemporary spectator within the historical regimes she investigates.

Our racial and aesthetic positions thereby take shape around highly charged signs, whose contemporary significance Walker holds up for reflection. In her 2010 graphite drawing *The moral arc of history ideally bends towards justice but just as soon as not curves back around toward barbarism, sadism, and unrestrained chaos* (Figure 26.3), Walker represents a public arena riddled with cruelty. Images of a burning cross, a rally of hooded KKK members, and a lynching crowd throng together with the figure of a black woman forced to perform fellatio on a white man, while holding the hand of another black woman. Amid this pandemonium, president Barack Obama stands in front of a lectern, delivering a speech.

Following Walker's comments on the work (Boucher 2012), the speech in question may be presumed to be the address on race Obama gave in Philadelphia in the spring of 2008. We can simultaneously see it as overlaid with themes found in other orations, however, especially in the presidential election victory speech made in Chicago, later that year, in which Obama used Martin Luther King Jr.'s famous metaphor of the arc of history, the trope on which Walker's title riffs, and that itself invokes the words of a nineteenth-century abolitionist.

Spatially, the drawing situates Obama in the very political sphere that he, as noted in the 2008 Philadelphia speech, has sought to move in the direction of a more perfect union. The work confronts the spectator with the sheer degree of brutality that renders the realization of social justice urgent. At the same time, the drawing points to the erosion of hopes for historical improvement centered on black icons such as Obama and King. The very forces that cry out for change come into play vehemently to quell the political efforts intended to achieve such change. Walker's work positions the viewer in a setting in which restrictions on the efficacy of official political action in a contemporary neoliberal state become visible. The drawing speaks to the power of iconic forms in

Figure 26.3 Kara Walker, *The moral arc of history ideally bends towards justice but just as soon as not curves back around toward barbarism, sadism, and unrestrained chaos*, 2010. Graphite and pastel on paper, 72 x 114 inches, 182.9 x 289.6 cm. © Kara Walker, courtesy of Sikkema Jenkins & Co., New York.

the political field—images of terror as well as images on which we stake our hopes for moral progress and our aspirations for ethical modes of address that will put an end to injustice. Highlighting the visual and affective dynamics of black iconicity (see Fleetwood 2011), Walker stresses their limits. She incites us to ponder society's investment in these images, while disturbing the binarism of ideal order and actual disorder informing aesthetic and political discourse.

Further Topics and Areas in Critical Race Feminist Aesthetics

The richness of critical race feminist aesthetics, in its practical and theoretical dimensions, stands out in Kara Walker's art. To further highlight the generativity of critical race feminist aesthetics, I will discuss several themes and areas within its scope.

Aesthetic Sustenance and Pleasure

Interconnected trajectories of racialized aestheticization and aesthetic racialization in many ways comprise vital kinds of well-being and sustenance, as Alice Walker makes clear in her famous essay, "In Search of Our Mothers' Gardens" (Walker 1983). Asking what it meant "for a black woman to be an artist in our grandmothers' time" (233), Walker celebrates a form of creativity that sustained her mother as she labored and raised a family in the US South at the beginning of the twentieth century. Working to keep her family afloat and to nourish her children under economically and emotionally exacting conditions, the mother was an avid storyteller, who told stories with an urgency that infected her daughter. In addition to this, the mother planted flowers, beautiful flowers, of many kinds, regardless of how shabby the house was that the family had to live in and no matter how rocky the soil turned out to be. Sunflowers would cover the holes in the walls. Accordingly, "even [Walker's] memories of poverty are seen through a screen of blooms—sunflowers, petunias, roses, dahlias, forsythia, spirea, delphiniums, verbena . . . and on and on. And I remember people coming to my mother's yard to be given cuttings from her flowers; I hear again the praise showered on her" (241). Explicitly reading her mother's creativity as a racialized practice, one that is shaped by gender and class, Walker describes a form of racialized aestheticization. This is a valuable tradition, one of which African American women, in Wlaker's view, should take explicit cognizance: knowing the socially grounded, personally and collectively vital creative capacities in question amounts to understanding "who, and of what, we black American women are" (235). Walker also emphasizes that it is necessary for black women artists of her own generation to identify with the "living creativity" they have inherited (237). This ability, she notes, is the creative spirit sustaining Phillis Wheatley, the anonymous quilters whose work is on display in the Smithsonian, as well as women who sing in church—makers who work in materials available to them (237–239). Walker, thus, outlines a valuable form of racialized aestheticization. This practice feeds into a process of aesthetic racialization.

Walker notes how her mother's habits of storytelling and gardening vitally nourished the mother's resilience and zeal for life. These aesthetic customs, accordingly, amount to a vibrant, indispensable form of aesthetic racialization: the mother's everyday artistic creativity has helped to render life livable to her. Further, the mother has passed on the creative impulse to her daughter. Walker recognizes her mother's creative capacity as a force within her own narrative art. Both daughter and mother, in Walker's narrative, participate in and propel a crucial strand of aesthetic racialization, carrying out a kind of intergenerational work that has linked together black women for a long time.

Given the social significance and economic power concentrated in processes of racialized aestheticization and aesthetic racialization these forces are subject to vehement debate. Kara Walker's works *The moral arc of history* and *A Subtlety* have occasioned intense polemics. Another set of controversies surrounds the dynamics of cultural appropriation.

Appropriation and Transculturation

In view of the widespread exchanges occurring across the bounds ordinarily ascribed to cultural traditions, the question arises: to what extent and under what conditions can ethically, politically, and aesthetically justifiable or even desirable forms of aesthetic racialization and racialized aestheticization traverse widely recognized cultural boundaries?

White Australian hip-hop celebrity Iggy Azalea (Amethyst Amelia Kelly) sings in what in common parlance is called a "blaccent." Adopting inflections and pronunciations connoting African American speech in the US South, she assumes for herself and her music a sound coded as black. Though her vocal style indexes some closeness to black lifeworlds, the sonic appearance she achieves does not necessarily register as black in a prosaically lived, richly experiential sense. Rather, she auditorily signals blackness as a corporately figured racial identity that is imagined to float freely from people's histories and bodies. By casting her lyrics in a transcultured black aesthetic form, Azalea participates in a mode of racialized aestheticization and invites her audience to do the same, namely, to draw for the public's self-fashioning on a repertoire of black idioms the global market makes available. Azalea's strategy of racialized aestheticization fuels a process of aesthetic racialization. As she infuses her music and persona with her black language, Azalea showcases an apparent proximity to black lifeworlds. The "blaccent's" racial connotations transfer to some extent to the star's artistic persona, investing it with positive, stereotyped features distilled from commercial images of US urban blackness, such as a sense of resilience, struggle, amicability, street-smarts, restraint, and cool, while filtering out a series of negative connotations.

Commentators accuse the star of co-opting blackness and appropriating a place that does not belong to her. They find fault with Azalea for failing to critique white privilege, and for a commercial exploitation of black women's "cultural performativity and forms of survival" in a system that side-rails their creativity, work, and needs (Cooper 2014). In view of the contemporary and historical abundance of contact across cultural boundaries (Hall 1994, 1996; Rogers 2006), the shifting and variable conditions for artistic production (Tate 2003), the for a select group highly lucrative institutionalization of hip-hop performances of black authenticity (Fleetwood 2011), and the relevance of multiple values and grounds for appeals to authenticity by which we can appraise putative cases of appropriation (Taylor 2016), proprietary notions of cultural registers reveal their limits in adjudicating the tenability of Azalea's vocal style. Indeed, we cannot straightforwardly assess procedures and sources of racialized aestheticization and aesthetic racialization in terms of conceptions of cultures as bounded entities. Azalea, furthermore, may be participating in a musical order in which claims to authentic enactments of aesthetic and racial subjectivity have come into question, a system that itself can be productive of new forms of critical cultural agency. Nonetheless, Azalea's strategy in several respects would appear to forego a commitment to an aesthetic politics purporting to critically transform invidious conditions of racialization and gendered imbalances of power on which she relies.

Noting that it is considered acceptable for the Rolling Stones to perform "'black' blues music" and implying that she should be given the same moral and aesthetic leeway that we supposedly unquestioningly grant to Keith Richards and Mick Jagger (Monroe 2013), Azalea indicates that she sees hip-hop as an art that is open to everyone, regardless of a person's racial background. Even if Azalea is correct that what it is fine for other whites to do, it is okay for her to do, the mere fact that others do it, or somehow escape being under fire for it (though this is debatable in the Stones' case [see Taylor 2016: 177–178]), of course, doesn't mean it really is right.

A contradiction in the star's position is that she combines a narrowly racialized notion of rap as demanding an African American vocal style ("it feels weird" to rap with an Australian accent [Monroe 2013]) with a pragmatic, self-serving notion of her own participation in the art. Azalea claims that as an artist she should have the "creative rein" to do whatever she wishes with her voice. Race, clearly, both does and does not count for her.

Fluidly shifting between racialized and postracial notions of music, Azalea downplays hip-hop's political dimension ("This is the entertainment industry. It's not politics" [Monroe 2013]). Her aesthetic politics of expedience serves herself, rather than (also) being conspicuously other-directed, targeting objectionable social structures, and seeking to answer to the needs and aspirations of the communities on whose cultural repertoires her transculturating modes are drawing.

And yet, the opportunistic aesthetic of Azalea's music doesn't supply the full story of the politics of her work, because uptake and context are indispensable ingredients of aesthetically engendered political meaning. The notions of racialized aestheticization and aesthetic racialization enable us to recognize moral, aesthetic, and political possibilities inherent in the deployment of what are considered others' cultural forms, while simultaneously acknowledging the complex, granular cultural forces, stances, and developments shaping given situations.

Aesthetics, Race, and the Everyday

Interlinked processes of aesthetic racialization and racialized aestheticization, as I have indicated, take shape around quotidian phenomena, including dress, architecture, design, narration, adornment, sugar, iconic images, and vocal styles. In contemplating the scope of collaborations and tensions between aesthetics and race and in thinking through their ethical, political, aesthetic, and economic potentialities, it is important to work with an adequately broad notion of the aesthetic.

The aesthetic is at work in all cultural arenas, as well as in our environments, both natural and humanly produced. Situating art in everyday life, the philosopher John Dewey (1934) underscored the encompassing reach of aesthetic matters. But broad conceptions of the aesthetic have been gaining traction among philosophers (Korsmeyer 1999; Saito 2007; Roelofs 2009, 2014; Kelly 2014; Taylor 2016) and cultural and literary theorists (Anzaldúa 1987; Jameson 1998; Johnson 1998; Moten 2003; Felski 2005). The aesthetic brings its manifold, sweeping presence to the realm of race. Given the ample, heterogeneous scope of aesthetic phenomena, we can expect them to encapsulate myriad racializing impulses.

Our conception of racial existence, likewise, will have to be adequately expansive and comprehensive to lend recognition to the fine-grained and wide-ranging ways in which aesthetic elements shape and are shaped by racial meanings, experiences, values, and forms.

The work by Kara Walker, Alice Walker, and Iggy Azalea I have discussed, along with the theoretical approaches by post- and decolonial theorists, philosophers of race, and critical race feminist aestheticians testify to the breadth and the intricacy of the entwinements of aesthetics and race in the planes of art, culture, and the quotidian organization of our lifeworlds.

Toward a Revised Repertoire of Aesthetic Concepts

Everyday social and material practices draw on aesthetic concepts. In other words, these practices deploy value-laden, sensory/experiential categories that structure aesthetic apprehension and meaning. Two aesthetic concepts that have received a good deal of attention for their operations within stratagems of racial perception and embodiment are beauty (West 1982; Du Bois 1986a; Johnson 1998; Taylor 1999, 2016; Cheng 2000; Roelofs 2014) and the sublime (Armstrong 1996; Gooding-Williams 2009). However, looking closely at strategies of bodily performance, forms of cultural engagement, and the multiple kinds of pleasure, invention, and critique that these modes introduce to our aesthetically mediated relationships with people and things, scholars have recently proposed new understandings of a range of aesthetic concepts, including those of the excessive, the comical, shine, the superficial, the zany, the cute, and the interesting (Cheng 2011a, 2011b; Fleetwood 2011; Ngai 2012). These theorists (to varying degrees, and at different levels of explicitness) have given these concepts a role in organizing the mutual imbrications of aesthetic and racial experiences, actions, and pleasures. Alerting us to qualities featured in non-Western traditions, including Japanese canons, and in artforms marginalized in the West, including Chicana visual art, scholars, further highlight the potentialities of categories such as those of the imperfect, the transient (Saito 2007), and the ephemeral (Pérez 2007). Given the hand that variable and evolving sets of aesthetic concepts have in trajectories of racialized aestheticization and aesthetic racialization, the organization these processes involve may be expected to shift from context to context, though, given the reach that aesthetic concepts, and especially vernacular ones, typically have *across* artforms, genres, and traditions (see Ngai 2012), unsuspected correspondences can also be anticipated.

We uphold racial constellations in the form of architectural infrastructures, stratagems of bodily and national policing, regimes of literacy, divisions of labor, patterns of environmental destruction and adjustment to climate change, artistic and theoretical canons, and curatorial and performance practices. As we explore how aesthetic routines participate in these and other racial formations, quite likely, additional pertinent aesthetic concepts and different kinds of sensory/experiential schemes undergirding modes of aesthetic creation, reception, and interaction will come to light.

Conclusion

The conception of interlinking processes of racialized aestheticization and aesthetic racialization I have elaborated in several cases and contexts illuminates the simultaneously aesthetic and racial dynamics of subject and culture formation. This view helps us to uncover the ways in which current entanglements of aesthetics and race take shape against the background of already existing interconnections. It elucidates how contemporary forms may channel or redirect historical forces, while also giving rise to new constellations. Not in the least, this outlook clarifies the depth and complexity with which aesthetic modalities fashion race, and race shapes the aesthetic.

Work on the entwinements of aesthetics and race sheds philosophical light on facets of experience, normativity, embodiment, and value. Exploring these dimensions, artists and theorists offer new conceptions of cultural life. Repertoires of aesthetic concepts are in motion. Interactions and overlaps between aesthetic and racial phenomena occur persistently across a host of divergent areas of analysis and praxis. This situation calls for the open-ended projects of a critical race feminist aesthetics, an agenda that remains on the look-out for the unpredictable, historically contingent, epistemic, political, and ethical forms that aesthetic meanings may give to race and that race can give to aesthetic existence.

Related Topics

Framing Intersectionality, Phenomenology and Race

References

Alston, V. R. (2011) "Cosmopolitan Fantasies, Aesthetics, and Bodily Value: W.E.B. Du Bois's *Dark Princess* and the Trans/Gendering of Kautilya." *Journal of Transnational American Studies* 3, no. 1. http://escholarship.org/uc/item/8r74n6wq.

Anzaldúa, G. (1987) *Borderlands/La Frontera: The New Mestiza*, San Francisco: Aunt Lute.

Armstrong, M. (1996) "'The Effects of Blackness': Gender, Race, and the Sublime in Aesthetic Theories of Burke and Kant." *Journal of Aesthetics and Art Criticism* 54, no. 3: 213–236.

Bernasconi, R. (1998) "Hegel at the Court of the 'Ashanti'," in S. Barnett (ed.), Hegel after Derrida, New York: Routledge, pp. 41–63.

Bhabha, H. K. (1994) *The Location of Culture*, New York: Routledge.

Boucher, B. (2012) "Kara Walker Artwork Censored at Newark Library." *Art in America Newsletter*, December 11. www.artinamericamagazine.com/news-features/news/kara-walker-newark-library/.

Burke, E. (1990) *A Philosophical Enquiry Into the Origin of Our Ideas of the Sublime and the Beautiful*, ed. A. Phillips, Oxford: Oxford University Press.

Cheng, A. A. (2000) "Wounded Beauty: An Exploratory Essay on Race, Feminism, and the Aesthetic Question." *Tulsa Studies in Women's Literature* 19, no. 2: 191–217.

———. (2011a) *Second Skin: Josephine Baker and the Modern Surface*, Oxford: Oxford University Press.

———. (2011b) "Shine: on Race, Glamour, and the Modern." *PMLA* 126, no. 4: 1022–1041.

Chow, Rey. (1998) "The Politics of Admittance: Female Sexual Agency, Miscegenation, and the Formation of Community in Frantz Fanon," in *Ethics After Idealism: Theory-Culture-Ethnicity-Reading*, Bloomington: Indiana University Press.

Cooper, A. J. (1998) "The Negro as Presented in American Literature," in Charles Lemert and Esme Bhan (eds.), *The Voice of Anna Julia Cooper*, Lanham: Rowman & Littlefield.

Cooper, B. (2014) "Iggy Azalea's Post-Racial Mess: America's Oldest Race-Tale, Remixed." *Salon*, July 15. www.salon.com.

Davis, A. Y. (1998) *Blues Legacies and Black Feminism: Gertrude "Ma" Rainey, Bessie Smith, and Billy Holiday*, New York: Random House.

Du Bois, W.E.B. (1904) "The Development of a People." *International Journal of Ethics* 14, no. 3 (April): 292–311.

———. (1971a) "African Culture," in Du Bois (1971d), pp. 464–484.

———. (1971b) "History of the Black Artisan From Africa to Emancipation," sections 2–4, in Du Bois (1971d), pp. 334–353.

———. (1971c) "The Negro in Literature and Art," in Du Bois (1971d), pp. 447–452.

———. (1971d) *The Seventh Son: The Thought and Writings of W.E.B. Du Bois*, Vol. 1, ed. J. Lester, New York: Random House.

———. (1986a) "Criteria of Negro Art," in Du Bois (1986e), pp. 993–1002.

———. (1986b) *The Souls of Black Folk*, in Du Bois (1986e), pp. 357–547.

———. (1986c) "The Sorrow Songs," in Du Bois (1986e), pp. 536–547.

———. (1986d) "Of the Training of Black Men," in Du Bois (1986e), pp. 424–438.

———. (1986e) *Writings*, ed. N. Higgins, New York: Library of America.

Eze, E.C. (1994) "The Color of Reason: The Idea of Race in Kant's Anthropology," in K.M. Faull (ed.), *Anthropology and the German Enlightenment: Perspectives on Humanity*, Lewisburg, PA: Bucknell University Press, pp. 200–241.

——— (ed.). (1997) *Race and the Enlightenment: A Reader*. Malden, MA: Blackwell.

Fanon, F. (1963) *The Wretched of the Earth*, trans. C. Farrington, New York: Grove.

———. (1967) *Black Skin, White Masks*, trans. C. L. Markmann, New York: Grove.

Felski, R. (2005) "The Role of Aesthetics in Cultural Studies," in M. Bérubé (ed.), *The Aesthetics of Cultural Studies*, Malden, MA: Blackwell, pp. 28–43.

Fleetwood, N.R. (2011) *Troubling Vision: Performance, Visuality, and Blackness*, Chicago: University of Chicago Press.

Gilroy, P. (1993) *The Black Atlantic: Modernity and Double Consciousness*, Cambridge, MA: Harvard University Press.

Gooding-Williams R. (2006) *Look A Negro! Philosophical Essays on Race, Culture and Politics*, New York: Routledge.

———. (2009) *In the Shadow of Du Bois: Afro-Modern Political Thought in America*, Cambridge, MA: Harvard University Press.

Hall, S. (1994) "Cultural Identity and Diaspora," in P. Williams and L. Chrisman (eds.), *Colonial Discourse and Post-Colonial Theory: A Reader*, New York: Columbia University Press, pp. 392–403.

———. (1996) "What Is This 'Black' in Black Popular Culture?" in D. Morley and K. Chen (eds.), *Stuart Hall: Critical Dialogues in Cultural Studies*, New York: Routledge, pp. 465–475.

James, R. (2010) *The Conjectural Body: Gender, Race, and the Philosophy of Music*, Totowa, NJ: Lexington Books.

Jameson, F. (1998) *The Cultural Turn: Selected Writings on the Postmodern 1983–1998*, London: Verso.

Johnson, B. (1998) *The Feminist Difference: Literature, Psychoanalysis, Race, and Gender*, Cambridge, MA: Harvard University Press.

Kant, Immanuel. (1951) *Critique of Judgment*, trans. J.H. Bernard, New York: Palgrave Macmillan.

Kelly, M. (2014) "Preface to the Second Edition," in M. Kelly (ed.), *The Encyclopedia of Aesthetics*, 2nd edition, Oxford: Oxford University Press, pp. xxi–xxx.

Korsmeyer, C. (1998) "Perceptions, Pleasures, Arts: Considering Aesthetics," in J.A. Kourany (ed.), *Philosophy in a Feminist Voice: Critiques and Reconstructions*, Princeton: Princeton University Press, pp. 145–172.

———. (1999) *Making Sense of Taste: Food and Philosophy*, Ithaca: Cornell University Press.

Lorde, A. (1984) *Sister Outsider: Essays and Speeches*, Freedom, CA: The Crossing.

Mignolo, W.D. (2007) "Delinking: The Rhetoric of Modernity, the Logic of Coloniality, and the Grammar of De-Coloniality." *Cultural Studies* 21, nos. 2–3: 449–514.

Monroe, J. (2013) "The Low End Theory." Interview with Iggy Azalea. *Complex Magazine*, September 16. www.complex.com/music/2013/09/iggy-azalea-interview-complex-cover-story.

Moten, F. (2003) *In the Break: The Aesthetics of the Black Radical Tradition*, Minneapolis: University of Minnesota Press.
Ngai, S. (2012) *Our Aesthetic Categories: Zany, Cute, Interesting*, Cambridge, MA: Harvard University Press.
Pérez, L. E. (2007) *Chicana Art: The Politics of Spiritual and Aesthetic Altarities*, Durham: Duke University Press.
Roelofs, M. (ed.). (2009) "Aesthetics and Race: New Philosophical Perspectives," special volume 2 of *Contemporary Aesthetics*. www.contempaesthetics.org.
Roelofs, M. (2014) *The Cultural Promise of the Aesthetic*, New York: Bloomsbury.
Rogers, R. A. (2006) "From Cultural Exchange to Transculturation: A Review and Reconceptualization of Cultural Appropriation." *Communication Theory* 16, no. 4: 474–503.
Saito, Y. (2007) *Everyday Aesthetics*, Oxford: Oxford University Press.
Spivak, G. C. (1999) *A Critique of Postcolonial Reason: Toward a History of the Vanishing Present*, Cambridge, MA: Harvard University Press.
———. (2012) *An Aesthetic Education in the Era of Globalization*, Cambridge, MA: Harvard University Press.
Tang, A. (2010) "Postmodern Repetitions: Parody, Trauma, and the Case of Kara Walker." *differences* 21, no. 1: 142–172.
Tate, G. (2003) *Everything but the Burden: What White People are Taking from Black Culture*, New York: Broadway Books.
Taylor, P. C. (1999) "Malcolm's Conk and Danto's Colors; or, Four Logical Petitions Concerning Race, Beauty, and Aesthetics." *Journal of Aesthetics and Art Criticism* 57, no. 1: 16–20.
———. (2016) *Black Is Beautiful: A Philosophy of Black Aesthetics*, Malden, MA: Blackwell.
Walker, A. (1983) "In Search of Our Mothers' Gardens," in *In Search of Our Mothers' Gardens: Womanist Prose by Alice Walker*, San Diego: Harcourt Brace Jovanovich.
West, C. (1982) "A Genealogy of Modern Racism," in *Prophesy Deliverance! Towards an Afro-American Revolutionary Christianity*, Philadelphia: Westminster Press.
Wynter, S. (1992) "Rethinking 'Aesthetics': Notes Towards a Deciphering Practice," in M. Cham (ed.), *Ex-Iles: Essays on Caribbean Cinema*, Trenton, NJ: Africa World Press, pp. 237–279.

27
JOKING ABOUT RACE AND ETHNICITY
Stephanie Patridge

What makes a racial or ethnic joke racist? Some might think that this very question relies on a confusion: jokes can't be racist, because they are a non-serious form of entertainment. When we tell or are amused by a joke, the thought goes, we are *only joking* (Connolly and Heydar 2005: 126). Two features of our practice of telling and being amused by jokes might be taken to support this thought. First, so-called racist jokes are sometimes told by members of the targeted group (e.g., Jewish folks tell Jew jokes, Polish folks tell "Polack" jokes, and African Americans tell black jokes). Second, we sometimes find jokes about racial or ethnic groups to which we don't belong funny, despite the fact that we don't believe that the joke's target is as the joke "says" it is. Consider, for example, the world's shortest joke: *Two Irishmen walk out of a pub*. Clearly, one needn't have any anti-Irish sentiment to find this joke funny. We need only be aware of a stereotype about Irish drinking habits to get the joke and find it funny.

Still, even the most stringent amoralist about jokes acknowledges that sometimes a joke isn't "just a joke" (Connolly and Heydar 2005). Our Irish joke, for example, might be told *because* the joker sees the Irish as a bunch of worthless drunks. Even worse, it might be told to an Irish youth in order to denigrate the youth because they are Irish. Most would agree that in cases like these the "joke" is racist as it is motivated by the joke teller's own personal racism, however we make sense of this, and it is made worse when it is deployed to harm. Observations like this might lead us to think that a particular joke-telling is racist just in case it is an expression of personal racism. In all other cases, a joke is just a joke.

Some philosophers of race will be attracted to a proposal like this because it relies on a conception of "racism" that is tied to an individual's actual attitudes (Garcia 2001) or beliefs (Appiah 1990). But, in our ordinary practice the term "racist" is applied in a more variable way by, particularly by those who are its victims, so as to include actions, social policies, and institutions when they operate to sustain and perpetuate racism (Blum 2002; Zack 1998). On this view, some actions are racist even though the agent is neither themselves racist, nor culpable for their action (indeed there need be no agent). Though I don't have space to argue the point here, I'm inclined to follow this more homely use of the term "racist" and include those activities, both personal and institutional, that perpetuate and sustain it among the things that we can properly call racist, and to reject a search for a univocal, reductive account of "racist" in favor of this more variegated account. My first goal here is to think through the various conditions under which telling and being amused by a racial or ethnic joke meets our ordinary conception of an act's being racist. I first consider empirical evidence that supports the claim that some tellings of a racial or ethnic joke harms the joke's target. Then, I consider some evidence to support the common suspicion that sometimes our joking and being amused is an expression of implicit bias and so an expression of personal racism. Finally, I'll offer a justification for another common thought, that there are some racial and ethnic jokes that white people simply shouldn't tell because their telling is racist, which is independent of issues of personal racism and harm. In closing, I'll consider a pragmatic objection to the variegated and permissive account of "racist" that I rely on, namely that we should reserve the term "racist" for the most egregious of acts so as to better eliminate all racist activities.

Jokes That Harm

Some claim that jokes aimed at historically oppressed groups promote prejudice and pernicious forms of discrimination (Blum 2002: 20; Carroll 2014: 242). For example, since African Americans have been and continue to be subject to widespread and diverse forms of unjust racial discrimination, both personal and institutional, it stands to reason that jokes that target them will support, sustain, and perpetuate such discrimination. Though some deny our ability to substantiate such claims (Cohen 1999: 9), there is a growing body of literature that shows that sometimes racial and ethnic jokes have this effect. For example, a Canadian study found that subjects rated Newfoundlanders, who are typically stereotyped as "dumb, as significantly more inept, foolish, dim-witted, and slow" after they read a series of "Newfie" jokes (Mail et al. 1934). More recent studies show that jokes about women (Ford et al. 2004, 2008; Romero-Sanchez et al. 2010) increase discrimination in subjects who score high for anti-female prejudice. This same effect has been shown to hold for jokes about Muslims among those who score high for anti-Muslim prejudice (Ford et al. 2014). Researchers hypothesize that this effect holds for any group about which society has "ambivalent attitudes," because prejudice is becoming unacceptable. In the United States, this includes many racial and ethnic groups, as well as sexual and gender groups. When the relevant prejudice is in a state of becoming unacceptable, the thinking goes, those who score high for the relevant prejudice tend to self-censor and not act on their prejudice. And jokes seem to be distinctive here. Similar subjects who read an anti-Muslim statement, instead of a joke, demonstrate no increased willingness to discriminate against Muslims. Jokes have a distinctive power to release prejudice into action (Ford et al. 2014).

Though researchers caution that we should avoid inferring too much from this data, as they don't know how significant or long lasting the effect is, that the subject reads a joke alone in lab conditions seems to gives us significant reason to be troubled by this phenomenon. Since humor is mostly enjoyed in groups, among those with whom we are comfortable enough to crack a joke, we might expect to find an even greater effect when the joke is told, say, in the pub among friends, rather than to ourselves in a lab. We might even find that the effect in these conditions holds for those who score lower for the relevant prejudice. Unfortunately, it isn't clear how we would design an experiment to test the effects of jokes in their natural habitat. The upshot of all of this is that we should avoid telling jokes that target certain racial and ethnic groups because doing so runs the risk of harming members of the joke's targeted group by promoting discrimination against them. To the extent that it is likely that such jokes will issue in these sorts of racial or ethnic harms, telling them is racist. Still, it is clear that there is more work to be done here.

Joking to Ally

Some whites might agree with everything I have said thus far, yet insist that they sometimes tell racial and ethnic jokes that don't express their personal racism, and don't perpetuate it. For example, whites sometimes tell racial or ethnic jokes to members of the targeted group to signal that they are not racist; they are friends and allies. My white students, for example, report telling black jokes to their African American friends with just such an intention. Some philosophers, however, point out that such jokes are likely to offend (Blum 2002; Mills 1987; Phillips 1984; Rodriguez 2014) and that we have a standing moral obligation to avoid sensitive subjects that will offend others unless we have a good moral reason for so doing (Phillips 1984). I'm not so sure. While we do avoid causing others offense, I'm not sure that this is always a *moral* requirement. Standup comedians, for example, consistently offend. Do they do something immoral? I doubt it. I suspect that our standing requirement to avoid offending others is a requirement of etiquette that in some cases becomes a moral one. So, if we are to rely on "causing offense" as a central normative notion here, we'll want to know if these jokes offend in a way that makes them racist. Some have argued that these kinds of offenses are distinctive because they are particularly hard to shake off. Such jokes target individuals *qua* members of a group, which makes them less personal, and more alienating, frustrating, and demeaning. For this reason they are both more harmful than other kinds of denigration humor, and they harm individuals *qua* members of a racial or ethnic group (Mills 1987; Rodriguez 2014). So, this line of reasoning continues, joking about race and ethnicity in multiracial or ethnic contexts is racist because it "perpetuates and sustains racism."

Still, some might insist that even if we accept this line of reasoning, sometimes whites can be fairly sure that no one will be offended. For example, my white students report that their friends of color join in the racial and ethnic joke telling, and this supports their contention that there is no offense in *these* cases. This certainly seems possible. But, we should be cautious about these sorts of inferences as there are powerful disincentives to complaining about racial or ethnic jokes, particularly for those who are members of the targeted group. Such jokes place an offended target in one of two positions: either stop the fun and be a killjoy, or let it go and take the offense "willingly." If the target decides to cry foul, the joker is likely to respond by saying things like "come on, I'm only joking. You know I'm not racist." This shifts the critical burden back to the offended, thereby undermining the legitimacy of their offense by challenging that it is ill grounded. Once the target has been put on their heels by this, they are now responsible for providing a cogent moral justification for the offense that either accuses a friend of racism or demonstrates that the offense is warranted, say, by proving that the joke is racist even if the teller isn't. Those who are commonly the target of denigration humor, for example, members of oppressed racial, ethnic, sexual, and gender groups, know all too well the consequences of complaint, and no doubt, "joining in the fun" is often a calculated decision to "take the offense willingly"; it just isn't worth it. For these reasons, this sort of joking often undermines the very bond that whites are trying to build. Hence, whites have fairly robust moral reasons to avoid telling racial and ethnic jokes in the presence of a member of the targeted group, as doing so may be racist. And, whatever reasons that whites might think that they have to tell such jokes—for example, it secures their status as allies—may very well be undercut (sometimes unbeknownst to them) as the joke backfires.

Still, even if the joke succeeds and no one is offended some empirical evidence suggests that jokes like this invoke stereotype threat. In one study, for example, blonde women scored lower on intelligence tests after having read a series of dumb blonde jokes (Seibt and Forster 2004) and it seems reasonable to think that a similar effect might hold for racial and ethnic jokes. Here again, however, it isn't clear how widespread or long-lasting the effect is. Still, since, whites cannot be sure that their friends of color are not offended or otherwise harmed by their racial and ethnic joking, they should avoid doing so because it might very well be racist.

Racial Jokes Without Malicious Will or Harm

Now, I'd like to set aside issues of personal racism and harm to ask a different question: are there some racial and ethnic jokes that white people shouldn't tell because it would be racist to do so irrespective of issues of personal racism and harm? To help see our way through this concern, consider the following guiding scenario: a group of white college students entertain each other by telling racial and ethnic jokes about groups to which they do not belong, including Hispanic jokes, African American jokes, and Jewish jokes. Further, consider that they honestly believe that they don't hold prejudicial attitudes toward any of the groups; they believe that they are just riffing on a theme. Moreover, though they think there is nothing wrong with entertaining each other in this way in principle, they would never tell *these sorts of jokes* in the presence of members of the targeted group because they honestly wouldn't want to hurt anyone. Are there resources to support the thought that their telling and being amused by these jokes in this context is racist?

Some might worry that my guiding scenario is at worst impossible and at best highly implausible, because in order to find racial and ethnic jokes funny at all, one must hold the relevant stereotype (de Sousa 1987; Bergmann 1986; Rodriguez 2014). But, our Irish joke suggests that in at least some cases one need only be aware that there is such a stereotype to find a joke funny. And, given that members of the targeted group seem to tell the very same jokes as a genuine expression of irony (Carroll 2014: 242), it seems at least conceptually possible that our white colleagues could do so as well. Still, we should grant that the likelihood of this scenario is lessened given the well-established fact that we live in white supremacist culture that subjects us to implicit biases that reflect its pernicious, racio-ethnic, hierarchical norms. There is overwhelming scientific evidence to demonstrate that we are subject to such biases (see, for example, Kelly and Roedder 2008; Kirwan Institute 2013, 2014). Though they are not accessible to us through introspection, racial and ethnic biases have a measureable and significant impact on our beliefs, affective attitudes, reasoning, and actions. This, no doubt, adds significant weight to the inductive inference that our white students are doing more than just joking. That is, it seems reasonable to suspect, as no doubt many will, that *these* jokers find *these* particular jokes funny (at least partially) because they have implicit, negative biases against the groups in question, and so what we have here probably isn't the good-natured fun that our white students think.

Little work has been done on the relationship between implicit biases and jokes. However, one study shows that those who score high for implicit racial bias against African Americans laugh harder at jokes about African Americans when told by a white comedian than those who scored lower for such bias (Lynch 2010). Adding to this, there is striking empirical evidence that shows that our implicit biases affect our attitudes and behaviors in other play contexts, such as video games and other virtual activities (Correll et al. 2002, 2007; Eastwick and Gardner 2008; Sadler et al. 2012). Further, given that we acquire implicit biases from cultural cues and messages that we receive via an unconscious process, conjoined with our earlier evidence that suggested that jokes put us in a non-critical mindset (Ford et al. 2013), we might worry that this activity of joke telling, particularly as it is among colleagues, will operate to strengthen implicit biases. So, telling these jokes in this context, unbeknownst to the jokers, may very well be an expression of personal, implicit racism and it may serve to further perpetuate it. Again, more work needs to be done here.

Granting the important role that implicit bias and issues of harm will undoubtedly play in a further developed account of racist jokes, I'd like to return to the question that I articulated at the outset of this section: might the telling of racial and ethnic jokes in the guiding case be racist independent of any connection to personal racism (explicit or implicit) or any attendant harms? That is, might the telling and being amused by these jokes in this context simply be racist? I think that answering this question is important for two reasons. First, it provides a fuller accounting of the normative considerations in play when we joke about race and ethnicity; not only in the context of jokes, but in other contexts where one would be inclined to say things like "I'm only kidding." And, since it is at least *possible*, even if we think unlikely, that our colleagues don't hold the relevant stereotypes even implicitly (again, our Irish joke suggests this) and, even if we could be convinced that they don't have such biases, at the very least I think that we would still have significant reservations about these jokes. I'd like to know why. Second, tracing out this line of reasoning may have a pragmatic benefit. As psychological strategy for evading criticism, whites are likely to acknowledge the empirical evidence on implicit biases and harm, yet underestimate the possibility of harm in their case while over-estimating their own lack of bias and imperviousness to acquiring or strengthening them. *They* are only kidding, and *everyone* knows it. So, if we pursue the issue of racist jokes to reduce the practice, then as a practical matter we should ask whether there is an argument not based in personal racism or harm, as this will be more convincing to whites.

Are there such resources? Philosophers of humor have largely ignored this question. So, we'll have to look elsewhere for normative resources to justify our discomfort with a scenario like this one. One place we might look is to the work being done on slurs in the philosophy of language. For example, we might be inclined toward a kind of prohibitionism about jokes modeled on the work of Luvell Anderson and Ernie Lepore on racial slurs (Anderson and Lepore 2013). Following their lead, we might think that the telling and being amused by a racial or ethnic joke is racist just in case members of the targeted group would prohibit it. While there is a lot to like about a view like this, not the least of which is that it shifts the normative power to the target, I see two worries as it applies to jokes. First is a bad faith worry. We can imagine a group that doesn't prohibit the relevant jokes because they have internalized pernicious, racialized messages about what kind of treatment is due to them. In a case like this, I doubt that we'd want to say that their mere failure to prohibit alters the fact that the jokes are racist. So, even if prohibitionism is on target, we'll still need more normative resources to capture a case like this. Second, we might worry that members of the targeted group aren't monolithic, and so it is hard to see what exactly is (or would be) prohibited by members of a group, particularly in joking contexts. Remember that some of my white students believe that they have permission, granted by their African American friends, to tell black jokes. And it is at least possible that they have such permission. But, I suspect there is still something to criticize here.

Ted Cohen suggests that these sorts of jokes bother us because they remind us that there are such stereotypes, which is something tragic (Cohen 1999: 80–81). On the basis of this, we might be inclined towards view of racial jokes modeled on the work of Elizabeth Camp on racial slurs (Camp 2013). Following her lead, we might think that the telling and being amused by a racial joke is racist just in case members of the joke telling group are made to "feel complicit in the speaker's way of thinking" (Camp 2013: 333). There is much to like about the resources we get from a view like Camp's, in particular it provides substantive moral reasons to avoid telling such jokes even if they are not told in the presence a member of the targeted group. But, it won't capture the joke-event that we consider here, as in our case no one is bothered. Our students' knowledge of the relevant stereotypes is the very presumption of their attempt at ironic joke telling; it is precisely what they find funny (or, so they claim).

On my view, what makes the telling of these jokes racist is that the activity expresses something like what Blum calls a public meaning (Blum 2002: 16–18), or what I have elsewhere called an incorrigible social meaning (Patridge 2011, 2013). Consider that our acts can be communicative: they can express or signal messages to others. These messages are *social* in that they come as a result of being deployed in a particular social world that has a particular social reality (both historical and current), so are local. They are *incorrigible* in that they cannot be altered by a mere act of will on our part, say by an attempt at ironic deployment. To help see this point, consider, an uncontroversial example, a person from the United States who gives the "A-Okay" gesture (when the index finger and the thumb form a closed circle) in Latin America—as Nixon mistakenly did in the '50s—not realizing that in this context its meaning is roughly that of giving someone the finger in the United States. Upon seeing this mistake, a friend might warn the clueless US citizen "don't do that here, it doesn't mean what you think it does." The meaning of this gesture is socially local and incorrigible. I take this to point to be perfectly familiar.

The fact that some acts express an incorrigible social meaning might help us to see racism that we might otherwise not. To help us see these resources as they apply to race more clearly, let us consider an example that I have mentioned elsewhere: a political cartoon that simianizes Desmond Tutu in order to criticize him (2013). Such an image is properly interpreted as racist. Obviously there is nothing intrinsically wrong with representing humans in animal form. The image of Desmond Tutu is racist because the context in which it is deployed is one in which Africans, those of African descent, and other disempowered racial and ethnic groups have been systematically demeaned by representing them as monkeys. Were the artist to respond to such charges by claiming that she intended to slight Tutu only personally, not racially, the image would still express a racist meaning because of the social context in which the image is deployed. The cartoon simply looks too much like images that have operated and continue to operate to systematically oppress those of African descent for this meaning to be resisted. So, we can reasonably say to the artist, "Look, I know you didn't mean it. But, you shouldn't depict people of color like that. It's racist."

How does this help us see the racism of our college students' jokes? Well, like the image of Desmond Tutu, some racial jokes express an incorrigible social meaning that is racist. Consider, for example, that white supremacy has been historically maintained, in part, by stereotyping members of racial and ethnic minorities in ways that makes them the proper object of mocking and humiliation, for example, that Jews have big noses, that African Americans are prone to crime, and that Hispanics are lazy. Further, jokes that trade on these sorts of stereotypes have historically played a role in this subjugation: whites have told and continue to tell them as an expression of an attitude of racial superiority. And, these sorts of jokes have historically served to maintain a pernicious, racialized social hierarchy: those who are the proper target for denigration humor on the bottom, and those who are entitled to tell such jokes on the top. Joseph Boskin (1987) helpfully makes a similar point about the Sambo character. When members of a group that occupies a privileged social position on the racio-ethnic social hierarchy, that is, whites, tell racial and ethnic jokes about members of groups that occupy positions on the social hierarchy that make them in the words of Charles Mills "subpersons" (1998), that is, persons of color, then these sorts of historical, contextual facts are relevant for understanding what the joke expresses, means, or is about (Hornsby 2000: 89–91). Like the cartoon of Desmond Tutu and the A-Okay sign in Latin America, our white students' jokes simply look too much like the perniciously told ones to not express a racist meaning.

Still, one might object that in the guiding case no one interprets the jokes in this way. While, in our A-Okay and cartoon of Desmond Tutu cases, individuals interpreted them as offensive (or, at the very least, warned that in public contexts they will be offensive). But, our jokers have, as it were, created a niche community where there is no one to interpret them as racist. Since, their jokes are not public in the relevant way; they are just jokes. This is, I think, a difficult challenge. Still, I don't think that what the joke expresses necessarily hangs on how people in fact interpret it. An act can express something pernicious, even when no one involved realizes that it does. For example, a male boss patting a female employee on her rear end might express contempt for women in the workplace, and so be sexist, even if neither of them realizes it because they don't have the conceptual repertoire of sexual harassment available to them (Hanslanger 2012). And, the case might be strengthened by considering our reactions to recent examples of white college students discovered in blackface. We find these sorts of activities offensive even though we often grant that the students don't intend to express contempt for African Americans, that is, they are just joking in this sense, and they don't have the requisite knowledge about the history of blackface to see why others would be offended (which they probably don't). Still, their wearing of blackface for entertainment has an incorrigible social meaning because it is deployed in a friend group that is situated in a wider cultural context. This cultural context is one that includes that actual contingent, history of racial oppression perpetuated by white actors playing that part of black characters in offensive ways while wearing of black face. Like whites in blackface, whites ironically telling black jokes unintentionally express a racist message, and for this reason their jokes are racist.

While I think that the analogy with blackface is helpful to convince us that appealing to the incorrigible social meaning of an action can help us to the see its racism, I also think that much more needs to be said about norms of interpretation to make the case more convincing. Specifically, we need to settle the question of what makes a meaning incorrigible rather than merely reasonable. If it is merely one among many reasonable interpretations, then it might be the case that our white colleges students' interpretation of their joking telling as ironic is also reasonable and hence, their joking isn't racist. I don't have space to fill this account fully, but elsewhere (2011) I have argued that it is the nature of the historical wrong, systemic historical racism, that requires us, due to obligations of sympathy and solidarity with its targets, to interpret the meaning thusly. But, we might follow Hanslanger in relying on what a "fully informed, rational judge" would say that the acts express (2012: 145). However, if we go this route, I'd argue that our ideal judge should have proper social and historical knowledge, and have a properly developed sense of empathy and sympathy with those who are the subject of the historical wrong at play. In fact, I might even argue that any ideal judge should be an actual embodied agent who has had the relevant lived experience of oppression, because this might be necessary to "see things aright." For the purposes of this essay, however, it is enough if we are convinced that the answer ultimately will center on the public or incorrigible social meaning of the telling of these jokes.

It is worth noting that the account that I provide is a socially contingent one that hinges on the particular socio-cultural history of how racial and ethnic groups have been systematically treated in a particular cultural context. But, it also hinges on the current socio-cultural status of a group in a given cultural context. This second feature helps to explain why we see a loosening of moral constraints on some ethnic jokes. In the United States, for example, the Irish have been subjected to pernicious forms of racism. One stereotype that has been deployed against the Irish is that they are a bunch of worthless drunks. However, in the United States the Irish have managed to shift their status from sub-human to human—they are often treated as paradigmatic instances of whiteness. This explains why our "world's shortest joke" seems much less offensive than a similar joke would be if told about, say, Mexicans. It invokes only a historical concern, not a current one. Though, of course, things might be different elsewhere, say, in England.

Appealing to the incorrigible social meaning of some jokes gains further support by the fact that it can make sense of the confusing features of racial and ethnic jokes that I mentioned at the outset of this essay. First, such jokes seem to lose their offensiveness when told by members of the targeted group. When a Mexican tells an anti-Mexican joke, it seems more reasonable to interpret the joke as ironic because the joking event looks sufficiently dissimilar from the historical act of joke telling as a tool of oppression as it is told by a member of the group that the joke targets. Second, it can make sense of the shifting norms around ethnic and racial jokes, as the offensiveness is set in part by considering both the actual history of how racio-ethnic denigration has played out in the a particular culture, and the current status of such groups. The same racial joke might be racist in one time period, and not another. Third, it can explain why a joke is offensive in one cultural context but not in another: telling our Irish joke in a bar in London carries with it a different, likely pernicious, incorrigible social meaning. Fourth, it can help explain why it is that sympathy seems required in some cases, but not in others. Sympathy is required with those who are currently subject to denigrating racial and ethnic stereotypes; it isn't required for those for whom the relevant racial or ethnic stereotype, even if held, doesn't serve as a tool for racial or ethnic denigration. Fifth, it helps to explain why racial and ethnic jokes are seen as more offensive than other types of denigration humor (though, of course, some non-racial tokens of denigration humor might be similarly offensive). Unlike some racial and ethnic jokes, ordinary instances of denigration humor, say when our friend makes fun of us for being overly analytical, and other types of offensive humor, like dead baby jokes, don't express offensive incorrigible social meanings.

Culpability

In this section, I'd like to pursue the question of culpability that I've largely avoided throughout this chapter. Let us consider the white college students. Have they inadvertently done something racist that, like our friend in Latin America, they are not culpable for? Or, like Nixon, do we think that they are culpably ignorant? I think that our white college students are morally insensitive to the incorrigible social meaning of their jokes, and their insensitivity is due to what Charles Mills calls "white racial blindness," a privileged, but defective, epistemic position that is partly, or even mainly, responsible for the continued perpetuation of white supremacy (2011). This is a feature of our shared, social life that whites have a substantive moral obligation to know about. So, our white students are guilty of a particular kind of moral obliviousness—white racial blindness—that renders them culpably ignorant to both the meaning of their jokes and their respective obligation to not entertain one another in this way. For this reason, our white students exhibit a culpable failure of sympathy and solidarity with the targets of their jokes, targets who know all too well what those jokes signify. A similar story might be told about at least some of the claims about the harm that racial and ethnic jokes can cause that I've considered here.

In light of the considerations I've laid out here, I think that we should follow Ronald de Sousa in identifying some jokes as default-racist (1987), and so reject Noël Carroll's claim that jokes, conceived of as types, lack evaluative properties (2014). In a particular socio-cultural context an otherwise racial joke has an incorrigible social meaning and so the telling of and being amused by it will generally express a racist viewpoint, except in cases where the joke is told ironically by a member of the group that the joke targets (though, even in these cases, bad faith worries loom). This is independent of the particular psychological facts of the jokers. So, some jokes are default-racist in that the telling and being amused by them in a particular socio-cultural context, except in certain narrowly prescribed circumstances, is racist and should be avoided. Further, as I have argued, whites are generally culpable for their failures in this regard.

On Being Racist and Being Racially Insensitive

In closing, I'd like to consider a pragmatic challenge to my acceptance of our variegated and permissive practice of the application of the term "racist." Some will be unhappy with calling many of the activities that I focus on here "racist," as they want to reserve this judgment for more egregious acts (Blum 2002; Anderson 2015). A more permissive use of the term, the practical challenge goes, will undermine our attempts to eliminate racism and white supremacy, and to achieve racial and ethnic justice. But, I think that we should be cautious about concluding too much by retreating to the lesser charge of racial insensitivity. To the extent that racial insensitivity renders one unable to be a racial ally, and serves to perpetuate, reinforce, and reflect white supremacy, I think that being racially insensitive just is a way of being racist. And, I think that for any of the joking events that I've considered here, we'd do better to say "hey, knock it off, those jokes are racist" than "hey, knock it off, those jokes are racially insensitive." I think is so in part because the worry that we currently face, at least in the United States, is not the undermining of the force of the term "racist" as Blum suggests, but the thought that we are post-racial (Shelby 2003: 125) and so we should all just lighten up about racial and ethnic jokes. But, I agree that if calling acts that are not an expression of personal racism racially insensitive is better able to achieve the dismantling of white supremacy, then I'm for it. If it isn't, then I'm not. I suspect that it isn't. Further, for those who reject the notion of "racist" that undergirds this chapter for what we might call metaphysical reasons, that is, the account is false, there is still something to be gained by attending to the normative resources that I set out in this chapter as they are morally salient and so relevant for thinking about the normativity of racial and ethnic jokes.

References

Anderson, L. (2015) "Racist Jokes." *Philosophy Compass* 10, no. 8: 501–509.
Anderson, L., and Lepore, E. (2013) "Slurring Words." *Noûs* 47, no. 1: 25–48.
Appiah, A. (1990) "Racisms," in David Theo Goldberg (ed.), *The Anatomy of Racism*, Minneapolis: University of Minnesota Press, pp. 3–17.
Bergmann, M. (1986) "How Many Feminists Does It Take to Make a Joke? Sexist Humor and What's Wrong With It." *Hypatia* 1, no. 1: 63–82.
Blum, L. (2002) *I'm Not a Racist, But . . . The Moral Quandary of Race*, Ithaca: Cornell University Press.
Boskin, J. (1987) "The Complicity of Humor: The Life and Death of Sambo," in J. Morreall (ed.), *The Philosophy of Laughter and Humor*, Albany: State University of New York Press, pp. 250–263.
Camp, E. (2013) "Slurring Perspectives." *Analytic Philosophy* 54, no. 3: 330–349.
Carroll, Noël. (2014) "Ethics and Comic Amusement." *British Journal of Aesthetics* 54, no. 2: 241–253.
Cohen, T. (1999) *Jokes: Philosophical Thoughts on Joking Matters*, Chicago: University of Chicago Press.
Conolly, O., and Heydar, B. (2005) "The Good, the Bad, and the Funny." *Monist* 88, no. 1: 121–134.
Correll, J., Park, B., Judd, C. M., and Wittenbrink, B. (2002) "The Police Officer's Dilemma: Using Ethnicity to Disambiguate Potentially Threatening Individuals." *Journal of Personality and Social Psychology* 83, no. 6: 1314–1329.
Correll, J., Park, B., Judd, C. M., Wittenbrink, B., Sadler, M. S., and Keesee, T. (2007) "Across the Thin Blue Line: Police Officers and Racial Bias in the Decision to Shoot." *Journal of Personality and Social Psychology* 92, no. 6: 1006–1023.
de Sousa, R. (1987) "When Is It Wrong to Laugh?" in J. Morreall (ed.), *The Philosophy of Laughter and Humor*, Albany: State University of New York Press, pp. 226–249.
Eastwick, P. W., and Gardner, W. L. (2009) "Is It a Game? Evidence for Social Influence in the Virtual World." *Social Influence* 4: 18–32.
Ford, T. E., Boxer, C., Armstrong, J., and Edel, J. (2008) "More Than 'Just a Joke': The Prejudice Releasing Function of Sexist Humor." *Personality & Social Psychology Bulletin* 34, no. 2: 159–170.
Ford, T. E., and Ferguson, M. (2004) "Social Consequences of Disparagement Humor: A Prejudiced Norm Theory." *Personality and Social Psychology Review* 8: 79–94.
Ford, T. E., Woodzicka, J. A., Triplett, S. R., Kochersberger, A. O., and Holden, C. (2014) "Not All Groups Are Equal: Differential Vulnerability of Social Groups to the Prejudice-Releasing Effects of Disparagement Humor." *Group Processes and Intergroup Relations* 17, no. 2: 178–199.

Garcia, J.L.L. (2001) "The Heart of Racism," in Bernard Boxill (ed.), *Race and Racism*, New York: Oxford University Press, pp. 257–296.

Gaut, B. (1998) "Just Joking: The Ethics and Aesthetics of Humor." *Philosophy and Literature* 22, no. 1: 51–68.

Goldberg, D. T. (2012) "Racist Culture," in Paul Taylor (ed.), *The Philosophy of Race*, New York: Routledge, pp. 243–266.

Hanslanger, S. (2012) "Language, Politics, and 'The Folk': Looking for 'The Meaning' of 'Race'," in P. Taylor (ed.), *The Philosophy of Race*, New York: Routledge, pp. 138–153.

Hornsby, J. (2000) "Feminism in Philosophy of Language: Communicative Speech Acts," in M. Fricker and J. Hornsby (eds.), *The Cambridge Companion to Feminism in Philosophy*, Cambridge: Cambridge University Press, pp. 87–106.

Jordan, A., and Patridge, S. (2012) "Against the Moralistic Fallacy: A Modest Proposal for a Modest Sentimentalism About Humor." *Ethical Theory and Moral Practice* 15, no. 1: 83–94.

Kelly, D., and Roedder, E. (2008) "Racial Cognition and the Ethics of Implicit Bias." *Philosophy Compass* 3, no. 3: 522–540.

Kirwan Institute for the Study of Race and Ethnicity. (2013) "State of the Science: Implicit Bias Review." http://kirwaninstitute.osu.edu/docs/SOTS-Implicit_Bias.pdf.

———. (2014) "State of the Science: Implicit Bias Review." http://kirwaninstitute.osu.edu/wp-content/uploads/2014/03/2014-implicit-bias.pdf.

Lynch, R. (2010) "It's Funny Because We Think It's True: Laughter Is Augmented by Implicit Preferences." *Evolution and Human Behavior* 31, no. 2: 141–148.

Mail, G.R., Olson, J.M., and Bush, J. (1934) "Telling Jokes That Disparage Social Groups: Effects on the Joke Teller's Stereotypes." *Journal of Abnormal and Social Psychology* 28: 345–365.

Mills, C. (1987) "Racist and Sexist Jokes: How Bad Are They (Really)?" *iReport From the Center for Philosophy and Public Policy*.

———. (1998) *Blackness Visible: Essays on Philosophy*, Ithaca: Cornell University Press.

———. (2012) "White Ignorance," in P. Taylor (ed.), *The Philosophy of Race*, New York: Routledge, pp. 243–266.

Patridge, S. (2011) "The Incorrigible Social Meaning of Video Games Imagery: Making Ethical Sense of Single-Player Video Games." *Ethics and Information Technology* 14, no. 4: 303–312.

———. (2013) "Exclusivism and Evaluation: Art, Erotica, and Pornography," in H. Maes (ed.), *Pornographic Art and the Aesthetics of Pornography*, Basingstoke: Palgrave Macmillan pp. 43–57.

Philips, M. (1984) "Racist Acts and Racist Humor." *Canadian Journal of Philosophy* 14, no. 1: 75–96.

Rodriguez, T. (2012) "Numbing the Heart: Racist Jokes and the Aesthetic Affect." *Contemporary Aesthetics*, 12. www.contempaesthetics.org/newvolume/pages/article.php?articleID=707.

Sadler, M.S., Correll, J., Park, B., and Judd, C.M. (2012) "The World Is Not Black and White: Racial Bias in the Decision to Shoot in a Multiethnic Context." *Journal of Social Issues* 68, no. 2: 286–313.

Seibt, B., and Forster, M. (2004) "Risky and Careful Processing Under Stereotype Threat: How Regulatory Focus Can Enhance and Deteriorate Performance When Self Stereotypes Are Active." *Journal of Personality and Social Psychology* 87: 38–56.

Shelby, T. (2003) "Review of Lawrence Blum's *I'm not a racist but . . .*" *Philosophical Review* 112, no. 1: 124–126.

Zack, N. (1998) *Thinking About Race*, Belmont: Wadsworth.

28
ANTI-BLACK RACISM
The Greatest Art Show on Earth
Janine Jones

The concept of the aesthetic derives from the concept of taste—often understood in the history of Western philosophy as that which enables us to discern beauty from non-beauty. In *The Cultural Promise of the Aesthetic*, Monique Roelofs understands the aesthetic as "an assembly of conceptually inflected, socially situated, multimodal, embodied practices" (2014: 2). Roelofs argues that Hume's and Kant's universalist accounts of aesthetic perception advance a notion of the public that emerges from "the hypothesis of shared appreciative capacities and the universally valid aesthetic judgments they warrant" (2014: 5). I understand the aesthetic, here, as pertaining to the assembly of which Roelofs speaks, anchored in discourses and experiences pertaining to the discernment of the beautiful and the non-beautiful, where such discernment targets the appearance of objects, and understands their deeper reality or meaning (when they are thought to have one) as stemming or inferable from their appearance. On my understanding of the aesthetic, the hypothesis claims that we possess shared capacities for discerning positive and negative aesthetic experiences, and, that the putative fact that these capacities (capacities of taste, we might call them) are universally shared is what warrants the aesthetic judgments that issue forth from them.

The hypothesis is compatible with the following proposition: the aesthetic provides symbolic and sensually responsive material that directs our movement with respect to objects in the world, and thereby assists in sustaining hierarchical structures by enriching our ideas of the ordering of categories and their members. Roelofs observes that evidence for the hypothesis is scant. Her views, in general, suggest that evidence for the proposition is extensive. Agreeing with Roelofs on both counts, I contend, however, that in places where we live, where more often than not we do not theorize our aesthetic experiences with a great deal of awareness—as we might when making an argument or deconstructing a discourse—the empirical conditions under which our racialized aesthetic and aestheticized racial experiences and evaluations take shape often remain concealed. Following Roelofs, I understand aesthetic racialization as occurring when "aesthetic stratagems support racist registers" and racialized aesthetics as occurring when "racial templates support aesthetic modalities" (2014: 29). Empirically observable conditions of systemic and other forms of racism may "disappear" behind aesthetic arrangements, where the latter may present themselves as being for aesthetic perception/appreciation only. Conversely, empirically perceivable conditions that appear to be solely about aesthetic schema may be grounded in and governed by non-apparent racial arrangements. Both types of disappearing acts are all the more likely to occur in lived experience because of the mutual saturation of race and aesthetics within sensually response-producing imagined materiality, which directs spontaneous somatic movement. Such complementary saturation leads Roelofs to claim that, on the one hand, we must aim to comprehend the workings of the aesthetic, because aesthetic schema and experience create the channels via which we produce and exchange racial passions, perceptions, and value; and that, on the other, we must seek to understand processes of racialization if we are to discern how and where such processes are grafted on to the aesthetic (2014: 29). But such comprehension and understanding often involves forms of theorization that take place within academic or academic-like spaces, where it is supposedly our task to examine our aesthetically racialized and racialized-aesthetic directed movements, even during theorizing.

Arguably, a significant factor in the preponderance of implicit racial bias (and of racial bias that masquerades as implicit, remaining unspoken until triggered, or of racism or racial bias that is not called out as such—see below) has to do with the conveyance of such bias through racialized aesthetic schema or aestheticized racial arrangements in the course of spontaneous, habitual, habit-producing somatic movement. One perspective from which to understand this idea is through an assertion Achille Mbembe makes in *Critique de la Raison Nègre*.

Mbembe understands that in order to operate at its very best, racism must function at the levels of affect, impulsion, and speculum: core elements of the infrastructure of racism. Thus, race must be presented not only through constituents of image, form, surface, and figure, but via a racial imaginary that structures these constituents into dynamic and comprehensible forms (Mbembe 2013: 57). In effect, what Mbembe lays claims to for race is an aestheticized racialization that depends on a type of image analyzed by Susanne Langer in *The Problems of Art*—the dynamic image. A dynamic image is a virtual object (a speculum) that is an apparition of *active* powers (Langer 1957: 5)—an expressive image made active by its sensually perceptible, response-directing materiality.

Race, *like other art forms* (e.g., dance) expresses "an idea of the way feelings, emotions, and all other subjective experience come and go—their rise and growth, their intricate synthesis that gives our inner lives unity" (Langer 1957: 7) and identity around discourses and realities of race. Transported through dynamic images, race structures subjective existence in us in such a way that it can be "conceptually known, reflected on, imagined and symbolically expressed in detail and to a great depth" (Langer 1957: 7–8). Dynamic art images, including racial ones, are public. Third-person accessible, they convey and facilitate inter-subjective communication. Dynamic images of black bodies presented through various processes of racialized aesthetics or aestheticized racialization are directly perceived and felt as threats: they can be as directly perceived and felt by an audience as is a bass played in a jazz club or in a symphony hall. Indirectly but immediately, black people, who have been socially constructed so that their physical bodies correlate in space and time with racist dynamic images, are themselves treated as the threats these images suggest or indicate they are. Social creation of such images takes different paths. Dynamic images have been grounded in purely imaginary structures of thought, such as those that place black people in biological relation to gorillas or chimpanzees in ways that other members of the biological family, *human being*, are not thought to stand. This type of creation has been effected through repetition of narratives and perceptual images, but also through the socially constructed built reality of segregated space, where black people have been concentrated in small places (slave ships, slave cabins, projects, prison cells, isolation cells within humungous prison complexes) and cut off from vital resources of the greater society. Actual segregated built realities have determined that a significant number of black people will be poorly educated, live in sub-standard conditions, and develop distinct behaviors and disparities in health—which can then be targeted, stigmatized and essentialized to create ready-to-use (tweakable) dynamic images for black people, in general. Racializing imaginaries essentialize their targets. What better way to essentialize black people than to create lived places that provide perceivable, third-person evidence that, for the most part, black people are inferior? Particular black people must *prove* to subjects, whose interaction with them is brokered through perceptions of black dynamic images, that they are innocent of the aspersions cast upon them—that they are the odd book not to be judged by its cover.

Slain Michael Brown may have been thought of as a "gentle giant" by his friends. But when physically positioned within Officer Darren Wilson's visual-imaginary field, Wilson imaginatively saw and felt a "demon," a "Hulk Hogan." A dynamic image appeared, which correlated with Brown's actual body in physical space. In order to understand anti-black racism, we must take seriously the dynamic image that Darren Wilson perceived and felt.

> Hulk Hogan, that's how big he felt and how small I felt just from grasping his arm.
> It looked like he was almost bulking up to run through the shots, like it was making him mad that I'm shooting at him.
> [He made] a grunting, like aggravated sound . . . I've never seen that. I mean, it was very aggravated . . . aggressive, hostile . . . You could tell he was looking through you. There was nothing he was seeing.
>
> (Bouie)

Let's also consider Charles Kinsey, the black therapist shot by a police officer in North Miami, in spite of the fact that he was lying on the ground with his hands in the air. When Kinsey asked the officer why he shot him the officer responded, "I don't know." Perhaps the officer didn't have words to express what he imaginatively saw and felt upon being confronted with a dynamic image correlated with Kinsey's actual body. Possibly a certain degree of cognitive dissonance occurred as the result of perceiving the dynamic image while divining the existence of some real person-body "behind" it. It would seem, however, that the cop went with the dynamic image as the relevant purveyor of reality.

The dynamic image of a black person (wordier, I really mean: the dynamic image of a black body, which through its active powers presents *effects* of the presence of a person), like the dynamic image presented by a dance performance, is given by physical realities: "place, gravity, body, muscular strength, muscular control, and secondary assets such as light, sound, or things . . . All of these are actual" (Langer 1957: 6). But in dance (as in the perception of dynamic images, correlated in space and time with black bodies) these actualities (e.g., an actual black person and her body) are not perceived. The more perfect the dance (or the more perfect the presentation of blackness in a context—the local or global environment or interaction between the two the less the actualities are perceived." (Langer 1957: 6).

Through the presentation of dynamic images, artworks succeed in presenting patterns that can be perceived, felt, and communicated. Dynamic images of anti-black racism—arguably Western modernity's greatest works of art—excel in this regard as narrative is an integral part of the racist art show, supplying fundamental ideas about what is being presented in dynamic forms. The fact that anti-black racist dynamic images can function at deep, non-discursive levels of emotional-cognitive uptake and absorption make it all the more difficult to challenge them discursively *during* episodes of lived experience. Moreover, and significantly, during lived experience some consciously seek strategies to occlude our awareness of the racism that dwells within and around us.

At a philosophy talk, I witnessed a philosopher suggest to a group of students that in order to avoid being the party pooper who points out that someone's racist assertion about black people or Hispanics *is* racist (e.g., black people are stupid; Hispanics are lazy) they might adopt a strategy that eliminates talk about racism altogether. Rather than maintain that an assertion made by one of the partiers is racist, they should argue that the assertion in question is false, because it is logically false. For example, it is logically false that birds fly, if we understand the statement as making a universal claim about birds, or, say, a generic claim about birds. The audience was taught how to use the logic of universal quantifiers or generics to make their case. I interpreted the speaker as—unwittingly or not—instructing the audience that (and how) we should seek to theorize some *lived experiences of race* in a way that erases race, in order to maintain an aesthetic of orderliness, "friendliness," and "civility" to name a few aesthetic promises we're supposed keep in some places. I use scare quotes to problematize the idea that friendliness and civility could be sought in a place where those who are attacked by racist statements are encouraged to pretend they feel nothing more than the misgivings attendant to logical falsehoods, while those who make racist statements are protected and can remain innocent of their own racism by turning their attention to the interesting world of logical fallacies. Per the recommended strategy, black and brown people, who already bear the burden of being a threat to the kind of etiquette mandated in such places by the dynamic images correlated in imaginary-perceived space with their physical bodies, must find ways to protect and nourish the innocence and well-being of white people. Thus, normative aesthetic orderliness, correlated with whiteness, is maintained. Disruption, correlated with blackness, is silenced.

Granted, the theoretical warrant for universally valid aesthetic experiences is thin. Nevertheless, within lived experience—where we spontaneously perceive, act, react, desire, move, and respond—it might *appear* to us that (1) we do in fact possess universally shared negative attitudes about black people, and (2) that our apparent shared aesthetic attitudes may appear to be not so much anti-black as merely *natural*, universal aesthetic responses to what black bodies *naturally* are, where our responses are understood as resulting in negative effects that turn out to work against black people. In the remainder of this chapter, I discuss two cases in which (1) and (2) have arisen within lived experience. Finally, I briefly present an out-of-academy response that struck anti-black racism at its aesthetic core.

The Opacity of White Light

And God said, Let there be light: and there was light.

> A television company is about to shoot a panel discussion before a studio audience. The producer, from the control room, is discussing with the floor manager in the studio how the audience looks in his monitor. The producer says something about the number of black people at the front of the audience. "You're worried there are not too many whites obviously there?," asks the floor manager. No, says the producer, it's nothing like that, a mere technical matter, a question of lighting—"it just looks a bit down."
>
> (Dyer, 1997: 82)

According to Richard Dyer, the producer's judgment, given in the epigraph, is purely aesthetic. "If he were to do it the usual way with a white audience, the image would look 'up': bright, sparkling" (1977: 82). But the image that looked down would have *looked down* not just to the producer but to almost all Western human perceivers brought up within the conventions of Western film-viewing. This observation provides good material for thinking about how the process of aesthetic racialization in the film industry gave rise to aesthetic judgments that seem to be about aesthetic experience only, and not to be about race at all. Such judgments seem to arise from a natural capacity most of us share. Therefore, such judgments may seem not to be anti-black, but merely judgments that express universal capacities of taste, which, unfortunately, give rise to thoughts and actions that work against black people.

Dyer remarks that lighting in filmmaking is almost always manipulated to make people the most important element in a shot, by focusing on their faces. That some faces are lit while others are not enables important people in a shot to be distinguished from their surroundings.

Dyer explains that in the *development* of lighting in film, whiteness was a monumental problem. Light didn't just shine a light on white skin. Light troubled *the colors* in white skin. Consider a highlight from Dyer's recounting of the history of film: "The earliest stock, orthochromatic, was insensitive to red and yellow, rendering both colors dark. Charles Handley, looking back in 1954, noted that with orthochromatic stock, 'even a reasonably light-red object would photograph black.' White skin is reasonably light-red" (1997: 91). The problem? White people came out black.

As if black-skinned white people were not problematic enough, lighting for whiteness had to contend with how white people *preferred* whiteness to be perceived. Citing Brian Winston, Dyer writes "it is 'preferred—a whiter shade of white'"; Dyer added, "Characteristically too, it is a woman's skin which provides the litmus test" (1997: 93). If white men have been thought to be exemplars of whiteness through their possession of mind, the litmus test suggests that white women are exemplars of whiteness through their bodies, which includes their faces.

In spite of all the problems that surfaced in the history of developing lighting for white skin, we are now compelled to see lighting as inherently non-problematic for white skin, but as particularly problematic for black skin: and of course, *it is*! Lighting was not developed for black skin.

"How does it feel to be a problem?" Apparently, feeling oneself to be a problem is something that white people, *qua* being white, are not supposed or allowed to feel, as we've seen above, in the discussion of how to keep parties polite. With a mendacious narrative of the history of film, we are left with the idea that white skin naturally promises an aesthetically pleasing result. Black skin, by contrast, inherently threatens film production. Both aesthetically and economically, great cost is incurred in compensating for the problems black skin poses. Thus, black skin appears to provide a reason *all on its own* against using black people in film. Hence, there is no need for white supremacist, anti-black racism in the film industry: light itself—a natural phenomenon—sheds light on who is aesthetically fair and who is aesthetic anathema. Light indicates what is aesthetically fair game for filming, and what ought to be left out in the dark, at the risk of offending *our* sense of aesthetics. Dyer's narrative undermines the official story by showing us how it should be recast as a story about aestheticized racialization. However, Dyer's revealed story is grounded in a larger historical narrative of racialized aesthetics.

> "I think the reason they do that is the boys . . . sometimes the boys could be more attracted to the Black girls, especially when it comes to body shape, and they think it's going to distract the boys, so they do tell the Black girls to cover up, because that's who the boys are looking at," Shamika said. "They are looking at the Black girls. They are looking at the White girls [too], but they're looking at their faces. They're not finna really cover up the White girls." It's notable that Shamika felt boys were attracted to White girls' faces but to Black girls' bodies. And that she didn't pause or skip a beat in explaining as much. "So if they're not looking at your face, what do you think are they looking at?" I asked. "They're looking at your butt or your boobs," Shamika responded.
>
> (Morris, 2016: 128)

Dyer told us that lighting in filmmaking is almost always manipulated to distinguish the important people from their environment—by way of the face. Mbembe has described the image ontology that reigns in racialized realms as "a regime of visuality that privileges the face. By seeing your face, I am interpellated. I'm expecting you to tell me something meaningful and then I'll respond: two subjects facing each other" (Mbembe, Rhodes seminar notes, 2014). Within racialized regimes, where faces are privileged as loci of meaning, indicating subjectivity and personhood, black people are reduced to *surfaces*. Surfaces, Mbembe asserts, hide *faces* (Rhodes seminar). But the extract above reminds us of the importance of analyzing racialized realms through multiple lenses of oppression. Black girls' and women's faces do not have the aestheticized racial purchase of their white female "counterparts." The occlusion of their faces is enacted by black males, who perceive them as surfaces, and reinforced by school authorities. Black girls and women are told to cover their offending surfaces in places (e.g., schools) where their surfaces are imaginatively perceived as posing aesthetic-sexual threats. (One cannot but wonder how a black Muslim girl, bearing a butt, boobs, and burkini, would fare in a place that would force her to uncover herself in order to satisfy its notion of feminine freedom while forcing her to cover herself up, in order to satisfy its notion of feminine decency.) In other places, these same surfaces promise some male or other sexual pleasure. As the black girl or woman is not interpellated, in or outside of film, as a person possessing the dignity of bearing a face, she can be raped and denied the dignity of being *someone* whose rape matters, although the logic for being denied dignity may differ. The logic of black males raping black females and the rape not mattering because the black girl or woman is not valued as a person *with a face*, is different from the logic of black females being raped by men of any race and the rape not mattering because black females are willfully submissive. In the first case, rape is recognized. Its value and meaning to the person raped is not. In the second, there is no recognition of a rape occurring to which value could be accorded. Regardless of the perpetrator or logic employed to deny dignity, given the racialized-gendered aesthetics of patriarchal realms, black girls and women lose face at least twice.

Combining Dyson's and Mbembe's analyses with multiple-lens reasoning, we understand that film developed within a larger racialized-gendered aesthetic realm, where black people's faces had already been differentially obscured depending on other factors, such as gender, class, and color. By reducing black people to surfaces, the wider, racist realm had pre-determined that they were not subjects: those who might have something meaningful to say to us or to each other. Following suit by developing lighting for white skin and white faces only, the film industry replicated the face-surface logic of the wider world. However, in hiding its replication story, it transformed an explicit logic of racializing aesthetics, operative in the wider world, into a logic of aestheticizing race, where light allegedly naturally shows the way to white faces. The narrative tells us that historically we have responded *appropriately* to the promise of aesthetic goods offered by the marriage of light and skin that is white, and to the threat of black skin, black as sin: rejected by light itself.

> *And why should one hab de white wife,*
>
> *And me hab only Quangeroo?*
>
> *Me no see reason for me life!*
>
> *No! Quashee hab de white wife too.*
>
> *Huzza, &c.*
>
> *For make all like, let blackee nab*
>
> *De white womans . . . dat be de track!*
>
> *Den Quashee de white wife will hab,*
>
> *And mass Jef. Shall hab de black,*
>
> *Huzza, &c.*
>
> (Lemire 1999: 14)

Even when we begin in a realm that explicitly racializes aesthetics we can be left feeling that, in the final analysis, we share some natural aesthetic capacity that responds to whiteness and rejects blackness. Quashee demands that he "hab de white wife too." Quashee demands a white wife on the grounds that Jefferson had declared all men equal. Using a multiple-lens analyses in our critical race theorizing, perhaps we ought to conclude that black women will only be equal when they can have a white wife too.

Eldridge Cleaver echoed Quashee's claim two centuries later, making a stake for freedom, for black men:

> I love white women and hate black women. *It's just in me, so deep that I don't even try to get it out of me anymore.* I'd jump over ten nigger bitches just to get to one white woman. *Ain't no such thing as an ugly white woman.* A white woman is beautiful even if she's baldheaded and only has one tooth. . . . *Sometimes I think that the way I feel about white women, I must have inherited from my father and his father and his father's father—as far as you can go into slavery.* I must have inherited from all those black men part of my desire for the white woman, because I have more love for her than one man should have. . . . They passed on their desire to me, they must have. . . . *But I'm stuck with myself* and I accept my own thoughts about things. For instance, I don't know just how it works, I mean I can't analyze it, but I know that the white man made the black woman the symbol of slavery and the white woman the symbol of freedom. *Every time I embrace a black woman I'm embracing slavery, and when I put my arms around a white woman, well, I'm hugging freedom.* The white man forbade me to have the white woman on pain of death. . . . Men die for freedom, but black men die for white women, who are the symbol of freedom. That was the white man's will, and as long as he has the power to enforce his will upon me. . . . I will not be free. I will not be free until the day I can have a white woman in my bed and a white man minds his own business. Until that day comes, my entire existence is tainted, poisoned, and I will be a slave—and so will the white woman.
>
> (1968/1991: 187–189, emphasis added)

Cleaver's declaration displays an entanglement of racialized-gendered aesthetics and racialized-gendered politics. For black men who have "inherited" the desire described by Cleaver, having a white woman in their bed—the type of female which, as a matter of racialized, gendered, aesthetic-ontological fact, *cannot* be ugly—is a matter of freedom and unfreedom: a matter of life and death. For a black man to act on such a desire at the time Cleaver wrote this piece (and even now in some places in the United States), was to sign his death warrant. But that's as it should be if it is true, as Cleaver claims, that black men die for white women. Quashee would have agreed with Cleaver: he sees no reason for living if he can hab only Quangeroo. Perhaps Quashee would speak of suicide if he could hab only de black woman with no European (or apparent European) ancestry, as Quangeroo possesses. In any case, Cleaver describes an inheritance he is stuck with. The inheritance determines racialized-gendered aesthetic sexual preferences and desires of some black men. "It's just in me" fosters the idea that Cleaver's desire is as natural as DNA (or as light on white skin). Beauty and ugliness are anchored in race via symbols and embodiments of freedom and unfreedom, thus linking them to the aesthetic via the politics of racial realities. Good evidence supports Cleaver's claim that white men made white women the symbol of freedom and black women the symbol of slavery, not to mention the living, bodily embodiment of its continuance in new forms. One such piece of evidence resides in the arguments of Thomas Jefferson, a beloved founding father and principle author of the US Declaration of Independence.

Jefferson had to explain why freed black people should be removed from the United States since wisdom had it that large numbers of people were the hope of America. In *Notes on the State of Virginia*, Jefferson popularized the rationalization of race as an aesthetic hierarchy of traits "with supposedly built in dynamics of sexual desire" (Lemire 1999: 27). The removal of blacks was supposed to guarantee that black and white people would remain "as distinct as nature has formed them" (1999: 27). How did Jefferson's argument go?

Jefferson claimed that the beauty of white race traits placed whites on top of a hierarchy of race. This central premise of Jefferson's argument was thought to be *proved* by the black preference for whites "as uniformly as is the preference of the Oranootan for the black women over those of his own species" (Lemire 1999: 28). The primary "physical distinctions [that] prove . . . a difference or race" (1999: 27) were skin color, hair, and smell. The perception that orangutans desire African women goes back to sixteenth- and seventeenth-century scientific theory. "Jefferson would have been familiar with the frontispiece of an English translation of Linnaeus titled A *Genuine and Universal System of Natural History*, featuring an orangutan snatching an African woman from her human mate" (1999: 28).

> To argue for removal in the face of emancipation is, in Jefferson's view, a moral imperative. . . . "The circumstance of superior beauty, is thought worthy of attention in the propagation of our horses, dogs, and other domestic animals; why not in that of man?"
>
> (1999: 28)

Maintaining that male orangutans desire black females and that black males desire white females (all female desire got lost), Jefferson, in effect, laid out the Chain of Being, which organized species by kind, and where black people and apes reside contiguously on the bottom of the hierarchy. Jefferson reimagined the ontological order of the chain as being epistemically accessed through the lens of racialized-gendered aesthetic evaluations, which were determined by the *natural* responsive capacity of sexual desire.

> He imagines that the chain is organized into biological kinds who are knowable as distinct through their relative beauty. And he envisions each race or species desiring to couple with that race or species above it on the chain out of "preference" for its greater beauty.
>
> (Lemire 1999: 28–29)

Thus, members of kinds can know—through third-person observation—the behaviors of members of their own kind and that of other kinds. Men can know—through reasoned observation about their aesthetic preferences mediated by their sexual desire—why different biological kinds are situated on the Chain of Being as they are, and why a kinds' members belong to the kind they belong to. On this scheme, I suppose that white men should really desire Mary, Mother of God, rather than white women, who are not above them *in any way*. In any case, in accordance with nature or God's commands, white males should not desire black or orangutan females. However, orangutan males should desire black females and black males should desire white females. Given these natural desires, at least two conclusions follow. Orangutans should try to engage black females sexually, if possible, and black males should try to engage white females sexually, where possible. Hence, black males are cast as a racial-aesthetic threat, *by nature*, to white women, and to a nation allegedly built by white women's white sons: black men *must* rape white females if they can. Black females—a foundational degenerative force—forcing white men to give in to their "boisterous passions" (Jefferson, Notes, Query XVIII, "On Manners")—are also racial-aesthetic threats to the nation. Indeed, Jefferson was laid open to accusations of failing to be truly white, because through his relationship with Sally Hemings, he manifested a type of deviance which purportedly augured the death of the foundling nation (Lemire 2009: 30).

What we should keep in mind here is that Jefferson's proof didn't have to mean that white people were enjoined to make discrimination against black people their *aim*. The proof could be understood as making explicit, through reasoned observation, nature or God's commands, and the consequences of not following them. As Lemire observes, significantly, laws were not required for getting people to conform to the logic of the proof. Aesthetic feeling and fear led individuals to conform in the constitution of an institution of anti-miscegenation.

> the depictions of inter-racial sex from New York, Pennsylvania, and Massachusetts indicate that many whites there clearly feared social and economic equality would follow political equality, New York, never had laws prohibiting inter-racial marriage, Pennsylvania overturned theirs in 1780, and Massachusetts would overturn theirs in 1843 . . . the numerous depictions of inter-racial couplings that dotted the Northern cultural landscape did the work of prohibiting inter-marriage by teaching whites that blacks are physically and socially inferior and to thereby treat them accordingly.
>
> (Lemire 1999: 2)

> When she passes she calls my attention, but her hair, there's no way no. Her *catinga* (body odor) almost caused me to faint. Look. I cannot stand her odor. Look, look, look at her hair! It looks like a scouring pad for cleaning pans. I already told her to wash herself. But she insisted and didn't want to listen to me. This smelly *negra* (Black woman). . . . Stinking animal that smells worse than a skunk.
>
> (Caldwell 2003: 18)

The above extract presents lyrics sung by former circus clown, Tiririca, who is currently a federal deputy for São Paulo, Brazil. In "'Look at Her Hair': The Body Politics of Black Womanhood in Brazil," Kia Caldwell examines ideals of female beauty in Brazil and their impacts on black women's subjective experiences. In the course of her exploration, Caldwell makes several crucial points. Consider a few, relevant to our discussion.

> Widespread beliefs regarding the inferiority and undesirability of Blackness have largely caused referential use of the terms *negro(a)* to be viewed as a form of insult and deprecation.
> "What is dirty is associated with Black, with color, and with Black men and women."
>
> (quoted in Caldwell 2003: 20)

Of all Brazilian social groups, Black women are the most profoundly impacted by Brazilian beliefs and prejudices regarding hair texture.

Of all the physical characteristics, it is particularly hair that marks "race" for women. . . . It is in the issue of hair that one sees a distinction between men and women and the differential social coding of race and ethnicity. Thus "race" is gendered.

(quoted in Caldwell 2003:21)

In Brazil, racialized gender hierarchies also classify women by dissecting their bodies and attributing certain physical features either to the category of sex or beauty. This dissection process assigns features such as skin color, hair texture, and the shape and size of the nose and lips (constituents of face) to the category of beauty, while features such as the breasts, hips, and buttocks are assigned to the sexual category. Given the Eurocentric aesthetic standards that prevail in Brazilian society, Black women have traditionally been defined as being sexual, rather than beautiful. Ironically, however, Black and Mulata women's association with sensuality and sexuality has been lauded as evidence of racial democracy in Brazil (Caldwell 1999; Gilliam 1998).

(Caldwell 2003: 20–21; addition in parenthesis mine)

Smoothing over—an aestheticizing process at the heart of *processing* black girls' and women's hair—often has a positive phenomenological valence in experience. Natural hairstyles, especially dreads—knotty dreads, as opposed to silky ones—may be experienced as symbols and embodiments of resistance: an unruly dread refusing to be ruled by radiant or chemical heat, which whatever the associated spiritual cost, damages hair *at its roots*. Resistance speaks to the idea of reclaiming one's roots, one's ancestors. Smoothing over reveals a great deal about the function of racist jokes (and logic, it would seem from our discussion above) to cover up racism.

"Look at Her Hair" trades in jokes that *smooth over* nexuses of race and aesthetics deployed to attack black girls and women, was not granted the privilege of being dissected in academic-like spaces *only*—allowing whiteness at large to go unscathed. It wasn't given the protection accorded spaces where racism wears the whiteface of logical fallacy. The song—defended by *the people* as a joke—"created an outcry amongst Black activists" (Caldwell 2003: 19). Their outrage led to a suit against Tiririca and Sony Music for racism.

The Center for the Articulation of Martinalized Populations (CEAP), . . . a non-governmental organization in Rio de Janeiro, requested that the Brazilian Public Ministry prohibit the music on the basis of discrimination against Blacks and women. A formal denouncement of racism was presented in July 1996 on article 20 of the 1989 Cao Law, which declared racism in the Brazilian media to be a crime.

(Caldwell 2003: 19)

My point: whatever might be revealed in academic-type spaces about the marriage between anti-black racism and aesthetics (and politics), black activist *movement*, understood broadly, is continually required to disrupt the somatic, habit-producing, anti-black racist *movements* of daily life, and make perceptible the fact that anti-black evaluations are not determined by innate, universal capacities of taste and *will not be* universally shared.

Further Readings

Cayton, H. R., and Drake, St. Claire. (1945, 1962, 1970) *Black Metropolis: A Study of Negro Life in a Northern City*, London: University of Chicago Press. See for further discussion of the construction of segregated places and their effects.

Duneier, Mitchell. (2016) *Ghetto: The Invention of a Place, the History of an Idea*, New York: Farrar, Straus and Giroux. See for extended discussion of the construction of segregated places and their effects, and a general discussion of the concept of *the ghetto* and historical lived realities of ghettos across historical times and locations.

Goff, A. (2008) "Not Yet Human: Implicit Knowledge, Historical Dehumanization, and Contemporary Consequences." *Journal of Personality and Psychology* 94, no. 2: 292–306. See for a discussion of the contemporary association between black people and apes.

Myrdal, Gunnar. (1944) *An American Dilemma: The Negro Problem and Modern Democracy*, New York: Harper and Brothers. See for further discussion of the construction of segregated places and their effects.

Taylor, P. C. (2016) *Black Is Beautiful: A Philosophy of Black Aesthetics*, London: Wiley Blackwell. See for extended discussions of nexuses between aesthetics, race, and politics, for further discussion of Thomas Jefferson's rendering of an aesthetic hierarchy of race traits and its political implications, and for further discussion of the significance of the aesthetics and politics of hair in anti-black racism, especially against black girls and women.

Wilderson, F. B., III. (2010) *Red, White, and Black: Cinema and the Structure of U.S. Antagonisms*, Durham: Duke University Press. See for further discussion of the construction of segregated places and their effects.

Yancy, G. (2008) *Black Bodies, White Gazes: The Continuing Significance of Race*, Lanham: Rowman & Littlefield. See Chapter 6 for Yancy's presentation of Dyer's discussion of how individuals are constructed through the use of light.

References

Bouie, J. "Michael Brown Wasn't a Superhuman Demon." *Slate*, November 26, 2014.

Caldwell, K. L. (2003) "Look at Her Hair: The Body Politics of Black Womanhood in Brazil," *Transforming Anthropology* 11, no. 2: 18–29.

Cleaver, E. (1968/1991) *Soul On Ice*, New York: Delta.

Dyer, R. (1997) "The Light of the World," in *White Essays on Race and Culture*, London and New York: Routledge, pp. 82–144.

Jefferson, T. *Notes on the State of Virginia.* http://press-pubs.uchicago.edu/founders/documents/v1ch15s28.html, accessed 8/15/15. (An extended discussion of racial hierarchy as determined by beauty and as known through proper sexual desire.)

Langer, S. K. (1957) *The Problems of Art*, New York: Charles Scribner's Sons.

Lemire, E. (2009) *"Miscegenation": Making Race in America*, Philadelphia: University of Pennsylvania Press.

Mbembe, A. (2013) *Critique de la Raison Nègre*, Paris: La Découverte.

———— Seminar Notes, Politics Department. Rhodes University, 2014.

Morris, M. (2016) *Pushout: The Criminalization of Black Girls in Schools*, New York: The New Press.

Roelofs, M. (2014) *The Cultural Promise of the Aesthetic*, New York, London, New Delhi, Sidney: Bloomsbury.

Part VII
ETHICS AND THE POLITICAL

29

RACISM

Luc Faucher

(Case 1) On the evening of June 17, 2015, Dylann Roof burst into the Emanuel African Methodist Episcopal Church and killed nine people, all African Americans. Roof's despicable action was not the result of a sudden and uncontrollable outburst that randomly targeted innocent churchgoers. Roof was, by his own admission, a white supremacist: on his website one could find a manifesto containing his (negative) opinions concerning African Americans and other racial groups as well as pictures of himself wearing a jacket with two white supremacist emblems: the flags of former Rhodesia and that of Apartheid-era South Africa. There was also a photo of Roof with a handgun and the Confederate flag. His actions on the day of the shooting, were planned and his goal was to ignite a civil war (Mindock 2015; Costa et al. 2015).

This is a clear, undisputable case of racism. Agreements on claims concerning racism are not always so easy to obtain. Take the following cases:

(Case 2) Roof's photo of himself in front of the confederate flag fuelled what has been called the "Confederate flag war." Some people suggested that the flag was an outdated symbol of racism and that it should be taken down. Polls showed that people were divided about the issue: according to one poll (Miller 2015), Americans were evenly split, 42% to 42%, over whether the flag was a racist symbol. Indeed, 42% of Americans did not see the flag as racist but rather as a symbol of Southern history. Interestingly, responses varied according to race. One-third of white Americans saw the flag as an emblem of racism, while another half saw it as symbol of the Southern heritage. More than 75% African Americans saw the flag as a racist symbol and only 10% saw it as a symbol of Southern heritage. The "Confederate flag war" resulted in the removal of the flag from the South Carolina State House as well as the decision of retailers, such as Wal-Mart, to stop selling merchandise with the Confederate flag on it.

(Case 3) On November 17, 2015, following the Paris terrorist shootings, a Muslim woman in Toronto was attacked and robbed while picking up her children. Two men approach the woman calling her a "terrorist" and telling her to go back to her country. They tore off her hijab and punched and kicked her repeatedly while she was on the ground. Needless to say, the woman was not a terrorist, and was born in Canada from parents who had immigrated 40 years ago. This is just one of the many Islamophobic acts that have happened since the Paris attacks (the *Huffington Post* listed 73 acts of this type in the month following the attacks; see Mathlas 2015).

(Case 4) On February 16, 2016, David Joseph, a 17-year-old unarmed African American male was shot by a police officer while running naked, allegedly acting erratically and chasing another male in an apartment complex in Austin, Texas (Ricke and Bien 2016). This happened in the wake of the previous shootings of unarmed African American males, like Michael Brown in Ferguson, Missouri, and Walter Scott in North Charleston, and the resulting surge of support for the Black Lives Matter protest movement. These cases have been perceived by many as either an expression of individual biases of white Americans against African Americans or an expression of broader racial biases of American society against African Americans. However, while in the latter cases the officers involved in the killing where white, in the case of Joseph, the officer was an African American and there is no evidence that the officer was overtly racist.

(Case 5) On March 9, 2016, a Manitoba First Nation (the Pimicikamak Cree Nation) declared a state of emergency after six suicides in two months and 140 suicide attempts in the previous two weeks of the month of March (for a population of 6,000). The reserve has an 80% unemployment rate and suffers from overcrowded housing, with no recreational facilities for its youth, and a poorly staffed nursing station. Referring to a shooting that took place two months earlier in a La Loche school of northern Saskatchewan, the Grand Chief Sheila North Wilson said that the epidemic of suicide was "the La Loche of northern Manitoba, except the shooter is society" (Baum 2016).

(Case 6) Finally, the 2015 census revealed the persistence of a difference in educational attainment between racial groups. For instance, according to the report from the Census Bureau, "a majority of Asians 25 years and older had a bachelor's degree or higher (54%). More than one-third of non-Hispanic Whites had a bachelor degree or higher (36%), 22% of Blacks had this level of education, as did 15% of Hispanics" (Ryan and Bauman 2016: 5). Commenting on the result of that census, data editor Lindsay Cook (2015) noted that among the factors that might account for these disparities are: differences in parents' attitudes toward education, time devoted to literary activities with family members in childhood, teachers' different expectations of children of different races, the quality of day care and schooling children have access to in their neighbourhood (see also Harper 2016).

Is the confederate flag "racist"? Is the case of the Muslim woman a case of racism or just xenophobia or bigotry? Can the shooting of an African American man by another African American man be explained by racism? Can a society be racist? Can differences between the educational attainment of various racial groups be explained by racism? I predict these questions won't garner agreement. There are many reasons why this is so. First, people are not always clear about what counts as racism and what can be racist (Can a flag be racist? Can a society be racist?). Second, when they are clear about the meaning of racism, they sometimes have different definitions about what counts as racism (sometimes because they have different explanatory or social projects). Third, claims of racism are "contested": because people do not like to be called "racist," they often resist being labelled as such. Fourth, (which also explains why claims of racism are contested), people are in different "epistemological positions"; they have access to or experience different realities. Because of that, some people might have different perspectives on the same events, so that they might end up framing them in different ways.

Getting clear on what racism is, is thus an important issue. But we should not be overly optimistic about the prospect of attaining agreement of the definition of racism. One reason for that is that the meaning of racism has evolved over time and needs to cover phenomena that it was not intended to cover initially. Some might not be aware of these new changes of meaning or might resist them for theoretical reasons (one such reason to resist change is the perceived danger of conceptual inflation, that is, the possibility that the concept will encompass so many different things which are different from each other that it ends up meaning "nothing"). Another reason is that people working on racism and providing definitions of the phenomena might have different research agendas that make it impossible to agree on such a definition. For instance, historians and sociologists might hold that society-specific cultural factors contribute to producing specific forms of racisms. If such is the case, racism is likely to take different forms, not necessarily being unified by much. Others, for instance moral philosophers, might be more interested by what is wrong with racism and will be quite happy to work with a generic version of racism that encompasses historic and sociologic variations.

In the following, I will present the different forms of racism that have been identified in the literature. I'll use this as a background for the discussion of the different philosophical accounts of racism. Philosophical accounts have generally a double objective: to capture the common (or core) use of the concept and to correct incorrect uses. As I will show, no account can pretend to capture all phenomena described as "racism" in the literature. I'll consider solutions to this problem.

What Is Racism?

If we are interested by racism, it is because of its negative effects on some individuals and on some groups. If racism never had led to any actions, had not created and perpetuated inequality between groups, it is uncertain we would care about it as much. It is not that there is a necessary link between racism and actions (as we will see later), but rather that because of its effects that racism has become important to track and to understand.

To say that someone or something is racist raises a flag or attracts attention to a kind of moral ill related to race. Claims of racism usually serve to deplore, denounce, or condemn a situation, an idea, an individual, and so forth. They are also ways to raise consciousness about the effects of some practices or behaviors on others. Often times, they are also a way to ask for a change (and/or a reparation from) either in the person (or group) who is accused of racism or in the situation that is qualified as racist. So racism is not a mere descriptive concept, it is a normative one. For instance, to say that an idea or a joke is racist is not just to say that it belongs to a class of ideas or a class of jokes (like one would say that this is an existentialist's idea or that this is a blonde joke). To say that an idea or a joke is racist is also to negatively evaluate that idea or that joke. As Arthur (2007) puts it, the concept of racism is a bit like the concept of "terrorist" or "genocidal": "the evaluative conclusion . . . is embedded in the concept itself. . . . Once we define a person as a terrorist, we have committed ourselves normatively" (12).

I have said that the concept of racism is a normative concept used to refer to a kind of moral ill, but we might want to be more specific. Racism is a moral ill that happens to an individual by virtue of the fact that he is perceived as belonging to a racial group (hereafter, a racialized individual), or to a group that it is perceived as a racial group (hereafter, a racialized group). So if a comet were to strike the earth and in the process eliminated a racialized group, this would not count as racism because it is not an ill that is caused to the group by virtue of being racialized; the latter is just bad luck happening to a racialized group. For something to count as racism, the fact that the individual or the group is racialized has to be a causal factor in the production of the event. But we might want to leave open until later the question of knowing if all moral ills that happen to individuals or groups by virtue of the fact that they are racialized should be labelled racism (Blum 2002a, 2002b, 2004; Garcia 2010).

Contemporary social sciences and philosophy have identified many different forms of racism. Though there are sometimes disagreements concerning the existence or the relative importance of these different forms of racism, I think it's worth mentioning them because they are the background against which the philosophical discussion takes place. I'll follow Zack's (2003; see also Atkin 2012) classification of the different forms of racism in what follows.

The first form of racism is classic or *mens rea* racism (sometimes called "overt racism"). Case 1 is an illustration of that kind of racism. It is grounded in a negative attitude (of hatred or contempt) or a combination of such attitudes (for instance, a mix of hatred and contempt) towards another racialized group that results in intentional actions/or inactions whose goal is to harm in one way or another (for instance, through violence, insults, or discrimination) racialized individuals or the racialized groups as whole.

In many countries, norms now favor the open expression of more egalitarian ideas and chastise the open expression of prejudice. While the extent to which this is true varies, old-fashioned, overt racism is nowadays frowned upon in many societies, enough that many people would not dare to openly express such attitudes. This has led racism to go underground, that is, to operating more covertly. Philosophers as well as researchers in psychology and social sciences have proposed different concepts seeking to capture the new forms racism is taking; I will mention a few in what follows.

Ikuenobe (2010) proposed two variations of classical racism: closet and tolerant racism. A *closet racist* is someone that "has the relevant racist beliefs and attitudes but does everything possible consciously to conceal them, but those racist attitudes and beliefs may be expressed occasionally, albeit inadvertently and unconsciously" (172). A closet racist has what psychologists call an "external motivation" not to discriminate or to respond without prejudice against other's racialized individuals (Amodio 2008). Someone is "externally motivated" if their motivation is to avoid negative reactions from others who may disapprove of prejudice rather than being motivated by internal standards (like the desire to be fair or equitable). A *tolerant racist*, for his part,

> has the relevant racist beliefs or attitudes, expresses them, but is willing to coexist with Blacks [or some other racialized group]. He will try not to openly oppress or discriminate against Blacks [or another racialized group]. But if he can get away with discriminating against them, he will do so.
> (Ikuenobe, 2010, 172)

A tolerant racist is someone who "just tolerates" the presence of racialized others, maybe because they think that their presence is necessary (to fill jobs that no one else wants to do) or because there is nothing they think they can do to change the multiracial state of the society they live in. A tolerant racist is not interested in forming friendships with, living in the same neighbourhood as, or doing everything possible to diminish the inequality suffered by other races. They might move to certain suburbs or neighbourhoods to avoid frequent contact with people of different racialized groups; they might hire only people of their own racialized group to work with; they might have their kids to go to a private school so as they'd stay with people of their own racialized group. As long as oppressed racialized groups stay "in their place," do not advocate for better or equal conditions, the tolerant racist is happy. They might also vote for a right-wing political party which projects, for instance, to build walls over the frontiers of its country to stop the flux of migrants from a particular racialized group that he dislikes.

Finally, there are many people who think that racism has mutated in contemporary society. Think of Case 3: is the case of the assaulted Muslim woman a case of xenophobia, or should we talk here of racism? (note the two are not incompatible; see Kim and Sundstrom 2014). Some have seen in Islamophobia a new form of racism that might be called *cultural racism* (Rattansi 2007). This racism is different because it does not use old racial categories, does not presume intrinsic biological differences, does not explicitly make reference to hierarchical positions of different groups. As Rattansi puts it, "the emphasis is on cultural difference and the genuine fears of ordinary citizens that their national character and, by implication, way of life may be in danger of being overwhelmed and marginalized [by different ethnic or religious groups]" (2007: 98). It might be argued that this is not enough to be considered racism. Indeed, some would claim that cultural racism is *racism* only when the group that is the object of negative feelings and/or discriminatory behaviors is "psychologically" treated as a "race" (one might say, is psychologically racialized), that is, that membership in the group is considered a basis for rich inductive generalizations, is inherited from parents, is rather immutable and so forth (Machery and Faucher, 2017; Mallon 2010; Moya and Boyd 2015).

Previously stated forms of racism involve individuals who are conscious of their racial beliefs and attitudes. The next forms of racism included involve *unacknowledged* forms of racism (Zack, 2003: 255; Atkin talks of "avert racism" to contrast it with "overt racism"; 2012: 118). There are two grand families of unacknowledged racism: *less-than-conscious racism* and *unconscious racism*. Let's start with the first family, which comprises *color-blind racism* (Bonilla-Silva 2006; Bonilla-Silva and Dietrich 2011), *laissez-faire racism* (Bobo and Smith 1995) and *symbolic racism* (Sears and Henry 2003). These theories are usually grounded in two observations: (1) overt racism has been on the decline in the American society in general since at least the second half of the twentieth century (this is true despite sporadic surges of overt expression of racism by some groups in the American society); (2) the disparities between racialized groups that were explained by overt racism are not disappearing. To explain this apparent paradox, sociologists and psychologists postulated that racism is taking new forms.

The new forms of racism share two features. They postulate that (1) because of the advancement of civil rights and the adoption of anti-discrimination laws, whites now believe they live in a "post-racial" or "color-blind" society where racial minorities are not suffering from discrimination or prejudice anymore (so any complaints about racial discrimination or any demands of positive discrimination to rectify racial injustice are perceived as unfounded and thought of as a way to bring back race in the fore, therefore can be seen as a form of racism); and (2) whites use socially available ideological "scripts," "frames," or sets of beliefs to explain and maintain disparities. These scripts, frames, or sets of beliefs are either exculpating whites of their responsibility for racial disparities and/or faulting cultural features of racial minorities for the existence of these disparities (for instance, blaming disparities on a lack of effort from their members, or loose family organization).

Individuals exhibiting these new forms of racism might not recognize their own racism, they might have what is sometimes called a "false-consciousness," rationalizing their negative affects toward other races by blaming members of these groups for their own condition. Moreover, their negative affects are not necessarily grounded in hate or hostility, rather, as Sears puts it, "it may be experienced subjectively as fear, avoidance, and a desire of distance, anger, distaste, disgust, contempt, apprehension, unease or simple dislike" (Sears 1988: 70; cited by Sears and Henry 2003: 260). Not being motivated by racial animus and resorting to abstract ideological concepts (like free market or laissez-faire), they might not recognize that their own actions perpetuate a system of racial domination. For this reason, it is legitimate to talk about "unrecognized" or less-than-conscious racism.

Aversive racism is different from the previous forms of racism because it is espoused by individuals who are often well-intentioned and ostensibly unprejudiced (for a recent review, see Pearson et al. 2009). Indeed, contrary to closet racists, aversive racists explicitly reject racists attitudes and beliefs and try to be fair and equitable in their actions. As Pearson and colleagues put it: "Aversive racists . . . sympathize with victims of past injustice, support principles of racial equality, and genuinely regard themselves as non-prejudiced, but at the same time possess conflicting, *often non-conscious*, negative feelings and beliefs about Blacks [or other races] that are rooted in basic psychological processes that promote racial bias" (2009: 3; my emphasis). Some explain cases like our Case 4 as the product of aversive racism. Police officers, white and black alike, have stereotypes about young black males, about the danger they represent, the likelihood that they carry guns, and so forth. Some think that it is the activation of such stereotypes that explain (at least partially) the asymmetry of shooting rates of black versus young white males (this is called the "weapon bias" or "shooter bias"; Payne 2006). So, to create a (fictional) example of how aversive racism would work, in Case 4, it would be possible to posit that perhaps Officer Freeman, who shot David Joseph, was not an overt racist nor a closet or tolerant racist, maybe that he was even working to advance the cause of Blacks in the United States. However, he might have harbored, unbeknownst to him, stereotypes about black males, and these stereotypes might have led him to overestimate the danger that Joseph posed, which led the officer to shoot him. These unconscious (or not perfectly conscious) stereotypes or attitudes are called "implicit biases" in social psychology, and they are thought to partly explain disparities in health, employment, housing, and education. While the size of these effects has been the object of a recent debate (see for instance, Greenwald et al. 2009; Greenwald et al. 2015; Oswald et al. 2013), the fact remains that despite the decline of overt racism, substantial discrimination and racial disparities persist.

The final form of racism that I will consider in this section is *institutional racism* or *structural racism*, a term introduced by Carmichael and Hamilton (1967) to refer to social, economic, or political inequalities disproportionally affecting a racialized group. This form of racism is called "institutional" or "structural" because it is thought that these inequalities are produced by social structures or cultural practices or political institutions (such as schools, health systems, voting laws, judicial nominations procedures, etc.) that create, perpetuate, or accentuate the unfair advantages of a dominant racialized group on a dominated one. Theorists of institutional or structural racism recognize the fact that *mens rea* or unacknowledged racism is often a factor in the production of the inequalities that they denounce, but these same theorists also state that these factors alone are not sufficient or necessary to produce racial inequalities. These theorists emphasize the fact that some inequalities depend, in part or in total, on social or political structures or institutions or practices, which, because of some of their features, give an unfair advantage to one racialized group over another. For instance, in Case 6, inequalities in educational attainment are thought to be caused by many factors: (a) attitudes of the parents toward education as well as the time they spend reading to their kids, (b) attitudes of the teachers (the fact that they have lower expectations of kids of certain racial groups than others), and (c) quality of the school attended by the children. Among those factors only (c) can be thought as being directly the result of institutional racism (some [Haslanger 2004] also argue that (b) might also be thought as being a form of institutional racism, since despite the good intentions of the teachers, their expectations lead to the perpetuations of an oppressive situation for some racial groups). Indeed, it has been shown that African Americans have access to lower quality schools because of housing discrimination. For a number of reasons (having to do with earning and assets, loan regulations, etc.), African Americans are often relegated to poorer neighbourhoods with less established, less well-equipped and staffed schools than those frequented by whites. Kids studying in those schools have less chance of getting the kind of support and environment they need to achieve good results in school. This is thought to be an important factor in educational disparities that will affect future income prospects that will prolong racial disparity.

As I said earlier, there are debates concerning the relative importance or even the existence of some of the forms of racism that I have mentioned in this section. For instance, some doubt that it makes sense to talk of aversive or unconscious racism (Arkes and Tetlock 2004; Garcia 2010) because phenomena thus qualified might be the result of shared stereotypes rather than racial animus. If the disparities are produced unintentionally by mechanisms that produce unfair advantages for a (usually dominant) racialized group, then it cannot be racism because it is not the result of racial animus (Garcia 2004). It seems therefore that what is at the root of some of disagreements concerning racism is the different conceptions people have of what racism is.

Philosophical Accounts of Racism?

In the previous section, I mentioned a number of phenomena that are called "racism" in the literature. I also pointed out that there are disagreements as to what really "counts" as racism. Disagreements of the latter sort are only possible if one holds that there is *a* concept of racism (one and only one) that is the right one. People who believe in the above, may hold one of two positions: either they assume that the above concept is the one that we folks share, or that the concept is significantly different from our folk concept (in that sense, this concept of racism would be "revisionist," in that it would be significantly different from our folk concept, and not necessarily capture the same phenomena; see Haslanger [2004] for an example of such a concept). Philosophers have until recently believed the former and they have tried to identify the core component(s) (sometimes called the "constitutive elements" or the "essence" or "nature") of our folk concept of racism through conceptual analysis. Conceptual analysis is a philosopher's tool and by using it, philosophers seek to provide the set of necessary and sufficient conditions for the application of a concept. A philosopher's proposed analysis is usually tested against what he thinks are common intuitions. Indeed, generally, a philosopher would propose a fictional or a real case (or many of them) where one condition deemed to be necessary for the application of a concept would be missing, or where all conditions deemed necessary would be present, and see if the concept is judged to apply in those circumstances, or if it generates counterintuitive consequences. If the latter, the proposed analysis would have to be rejected (or modified substantially).

Before presenting the different philosophical accounts of racism, it has to be noted that trying to identify the core components of racism is something different from studying the forms that racism takes in different places or at different times (the latter being what historians and sociologists set out to do). Philosophers using conceptual analysis often explore the "limits" of our concepts by using imaginary cases to test our intuition; while historians, psychologists, and sociologists are interested in "real" cases, and are happy with operational definitions that capture the phenomena they are trying to explain (without being exhaustive or trying to capture the "essence" or "nature" of the concept). So, it is possible that philosophers will find the later definitions to be lacking. I think it would sometimes be unfair to accuse historians, psychologists or sociologists of failing to spell out the necessary and sufficient conditions for something to be racist: they are, so to speak, playing a different game than philosophers. At other times, philosophers might be disturbed by an extension of the use of the concept to cases that they think are not racism; it is there that one encounters real and substantial points of disagreement. One question that such disagreements raise is "By virtue of what do philosophers think that they can impose a particular definition of racism?" I won't try to answer that question here, but that is something one might want to hold in mind while considering various arguments for or against certain definitions of racism.

There are two grand families of philosophical accounts of racism: one locates the core elements of racism in individuals (we can call these accounts "agent-based" or "input accounts"), while another locates them in the effects of certain actions or processes (for this reason we can call these "output accounts"). Until recently, philosophers have mainly been concerned with the first family of accounts of racism.

There are three types of agent-based accounts: the doxastic, the behavioral, and the affective/volitional account. I will present them shortly in what follows; then I'll explain what their limitations are (I am expanding here on work I have previously done with Edouard Machery; Faucher and Machery 2009).

According to the proponents of a pure version of the doxastic account such as, for example, Zack (1999) or Shelby (2002), a necessary and sufficient condition for racism is a set of beliefs (that includes minimally the belief that there are races). For instance, according to Zack, racial thinking is fairly recent, dating from the eighteenth century. Race is at the center of a cluster of ideas (a kind of theory) proposed by philosophers like Hume or Kant to explain human difference, ideas which have since been used to rationalize European domination of other groups of humans. Zack also thinks that these ideas are articulated in the form of Kuhnian paradigms, ensconced in sets of beliefs (some concerning the existence of race, some others about the specific groups called "races"), as well as ways of seeing and categorizing, and so forth. As she puts it:

> The ingredients of a racial paradigm at any given time would include a taxonomy of race, the criteria for membership in different races and their application to individuals, social customs and laws that pertain to race, moral beliefs about different race relations, expectations for change in social areas pertaining to race, ideologies of race, and beliefs about the connections between physical race and human physical attributes.
>
> (Zack 2002: 110)

According to Zack, racism depends first and foremost of the acceptance of the racial paradigm (and as for scientific paradigms, the racial paradigm can rationally be maintained in the face of counter-evidence, that is, until such counter-evidence does become so overwhelming that it is not possible to hold to it anymore).

Shelby for his part thinks of racism as a type of ideology. As he puts it, "ideologies are widely accepted illusory *systems of beliefs* that function to establish or reinforce structures of social oppressions" (2002: 415; my emphasis). What seems to distinguish ideologies from other sets of beliefs is their function, which is to rationalize oppression. The precise content of the ideology underlying racism is rather dynamic in that "with the possible exception of the belief in the reality of races, no one belief is essential to the legitimating function of the belief system" (2002: 417).

Shelby's theory can be conceived as a pure form of the doxastic approach. While according to other "impure" forms, including Zack's previously cited and Appiah's (1990), racism essentially involves believing in a particular set of propositions. They also involve having specific dispositions with respect to these beliefs (see also Lengbeyer 2004). To be racist, people must believe that races exist (a belief sometimes called "racialism") and that they are morally significant (either because races are correlated with morally significant properties, or because races are intrinsically morally significant). As Appiah noted (1990: 8; our emphasis), the dispositions themselves consist of

> assent[ing] to false propositions, both moral and theoretical, about races—propositions that support policies or beliefs that are to the disadvantage of some race (or races) as opposed to others . . . and *to do so even in face of evidence and argument that should appropriately lead to giving those propositions up.*

Racism would thus be a combination of false beliefs (for example, in the inferiority of one group compared to another) and of a cognitive resistance to rational revision of those beliefs in light of countervailing evidence.

The behavioral account insists that racism essentially involves behaving or being disposed to behave in a way that is harmful to the members of a racial group. Michael Philips has proposed a version of this model in which the expression "racist" is used in "a logically primary sense" to qualify actions (what he calls "Basic Racist Acts"). Thus, he wrote:

> P performs a Basic Racist Act by doing A when: (a) P does A in order to harm Q because Q is a member of a certain ethnic [or racial] group; or (b) (regardless of P's intentions or purposes) P's doing A can reasonably be expected to mistreat Q as a consequence of Q's being a member of a certain ethnic [or racial] group.
>
> (1984: 77)

He continues:

> Note that, on this account, P's motives, beliefs, feeling, or intentions need not be taken into account in determining that P performed a racist act.
>
> (1984: 77)

I take Philips to mean that there can be cases of "neglectful racism," where someone hurt someone else unintentionally as a consequence of that person being a member of a particular race, but should had known better. For instance, imagine that you have been reading a lot about implicit biases in hiring and that you are just about to open a position in your company. Imagine further that someone looking at your hiring process finds out that you have been discarding certain candidates on the basis of their race (for instance, you found all sorts of reasons not to hire candidates that have Asian-sounding names). Because you knew about potential biases and did nothing to prevent them, you are responsible for the harm caused by your actions, and because this harm specifically affects members of a racial group and was done by virtue of the fact that they were thought to belong to that group, your actions might be said to be racist (for a detailed discussion of examples of that kind in conjunction with responsibility, see Washington and Kelly 2016). More generally, Philips could refer to the fact that we hold people to certain standards concerning their actions and that, in some cases, we expect people to know about the effects of their actions on racial others (and to avoid them or to accept being blamed for not doing so; Glasgow 2016; Watson 1996; Zhang 2016).

In his book *Racism: A Short History*, Fredrickson has defended another version of the behavioral model:

> Racism exists only when one ethnic group or historical collectivity dominates, excludes or seeks to eliminate another on the basis of differences that it [the first group] believes are hereditary and unalterable.
>
> (2002: 170)

In Fredrickson's version of the behavioral account as in the doxastic account, racism involves believing in the existence of racial differences; however, in contrast to the doxastic model, this belief must be entertained by an ethnic group or by a collectivity that is able and disposed to act against another group. Behavior is thus essential to racism: without it, one cannot truly talk of racism; there is only racialism. Commenting on and endorsing Appiah's distinction between racialist and racist, Fredrickson wrote (for a similar account, see Goldberg 1990):

> Racialists do not become racists until they make such convictions the basis for claiming special privileges for members of what they consider to be their own race, and for disparaging and doing harm to those deemed racially Other.
>
> (2002: 154)

While the behavioral account emphasizes people's behavior and the doxastic account emphasizes people's beliefs, the *affective/volitional account* (sometimes also called the "attitudinal account"; Glasgow 2009) posits that either emotions or non-cognitive dispositions are at the core of racism. There are two main versions of this account. Accordingly, one is racist if:

1. They display some form of antipathy or disregard, mostly, but not necessarily (see Dixon et al., 2012) in the form of specific negative emotion(s) (like hate, contempt, distrust, or fear) or some disposition to have this emotion or these emotions toward members of a specific racialized group, such that they will be motivated to act (or not to act) in ways that will negatively impact them (for proponents of this view, see Arthur 2007: 17; Faucher and Machery 2009; Kim and Sundstrum 2014); or
2. They have a host of non-cognitive mental states that can be understood as a lack of concern, callous indifference, or ill-will against members of a specific race (Garcia [2011, 255] thinks that (1) above is racism only when it reduces to (2) and that (2) also includes states that are not affective).

In a paper written with Edouard Machery (Faucher and Machery 2009), we defended a version of (1). Using this version of the affective/volitional account, some important cases of racism (but not necessarily all cases) are the result of negative emotions like hate, contempt, moral indignation, or fear towards target racialized groups. This account is based on a socio-functional approach to emotions (for a short presentation of such an approach see Neuberg and Schaller 2016). According to a functional approach to emotions, each emotion (fear, disgust, anger, embarrassment, etc.) is a specific response (or a set of coordinated responses) to a specific problem. The socio-functional approach to emotions is a version of the functional approach. In contrast to other functional approaches, which focus more on the problems posed by the physical environment (e.g., avoiding toxic food), it highlights the problems that we encounter in our social life. The problems posed by members of other groups to our own group are among these problems. Some emotions constitute an answer to those problems by signaling that some action is needed to solve these problems and by motivating the form of appropriate action. The emotions evoked by a particular racialized group should thus correspond to the problems that that group is seen as posing to members of another racialized or social group. Because a given racialized group might be seen as posing several problems, it might evoke a combination of emotions. It is also plausible that different racialized groups can be seen, by the very same group, as posing different types of problems (contamination, physical danger, economic danger, etc.). Thus, such distinct racialized groups should evoke different emotions (disgust, fear, indignation, or anger). Further still, sub-groups within these groups may be seen as posing different problems and may thus themselves evoke different emotions. For instance, in the United States, it is plausible that young African American men evoke fear, while African American women evoke a different emotion unrelated to fear. It is also possible that the problems a group is seen as posing may vary by location. This version of the affective/voltional theory is thus a solution to a problem of usual accounts of racism that has been identified by Kim and Sundstrum according to whom

> accounts of racism tend to have a generality that obscures important particularities of group-specific types of racism: e.g., the genocide-based racism against Native Americans differs notably from the slavery-based racism against African Americans, and the racist anti-Semitism directed at Jews is distinct in expression and historical effect.
>
> (2014: 21)

This version of the affective/volitional account aims to correct this lacuna by positing different forms of racism tied with different contexts.

The previous form of the affective/volitional account is at present not the dominant one. The most influential version of it is found in a series of articles written by Garcia (1996/2003, 1997, 1999, 2004, 2010, ms) in which he defends a version of (2) above. He has proposed that a behavior (an institution, a thought, etc.) is racist if and only if it results from (or is maintained by) a vicious attitude, namely hate or malevolence (but also of lack of benevolence, disdain, or callous indifference) toward the members of a particular race, and that a person is racist if and only if she feeds on this hate and malevolence. As he has put it, "in its central and most vicious form, it [racism] is a hatred, ill-will, directed against a person or persons on account of their assigned race" (1996/2003: 259). As Garcia puts it, his account "concentrates on the disposition of certain volitions, along with desires, preferences, choices, and affective states" (2010: 253). For him, what underlies racial judgments and actions deemed to be racist is malevolence, a "deformation of character" (2004: 41) that is opposed to benevolence and justice (as he sometimes puts it, opposed to "benevolent love") and which leads to disregard of the welfare of racial others. Importantly for later discussion, Garcia posits that one does not need to have beliefs about the existence of races to have a vicious attitude toward members of a particular race (2001: 134).

Each of the previous accounts can be criticized on the grounds that it does not capture each and every aspect of racism. First, contrary to what advocates of the doxastic account assert, it does not appear to be necessary to believe in the existence of races to be racist. Someone can sincerely profess that races do not exist, and yet still be racist if they have a malevolent attitude toward a particular racial group. Indeed, this is the reason why doxastic accounts do not fare very well with the new forms of racism I mentioned in the previous section (like color-blind racism or symbolic racism). These new forms of racism are predicated on the idea that nowadays agents believe that biological races do not exist, but still entertain negative attitudes towards racialized groups.

Second, and to counter Fredrickson's behavioral account, it seems quite conceivable that we would think of someone as a racist even if they were powerless and could not harm the members of another racialized group, provided that they demonstrated hate or lack concern for the other racialized group. For instance, one could imagine someone living in an isolated area, without any contact with members of a specific racialized group, yet we would consider that person to be racist if they had a vicious attitude toward them (Garcia 1996/2003: 268). We also might want to say that the tolerant racist we mentioned in the previous section is "racist," even if they structure their environment and control their actions in such a way that their racism would not have any effect on anyone.

More generally, behavioral accounts suffer from two types of problems. First, in many cases, it is not exactly clear what can reasonably be expected of someone (recall that the second part of Philips's definition implies that someone is racist if it could be expected that their actions would have a negative impact on members of a racialized group), and who is entitled to settle the question (Garcia 2001). For instance, would well-intentioned teachers who, to counter the malnutrition of their mainly black students, proceed to distribute milk (not knowing that it is likely that many of their students are lactose intolerant), reasonably be expected to know about their students' lactose intolerance—therefore should these teachers be considered racists? Second, behavioral accounts do not fare well with reverse discrimination (that is, discrimination against members of a dominant group in favor of members of a discriminated group; see Gracia 2010 on these questions).

Third, affective/volitional accounts face a problem with "benevolent" forms of racism (sometimes also called "paternalistic racism"; see Dixon et al., 2012). A benevolent racist is someone who thinks that members of a racialized group R are inferior (either morally or intellectually) and need to be taken care of. Though it is obvious that benevolent racism can be harmful, it is easy to imagine—despite Garcia's assessment that benevolent racism is necessarily malevolent (Garcia 1997, 2001)—cases of benevolent racists who have a really pure heart (for instance, someone brought up to believe that members of another racialized group were unable to govern themselves and were better of governed by members of "a more able race"). Accounts similar to Garcia's also face another problem: it is not clear if one can have ill-will against members of a racial group without having any beliefs (Shelby 2002; Mills 2003). At the minimum, one must believe that these individuals belong to a racial group. Accounts like Faucher and Machery are better equipped to face that kind of problem since they are built around the idea that racism is shaped by what individuals believe about the specific dangers posed by racialized groups. Unfortunately, they face other problems: for instance, one can imagine the case of someone who has no negative feelings toward members of race R, but who has been raised to believe that the other racialized group is inferior in some way (for example, they think that members of race R are lazy). This belief will produce a host of negative effects, like depriving members of this race R of work, or bonuses related to work performance, and so forth, that one might want to consider as a form of racism.

Because of these limitations, it is hard to figure out where racism is really located (in the mind, in the heart, or in the actions of agents); Glasgow calls this the "location problem" (2009: 69). If this problem is not solved by the accounts mentioned above, it is also not solved by hybrid accounts in which racism is seen as being a combination of the elements of the individual accounts. For instance, Corlett (1993, 2003) and Dummett (2004) have proposed understanding racism as a combination of prejudice (i.e., a negative attitude) and behavior (i.e., discrimination). Though these accounts might better capture the kind of phenomena that got people interested in "racism" in the first place, or the phenomena that are most socially relevant (if racism had been confined to powerless individuals living on desert islands, racism would not be a pressing issue), they end up excluding more cases than non-hybrid accounts of the kind we mentioned in the previous paragraph (the more elements one adds to our definition, the more restrictive it is). Another possible solution to the problem, which avoids the previous objection to hybrid accounts, is a disjointed analysis: for instance, an analysis of racism as the product of either inferiorization or antipathy (Blum 2002a; 2002b). Glasgow faults this kind of solution for not being able to accommodate all cases of what we consider racist: for instance, stereotypical remarks concerning a racial group coming from someone with a pure heart and who harbors no beliefs in racial inferiority of that racial group. In such a case, Glasgow argues, the remark would be racist, even if the person uttering it is not. It is not clear that this could not be patched by adding more elements in the disjunction. But then, one would run the risk to trivialize the concept of racism as it would lose its precise meaning.

A more general problem for agent-based accounts comes from cases of institutional racism. It is generally admitted that some cases of institutional racism are forms of racism by virtue of the intentions of those who built the institutions in the first place, or those who help maintain them now. Yet some cases of institutional racism cannot be so explained. For instance, imagine university admission policies that would privilege students from specific high schools (because students from these high schools are more likely to have success at the university level) and that, as a side effect that was not foreseen by those who adopted the policies, it results in harming students from a particular racial minority that has an historical background of racist mistreatment (Atkin [2012] calls these forms of racism "indirect"). According to agent-based accounts, these policies would not be racist if they were adopted (or maintained) via a process involving no racist beliefs, malevolent motives, or individual behaviors that could be labeled racist. However, some might want to insist on calling the policies "racist" (Glasgow 2009: 76).

At this point, it seems that different accounts can accommodate different intuitions about what is racist and what is not, but that no accounts can accommodate all of our intuitions. The solution to this situation might be either to abandon the idea of producing a unifying account that would encompass all our intuitions or to produce a different one. I'll come back on the first solution at the end of this section; let's look at the second solution for now.

Some philosophers have proposed a type of account that does not try to locate racism inside the agent, but rather in the effects something or someone has on people of a particular race(s). For instance, Glasgow has proposed that something or someone is racist if and only if that thing or person is disrespectful towards members of a racialized group *qua* members of that group (we can call his approach "the racial disrespect" view; for a similar account, but in terms of disregard, see Taylor 2004) According to Glasgow, this kind of account can accommodate all of the various agent-based cases, plus cases not covered by them (like the peculiar form of institutional racism I mentioned earlier or the behaviors caused by unconscious biases). As he puts it: "One of the reasons that disrespect is a useful *analysans* for racism is that disrespect is abstract enough to take as many forms as racism takes" (Glasgow 2009: 92). One problem with this analysis is that it might be over-inclusive as there are many disrespectful acts that we might not want to call racist, for instance, the fact of feeling uneasy in the presence of someone perceived as belonging to another race might be interpreted as disrespect. Another problem, noted by Garcia (ms), is that according to some analyses, disrespectful acts depend on the imputation of mental states of an agent, more specifically, they seem to flow from an attitude of disrespect. If so, the racial disrespect account is not really different from the input-based account.

Given that all the accounts we presented in this section suffer from some defects, and that none seem to capture all our intuitions, one might be tempted to give up the idea that "racism" refers to a set phenomenon that could be captured by one and only one analysis. This is a strategy adopted by Haslanger (2004). She observed that:

> Persistent institutional injustice is a major source of harm to people of color. Of course, moral vice—bigotry and the like—is also a problem. But if we want the term "racism" to capture all the barriers to racial justice, I submit that it is reasonable to count as "racist" not only the attitudes and actions of individuals but also the full range of practices, institutions, policies, and such like that, I've argued, count as racially oppressive.
>
> (2004: 122)

For this reason, she recommends a "mixed approach," one "that does not attempt to reduce either agent or structural oppression to the other" (Haslanger 2004: 107; for a similar position, see Goldberg 1990). Her account is different from Blum's disjunctive account in that, contrary to Blum who tries to ground his analysis in both history and current folk use, Haslanger's talk of racial structural or institutional oppression is explicitly revisionary. It could also be used opportunistically in different situations or context. Maybe one would want to distinguish different meanings of racism (racism1, racism2, etc.) in order to identify the different racial factors involved in the production of racial injustice or racial ills. So, we might agree that we use the term "racism" to signal situations of moral import, it is possible to argue that different forms of racism could be wrong for different reasons (we might call this thesis "moral pluralism" and oppose it, to "moral monism" which would consider all cases of racism wrong for the same kind of reason). If you look at Cases 1–6 and agree to see in them some forms of racism, you might easily find different reasons to consider them morally wrong or immoral. Cases 1 and 3 involve vicious attitudes; Case 2 has been historically associated with vicious attitudes (and it might still be); while Cases 4, 5, and 6 are wrong because they perpetuate injustice. If such is the case, some expressions of racism can be wrong for more than one reason. But also, the absence of one form of moral ill should not be taken as a guarantee of the absence of the other(s). For instance, arguing against the sufficiency of Garcia's account, Haslanger (2004) insightfully observes that: "love, certain kinds of respect, and tolerance are no guarantee of justice. A moment of reflection on sexism can reveal that. For women, love and respect have often been offered as a substitute of justice, and yet unjust loving relationships are the norm, not the exception" (122).

Conclusion

There are reasons to think that we will never agree on what racism is, and I think it would be sobering if we could agree on that. One reason why I think it would be important to recognize this (other than the ones mentioned in the previous sections), is the question of trying to establish who is right and who is wrong about the meaning of the term would be foregrounded by the question of identifying the different kinds of moral ills that are involved in the different phenomena people call racism. One advantage of adopting such a policy, as Lawrence Blum once observed (2004: 77), would be to attract attention to the larger class of "moral ills" which have been neglected by philosophers.

References

Amodio, D. M. (2008) "The Social Neuroscience of Intergroup Relations." *European Review of Social Psychology* 19: 1–54.

Appiah, K. A. (1990) "Racisms," in D. T. Goldberg (ed.), *Anatomy of Racism*, Minneapolis: University of Minnesota Press, pp. 3–17.

Arkes, H. R., and Tetlock, P. E. (2004) "Attributions of Implicit Prejudice, Or 'Would Jesse Jackson "Fail" the Implicit Association Test?'" *Psychological Inquiry* 15, no. 4: 257–278.

Arthur, J. (2007) *Race, Equality, and the Burden of History*, Cambridge: Cambridge University Press.

Atkin, A. (2012) *The Philosophy of Race*, Durham: Acumen.

Baum, K. B. (2016) "Manitoba Community Seeks Answers as Youth Suicides Soar." *Globe and Mail*, March 11. Updated March 12 (www.theglobeandmail.com/news/national/a-community-seeks-answers-as-youth-suicides-soar/article29199297/).

Blum, L. (2002a) "Racism: What It Is and What It Isn't." *Studies in Philosophy and Education* 21: 203–218.
———. (2002b) *"I Am Not a Racist But . . .": The Moral Quandary of Race*, Ithaca: Cornell University Press.
———. (2004) "What Do Accounts of 'Racism' Do?" in M. P. Levine and T. Pataki (eds.), *Racism in Mind*, Ithaca: Cornell University Press, pp. 56–77.
Bobo, L. D., and Smith, R. A. (1995) "From Jim Crow Racism to Laissez-Faire Racism: The Transformation of Racial Attitudes," in W. E. Katkin, N. Landsman and A. Tyree (eds.), *Beyond Pluralism: The Conception of Groups and Group Identities in America*, Urbana: University of Illinois Press, pp. 182–220.
Bonilla-Silva, E. (2006) *Racism Without Racists: Color-Blind Racism and the Persistence of Racial Inequality in the United States*, 2nd edition, Lanham: Rowman & Littlefield.
Bonilla-Silva, E., and Dietrich, D. (2011) "The Sweet Enchantment of Color-Blind Racism in Obamerica." *Annals of the American Academy of Political and Social Science* 634: 190–206.
Carmichael, S., and Hamilton, C. (1967) *Black Power: The Politics of Liberation*, Harmondworth: Penguin.
Cook, L. (2015) "U.S. Education: Still Separate and Unequal," *U.S. News*. www.usnews.com/news/blogs/data-mine/2015/01/28/us-education-still-separate-and-unequal.
Corlett, J. A. (1993) "Racism and Affirmative Action." *Journal of Social Philosophy* 24(1): 163–175.
———. (2003) *Race, Racism and Reparations*, Ithaca: Cornell University Press.
Costa, R. et al. (2015) "Church Shooting Suspect Dylann Roof Captured Amid Hate Crime Investigation." *Washington Post*, June 18 (www.washingtonpost.com/news/morning-mix/wp/2015/06/17/white-gunman-sought-in-shooting-at-historic-charleston-african-ame-church/?utm_term=.c48960e24a83).
Dixon, J., M. Levine, S. Reicher and K. Durrheim (2012) "Beyond Prejudice: Are Negative Evaluations the Problem and is Getting us to Like One Another the Solution?". *Behavioral and Brain Sciences* 35 (6): 411–425.
Dummett, M. (2004) "The Nature of Racism," in M. P. Levine and T. Pataki (eds.), *Racism in Mind*, Ithaca: Cornell University Press, pp. 27–34.
Faucher, L., and Machery, E. (2009) "Racism: Against Jorge Garcia's Moral and Psychological Monism." *Philosophy of the Social Sciences* 39, no. 1: 41–62.
Fredrickson, G. (2002). *Racism: A Short History*, Princeton: Princeton University Press.
Garcia, J.L.A. (1996/2003) "The Heart of Racism." *Journal of Social Philosophy* 27, no. 1; reprinted in B. Boxil (Ed.), *Race and Racism*, Oxford: Oxford University Press, pp. 257–296.
———. (1997) "Current Conceptions of Racism: A Critical Examination of Some Recent Social Philosophy." *Journal of Social Philosophy* 28: 5–42.
———. (1999) "Philosophical Analysis and the Moral Concept of Racism." *Philosophy and Social Criticism* 25: 1–32.
———. (2001) "Racism and Racial Discourse." *Philosophical Forum* 32, no. 2: 125–145.
———. (2004) "Three Sites for Racism: Social Structures, Valuing, and Vice," in M. P. Levine and T. Pataki (eds.), *Racism in Mind*, Ithaca: Cornell University Press, pp. 35–55.
———.(2010) "Racism, Psychology, and Morality: Dialogue with Faucher and Machery." *Philosophy of the Social Sciences* 41 (2): 250–268.
———.(2010) "Racism: Negative and Positive?" *Monist* 93, no. 2: 208–227.
———. (2011) "Racism, Psychology, and Morality: Dialogue With Faucher and Machery." *Philosophy of the Social Sciences* 41, no. 2: 250–268.
———. ms. "Racist Disrespect in Moral Theory: Dialogue with Glasgow".
Glasgow, J. (2009) "Racism as Disrespect." *Ethics* 120: 64–93.
———. (2016) "Alienation and Responsibility," in M. Brownstein and J. Saul (eds.), *Implicit Bias and Philosophy*, Vol. 2, Oxford: Oxford University Press, 37–61.
Goldberg, D. T. (1990) "Racism and Rationality: The Need for a New Critique." *Philosophy of the Social Sciences* 20, no. 3: 317–350.
Greenwald, A. G., Banaji, M. R., and Nosek, B. A. (2015) "Statistically Small Effects of the Implicit Association Test Can Have Societally Large Effects." *Journal of Personality and Social Psychology* 108: 553–561.

Greenwald, A. G., Poehlman, T. A., Uhlmann, E., and Banaji, M. R. (2009) "Understanding and Using the Implicit Association Test: III. Meta-Analysis of Predictive Validity." *Journal of Personality and Social Psychology* 97: 17–41.

Harper, Shaun R. (2016) "No, Protesters Who Point Out Campus Racism Aren't Silencing Anyone." *Washington Post*, March 10 (www.washingtonpost.com/posteverything/wp/2016/03/10/protests-against-campus-racism-dont-threaten-free-speech-they-embrace-it/?utm_term=.27fc20d1457d).

Haslanger, S. (2004) "Oppressions: Racial and Other," in M. P. Levine and T. Pataki (eds.), *Racism in Mind*, Ithaca: Cornell University Press, pp. 97–123.

Ikuenobe, P. (2010). "Conceptualizing Racism and Its Subtle Forms." *Journal for the Theory of Social Behaviour* 41, no. 2: 161–181.

Kelly, D., Faucher, L., and Machery, E. (2010) "Getting Rid of Racism: Assessing Three Proposals in Light of Psychological Evidence." *Journal of Social Philosophy* 41, no. 3: 293–322.

Kim, D. H., and Sundstrom, R. R. (2014) "Xenophobia and Racism." *Critical Philosophy of Race* 2, no. 1: 20–45.

Lengbeyer, L. A. (2004) "Racism and Impure Hearts," In M. P. Levine and T. Pataki (eds.), *Racism in Mind*, Ithaca: Cornell University Press, pp. 158–178.

Machery, E., and Faucher, L. (2017). "Why Do We Think Racially? Culture, Evolution, and Cognition". *Handbook of Categorization in Cognitive Science*, 2nd edition, Elsevier, 1135–1175.

Mallon, R. (2010) "Sources of Racialism." *Journal of Social Philosophy* 41, no. 3: 272–292.

Mathlas, C. (2015) "A Running List of Shameful Islamophobic Acts Since the Paris Attacks," *Huffington Post*, November 20. Updated December 16.

Miller, M. E. (2015) "Can We All Agree That the Confederate Flag Is Racist? Apparently Not, According to Poll." *Washington Post*, July 1.

Mills, C. (2003) "Heart's Attack: A Critique of Jorge Garcia's Volitional Conception of Racism." *Journal of Ethics* 7: 29–62.

Mindock, C. (2015) "Charleston Shooting Racial Motivation? Dylann Storm Roof Told Black Neighbor He Planned On Killing." *International Business Times*, June 8 (www.ibtimes.com/charleston-shooting-racial-motivation-dylann-storm-roof-told-black-neighbor-he-1974050).

Moya, C., and Boyd, R. (2015) "Different Selection Pressures Give Rise to Distinct Ethnic Phenomena: A Functionalist Framework With Illustrations from the Peruvian Altiplano." *Human Nature* 26, no. 1: 1–27. doi:10.1007/s12110-015-9224-9.

Neuberg, S. L., and Schaller, M. (2016) "An Evolutionary Threat-Management Approach to Prejudices." *Current Opinions in Psychology* 7: 1–5.

Oswald, F. L., Mitchell, G., Blanton, H., Jaccard, J., and Tetlock, P. E. (2013) "Predicting Ethnic and Racial Discrimination: A Meta-Analysis of IAT Criterion Studies." *Journal of Personality and Social Psychology*, 105, no. 2: 171–192.

Payne, B. K. (2006). "Weapon Bias: Split Second Decisions and Unintended Stereotyping." *Current Directions in Psychological Science* 15: 287–291.

Pearson, A., Dovidio, J., and Gaertner, S. (2009) "The Nature of Contemporary Prejudice: Insights From Aversive Racism." *Social and Personality Psychology Compass* 3: 1–25.

Philips, M. (1984) "Racist Acts and Racist Humor." *Canadian Journal of Philosophy* 14: 75–96.

Rattansi, A. (2007) *Racism: A Very Short Introduction*, Oxford: Oxford University Press.

Ricke, C., and Bien, C. (2016) "APD Fires Officer Who Shot, Killed David Joseph." *KXAN*, March 21 (http://kxan.com/2016/03/21/officer-freeman-waives-right-to-hearing-in-17-year-olds-death/).

Ryan, C. L., and Bauman, K. (2016) "Educational Attainment in the United States: 2015." *Populations Characteristics: Current Population Reports*, U.S. Census Bureau.

Sears, D. O. (1988) "Symbolic Racism," in P. Katz and D. Taylor (eds.), *Eliminating Racism: Profiles in Controversy*, New York: Plenum Press, pp. 53–84.

Sears, D. O., and Henry, P. J. (2003). "The Origins of Symbolic Racism." *Journal of Personality and Social Psychology* 85, no. 2: 259–275.

Shelby, T. (2002) "Is Racism in the Heart?" *Journal of Social Philosophy* 33: 411–420.

Taylor, P.C. (2004) *Race: A Philosophical Introduction*, Malden, MA: Polity Press.
Washington, N., and Kelly, D. (2016) "Whose Responsible for This? Moral Responsibility, Externalism, and Knowledge About Implicit Bias," in M. Brownstein and J. Saul (eds.). *Implicit Bias and Philosophy*, Vol. 2, Oxford: Oxford University Press.
Watson, G. (1996) "Two Faces of Responsibility." *Philosophical Topics* 24, no. 2: 227–248.
Zack, N. (1999) "Philosophy and Racial Paradigms." *Journal of Value Inquiry* 33: 299–317.
———. (2002) *Philosophy of Science and Race*, London: Routledge.
———. (2003) "Race and Racial Discrimination," in H. Lafollette (ed.), *The Oxford Handbook of Practical Ethics*, Oxford: Oxford University Press, 245–271.
Zhang, R. (2016) "Attributability, Accountability, and Implicit Attitudes," in M. Brownstein and J. Saul (eds.), *Implicit Bias and Philosophy*, Vol. 2, Oxford: Oxford University Press.

30
ON RACE AND SOLIDARITY
Reconsiderations
Lucius Turner Outlaw (Jr.)

Racial Solidarity?

If there are no "races"—that is, if notions that the human species is distinguished by diverse self-reproducing, bio-culturally related groupings of individuals who share the distinguishing characteristics of supposed raciality are erroneous since, empirically, there are no groupings that fulfill the notions—then notions of *racial solidarity* are likewise misguided, perhaps even immoral in important instances (e.g., when fostering such solidarity is for purposes determined unjust). The work to be done, then, seems that of identifying, explaining, and critiquing the misguided notions in keeping with efforts to promote the cessation of efforts to forge and/or sustain such forms of solidarity.

Numerous notions of raciality have been explored in various fields of natural and social sciences, and in socio-political life, and found inadequate. Recent debates among academic philosophers regarding the viability—or lack thereof—of such notions have given rise to sufficient research and scholarly activities as to generate a new disciplinary subfield, "Philosophy of Race." And among philosophers, too, many are convinced there are no "races" or, at the very least, that referring to or regarding groupings of individuals as "races" should cease given all of the harm that has ensued by way of nefarious deployments of the notions.

Still, there some among philosophers, and among practitioners of various sciences—natural, social, and humanistic—and arts who argue for continuing to regard particular forms of bio-culturally related groupings as "races," and as retrospectively and prospectively of substantial anthropological significance, though notions of raciality, many are convinced, do need careful rehabilitation. For some among this disparate aggregate of racialists, revised conceptualizations of raciality are important resources for understanding the emergence and dispersive, evolving developments of the human species across expanses of times and spaces into bio-culturally diverse populations, these populational diversities having become crucial to the evolutionary well-being of our species as well as the sources of so very much that has been, and can be even more, enriching of life lived in critical appreciation of the riches while attenuating the inevitable and promoted conflicts.

I count myself among those endeavoring to understand the developments of the formation and maintenance of such relatively distinctive groupings for which some (though by no means all) forms and intensities of relations of solidarity have been anthropologically contingent necessities.[1] In what follows I offer a sketch of an approach towards such an understanding, one that, if viable, might serve as a context for a fuller exploration of forms of "racial solidarity" worth fostering in the present and future. First, how best to understand human beings . . .

What Is "Man"?

> it is evident that the state is a creation of nature, and that man is by nature a political animal. And he who by nature and not by mere accident is without a state, is either a bad man or above humanity.
> (*Politics* 1973d: 598)

Aristotle's characterization of "man" as a "political animal" is all too familiar. His characterization, however, was not what, today, is often meant when describing someone as "political": namely, that they engage in self-serving, or unfair group-favoring, partisan, agonistic, adversarial activities in the realm of politics rather than seeking "the common good," and in contrast to other modes of behavior appropriate to other, supposedly non-political, realms of life (private life, non-political social life, economic life). Rather, for Aristotle all of shared human living—that is, all of life lived in association with others—constituted "political" life, which, in the "highest" form of associated living in a state, was best structured by terms and principles of ordering that were explicated in a constitution. Only gods or beasts live otherwise, or alone, he reasoned.

For Aristotle, then, political life was characteristic of the human species *by nature*: it was the outcome of processes of development that actualize and realize potentialities definitive of our species. (The *nature* of a thing or being is what it is when it is "most fully developed" and that distinguishes it as the *kind* of thing or being that it is.) And in humans that developmental process began in the foundational unit of the nuclear family (male and female producing offspring), continued through collections of families into villages, and reached its fullness when villages came together to form a state (*Politics* 1973d: 596–598).

How was it for Aristotle that humans "by nature" developed in this way? It was because, as was the case for living beings of all kinds, humans have an "innate impulse to change":

> Of things that exist, some exist by nature, some from other causes. "By nature" the animals and their parts exist, and the plants and the simple bodies (earth, fire, air, water)—for we say that these and the like exist "by nature."
>
> All the things mentioned present a feature in which they differ from things which are *not* constituted by nature. Each of them has *within itself* a principle of motion and of stationariness (in respect of place, or of growth and decrease, or by way of alteration) . . . nature is a source or cause of being moved and of being at rest in that to which it belongs primarily, in virtue of itself and not in virtue of a concomitant attribute.
> (Aristotle, *Physics* 1973c: 122–123, emphasis in original)

"Man," then, as a kind of living being, has within itself "the source of its own production" (Aristotle, *Physics* 1973c: 123). Beings that are "by nature" have definitive, inherent properties that make for—are a *cause* of—developmental changes; and the understanding of this particular cause—*nature*—was the effort of Aristotle's *Physics*.

Thus, for Aristotle the understanding of "man" as a political animal could not be achieved by examining political life alone. Rather, "man" had also to be understood as a particular kind of living being *of* nature, *by* nature. And, understood, as well, in terms of how best—given a full understanding of "man" as a being of nature with inherent principles of motion (movement and rest) and of change or alteration (growth and decline) that persists in associations of interrelated levels of complexity (nuclear family; collections of nuclear and extended families constituting villages; collections of villages constituting a state)—the relations comprising the associations of political life should be oriented, forged, and regulated, and to what ends. The effort to achieve and articulate this understanding was the work of Aristotle's *Ethics*: determining how normative ordering could and should be achieved and sustained through intelligently guided, intensively habit-forming practices that would subsequently structure and order ethical choices and behavior (Aristotle, *Nicomachean Ethics* 1973b: 337–581).

More still was required: an understanding of the particular part of the makeup of the human animal that was the "source of its own production" of motion and change, and in terms of which the ethical ends of living, individually and in association with others, could be achieved if that particularly important part were properly ordered: an understanding of the *soul* of "man," the work Aristotle pursued in *De Anima* ("On the Soul"):

> the soul must be a substance in the sense of the form of a natural body having life potentially within in. But substance is actuality and thus soul is the actuality of a body . . . the soul is the first grade of actuality of a natural body having life potentially in it. The body so described is a body which is organized . . . If then, we have to give a formula applicable to all kinds of soul, we must describe it as the first grade of actuality of a natural organized body.
> (Aristotle, *De Anima* ("On the Soul") 1973a: 182)

The soul, further, was that which provided living things "the power of self-nutrition," growth, and decay (Aristotle, *De Anima* ("On the Soul") 1973a: 184–185). But in living things that were animals, the soul provided, in addition, "sensation, thinking, and motivity" (p. 185). Overall, Aristotle reasoned, animal souls were composed of four powers or faculties: growth and decay; desire or appetites; sensation; movement; and, most importantly for "man," a fifth faculty or power: that of thought (p. 187).

Also to be understood in contenting with "man" was the orderliness encompassing the categories of things and beings, particularly the orderliness of the development definitive of each *kind* of being from emergence (birth) through development (maturation) to decay (death); and the orderliness of non-living nature—even the cosmos as then experienced and thought—such that, for Aristotle, from the lowest to the highest kinds of beings, each kind, so, too, the whole, was *reasonable* because each was, thus all were, defined by definite causal *ends* or *purposes* (functional imperatives) that were implicit in each kind's form and origin, and that gave directional shape to the motion and/or development appropriate to each kind, thus to each individual of each kind. The *Metaphysics*, as well as the *Physics*, were studies through which Aristotle worked out his notions of the four fundamental *causes* (*form, nature, matter,* and *end*) that accounted for orderly development and, in the case of animals, accounted for cross-generational persistence through the recurring and overlapping processes of birth, maturation, decay, and death, all managed, in the case of "man," through the associations constituting political life. These cross-generational processes, though predicated on the mortality of each generation, made for the seeming immortality of "man" through the contingent potentiality of the infinity of the cross-generational continuation of the species. Of fundamental importance to such processes was the *end*: that *toward which* the processes tended that, accordingly, gave shape and direction to the processes.

It was the confluence of these lines of reasoning that led Aristotle to conclude that "man is by nature a political animal," and to conclude that the formation of states is the highest end, or fullest possible development of the potentialities, of the human animal:

> Every state is a community of some kind, and every community is established with a view to some good; for mankind always act in order to obtain that which they think good. But, if all communities aim at some good, the state or political community, which is the highest of all, and which embraces all the rest, aims at good in a greater degree than any other, and at the highest good.
> (*Politics* 1973d: 595)

The point of this truncated rehearsal of several of Aristotle's interrelated studies was for the purpose of highlighting just this important point: that the studies were *interrelated* and intended to provide a comprehensive account by drawing on a number of fields of study each pertinent to considerations of "man." An understanding of "man" as a "political animal" required a combination of insights from several different lines of inquiry: politics; what most closely approximates what came to be called "psychology" (studies of the "soul"); functional, teleological developmental biology; what has come to be called "ethology" (study of animal behavior, that characteristic of "man" especially); metaphysics (the consideration of *substance* and being *qua* being); physics (studies of matter, of living beings especially); studies of the normative ordering of "political" life, of human associations in bio-social, bio-cultural reproductive collectives from nuclear families to states: that is, ethics.

Aristotle was on to something significant in terms of endeavoring to produce insightful, comprehensive understandings of "man" through a unifying confluence of these related lines of inquiry via a number of methods of inquiry (methods, he insisted, that were always to be forged and pursued, the conditions to be met to produce knowledge, in keeping with the nature of the subject matter). I dare say that today too few efforts to wrestle with challenging subjects of socio-political life, especially by many philosophers, are ever fueled by aspirations to produce a similarly comprehensive understanding of our species as a contextual and foundational prerequisite for understanding important aspects of political life. Or even dare to aspire for such. If not dismissed outright, such an aspiration would likely face passionate criticism from many (producing much heat, as it were, but little, I think, in the way of informed understanding), especially if the understandings pursued involve efforts to have evolution-focused accounts of biological and cultural developments provide explanatory foundations for understandings of the sociological, political, ethical, intellectual, and aesthetic activities and productions of humans. Such understandings would have important implications for addressing questions of the veracity and integrity of deliberately "philosophical" explorations and declarations regarding *Homo sapiens*, especially those efforts in service to intentions to establish normative guidance secured by "right reasons/reasonings" that satisfy rules of logic(s) applied to or derived from non-empirical "ideal" considerations.

This is especially the case when many philosophers (though not just philosophers . . .) endeavor to grapple with problems involving matters of *race* (see, for example, Banton 1998). For reasons easily understood, many who consider "race" have taken flight from affirmative considerations of group-shared biological, socio-cultural, even psychological characteristics as conditioning factors in the composition of populations identified (or mis-identified) as races, and as conditioning factors in the way those thought to be members of a historically bio-culturally interrelating, supposedly racial population go about their lives. Out of opposition to centuries of forms of practices of racism—from racialized enslavement and genocide to what today are characterized as "micro-aggressions"—to a large extent such practices have been condemned as unjust and immoral, justified, in large part, by appeals to supposedly widespread scientific consensus that "there are no races." Often such justifications of oppositions, even to affirmative considerations of racial groupings, are enforced by strenuous policing criticisms supposedly secured by appeals to frequently unspecified, but nonetheless supposedly authoritative, "science"—as in such claims as "there is no 'science' to notions of *race*"—or by resorting to the *ad hominem* declaration that "no 'reputable' scientist has claimed or would claim that there are races." All too often such appeals fail to account for just what settled conclusions have been produced by which enterprise(s) of scientific knowledge production, or fail to account for how a scientist's supposed lack of reputation is determined, and by whom. Much too infrequently there has been too little reasoned, measured, productive debate regarding the propriety of considering certain groupings of humans as "races," considerations supported by conclusions based on relatively well-settled and integrated disciplinary, interdisciplinary, and cross-disciplinary theoretical and empirical work challenged by mutually respectful disagreements.

Reconsiderations are needed by many philosophers, I among them, who are concerned with matters having to do with racialized populations, reconsiderations that draw on and integrate pertinent knowledges that continue to enrich understandings of the histories of the emergence and ongoing evolution of developmental *Homo sapiens* during migratory radiations from locale(s) of emergence to settlings in, and adaptations to, the various geographical settings in which our world's various civilizational populations and peoples developed and produced the diversity of still-evolving genotypes, phenotypes, and cultural legacies that enrich and sustain our species. Productions and refinements of these knowledges are well underway in a number of disciplines across the natural and social sciences, though with much too little impact on the thinking of many philosophers, while efforts to contend with, and to work against, *racisms* continue and, by necessity in too many instances, are intensified. With assistance from considerations of these pertinent knowledge-producing efforts, the reconsiderations of philosophers concerned with "race" matters might well avoid the hyper over-reaction to *racism* manifested in efforts to ignore, rather than understand thoroughly, the significance of self-reproducing bio-cultural groupings of developmental human beings subject to, while actively contributing to, the adaptive evolution of our species. If understanding our bio-culturally diverse species as *by nature* political in something of an Aristotelian sense for which modes of solidarity are an anthropological necessity for persistent contingent existence, pursued and sustained by way of reproductive groupings forged and sustained by various forms and intensities of shared investments in socially bonding associational identities and obligations, we might, then, be compelled to reconsider how solidarity at "racial" group levels has, too, been *by nature*. Still, it must be emphasized that such a conclusion compels no endorsement of any and all forms and agendas of "racial solidarity." Other considerations must be satisfied before endorsements are warranted. Meanwhile, towards a reconsideration of the "political nature" of our species . . .

Human Sociality

Though we are a long way from Aristotle by thousands of years when measured by the average longevity of individual human lives, there are many researchers who endeavor to understand the emergence and continuing developing existence of *Homo sapiens*, among other species, not only as both biological *and* social (or political, in Aristotle's sense), but through enlarged and enriched, though quite complicated, theories, experiments, and comparative studies of human and other social species in order to determine and understand species-specific interrelated phylogenetic, ontogenetic, and socio-cultural developments. And to be noted, the understandings of such developments are forged through disciplines structured by appropriately vetted norms and practices of knowledge-production constitutive of enterprises of scientific investigation (among them paleontology, entomology, archaeology, ecology, cognitive neuroscience, developmental cognitive psychology, social psychology, human genetics, history, and evolutionary biology, among others), all sharing, more or less, core theoretical notions of *development by way of survival through adaptive evolution*.

Of course, the foundational notions of evolutionary development (by "natural selection") were initially worked out and articulated by Charles Darwin (1859) in his historic publication *On the Origin of Species By Means of Natural Selection, or the Preservation of Favored Races in the Struggle for Life*. A contemporary effort toward a more comprehensive account (quite similar to Aristotle's account of "man's" development from families through tribes to states and empires), an effort bolstered by substantial findings produced by refined and well-tested theories and comparative empirical studies, and amplified by ongoing speculations developed since 1859, and much enhanced by further refinements of the axial synthesis of continuously accumulating, more or less settled scientific discoveries and understandings of the nature of, and changes to, the human genome as a (not the only) principal means by which evolutionary adaptations are fostered, has been offered by Edward O. Wilson in several works. Particularly noteworthy are his *The Social Conquest of the Earth* (Wilson 2012) and the mammoth *Sociobiology: The New Synthesis* (Wilson 2000) in which he endeavors to produce a synthesis (*consilience* is Wilson's preferred concept; Wilson 1999) of the findings that, together, are offered as the most comprehensive and integrated articulation of the disciplinary complex of *sociobiology* (see also Wilson and Wilson 2007).

E. O. Wilson is a controversial figure, to say the least. I do not draw on his work because I am convinced that his attempted comprehensive synthesis is settled and authoritative, or fully convincing. It is neither of these. However, his efforts do provide a broad and rich heuristic framework of multidisciplinary, multilevel evolutionary considerations in the context of which I can explore continuing efforts at reconsideration of particular cross-generational bio-cultural populations often referred to (frequently imprecisely and, too often, perniciously) as "races." Wilson's is a framework that has the virtue, among others, of daring toward synthesis or *consilience*, having reached a conclusion, reminiscent of Aristotle, which serves as fruitful heuristic platform for my reconsiderations. In his words (Wilson E.O. 2000: 553), "The building block of nearly all human societies is the nuclear family." From this building block, kinship systems are developed as family-members leave the nuclear unit to form new, linked families, and as linked families form bands and tribes.

> As societies evolved from bands through tribes into chiefdoms and states, some of the modes of bonding were extended beyond kinship networks to include other kinds of alliances and economic agreements. Because the networks were then larger, the lines of communication longer, and the interactions more diverse, the total systems became vastly more complex. But the moralistic rules underlying these arrangements appear not to have been altered a great deal. The average individual still operates under a formalized code no more elaborate than that governing the members of hunter-gatherer societies.
> (Wilson E.O. 2000: 554)

These strong similarities in the developmental accounts of Aristotle and E.O. Wilson—though there are quite substantial differences in the knowledges, and in the methods of knowledge-production, that are synthesized into their respective accounts—have sufficient heuristic promise as to persuade me to draw on their efforts to aid in reconsidering how best to approach matters of the history of development of humans as a distinctive kind of *social* species that, in persisting, has evolved relatively distinctive bio-cultural populations and sub-populations often characterized as "races," in part on the basis of presumptions that members of such groups share the conditions and factors, and processes of development, that determine the persistence and/or dissolution of the characteristics shared to a sufficient degree by enough members of the populations as to be taken as bases for identifying and regarding the populations as comparatively distinct in several evolutionarily significant ways.

***

Ours is a species for which associational existence is a definitive characteristic, though we are not thereby unique: there are *many* other species (20,000 among insects, among other species, Wilson asserts) characterized by what biologists term *eusociality* or "'true social condition'. Members of a eusocial animal group . . . belong to multiple generations. They divide labor in what outwardly at least appears to be an altruistic manner" (Wilson E.O. 2012: 109). Still, according to Wilson, among animal species two developments stand out regarding eusociality, the consequences of cause and effect (evolution): land-based animals are dominated by those with the most complex social systems; and the evolutionary *rarity* of the eusocial species (p. 109). Across millions of years of theorized evolution of life on planet earth, from among all of the eusocial species, and from among the several ancestor species (*Homo florensiensis*, *Homo neanderthalensis*, and "Denisovans" that were, it is speculated, vicariant to the Neanderthals), *Homo sapiens* "emerged in the last several hundred thousand years and spread around the world only during the last sixty thousand years" (p. 15). And from the theorizing reconstructions of this evolutionary history, a stunning, sobering conclusion:

> By one means or another, through competition for food and space or outright slaughter or both, our ancestors were the future exterminators of this [the Neanderthals] and any other species that arose during adaptive radiation of *Homo* . . . In the process, all other human species encountered were swamped and erased.
>
> (p. 10)

(Regarding this, *much* to be considered . . .) And, Wilson takes care to note:

> Human beings create cultures by means of malleable languages. We invent symbols that are intended to be understood among ourselves, and we thereby generate networks of communication many orders of magnitude greater than that of any animal. We have conquered the biosphere and laid waste to it like no other species in the history of life. We are unique in what we have wrought . . . We are an evolutionary chimera, living on intelligence steered by the demands of animal instinct . . . Humanity is a magnificent but fragile achievement.
>
> (2012: 13)

Ours is, then, a fragile *social* species, a species of various scalings of socially bonded *groupings* of *individuals*, that emerged evolutionarily out of conditions on the landmass now long called "Africa," from which, over tens of thousands of years, small bands radiated out, settling along the way, the survivors reproducing while adapting to new environments with new bands of successive generations moving further, settling, adapting, reproducing, and giving rise to still more bands migrating to other areas of the planet. Survival of the bands of individuals through adaptations to new environments was predicated on *sociality*: transgenerational groupings formed by alliances (to construct settlements or "nests"; forming teams to secure food, particularly in the form of non-human animals that when consumed fulfilled the evolving need for protein); groupings structured by emotionally charged identities (that established the meaningfulness of natal and related groupings, and of individuals within the relationships) and in which individuals evolved to make good judgments of the intentions of others (within natal and related groupings, especially), and planned and executed strategies of interactions—all of these endeavors being made suitable to environments through adaptations (Wilson E. O. 2012: 20). Bonding and cooperation among individuals *and* groupings, then, were fundamental to meeting the needs of survival, thus to the evolutionary development and persistence of the various forms of human sociality. Hence, the development of emotionally charged social intelligence—that is, "a sharp sense of empathy"—became crucial to the evolution of our *Homo* species. And, Wilson emphasizes, settlements—in the form of campsites early on—that became sites ("nests") of concentrated groupings that necessitated protection and compelled *social cohesion*, were especially crucial factors. It was this cohesion that "launched the final drive to modern *Homo sapiens*" (p. 44). It is forms of this supposed "cohesion" that have been explored by many thinkers by way of accounts of "solidarity."

Conceptions of "the" or "a" biological *individual* are being challenged by recent research findings, most notably in work reconsidering the division between humans and other sentient beings, such as animals, and what distinguishes individualism—anatomically, physiologically, or in terms of symbionts (Gilbert, Sapp, and Tauber 2012: 325–326). Still, in stressing the evolutionary significance of the "eusociality" of our species, the importance of "individuals"[2] must not be overlooked. For in accounting for (theorizing) eusocial evolution, Wilson and others have concluded that the evolutionary dynamics that have been at work in the creation of new groupings by humans, at present and stretching back into prehistory, have involved multileveled processes of selection: that is, have been "driven by both individual and group selection" (Wilson E. O. 2012: 52). And the processes of "selection" at work were affecting the genome, of "individuals" and of the groups, the sources of the driving forces being the natural environments in which the out-radiating groups had settled, and the likewise evolving socio-cultural practices forged, sustained, and modified in responses to environments that are both human-modified natural and human-made cultural—and, consequently, are dynamic. Both modes of evolution, genomic and socio-cultural, were mutually conditioning, it is theorized, and were affected by contacts with other, comparatively distinct groups. Both modes, and their interactions, are now being explored guided by the heuristic notions and theories of *gene-culture co-evolution* (2012: 195–210).

Theories of bio-social evolution(s) are offered to account for (to explain) the group-based cultural and genetic *diversities* that emerged by way of the out-radiating groupings that settled in different geographic environments thus producing, over the course of tens of thousands of years, the evolutionary formation of anthropologically relatively distinct (culturally, phenotypically, and genotypically) sub-populations of *Homo sapiens* that came to be called "races"—or termed "geographic races" by some population geneticists and other researchers—though these "races" were/are *not* internally homogeneous genetically or phenotypically. Still, over the course of tens of thousands of years, the adaptive radiations and settlements of *Homo sapiens* have resulted in our being a species (but by no means the only such species) that is notable for substantial intraspecie diversities. And to good ends: for Wilson (and I agree): "In evolution, from diversity comes opportunity" (*Social Conquest*, 2012: 27). The crucial importance of this diversity is expressed forthrightly by Wilson, but, against the backdrop of much too much nefarious history, it is how he positions indigenous peoples of Africa in doing so that is *quite* astounding and worth quoting at great length:

> The ancestors who achieved the breakout from Africa and conquered Earth were drawn from a diverse genetic mix. Throughout their evolutionary past, during hundreds of thousands of years, they had been hunter-gatherers. They lived in small bands, similar to present-day surviving bands composed of at least thirty and more than a hundred or so individuals. These groups were sparsely distributed. Those closest to each other exchanged a small fraction of individuals each generation, most likely females. They diverged genetically enough that the entire ensemble of bands (the metapopulation, as biologists call such a collectivity) was far more variable than the indigenous humans destined to achieve the breakout.
>
>   That difference persists. It has long been known that Africans south of the Sahara are far more diverse genetically than native peoples in other parts of the world . . .
>
>   It has not escaped the attention of human biologists and medical researchers that the genes of modern-day Africans are a treasure house for all humanity. They posses our species' greatest reservoir of genetic diversity, of which further study will shed new light on the heredity of the human body and mind. *Perhaps the time has come, in light of this and other advances in human genetics, to adopt a*

> *new ethic of racial and hereditary variation, one that places value on the whole of diversity rather than on the differences composing the diversity. It would give proper measure to our species' genetic variation as an asset, prized for the adaptability it provides all of us during an increasingly uncertain future. Humanity is strengthened by a broad portfolio of genes that can generate new talents, additional resistance to diseases, and perhaps even new ways of seeing reality. For scientific as well as for moral reasons, we should learn to promote human biological diversity for its own sake instead of using it to justify prejudice and conflict.*
>
> (Wilson E.O. 2012: 80–81 (emphasis added))

Wilson has concluded that "groupism," the propensity of *Homo sapiens* to "form groups, drawing visceral comfort and pride from familiar fellowship, and to defend the group enthusiastically against rival groups," is one of the "*absolute* universals of human nature and hence of culture" (Wilson E.O. 2012: 57 (emphasis added)). Once groups are formed, their boundaries are flexible, with members developing loyalties to other groups, and with groups admitting as members others (recruits, allies, converts, honorary inductees, traitors from rival groups (p. 57)). The propensity toward groupism, Wilson reasons, is a biological product of forces of selection acting on the group that produces an instinct for group formation, and is as much an evolutionary aspect of the psychological makeup of modern groups as is theorized was the case for tribes of ancient history and prehistory. Consequently, he concludes, "[p]eople must have a tribe" (p. 57).

Of course, Wilson's conclusion is questionable, thus requires more compelling evidence to be convincing. Nonetheless, modern humans are hardly without social groupings—contrary to centuries of philosophical celebrations of various forms of *individuality* and *individualism* as the ethically preferred model of human living—but live much more complex group-ordered lives, navigating a social world not of a single tribe, "but rather a system of interlocking tribes" (Wilson E.O. 2012: 57) that, in some case, have spanned continents and centuries. The theory of evolutionary eusociality provides a path toward an explanation, perhaps, of why virtually all of the world impacted by European and Euro-American Modernities, for example, have been structured vertically and horizontally by systems of interlocking tribes ordered by conceptions—and correspondingly by horizontal and vertical valorizations—of raciality in combination with other group-life and world-ordering systems of meaning and practices (religion, economies, territoriality, etc.): namely, conceptual and practical schemes constituting White Racial Supremacy. Modern racialisms are but forms of tribalism, we might say, scaled up to nation-state, multistate ("Europe," for example), and ancient and modern empire formations (nation-states and their colonies and territories). We might consider racialisms as historically contingent socio-cultural developments out of a powerful species-specific instinctual propensity or "prepared learning" ("the inborn propensity to learn something swiftly and decisively" (2012: 59)) for in-group biases that seem likely to be consequences of adaptations on the group level. Racialisms, therefore forms of racism, are *constructed* (socio-culturally) out of this propensity, not *determined* by it genetically, though Wilson is convinced that "different parts of the brain have evolved by group selection to create groupishness" (2012: 61).

Still, it must be insisted, individuals can (and do!) defect from the tribe, can become traitors to a tribe's racialism and racism. Moreover, the terms and valences of group life are always subject to entropy and revision. These, too, apparently, are among the evolved characteristics of the eusociality our species, the complete list being:

- Intense competition between and among groups;
- Instability of group composition;
- Perfecting of quick, expert reading of the intentions of others;
- Perpetual, unavoidable conflict between the products of group selection (honor, virtue, duty) and the products of individual selection (selfishness, cowardice, hypocrisy);
- Much of culture emerges from this clash between what has been produced, or conditioned significantly, by group selection and that produced or conditioned by individual selection (Wilson E. O. 2012: 56).

Homo sapiens eusociality, Wilson concludes, is instinctual, a consequence of advantageous mutations of the human genome, of natural selection, and cultural adaptations because the affected grouped individuals that adapted and survived challenges to existence produced offspring to which they conferred, genetically and culturally, the advantageous adaptations. "Natural selection" are the processes by which environmental conditions affect a gene or an arrangement of genes or alternative genes (alleles) in the heredity code such that a trait or combination of traits encoded by the affected gene, genes, or alleles becomes, or ceases to be, advantageous for successful living, individually and socially, and for reproducing and nurturing offspring. Processes of selection are multilevel, acting "on genes that prescribe targets [trait or combination of traits] at more than one level of biological organization, such as cell and organism" (Wilson E. O. 2012: 162).

The "selection" processes affect both individuals and groups of individuals; however, "Traits that are acted upon exclusively by selection between groups are those emerging from interactions among members of each group" (Wilson E. O. 2012: 163). To be noted, as well, is that relationships involving genes or combinations of genes and particular traits are quite complex: in some instances the trait(s) may be completely encoded by a gene or gene combination; in other instances the trait(s) is (are) only partially gene-encoded and may be subject to other conditions. In short, the trait(s) may be phenotypically plastic, differing in manifestation and effect though linked, in some way(s), to the same or similar genotype(s) (genes or combinations of genes). (These conditions explain, in significant part, why persons with more or less similar phenotypic features are regarded as being members of the same racial or ethnic group though, on examination, it turns out that within the purported group the members have different frequencies and/or combinations of genes: that is, there is substantial genomic variety among phenotypically similar members of the identified group (p. 163).)

This listing of features of *Homo sapiens* eusociality and discussion of the formative role of evolution by natural selection would hardly satisfy Aristotle as an explanation, that is, as a full account of the *causes* of eusociality, surely not the *why* or *end*. Producing such an account involves a number of related massive tasks, not yet completed, not even by Wilson, who is fully cognizant of what is required. As he notes,

> The evolutionary origin of any complex biological system can be reconstructed correctly only if viewed as the culmination of a history of stages tracked from

start to finish. It begins with empirically known biological phenomena in each stage, if such is known, and it explores the range of phenomena that are theoretically possible.

(Wilson E. O., *Social Conquest* 2012: 183)[3]

Wilson has a theory of these "stages" of evolution, still to be verified empirically, including by experimentation, and by comparison to the evolutions of other eusocial species. His list of stages (truncated):

1. The formation of groups . . .;
2. The occurrence of a minimum and necessary combination of preadaptive traits in the groups, causing the groups to be tightly formed . . .;
3. The appearance of mutations that prescribe the persistence of the group . . .;
4. In the insects, emergent traits caused by either the genesis of robot-like workers or the interaction of group members are shaped through group-level selection by environmental forces;
5. Group-level selection drives changes in the insect colony life cycle and social structures . . . (Wilson E. O. 2012: 187).

Clearly, much of this theory relies on studies of eusocial insects, other invertebrates, and vertebrates, not of humans (Wilson E. O. 2012: 187). How, Wilson asks (and we must ask), to explain more fully—to explicate the *causes of*—the *extraordinarily rare* evolutionary development and persistent eusociality of *Homo sapiens*, taking into account both genetic and cultural processes?

Very much in keeping with Aristotle's investigations, Wilson devotes a chapter to the question "What is Human Nature?" (Wilson E. O. 2012: 191–211). It is not to be found in the genes, he reasons, nor defined by the cultural "universals" of social behavior and institutions found in all of hundreds of closely studied human societies (2012: 192). Rather:

If the genetic code underlying human nature is too close to its molecular underpinning and the cultural universals are too far away from it, it follows that the best place to search for hereditary human nature is in between, in the rules of development prescribed by genes, through which the universals of culture are created.

Human nature is the inherited regularities of mental development common to our species. They are the "epigenetic rules," which evolved by the interaction of genetic and cultural evolution that occurred over a long period in deep prehistory. These rules are the genetic biases in the way our senses perceive the world, the symbolic coding by which we represent the world, the options we automatically open to ourselves, and the responses we find easiest and most rewarding to make.

(Wilson E. O. 2012: 193)

What have we, so far, in terms of a sketch of an evolutionary account of human sociality? *Homo sapiens* is an evolved and evolving, widely dispersed, genomically and socially dynamic metapopulation of likewise genomically and socially dynamic, relatively distinct subpopulational groupings the "individuals" of which share variants of a species-specific genome that is composed of genes and alternate alleles, some of which prescribe and others that regulate gene expressions but do not themselves prescribe, all of which are subject to mutations, alterations of combinations during reproduction, and to natural selection. Individuals within particular subpopulations tend to share (more or less) epigenetic rules that regulate changes in gene activity and expression but are not dependent on gene sequences (Wilson E. O. 2012: 204) and that function to "prepare" the human individuals and groups for instances of learned behavior (e.g., lactose tolerance; incest avoidance; evolved and inherited systems of perception that condition the evolution of color vocabularies; the "Westermarck effect," which is "the avoidance of sexual activity among closely related individuals who remain within their natal group" (2012: 200)); the capability of "shared intentionality" or "the ability to participate with others in collaborative activities with shared goals, and intentions" (Tomasello, Carpenter, Call, Behne, and Moll 2005: 675); and evolving cultural practices, which, drawing from Wilson, we understand as *ultimately* caused by the evolving genome, but not *proximately* caused by the genome[4]—that can, in various instances, in Wilson's words, "smother genetic evolution" (2012: 197), but not arrest the process altogether.

The singularity of the persisting (so far . . .) eusociality of *Homo sapiens* is marked by the development of many factors, greater by several magnitudes than those of any other known eusocial species, and further distinguished by their varieties in terms of cultures; languages; religions; and schemes of morality, creative arts, and technologies, among more than a few factors. One key to all of these developments has been the inheritance of a much-evolved brain with an extraordinarily complex, not-yet-fully-understood architecture and operations that make for, among other processes, various modes of mindfulness and communication that affect behavior. The brain was central to what Wilson theorizes was "the driving force that led to the threshold of complex culture":

> It appears to have been group selection. A group with members who could read intentions and cooperate among themselves while predicting the actions of competing groups, would have an enormous advantage over others less gifted. There was undoubtedly competition among group members, leading to natural selection of traits that gave advantage of one individual over another. But more important for a species entering new environments and competing with powerful rivals were unity and cooperation within the group. Morality, conformity, religious fervor, and fighting ability combined with imagination and memory to produce the winner.
> (Wilson E. O. 2012: 224)

The significance of sociality for brain evolution has become the focus of intense research with results seeming to provide confirmations of the heuristic notion-cum-testable hypothesis of the "social brain":

> The broad interpretation of the social brain hypothesis is that individuals living in stable social groups face cognitive demands that individuals living alone (or in unstable aggregations) do not. To maintain group cohesion, individuals must be able to meet their own requirements, as well as coordinate their behavior with other individuals in the group. They must also be able to

defuse the direct and indirect conflicts that are generated by foraging in the same space.

(Dunbar and Shultz, *Evolution in the Social Brain* 2007: 1345)

From their research, Dunbar and Shultz conclude "the key selection pressure promoting the evolution of large brains is explicitly social" (*Evolution in the Social Brain* 2007: 1345), and that "it may have been the cognitive demands of pairbonding that triggered the initial evolution of large brains across the vertebrates. More important, pairbonding is the issue, not biparental care" ((*Evolution in the Social Brain* 2007: 1346); see also (Dunbar 2003)).

Why? Because, possibly, reproductive pairbonds are especially demanding and risky, thus impose substantial computational demands (choosing mates of good quality who will be both loyal and contribute substantively to child-rearing across the length of a monogamous relationship); and, possibly, because "postnatal parental investment requires very close coordination and behavioral synchrony . . . the pair needs to regulate its activities so that each has enough time for feeding and rest. That will usually necessitate some degree of activity synchronization" (Dunbar and Shultz 2007: 1346). These considerations are consistent with quite similar considerations by Tomasello et al. (2005) of the evolutionary significance of synchronized or shared intentionality in developing and sustaining social cognition. As they note, "The result of participating in these activities is species-unique forms of cultural cognition and evolution, enabling everything from the creation and use of linguistic symbols to the construction of social norms and individual beliefs to the establishment of social institutions" (Tomasello, Carpenter, Call, Behne, and Moll 2005: 675).[5] And consistent with conclusions drawn from considerations of field and laboratory research by Joan B. Silk, another proponent of the social brain hypothesis: "New evidence indicates that the competitive success and reproductive performance of individuals in primate groups is affected by the nature and quality of the relationships that they form" (Silk 2007: 1347).

A striking conclusion drawn from these converging lines of research is that it was the evolving sociality of situated groups that drove the evolution of the *Homo sapiens* brain, which ratcheted up human capabilities by several magnitudes and has been a key resource for the inventiveness at the heart of cultural creativity. As Tomasello (2006: 205) concludes, "None of the most complex human artifacts or social practices—including tool industries, symbolic artifacts, and social institutions—were invented once and for all at a single moment by any one individual or group of individuals." Rather, various cultures are cumulative cultural *systems* (Tomasello 2006: 205),[6] which in turn, become major forces driving *Homo sapiens* life and evolution as yet-to-be-fully-understood complements to evolution of the genome (Levinson 2006).

To be noted: cultural systems are not completely independent of evolutionary genomic influences. However, the influences, in various instances, are, as noted by Wilson, mediated by epigenetic rules and by institutionalizations of cultural practices (norms guiding mate-selections, dietary practices, food productions, for example) that, as well, affect the genome (again, through diets, patterns of activity, impacts on the environment, etc.) (Francis 2011). A successfully adapting trans-generational group or complex of related groups must have in the arsenal of its cultural systems institutionalized strategies and social mechanisms by which to meet and resolve challenges to the groups' survival: "these mechanisms also depend on biological underpinnings: the ability to inhibit private interest, to pull together in times of stress, and also more generally the cognitive abilities that make long-term communal planning possible" (Levinson, *Introduction: The Evolution of Culture in a Microcosm* 2006: 32).

Cultural systems, as noted when considering the processes of "ratcheting" by which such systems are thought to be developed, are subject to and consequences of particular forms of evolution: that is, the elements of cultural systems, once acquired, can be transmitted by way of teaching and learning (also parts of the cultural system) across generations with modifications (revisions, new inventions, borrowings from other cultures, or losses), thus are thought by some to be subject to distinctive forms and forces of selection (Levinson, *Introduction: The Evolution of Culture in a Microcosm* 2006: 3). In other words, cultural systems are sustained by retention and usage by the encultured actors of the social group(s) who are the systems' carriers and modifiers. As well, a cultural system might become maladaptive in some circumstances, thus putting at risk the survival and viability of the groupings, or portions of them. And all of this while the genome is subject to evolutionary pressures, some of which have been initiated by cultural practices. Hence, the need for considerations of "gene-culture coevolution" or "twin-track" theories of gene-culture evolution (Levinson 2006: 3). The upshot of the theories is that "the interaction between culture and genome in humans has produced an extraordinary symbiotic hybrid, yielding a quantum leap in adaptational flexibility, which allows humans to exist in every niche on the planet and beyond" (2006: 5). Cultural systems are, consequently, *both* relatively unique and similar.

However, it is crucial to note that not all theorists of cultural evolution conceptualize the processes using models of genomic evolution. An explanatory approach to evolutionary understandings of *Homo sapiens* more robust than that of Wilson is offered by the theorizing of Eva Jablonka and Marion J. Lamb: namely, that evolution is a consequence not just of "two tracks" interrelated, but, rather, of interrelated developments and processes in *four* dimensions: genetic, epigenetic, behavioral, and symbolic (Jablonka and Lamb 2014). They regard all four dimensions as "inheritance systems," that is, as structured *systems* through which developments occur, are transmitted and acquired (inherited), in the case of behavior and symbolic activities, especially, by way of *socially mediated learning* that results in "reconstruction in an ancestor's behavior or preferences in its descendants" (Jablonka and Lamb 2014: 156). And in both inheritance systems (behavioral and symbolic) social learning predominates. Hence, the evolution involves *culture*: "the system of socially transmitted patterns of behavior, preferences, and products of animal activities that characterize a group of social animals" (production and transmission, for example, of knowledge, habits, preferences, skills, culinary traditions, group histories, identities, etc., and, through socially mediated learning, the production and transmission of *new* traditions, identities, etc.).

All of these transmitted developments are "to a large extent independent of genetic variation" (Jablonka and Lamb 2014: 159). Rather, the carrying weight, so to speak, is borne not by genes, but by the meaning-informing, meaning-conveying sign and symbol systems of a given culture.[7] For Jablonka and Lamb, as for Wilson and other theorizing researchers, the most distinguishing feature of *Homo sapiens* eusociality remains "the way we organize, transfer, and acquire information . . . our ability to think and communicate through words and other types of symbols," these systems having become especially adaptive in enabling "the construction of a shared imagined reality" (Jablonka and Lamb 2014: 189, 197) and "forward planning" while also providing resources by which to manage the experiences of a dynamic and diverse world by grouping things into relatively distinct categories, among these color categories, shape categories, etc. (Jablonka and Lamb 2014: 173). Language is crucial to this categorization: "There is a core set of categories that are identifiable in all languages, although the way that they are indicated grammatically varies from language to language. In addition, different languages may structurally distinguish some categories that are not distinguished in others" (Jablonka and Lamb 2014: 300). A most pertinent example: how color categories came to be used to signify and symbolize "races" in the Modern West, but through differing schemes of racialized categorization being constructed in different polities (e.g., the United States of America, Brazil, South Africa . . .).

It is within this *Homo sapiens* geographically distributed evolutionary genome-epigenomic-behavioral-symbolic (bio-cultural) nexus of populational sociality that the species-particular forms of psychological and cognitive systems and processes have been developed and actualized in forming groupings (geographic races), culture-societies, and polities in the occupied locales into which our migrating ancestors moved and settled, then produced successive generations that continued the settle-move demographic dispersals in spreading and adapting to various environments of planet earth. By some accounts, these developments resulted in the development of the "five continental races": Africans, East Asians, Caucasians, Native Americans, and Australian aborigines, including the people of New Guinea (Wade 2014: 94). Although Wade cautions that "portioning human variation into five continental races, is to some extent arbitrary," he nevertheless concludes, "But it makes practical sense. The three major races are easy to recognize. The five-way division matches the known events of human population history. And most significant of all, the division by continent is supported by genetics" (Wade 2014: 93–94).[8] More needs to be said, however, about just what is the basis of the attribution of a notion of *raciality* to these groupings, though I am willing to forgo arguing for the nomenclature here while holding on to the accounts that trace the historical formations of the continental groupings. More pertinent is to consider the *something* that constitutes the *sociality* that continues to make of such forms of groupings of individuals much, much more than an aggregate of monads. Sociality is *by nature*. But, what is the "stuff" of sociality?

Relations, certainly. Particular forms and intensities of relations between and among "individuals" of eusocial species are both contingent *and* necessary: "contingent" in that neither their formation nor their persistence is necessary; "necessary" in that no "individual" comes into existence on its own, nor can care for itself across the long years of precarious existence that must be negotiated successfully if the "individual" is to develop from totally dependent newborn to an only partially independent and self-sustaining adult. The sustaining of life through development, from initiation in utero to death in old age, *requires* enablement by and complementarity with other humans within social (or Aristotelian *political*) networks, *necessarily*. And the processes by which new human life is created are the *most* intimate, and the most foundational to the persistence and evolution, of the species, thus, though embellished in their practice with cultural variety, are species-universal. So, too, the caring for, nurturing, of newborns. And none of these relations and their constitutive practices are consummated or sustained in keeping with the speculations of sociality as a function or consequence of strictly rationalist "contractual" arrangements between mature, "free," and "equal" negotiating, self-interested *individuals*. The persuasive arguments have been made disclosing that the supposed "contracting" between abstract, reasoning, free "individuals" in the formation and maintenance of decidedly "modern," supposedly democratic polities were *thoroughly* invested with social-ordering schemes of institutionalized meanings, characterizations, and practices involving considerations of sex and gender (Pateman 1988) and of race (Mills 1999).

We should think of sociality, then, not as an addition to the life of free-standing persons that is a consequence of relations deliberately forged "contractually" by "free individuals" (or by pre-social "individuals" who came before them) who have somehow (unaccountably) grown to contract-making maturation on their own. Rather, we should think of sociality as *co-constitutive of* individuality: as the enabling matrix in which "individuals" *come to be* and are sustained while having their development forged into a relatively unique group(s)-networked "individual" who is group(s)-forged out of genomic substrates and cultural matrices bequeathed by socially networked significant others making the investments in order that there continue *to be* related and relating others. More succinctly still: "Even genetic and developmental interactions within a single individual can be regarded as social, since the organisms of today are now known to be the social groups of past ages" (Wilson and Wilson 2007: 329). Of course, there is no possibility of determining the detailed *how* of the initial emergence of the various lines of decent from which our species evolved. Suffice it to say, once "the threshold of eusociality" was "crossed" (heuristic notions at best . . .) sociality was not, is not, an independent element that may or may not be present.

What, further, is *sociality*? In one sense, the term seems a poor resource for the distinguishing work that is called for in explaining, if you will, "the ties that bind": for explaining how it is, in particular, that "individuals" connect with, become "bonded" to, other networked "individuals" in anthropologically specific ways that provide conditions of possibility for sustaining, cross-generational life, thus for adaptive survival. But the sense of the term only seems inadequate if the search is for *sociality* as an independent, non-essential, or even corrupting addition to free and self-sufficing "individuals" as a contractual option.[9] Instead, ours is a species that is *by nature* social: that is, is composed of *groupings* of "individuals" whose very being and persistence *require* sustained and sustaining relationships with others. Moreover, we would do well, even, to rethink and revise our notions of "individuality" as characterizing an autonomous, biologically self-contained, and singular *person* determined as such anatomically, physiologically, genomically, and developmentally and think, instead, of "individuals in cooperative and competitive relationships" that constitute/are constituted by "organic *systems*."

The rethinking is being compelled by findings from new lines of research guided by system-focused paradigms and aided by new technologies that

> continue to dramatically transform our conceptions of the planet's biosphere. The research has revealed not only a microbial world of much deeper diversity than previously imagined, but also a world of complex and intermingled *relationships*—not only among microbes, but also between microscopic and macroscopic life . . . Symbiosis is becoming a core principle of contemporary biology, and it is replacing an essentialist conception of "individuality" with a conception congruent with the larger systems approach now pushing the life sciences in diverse directions.
>
> (Gilbert, Sapp, and Tauber 2012: 326)

In short, the discovery of symbiosis is providing a counter to "the notion of essential identity" (Gilbert, Sapp, and Tauber 2012: 326).[10] Subsequently, systems, and systems-of-systems, should command our attention, *groupings* of rethought-"individuals" being one form of systems-of-systems.

Of course, there will still be need for important distinctions to be made, for rethought-*individuals* differ in more or less significant ways that are, in important instances, crucial to the roles played and contributions made to the prospects for the adaptive survival of our species. In sex-selection and sexual reproduction, for example; in the female-male pair-bonding that, with *Homo sapiens*, is a precursive condition that enhances the prospects of a structuring relational social context that provides for well-being in the foundational units of human sociality: nuclear, then extended, families. Females and males have evolved for crucial roles (male to female; female to female; male to male) with genetic and epigenetic substrates out of and on which are developed the complex repertoires of brain-coordinated, culturally influenced hormonal, emotional, psychological, homeostatic, sensory-motor, and cognitive systems that make for the always culturally conditioned, emotionally loaded *relations* that have been crucial to human sociality across centuries. Recall that for Wilson and other sociobiologists, "eusociality" involves a *group* that is composed of members; that spans *multiple generations*; whose members are "prone to perform *altruistic acts* as part of their *division of labor*" (Wilson E.O. 2012: 16 (emphasis added)). In an important sense, then, "sociality" refers to all of those "elements" of dynamic *biological and socio-cultural relationality*, the consequences of multilevel selection, as well as of cultural evolutions, as human bio-cultural reproductive groupings survived across generations by adapting successfully to different continental and smaller-scale natural and politicized environments.[11]

And to be reiterated: adaptive evolution involves the enormously significant cultural contributions, creations of an evolved social brain. Among those creations are legitimated social norms and abstracted/abstract "principles" (ethics, for example) fashioned by humans as conceptual tools with which to order various aspects of social life.[12] The forging and articulation of the tools are institutionalized social practices. As is clear with social rituals, often the articulations are embellished with emotional loadings and often are mediated during culturally specific times or periods of life, all the more to enhance the "stickiness," we might say, for retention by individuals for the good of the social whole: the emotional as well as cognitive loadings that heighten the meaningfulness of articulations that are embraced by socially linked persons as more or less definitive of who they take themselves to be; of their place(s) in the world; of their historicity: lived, imagined, desired. It is this "stickiness" that makes for the "bonding attachments" between and among "individuals," that makes for the sociality quite often pursued for clarification and normative management by philosophers, sociologists, anthropologists, and political scientists, among others. The term and concept long use to denote and connote this "stickiness" and its varying degrees of attachment and bonding are "solidarity," *solidarity*.

"Solidarity"

It has become apparent that we lack adequate language with which to describe relationships, yet bondedness is precisely what primate sociality is all about. Intuitively, we know what we mean by bondedness because we experience it

ourselves, and we recognize it when it happens. The problem, perhaps, is that bondedness is an explicitly emotional experience and language is a notoriously poor medium for describing our inner, emotional experiences.
(Dunbar and Shultz, *Evolution in the Social Brain* 2007: 1346)

While there are many meanings and uses of "solidarity," common to many is the idea of "a mutual attachment between individuals, encompassing two levels: a *factual* level of actual common ground between the individuals and a *normative* level of mutual obligations to aid each other, as and when should be necessary" (Bayertz 1999: 3; see also Laitinen and Pessi 2014). Another sense of the term explored by Bayertz is that relations of solidarity constitute "the inner cement holding together *a society* . . . central elements of such a cohesion include a common descent and history, a common culture and way of life, and common ideals and goals" (p. 9; see also Salmela 2014). Very much in this regard, notions of raciality have long served to mobilize rationalizing cognitive and emotionally charged bio-social and cultural preferences in order to forge and sustain groupings of varying scalings both vertically (in terms of genealogies) and horizontally (across politicized geographies). The European Modernities have been paradigmatic instances of such constructions, decisive in their global impacts as worldviews by way of which non-European racialized populations were subjected to genocidal decimation, others to enslavement and oppressive colonization.[13]

To conclude, as did Aristotle, that humans are *by nature* political is to conclude that humans are by nature *social* beings emotionally connected with varying degrees and forms of solidaristic intensity: by anthropologically contingent necessity, individuals live as members of one or more groupings of individuals of the same species and are organized in a cooperative manner facilitated, primarily, by reciprocal communication (Wilson E.O. 2000: 7). And if both Aristotle and Wilson are correct in theorizing that the foundational units of social life have been nuclear and extended families— foundational in that it is within such a grouping that, heretofore, new beings have been created, receive primary life-sustaining nurturance and the cultivation of such primary nurturance—then of particular importance to foundational sociality are the complex, dynamic ways in which genetic relations (the passing of genes from parents to offspring, thus the genomic constitution of "individuals") condition (though not determine in every instance) individual behavior and social relations (cognitively, emotionally, psychologically, culturally), even as social relations are governed by the logics of group socio-cultural norms and institutions, *not* by genes. Both Aristotle and Wilson seek understandings that grasp the *developmental* and *integrated complexities* of our species-being that make for sociality ("political life" for Aristotle; "eusociality" for Wilson) while also accounting for those aspects that, when compared to other species, render ours particularly unique. For both theorists, understanding the developmental histories of living beings was, is, foundational.

For *Homo sapiens*, solidaristic sociality has been definitive of the formation and persistence of continentally dispersed and settled *populational* groupings comparatively distinct genomically and socio-culturally though indisputably all of the same species. For more than six hundred years, pernicious mobilizations of the distinctivenesses through conceptual and social systems fostering solidarity predicated on notions of supposed *racial* differences as definitive of the populations have ratcheted up the evolutionary persistence of the differences, of their *meanings*, by embedding *racial* considerations in the social and cultural systems that have become of primary significance for human evolution. The anthropologically contingent necessity of solidaristic sociality required for the evolutionary persistent of *Homo sapiens* continental populations came to be characterized as "racial."

Even so, there was, is, no evolutionary necessity that such characterizations be *racist*. Accordingly, it is not *necessary* that forgoing considering these populations as "races" is the only, or even the best, means for contending with racism. Certainly, I am convinced, there are compelling evolutionary imperatives for fostering the diversities constitutive of the populations: they are *crucial* to the adaptive survival of our species. And to this end, we desperately need the cultivation of solidarity within and among racialized groupings, while together working to curtail the laying-to-waste of our species and our planet-home that have been characteristic of our species-made species-being for far too long . . .

Notes

1 For a critique of different forms, intensities, and agendas of among and on behalf of black folks, see Tommie Shelby's *We Who Are Dark: The Philosophical Foundations of Black Solidarity* (2007).
2 Conceptions of "the" or "a" biological *individual* are being challenged by recent research findings:

> Animals cannot be considered individuals by anatomical or physiological criteria because a diversity of symbionts are both present and functional in completing metabolic pathways and serving other physiological functions. Similarly, these new studies have shown that animal development is incomplete without symbionts. Symbionts also constitute a second mode of genetic inheritance, providing selectable genetic variation for natural selection . . . Recognizing the "holobiont"—the multicellular eukaryote plus its colonies of persistent symbionts—as a critically important unit of anatomy, development, physiology, immunology, and evolution opens up new investigative avenues and conceptually challenges the ways in which the biological subdisciplines have heretofore characterized living entities. (Gilbert, Sapp, and Tauber, 2012, pp. 325–326)

3

> The evolutionary origin of any complex biological system can be reconstructed correctly only if viewed as the culmination of a history of stages tracked from start to finish. It begins with empirically known biological phenomena in each stage, if such is known, and it explores the range of phenomena that are theoretically possible. Each transition from one stage to the next requires different models, and each needs to be placed in its own context of potential cause and effect. This is the only way to arrive at the deep meaning of advanced social evolution and the human condition itself. (Wilson E. O., *Social Conquest*, 2012, p. 183)

4

> When thinking about evolution by natural selection, a crucial and necessary distinction to make is between *proximate causation*, which is how a structure or process works, and *ultimate causation*, which is why the structure or process exists in the first place. (Wilson E. O., *Social Conquest*, 2012, p. 164)

5

> We propose that the crucial difference between human cognition and that of other species is the ability to participate with others in collaborative activities with shared goals and

intentions: shared intentionality. Participation in such activities requires not only especially powerful forms of intention reading and cultural learning, but also a unique motivation to share psychological states with others and unique forms of cognitive representation for doing so. The result of participating in these activities is species-unique forms of cultural cognition and evolution, enabling everything from the creation and use of linguistic symbols to the construction of social norms and individual beliefs to the establishment of social institutions. (Tomasello, Carpenter, Call, Behne, and Moll, 2005, p. 675)

6

> What distinguishes human culture from that of chimpanzees and other species is the existence of the "ratchet" effect. The basic idea is that the cultural traditions and artifacts of human beings accumulate modifications over time. Basically none of the most complex human artifacts or social practices—including tool industries, symbolic artifacts, and social institutions—were invented once and for all at a single moment by any one individual or group of individuals. Rather, what happened was that some individual or group of individuals first invented a primitive version of the artifact or practice, and then some later user or users made a modification, an improvement, that others then adopted perhaps without change for many generations, at which point some other individual or group of individuals made another modification, which was then learned and used by others, and so on over historical time. This process of cumulative cultural evolution requires not only creative invention but also, and just as important, faithful social transmission that can work as a ratchet to prevent backward slippage, so that the newly invented artifact or practice may preserve its new and improved form at least somewhat faithfully until a further modification of improvement comes along. The outcome is that human beings are able to pool their cognitive resources in ways that other animal species, whose cultural traditions do not ratchet up in complexity over historical time, are not. (Tomasello, 2006, p. 205)

7 On the crucial differences between "signs" and "symbols," see (Berger and Luckmann, 1966).

8

> The first step in making sense of human variation and the emergence of races is to follow the historical succession of major population splits . . . the first such split occurred when a small group of people left northeast Africa some 50,000 years ago and populated the rest of the world. The first major division in the human population is thus between Africans and non-Africans . . . Among the non-Africans, there was an early division, whose nature is still poorly understood, between Europeans and East Asians . . . Australian aborigines can reasonably be considered a race although a minor one in terms of population size, because of their distinctness, antiquity and the fact that they inhabit a continent . . . American Indians, the original inhabitants of North and South America, can also be considered a race . . . Such an arrangement, of portioning human variation into five continental races, is to some extent arbitrary. But it makes practical sense. The three major races are easy to recognize. The five-way division matches the known events of human population history. And most significant of all, the division by continent is supported by genetics. (Wade, 2014, pp. 93–94)

9 For an informative discussion of the function of social bonds as determined by field and laboratory studies of social cognition as the basis for social behavior in primate groups, see Silk, 2007.

10

> We report here that the zoological sciences are also finding that animals are composites of many species living, developing, and evolving together. The discovery of symbiosis throughout the animal kingdom is fundamentally transforming the classical conception of an insular individuality into one in which interactive relationships among species blurs

the boundaries of the organism and obscures the notion of essential identity. (Gilbert, Sapp, and Tauber, 2012, p. 326)

11 Accounting for "evolution" across the "four dimensions" of genomic (genomic, epigenomic) and socio-cultural (behavioral, symbolic) systems (Jablonka and Lamb, 2014) is more than can be accomplished on this occasion. For further enlightening discussion with rich bibliographic resources, see Richerson and Boyd (2005); and for a helpful discussion and assessment of various approaches to theories of "cultural evolution," see Lewens (2015).
12 For an especially insightful discussion of "conceptual systems of universe maintenance" in the context of the discussion of the significance and functions of "legitimation" in social life, see the seminal work by Berger and Luckmann (1966).
13 For an illuminating critical reconstruction of an impactful deployment of such a worldview see (Smedley and Smedley, 2011).

References

Aristotle. (1973a) "De Anima (On the Soul)," in R. McKeon (ed.), *Introduction to Aristotle* (J. Smith, Trans.), 2nd edition, Chicago: University of Chicago Press, pp. 155–245.
———. (1973b) "Nicomachean Ethics," in R. McKeon (ed.), *Introduction to Aristotle* (W. D. Ross, Trans.), 2nd edition, Chicago: University of Chicago Press, pp. 337–581.
———. (1973c) "Physics," in R. McKeon (ed.), *Introduction to Aristotle* (R. K. Gaye, and R. P. Hardie, Trans.), 2nd edition, Chicago: University of Chicago Press, pp. 113–144.
———. (1973d) "Politics," in R. McKeon (ed.), *Introduction to Aristotle* (B. Jowett, Trans.), 2nd edition, Chicago: University of Chicago Press, pp. 583–659.
Banton, M. (1998) *Racial Theories*, 2nd edition, Cambridge: Cambridge University Press.
Bayertz, K. (1999) "Four Uses of 'Solidarity'," in K. Bayertz (ed.), *Solidarity*. Dordrecht, Netherlands: Kluwer, pp. 3–28.
Berger, P. L., and Luckmann, T. (1966) *The Social Construction of Reality: An Treatist in the Sociology of Knowledge*, New York: Anchor Books.
Darwin, C. (1859) *The Origin of Species by Means of Natural Selection, or the Preservation of Favored Races in the Struggle for Life*, London: John Murray.
Dunbar, R. I. (2003) "The Social Brain: Mind, Language, and Society in Evolutionary Perspective." *Annual Review of Anthropology* 32: 163–181.
Dunbar, R. I., and Shultz, S. (2007, September 7). "Evolution in the Social Brain." *Science, New Series* 317, no. 5843: 1344–1347.
Francis, R. C. (2011). *Epigenetics: How Environment Shapes Our Genes*, New York: W. W. Norton.
Gilbert, S. S., Sapp, J., and Tauber, A. I. (2012, December). "A Symbiotic View of Life: We Have Never Been Individuals." *Quarterly Review of Biology* 87, no. 4: 325–340.
Jablonka, E., and Lamb, M. J. (2014). *Evolution in Four Dimensions: Geneic, Epigenetic, Behavioral, and Symbolic Variation in the History of Life*, Cambridge, MA: MIT Press.
Laitinen, A., and Pessi, A. B. (2014). "Solidarity: Theory and Practice: An Introduction," in A. Laitinen and A. B. Pessi, eds., *Solidarity: Theory and Practice*, Lanham: Lexington Books, pp. 1–29.
Levinson, S. C. (2006) "Introduction: The Evolution of Culture in a Microcosm," in S. C. Levinson and P. Jaisson (eds.), *Evolution and Culture: A Fyssen Foundation Symposium*. Cambridge, MA: MIT Press, pp. 1–41.
Lewens, T. (2015) *Cultural Evolution: Conceutual Challenges*, Oxford: Oxford University Press.
Mills, C. (1999) *The Racial Contract*, Ithaca: Cornell University Press.
Pateman, C. (1988) *The Sexual Contract*, Stanford, CA: Stanford University Press.
Richerson, P. J., and Boyd, R. (2005) *Not by Genes Alone: How Culture Transformed Human Evolution*, Chicago: University of Chicago Press.
Salmela, M. (2014) "Collective Emotions as the 'Glue' of Group Solidarity", in A. Laitinen, and A. B. Pessi (eds.), *Solidarity: Theory and Practice*, Lanham: Lexington Books, pp. 55–87.

Shelby, T. (2007) *We Who Are Dark: The Philosophical Foundations of Black Solidarity*, Cambridge, MA: Belknap Press.
Silk, J. B. (2007, September 7). "Social Components of Fitness in Primate Groups." *Science*, New Series 317, no. 5843: 1347–1351.
Smedley, A., and Smedley, B. D. (2011) *Race in North America: Origin and Evolution of a Worldview*, 4th edition, Boulder: Westview Press.
Tomasello, M. (2006) "Uniquely Human Cognition Is a Product of Human Culture," in S. C. Levinson and P. Jaisson (eds.), *Evolution and Culture: A Fyssen Foundation Symposium*, Cambridge, MA: MIT Press, pp. 203–217.
Tomasello, M., Carpenter, M., Call, J., Behne, T., and Moll, H. (2005, October). "Understanding and Sharing Intentions: The Origins of Cultural Cognition." *Behavior: Brain Sciences* 28, no. 5, 675–735.
Wade, N. (2014). *A Troublesome Inheritance: Genes, Race and Human History*, New York, NY: Penguin Press.
Wilson, D. S., and Wilson, E. O. (2007, December). "Rethinking the Theoretical Foundation of Sociobiology." *Quarterly Review of Biology* 82, no. 4: 327–348.
Wilson, E. O. (1999) *Consilience: The Unity of Knowledge*, New York: Vintage Books.
———. (2000) *Sociobiology: The New Synthesis*, Twenty-Fifth Anniversary Edition, Cambridge, MA: Belknap Press.
———. (2012). *The Social Conquest of Earth*, New York: Liveright.

31
RACE, LUCK, AND THE MORAL EMOTIONS

Samantha Vice

Introduction

However we understand "race", our own racial classification has a deep connection to our identity and character, and to our prospects and success in the world. How should we think about this aspect of ourselves? Even if we repudiate racial classifications for the damage they have done or hope for a non-racial future, we are racially classified now whether we like it or not. Race might not be biologically real but it is socially real for all that. This chapter explores whether there are better and worse ways—more or less virtuous ways—of responding to our racial identity.

In this complex debate, I need to set out some basic commitments at the start. First, I speak of "virtuous responses" and "character" in a way that should be compatible with any moral theory of right and wrong action. My concern is with a normative inquiry that is focused on character rather than action, and in particular, with our evaluations of a person's character as more or less appropriate and praiseworthy—that is what I shall mean by "virtuous." I say nothing about whether a "virtue ethics" should replace or supplement traditional theories of right and wrong action. Aristotle's notion of a (virtuous) character is still useful and standard: the set of stable and reliable dispositions to act, think, and feel in certain ways, which are responsive to practical reason (1953: Bk 2). Unlike "personality," a term we usually use to pick out the idiosyncratic features which distinguish us from one another, "a virtuous character" picks out traits that express the excellences characteristic of humans per se. In this chapter, I focus on the whole on our emotional responses to our own racialized, more or less virtuous characters, though as we shall see, assessing those requires reference to our cognitive responses to our situation.

Second, although I look at both blacks' and whites' responses to their racialized characters, when it comes to disentangling the ethical implications I am mostly concerned with the responses of whites. This carries the risk of putting white people at the center of ethical inquiry, where they have been for far too long, to disastrous effect. My reasons for concentrating on white experience yet again are personal, philosophical, and ethical: personally, it is uncomfortable and probably inappropriate to make comments on how those in another racial position should feel, especially when I speak from a position of privilege. On the whole, therefore, I speak as a white person about whites' emotional responses, and when I make a claim about blacks' responses, I am calling on black writers. The philosophical issues explored here of course have general features, but I hope to show that the position of whites brings with it distinctive puzzles about responsibility, luck, and identity. Being black will bring its own puzzles in this domain, but I leave this to others to explore. Ethically, whiteness has created plenty of opportunities to evade responsibility for a racially unjust world, so whites' sense of being basically decent people is more at stake.

Finally, I use the label "black" in the inclusive political sense still standard in post-apartheid South African political and theoretical discourse, to refer to a variety of identities that have occupied an inferior racial position. So in this inclusive sense, "black" applies to people of various ethnic and national origins—African; Afro-Caribbean, and South Asian in the UK; African Americans and Asian Americans, American Indians, and Latino/as, in the United States; people of mixed race. Particular black identities may have significantly different racial experiences, but "black" is still a politically and morally powerful category.

Race and Luck

A crucial aspect of this exploration is that whether we are black or white, privileged or not, most of us have no control over the way we are racially classified in a racialized world. Unless we are able to pass for another race, our race is not something we can opt out of, and conscious attempts to do so usually lead to debilitating psychological contortions and fraught relations. (On passing, see Piper 1992; and consider the controversial case of Rachel Dolezal, the ex-president of the NAACP chapter in Spokane, Washington, a white woman who identifies as black, and who successfully passed as black until her dramatic exposure in 2015). I may not personally identify with what "whiteness" means, for example, and I might want to repudiate that identity, but in this world I am white and am treated as white. For most of us, our race has enormous implications for our lives, inclining them in a certain direction and into a certain shape from birth. Our race provides us with a greater or lesser array of options from which we can create, develop and understand our adult selves, and it brings attendant advantages and disadvantages. Being born black in apartheid South Africa meant that many options were automatically foreclosed, that your future was radically restricted in more than just legal ways. That is an extreme example, but blacks in most parts of the world still lead far less flourishing lives than their white fellow citizens, with violence, incarceration, and poverty blighting many lives. On the other hand, the undoubted social, political, and economic privilege of whiteness can be double-edged and bring its own burdens, as José Medina (2013) shows: those cushioned in the blindness and arrogance of privilege often lack the skills and insight which the less privileged are forced to acquire and which often put them in at least a better epistemic position. The luck of being born black or white therefore has pervasive consequences, negative and positive, for all aspects of our lives.

Race is also, to use the influential terms introduced by Bernard Williams (1981) and Thomas Nagel (1979), a matter of *moral* luck (for a survey of the debate, see Nelkin 2013). Even though our race is not under our control—and hence is a matter of luck—it has implications that are in the realm of normativity. It greatly influences who we become and we still seem to be responsible for our characters and lives; they seem appropriate objects of moral evaluation. The extent of the influence of race on our characters may not be apparent to us and we may need to learn it for ourselves, or be "conscientized" by others into an understanding of race's meaning (as whiteness studies and black consciousness movements attempt to do). It may be easy to understand and sympathize with some of the morally problematic character traits that arise out of being a certain race, and sometimes we may not be blamed for them. For instance, the unconscious adoption of white standards by some blacks, and the shame that accompanies not living up to them, is understandable but still morally problematic. We do not blame them, but we still evaluate their lives as worse than they could be. In contrast, the complacence and arrogance that typically accompanies being white does not seem to be excused by whites' lack of control over their race; we judge that they are answerable for these traits and that they should try to change them. Whether or not people are open to blame, then, they can still be held responsible for the characters that race might have influenced, and for at least some of their effects in the world.

So it is a matter of luck that we are born white or black in a racist world, but a matter of moral luck that our character is influenced by our race. Despite talk of luck, however, the general patterns of influence of race on our lives are not accidental—in this world we are from birth enmeshed in systems of privilege, opportunities and deprivations. Claudia Card calls the results of this system the "unnatural lottery" (1996, after Rawls 1973), which Lisa Tessman (2005: 13) explains as those "circumstances that are systematically arranged and that tend to affect people as members of social groups." The unnatural lottery affects our characters in patterned ways that can be explained by our position in those non-accidental systems. We can call the luck that affects character formation "constitutive luck" (after Williams 1981 and Nagel 1979), and the luck coming from the unnatural lottery "systemic luck" (Tessman 2005: 13). The most relevant kind of luck for our purposes is, then, a combination of systemic and constitutive luck. My being white may not be under my original control, but the fact that *I*, because white, was influenced in certain ways and became recognizably a certain kind of person is something we can explain and predict given white supremacy. The character traits I then develop under these systematic conditions are open to moral assessment.

Of course—and as we shall see, this makes the issue tremendously tricky—each one of us is not only what systemic constitutive luck has made of us. Race does not exhaust our identity; it does not exhaust what can be said of us, nor how we can be evaluated. Each one of us is far more than this. We may display types of traits that can be correlated with occupying a particular position in a racialized world, but we are each also individuals, and this can unsettle easy categorizations. Some of us might escape the patterns of character development and life trajectories that the unnatural lottery predicts for us; some might struggle for years to overcome them. It is a symptom of a *racist*, and not just racialized, world to treat people as only, or essentially, their race. These two thoughts—that we are importantly what our racial positions have made us, and that we are also importantly more than this or, sometimes, not this—complicate the "moral" dimension of moral luck. They complicate the kind of assessment and range of responses we think is appropriate towards ourselves and others as black or white. I will explore this complexity after setting out a framework for understanding the emotions.

The Moral Emotions and Responsibility

My concern in this chapter is with how we respond emotionally to our own characters in the light of racial luck, and with what those self-directed responses, in turn, express about ourselves. To have a character is to respond to ourselves and the world in patterned and stable ways that express our core commitments. At the same time, our characters are partly constituted by the way we respond, and we can develop or change ourselves insofar as we can change those emotional responses. The influence between character and emotion therefore goes both ways.

The view in this chapter assumes that we have some significant control over our characters and emotional responses, and that they are appropriate objects of moral assessment. I will not say too much about responsibility for character. Skepticism about responsibility here would undermine our most basic moral practices: One of the ongoing and arduous tasks of an ethical life is to develop and improve one's character, and a moral community is constituted by moral agents who are answerable to each other not only for what they do but also, in certain respects, for the kinds of people they are. As Peter Goldie (2004: chapter 4) notes, character traits are reason-responsive—generous people, for example, respond to reasons for being generous which the parsimonious fail to see or heed.

The very notion of the moral emotions also includes reason-responsiveness and brings moral evaluation with it. The moral emotions are those that respond to, incorporate, or express moral assessments—examples are shame, guilt, and remorse; resentment, indignation, and bitterness; certain kinds of pride and praise; self-satisfaction and esteem of others. For example, most of us will feel shame if we do something that falls below the standards we accept for ourselves and that reflects badly on ourselves. If we do something we accept to be morally wrong, we feel guilt or remorse for our actions, even if our sense of our basic decency remains relatively unscathed (Taylor 1985). We can resent our weaknesses and take pride in our achievements; we can hold ourselves in contempt, or be gentle with ourselves. Our experiencing or not experiencing these emotions is also open to the moral assessment of others, who can judge emotions to be uncalled for, or commendable, and who can hold to account those who fail to feel remorse or are utterly shameless in circumstances that warrant it.

One mark of the emotions, however, seems to be their passivity, their not being directly "up to us." We cannot just choose to feel ashamed, or proud, or grateful. How, then, can our feeling them reflect well or badly on ourselves? We could wish that they weren't the way they are, certainly, but it hardly seems fair that *we* be evaluated for having them. While it is true that we cannot, on the spot, choose how we feel, emotions are not simply sensations like pain or itchiness, or instinctual reactions like disgust or being startled. Most philosophers agree that the emotions have some kind of cognitive dimension, though they differ greatly in the details. We need not hold the strong view that emotions are essentially beliefs or judgments to accept that emotions are directed at something, that they are *intentional* states that respond to and inform us about the world, and are therefore in the realm of reasons. (Cognitive theories of the emotions can take many forms; see de Sousa 2014 and Deonna and Teroni 2012 for helpful surveys.) If our beliefs, perceptions or evaluations of the world change, usually—and properly—so do our emotions. If they do not, we think the situation odd or pathological or at least unfortunate. An emotion which proves impervious to change—an *idée fixe*—we judge to be inappropriate precisely because it is insensitive to the very evidence that would undermine it. About our emotions, then, we can ask a range of questions that show their reason-responsiveness: Are they based on false beliefs? Are they out of proportion to reality? Are they (or do they include) faulty perceptions or assessments of the situation? More deeply, we can ask about the kinds of temperament, attitudes, or character that they express: are they expressions of a fundamental malice, pessimism, or generosity, for instance? These are all questions we can ask of ourselves and of others. Even if we cannot immediately change them, and even if initially we simply find ourselves with an emotion, in the light of this cognitive dimension it is most of the time possible to change or slowly eradicate our emotions by changing our assessments, perceptions or beliefs, and by working longer term on our characters.

I will assume for this chapter, too, that the assessment of our emotions is moral and not only broadly ethical or rational. That is, we assess our emotions not just as valuable or good to have, or as fortunate or unfortunate, and not just as rational or irrational, but as appropriate in a deontic sense—meriting esteem, blame, or censure, rather than simply repulsion or admiration. We can be held accountable for them before others and we can be morally wrong in how we feel, not just irrational or lacking some other value. Even though I cannot immediately—just like that—stop feeling resentful or guilty, I can be morally assessed for what I do with those emotions and for how I work on them. So this chapter accepts that there is such a thing as moral luck (not an uncontroversial assumption—see Nelkin 2013: §4), and accepts that we can be morally evaluated for our characters and for having, or failing to have, certain emotions, even though they are only indirectly under our control.

We can give some defense of this framework by noting a point that I will return to, that there are other aspects of ourselves that are not under our control but that we still assess morally—our natural temperament, dispositions, and abilities, for instance. If we exempt emotional responses from evaluation because we find ourselves with them, so, too, will a range of other evaluations have to be jettisoned. Understanding why it matters that our emotional reactions be a certain way will also partly justify this framework. One reason it matters is that our emotional dispositions are a defining part of our characters—we are irascible, or optimistic, or shameless, or generous, and this tells us something important about who we are and, if we are at all self-reflective, we think it can reflect well or badly on ourselves. It probably does not say everything morally important about us (we might, for instance, do what we take to be right without feeling inclined and with no emotion, and that can be praiseworthy), but it is a familiar and deep aspect of ourselves and moral evaluation. Finally, and as I go on to explore, we might think that if we do not have certain emotional moral responses then our understanding is lacking too, and we display both a moral and epistemic failure.

Race and the Moral Emotions

What, then, are the range of emotional responses that apply to our sense of self as white or black, and, more particularly, to our understanding of ourselves as racially privileged or oppressed, in light of the constitutive and systemic luck involved in these identities? And how do we ethically assess these responses?

Moral agents who recognize injustice and unfair privilege would naturally respond with some degree of emotion, even if it is not sustained at a high pitch (it probably could not be without risking mental health and, as Tessman explores (2005: chapter 4), part of virtue is finding the "mean" between indifference and a self-destructive immersion in suffering). We would feel some anger and sadness towards the injustices of the world, even if only when we dwell consciously on them or our attention is demanded by circumstances. Further, recognition of the long-lasting and damaging systems that we all find ourselves inhabiting (some comfortably, others painfully), seems to call for certain responses towards ourselves as well.

It seems plausible to say—though, as we shall see, it is certainly not uncontroversial—that whites should feel some kind of discomfort even if they have not performed any obviously racist acts. I will explore this claim throughout the chapter, but we can give some schematic reasons in support of it to begin with. First, white people belong to a group that is responsible for the atrocities of slavery and, in South Africa, for apartheid, the socio-economic effects of which are still felt. As members of the group, most of them benefit from that history and from the ongoing unjust distribution of resources that is its legacy. While a full defense of the claim that whites are still beneficiaries of racial injustice would require empirical evidence, the claim is plausible enough to be an assumption in the rest of this chapter. (One piece of evidence is that the percentage of whites living in poverty in South Africa is less than 1%.) Second, the injustice of the current distribution is maintained over generations as already privileged whites pass down their goods to their descendants; and so third, it could be said that white privilege is gained and maintained at the expense of others.

Fourth, privilege is not only material. Whites are favored in all sorts of subtle and not so subtle ways (McIntosh 1988), and are protected from the everyday dangers and annoyances that accompany many black lives. Furthermore, most whites will display habitual, often unconscious, ways of being in the world that Marilyn Frye (1992) influentially terms "whitely" (and see Sullivan 2006; McIntosh 1988; Matthews 2012). These habits, which are as clear to non-whites as they are often invisible to whites, demonstrate their ease in a world that continuously accommodates and validates them. For example, whites assume that their way is the universal way of being, are confident in their abilities and future success, and assume that things will go their way. Many whites will also be whitely, even if they do not perform crudely racist acts or say blatantly racist things. And once this is brought to their attention, most will not be happy to recognize those habits in themselves.

The target of our discomfort can be difficult to put a finger on, however. Some of the habits mentioned above are not problematic in themselves (e.g., confidence and expectation of success), and many of the goods that whites enjoy routinely should accrue to everyone (Gordon 2004: 175; Blum 2008: 310). In a world without systemic inequalities, much of what we think of as privilege now would simply be what is due to all of us as moral agents and citizens. Our discomfort, then, must have something to do with the thought that whites' ease of being is at the expense of others' discomfort or relegation, and with the complacency that they take towards their good luck. Some of the "privilege" of white privilege is therefore only negative in a context of racial inequality, and it is in this negative sense that I will use the term.

It also seems plausible to say that blacks would appropriately feel not only anger, resentment, or bitterness at white people and at their disadvantaged position in a white supremacist world, but also emotions towards themselves as positioned in that system—sadness for possibilities they might never experience, a need to come to terms with a life that is not how it could have been, mourning a loss of trust in others and the constant vigilance needed to avoid trouble. Someone might also recognize in himself problematic habits of behavior and thought. He might not like, for instance, the fact that he defers to whites or unthinkingly accepts their judgments about himself, and this might occasion shame. He has fallen below his own reflectively endorsed standard of not deferring to white standards, even as they still influence him. Such negative emotions need not always be debilitating and inappropriate. They can, for example, be mobilized by leaders in social justice movements, as they arguably were in South Africa's Black Consciousness Movement (Biko 1987), and thus be put in the service of justice. If they are turned outwards and responsibly guided, they can be instrumentally valuable, and so ensure that blacks do not become indirect agents of whiteliness themselves by satisfying white norms. However, many also feel understandable, yet ultimately *inappropriate* emotions of self-contempt, hopelessness, or shame, which are grounded in their acceptance of the standards of the privileged. An important part of the liberation struggle for blacks has been to understand and change those negative self-directed emotions (Fanon 2008).

At the least, then, we do not condemn self-directed negative responses of some kind from whites. In contrast, while we understand that blacks might also, perhaps unconsciously, be harsh towards themselves, we judge those feelings to be sadly inappropriate when they are not utilized for the ends of justice. (I have these cases in mind in what follows.) We seem to have reached an uncontroversial and perhaps banal conclusion: negative and judgmental emotional responses to the self *qua* privileged are appropriate, but to the self in a less privileged position they are not, and this is because of the badness of oppression and privilege. Those in the non-privileged position should not be harsh towards themselves. They are in a morally bad position because their flourishing and dignity is undermined, but it is not morally bad in the sense of their being perpetrators or beneficiaries of injustice. Those in a privileged position should at least feel discomfort about themselves *qua* privileged because privilege is morally bad, because they benefit in systematic and predictable ways that contribute to reinforcing injustice.

Which moral emotions would be appropriate to whites' compromised position? Shannon Sullivan (2006) reminds us of the difficulty of eradicating whitely habits, many of which operate without our awareness. For many in South Africa, habits of whiteliness and the racism inherited from apartheid are difficult to recognize, let alone dislodge. They will sometimes be expressed as fairly straightforward racism, even though whites may be unaware of it and even though they might express their disapproval of racism. Coming to realize that their own behavior is racist, when they know that racism is considered wrong, would naturally lead to guilt; realizing that *they* are racists would lead to shame. Those whites who are not racist in an obvious sense, but who are aware of their ingrained whitely habits and who try actively to resist them, present a more complicated case. Perhaps, minimally, they would feel something akin to what Williams (1981) calls agent-regret. For Williams, this is regret for being part of a causal chain that resulted in harm, even if one had no control over it and did no wrong intentionally. We would not judge a person generously if she felt nothing in such unfortunate circumstances. Similarly, it is appropriate that whites should at least regret their fortunate position in a structure that perpetuates racial injustice, even though being in that position is a matter of bad moral luck. More strongly, and controversially, perhaps it would be fitting for them to feel *shame*: we cannot approve of the habits of whiteliness when they are pointed out to us—we do not want to be those kinds of complacent and arrogant people. We do not want to perpetuate an unjust system from a position of privilege, and flourish at the expense of those less privileged in that system. In both these respects, we are falling below our own standards for virtue (Vice 2010). Finally, perhaps *guilt* for flourishing at the expense of others would also be appropriate. Not actively resisting an unjust regime, continuing to enjoy its fruits, and passing them down to the next generation, are also plausible grounds for guilt: "I am guilty by virtue of my relationship to wrongdoing, a relationship that I did not create but have not severed either," Sandra Lee Bartky writes (1999: 41). She notes that this means rejecting the intuitive link between guilt and intentional wrong-doing: "one can be guilty *without having done anything wrong*" (Bartky 1999: 41; and see Vice 2010). Insofar as whites might not be able fully to escape their entanglement with injustice—merely by being white, the world accommodates them—some uncomfortable emotions might be something they have to live with.

Some such painful emotions are the natural and proper responses to a deepening understanding of a racialized world in which one is privileged, and so have "an affective dimension that is inextricable from a cognitive dimension" (Bartky 1999: 40). Feeling them expresses one's understanding of the situation; so we can see how they are intentional, reason-responsive states, directed towards a phenomenon evaluated as bad. They also express something about the kind of person one is—for instance, that one has enough sense of justice to respond with pain to the recognition of one's privileged, unearned position. On the other hand, if one is the recipient of injustice one can certainly feel pain *for* oneself—and coming to terms with one's position might require acknowledging it—but hardly pain *at* oneself. A racialized and racist world is bad for one and not sought out.

These conclusions strike me as plausible and correct, and I want to retain them. However, matters become more complex once we recall moral luck. We have accepted that privilege is attendant on being white, and disadvantage attendant on not being white, and over the origins of neither racial identities do we have control. On the view so far, moral luck is *asymmetrical*: the luck of being white brings with it appropriately negative self-directed emotions, but the luck of being born black does not. The fact of luck, therefore, does not warrant only one set of responses, but is *asymmetrical*. We thought earlier that this was banally true, but perhaps it is not true, or at least not banally so. Could a white person not say, "I'm sorry about the injustices of the world, but I didn't choose to be white and I have no control over the fact of being white. I will certainly avoid actively being unjust or racist myself; I will try to change my whitely habits and I will try to contribute to social justice where I can. I am as unhappy and angry with the state of the world as you are. But it is not my fault and there is no reason for me to feel bad about *myself*." Just as the black person did not choose her position, nor did the white person, and if self-directed negative emotions are inappropriate in the one case, so are they in the other. I shall call this the "symmetry response." Note that it does not say that whites need not feel any emotions about the racialized world they inhabit and benefit from, only that they need not feel *self*-directed negative emotions.

The apparently uncontroversial thesis that responses to one's racial moral luck are justifiably asymmetrical is therefore put under pressure by the notion of luck, which leads us to consider the symmetry response. Both asymmetry and symmetry defenders can agree that there is bad luck for blacks and whites. It is (one kind of) bad luck to be born white—because it typically puts one on the side of injustice and privilege, develops whitely habits and epistemic and ethical vices, and opens one to criticism for benefitting from an unjust system. It is a different (certainly worse) kind of bad luck to be born black—because it typically puts one in the position of an inferior, radically reduces one's life choices, and opens one to a variety of humiliating and difficult situations. However, the symmetry response says that while one might rightly condemn the *world* that makes these different positions likely, it would be inappropriate to condemn the *self*, whether white or black. This of course only covers cases in which whites have not intentionally acted in racist or harmful ways, but it can allow that feeling agent-regret for being unintentionally embedded in a system that is harmful to others is not unreasonable. It therefore does not completely reject the applicability of the notion of moral luck to one's racial identity. Rather than agent-regret, then, the symmetry response targets shame in particular, and perhaps guilt, if we disentangle guilt from intentional action in the way suggested above.

How can we reply to the symmetry response? It is correct, but not enough, to point out that whiteliness is hard to eradicate and will probably indelibly stain one's character and affect one's actions; and it is correct, but also not enough, to point out that one continues to benefit in non-accidental and predictable ways from the unjust system into which one did not choose to be born. These are true, but they might not satisfy the supporter of symmetry. First, as we granted, it might be said of some whitely habits and privileges that they are pernicious only in a system that considers whiteness the norm. All white people should try not to harm others through these habits and be as attentive to their workings as possible; they should support political and social change, and in that way, systemic change. That is all that can be expected. Second, as noted earlier, we benefit in all sorts of ways from features of ourselves we did not choose and which are distributed unevenly—being talented in areas that have social status and bring economic rewards; being highly motivated and energetic; thriving on the competitiveness and aggression that characterize many influential professions; having sturdy mental and physical health; being temperamentally optimistic. Many have tried to think of ways of leveling that playing field, but it is impossible without massive interference in private lives. Merely benefiting does not yet justify feeling bad about oneself unless one should—and this is crazy—also feel bad about one's rewards in all aspects of the natural lottery of our origins (see Rawls 1973: 101ff; and for a discussion of the liberal response to the lottery, see Kymlicka 1992: chapter 3).

These last claims of the defender of symmetry contain something that is true, and I will return to them, but nonetheless, proponents of asymmetry are unlikely to be persuaded. Could they then reply to the symmetry response by weighing the *bad* moral luck of being white against the *good* moral luck of being white? The "natural lottery" of their origins included inherited privilege, after all. Whites may have the bad luck to be placed in a position of privilege at others' expense, but of course that position is also, and in ways more morally relevant, a matter of good luck for them. Their lives are eased and improved in innumerable ways, which ethically outweigh the epistemic deficiencies that Medina (2013), for instance, explores. They might not have chosen this fortunate position, but surely it means *something*? It seems callous to deny this, but a proponent of symmetry might, in a third response, refuse to accept that their flourishing *qua* white is evidence of an unjust system of white privilege, or that white privilege is unjustly expensive to others. Earlier we noted that a symmetry proponent could say that whiteness is only problematic in an unjust system, so we should pay attention to that system. But a different response is to reject the work that "system" is doing in this debate. In any society, some people will flourish and others will not, and we cannot blame a system if we want to retain notions of agency, integrity, and responsibility. If whites predominately flourish over blacks, this may be a result of morally relevant features like hard work and diligence which everyone in principle can cultivate. There is a kind of envy at work here, they might say, that is chary of the good fortune of others.

This view appeals to the value of people taking responsibility for their lives and not blaming others for their failures. Again there is something right in this, which I shall explore in the next section. But we can already argue that this very individualistic view misses ethically important aspects of privilege and ethical agency. It does not acknowledge how deeply we are embedded in, and supported by, our social, economic, and racial backgrounds. Being white brings with it a backdrop of security and opportunities that enhances any abilities whites might have, and which is absent for many blacks. It is arrogant and self-serving to insist that whites are successful by dint of their own pure efforts and hard work alone, and it is unjust to those whose lack of worldly success has little to do with abilities, motivation, or assiduity. Such a view reveals a blindness to the patterns of distribution of benefits and burdens; it is not an accident that whites tend to live materially and socially better lives than blacks. Their fortunate position in a system that already favors them helps to maintain patterns of injustice; privilege is passed down generations, and the children of the privileged start off in a better position to acquire social and material goods. The system in which they live ensures that they benefit while others struggle, and, more strongly, a case could be made that this benefit *depends* on there being a group that is less privileged and which can support that privileged lifestyle (for example, by providing cheap domestic labor, and by being less prepared than the privileged for the middle-class job market). An appropriate response to this understanding would be painful. We therefore have reason to evaluate such complacent responses to one's own good fortune and the lack of appropriate moral emotions towards oneself as a beneficiary of injustice as lacking virtue. As we shall see further below, for whites to reject the symmetry response and accept the appropriateness of feeling uncomfortable about themselves can itself be a virtuous response to a vicious socio-political position.

In this section, I have explored the implications of taking moral luck seriously in the discussion about racial identity. At first glance it seems that such luck renders self-directed emotions of blame and guilt from both whites and blacks inappropriate. However, I suggested in return that this symmetry response ignores the nature of systematic white privilege. White people's relative success in the world is ill-gotten, inherited through an unjust system and enabled by the secure structures of their lives. Acknowledging this should occasion *some* discomfort towards the white self who benefits in this way. This is one reason to reject the symmetry response, but there is more to say about the complex nature of selfhood and ethical agency, which shows both what is attractive about that response, and where it goes wrong.

Identity, Group Membership, and Responsibility

Both the critic and defender of negative self-directed emotions can press more deeply on the fundamental notions of identity and responsibility. At issue is how a person appropriately responds to *her own individual self*, for which she is responsible, *as a member of a socially relevant group*, membership of which is not under her control. While I focus on the moral situation of whites, the issue is just as pressing, in a different way, for blacks, who have for so long had their particularity denied by stereotypes and shallow assumptions.

When considering group oppression and privilege different aspects of ourselves are forced into a destabilizing juxtaposition. I am uniquely I, but I am also a white woman, and more particularly, a white South African who grew up under apartheid and came to adulthood in the early days of the democracy. Am I responsible for the ongoing patterns of meanings of my racial identity, even as I try not to be unjust? Is my group membership a morally relevant feature of myself, to which appropriate emotions are called for? Putting aside individual vices, the line of thought in this context is that it is *as a white woman* that the unique *I* should feel some kind of discomfort. In a racialized world, in which whites historically have been either oppressor or privileged, it is difficult to think—and would be disingenuous if thought—that one's race is not a morally relevant feature of oneself.

The acceptance of race as morally relevant to one's own individuality and identity will be expressed through the range of moral emotions explored in the previous section. That one does, in fact, feel uncomfortable emotions about *oneself-as-a-member-of-a-group* therefore depends on one's identification of oneself as a member of that group, even as one rejects the standards that govern or partly constitute it. However, what if one refuses that identification, or refuses its moral significance? Someone could say, "Yes, I am white (or black or lesbian or Jewish), but that is of no moral or existential importance to me. I choose to ignore or repudiate its meaning and I refuse to live by the scripts of whiteness (or blackness or homosexuality or Jewishness)" (on "scripts," see Appiah 2005: 110). Can we say to this person that she has gone wrong?

We are brought to the fundamental issues of what it is that constitutes a person in a morally significant way and what a person should accept about herself in order to live virtuously. So, who am *I*? Only those features I choose or have control over, only my autonomous self? That cuts out most of ourselves as counting as ourselves, if we accept that much of our temperament and dispositions are set down in childhood, and that the natural talents and abilities by which we make a living and define ourselves are not up to us (though their development may be). As Nagel expresses it, taking constitutive luck to its extreme threatens to shrink "the area of genuine agency" to "an extensionless point" (1979: 35). Confronting such an unpalatable conclusion, most of us nonetheless accept those features as part of ourselves and also as appropriately open to ethical evaluation. At the same time, however, we usually do not wish to be utterly defined, or most significantly defined, by any feature of ourselves, even those that play as deep a role in our lives as gender, sexual orientation, or race. For most of us, such features and even our chosen commitments remain but one aspect of ourselves. Persons are complex and unique and it is right that no single feature of them be taken as decisive for identity or for moral evaluation. In this respect there is truth in the symmetry response's reluctance to accept the asymmetry of black and white moral luck.

These thoughts are understandable, important, and, I think, correct. One of the most odious aspects in the history of racism is how complex, unique people were reduced to their race and physiognomy, and how their potential and capacities—and so the narratives their lives could follow—were restricted by the narrow perceptions and power of others. However, some refuse to accept that their group membership is "themselves" in any morally relevant and identity-conferring sense at all. I *belong*, possibly, to many groups, but I *am* not any of the defining features of those groups, unless I choose to make them personally relevant. Many whites seem to have something like this in mind when they refuse to feel guilty about apartheid or slavery or the radically reduced life chances of blacks in many racialized settings. "Other white people may have done horrendous things," they may say, "but I haven't done anything horrendous and I don't have to identify myself with *those* white people and share their guilt. My whiteness is an arbitrary physical feature of me and, like my hair or eye color or my height, carries no moral significance unless I choose to make it so."

This response is characteristic of the whiteliness that many people still refuse to see in themselves. One of the typical features of whiteliness in many parts of the world is that it is invisible to white people, in the sense of setting white standards and ways of being as an unrecognized norm: I am not white, I am just *I*, and my ways of doing things are not parochial, but universal (e.g., Dyer 1997 and the essays in Rasmussen et al. 2001). In a white supremacist world, refusing one's white identity is a sign of privilege: I do not feel white as opposed to anything else and being white is not significant, just because whiteness is never made an issue. This nonchalance is impossible for most black people. The refusal to acknowledge the moral and political significance of being white is therefore nothing to be proud of or indifferent towards. It is, rather, a sign of something morally and epistemically amiss—a sign of willful ignorance, woeful naïvety, genuine lack of understanding of the workings of race, or callous indifference to other people's struggles, none of these is a sign of virtue. The logic of whiteliness therefore suggests some reasons why we could think that whites who do not identify their whiteness as a morally relevant feature of themselves are morally lacking.

Coming to acknowledge this will require and be an instance of what Claudia Card (1996) calls "taking responsibility for" our character (and, in a more restricted context, see Wolf 2001: 10). As we saw in the previous section, proponents of the symmetry response correctly wish to retain responsibility, and take it as a reason *against* asymmetry. However, a deeper understanding of ethical responsibility in fact supports asymmetry. As noted, we can take responsibility for many aspects of ourselves for which we are not originally responsible. My temper is naturally bad, say, so I try to control it, or my itinerant and insecure childhood made me anxious about change, but I try to prevent this getting in the way of adventure. Similarly, regardless of whether we had initial control over our racial identities and over the kinds of characters we developed as a result— whitely or submissive or bitter or angry—we can still evaluate ourselves and then take steps to make ourselves more into the kinds of people we reflectively endorse. Mature moral agency requires taking responsibility for the aspects of ourselves that, while not under our original control, are constitutive of ourselves. It is what we make of what we are given that matters ethically.

Making ourselves better will take time and effort; habits stemming from our systemic constitutive luck will be difficult to dislodge, and some may work beneath the level of conscious awareness (Sullivan 2006: 4). As Card writes, we "develop responsibility as a virtue by first *taking* responsibility in ways that outrun our apparent present worthiness to do so and then carrying through successfully" (1996: 27). Sometimes, being motivated to do this at all will also be a matter of luck (1996: 27). It is—just—possible that some whites may never enter a world different enough from their own to be spurred on to self-reflection and to reach an understanding of the non-white world. Such seclusion is unusual—the world *will* impinge, however inconveniently—and then we show the worthiness or deficiency of our characters by the way we respond. Responding with shame or guilt towards one's white self, and deep sadness towards the world that helped to create that self, says *something* positive about one—besides self-knowledge and a degree of autonomy, those emotions express caring or solidarity, acknowledgement of racial injustice, and a sincere desire to be better than our race makes us. Taking responsibility for one's whiteness will also indicate a willingness to open oneself to unpleasant emotions. One does not decide to feel, nor set out to feel—that would be artificial and, sometimes, perverse—but still, one accepts that one will feel in new and uncomfortable ways as one's understanding of the racial world and one's position in it deepens.

So it will no doubt be difficult for whites to take responsibility for their racial identity and habits, and they may have their sense of being basically decent severely eroded in the process. It is itself an ethical *choice* and ethical step to take up the responsibility that will allow for further ethical change. Margaret Urban Walker writes that being accountable and bearing responsibility for what might have befallen us by luck "means exposure to possibilities of criticism, rebuke, and punishment; to valid demands of reparation, restoration, or compensation; to proper expectations of regret, remorse, self-reproof, and self-correction" (1991: 24). In this field of assessment, she says, we can be expected "to muster certain resources of character to meet the synergy of choice and fortune" (1991: 19). In the process, temptations to "self-deception, self-indulgence, and wishful thinking" will need to be overcome (1991: 20). And if Aristotle is correct, and we acquire the virtues by exercising them (1953: Bk 2), we can in the arduous process of taking responsibility for ourselves, accepting the pain of our emotional self-assessment, and coming to a deeper awareness of the world we share with others, become ourselves a little better.

Conclusion: Self and Others

Luck has played a large role in making us who we are, but as the vast literature on the subject shows, our intuitions are often divided on its moral significance (see the essays in Statman 1993). On the one hand, if luck originally distributed benefits and burdens unfairly but still systematically, some of the burden of responsibility for my character seems removed from me. This is the aspect of the problem which advocates of the symmetry response attend to. On the other hand, to *be* a self at all is to be the confluence of properties, features, histories over which we had no original control. We are constituted originally by luck, but that constitution then becomes who we are. How can we *not* be responsible for the self that arises from them? To repudiate responsibility is to repudiate being a self and all control over our future development.

"Taking responsibility" is a notion that should be amenable to those of an individualistic temperament, some of whom would be attracted to the symmetry response. However, we can take responsibility for ourselves as members of groups as much as for ourselves as individuals who are never fully defined by that membership. Both show an awareness of a racialized reality. The willingness to accept the emotions that naturally accompany this awareness, and to respond with clear vision, self-knowledge and the beginnings of some integrity in a racialized world, is one kind of virtue. It includes the morally necessary step of taking up what Thomas Nagel (1991) calls the "impersonal" stance towards ourselves—seeing ourselves as one of many people, all equally morally important, and I would add, seeing ourselves *as others see us*, and in relation to others. In many contexts, too large a concern with how we appear to others is not virtuous, but when considering our position in a racist and racialized world it is, I think, appropriate. Many whites do not realize how they appear to non-whites, "what white looks like" to blacks, to use the title of George Yancy's collection (2004). Taking responsibility requires seeing ourselves as others see us and admitting the justice of that vision: it is to admit our implication in a world we may not have chosen, but which we help to maintain. And it can be the start of an apology to those others for our position of privilege over them, chosen or not.[*]

Note

[*] My thanks to Ward E. Jones and Paul Taylor for their helpful comments, and to the National Research Foundation for its ongoing support of my research.

References

Appiah, Kwame Anthony. (2005) *The Ethics of Identity*, Princeton: Princeton University Press.
Aristotle (1953) *The Nicomachean Ethics*, trans. J.A.K. Thomson, Harmondsworth: Penguin.
Bartky, Sandra Lee. (1999) "In Defense of Guilt," in Claudia Card (ed.), *On Feminist Ethics and Politics*, Lawrence: University Press of Kansas, pp. 29–51.
Biko, Steve. (1987) *I Write What I Like*, Oxford: Heinemann.
Blum, Lawrence. (2008) "White Privilege: A Mild Critique." *Theory and Research in Education* 6, no. 3: 309–321.
Card, Claudia. (1996) *The Unnatural Lottery: Character and Moral Luck*, Philadelphia: Temple University Press.
Deonna, Julien A., and Teroni, Fabrice. (2012) *The Emotions: A Philosophical Introduction*, London: Routledge.
de Sousa, Ronald. (2014) "Emotion," in Edward N. Zalta (ed.), *The Stanford Encyclopedia of Philosophy*. http://plato.stanford.edu/archives/spr2014/entries/emotion/.
Dyer, Richard. (1997) *White*, New York: Routledge.
Fanon, Frantz. (2008) *Black Skin, White Masks*, trans. Richard Philcox, New York: Grove Press.
Frye, Marilyn. (1992) "White Woman Feminist," in *Willful Virgin: Essays in Feminist Theory*, Freedom, CA: Crossing Press, pp. 147–169.
Goldie, Peter. (2004) *On Personality*, London: Routledge.
Gordon, L. (2004) "Critical Reflections on Three Popular Tropes in the Study of Whiteness," in George Yancy (ed.), *What White Looks Like: African-American Philosophers on the Whiteness Question*, New York: Routledge, pp. 173–193.
Kymlicka, Will. (1992) *Contemporary Political Philosophy: An Introduction*, Oxford: Clarendon Press.
Matthews, Sally. (2012) "White Anti-Racism in Post-Apartheid South Africa." *Politikon* 39, no. 2: 171–188.
McIntosh, Peggy. (1988) *White Privilege and Male Privilege: A Personal Account of Coming to See Correspondences Through Work in Women's Studies*. Wellesley, MA: Center for Research on Women.
Medina, José. (2013) *The Epistemology of Resistance: Gender and Racial Oppression, Epistemic Injustice, and Resistant Imaginations*, Oxford: Oxford University Press.
Nagel, Thomas. (1979) "Moral Luck," in *Mortal Questions*, Cambridge: Cambridge University Press, pp. 24–38.
———. (1991) *Equality and Partiality*, New York: Oxford University Press.
Nelkin, Dana K. (2013) "Moral Luck," in Edward N. Zalta (ed.), *The Stanford Encyclopedia of Philosophy*. http://plato.stanford.edu/archives/win2013/entries/moral-luck/.
Piper, Adrian. (1992) "Passing for White, Passing for Black." *Transition* 58: 4–32.
Radzik, Linda. (2009) *Making Amends: Atonement in Morality, Law, and Politics*, Oxford: Oxford University Press.
Rasmussen, Birgit, Nexica, Irene J., Wray, Matt and Klineberg, Eric. (2001) *The Making and Unmaking of Whiteness*, Durham: Duke University Press.

Rawls, John. (1973) *A Theory of Justice*, Oxford: Oxford University Press.

Statman, Daniel (ed.). (1993) *Moral Luck*, Albany: State University of New York Press.

Sullivan, Shannon. (2006) *Revealing Whiteness: The Unconscious Habits of Racial Privilege*, Bloomington: Indiana University Press.

Taylor, Gabriele. (1985) *Pride, Shame, and Guilt: Emotions of Self-Assessment*, Oxford: Clarendon Press.

Tessman, Lisa. (2005) *Burdened Virtues: Virtue Ethics for Liberatory Struggles*, Oxford: Oxford University Press.

Vice, Samantha. (2010) "How Do I Live in This Strange Place?" *Journal of Social Philosophy* 41, no. 3: 323–342.

Walker, Margaret Urban. (1991) "Moral Luck and the Virtues of Impure Agency." Metaphilosophy 22, nos.1–2: 14–27.

Williams, Bernard. (1981) "Moral Luck," in *Moral Luck*, Cambridge: Cambridge University Press, pp. 20–39.

Wolf, Susan. (2001) "The Moral of Moral Luck." *Philosophic Exchange* 31, no. 1: 1–16.

Yancy, George (ed.). (2004) *What White Looks Like: African-American Philosophers on the Whiteness Question*, New York: Routledge.

32
RACISM AND COLONIALITY
The Invention of "HUMAN(ITY)" and the Three Pillars of the Colonial Matrix of Power (Racism, Sexism, and Nature)

Walter D. Mignolo

I

The issue at stake is social classification, which includes social class. Racism is not exactly what catches the eye. On the surface, racism is a question of content and identification based on biological markers (blood, skin color, hair, and nose shape, as well as language, religion, nationalities). Beneath the surface are the principles of classification and ranking that sustain and characterize racism. Racism is one fundamental aspect of the logic of coloniality: someone who has the privilege to classify and someone who has to endure classification.

The foundation of modern racism is tantamount to the foundation of sexism and the invention of nature to classify the marvelous multiplicity of life on the planet. I will refer to it as "naturism" in parallel with racism and sexism. The logic of racial, sexual, and natural classification is the same.

The logic of racial, sexual, and natural classification is the same. It presupposes a point of reference: the invention of the Human in relation to which lesser religious and ethnic human entities were identified and described. There were neither Human nor humans before the European Renaissance. Greeks named the species *Anthropos*, Chinese *Ren*, Quechua *Runa*. In the Persian version of the Qur'an there were *Bashar* and *Insan* (see below), and we can go on and on. We cannot say that all could be simplified by saying that we are all Humans for it may not be accepted to say that we are all Ren or Runa or Bashar/Insan. Reducing Human to size, divesting it from its pretense to universality, implies accepting it as a regional name in a pluriversal universe of meaning.

The idea of Human in Western civilization presupposes masculinity, which set the standards for classifying sexual lesser humans. Sexual classification had further ramifications. The invention of Women in Medieval Europe created a double hierarchy:

woman lesser than man and witches lesser than woman (Federici).[1] Sexual lesser humans are Women: both necessary women for regeneration of the species and unwanted and expelled women (witches, sexual workers). But sexual lesser humans are also Man and Woman with "abnormal" sexual preferences. Simultaneously Nature was invented and distinguished from Culture. Culture characterized Human/Man while Nature framed the realm of animal, vegetal, and mineral. The Chain of Beings located Human/Man at the top of the world created by God and so the classification established, while at the same time, a hierarchy among beings. By the same token, since Culture is what Humans do, Nature became the facto surrogated to Human cultivation and, later on, exploitation.

The foundational classification focused on entities, that is, on *beings* instead of on *vincularidad* (inter-relationship) facilitating the double operation of classifying and ranking. At the same historical moment, all civilizations in what would become the New World and then America lived in an ontology of *vincularidad* (better yet, in an oxymoronic [e.g., relations are not entities but connections and flows between and through identities] vincul-ontology or inter-relation-ontology) since everything was related to everything. "Nature" was un-imaginable, for what "existed" was the flow of energy among all living organisms, including rock and mountains. Co-existing ontologies presupposes co-existing cosmologies or, if you prefer, epistemologies. As we know one cosmology began to displace and delegitimize other cosmologies—first in the Americas and the Caribbean, then in Africa and in Asia. Human was the category at the center of a cosmology created by living organisms that conceived themselves as Human.

Both operations and their particular manifestation self-placing Human at the center and establishing racial, sexual and nature/culture frontiers, generated the effect of totality of knowledge building an image of the world through the disciplines of theology first and secular philosophy and science later. Art and literature were included in that totality, while aesthetics became a philosophical discourse to legitimize competency to admire the beautiful and the genius of the artist and the sublime spectacles of nature. Here nature maintains its separation from the human artist, although it is not only there to be dominated but to be admired. Understanding nature, in the sixteenth century, meant to understand the greatness of its Creator.[2] But by Kant's age, the Creator was de-goded and the sublime was a business of the individual in front of majestic *nature*. All contributed to totalize knowing and sensing, which together with the theological Christian belief system from the previous century, covered all aspects of Human and the experiences that Human set up for himself. The rest was left in the dark or outside the totality. The same narrative continues today with different content: the beauties of economic growth and technological innovation are identified flying objects hiding the consequences of their flight.[3]

Where I am coming from and going with this argument? My argument here is decolonial. Albeit my training was in philosophy, literature, and semiology, the argument that unfolds requires un-disciplinary decolonial thinking. Otherwise, I would be trapped in debating the *content of the conversation* but leaving the *terms of the conversations* intact. Not only that decolonial thinking cannot be reduced to any given discipline; it is also the case that the disciplines are complicit in creating and maintaining the classifiers (enunciations, terms of the conversation) and the classified (the enunciated, contents of the conversation). Consequently, decolonial thinking to be decolonial has to constantly engage processes of delinking from disciplinary strictures and control.

Reasoning in this way (that is, reasoning decolonially) helps us (readers and myself) to understand the fictionality of Western epistemology behind its claims to truth; an epistemology that created the distinction between facts and fictions, fictions and truths, fiction and reality as if these pairs were two independent entities and not pairs that sustain Western cosmology (narratives of the creation of the world and of the species that tells the story of the creation of the world and of the species) and epistemology (basic assumptions and legitimization of knowing and knowledge within the cosmology of a species that imagine itself as universal). Once the mask is lifted it becomes understandable that ontologies are created by epistemologies (or in more general terms, by cosmologies), and that racism, sexism, and naturism are epistemic categories inventing ontologies (that is, entities).

The complicity of racism (as well as of sexism and naturism) with coloniality will subsist as far as knowledge and understanding is secured by the *Human* control of the enunciation. The question is not to de-humanize the *human* but shifting from the historical, economic, legal, philosophical languaging that secured the belief that the world is composed *of beings* (entities) instead of *vincularidad* of life (inter-relationality of the living), but shifting from *Being* to *vincularidad*. Once *vincularidad* displaces *Being* to the background, the lines traced by Human/Man to project Himself as the standard and the model to which all racially and sexually lesser humans shall aspire (to gain Heaven after death or the heaven of Material Possessions) and nature is no longer seen as a place to be superseded by culture, racism, sexism, and naturism would vanish simply because they would no longer be necessary.

At that point Human would become human (without a capital h) and Man would be dissolved in the complementarity of feminine and masculine dimensions of all living organisms and in the cultural pluriversality of languaging living organisms. And at this point ontology is no longer necessary because ontology refers to *entities* and not to *inter-relationality* (*vincularidad*). Ontology (the discourse on entities, on beings) is displaced and relation-logy (the discourse on relations) comes to the foreground. For, to conceive *vincularidad* ontologically would be to kill inter-relationship and reduce it to an entity rather to a constant movement.

II

In what follows I examine several instances to reveal the logic underlying the invention of racial, sexual (among human beings) and natural differences (naturalism) among the species of *languaging living organisms*[4] and the difference that a numerical minority of these organisms, through languaging, separated themselves from nature.

The English word "human" is one among many in the world of linguistic diversity to name the entity with which the one who names identify him as such. It was not someone "lesser human" who invented the concept of Human for two reasons. One because lesser humans cannot exist without Human as the point of reference and two because whomever identifies him or herself with a given entity would not identify himself or herself as lesser. "Human" is not the name for an already existing entity but a noun that in the act of naming creates the entity that is so being named. It was only for Latin speakers and their future fellow speakers of vernacular European languages, that "Human" will remain the standard from where to name lesser humans and a separated entity, nature, upon which culture was and continues to be built. "Human," from Latin "humanus," was the translation of the Greek "anthropos."

anthropo—

—, anthrop—a combining form meaning man, human being, as in *anthropology*, *anthropormorphic*; borrowed from Greek *anthrōpo -*, combining form of *anthropos* man, human being.[5]

What is crucial to understand here is that both, "Hu/Man" are European Renaissance concepts that appropriated (and "westernized") *anthropos*. With time, *anthropos* came to denote the *differences* within the same living organism species with lesser "hu/mans" and that for a multiplicity of reasons (e.g., blood, skin color, religious belief, nationality, languages, sex, sexual preferences) sustaining narratives that created and replicate differences: *humanitas* and *anthropos* are two Western concepts and we see in them the deep structure of racism, sexism, and naturism. The seed of racism (one among the multiplicity of differences that allowed Human to stand tall and manage) was planted and the belief in that *human* was the universal name for the species was established: epistemology surrendered to ontology and ontology was assumed to be independent of epistemology. This was and still is coloniality of knowledge and of being. Those who established the *terms of the conversation* did not place themselves either among the *anthropos* or closer to *nature*, but, obviously, among the *Humans* who had the epistemic privilege of classifying and ranking themselves among all imaginable entities and preventing, at the same time, being classified.

nature (n.)

About 1275, bodily processes, restorative powers of the body; later, innate character or disposition (about 1380), and inherent creative power or impulse (about 1385); borrowed from Old French *nature*, and directly from Latin *nātūra* birth, character, from *nasci* be born: see NATIVE.

The meaning of the material world, the features and products of the earth is first recorded in 1662. The use of nature in the sense used inhuman nature is found in 1526. (Italics mine, WM)[6]

"Restorative powers of the body": but not only Man/Human have bodies, plants have bodies, fish have bodies, birds have bodies, vegetables have bodies, and fruits have bodies. That is, every living organism has a "body" that lives and dies. It is the materiality of the living that constitutes the "body." And the second definition of "nature" refers to "creation, the universe." I bet that Man/Human have been also created with the universe but many times "they" (Man/Human) act as if they are only "observing" (with telescopes or experiments) the creation of the living.

But "nature" which certainly was there much before "human" did not come to the world with its own identification. It was identified by the type of organism that "nature" itself created! "*Cria cuervos y te sacaran los ojos*" ("Nurture crows and they will peck your eyes out") goes a popular dictum in Spanish.

"Nature" and "human" were born at the same time, even if life on earth and the universe and living organism walking on two extremities were there much before the invention of "human" and "nature" obtained. The need to uncouple the name from the referent is always already a basic decolonial epistemic and philological move. For it was the invention of the category "human" that prompted the category "nature" to distinguish "human culture" from the "natural world." The trap had been set up during late European Middle Age and the imperial/colonial expansion of Western Europe and Renaissance ideas.

It all amounts to the fact that if you control knowledge, you can allocate meaning; and if you are able to allocate meaning you can also control the economy and allocate money. If then you belong to the sectors that control meaning and money, you are set up to believe that you are Human and those you consider equal are Human too, but the rest are not quite. So that the rhetoric of modernity consists in constantly producing "the rest"; and coloniality is the mechanism that secures keeping the rest beyond the dividing line. If you assume, for instance, and your assumptions are legitimized by ethical, philosophical and political discourses that *life* on the planet could be classified as *nature*, and nature is something you are not and it is irrelevant to your life and self-interests, then you could go ahead and extract all *natural resources* you need to maintain your privileges and to allocate meaning and money.

III

Following the same logic, the anthropocene was invented at the beginning of the twenty-first century. There was no anthropocene before the year 2000, more or less.

The anthropocene is indeed a welcome addition to the fictional vocabulary naming the species of organisms to which he who names belong. It is also a welcome addition because Human (always since the European Renaissance) were depicted as good guys: they were the agents of conversion to Christianity and the fight against the Devil and Evil, the agents of the civilizing mission, the agents of development and modernization, and the agents of the march towards socialism. But the anthropocene singles out the agents of the era of the bad guys of the narrative; the guys that contributed to degenerate life on earth—all of us, so it seems. There is no escape from the damage the agents of the anthropocene era caused to the planet. We are all bad guys, not only those self-identified as Humans.

To be clear, the anthropocene has been proposed to delimit a special era in the history of planet earth. This particular era is added to Pleistocene, Pliocene, and Holocene and it singles out the time in which "human activities started to have a significant global impact on Earth." Human beings had no distinguished roles in the previous era, for such creatures (our ancestors) did not even biologically (and not only semantically) exist. The specificity of the definition is "significant global impact on Earth System."

The anthropocene was invented by Earth System's scientists. The earth is—for them—conceived as a system of interlinking and interacting "spheres" of processes and phenomena. Earth system *science* embraces chemistry, physics, biology, mathematics, and applied sciences in transcending disciplinary boundaries to treat the Earth as an integrated system and seeks a deeper understanding of the physical, chemical, biological, and human interactions that determine the past, current, and future states of the Earth.[7] Interestingly enough, the earth's conception in earth system science coincides with current version of millenarian cosmological and philosophical in many civilizations on the planet before the advent of the Human in the European Renaissance, the ancestors of today's scientists.

And there is more. *Chakana* is the overarching scheme of Andean millenarian philosophy. Life requires a cyclical mutation of the seasons (summer, winter, fall, spring). Each season corresponds to one dimension of *Chakana*. When the seasons are in consideration because of the harvest and the fundamental needs of survival, the center of the Chakana is occupied by "Life" (Kawsay). But the four dimensions of the Chakana could also be interpreted in relation to labor. Thus, in this regard, one dimension of the Chakana would be Munay (Spiritual dimension). Another dimension is Atiy-Yuyah (also Ushuay) (Political and organizational dimension of the communal); a third dimension would be Ruray (Building, doing, economy in narrow sense, working to leave) and the fourth Yachay (Wisdom, knowledge, epistemology). When the doing of Runa is considered the center of the Chakana "Wisdom" (Kawsay).[8]

The fact that the same word, Kawsay, means Life and Wisdom means that to live it is necessary to know and knowing is living. Thus the concept of "Sumak Kaway" meaning "Life in plenitude and harmony" (translated as Buen Vivir, Good Living), implies that just paying attention to one dimension (Ruray), and forgetting the rest leads to disharmony and an unbalanced world order. And that is what happened precisely with the advent, during the Renaissance, of a cosmology in which living organisms that defined themselves as Human and from there they invented Racism, Sexism, and Naturism, began a process of disequilibrium and disharmony that lead to inequalities, violence, wars, and the deterioration of the niche of all living organisms of the anthropocene era.

If Earth System Science conceived the Earth as a system of interlinking and interacting "spheres," so did all Pueblos Originarios of the Americas since we have knowledge about them. One case will be the just described Chakana, the master symbol of Andean epistemology, providing one specific example of the interlinking and interacting domains of spheres of life. Chakana is not buried in the forgotten past; it was never forgotten by Indigenous people; and it is well and alive today, co-existing with Earth System Science. The Chakana and Earth System Sciences are both creations of human beings based on different cosmologies. Earth System Sciences are ingrained in Western cosmological history, while the Chakana is ingrained in Andean cosmological history. The technicalities that distinguish one from the other are not relevant here. What counts are the vision that emanates from each of them. The difference is radical.

And if the anthropocene is the era in which human beings began to have a significant global impact on earth, then we have to assume that there was a time in which the living organisms that eventually would be identified as "human beings" and later framed in the "anthropocene era" were living organisms without one common and universal name but were not having a significant impact on earth. Following this reasoning, one may ask if the story of the emergence of "human beings" on the planet coincides or not with the anthropocene era.

Furthermore, if the focus is on "era" and not on the actors (presumably "human beings"), there is not much concern about the agents that characterize the era. The concern is on the time frame: when did it begin and where? But if the focus is on the agency, the question cannot be avoided: was/is the anthropocene female or male; yellow, black, or white; straight, gay, or transsexual; Muslim or Christian, Buddhist, Confucianist, the non-Specified Indigenous beliefs, and so forth? Or perhaps an android? Racism and sexism, in its variegated forms should not be a concern if we focus on anthropocene as an era. But we cannot focus on the era without focusing on the agency. And that is the difference between the Anthropocene on the one hand and the Holocene, Pleistocene and Pliocene on the other. The anthropocene era is the work of the Anthropos while there is no Pleisto or Holo agents identified in these other two eras.

The circumstance that the anthropocene is an era is not universal: it is an era for the scientists of earth system sciences, their followers and believers.

It doesn't make any sense from the perspective of indigenous cosmologies! How can they be counted in the era of the anthropocene and responsible for damaging the earth system when indigenous people considered "Mother earth" what scientist leveled "earth system?"

What I am strongly arguing is that the anthropocene era *could not be but another fiction* of Western epistemology and Western civilization reflecting on its own selfish history and counting among the guilty party people who have been always respectful of Mother Earth now converted into a System. The anthropocene, in other words, is another North Atlantic universal fiction pretending to be universal truth. It belongs to the same underline logic that divided nature from culture and that erases the classification that, in the era of the anthropocene, divided Humans from lesser humans.

Now the question is whether the anthropocene(s) equals human beings or the actors of the anthropocene era are or are not human beings? It seems implied in the conceptualization of the era that the actors are human beings in one of their aspects: their/our doings to damage planet earth, so that there are three meta-narratives: one is the story of when human beings appeared on earth till today; the second is shorter in time, it is the appearance of the Human (European Renaissance) that built its own metanarrative distinguishing itself from human of color, from non-man (woman) and from non-heterosexual human beings of all color including white.

But let's look closer at the ambiguous relations now between human beings and the actors of the anthropocene era. The advent of human beings (that is, the history of human beings after the concept of the Human was created) seems to be the general assumption. For example, Roger Bradbury's assumption in his *New York Times* op-ed of July 13, 2012:

> Coral reefs will be the first, but certainly not the last, major ecosystem to succumb to the Anthropocene.[9]

Here anthropocene seems to refer to both the era and the actor. In that case the anthropocene is the human with small h, our ancestors. Or is it perhaps the Human, the ancestors for the scientists that invented the anthropocene? Hard to believe that it would be the Human because the Human only did good things: to Christianize, to civilize, to develop, to promote democracy and peace on earth even if violence was necessary. The Human is also the inventor of racism, sexism and naturism, but, could it be the agent damaging the earth system?! Bradbury's article generated a heated discussion about whether coral reefs would succumb or not. No one, however, paid any attention to the anthropocene that would succumb to the Anthropocene (with capital A). In this case, the Anthropocene is not an era, but an agency, someone who destroys coral reef. Thus, the Anthropocene is a human being, or something like that. Let me repeat: if this is the case, then the anthropocene era begins with advent of the human species on earth, and the advent of the human species on earth marks the beginning of the anthropocene era. But all of these narratives are narratives of one and the same ontology: the world imagined through Western scholarship.

At this point, the anthropocene-agent can no longer remain an unspecified walking subject framed in a geological era. If as it is known *anthropos* is the Greek word for what became then *humanus* in Latin and *cene* is "new," the new geological era is the era where the *anthropos* began to leave its mark on planet earth. When exactly and where that era began is a matter of debate. And since the anthropocene is an invention, a fiction, so it would be the temporal location of its rapacious behavior.

IV

Let me remind you that I am exploring racism and coloniality. Racism as the consequence of hierarchical classifications; and arguing that hierarchical classification is not ontological (that is, that the classification I am talking about came with human beings on earth, whether anthropocene era or not) but epistemological. And further claiming that the origination of the classification (not of the classified) was the European Renaissance and the invention of the concept of Human (Man1 in Wynter's argument).[10] Now, this is important. We do not have the point of origination of the anthropocene era but the origin of the system of classification that made possible, 500 years later, the invention of the anthropocene era.

As far as Human (Man1) and Humanity are Western inventions (and I mean, the genealogy from Greek to Latin to modern European vernacular and Imperial languages), they are manifestations of the self-consciousness that (at least) all languaging living organisms have of them; and can express it in sign systems, visual and/or audible.[11] What is common to all known communities of this kind living on planet earth, past and present, is precisely the self-consciousness of themselves as a group, as a community and as an individual within the group that share (through conversations and physical and visible signs) the memories of the group. When a community at a certain stage of its organization reaches the point of collective self-consciousness, the community builds narratives of their common heritage.

What is "universal," then (and this is very crucial for all other domains of lived experience, their conceptualization, naming, unfolding, and preservation) is not the ideas of Human and Humanity but the self-consciousness of living organisms engaging in conversations about themselves as being "x" and member of a larger community of "xs."

While I was in Hong Kong (the first semester of 2012), I entertained conversations with Chinese friends and colleagues asking how they expressed their self-consciousness of being on the one hand the species of "x" and on the other of being Chinese, a national specification of the global "x". I was informed several times that in Mandarin, there is a concept Ren (just in passing, in Quechua there is the concept of Runa equivalent to Ren and humanity in Latin and European languages), visibly expressed as in Figure 32.1.

Ren was the self-consciousness of people who inhabited the center of the nested rectangles, according to territorial imagination in Ancient China (Incas modeled the territory as diagonal of an open square). There is more to say about the five nested rectangles and who inhabited them. But I will not go there.[12] The point to note is that the

人

Figure 32.1 Ren

figure of the nested rectangles was invented by people who inhabited the center. This is indeed a "universal" or global feature of communities building narratives of the creation of the world and of their heritage and spatial organization of their territoriality.[13]

- "Dongyi," referred to people outside the center, inhabiting the lands where the sun rises (dong);
- "Nanman," referred to people outside the center who inhabited the land to the left from where the sun rises (nan);
- "Xirong," referred to people outside the center who inhabited the land where the sun sets (xi means);
- Beidi," referred to people inhabiting the lands to the right from where the sun sets: barbarians in the north (bei).

We could go around and make similar observations based on ancient Arabic, Persian, Nahuatl and Kechwa/Aymara, Hindi and Bengali, Wolof and Bambara, and so forth. I won't pursue these analogies here. I wanted to name them to remind you that *humanity* is one among many regional concepts that communities built to express the consciousness of themselves as people and their genealogy). The problem emerged at the moment in which humanity became the concept that brought together coloniality and racism and it became the only concept that is at once local and became global (or universal) and in so doing demoted the "centrality" that other civilizations have of themselves.

The point is that once "humanity," became the self-referential concept of the newest civilization on the planet (Western civilization is only 500 years old) came into the picture, it managed to project its own regional self-consciousness into a planetary one. The "success" in universalizing the concept of humanity was devastating; for it is upon it that modern/colonial racial classification (including the racialization of life reducing it to nature) was founded. As we know it, racial classification is tantamount to racism.

Why I am saying that the concept of humanity was the foundation of racism? Because racism is not a question of skin color or the purity of your blood, but a classificatory system that takes a definition of the "human" and humanity to rank "lesser" beings in need of be lifted up: Christianized, civilized, developed, organized themselves in multiparty system and built a civil society that votes, and so forth. Western humanity became the exemplar of the species while at the same time set up to classify and rank people of the world taking the idea and the ideal of humanity as points of reference. Thus, the global age and the concept of humanity are two sides of the same coin: the historical foundation of global coloniality.

Let's explore other naming of the walking entities that the Greek named *anthropos* and the Romans *humanus*. These two names, remember, are very local like any other at their time. Their promotion to universality has to do with the consolidation and expansion of Western civilization, which was a specific time and place of the anthropocene era in which the walking entities who could engage in conversations named themselves *anthropos and then humans*.

All known storytelling on the creation of the world (including sacred books like the Bible and the Qur'an) and of the living species to which the narrators of the origin of the world and of their selves belong, aim and claim the totality. The narrators of the Popol Vuh, of the Legend of the Fifth Sun, the many cosmological narratives in Ancient China or Ancient India or any other you would like to consider, wouldn't aim the totality, that is, what Christian philosophers of the Middle Age formulated in terms of "universals." Universals, then, is a philosophical formulation within one specific cosmology (Christian) of the totality to which this cosmology, as any other cosmology, aims.[14] The problem with "the problem of the universals" is not from aiming at the totality, but that it became totalitarian. What this means is that it erased or disavowed similar claims in other cosmologies. *From being a local totality it became a universal totality* (as redundant as it may sound).

To sustain my argument I provide here conceptualizations of languaging living organisms, one from Persian and the other from Kechua. Notice that by "languaging living organisms" I describe a species of the animal kingdom that in the West was conceptualized as Human but not in other civilization contemporary or previous to the European Renaissance.

Ali Shari'ati's discussions of the *Holy Qur'an* makes a distinction between *Bashar and Insan*. By using *Bashar*, the Qur'an is talking about the two-footed creature that emerged at the end of the evolutionary chain . . . *Bashar* is that particular being that contains physiological, biological and psychological characteristics which are shared by all men . . . On the other hand *Insan* is that unique and enigmatic being that has a special definition that does not apply to any other phenomenon in nature . . . *Bashar* is "being" while *Insan* is becoming (Italics mine).[15]

I double-checked Shari'ati's definition of both terms (since I speak neither Arabic nor Persian), with Hamid Dabashi, Persian scholar and intellectual, who confirmed through an email conversation:

BASHAR and INSAN—both mean "human" in slightly different senses—they are both Arabic/Qur'anic that have entered Persian too.
BASHAR is the generic name for the corporeal body of the organism that becomes a person;
INSAN is the generic name for the disposition of the organism or person, to become a member of the community of organism in which is born.

Members of the species are all equals as BASHAR, but they/us become different as INSAN. If I had to translate this idea to Western vocabulary I would say that humans are not being but "becoming." Organisms that "become" cannot become in isolation, by themselves. Not only the organism needs the assistance of its "parents" (and mainly the mother) until it can be on its own, but it needs the niche (air, water, food, light, etc.), that is, needs to be inter-relational with life beyond itself and the "parents." Thus BASHAR/INSAN could not be translated as "human being." Being underscores the entity while becoming underscores inter-relationality.

If we move from Persian to Quechua we would encounter that the noun Runa is often translated to modern European vernacular languages, like "human" or "human being." But Runa is quite different from Man/Human. Man/Human as we have seen self-fashioned himself (perhaps I should say itself), by cutting the links with "nature" and by the eighteenth century with God, an act of degoding (in Sylvia Wynter's vocabulary) and by setting up the rule of divisions between two things that are or are represented as being opposed or entirely different: Man and Woman, Human and Nature; Life and Death; Day and Night, Matter and Spirit; Mind and Body, and so forth.

Runa cannot be flatly translated to Man/Human and vice-versa for the two reasons that have to do with power differential than with the problems of the incommensurability of translation. People who conceived their own awareness of living organisms as Runa (similarly and parallel to other people who conceived themselves as Man/Human or still other Bashar/Ensan, and still others conceive themselves as Ren [人的]), aimed at universality from their local universe of meaning. Let's take Runa, to make a long story short, since we have already said something about Persian Bashar/Ensan.

Runa was and still is conceived in relation and "convivencia" (a literal translation would be "living-with-other-living-entities", but is generally translated as coexistence or conviviality) with *huacas* (deities, entities of the sacred sphere) and *sallqa* (every living organisms), and the Apu (the tutelary spirit that inhabit the snowed picks of the mountains). All of that is also weaved (for the metaphor of "tejido" is common to express "convivencia" and *vincularidad*. "Convivencia" furthermore is convivencia in the "Convivencia" (conviviality) furthermore is convivencia in the *ayllu* (equivalent to *oykos* in ancient Greece), a fluid structure of convivencia (conviviality). The *ayllu* is a fluid structure of kinship, but kinship not only among Runas, but also among *huacas*, *sallqa*, and *Apu*.[16]

In consequence, by translating Runa into Man/Human you erase convivencia of the living and the spiritual world and you "endow" Runa with the same violence that Man/Human have enacted to define themselves and, when projected towards Tawantinsuyu during the conquest and colonization, you continue the erasure that Man/Human started during the Renaissance in Europe and in the process of epistemic conquest and colonization of the world. In such translation you would imply that Runa is separated from Nature, which is an aberration. Now, convivencia is not necessarily pacific, but it is a struggle in search of balance and harmony. Andean philosophy had the concept of *tinku* and *ayny*. Tinku and ayny bring opposite but complementary elements in relation, as we see more below.[17] Struggling in search of balance and harmony is not the same than violence and war to secure development and democracy. Racist logic (and therefore coloniality) is embedded in politics.

Now, taking a cursory look at Daoism, one learns that *Qi* cannot be translated as *nature* but rather as *energy*. The energy of the living, of life in the universe and the energy that made possible living organisms that were able to self-define themselves in relation to all other organisms in *convivencia* (living and co-existing with other organisms that live and co-exist with us who are describing ourselves in relation to other organisms.) In some case, the relation is convivial, on other antagonistic.

Qi is the energy and principle of harmony expressed in the complementarity of *yin-yang*: there is no *yin* without *yang*, there is no masculine without feminine, there is no day without night, there is no life without death (I already said that), and so forth. Like indigenous cosmologies in the great civilizations of the Americas, yin-yang (like *Tinku* in Andean indigenous philosophy) is the constant search for harmony and equilibrium and the goal of living organisms endowed with the capacity to define themselves/ourselves as a particular entity in convivial or agonic relations with other living organisms.

The diversity of the living that Western epistemology racialized and reduced to *nature* has a different conceptualization in Taoist or Daoist philosophy. In these philosophies the diversity of the living doesn't exclude the spiritual and the social and therefore it makes no sense reducing it to *nature*. It is very similar to Andean philosophy: *sallqa* doesn't exclude *Runa* and *huacas* as in fact, *apu* is at once *sallqa* and *huaca*. So that the struggles of *yin* and *yang* in search of plenitude and harmony, not of development.

In Quechua language and Andean philosophy, *yanintin* and *masintin* are parallel to *yin* and *yang*.[18] What they have in common is to acknowledge that there cannot be A without its opposite B: there is no day without night, no masculine without feminine, no good without bad, and so forth. The search for balance and harmony is a search, is a struggle. It is not a given, a pacific conviviality without efforts. However, once you acknowledge that there cannot be one without the other, you have two options at least: either you try to eliminate what you declare to be opposite and did not let it be; or you recognize that you cannot eliminate or dominate forever your opposite: you could eliminate some of its manifestations but not its energy and living force. If you are trying to eliminate and control the opposite you enter the realm of *war*; if you search for harmony and balance, you enter the realm of *struggle* in search of harmony rather than *war* in search of elimination or total control.

V

We can go on an on surveying cosmologies shattered by the cosmology of one God, binary oppositions and isolated rational individuals looking for their own interest and supporting democratic governments elected by vote. That is at the same time the cosmology founded on racism, sexism, and naturism.

What matters is the need to reset the goals and visions of life on the planet. The search for balance and harmony shall displace development and growth conceived only economically without attention to the growing of unbalance and disequilibrium of communal life and life on the planet. This statement and the argument that proceeds are the result of decolonial thinking and, in this case, oriented toward decolonizing knowledge and being.

Thus, decoloniality of knowledge and of being presupposes that the analytic that I went through in this chapter aims to delink and liberate us from the ontology of beings (and one of the consequences, the isolated self-interested individual of modernity) and to relink it to "vincularidad of the living and of life." Changing the terms of the conversation requires engaging in living story telling that delink from the belief in development, economic growth, manifest destinies and divine privileges to enact violence to keep the world in peace.

Notes

1 See Sylvia Wynter's compelling argument excavating the historical foundations of Hu/Man1 (the European Renaissance) and Hu/Man2 (the European Enlightenment): "Unsettling the Coloniality of Being/Power/Truth/Freedom: Towards the Human, After Man, Its Overrepresentation—An Argument," *New Centennial Review* 3, no. 3 (2003): 257–337.
2 See my "Commentaries" to the English translation of José de Acosta's *Natural and Moral History of the Indies*, trans. Frances Lopez-Morillas, ed. Jane E. Mangan (Durham: Duke University Press, 2002), 451–518.
3 Kishore Mahbubani and Lawrence H. Summers, "The Fusion of Civilizations: The Case for Global Optimism," *Foreign Affairs* 95, no. 3 (2016): 126; Klaus Schwab, *The Fourth Industrial Revolution*. Geneva: World Economic Forum, 2016.

4   The reader shall keep in mind that by "languaging living organisms," I am referring to the set of living organisms that were once conceived of as "human" and lately as "post-human," and singling out an era, the anthropocene era, in which such living organisms called "human" began to impact the balance of life in which the species of languaging living organisms emerged on planet earth.
5   *The Barnhart dictionary of etymology*, Robert K. Barnhart, editor, New York: H. W. Wilson Co., 1988.
6   *The Barnhart dictionary of etymology*, Robert K. Barnhart, editor, New York: H. W. Wilson Co., 1988.
7   Martin Ruzek, "Earth Science in a Nutshell," *Starting Point: Teaching Entry Level Geo-Science*, National Digital Science Library, n.d.
8   The popularized "Buen Vivir-Sumak Kawsay" is most of the time a version of non-Indigenous intellectuals alien to the senses, knowing and reasoning from Chakana's philosophy. From Indigenous philosophy, Chakana is not an entity but the shape of the energy of thinking, sensing, and living; "Sistema de Vida Andino."
9   Roger Bradbury, "A World Without Coral Reefs," *New York Times*, July 13, 2012.
10 Wynter, "Unsettling the Coloniality."
11 Languaging Maturana
12 Joseph Needan and Wang Ling, *Science and Civilization in China* (Cambridge: Cambridge University Press, 1969).
13 Marshall G. S. Hodgson, "In the Center of the Map: Nations See Themselves as the Hub of History," in *Rethinking World History: Essays on Europe, Islam, and World History*, ed. Edmund Burke III (Cambridge: Cambridge University Press, 1993), 29–34.
14 For the continuity of the topic in contemporary philosophy, see *The Problem of Universals in Contemporary Philosophy*, ed. Gabriele Galluzzo and Michael J. Loux (Cambridge: Cambridge University Press, 2015).
15 Najibullah Lafrai, *Revolutionary Ideology and Islamic Militancy: The Iranian Revolution and the Interpretation of the Quran* (London: I. B. Tauris, 2009), 128.
16 Grimaldo Rengifo Vázquez, "The *Ayllu*," in *The Spirit of Regeneration: Andean Culture Confronting Western Notions of Development*, ed. Frédérique Apffel-Marglin with PRATEC (London: Zed Books, 1998), 89–123.
17 A similar conceptualization was at work in Aztec philosophy. See James Maffie, "'We Eat of the Earth Then the Earth Eats Us': The Concept of Nature in Pre-Hispanic Nahua Thought," *Ludis Vitalis* 10, no. 17 (2002): 5–19.
18 Tristan Platt, "Mirrors and Maize: The Concept of Yanantin Among the Macha of Bolivia," in *Anthropological History of Andean Polities*, ed. John Murra, Nathan Wachtel, and Jacques Revel (Cambridge: Cambridge University Press, 1986), 228–259. See also Deisy Nuñez del Prado Béjar, "Yanintin y masintin. La cosmovisión Andina," in *Yachay: Revista Científica de la Universidad Andina del Cusco*," 1 (2008): 130–136.

This is similar in Aztec philosophy (see note 17), where the goal was to strive for balance and harmony. And they sacrifice human beings, you could object. The belief was to sustain the life of the sun rather than to advance democracy, for example, or to sustain development. The *Internet Encyclopedia of Philosophy* provides this helpful insight and bibliography information:

> Because of this I suggest Nahua philosophy is better understood as a "way-seeking" rather than as a "truth-seeking" philosophy. "Way-seeking" philosophies such as classical Taoism, classical Confucianism, and contemporary North American pragmatism adopt as their defining question, "What is the way?" or "What is the path?" In contrast, "truth-seeking" philosophies such as most European philosophies adopt as their defining question, "What is the truth?" (James Maffie, "Aztec Philosophy," *Internet Encyclopedia of Philosophy*, n.d.)

Similar arguments can be found in David L. Hall and Roger T. Ames, *Thinking from the Han: Self, Truth and Transcendence in Chinese and Western Culture* (Buffalo: SUNY Press, 1998).

References

Béjar, Deisy Nuñez del Prado. (2008) "Yanintin y masintin: La cosmovisión Andina." *Yachay: Revista Científica de la Universidad Andina del Cusco* 1: 130–136.

Bradbury, Roger. (2012) "A World Without Coral Reefs." *New York Times*, July 13.
Galluzzo, Gabriele, and Loux, Michael J. (2015) *The Problem of Universals in Contemporary Philosophy*, Cambridge: Cambridge University Press.
Hall, David L., and Ames, Roger T. (1998) *Thinking From the Han: Self, Truth and Transcendence in Chinese and Western Culture*, Buffalo: State University of New York Press.
Hodgson, Marshall G. S. (1993) "In the Center of the Map: Nations See Themselves as the Hub of History," in *Rethinking World History: Essays on Europe, Islam, and World History*, ed. Edmund Burke III, Cambridge: Cambridge University Press, pp. 29–34.
Lafrai, Najibullah. (2009). *Revolutionary Ideology and Islamic Militancy: The Iranian Revolution and the Interpretation of the Quran*, London: I. B. Tauris.
Maffie, James. (2002) "'We Eat of the Earth Then the Earth Eats Us': The Concept of Nature in Pre-Hispanic Nahua Thought." *Ludis Vitalis* 10, no. 17: 5–19.
———. (n.d.) "Aztec Philosophy," in *Internet Encyclopedia of Philosophy*.
Mahbubani, Kishore, and Summers, Lawrence H. (2016) "The Fusion of Civilizations: The Case for Global Optimism." *Foreign Affairs* 95, no. 3: 126.
Maturana, Humberto. (1991) *El Sentido de lo Humano* Dolmen Ediciones. Santiago de Chile.
Mignolo, Walter. (2002) "Commentaries," in José de Acosta (ed.), *Natural and Moral History of the Indies*, trans. Frances Lopez-Morillas and ed. Jane E. Mangan. Durham: Duke University Press, pp. 451–518.
Needan, Joseph, and Ling, Wang. (1969) *Science and Civilization in China*, Cambridge: Cambridge University Press.
Platt, Tristan. (1986) "Mirrors and Maize: The Concept of Yanantin Among the Macha of Bolivia," in John Murra, Nathan Wachtel, and Jacques Revel (eds.), *Anthropological History of Andean Polities*, Cambridge: Cambridge University Press, pp. 228–259.
Ruzek, Martin. (n.d.) "Earth Science in a Nutshell." *Starting Point: Teaching Entry Level Geo-Science*. National Science Digital Library.
"Sistema de Vida Andino." http://image.slidesharecdn.com/alliwapazmio-110824161232-phpapp01/95/kichwahablantes-del-ecuador-28-728.jpg?cb=1314202478.
Schwab, Klaus. (2016)*The Fourth Industrial Revolution*, Geneva: World Economic Forum.
Vázquez, Grimaldo Rengifo. (1998) "The Ayllu," in Frédérique Apffel-Marglin with PRATEC (ed.), *The Spirit of Regeneration: Andean Culture Confronting Western Notions of Development*, London: Zed Books, 89–123.
Wynter, Sylvia. (2003) "Unsettling the Coloniality of Being/Power/Truth/Freedom: Towards the Human, After Man, Its Overrepresentation—an Argument." *New Centennial Review* 3, no. 3: 257–337.

33
WHITE SUPREMACY
Charles W. Mills

The term *white supremacy* is ambiguous. Some speakers use it to refer to a particular sort of social structure, one characterized by white domination; others use it to refer to a particular variety of white racism, the kind that justifies such a social structure; while for others, the term can be used to denote both. In this chapter, I will focus on white supremacy as social structure, though, as I have argued elsewhere (Mills 2003), it might be better thought of as socio/political/economic structure.

But why include a chapter on white supremacy in a philosophy reference work (as against a social science text) in the first place? The point is to enable a better understanding of the workings of race. Whatever one's metaphysical view of race (eliminativist, naturalist, social constructionist, hybrid social-natural position), the history and significance of white racial domination cannot be denied, even if people's views on the ontological implications of that domination will diverge. Both from a descriptive point of view, then, in understanding the interplay between the social order and race (however conceived of), and from a normative point of view, in terms of social justice, a theorization of racial domination in general and white supremacy in particular (as the most important form, historically, of racial domination) is crucial. Like Marxism and feminism, its better known philosophical counterparts for class and gender theory, critical philosophy of race is generally predicated on the assumption that the most fruitful way to do philosophy is to start with human beings in their embodied identities and embedded socio-historical positioning (Alcoff 2006). A genuine illumination of the realities of the human condition, both descriptive and prescriptive, requires the construction of non-idealizing abstractions that do not ignore the architecture of social oppression (Cudd 2006). Marxism and feminism in their various incarnations have tried to make this case plausible for class society and patriarchal society. Mapping a white supremacist social order can thus arguably be seen as a complementary task for the philosophical theorization of race.

In developing a critical conceptualization of white supremacy, I suggest that the best strategy is to draw on popular usage (so as to maintain some continuity with the everyday sense) while revising it where necessary in the light of a more sociopolitically informed understanding of the history of race. Developing a grasp of the essential features of the phenomenon may thus require breaking with conventional analyses in certain respects.

In this spirit, then, I propose the following characterization of white supremacy. White supremacy is (1) a particular kind of oppressive social system, sub-national or national or international, coming into existence (2) in a time period in which race has emerged as a significant social category and social reality, and (3) whiteness and nonwhiteness are recognized racial identities, and (4) whites have and exert differential power in creating and controlling the evolution of the social system in question, and/or in blocking changes to it that would substantially reduce their domination, whose end is originally (5) the systemic, significant, and illicit differential advantaging of all or most whites as a group with respect to nonwhites as a group in various important social spheres.

Let me now go through each of these conditions in detail.

White Supremacy as Historically Existent and Oppressive

First, then, *white supremacy* is intended to designate a social system, or set of social systems, that were uncontroversially historically existent at one time and are either, in different guise, *still* existent today (though this is obviously a more controversial claim), or that have at least left a racial legacy the understanding of which requires the concept. The clear-cut cases, frequently compared with each other because of their history of explicit and formal juridical subordination of nonwhites, are the United States and apartheid South Africa (Fredrickson 1981; Marx 1998; Jung, Costa Vargas, and Bonilla-Silva 2011). However, I would claim that a broader and more useful concept that is still tracking the crucial features of the phenomenon under investigation can be produced by dropping as a prerequisite the stipulation often associated with it of *de jure* white privileging. In the more extensive sense that includes *de facto* domination, the European nations and the Euro-colonial world in general can be seen as white supremacist, insofar as "whites" were (are) dominant over and privileged with respect to people of color across the planet (Mills 1997; Winant 2001). So white supremacy was originally (and is still . . . ?) global, the famous international "color-line" identified more than a century ago by W.E.B. Du Bois (2007 [1903]) that is now increasingly the subject of research in critical International Relations (IR) theory (Lake and Reynolds 2008; Anievas, Manchanda, and Shilliam 2015; Vitalis 2015).

By contrast with an analysis that focuses just on individual racism, then, or even on an institutional racism framed withal as socially deviant, *white supremacy* as a term has much more far-reaching implications. It is claiming that white domination can be found across entire social systems, indeed the world, with major ramifications in multiple spheres. As such, the concept challenges both orthodox mainstream liberal understandings of the Western social order that frame race and racism as "anomalies" to an inclusivist liberal democracy and orthodox Marxist understandings that reduce racial domination to capitalist class domination. *White supremacy* is thus both descriptive and (negatively) normative, in that it asserts the historic existence of such social systems and indicts them for their *injustice*, as against the neutral or approbative characterizations typical of the past (Stoddard 1920). (Compare the feminist appropriation from male political theory of the term *patriarchy*, and its similar negative revalorization.) A racially supremacist social order is one that should be morally condemned by us, one that we should be seeking to dismantle.

Correspondingly, such a reconceptualization has dramatic normative implications for Western political philosophy, whether in the mainstream Anglo-American analytic tradition or the Critical Theory tradition. John Rawls (1999: 6–7, 8) famously shifted the focus of political philosophy from the issue of political obligation to the issue of the justice of the "basic structure" of society, which he pointed out has such a profound determinant effect on people's life chances. But his theory of justice took distributive justice in perfectly just, "well-ordered" societies of "strict compliance" as its starting point, and he never moved on to the exploration of "compensatory justice" in unjust societies, which he himself conceded was one of the "pressing and urgent matters" of "partial compliance theory."

Neither he nor his innumerable disciples and commentators over the past 45 years (see, for example, Mandle and Reidy 2014) have made any attempt to theorize the moral challenge posed by white supremacist societies, with racialized "basic structures," despite the fact that all of the Anglo settler states (the United States, Canada, Australia, New Zealand, South Africa) can arguably be so characterized (Fredrickson 1981; Goldberg 2002; Pateman, in Pateman and Mills 2007: chapter 2; Carey and McLisky 2009; Vickers and Isaac 2012). Albeit in a different idiom, Continental Critical Theory is likewise supposed to be concerned about emancipation from oppressive social structures. Yet race, colonialism, and white racial domination's repercussions for Europe and the Euro-colonial world it created have been consistently marginalized in this literature also (McCarthy 2009; A. Allen 2016), despite Lucius Outlaw's (1990) call more than a quarter-century ago for a Critical Theory of "race." In neither body of work, then, is white supremacy recognized as a system of domination in itself, and the correction of racial injustice and racial oppression prioritized as a central imperative.

The Emergence and Periodization of Race

To put white supremacy into its historical context, we need to turn to the more general issue of the emergence of race as a social category. Note that even if racial naturalism is correct (races as socio-independent biological entities), races might not have been *recognized* as existent. So a periodization of race (in this case as an acknowledged social category) would still be appropriate, and this obviously holds *a fortiori* if social constructionism is in fact the correct position on the metaphysics of race.

Suppose we are in a historical epoch, T1, before racial categorization has begun. Then we could not even have racism, let alone racial domination. Racism, whether conceptualized in affective/volitional terms, as in Jorge Garcia's (1996) work (racism as *ill-will*), or in cognitivist/doxastic terms, as in Tommie Shelby's (2002; 2003) work (racism as *ideology*), requires the idea of races: the human race as divided into R1s, R2s, R3s . . . But even when race, R, as a concept enters the world as a self- and other-categorization, this is only a necessary, not a sufficient condition, for racism. For it is possible that the R2s, say, could be viewed without ill-will by the R1s, and/or as racial equals, without claims of hierarchical superiority/inferiority. (Admittedly, this would not be so for Sally Haslanger's [2012] recommended conceptualization of race, which builds domination directly into the concept.)

Moreover, the advent of racism need not lead to R-domination, since while the R1s and R2s could regard each other in racial and racist terms, neither might have the power to subordinate the other. So the establishment of a particular variety of R-supremacy— say this happens at T2—requires (a) the existence of race as a category and identity under which the relevant groups understand themselves (b) racist feelings of, for example, R1s toward R2s and/or racist beliefs about R2s by R1s (c) the subordination of (all or some of) the R2s by the R1s in a process significantly shaped, whether initially and/or subsequently, by R1 racism.

The point of specifying these criteria is to rule out as R-supremacist a situation where, say we (as time-traveling anthropologists from the twenty-second century exploring, with the help of a generous research grant, the T1 epoch) discover societies in which groups categorizable for *us*, by *our* norms, as R1s and R2s, are in hierarchical social relations, but have no concept of race themselves. So those who are (for us) the R1s do not exhibit racism against those who are (for us) the R2s and have not been motivated by such sentiments or ideologies in establishing and/or maintaining the social order, though they may have negative anti-R2 sentiments/ideologies of other kinds. Racial domination, I am contending, requires the intersubjective recognition of race by the members of the society *themselves*, by the standards of *their* time, in order for it to count as such. And the reason for the time hedge ("whether initially and/or subsequently") is to accommodate the possibility that race and racism are not initially crucial to the process of social subordination, but become so in the consolidation of the system. Some theorists have argued, for example, that anti-black racism is more the consequence than the cause of Atlantic slavery, the original motivation being simply pecuniary (E. Williams 1994 [1944]; Shelby 2002). So Atlantic slavery could *become* racial slavery, part of a system of white domination, without necessarily having begun as such.

This has all been very abstract, since I wanted to illustrate the more general potential scope of the idea of R-domination, whether in our own planetary timeline or possible alternative timelines. What, however, is the actual history? Two main competing periodizations can be found in the literature: race and racism as distinctly modern, or at the oldest, dating to the late medieval epoch (Hannaford 1996; Fredrickson 2015 [2002]) and race and racism as going back to the ancient world (Isaac 2004; Eliav-Feldon, Isaac, and Ziegler 2009).

For the former, racism is primarily Western in origin, a creation of European expansionism, so that racial categories and whiteness would be more or less coeval. Thus Nell Painter's *History of White People* (2010: 1) contends that in antiquity "neither the idea of race nor the idea of 'white' people had been invented, and people's skin color did not carry useful meaning." But others disagree. Benjamin Isaac argues in his *Invention of Racism in Classical Antiquity* (2004) that race and racism do indeed go back to the classical period, but that this was a non-color-coded racism, in which Greeks, as naturally free, were contrasted to naturally servile Persians. So on this account, the emergence and periodization of race would need to be separated from the emergence and periodization of whiteness. We would have had Rs and the belief in an R1/R2 hierarchy that did not include "whites." Had such racial consciousness been sufficiently widespread, Alexander the Great's later conquest of the Persian Empire would have resulted in a racial social order in the classical world: R1-supremacy under the aegis of an unambiguously racialized Hellenization.

The Emergence, Periodization, and Scope of "Whiteness"

The arrival of white supremacist systems on the planet, then—say this happens at T3—requires the emergence of "whiteness" as a racial category, not just the emergence of race, and, apart from the establishment of relations of domination between R1s and R2s where R1s are "white," the intersubjective role of this identity in creating and/or perpetuating the system. As argued above, it is not enough for those in the dominant group to be retrospectively characterized by *us* as having this identity; they have to think of *themselves* this way. Conquest of dark-skinned non-European non-Christians by light-skinned European Christians does not suffice to establish white supremacy if race is absent from the latter's own self-characterization—if, say, religion is the sole pertinent identity for them.

Given this stipulation, the European conquest and gradual establishment over several hundred years of relations of colonial and imperial domination over the rest of the world will not be coextensive with the spread of a subjugating whiteness. The question—and this is an empirical question, though obviously with a conceptual aspect—will be when and where whiteness and a corollary nonwhiteness as significant identities actually arise in specific locations L. Moreover, even when whiteness does eventually emerge, not all Europeans will automatically share in it. So white supremacy in location L1 may privilege a less extensive population of "whites" than white supremacy in location L2. (I specify location rather than country since white supremacist systems are not necessarily coextensive with a nation. If the country is large enough, one could find regional variations, so that in one nation white supremacist systems could coexist with non-white-supremacist systems.) It could even be logically possible, at least in a constructionist ontology, for the white populations in different locations on the planet to be defined/"constructed" completely differently, so that there would be no overlap among them. I know of no actual historical examples of this kind, but it is an instructive illustration of the possibilities opened up by an anti-naturalist metaphysics.

We also have to take into account intra-epochal/intra-T3 variations in and evolutions of whiteness, whether globally or locally. For example, the acceptance into whiteness of, say, previously excluded R2s, as well as the possibility of the expulsion from whiteness of previous R1s now relegated to R3 status. On an alternative Earth, it might have been the case that white supremacy never came into existence at all. Some other ethnic/national/continental group might have become hegemonic, establishing brownness as the superior R1 category and brown supremacy as the global system. Or consider the possibility, on our own Earth, of a conceivable future timeline, of a T4 post-whiteness, in which—whether through widespread miscegenation, or just revisionist categorization—whites disappear altogether as a racial category and white supremacy with it.

On our own Earth, the actual historical pattern has been a core "whiteness" (roughly Anglo) that is generally recognized across the world, in keeping with Srdjan Vucetic's (2011) judgment that the "Anglosphere" (the British and American empires) has historically been the most important of the Euro-dominant imperial orders. Controversy then centers on the "off-whiteness" or (depending on the theorist) even "non-whiteness" of other Europeans and Euro-descended immigrant groups, whether in their own country or in immigrant destinations. Consider, for example, the cases of the Irish in Britain; English versus French populations in Canada; Italians, Greeks, and Slavs a century ago in the United States, or Hispanic whites today; the Portuguese in the Caribbean; Anglo-Celtic versus NESB (Non-English Speaking Background) European immigrants to Australia; Euro-descendant populations in the self-conceived *mestizo* "racial democracies" of Latin America; Jews across the planet. How "white" and privileged are they respectively in different times and places? Again, it must be emphasized that this is not an a priori but an empirical/conceptual question, requiring both historical research and careful theoretical analysis to be settled (Andrews 2004; Garner 2007; Carey and McLiskey 2009; T. W. Allen 2012; Vickers and Isaac 2012; Telles 2014; Watson, Howard-Wagner, and Spanierman 2015).

In the United States, where "critical whiteness studies" has been most extensively developed, the racial status of the Irish, for example, has been the source of ongoing dispute. One of the most famous books of the 1990s that established this literature was Noel Ignatiev's *How the Irish Became White* (2008 [1995]), the titular claim that Irish immigrants to the United States were not originally categorized as whites, and so could not have been part of white supremacy (see also T. W. Allen 2012). Comparable claims, inspired by Ignatiev's book, would later be made about Jews and other "European ethnics" from eastern and southern Europe (Slavs, Greeks, Italians, etc.) (Jacobson 1998; Roediger 2005). But some scholars have argued, against this line of analysis, that the appropriate conclusion was not that the Irish, Jews, and other immigrant Euro-"ethnics" were actually nonwhite in the United States, but rather that they were *inferior* whites (Guglielmo 2004). In other words, while located on a lower rung of an intra-white hierarchy of races, they were nonetheless still white, and as such positioned above the unambiguously inferior nonwhites, such as blacks and Native Americans. Indeed, early twentieth-century categorizations of Europeans, though later abandoned, differentiated several "white" races within Europe itself (for example, Nordics, Alpines, Mediterraneans) (Painter 2010).

However, even if the "inferior white" rather than "nonwhite" verdict is sustained, such heterogeneities in the category remind us that not all whites can be said to share equally in the power relationships and benefits provided by "whiteness"—an "intersectionalist" point that needs to be generally borne in mind, and applying, of course, not merely because of intra-white "ethnic" differentiation but also gender and class differentiation. From first-wave feminism onward, white women have depicted themselves as subordinated by white men, and in some cases have analogized their experience to racial oppression (De Beauvoir 2011). If you cannot vote, cannot hold political office, and cannot (because of the concept of "coverture") have a legal personality separate from your husband's, can you really be said to be equal power-holders in, equally complicit with, and equal beneficiaries of white supremacy? But critics, especially women of color, have retorted that white women do benefit from this system, even if not to the same extent as males, that historically they have offered little resistance to it, and that over the last century they have attained much more power than previously, so that the indictment of complicity is indeed justified (Roth 2004).

Somewhat comparably, class differences within the white population—highlighted in the United States by the contemptuous designation of "white trash" for those in the lower Euro-American echelons (Eisenberg 2016)—have standardly been cited by white Marxists in particular as showing that it is the ruling class, not "whites" as an undifferentiated group, who should be seen as the real creators and movers of the racial order (if it is even conceded that it is a "racial" order). On this diagnosis, white workers and the white poor—far from benefiting from white supremacy—are actually likewise its victims, since race has been used to weaken the trade union movement, keep down wages, and pre-empt the development of a powerful oppositional force against capital (T. W. Allen 2012). Again, critics have replied that such political analyses ignore the history of white working-class agency in making and affirming a white identity for themselves, keeping nonwhites out of unions, and generally signing on to rather than rejecting the "wages of whiteness" in their multiple aspects (Roediger 2007). Hence the long, often bitter debate from the late nineteenth century onwards between the white left and black radicals—sometimes from within, often from outside, white socialist and communist parties—about what theoretical framework should be employed to bring race and class together, how or if white racism can be overcome, and whether the "whiteness" of the white working-class is ultimately more causally and explanatorily significant than their identity as workers.

Having and Deploying Differential White Power

The specifics of the genealogy and reproduction of the system are thus crucial to its identity. Access to, and use of, differential white power in the creation/maintenance of the white supremacist social order needs to be part of its conceptualization. For it is at least logically possible that contingent circumstances might so conspire as to advantage (those categorized as) whites in the social order, though they did not contrive to bring about this state of affairs themselves, nor do they block attempts to dismantle the resulting social system. Imagine, say, a natural disaster that only affects some parts of the country and the racialized nonwhite populations living there (by stipulation not because of racialized causality). Then a situation of radical comparative white advantage and nonwhite disadvantage could be nationally created that has nothing to do with "white" causality. (By contrast, the 2005 Hurricane Katrina calamity in New Orleans could legitimately be characterized as a "social" rather than natural disaster because of course it was precisely *as a result* of a previous history of racism, segregation, and governmental indifference to their fate that poor African Americans in the city were so vulnerable, and thus so differentially and disastrously affected.) So, especially if whites seek to equalize these differences, I would not term such a society or sub-national system a white supremacist one. White supremacy as a negative normative description implies oppression, as emphasized from the start, and this is different from a social formation accidentally created that whites are happy to reform.

In our actual world, of course, differential European power (bracketing the question of when it became "white") was originally blatantly manifest in the uncontroversial form of the violence of the military subjugation of non-Europeans, even if this history is now increasingly subject to what has been called "postcolonial forgetting." In the conquest of the Americas, North, South, and Caribbean, in Africa and Asia, in Australasia, wars were fought with indigenous populations, in some cases genocidal, to take their land and/or subjugate them to European rule and/or displace them for the installation of white settler communities. The racial slavery of the Atlantic slave societies required ongoing coercion, a watchfulness for the dangers of slave rebellion, and a corresponding willingness both to use pre-emptive punishment and to retaliate with massively disproportionate force against local insurrections. Even after emancipation, freed blacks across the Americas, denied equal resources and equal opportunities to achieve material well-being, were perceived as a potential threat to the social order, to be constantly monitored and subjected to imprisonment and punishment.

In the United States in particular one also needs to take into account the role of white race riots and lynchings in terrorizing the black population, where in a sense the white citizenry as a group are authorized (through the non-intervention or merely token punishments by official bodies) to take up a parastatal capacity to maintain racial order. And across the colonial world, of course, armies, militias, national guards, and a politicized police force were formally delegated with the task of suppressing indigenous resistance. Nor is this a matter of the remote past, if one recalls that colonial wars and counter-insurgency campaigns against national liberation movements (Vietnam, Algeria, Kenya, Portuguese Africa, South Africa) were still being fought only a few decades ago, or that blacks and Amerindians in the Americas, and indigenous peoples in Australia, continue even today to be differentially subject to police violence and to be disproportionately represented in the prison system. As David Theo Goldberg (2002) has argued, the idea of a racial state should not be limited to what are usually represented as the "outlier" cases of Nazi Germany, apartheid South Africa, and the American Old South. Rather, insofar as the modern state presides over and facilitates inequitable treatment by race—whether through active intervention or non-intervention when a genuine commitment to racial equality would have mandated it—it is in general a racial state.

Not all whites, of course, were/are involved in such wars and other overtly repressive measures, and in some cases sections of the white citizenry protested and politically organized against them (abolitionist, anti-imperialist, anti-colonial, anti-war, and civil rights movements). But usually the majority of the white population were content to go along with these policies, thereby arguably giving them their "tacit consent."

However, power can also be "softer," manifest not in overt violence but, for example, in a two-tiered juridical system with one set of legal rules for whites and another set for people of color, whether formally, as under American Jim Crow and European colonial rule, or informally, as in the post-colonial and post-civil rights epoch. Economic constraint—the necessity of making a living in societies controlled by whites—also "materially" limited options for people of color, whether because of the threat of outright dismissal from one's job for any would-be activists agitating for social reform, or simply the overwhelming daily burden of trying to find the wherewithal to keep oneself and one's family alive, that left no time for any activity other than that aimed at simple survival.

Finally, across all these societies it was generally the case that government-run educational systems and the popular media, as well as the organizations of civil society, acted as agents of legitimation for the existing white order, creating what Antonio Gramsci would have termed a white "hegemony." Or, in Miranda Fricker's (2007) more recent conceptualization, an epistemic universe in which the derogation as credible knowers of nonwhites saying the "wrong" thing, and the vigilant pre-emptive exclusion or targeted eradication (where pre-emption had somehow failed) of oppositional anti-racist hermeneutical ideas and frameworks, made systemic white epistemic injustice the cognitive norm. A white "epistemology of ignorance" would govern social cognition, affecting not merely whites as the beneficiaries of the system but also people of color as potential resisters of it (Sullivan and Tuana 2007). "Whiteness" would eventually become not merely a set of political and socioeconomic power-relationships, but a kind of ontological and epistemic state imbued with its own worldview-shaping power, a carrier of epistemic violence, a "racial frame" for understanding social reality (Feagin 2010). As a way of being, as a form of life, whiteness in this sense now itself constitutes one of the most formidable obstacles to a more equitable racial order, operating as it does at the most basic cognitive, affective, and phenomenological level (Dyer 1997; Yancy 2008; Alcoff 2015).

The Advantaging of Whites

Finally, it is natural to run together white power and (what is now called) white privilege. But we need to separate them if only for the purposes of analytic clarification and testing our intuitions.

Consider a somewhat sociologically implausible scenario: whites have differential power in the society, but do not use this power to advantage themselves. So we would have white domination—which for some would be enough to count as white supremacy—without systemic white privilege, at least in all its familiar forms. (Differential political access can itself be seen, obviously, as "privilege.") Whites would be benevolent rulers, racial paternalists, seeking to ensure, without racial favoritism, that all races in the social order prosper equally.

Should this count as a situation of white supremacy? The problem is, of course, that our linguistic intuitions on such matters are shaped by the actual history, and perhaps close counterfactual variants of that history that are in neighboring rather than distant worlds. So we are intellectually handicapped in considering such a scenario because no historical societies of this kind have ever existed. But, freeing our imaginations from the bonds of the actual, what would we say of this situation as a hypothetical? Here we enter the realm of the stipulative, and my own intuitions might not match the intuitions of others. But I think that "privilege" as systemic significant differential white advantage is too closely tied to the concept of white supremacy in common parlance for this component to be regarded as logically expendable. So a system of white domination where whites control the social order but nonwhites have the same access and opportunities, income and wealth, as whites would not, I think, count in everyday parlance as white supremacist, and should not so count for us.

The "illicit" in "illicit differential advantaging" obviously also needs specification. If it were really the case—as of course it is the case in the white racist imaginary—that whites were at the top of the social order because of being smarter and of more industrious character than everybody else, then it would be harder to justify using *white supremacy* in a pejorative way (though a Rawlsian [1999] could still argue for the irrelevance of racial "desert" of this kind). "White supremacy" would then just be a recognition that whites are in fact supreme, the superior race on the crucial metrics. So the claim has to be that differential white advantage is unfair because white pre-eminence does *not* in fact stem from such factors but rather from the violation of nonwhite rights, both currently and historically. The strongest case will be if it is Lockean "negative" rights—rights to life, liberty, and property—that can be shown to have been violated, since these are the rights uncontroversially recognized as legitimate in the liberal tradition. Libertarian Robert Nozick (2013 [1974]: 149–153, 344n2), for example, incorporates rectificatory justice into his Locke-inspired theory of justice, and—in an admittedly brief discussion—seems to be open to the possibility that reparations for wrongs done to black Americans could be justified. What would have to be established is that the present-day conditions of African Americans can plausibly be demonstrated to constitute, through inherited disadvantage, an ongoing transgression of Lockean rights. Positive "welfare" rights, by contrast, are highly contested, and would be repudiated by the political right as social democratic/"socialist" rather than liberal.

Note also that I have specified "significantly." The justification here is that—if we imagine social variables readily quantifiable such as educational attainment, employment profiles, income, wealth, poverty rates, imprisonment, life expectancies, and so forth—it would seem odd to label a system white supremacist if the white "edge" was generally minute, only, say, in the region of 0.1%. White privilege must be substantial for the judgment of white supremacy to be appropriate (L. F. Williams 2003; Oliver and Shapiro 2006).

However, such privilege does not require, of course, that *all* whites should be positioned above *all* people of color on the relevant metrics. (The poorest-off whites would then be located above the best-off nonwhites.) Rather, it just requires that whites as a group (as measured by averages, medians, horizontally displaced racial distribution curves, pairwise comparisons of corresponding racial deciles or quintiles, etc.) be so favorably located. Moreover, as earlier pointed out with respect to ethnicity, gender, and class, the white population will need to be disaggregated to take account of intra-white differentiations. If at some point the average or median metric for "whites" as a group begins to conceal intra-group differences so great that some significant component (say, the white working class) ceases to be significantly positioned above its nonwhite equivalent, then we might begin to question the appositeness of "white supremacy" as an accurate overall characterization.

Further complications arise if more than one nonwhite race exists, as of course will generally be the case. If we have, say, not just whites/R1s and R2s, but also R3s and R4s, how might different possible R combinations on the axes of power and benefit change our judgment of the appropriateness of the judgment of white/R1-supremacy?

If the R1s rule monoracially, and the R2s, R3s, and R4s are equally located at the bottom of the social ladder (R2 = R3 = R4), then R1-supremacy is obviously still the right assessment. Similarly (I would claim) if the R1s rule monoracially, and the other races are arranged in an R2 > R3 > R4 hierarchy of benefit, since white/R1-supremacy need not imply the *equal* disadvantaging of nonwhites/non-R1s. The R2s, let us say, are "model minorities," held up as an admonitory example to the feckless R3s and R4s.

But what if the R2s have advantages *equal* to the R1s (while still lacking political power)? Can this still be represented as a state of R1-supremacy (since the R1s still control things), or does this category now need to be qualified? (A problem in such analytic logical permutations is, of course, that in real-world scenarios, variables that are logically separate may be causally linked. No Marxist would find credible the idea that a group with equal economic advantages, if that implies wealth and economic property, could be shut out of political power for long.) Or suppose the R2s do come to share political power, not just economic advantages, with the R1s. Can we still characterize the society as R1-supremacist, on the grounds, say, that the R2s are now, effectively, the *same* as the R1s?

This is by no means a purely hypothetical scenario. Eduardo Bonilla-Silva and David Dietrich (2008), for example, have predicted that the United States, having been the paradigm white supremacist state for most of its life, is moving towards the Latin model of racial hierarchy, *pigmentocracy* in the classic formulation (Telles 2014). So "whiteness" would be rewritten and expanded as a category to admit groups currently not counted as white. Should we say that it would then be tautological to represent the society as still white supremacist, since "whiteness" is just being circularly defined to denote the race at the top? Or can we say that it is not tautological, because there are independent criteria for what it is to be an R1/white, and these other groups have now met these criteria? (Think of the traditional category of the "honorary white.")

A related issue is that a society could continue to be black- and/or Amerindian-subordinating, or, more generally, R3/R4-subordinating, even while "whiteness"/R1-ness was being expanded, or even if the R1s were displaced altogether by the R2s, say. Just as the existence of anti-black and anti-Amerindian racism is independent of the existence of racism against other people of color, so black- and Amerindian-subordinating societies could have a change of racial personnel in the privileged socio-racial categories, while still maintaining blacks and indigenous peoples at the bottom of the social ladder. If in Latin America, for example, mulatto, mestizo, and other mixed ethnoracial groups were elevated all the way up to an equal status with "whiteness," leaving "unmixed" blacks and Indians at the bottom, this might no longer count as white supremacy, but it would obviously still be a society of racial inequality and injustice. So perhaps in addition to the abstract category of R1-domination, where whites have traditionally occupied the R1 slot, we also need to develop the abstract category of R3/R4-subordination, where a particular global history makes particular racial groups the likely occupants of this bottom position in the racial order.

In mainstream scholarship and everyday parlance, white supremacy is usually restricted temporally to the historical epoch of *de jure* racism, and taken to be paradigmatically represented by the American Old South and South African apartheid. The corollary is a reluctance, or outright refusal, to concede the accuracy of the characterization outside of such cases. But if, as I would claim, the essence of white supremacy is significant and structural illicit white privileging in a social system of white-over-nonwhite domination, then we can legitimately conclude that the scope of the concept is much broader than commonly acknowledged, both in time and space, and of obvious importance for theorizing the sociopolitical and normative. *White supremacy* needs to be added to the philosophical lexicon not just of critical philosophy of race but social and political philosophy in general.

Related Topics

Chapters 7, 11, 12, 13, 17, 28, 31, 36

References

Alcoff, L.M. (2006) *Visible Identities: Race, Gender, and the Self*, New York: Oxford University Press.
———. (2015) *The Future of Whiteness*, Malden, MA: Polity.
Allen, A. (2016) *The End of Progress: Decolonizing the Normative Foundations of Critical Theory*, New York: Columbia University Press.
Allen, T.W. (2012) *The Invention of the White Race*, 2 vols., 2nd edition, New York: Verso.
Andrews, G.R. (2004) *Afro-Latin America, 1800–2000*, New York: Oxford University Press.
Anievas, A., Manchanda, N., and Shilliam, R. (eds.) (2015) *Race and Racism in International Relations*, New York: Routledge.
Bonilla-Silva, E., and Dietrich, D.R. (2008) "The Latin Americanization of Racial Stratification in the U.S.," in R.E. Hall (ed.), *Racism in the 21st Century: An Empirical Analysis of Skin Color*, New York: Springer.
Carey, J., and McLisky, C. (eds.) (2009) *Creating White Australia*, Sydney: Sydney University Press.
Cudd, A.E. (2006) *Analyzing Oppression*, New York: Oxford University Press.
De Beauvoir, S. (2011) *The Second Sex*, trans. C. Borde and S. Malovany-Chevallier, New York: Vintage.
Du Bois, W.E.B. (2007 [1903]) *The Souls of Black Folk*, ed. B.H. Edwards. New York: Oxford World's Classics.

Dyer, R. (1997) *White*, New York: Routledge.

Eisenberg, N. (2016) *White Trash: The 400-Year Untold History of Class in America*, New York: Viking.

Eliav-Feldon, M., Isaac, B., and Ziegler, J. (eds.) (2009) *The Origins of Racism in the West*, New York: Cambridge University Press.

Feagin, J.R. (2010) *The White Racial Frame: Centuries of Racial Framing and Counter-Framing*, New York: Routledge.

Fredrickson, G.M. (1981) *White Supremacy: A Comparative Study in American and South African History*, New York: Oxford University Press.

———. (2015 [2002]) *Racism: A Short History*, Princeton: Princeton Classics.

Fricker, M. (2007) *Epistemic Injustice: Power and the Ethics of Knowing*, New York: Oxford University Press.

Garcia, J.L.A. (1996) "The Heart of Racism," *Journal of Social Philosophy* 27, no. 1: 5–45.

Garner, S. (2007) *Whiteness: An Introduction*, New York: Routledge.

Goldberg, D.T. (2002) *The Racial State*, Malden, MA: Blackwell.

Guglielmo, T.A. (2004) *White on Arrival: Italians, Race, Color, and Power in Chicago, 1890–1945*, New York: Oxford University Press.

Hannaford, I. (1996) *Race: The History of an Idea in the West*, Baltimore: Johns Hopkins University Press.

Haslanger, S. (2012) *Resisting Reality: Social Construction and Social Critique*, New York: Oxford University Press.

Ignatiev, N. (2008 [1995]) *How the Irish Became White*, New York: Routledge Classics.

Isaac, B. (2004) *The Invention of Racism in Classical Antiquity*, Princeton: Princeton University Press.

Jacobson, M.F. (1998) *Whiteness of a Different Color: European Immigrants and the Alchemy of Race*, Cambridge, MA: Harvard University Press.

Jung, M., Costa Vargas, J.H., and Bonilla-Silva, E. (eds.) (2011) *State of White Supremacy: Racism, Governance, and the United States*, Stanford: Stanford University Press.

Lake, M., and Reynolds, H. (2008) *Drawing the Global Colour Line: White Men's Countries and the International Challenge of Racial Equality*, New York: Cambridge University Press.

Mandle, J., and Reidy, D.A. (eds.) (2014) *A Companion to Rawls*, Malden, MA: Wiley Blackwell.

Marx, A.W. (1998) *Making Race and Nation: A Comparison of the United States, South Africa, and Brazil*, New York: Cambridge University Press.

McCarthy, T. (2009) *Race, Empire, and the Idea of Human Development*, New York: Cambridge University Press.

Mills, C.W. (1997) *The Racial Contract*, Ithaca: Cornell University Press.

———. (2003) "White Supremacy as Sociopolitical System," in C.W. Mills, *From Class to Race: Essays in White Marxism and Black Radicalism*, Lanham: Rowman & Littlefield.

Nozick, R. (2013 [1974]) *Anarchy, State, and Utopia*, New York: Basic Books.

Oliver, M.L., and Shapiro, T.M. (2006) *Black Wealth/White Wealth: A New Perspective on Racial Inequality* (10th anniversary edition), New York: Routledge.

Outlaw, L., Jr. (1990) "Toward a Critical Theory of 'Race'," in D.T. Goldberg (ed.), *Anatomy of Racism*, Minneapolis: University of Minnesota Press.

Painter, N.I. (2010) *The History of White People*, New York: W.W. Norton.

Pateman, C., and Mills, C.W. (2007) *Contract and Domination*, Malden, MA: Polity.

Rawls, J. (1999) *A Theory of Justice*, Revised edition, Cambridge, MA: Harvard University Press.

Roediger, D.R. (2005) *Working Toward Whiteness: How America's Immigrants Became White—the Strange Journey From Ellis Island to the Suburbs*, New York: Basic Books.

———. (2007) *The Wages of Whiteness: Race and the Making of the American Working Class*, Revised and expanded edition, New York: Verso.

Roth, B. (2004) *Separate Roads to Feminism: Black, Chicana, and White Feminist Movements in America's Second Wave*, New York: Cambridge University Press.

Shelby, T. (2002) "Is Racism in the 'Heart'?" *Journal of Social Philosophy* 33, no. 3: 411–420.

——— (2003) "Ideology, Racism, and Critical Social Theory," *Philosophical Forum* 34, no. 2: 153–188.

Stoddard, L. (1920) *The Rising Tide of Color Against White World-Supremacy*, New York: Charles Scribner's Sons.

Sullivan, S., and Tuana, N. (eds.) (2007) *Race and Epistemologies of Ignorance*, Albany: State University of New York Press.

Telles, E. E. (2014) *Pigmentocracies: Ethnicity, Race and Color in Latin America*, Chapel Hill: University of North Carolina Press.

Vickers, J., and Isaac, A. (2012) *The Politics of Race: Canada, the United States, and Australia*, 2nd edition, Toronto: University of Toronto Press.

Vitalis, R. (2015) *White World Order, Black Power Politics: The Birth of American International Relations*, Ithaca: Cornell University Press.

Vucetic, S. (2011) *The Anglosphere: A Genealogy of a Racialized Identity in International Relations*, Stanford: Stanford University Press.

Watson, V., Howard-Wagner, D., and Spanierman, L. (eds.) (2015) *Unveiling Whiteness in the Twenty-First Century: Global Manifestations, Transdisciplinary Interventions*. Lanham: Lexington Books.

Williams, E. (1994 [1944]) *Capitalism and Slavery*, Chapel Hill: University of North Carolina Press.

Williams, L. F. (2003) *The Constraint of Race: Legacies of White Skin Privilege in America*, University Park: Penn State University Press.

Winant, H. (2001) *The World Is a Ghetto: Race and Democracy Since World War II*, New York: Basic Books.

Yancy, G. (2008) *Black Bodies, White Gazes: The Continuing Significance of Race in America*, Lanham: Rowman & Littlefield.

Part VIII
POLITICS AND POLICY

34
ON POST-RACIALISM
Or, How Color-Blindness Rebranded Is Still Vicious

Ronald R. Sundstrom

Introduction

During the 2008 election of President Barack Obama, idealistic talk that America was on the verge of entering a post-racial age was at its apogee. A set of demographic changes was apparent in America and the nation was poised to elect its first African American president. The feeling that the United States was back on the trajectory of the arc of justice was electric, and faith in individualism, with its ties to the distant ideal of color-blindness, felt vindicated. Andrew Delbanco put it this way: "there was suddenly a sense that one could believe in a 'post-racial' future without being a dupe or a chump" (Delbanco 2008).

Post-racialism conveys the idea that we in significant part had somehow risen above race and racism and heralded the tipping point of a demographic and cultural trend. The nation's racial habits, according to this view, have been destabilized by the browning of America; a shift resulting from the growth of the non-white population in the United States, along with increased patterns of immigration from Mexico and Latin America, the rise of multiracial or mixed-race identification, and higher rates of cross-racial or ethnic intimacies (Hoschild et al. 2011; Pew 2015). This is post-racialism as a description and what it intends to describe is a trend in demographics and self-conception. Alternatively, the idea of post-race is offered as a normative ideal that is a prescription for society's racial ills, and what it prescribes is a guiding vision of transcendence from racial beliefs, categories, and habits (Hollinger 2008, 2011; Lind 1996). Post-racialism either as description or prescription is presented as an epoch-defining intervention, a movement that is happening *now*.

This good post-racialism was chased away by a train of racially charged conflicts, such as the protests after the killing of Oscar Grant by a Bay Area Rapid Transit police officer on New Year's Day of 2009, and then the #BlackLivesMatter protests that spanned from September 2014 through January 2015. Critics of the post-racial idea and ideal pointed to these painful events, as well as to a standard array of sociological indicators, such as rates of incarceration and disparities in education and employment, that clearly demonstrated that race still matters. Insisting otherwise in the face of these facts is to give a naïve version of post-racialism.

As stunning a counter-example as the protests were, a satisfactory response to post-racialism as an *ideal* requires more than pointing out the inaccuracy of the *idea* as a sociological and demographic trend. An adequate response, as Paul C. Taylor made clear, would identify what it gets right, but also answer how it is deficient as a normative ideal and how those deficiencies continue to taint the best-intentioned liberal post-racial ideals and activism (P.C. Taylor 2014). Responses to the ideal of post-racialism have not done that; instead they have concentrated on its deleterious consequences on civil rights law and social policy, and its use by naïve, cynical, or partisan political actors. It is accused of playing into the hands of white privilege, institutional racism, not confronting the real problems posed by implicit biases against non-whites, and justifying the reactionary political project of denying or neglecting the consequences of America's racial history that aims at limiting or repealing civil rights legislation. More is needed to fully respond to the post-racial, so I add two criticisms: post-racialism as a normative ideal depends on a pastiche of history that invites the problems outlined above and that it leads to the vice of disrespecting persons.

Types of Post-racialism and Their Relation to Color-Blindness

Commonsense seems to undermine the veracity of the post-racial trend, but before those objections are reviewed the variations of the idea as a trend should be considered. There have been several useful typologies of postracialism. The typology presented here follows Lawrence Bobo's (2011b) account, but also draws from those of Howard McGary (2012), Paul C. Taylor (2014), and Kathryn Gines (2014). This typology of postracialism holds (1) that the salience of black victimhood narratives is diminishing because of the decline in significant instances of explicit racism. Our society is postracial, under this view, because it is post-racism. The other (2) has it that our society has become post-racial because of the demographic shifts outlined in section one.

This second claim may involve or not the previous claim of post-racism; however, post-racialism is distinct from post-racism. Advocates of post-racism believe we are in this new epoch but that many (usually people of color) still identify with racial categories out of bad faith and self-interest (D'Souza 1995). In contrast to that view, most Americans think that the nation is developing new racial habits, but that forms of racism based on historical forms of discrimination and domination persist to some degree (Cohen 2011). All the same, when the idea of post-racialism as a trend is paired with post-racism—this coupling was prevalent in contemporary US politics until disrupted by the killings of black men that inspired the #BlackLivesMatter movement—then it takes the form of a strategy, for example, a rhetorical tactic used to oppose the continuation of race-conscious social policy (Bonilla-Silva 2003; Barnes 2010).

Claims of post-racialism and color-blindness as a trend, as is apparent even from a cursory review of current sociological studies, suffer from a lack of consistent evidence. Such claims are hopelessly naïve and willfully ignore evidence of the role of race in the United States. The United States did not quit its old racial habits and emerge anew after Obama's election (Bobo 2011a, 2011b, King and Smith 2011; Gooding-Williams and Mills 2014). Racial and ethnic lines across our communities persevere, yet post-racialism appeals to a broad audience of Americans exhausted by race talk (Hutchinson

2009). Exhaustion does some work in explaining the popularity of post-racialism and color-blindness, but the appeal of these ideas also points to their status as ideals for how we should act and whom we ought to become as individuals and a people. This is why Bobo counts (3) recent color-blind rhetoric as a third version of post-racialism (cf. McGary 2012; Gines 2014).

Color-blindness has similar descriptive and prescriptive branches, but as with post-racialism its status as an ideal is independent of its truth as a descriptive claim. The ideal of color-blindness has been offered in many versions, but two are commonly encountered. The first type is narrow and concerns whether race or ethnicity should play any role in the formation and administration of law and public policy. The other type is more ambitious since it asserts that race and ethnicity are morally irrelevant social identities and should make no moral, social, political, or legal difference in a person's life (Sundstrom 2008: 37–64). This is the normative core of color-blindness.

So as not to be naïve, the best proponents of the ideal of color-blindness affirm that the value of equal moral standing of individuals *qua* individuals is best realized in ethical decision-making, and related law and public policy, by being sensitive to race. Color-conscious law and public policy can identify, limit, and prevent ethnic and racial discrimination; it can ensure equal access to opportunity; address economic and social disparities due to past racial discrimination; and encourage individuals from all groups to participate in the political, economic, and cultural life of the nation (Boxill 1992; Dworkin 2000). This moral and political point is an extension of political theorist Amy Gutmann's view that "What's right about color-consciousness . . . is also the partial truth of color-blindness: all human beings regardless of their color should be treated as free and equal beings, worthy of the same set of basic liberties and opportunities" (Gutmann 1996: 112–113).

In contrast to older forms of color-blindness, Bobo claims that something like the more ambitious version of color-blindness with its future orientation is at the heart of post-racialism, that it "is intended to signal a hopeful trajectory for events and social trends, not an accomplished fact of social life" (Bobo 2011b: 13). This claim is exemplified by the arguments of David Hollinger, one of the most prominent proponents of post-racialism, who insists that it is distinct from color-blindness, which he calls "abstract" and associates with erroneous descriptive claims or policy debates (Hollinger 2011: 176). Nevertheless, the bad associations aside, color-blindness can and has been asserted as an ideal—this then is not a distinction that holds up. Post-racialism, however, does mark the period after President Obama's election, which is the focal point for current discussions about color-blindness and post-racialism; so, post-racialism is, in a sense, a re-branding of color-blindness in an age especially attuned to the craft of brand design that is fond of tagging as "innovative" or "disruptive" ideas with the prefix "post."

The moral core of color-blindness, and by extension, post-racialism, as stated above is the robust claim that holds that ethnic and racial categories are irrelevant moral characteristics and should have no role in moral decision-making. This position is sometimes tied to the idea of racial eliminativism, which is the idea that the idea of race is nonsensical, that "races" do not exist, and that we should eliminate race-talk in our language and from our practices in all spheres of life. Post-racialism, however, as a trend or ideal is distinct from questions about whether there is any "there" there when it comes to race or whether we are obliged to abandon or conserve the use of those distinctions.

Nevertheless, the ontological debates about racial categories and identifications affect the position of the parties in the debate over post-racialism.

Howard McGary, therefore, (2012) considers the (4) ontological position of racial eliminativism to be a form of post-racialism because the skepticism about racial identifications inherent in eliminativism conceptually legitimize post-racial trends and the ideal. This makes sense since post-racialism in the long-term will aid eliminativist goals, but insofar as eliminativism stands in for the ontological claim that race is not real, then post-racialism is distinct from it because one could hold that racial identitfications are in some sense real (for example as social categories or even have some distant genetic basis) yet support post-racialism.

Post-racialism, with its conceptual ancestry in color-blindness, is most interesting and defensible as a prescriptive normative ideal. It is untouched by the relative weaknesses of its descriptive forms, and its proponents do not take seriously rebuttals that rely on pointing out the errors of the descriptive claims (P.C. Taylor 2014). David Hollinger laid out a clear version of this ideal in his reaction to President Obama's election. He wrote:

> At the center of that challenge is a gradually spreading uncertainty about the significance of color lines, especially the significance of blackness itself. Blackness is the pivotal concept in the intellectual and administrative apparatus used in the United States for dealing with ethnoracial distinctions. Doubts about its basic meaning, boundaries, and social role affected ideas about whiteness, and all other color-coded identities. These uncertainties make it easier to contemplate a possible future in which the ethnoracial categories central to identity politics would be more matters of choice than ascription; in which mobilization by ethnoracial groups would be more a strategic option than a presumed destiny attendant upon mere membership in a group; and in which economic inequalities would be confronted head-on, instead of through the medium of ethnorace.
>
> (Hollinger 2008: 1033)

Hollinger's ideas echo Delbanco's (2008), and both proclaim the race-less value of universal individualism and the new credibility of post-racialism. Key here are the ideas that (1) there is a challenge to racial practices exemplified in the president's election that has spread uncertainty about our practices, (2) these uncertainties have made it easier to imagine a future beyond race and ethnicity, (3) where ethnic and racial ascriptions are loosened and become more voluntaristic, and which (4) make it easier to confront economic inequalities. For those who agree with Hollinger and Delbanco, President Obama's election further loosened the grip that race has on us.

The Post-racial Trend Energizes the Ideal

Post-racial ideals depend on the assumption that there are post-racial trends and they will affect how our future society will organize itself. But the trend does not have to be true for true believers to hold onto the ideal. I leave the analysis of the empirical validity of the post-racial trend for social scientists to hash out and for another venue (Sundstrom, forthcoming). Yet, what should be recognized are the strong conceptual ties between post-racialism as trend and idea. The ideal cannot be cleanly dealt with by criticizing the trend, but the former is energized and depends on its plausibility because of the latter. The post-racial ideal is not a view from nowhere; its descriptive elements—with all its weaknesses—intersects with the prescriptive. It is encouraged by shifts in racial attitudes and practices: the rise of the mixed-race movement and pride in mixed-race identity; the demographic growth of interracial marriages and aggressive assertions of the social legitimacy and vitality of interracial families and friendships; and demographic growth of immigrants and trans-national families (Jones and Bullock 2012; P. Taylor 2014). The United States of America is changing—social networks and boundaries are shifting—and the post-racial ideal is emerging from this change (Hochschild et al. 2011).

As a general trend, the demographic changes motivating the post-racial idea are impressive, but there are specific differences between groups that should give us pause. There are regional and group differences among those who claim more than one race, and similar differences show up in rates of ethnic and racial intermarriage (Fishman et al. 2008; Lofquist 2012; Taylor et al. 2012; Jones and Bullock 2012). Additionally there are significant differences in attitudes among Millennials about post-racialism. While white youth tend to think that society is at or in near a post-racial moment, black youth remain deeply unconvinced (Cohen 2011: 198). If the national changes hinted at above can be fairly called post-racial, then post-racialism as such is a minor note and does not describe the lives or practices of most Americans, especially among black Americans (Bobo 2011b).

It is possible that whites and blacks are behind the post-racial curve, but it is more likely, especially among blacks, that they do not see enough change in American racial practices to encourage the uptake of post-racialism. While attitudes and some practices are breaking up, significant patterns of racial disparity and discrimination have not changed enough to justify calling our age post-racial (Cole 1999; Alexander 2010; Bobo 2011b; King and Smith 2011). As Hochschild et al. (2011) show, the persistence of these disparities, along with instances of individual and systemic discrimination, is a drag against the post-racial trend, and their entrenchment means that post-racialism is not a universal trend.

Instrumental and Ideological Objections Against the Post-racial Ideal

Leaving behind the trend, let us consider the soundness of the post-racial ideal. The first three objections against the ideal that follow address how such rhetoric is employed and its practical consequences; as such, they are instrumental objections, so they do not touch the core of the post-racial ideal, yet they lengthen the shadow of suspicion over post-racialism that the criticisms of the post-racial trend initially cast. A fourth objection questions the very idea of color-blindness, and the fifth objection claims that post-racialism is an ideology implicitly skewed toward racial injustice.

The first criticism is instrumental and asserts that talk of post-racialism as both trend and ideal encourages the proponents of color-blind law and policy and those who seek to continue the rollbacks on civil rights advances. Color-blindness as a policy position is a key tool and goal in the long-running American conservative political project focused on rolling back civil rights gains, as well as the related gains of the New Deal, preserving white privileges, and delegitimizing the very idea of the liberal welfare state and its social programs; often the color-blindness that is referenced in such tactics is the naïve or cynical sort, rather than the ideal based in justice and the moral equality of persons and democratic equality of citizens (Steinberg 1995; Haney-López 2006). Now post-racialism as trend and ideal adds another arrow in their quiver—an arrow that has been repeatedly shot, such as in the recent weakening of the Voting Rights Act. The idea that the application of law and public policy in the United States, even after *Brown vs. Board of Education* or the passage of the Voting Rights Act, has been color-blind is patently false. Society is not color-blind, so to insist on color-blindness is to not fully address past racial wrongs and to leave vulnerable populations open to the damaging forms of color-consciousness that the proponents of color-blindness dream that the nation has put behind it. Color-blindness is a hustle that brings easy relief and feelings of righteousness to those who are troubled with racial exhaustion; and for those who suffer from the effects of racial bias and oppression it is a setup with catastrophic consequences. Therefore, according to the advocates of color-consciousness, society must be sensitive to race to adequately detect and address discrimination based on skin-color, ethnicity, and race.

The second criticism is also instrumental and contends that the political right has narrowly applied color-blindness to American life. As an ideal, it has largely been implemented in law and public policies. The proponents of color-blindness, following Justice Harlan's view that while the law "regards man as man," have been silent and even hostile to the application of color-blindness in other spheres of the lives of citizens, in particular the social and private spheres of individuals. Contrary to Martin Luther King Jr.'s vision of color-blindness—a vision that applied to the private as well as public life—the typical supporters of color-blindness in law and public policy have even defended the right of individuals to discriminate in their private and social lives. Furthermore, they have defended the right of the state to engage in some forms of color-conscious racial profiling in domestic policing and monitoring against international terrorism and, of course, migration. Thus, the proponents of color-consciousness see in color-blindness a double-hypocrisy: first, color-blindness ignores the social-historical role of race in the United States, and second, it leaves the private and social sphere of individuals untouched as a vector of explicit racism or implicit bias. Post-racialism, as trend and ideal, plays right into this double play.

The third instrumental objection against the post-racial ideal is how it supports the American vice of evading discussions about racial injustice. There are accusations of racism, largely personal and having to do with an idiotic, lascivious, or vicious comment by some influential somebody, and references to our racial divisions among old- and new-media pundits, but what has been missing—except in times of crisis—are discussions of serious racial disparities. This is a symptom of racial exhaustion but also what Charles Mills so memorably described as an epistemology of ignorance about race in America (Mills 1997, 2007). Our presumptions about racial inferiority and superiority, cultural development, and justice, in turn justifies racial injustice and the disparities that come with it—the classic paternalistic defenses of slavery, dispossession and displacement, colonialism, and Jim Crow segregation as being good for the American Indians, blacks, natives, so on are prime examples of racial epistemologies of ignorance in action. These epistemological stances have shifted through time to focus on, for example, the threat immigration from Mexico, Central and south America, or have recycled old accusations—they are lazy, disease-ridden, and criminal—and combined to form accusatory labels, such as the welfare queen, illegal, or thug, which are used as ammunition against color-conscious programs, and accompanied arguments that color-consciousness was unfair and unjust and that the disparities are the fault of those that suffered them.

Representations of the post-racial trend and ideal encourages contemporary epistemologies of ignorance about race because the suggestive statistics offered in its support confirm the belief that race no longer matters, and the ideal does so because it encourages the application of naïve forms of color-blindness, a form that does not address racial disparity. Moreover, given the demographic shifts of the browning of America, this leads to more than an epistemology of ignorance in the service of retaining white privilege and ignorance, it serves as succor for those of us on the beneficial side of post-racialism. What post-racialism offers is not just a "white-washing"—an obscuring or hiding of injustice in the service of white privilege—it also offers a "color-washing" of those disparities. The increase in diversity in the United States lulls the nation into thinking that our racial conflicts have largely dissipated and controversial color-conscious policies are no longer needed or justified (Sundstrom 2008).

Related to the instrumental objections and leading to the ideological one, is the fourth, and conceptual, criticism that rejects the possibility of a race-less perspective in the first place. This objection is registered here because it is frequently referred to in the discussion as a trump card; that is, color-blindness in a world where skin color, ethnicity, and race matter in many different aspects in lives of the citizens and residents of the United States is an artificial, forced, and illusory perspective—it is truly a view from nowhere. This is a point as much about the foundations of human experience and knowledge as it is about practical interactions with the world. Individuals cannot take on a race-less, or for that matter a gender-less, perspective, especially on matters involving those social identities. We live in and through our bodies and minds interacting with other people (Alcoff 2006). To this I would add, it would require thinking and feeling independently from our minds, with our associated emotions, explicit and implicit attitudes, and thought processes that have been formed by our social environments. To be color-blind we would have to get out of ourselves. And just as that is presently impossible, so is post-racialism.

As much as this conceptual objection rightfully warns us against false universal perspectives, the objection is hyperbolic in that it overstates our conceptual limits to ridiculous effect—potentially ending in solipsism—and the goal of the color-blind and post-racial ideal, which can be framed as a practical and reasonable ideal. The accusation that being color-blind or taking on a race-less perspective is impossible is vulnerable to the retort that color-blindness, as applied to race, need not be literal. Policy can and has been implemented in a manner that approximates the ideal of color-blindness. Justice, or even the administration of government institutions on all levels, has not been color-blind but that is the goal (Cole 1999; Alexander 2010). Although this objection applies a necessary break to the excesses of color-blindness, it is not definitive, and so the fifth objection deserves the most attention.

Beyond being a delusion or merely misapplied as a political tool, Sumi Cho (2009) and Eduardo Bonilla-Silva and David Dietrich (2011) argue that the rhetoric of post-racialism is itself an ideology or part of a larger color-blind ideology that intends to minimize racism and justify the end of color-conscious civil rights policies. This is the fifth and most serious objection since it turns the very idea of post-racialism as an ideal on its head; it asserts that post-racialism is part of a system that seeks to diminish recognition for the presence and enduring effects of personal and systemic racism, preserve white privilege and the systemic racism that support those privileges, roll back civil rights gains, and de-legitimate racial identity as a progressive organizational focus. It builds off of earlier arguments that color-blindness is an ideology that preserves white privilege and non-white racial oppression (Bonilla-Silva 2003; Haney-López 2006).

The central features of color-blind racism, according to Bonilla-Silva, are abstract liberalism, cultural racism, minimization of racism, and naturalization; these features interact and serve as "frames" by which those committed to color-blind ideology understand racial identifications and politics (Bonilla-Silva 2003; Bonilla-Silva and Dietrich 2011: 192). The first "frame," abstract liberalism is understood to involve disembodied and otherwise decontextualized principles of classical liberalism or (loosely) deontological ethical principles, such as individual rights, personhood, or equality, or even rationality to argue against race-sensitive law and public policy. For example, consider Chief Justice Roberts's assertion in *Parents Involved in Community Schools v. Seattle School District No. 1* (551 US 701) that "the way to stop discrimination on the basis of race is to stop discriminating on the basis of race." His view, as with liberal ideals naïvely applied, are unhinged from the practical exigencies of rectifying or curtailing ethnic and injustice. The second frame, cultural racism holds that the problem with the group in question is not their biological inferiority, but their culturally embedded habits, practices, and customs; for example, the old American habit of blaming poor people of color for their own social, political, and economic disparities. The minimization of racism, the third frame, follows from the first two frames, because if society's basic social structures and political culture is fair, and if the fault lies with the cultural practices of the group, then race and racism does not matter. The final frame, naturalization, holds that ethnic and race-based biases and preferences, as long as they happen in the private or social spheres (e.g., in the bedroom, home, clubhouse, church), are somehow natural and should not be subject to social engineering (Bonilla-Silva, 2014). Obviously, this frame is in tension with the presumptive race-neutrality of the other frames, but post-racialism as ideology strives for justification of racially self-interested action and not conceptual consistency. This ideology is especially punishing, because it entrenches and solidifies racial disparities and domination, and provides, as its critics point out, intellectual cover for injustice and balm for our social guilt.

A Liberal Defense of the Post-racial Ideal Against the Ideological Objection

Color-blindness has been used as a tool in political strategies to roll back the Civil Rights advances, and it has been used by ideological warriors, committed to preserving white racial and class privileges. Hollinger's version of the post-racial ideal, however, explicitly disavows naïve or cynical applications of color-blind policy; the core of it concerns the loosening of racial identification and ascription, which track demographic trends and attitudes, therefore the first four objections deliver only glancing blows to serious versions of post-racialism (Hollinger 2008, 2011). Let us then turn to the fifth objection.

A full response to the ideological objection begins with admitting that the post-racial ideal is a historically aware, non-naïve liberal ideal. It is consistent with the values of personal autonomy, liberty, and toleration at the heart of liberal political theories, and is ideological in the sense that it promotes and is underwritten by those and other related values (e.g., civil rights, democratic rule by consent, civic participation, and political transparency), but it is not necessarily committed to the follies of what Bonilla-Silva labels "abstract liberalism"—a false universalism, or a particularism that pretends to be universal—nor is it committed to cultural racism, the minimization of racism, or what he terms "naturalization."

The value of personal autonomy, in particular, evident in Hollinger's and Delbanco's defense of post-racialism, is at the heart of the post-racial ideal, because the implication is that individuals will have greater personal autonomy as they are freed from sometimes unwelcome ascribed racial scripts that limit their behavior and their life chances. This position certainly has ramifications for debates over the conservation of ethnic and racial identifications, but it does not necessarily serve the interests of color-blind ideology (for example, the loosening of racial scripts assaults the biases and assumptions that often come with racial ascriptions—persons with X-identifications do not or should not participate in Y-activities, and should be prevented from doing so), which is often hypocritically silent about race-sensitive mores in the private sphere. Certainly, the ethnic and racial loosening implication of the post-racial ideal has been used for ideological purposes, but other related ideals have been used as grist for the reactionary mill. Frederick Douglass's liberal, civic republican and Christian arguments for abolition, Martin Luther King Jr.'s evocation of the dream of liberty from racial oppression and racial unity, and even Malcolm X's emphasis on self-help are used to argue against color-conscious policies, but such misinterpretations do not justify scorning the original ideas. Furthermore the complaint against "new" or "liberal" racism, as for racism in general, concerns how what is morally and rightfully *due* to individuals and communities is denied; what is new in "new racism" is the use of sub-text, coding, or dog-whistle strategies to effect those denials and to ignore explicit racism or implicit bias (Haney-López 2014). At the center, then, of the objection to racism are the liberal assumptions of personhood, individual rights, moral and personal autonomy, non-domination, and equal justice and civic belonging, and that social goods are due to individuals regardless of their ethnic or racial identifications, gender, class, sexuality, or level of ability—all of this is affirmed by the first implication of the post-racial ideal.

This pertains to Bonilla-Silva's frame of abstract liberalism; certainly liberalism in the abstract and the applied is implicated in the history of racism. Charles Mills and Carole Pateman have forcefully argued that the foundational social contract theories includes gender and racial contracts that have built in the domination of women and non-white, non-Europeans into the terms of the contract (Pateman 1988; Mills 1997; Pateman and Mills 2007). The components of liberalism, however, have been some of the principal tools in the enduring effort of moral and political suasion and physical struggle over domination. As Amy Gutmann recognized, color-blindness and color-consciousness are methods that meet in the middle. Thus, we can dismiss facile associations of the post-racial ideal with equally facile objections against abstract liberalism, racial progress, race-neutral universalism, silly applications of moral equivalence between uses of race, and so on. When one takes a liberal position that does not mean they are ipso facto implicated in color-blind racism.

Another aspect of Holligner's post-racial ideal is its assertion that class is more important than race at our present historical juncture, and thus that economic inequalities should be confronted head-on instead of through the proxy of race; this implication does assume that race is not necessarily central to understanding and responding to the economic and political inequalities that track race, and that focusing on race may even be an obstacle for dealing with those disparities (Michaels 2006; Cashin 2014). This view comes close to what the critics accuse of doing: it minimizes racism. However, it only falls prey to this problem if it is applied naïvely. On particular issues, the centrality of race, and how closely some inequality tracks race is an empirical issue, so interested parties should act accordingly. There may be particular issues that deserve wholly or largely a class-based (or gender- or sexuality-based) approach, because that targets those most effected, and not—as the critics of post-racialism assert—because this is most the politically palatable approach.

Even so, economic inequalities intersect with ethnicity and race. Taking any one of these variables out of the analysis would miss crucial facts about how those inequalities play out on the ground. What is more, taking wealth as an indicator that grapples with inequality head-on, it is apparent that to understand how race matters, we need to see how race works within class (Kochar et al. 2011; McKernan et al. 2013; Shapiro et al. 2013). Therefore, Hollinger's post-racial ideal is too closely associated with his view of post-racial trends, and can lead to what Bonilla-Silva calls the minimization of racism. To recover from this fumble, a stronger version of the ideal adjusts, but does not drop, the second implication: some disparities, indeed, must be confronted head-on via class, gender, sexuality, or place, but that does not mean intersectionality or the relevance of race is denied.

All in all, none of the criticisms of post-racialism as an ideology fully touch the core message of serious post-racialism; even Hollinger's sloppy assertion that race obscures dealing with inequality head-on does not directly undermine the core idea. The ideal expresses the hope that ethnic and racial identification will become more voluntarily rather—along with the scripts that come with them—imposed on individuals and communities. Anthony Appiah, although he has not espoused post-racialism, has articulated the aims that smart post-racialists most identify with; he argues that we should take individual autonomy seriously, recognize the limiting power of the ascription of identifications (what most call identities), while recognizing their value and use in beating back domination, and move to loosen their hold over individuals' lives. He advocates for the position that lives be "not too tightly scripted," and "not too constrained by the demands and expectations of others (Appiah 1996, 2005). Appiah advocates that society help to increase the autonomy of individuals from the constraints of identity ascriptions—he calls this "soul making"—and lead its citizens to consider such identifications as voluntary and recreational, and that their identities and interests are complex, multifarious, and they cut across groups. These are the fruits of the universal individualism that Holligner and Delbanco celebrated after Obama's 2008 election, and this vision, as well as Appiah's analysis of racial ascriptions, were inspired by John Stuart Mill's vision of individual liberty and experiments with living (Mill 1977).

Instead of being ideologically at odds with racial justice, this vision is emphatically affirmed by critics of post-racialism like Cathy Cohen; for example, when she approvingly quotes john a. powell's claim that "equal membership in the political community" requires "expanding the choices that people have to lead lives they value" (Cohen 2010: 233; powell 2004: 969). This entails supporting the development of their capabilities and giving them equal access to resources and opportunities, which ultimately should, Cohen and powell hope, lead to "an environment in which people can develop their potential and lead productive, creative lives in accord with their needs and interests" (Cohen 2010: 233; powell 2004: 969).

A Historical and Realist Objection Against the Post-racial Ideal

The values at the heart of the post-racial ideal are worthy and they harmonize with the American narrative of racial progress, so the idea of a time and place that is post-racial seems reasonable and credible utopia. Delbanco and Holliger affirm this vision because race no longer seems like an insurmountable obstacle to progress. However, the narrative of American progress on racial issues, and the time and place it imagines, are the key weaknesses of the post-racial ideal. Together these two elements (time and place) serve a political mnemonic that the post-racial ideal leans on for conceptual support; without them, the ideal loses its feasibility and reasonableness (P.C. Taylor 2014).

Post-racialism marks the rupture with racialism, or the time of traditional racial practices, and serves to convince us to work toward ending racial practices in the present and to fulfill a post-racial future. The ideal offers us, according to Taylor, a pragmatic and prophetic opening through which we can escape the hold that racial practices have over us. Post-racialism is pragmatic insofar as it is a reasonable response to demographic trends and is responsive to the need for, at least temporary, color-consciousness, and it is prophetic because it summons a new world that it discerns in the pattern of American history, particularly in the African American civil rights movement (P.C. Taylor 2014: 18). The grand narrative of the American Civil Rights movement, in its typical post-1964 form, emphasizes the overcoming of the divisions of racial identifications as much as it emphasizes addressing serious racial injustices. It has an abiding hold on many white liberals and conservatives.

The grand Civil Rights narrative started off as a critical history that was meant to free Americans from the previous monumental narrative of the founding of America that was innocent of racial wrongs. In turn the critical narrative that challenged the old with its own key events, for example Martin Luther King Jr.'s protest in Birmingham and the crossing of the Edmund Pettus Bridge in Selma became set pieces in standard tales of the arc of American history. The critical history, in the hands of commentators and politicians interested in telling a national narrative, became a historical pastiche (Jameson 1991: 17).

Pastiche, maybe, but it is pastiche with an invigorating purpose. In Nietzsche's early view in *On the Advantage and Disadvantage of History for Life* (1980), what historian William Hardy McNeil labeled as "mythistory" is addressed. As Nietzsche delineated, monumental histories emerge from the fragments left over from the destructive work of critical history, and they serve as the basis and model for activity and striving, which monumental histories inspire and fortify. Thus, we see in the American political traditions celebrations of the usual cast of characters—Thomas Jefferson, Theodore Roosevelt, Franklin D. Roosevelt—but when it comes to imaginings of national unity, courage, and moral foresight, none is more prominent than Lincoln and Martin Luther King Jr. These "profiles of courage" and civic virtue serve as models for moral and political formation. Further, a big part of the enabling and ennobling power of monumental history is the role of ignoring and forgetting in its formation of its invigorating monuments—they must capture what we deem as the essential message or moment and leave off the rest as dross.

But whose history will be kept in the dark so that others may live? The selective use of forgetting is at the core of Taylor's complaint against how the grand narrative obscures relevant details that run counter to the story of the myth. A significant fallout of this grand narrative, however, is the view that African Americans—the trouble started with the black Muslims of Chicago and the Black Panthers of Oakland—and other groups that followed the lead of the Black Power movements (e.g., feminist, Latino/Hispanic, Asian American, and the LGBT movement) broke away from the genius of the trajectory in their turn to identity politics (Glazer and Moynihan 1970; Michaels 2006). This view, in turn, obscures relevant details that run counter to the story of the myth; for example, the role of community organizing that was explicitly color-conscious and drew on the rising rhetoric of black power, or of the role of an under-appreciated diverse movement, especially of women, and the depth and persistence of racial disparities. President Obama drew on this narrative in his few speeches about race; notably in his pre-election March 18 "speech on race" and his first inaugural address. However, he expressed less enchantment for mythistory in other addresses. In some cases, Obama spoke of racism being in the country's "DNA," even though he still defended the basic idea that there has been progress on racial justice. America's mythistory of racial progress undermines the social and political strategies used to produce the myth in the first place.

The prophecy of a time and place in America without race lacks credibility, especially for those who suffer from racial oppression, because it is not feasible and is based on a deeply biased reading of history. Some variants of cognitive framing have implications for understanding the political meaning and role of historical narrative (Tenbrunsel and Messick 2004; Wohl et al. 2006; Bazerman and Tenbrunsel 2011). This is where the historical objection converges with Derrick Bell's view of "racial realism" (Bell 1992: 92 and 101); specifically his criticism of jurisprudence that "reifies" and "deifies" legal ideals, forgetting that they are in fact abstract ideals that are either not or imperfectly applied in the present non-ideal world, and regarding them with moral absolutism that offers their proponents an appearance of moral purity while preserving the effects, and enabling the continuation, of racial injustice. All the other objections against the post-racial trend and ideal converge on this realism that is awake to the hard truths of American history: America is not post-racial, post-racial trends are not general, the ideal is an instrument for rolling back civil rights advances and ignoring disparities, a post-racial perspective—as with a color-blind one—is impractical, and whether intentionally or implicitly it has served the purposed of a racially dominating ideology.

A Disruptive Defense of the Post-racial Ideal

Post-racialism need not wither in the face of the historical-realist objection; it has access to a harsher defense than the liberal response. It is one that is motivated by a Nietzschean view of monumental history, is not bothered by the critiques of the monumental history that post-racialism depends upon, and refuses to take into consideration the concerns of the opposition. It challenges historiographical objections by refusing responsibility for the old precisely because it seeks to make the new. This response sees the post-racial trend and ideal as explicitly creatively destructive. It sees post-racialism as going beyond, over, and setting aside old racial practices. Dialogue and participation are not its central values; instead it taps into the churning forces of modernity for justification of change, and it takes inspiration in the heroic emergence of the new from disruption. An example is Ralph Waldo Emerson's (1983) view of race and the "fate" of those used and oppressed for the sake of historical progress.

There is more than a little bit of arrogant, self-pleasing cruelty in this presumptively transcendent stance. It speaks from the position of the assumed victor, the one that can ride out the churn of history and emerge in a new epoch. There are few if any who accept this sort of adventurism, but some do (Hill 2013). Post-racialism as an ideal may be an ideology in this case, but not one of racial subterfuge and domination, but a self-overcoming one that is attempting to shift the social paradigm. The post-racial ideal is again evoked and the nation is invited to move toward the future. What the destination of this movement is, is unknown and anxiety is to be expected.

Post-racialism is Vicious

The disruptive version of the post-racial ideal departs from the liberal post-racial ideal. As with the liberal version, it does not assume that society is now post-racial, but it has a skewed relation with the moral ideal at its core—of equal dignity and treatment regardless or racial identification—because the disruptive version allows that the perspectives and interests of those not on board with its prophetic vision be left aside. This means that the disruptive post-racial ideal shares the practical weaknesses of the liberal post-racial ideal version. But while that critique might give the reasonable holder of the liberal post-racial ideal pause, the disruptive version is not stopped, because its proponents may be willing to embrace the loss that would accompany its realization. Some people would lose in its view, but those who do not allow themselves to be transformed in its light would be seen as regressive and conceptually left behind as we move to create a post-racial world.

Thrilling stuff—but it is easy to be thrilled because it is assumed to be someone else's pain. It should not be surprising then that those who hold the life forms the position seeks to abandon fight back. This brings up another objection against both the liberal and disruptive versions of post-racial ideal: they are vicious. They disrespect the moral status of those whose lives would be made worse by the implementation of policy guided by post-racial ideals, because it would add to conditions of deprivation and domination by ignoring those conditions or the social dynamics, instruments, and institutions that create and maintain those conditions. The liberal post-racial ideal in particular is therefore led into a contradiction its reasonable proponents must attend to. If the post-racial ideal takes the moral equality of individuals seriously, then it should not dismiss the means by which ethnic and racial discrimination is understood and addressed. Otherwise, the ideal would not be reasonable and could not possibly attract the support of those suffering from such injustice. If, however, the post-racial ideal includes a call to ignore and forget those left behind, then this disruptive version is not just misguided, it is vicious. It disrespects persons who suffer ethnic and racial discrimination and oppression, by ignoring the non-ideal conditions that plagues their lives, and fails to give them equal regard.

This gets to the sharp feelings that critics of both color-blindness and post-racialism have about those ideas. They are vicious in their disregard for the effected persons and the challenges they face in their present places and times. Michelle Alexander, the legal scholar, offered one of the best succinct statements of this ethical failure:

> Colorblindness has inspired callousness. When people say, "I don't care if he's black," what they're really saying is that they're not willing to view his

> experience in racial terms. . . . Not caring about a person's race is presented as some kind of virtue, as if it will lead us to act in fair and nondiscriminatory way. In fact, not caring can be a form of cruelty.
>
> (Alexander 2011: 7)

Color-blindness and the post-racialism that builds off it are not virtuous positions; they are positions one stakes out that lead to ignoring morally relevant features of social life. Even in the face of mass violence they can prevent those who are naïvely or ideologically committed to them from seeing the bloody truth. Witness the politicians and pundits, like Senator Lindsey Graham, who after the killings at Emanuel A.M.E. Church stumbled in his attempts to explain the tragedy in a way that his white conservative base would find appealing by saying that the murder had been targeting Christians. He shamelessly refused to recognize the innocent dead as black and the victims of racial violence. Only after being rebuked on social media did he acknowledge the victims and their church as being targeted because they were black while still warping his sympathetic words for political ends by calling the murderer a "racial jihadist" (Parker 2015). Such are the evasions of color-blindness and the moral failure of post-racialism that we have a moral imperative to reject the latter, and to apply the former judiciously in the service of preventing or rectifying racism and distributive injustice.

References

Alcoff, Linda Martín. (2006) *Visible Identities: Race, Gender, and the Self*, New York: Oxford University Press.
Alexander, Michelle. (2010) *The New Jim Crow: Mass Incarceration in the Age of Colorblindness*, New York: New Press.
———. (2011) "Throwing Away the Key: Michelle Alexander and How Prisons Became the New Jim Crow." Interview by Arnie Cooper. *Sun*: 4–12.
Appiah, Kwame Anthony. (1996) "Race, Culture, Identity: Misunderstood Connections," in Kwame Anthony Appiah and Amy Gutmann (eds.), *Color Conscious: The Political Morality of Race*, Princeton: Princeton University Press, pp. 30–105.
———. (2005) *The Ethics of Identity*, Princeton: Princeton University Press.
Barnes, Mario L., Erwin Chemerinsky, and Trina Jones. (2010) "A Post-Race Equal Protection?" *Georgetown Law Journal* 98, no. 4: 967–1004.
Bell, Derrick. (1992) *Faces at the Bottom of the Well: The Permanence of Racism*, New York: Basic Books.
Bazerman, Max H., and Tenbrunsel, Ann E. (2011) *Blind Spots: Why We Fail to Do What's Right and What to Do About It*, Princeton: Princeton University Press.
Bobo, Lawrence D. (ed.) (2011a) "Race, Inequality, and Culture" [Special issue]. *Daedalus* 140, no. 2 (Spring).
———. (2011b) "Somewhere Between Jim Crow & Postracialism: Reflections on the Racial Divide in America Today." *Daedalus* 140, no. 2: 11–36.
Bonilla-Silva, Eduardo. (2003) *Racism Without Racists: Color-Blind Racism and the Persistence of Racial Inequality in the United States*, Lanham: Rowman & Littlefield.
Bonilla-Silva, Eduardo, and Dietrich, David. (2011) "The Sweet Enchantment of Color-Blind Racism in Obamerica." *Annals of the American Academy of Political and Social Science* 634: 190–206.
Boxill, Bernard R. (1992) *Blacks and Social Justice*, Lanham: Rowman & Littlefield.
Cashin, Sheryll. (2014) *Place, Not Race: A New Vision of Opportunity in America*, Boston: Beacon Press.
Cho, Sumi. (2009) "Post-racialism." *Iowa Law Review* 94: 1589–1649.
Cohen, Cathy J. (2011) "Millennials and the Myth of the Post-Racial Society: Black Youth, Intra-Generation Divisions and the Continuing Racial Divide in American Politics." *Daedalus* 2, no 2: 197–205.

———. (2010) *Democracy Remixed*, Oxford: Oxford University Press.
Cole, David. (1999) *No Equal Justice: Race and Class in the American Criminal Justice System*, New York: New Press.
Delbanco, Andrew. (2008) "A Fateful Election." *New York Review of Books* 55, no. 17. Last modified November 6. www.nybooks.com/articles/22017.
D'Souza, Dinesh. (1995) *The End of Racism: Principles for a Multiracial Society*, New York: Free Press.
Dworkin, Ronald. (2000) *Sovereign Virtue: The Theory and Practice of Equality*, Cambridge, MA: Harvard University Press.
Emerson, Ralph Waldo. (1983) "Fate," in Joel Porte (ed.), *Essays & Lectures*, New York: Library of America, pp. 943–968.
Fishman, Raymond, Iyengar, Sheena S., Kamenica, Emir, and Simonson, Itamar. (2008) "Racial Preferences in Dating." *Review of Economic Studies Limited* 75, no. 1: 117–132.
Gines, Kathryn T. (2014) "A Critique of Postracialism: Conserving Race and Complicating Blackness Beyond the Black-White Binary." *Du Bois Review: Social Science Research on Race* 11, no. 1: 75–86.
Glazer, Nathan, and Moynihan, Daniel P. (1970) *Beyond the Melting Pot; the Negroes, Puerto Ricans, Jews, Italians, and Irish of New York City*, 2nd edition, Cambridge, MA: MIT Press.
Gooding-Williams, Robert, and Mills, Charles W. (2014) "Race in a 'Postracial' Epoch" [Special issue]. *Du Bois Review* 11, no. 1 (Spring).
Gutmann, Amy. (1996) "Responding to Racial Injustice," in Appiah K. Anthony and Amy Gutmann (eds.), *Color Conscious: The Political Morality of Race*, Princeton: Princeton University Press, pp. 106–178.
Haney-López, Ian. (2006) *White by Law: The Legal Constructions of Race*, New York: New York University Press.
———. (2014) *Dog Whistle Politics: How Coded Racial Appeals Have Reinvented Racism and Wrecked the Middle Class*, New York: Oxford University Press.
Hill, Jason D. (2013) *Civil Disobedience and the Politics of Identity: When We Should Not Get Along*, New York: Palgrave Macmillan.
Hochschild, Jennifer L., Weaver, Vesla M., and Burch, Traci. (2011) "Destabilizing the American Racial Order." *Daedalus* 140, no. 2: 151–165.
Hollinger, David A. (2008) "Obama, the Instability of Color Lines, and the Promise of a Postethnic Future." *Callaloo* 31, no. 4: 1033–1037.
———. (2011) "The Concept of Post-Racial: How Its Easy Dismissal Obscures Important Questions," *Daedalus* 140: 174–182.
Ifill, Gwen. (2009) *The Breakthrough: Politics and Race in the Age of Obama*, New York: Doubleday.
Jameson, Frederick. (1991) *Postmodernism, or, the Cultural Logic of Late Capitalism*, Durham: Duke University Press.
Jones, Nicholas A., and Bullock, Jungmiwha. (2012) "The Two or More Races Population: 2010 Census Briefs." U.S. Department of Commerce Economics and Statistics Administration and U.S. Census Bureau, C2010BR-13. Washington, DC.
King, Desmond S., and Smith, Rogers M. (2011) *Still a House Divided: Race and Politics in Obama's America*, Princeton: Princeton University Press.
Kochhar, Rakesh, Fry, Richard, and Taylor, Paul. (2011) "Wealth Gaps Rise to Record Highs Between Whites, Blacks and Hispanics." *Pew Social & Demographic Trends*. Last Modified on July 26. www.pewsocialtrends.org/2011/07/26/wealth-gaps-rise-to-record-highs-between-whites-blacks-hispanics/.
Lind, Michael. (1996) *The Next American Nation: The New Nationalism and the Fourth American Revolution*, New York: Free Press Paperbacks.
Lofquist, Daphne, Lugaila, Terry, O'Connell, Martin, and Feliz, Sarah. (2012) "Households and Families 2010 Census Briefs." U.S. Department of Commerce Economics and Statistics Administration and U.S. Census Bureau, C2010BR-14. Washington, DC.
McGary, Howard. (2012) *The Post-Racial Ideal*, Aquinas Lecture, Vol. 76, Milwaukee: Marquette University Press.
———. (2008) *The Browning of America and the Evasion of Social Justice*, Albany: State University of New York Press.

McKernan, Signe-Mary, Ratcliffe, Caroline, Steuerle, Eugene, and Zhang, Sisi. (2013) "Less Than Equal: Racial Disparities in Wealth Accumulation." Urban Institute. Last Modified April 26. www.urban.org/research/publication/less-equal-racial-disparities-wealth-accumulation.

Michaels, Walter Benn. (2006) *The Trouble With Diversity: How We Learned to Love Identity and Ignore Inequality*, New York: Metropolitan Books.

Mill, John Stuart. (1977) *On Liberty: Collected Works of John Stuart Mill*, ed. John M. Robson, Vol. 28, Toronto: University of Toronto Press.

Mills, Charles W. (1997) *The Racial Contract*, Ithaca: Cornell University Press.

———. (2007) "White Ignorance," in *Race and Epistemologies of Ignorance*, eds. Shannon Sullivan and Nancy Tuana, Albany: State University of New York Press, pp. 13–38.

Nietzsche, Friedrich Wilhelm. (1980) *On the Advantage and Disadvantage of History for Life*, Indianapolis: Hackett.

Obama, Barack H. (2015) Interview with Mark Maron, *WTF*, podcast audio, June 22, http://potus.wtfpod.com/podcast/episodes/episode_613_-_president_barack_obama/.

Parker, Ashley. (2015) "Returning Home to Console, Lindsey Graham Joins the Mourning," *New York Times*, June 19. www.nytimes.com/2015/06/20/us/politics/returning-home-to-console-lindsey-graham-joins-the-mourning.html?ref=topics.

Pateman, Carole. (1988) *The Sexual Contract*, Cambridge: Polity.

Pateman, Carole, and Charles W. Mills. (2007) *Contract and Domination*, Malden, MA: Polity.

Pew Research Center. 2015. "Multiracial in America: Proud, Diverse and Growing in Numbers." Washington, DC: 1–153. Last Modified June 11. www.pewsocialtrends.org/2015/06/11/multiracial-in-america/.

powell, john a. (2004) "Symposium: The Needs of Members in a Legitimate Democratic State." *Santa Clara Law Review* 44: 969–997.

Shapiro, Thomas, Tatjana Meschede, and Sam Osoro. (2013) "The Roots of the Widening Racial Wealth Gap: Explaining the Black-White Economic Divide." Institute on Assets and Social Policy, Research and Policy Brief. Last modified February 2013. http://iasp.brandeis.edu/pdfs/Author/shapiro-thomas-m/racialwealthgapbrief.pdf.

Steinberg, Stephen. (1995) *Turning Back: The Retreat From Racial Justice in American Thought and Policy*, Boston: Beacon Press.

Sundstrom, Ronald R. (2008) *The Browning of America and the Evasion of Social Justice*, Albany: State University of New York Press.

———. (Forthcoming). *The People's Republic: Equality, Integration, & the City*.

Taylor, Paul. (2014) *The Next America: Boomers, Millennials, and the Looming Generational Showdown*, New York: PublicAffairs.

Taylor, Paul, Wendy Wang, Kim Parker, Jeffrey S. Passel, Eileen Patten, Research Assistant and Seth Motel. (2012) "The Rise of Intermarriage Rates, Characteristics Vary by Race and Gender." *Pew Research Center*. Last modified February 16. www.pewsocialtrends.org/2012/02/16/the-rise-of-intermarriage/.

Taylor, Paul C. (2014) "Taking Postracialism Seriously: From Movement Mythology to Racial Formation." *Du Bois Review: Social Science Research on Race* 11, no. 1: 9–25.

Tenbrunsel, Ann E., and David M. Messick. (2004) "Ethical Fading: The Role of Self-Deception in Unethical Behavior." *Social Justice Research* 17, no. 2: 223–236.

Wohl, Michael J. A., Nyla R. Branscombe and Yechiel Klar. (2006) "Collective Guilt: Emotional Reactions When One's Group Has Done Wrong or Been Wronged." *European Review of Social Psychology* 17, no. 1: 1–37.

35
PHILOSOPHY OF RACE AND THE ETHICS OF IMMIGRATION
José Jorge Mendoza

Introduction

In recent years, moral and political philosophers have shown a growing interest in the ethics of immigration. This interest has produced a substantial literature that looks at whether a state's right to control immigration can be outweighed by any moral obligations it might have to open its borders. Yet, despite the fact that many of today's liberal democratic states have at some point employed race-based immigration restrictions and currently employ what some consider racist immigration enforcement practices, this literature has only superficially dealt with issues of race and racism.

Philosophers who specialize in issues of race and racism have also demonstrated a growing interest in immigration. These philosophers, however, have been more concerned with showing how race-neutral immigration policies can nonetheless generate discriminatory outcomes. In doing so they have developed a variety of interesting and competing strategies for how to think about and condemn this kind of discrimination. Yet, despite all the work that's been done on immigration from a philosophy of race perspective, its implications for an ethics of immigration have largely been underdeveloped.

This chapter is therefore an attempt to do two things. First, provide a general overview of the philosophical literature on immigration from both an ethics of immigration and philosophy of race perspective. Second, make a case that putting these two literatures into conversation would be fruitful. In particular, that it could provide an underappreciated argument for limiting the discretion states are normally thought to enjoy with respect to immigration.

Discrimination and the Ethics of Immigration

The literature on the ethics of immigration can largely be broken down into two camps: those that favor a state's presumptive right to exclude immigrants (Walzer 1983; Miller 2005, 2008) and those who oppose this right by appealing to principles of universal equality and/or individual freedom (Cole 2000; Carens 2013). This section will primarily focus on the former—those who support a state's presumptive right to control immigration—because this position has had the hardest time in dealing with racism in immigration policy. This is not to say that there are not some who believe that the open borders position also suffers from a similar difficulty—that opening borders might exacerbate inequalities among racial groups (Higgins 2013)—but such a view seems to misunderstand how immigration policy can be the source of racism (Mendoza 2015b). A state's immigration policy is the source of racism to the degree that it uses race to deny persons entry, favors them for admission at the expense of others, or uses it to determine when, where, how, and to what degree immigration laws get enforced. A world with open borders (i.e., a world where everyone has the *right* and not merely a *privilege* to be present) might not be a world without racism, but it would be a world where immigration policy is not one of its sources.

If we limit our discussion to proponents of a state's presumptive right to control immigration, then the place to start is with the second chapter of Michael Walzer's *Spheres of Justice*. In that chapter, Walzer provides a compelling argument that: "Across a considerable range of the decisions that are made, states are simply free to take in strangers (or not). . . . Admission and exclusion are at the core of communal independence" (Walzer 1983: 61). In other words, a state's ability to control its borders (e.g., immigration) is essential to its claim to be self-determined. Assuming that states have a right to be self-determined, it naturally follows that they ought to have the right to control immigration.

Walzer is clear that this right is only presumptive, meaning that it can be defeated in extreme cases such as when "needy outsiders whose claims [in justice] cannot be met by yielding territory or exporting wealth [and] can be met only by taking [them] in" (Walzer 1983: 48). Walzer is also clear, however, that his account does not morally or politically prohibited states from adopting discriminatory (e.g., racist or sexist) immigration policies. Walzer recognizes this difficulty and even concedes that on his account some modified version of the notorious "White Australia Policy"—a 70-year policy that favored northern European immigrants while discouraging or preventing the immigration of non-whites into Australia—would be permissible (Walzer 1983: 46–47).

In the United States, a similar justification was used to defend some of the country's most disconcerting immigration polices. For example, when the Supreme Court upheld the constitutionality of the Chinese Exclusion Act, it did so by stating that:

> the United States, through the action of the legislative department, can exclude [non-citizens] from its territory is a proposition which we do not think open to controversy. Jurisdiction over its own territory to that extent is an incident of every independent nation. It is a part of its independence. If it could not exclude [non-citizens] it would be to that extent subject to the control of another power.
>
> (*Chae Chan Ping v. United States*)

In this case, the Supreme Court justified a racist immigration policy through a line of reasoning that mirrors Walzer's: independent states have a right to exclude non-citizens and it is morally and politically irrelevant (so long as the non-citizens in question are not refugees) on what grounds, including racist grounds, they base their criteria for exclusion.

Most philosophers, even those who are sympathetic to the idea that states have a presumptive right to control immigration, are uncomfortable with this implication in

Walzer's account. Yet coming up with a way to avoid it while also consistently defending a state's right to exclude non-citizens has proven difficult. David Miller, for example, has tried to temper his own nationalist position by proposing that characteristics such as race, ethnicity, sex, and gender should not be used as criteria for exclusion because "[for immigrants to] be told that they belong to the wrong race, or sex (or have hair of the wrong color) is insulting, given that these features do not connect to anything of real significance to the society they want to join" (Miller 2005: 204).

While this is a laudable attempt to resolve the problem, many people have found it unsatisfying. For example, Christopher Heath Wellman has responded to Miller by stating:

> as much as I abhor racism, I believe that racist individuals cannot permissibly be forced to marry someone outside of their race . . . [therefore] why does [a state's presumptive right to control immigration] not similarly entitle racist citizens to exclude immigrants based upon race.
> (Wellman 2008: 138)

In other words, if a state has a right to exclude potential immigrants, why should it matter that non-citizens are insulted by the criteria a state chooses to use? We do not, for example, think that a person has a duty to marry someone simply because declining their marriage proposal would be insulting.

In response to this, Michael Blake has presented an interesting and original alternative. Blake argues that "In all cases in which there are national or ethnic minorities . . . to restrict immigration for national or ethnic reasons is to make some citizens politically inferior to others" (Blake 2003: 232–233). In other words, discriminatory immigration policies should be rejected not because they are insulting to non-citizens, but because discriminatory policies can undermine the social and civic standing of citizens who happen to share the race, ethnicity, religion, sex, or gender that is being excluded (i.e., it is a violation of political equality).

Philosophers who endorse a state's presumptive right to control immigration, such as Wellman, have now come to adopt some version of Blake's argument. Wellman, for example, writes that: "whether or not we are sympathetic to the idea of a state designed especially to serve a specific racial, ethnic, or religious constituency, such a state is not exempt from the requirement to treat all its subjects as equal citizens" (Wellman 2008: 141). And even Walzer would seem amenable to this idea, as he has stated that "no community can be half-metic, half-citizen and claim that its admissions policies are acts of self-determination or that its politics is democratic" (Walzer 1983: 62). Philosophers who support a state's presumptive right to control immigration therefore believe they have found an agreeable solution to their problem with discriminatory immigration policies. So long as the criteria for admissions and exclusions are neutral with regard to such factors as race, ethnicity, religion, sex, and gender, a state can maintain its discretionary control over immigration without generating discriminatory outcomes.

This is not an unreasonable conclusion, but if critical race theory has taught us anything it's that laws that might appear neutral on the surface can nonetheless generate racist outcomes (Delgado and Stefancic 2012). The easiest and least controversial example are the laws that undergirded Jim Crow segregation. On the surface, these laws claimed to respect the equality of citizens, yet in their implementation they degraded the civic standing of a particular racial group (i.e., African Americans) to a point where members of that racial group could no longer be considered equal citizens. This insight from critical race theory presents a potential difficulty for proponents of a state's right to control immigration: what reason do we have for believing that something analogous will not take place with respect to immigration policy? A state's immigration policy might appear neutral on the surface, thereby satisfying Blake's constraints, but in its implementation it might nonetheless generate discriminatory outcomes.

In this regard, the history of US immigration policy is again insightful. As already mentioned, the United States once had an explicitly racist immigration policy that it justified on grounds of self-determination. This policy, however, came to an end in 1965 when the United States repealed the racist elements of its prior policy and instead adopted a race-neutral immigration policy. This was done not because the prior racist policy was insulting to foreigners, but because it negatively impacted the civic standing of citizens of non-northern European ancestry (Roediger 2006). In short, the history of US immigration policy closely follows the trajectory in the ethics of immigration that took us from of Walzer to Blake.

Therefore, if neutrality were enough to preclude an immigration policy from having discriminatory outcomes, this should have been borne out in post-1965 US society. Instead, the implementation of a neutral immigration policy had the effect of eroding the civic standing of Latino/as and Middle Eastern Americans. For example, after 1965 immigration enforcement agents began to use "Mexican appearance" as a basis for stopping and interrogating persons over their immigration status. This practice was so endemic that by the mid-1970s it was challenged twice in the Supreme Court. In both cases, however, the court ruled that "Mexican appearance" was not necessarily a racial demarcation and that its use was justifiable given the sudden increase in undocumented immigrants from Mexico (*United States v. Brignoni-Ponce; United States v. Martinez-Fuerte*).

More recently, the United States has adopted an internal enforcement strategy known as "attrition through enforcement." This strategy aims to reduce the number of undocumented immigrants living in the United States by employing harsh domestic policies that makes life so difficult for undocumented immigrants that they begin to "self-deport" (Vaughan 2006). Following this strategy, various laws have been passed at both the state (Schuck 1995; State of Arizona Senate) and national level (1996 Illegal Immigration Reform & Immigrant Responsibility Act; 1996 Personal Responsibility and Work Opportunity Reconciliation Act) that deny undocumented immigrants access to social services, driver's licenses, and in-state college tuition, while at the same time deputizing local police to perform immigration enforcement duties and compelling employers to use various verification methods to insure the legal status of their employees.

Stopping and interrogating people based on a "Mexican appearance" and deploying strategies such as "attrition through enforcement" might make the implementation of US immigration policy better and more efficient, but it has the consequence of disproportionally affecting the civic standing of Latino/a citizens. More than any other segment of the citizenry, Latino/a citizens have been ensnared or have had their lives made difficult by this kind of enforcement (Lovato 2008; Sánchez 2011; Mendoza 2014). In this respect, the implementation of immigration policy fails to give Latino/a citizens equal consideration, even though the policy is on its face neutral.

Another community that has been disproportionally affected by recent US immigration policies has been the Middle Eastern and South Asian American community. Shortly after the 9/11 attacks on the World Trade Center, US immigration policy underwent a drastic change. Seeing as all 19 terrorist hijackers were (a) foreign nationals who had entered the United States legally and (b) were connected to a radical Islamic terrorist group (i.e., al-Qaeda), the US government made immigration enforcement a central component of its revamped national security strategy. Under the auspices of national security, the United States passed various measures aimed at helping agents identify immigrants who might be linked with or sympathetic to radical Islamic terrorist groups. The result is that citizens of Middle Eastern or South Asian descent—or of the Islamic faith in general—have been disproportionately targeted by these changes (e.g., increased warrantless surveillance and stricter requirements for reentry), even though these changes in law are technically supposed to be non-racist (Kayyali 2006).

Philosophers working on the ethics of immigration have had little to say about this kind of discrimination. In part this has been because the discrimination described has more to do with the enforcement of immigration policy than with the actual criteria used for determining admissions and exclusions. In other words, they believe that simply showing that a state fails to enforce its immigration policy in a fair or just manner tells us nothing about whether a state does or does not have the right to control immigration (Mendoza 2015a). Still, the kind of discrimination that arises from the implementation of neutral immigration policies should not be ignored. In this respect, philosophers of race have done a tremendous job. I therefore turn to this literature in the following section with the aim of accomplishing two things. First, to outline the debate over immigration that has taken place within this literature. Second, to suggest that it offers an insight that philosophers working on the ethics of immigration have overlooked; that immigration justice should have some connection to enforcement, and that in making this connection we will find an underappreciated basis for circumventing the discretion states are normally thought to enjoy over immigration.

Immigration and the Philosophy of Race

While moral and political philosophers have come to the issue of immigration in an attempt to resolve the tension between liberal principles and democratic self-determination (Benhabib 2004), philosophers of race have come to this issue in an attempt to account for the kind of discrimination that particular groups, such as Latino/as and Middle Eastern and South Asian Americans, have encountered in so-called post-racial societies (Taylor 2013: 181–204). This section provides an overview of the latter, arguing that philosophers of race have typically employed one of two competing strategies in accounting for this kind of "post-racial" discrimination. One strategy has been to expand or redefine our shared conception of race so that this discrimination can be classified as a kind of racism. The second strategy has been to classify this discrimination as something other than racism (e.g., xenophobia) and argue that condemnations of it should be on par with condemnations of racism. This section concludes by suggesting that, despite their apparent differences, philosophers of race have located a source of this discrimination in the discretionary enforcement states are allowed to have over immigration. Thereby suggesting that the enforcement of immigration policy should matter to an ethics of immigration and that philosophy of race offers some unexplored reasons as to why the discretion states have over immigration should be circumvented.

It seems fair to say that Latino/as and Middle Eastern and South Asian Americans suffer from a particular form of discrimination in the United States. The question, however, is whether this discrimination counts as a form of racism. The answer to this question depends heavily on how one answers a prior question: do Latino/as and Middle Eastern and South Asian Americans count as racial groups in the proper sense of the term "race"? Some might argue that Latino/as and Middle Eastern and South Asian Americans clearly constitute ethnic groups, but it's not clear that they therefore constitute racial groups. Ethnic groups and racial groups, after all, are not necessarily the same. This is clear from the fact that people can belong to different racial groups (e.g., White, Black, Native American, or Asian), while nonetheless belonging to the same ethnic group (e.g., Latino/as). If this is the case, then it seems like a mistake to condemn the kind of discrimination faced by Latino/as and Middle Eastern and South Asian Americans as racist. But if it's not condemnable as racism, then is this kind of discrimination weighty enough to override a state's right to control immigration?

One way to answer this concern is to say that this discrimination is a form of racism. In order to do that, however, there needs to be some kind of account that can explain why or how our shared conception of race should be expanded or redefined so as to include groups such as Latino/as and Middle Eastern and South Asian Americans. In *Towards a Political Philosophy of Race*, Falguni Sheth provides such an account. According to Sheth, it is inaccurate to think of race in strictly biological, cultural, or even socially constructed terms. On her account, races are made up of those segments of the polity whose beliefs, values, and behaviors are perceived as a threat to the authority of the sovereign, what she terms the "unruly," and who are at the same time vulnerable to sovereign power.

By defining race in this broad way—as a perceived threat to sovereignty that is nonetheless vulnerable to it—Sheth is suggesting we expand our shared conception of race. Our current conception of race, she argues, is only the product of a more complicated process, and by failing to pay attention to this process we have missed what is really essential to racial formation (Sheth 2009). The larger argument that Sheth is concerned with making is that racism is inherent to all liberal political projects. Whether Sheth is correct about this or not is irrelevant for our purpose. What is important is her claim that we should expand our notion of race in order to better and more accurately capture the wrong that transpires when a state uses its discretionary power to coercively enforce immigration policy.

The payoff in adopting an account like Sheth's is clear; it lets us condemn the current treatment of Latino/a and Middle Eastern and South Asian Americans as kind of racism. It also hints at a possible solution to this treatment by suggesting that if the combination of misrecognition (e.g., viewing Middle Eastern and South Asian Americans as "unruly") with the unchecked coercive use of state power (e.g., making Middle Eastern and South Asian Americans vulnerable through the discretionary enforcement of immigration laws) are the source of this racism, then we should find ways to check these powers and be suspicious of any attempt to regard vulnerable groups as threats to national security.

A problem for such an account, however, is that there are many exceptions to it. For example, during a period that is now commonly referred to as the Quasi-war with France, President John Adams signed into law a set of bills that have collectively come to be known as the Alien and Sedition Acts. These bills were aimed at rooting out the "Jacobin threat," which French immigrants were believed to pose. Among other things, these Acts allowed the president to imprison or deport any non-citizen who was considered "dangerous" or a citizen of a hostile nation and made any speech critical of the US government into a punishable offense. Even though these Acts were supposed to target a people of a particular nationally, their real aim was to enhance the powers of the federal government at the expanse of basic liberties. As Thomas Jefferson astutely pointed out at the time: "the friendless alien has indeed been selected as the safest subject of a first experiment: but the citizen will soon follow, or rather has already followed; for, already has a Sedition Act marked him as its prey" (Jefferson 2015: 553–554).

Similarly, at the turn of the twentieth century various immigration laws were passed that banned or called for the deportation of communists and anarchists. In part these laws received a lot of public support because an anarchist had been responsible for assassinating President William McKinley in 1901. These laws were challenged in the courts, but ultimately the Supreme Court justified them and even allowed for the indefinite detention of communist or anarchist immigrants because these were matters of immigration (where the federal government is believed to have complete discretionary control) and because these immigrants posed a threat to national security (*United States ex rel. Turner v. Williams*).

These two scenarios, the French "Jacobins" and the communist/anarchists, present a problem for Sheth's account. They are both examples of how sovereign power is consolidated by scapegoating a particular vulnerable segment of the population, which is made to appear as a threat to national security. In other words, they both fit her definition of a vulnerable and *unruly* segment of the polity. Therefore, if Sheth's account were correct, French "Jacobins" and communist/anarchists would not just count as national or ideological groups, but should also be considered racial groups. Such a conclusion, however, seems bizarre and it's unclear whether or not Sheth would endorse it given that these are not examples she chooses to focus on.

When faced with this objection there are two ways to proceed; either double down on the project of expanding/redefining the notion of race or abandon this approach and look for another way to condemn this kind of discrimination. In *Biopolitics of Race*, Sokthan Yeng takes the doubling-down approach. Yeng, like Sheth, adopts a Foucauldian notion of "state racism." The notable difference between the two accounts, however, is that Yeng's conception of race is explicitly much broader. For Yeng a social group becomes a "race" when the group is deemed unhealthy and therefore a threat to the life of the nation. On this account, states no longer need to deploy explicitly racist policies to get the kind of immigration they want. Instead states employ a kind of racism where immigrants are excluded or deported on grounds that they are a threat to the nation's life. This allows states to continue excluding or placing more enforcement on groups they find socially undesirable while at the same time avoiding the charge of racism.

On this account, Latino/as constitute a race because they are seen as a drain on public resources—in particular on healthcare services—and therefore a threat to the welfare of the nation. Similarly, people of Middle Eastern and South Asian descent constitute a race because Islam (i.e., the religion they are most closely identified with) is considered a threat to Western civilization and in particular the United States. Increased restrictions and enforcement on these groups is therefore not condemned as racist because they are said to be pursuant of worthwhile and racially neutral objectives.

The advantage of adopting an account like Yeng's is similar to adopting Sheth's; it explains why the discrimination faced by Latino/as and Middle Eastern and South Asian Americans is racist even though it results from the implementation of race-neutral immigration policies. Yeng's account, however, has the added advantage of being able to avoid the objection leveled against Sheth—of avoiding similarly situated social groups (e.g., Jacobins and communist/anarchists) from counting as races. Yeng avoids this difficulty by embracing it. For her, these and other similarly situated groups should be considered races, in that

> classifications of race are expanding because state racism emphasizes the need to reject or problematize any group, which threatens the health of the nation . . . This line of thinking allows disparate individuals to be organized into races through a wide variety of identifying markers such as their religious affiliation, sexual orientation, or gender.
>
> (Yeng 2013: 10)

In short, not only is there no problem on her account with Jacobins, communists, and anarchists constituting races, but any group that is perceived as a threat to the health of the nation can come to constitute a race.

There are two obvious problems with such an account. The first is the pragmatic concern that expanding the concept of race might not so much help to legitimate other less recognized forms of discrimination as much as it might take away from the seriousness of racism. Second, while the difference between racism and ethnic discrimination can at times be almost negligible, it seems like a stretch to say that there is no fundamental difference between racism, sexism, or homophobia. In fact, even the work on intersectionality, which tries to bring these different forms of oppression and discrimination together, rests on the assumption that there is some notable difference between them.

If these concerns outweigh the benefits that expanding/redefining race and racism might have to offer, then an alternative approach could be to put less emphasis on trying to make this kind of discrimination fit traditional models of racism and instead highlight its uniqueness while nonetheless arguing that it should be as condemnable as racism. In a series of articles, Ron Sundstrom and David Kim have exemplified this alternative strategy. They have argued that the discrimination suffered by Latino/as and Middle Eastern Americans is best understood as xenophobia. According to them, xenophobia is a form of "civic ostracism" which can be described as:

> a subjective belief or affect, usually from the perspective of an individual who is in their imagination, fully rooted in the nation, that some other person or group cannot be a part of that nation. These strangers cannot be authentic participants of the cultural, linguistic, or religious traditions of the nation they inhabit; they do not derive from soil of the nation's land or the blood of its people.
>
> (Sundstrom 2013: 71)

Because xenophobic projects are distinct from racist projects, and in fact are sometimes celebrated as a common national cause that brings different racial groups together, these projects are not always seen as objectionable. According to Sundstrom and Kim, this is how the implementation of race-neutral immigration policies nonetheless generates discriminatory outcomes for Latino/as and Middle Eastern and South Asian Americans.

Sundstrom and Kim defend their position by first raising two objections to the earlier strategy of expanding/redefining the concept of race. First, they worry that expanding/redefining race would lead to a homogenized (i.e., monistic) conception of racism. According to Sundstrom and Kim, a homogenized conception of racism is problematic in that combating racism requires an understanding of its particular context (i.e., where and how it is situated). For example, combating racism in the United States would require understanding the history of slavery and how race has been mostly defined through a black/white binary, while combating racism in a place like Mexico would require understanding the history of Spanish colonialism and the triangulated relationship between Europeans, Native Americans, and Africans. Monistic conceptions of racism, on the other hand, try to simplify and over-generalize these complicated forms of racism and in so doing overlook the fine-grained differences that distinguish particular forms of racism. For this reason, Sundstrom and Kim instead advocate for what they call a pluralistic account of racism.

Sundstrom and Kim's second objection to the earlier strategy is that a homogenized account of racism tends to subsume and obscure important concepts such as xenophobia and nativism. So even though some expansive notions of racism, such as Sheth's and Yeng's, might claim to account for the harms and injustices usually associated with xenophobia and nativism, Sundstrom and Kim believe that these expansive notions actually help to "shelter" rather than combat these forms of discrimination. So even though racism and xenophobia might at times overlap and historically have tended to come together, for Sundstrom and Kim there are important differences between these two concepts.

> Civic outsiders are not necessarily racial outsiders. Although most racial outsiders were deemed ipso facto to be civic outsiders, this convergence does not hold up. In the United States, for example, Native Americans and African Americans were explicitly not included in the nation. Over time, however, those groups, among others, were granted, under paternalistic and dominating conditions, a degree of civic insider status. This insider status was, of course, limited, exploitative, and degrading ... We do not mean to make too much of this civic insider status, but to be inside is not to be outside.
> (Sundstrom and Kim 2014: 34)

Understanding this difference, Sundstrom and Kim believe, allows us to see why people of color, who otherwise are conscious of the racism within their society, are nonetheless susceptible to nativist rhetoric.

The two strategies outlined so far have been presented as diametrically opposed. This was done in order to accentuate their differences and also highlight what is at stake in choosing to classify a particular kind of discrimination as either racial or xenophobic. This is not to say, however, that there are not various positions that fall somewhere in between. For example, Grant J. Silva and George N. Fourlas have each staked out interesting positions that straddle these two strategies. Both of them share the worries expressed by Sundstrom and Kim—that expanding the concept of race in ways that theorists such as Sheth and Yeng suggest might dilute (rather than improve) our understanding of racism—but they also worry that the concept of xenophobia is not rich enough to capture the kind of discrimination suffered by Latino/as and Middle Eastern and South Asian Americans.

While their accounts differ in emphasis, Silva and Fourlas are both in agreement—drawing from the work of Frantz Fanon and Edward Said, respectively—that modern racism finds its roots in Western colonialism and orientalism. They also note that Western colonialism and orientalism has largely shaped the patterns and official policies of migration in most (if not all) Western countries. Therefore, they conclude (*pace* Sundstrom and Kim) that racism or at least some version of white supremacy undergirds the "perpetual foreigner" experience that Latino/as and Middle Eastern and South Asian Americans are forced to undergo in places like the United States (Fourlas 2015; Silva 2015).

As for my own sympathies, they are much closer to Sundstrom and Kim's position (Mendoza 2010, 2014), but by no means do I think they are the final word. In fact, the purpose of this overview has been not so much to settle the issue once and for all, but to show how despite apparent differences there are some fundamental points of agreement. First and foremost, there is a near consensus that certain communities (regardless of whether we want to think of them in racial, ethnic, or national terms) are disproportionately targeted by the surveying, interrogation, apprehension, and detainment that goes along with the enforcement of a state's immigration policy, even when that policy is supposed to be neutral. Second, that when this happens citizens who belong to these communities are not only not receiving equal treatment by the state, but also come to be socially and civically ostracized. While these points of agreement might not seem like much, when brought to bear on an ethics of immigration they raise an underappreciated difficulty for proponents of a state's right to control immigration. These points suggest that the enforcement of immigration policy does make a difference in determining how much discretion a state should have in matters of immigration and that the discretion it has should be minimal.

This conclusion is derived from the following argument. If immigration enforcement can generate the same kind of deleterious effects on the status of citizens as discriminatory admissions and exclusions criteria, then it stands to reason that supporters of a state's presumptive right to control immigration should have something to say about this potentially adverse consequence. The most obvious way to account for it would be to expand Blake's argument into matters of enforcement. If we recall, Blake's argument precluded the use of discriminatory criteria for the sake of political equality, but so long as this was the case a state could maintain discretionary control over immigration. Given the parallel between the two potential harms, why would Blake's argument not lead to a similar outcome with respect to immigration enforcement?

The reason it will not have a similar outcome is that enforcement is far less malleable than admissions and exclusions criteria. What made Blake's original argument so attractive was that it never compromised a state's discretionary right to disassociate itself from non-citizens. This, however, is not possible with respect to immigration enforcement. Enforcing immigration policy requires that a state disaggregate non-citizens (specifically undocumented immigrants) from citizens in a society where they are deeply intertwined.

What philosophers of race have shown us—in various and at times conflicting ways—is that disentangling these two groups can lead to certain communities of citizens (e.g.,

Latino/as and Middle Eastern and South Asian Americans) not having their rights as citizens properly respected. In an effort to avoid this outcome, legitimate states need to make sure that immigration enforcement meets at least two standards. First, enforcement should not single out any particular community, but make sure the burdens of enforcement are shared equally among all citizens. Second, because some intrusions by the state are in themselves excessive, even if they are shared by all citizens (e.g., warrantless surveillance, random interrogations into one's legal status and indefinite detention), certain protections need to be in place to shield citizens from these potential excesses.

In short, if something like Blake's argument is applied to immigration enforcement, it seems that something like these two standards (e.g., equality of burdens and universal protections) would be implied. This might not present much of a problem for Blake, as he believes that a state's right to control immigration can at times be outweighed by other considerations (Blake 2012), but it does pose a problem for those who don't. These two standards form a canopy that not only protects the equal rights of citizens, but also protects non-citizens (including undocumented immigrants) from a state's enforcement apparatus. In short, one of the consequences of a state respecting the political equality of citizens in matters of enforcement is that its control over immigration becomes less discretionary and more circumscribed (Mendoza 2014: 76–79).

Conclusion

To be clear, the position I advance in this chapter is not that philosophers who defend a state's presumptive right to control immigration are somehow racist or xenophobic. This chapter is meant to be an invitation to moral and political philosophers who are concerned with the issue of immigration to engage with more of the work being done in philosophy of race. It is also meant as an invitation to philosophers of race to apply their insights into the nature of discrimination toward an ethics of immigration and see what implications this might have. The route I have suggested for doing something like this is to argue that regardless of whether one wants to call it racism, xenophobia, or something else, the potential for discrimination that arises from immigration enforcement is weighty enough that an ethics of immigration should take it into account and that it justifies circumventing the discretion states are normally thought to enjoy with regard to immigration.

Further Readings

Bonilla-Silva, E. (2014) *Racism Without Racists: Color-Blind Racism and the Persistence of Racial Inequality in America*, Lanham: Rowman & Littlefield. This book provides an account of "color-blind racism" in the contemporary United States and argues that the conventional bi-racial structure of the United States is being replaced with a tri-racial structure. In this tri-racial structure, certain immigrant groups will be given "honorary white" status and in this capacity serve as a third racial group that buffers whites from blacks.

Chavez, L. (2008) *The Latino Threat: Constructing Immigrants, Citizens, and the Nation*, Stanford: Stanford University Press. This book carefully examines the public discourse and media portrayals of Latino/as in an effort to show why and how they have come to be seen as a threat to the nation.

Gracia, J. ed. (2007) *Race or Ethnicity? On Black and Latino Identity*, Ithaca: Cornell University Press. This book offers a collection of philosophical essays that debate the difference (if any) between race and ethnicity.

Jamal, A. and Nadine, N. eds (2008) *Race and Arab Americans Before and After 9/11: From Invisible Citizens to Visible Subjects*, Syracuse: Syracuse University Press. This book offers a collection of essays that try to account for how the Arab American community in the United States, which has historically been regarded as racially white, has come to be regarded as racially non-white.

López, I. (1997) *White by Law: The Legal Construction of Race*, New York: New York University Press. This book provides an excellent account of how "whiteness" in the United States was constructed through various court cases, especially those dealing with immigration law.

Ortega, M. and Alcoff, L. eds. (2009) *Constructing the Nation: A Race and Nationalism Reader*, Albany: State University of New York Press. This book offers a collection of essays that explore the connection between race and nationality, specifically in the United States after 9/11.

References

1996 Illegal Immigration Reform & Immigrant Responsibility Act, H.R. 3610; Pub.L. 104–208; 110 Stat. 3009–3546. 104th Cong. (September 30, 1996).

1996 Personal Responsibility and Work Opportunity Reconciliation Act, H.R. 2260; Pub.L. 104–193; 110 Stat. 2105. 104th Cong. (August 22, 1996).

Benhabib, S. (2004) *The Rights of Others: Aliens, Residents, and Citizens*, Cambridge: Cambridge University Press.

Blake, M. (2003) "Immigration," in R.G. Frey and Christopher Heath Wellman (eds.), *A Companion to Applied Ethics*, Oxford: Blackwell, pp. 224–237.

———. (2012) "Immigration, Association, and Antidiscrimination." *Ethics* 122, no. 4: 748–762.

Carens, J. (2013) *The Ethics of Immigration*, New York: Oxford University Press.

Chae Chan Ping v. United States, 130 US 581 (1889).

Cole, P. (2000) *Philosophies of Exclusion: Liberal Political Theory and Immigration*, Edinburgh: Edinburgh University Press.

Delgado, R., and Stefancic, J. (2012) *Critical Race Theory: An Introduction*, 2nd edition, New York: New York University Press.

Fourlas, G. (2015) "Being A Target: On the Racialization of Middle Eastern Americans," *Critical Philosophy of Race* 3, no. 1, pp. 101–123.

Higgins, P. (2013) *Immigration Justice*, Edinburgh: Edinburgh University Press.

Jefferson, T. (2015) "Resolutions Adopted by the Kentucky General Assembly," in Barbara B. Oberg and J. Jefferson Looney (eds.), *The Papers of Thomas Jefferson Digital Edition*, Charlottesville: University of Virginia Press.

Kayyali, R. (2006) "The People Perceived as a Threat to Security: Arab Americans Since September 11," *Migration Policy Institute*, July 1. Accessed May 21, 2015. www.migrationpolicy.org/article/people-perceived-threat-security-arab-americans-september-11.

Lovato, R. (2008) "Juan Crow in Georgia," *Nation*, May 26. Accessed December 21, 2014. www.thenation.com/article/juan-crow-georgia.

Mendoza, J. (2010) "A 'Nation' of Immigrants." *Pluralist* 5, no. 3: 41–48.

———. (2014) "Discrimination and the Presumptive Rights of Immigrants." *Critical Philosophy of Race* 2, no. 1, 68–83.

———. (2015a) "Enforcement Matters: Reframing the Philosophical Debate Over Immigration," *Journal of Speculative Philosophy* 29, no. 1: 73–90.

———. (2015b) "Does Cosmopolitan Justice Ever Require Restrictions on Migration?" *Public Affairs Quarterly* 29, no. 2: 175–186.

Miller, D. (2005) "Immigration: The Case for Limits," in Andrew I. Cohen and Christopher Heath Wellman (eds.), *Contemporary Debates in Applied Ethics*, Malden, MA: Blackwell, pp. 193–206.

———. (2008) "Immigrants, Nations, and Citizenship," *Journal of Political Philosophy* 16, no. 4: 371–390.

Roediger, D. (2006) *Working Towards Whiteness: How America's Immigrants Become White*, New York: Basic Books.

Sánchez, C. (2011) "On Documents and Subjectivity The Formation and De-Formation of the Immigrant Identity." *Radical Philosophy Review* 14, no. 2: 197–205.
Schuck, H. (1995) "The Message of Proposition 187." *Pacific Law Journal* 26: 989–1000.
Sheth, F. (2009) *Toward a Political Philosophy of Race*, Albany: State University of New York Press.
Silva, G. (2015) "Embodying a 'New' Color Line: Racism, Anti-Immigrant Sentiment and Racial Identities in the 'Postracial' Era." *Knowledge Cultures* 3, no. 1: 65–90.
State of Arizona Senate, Forty-Ninth Legislature, Second Regular Session 2010, *Senate Bill 1070*.
Sundstrom, R. (2013) "Sheltering Xenophobia." *Critical Philosophy of Race* 1, no. 1: 68–85.
Sundstrom, R., and Kim, D. (2014) "Xenophobia and Racism." *Critical Philosophy of Race* 2, no. 1: 20–45.
Taylor, P. (2013) *Race: A Philosophical Introduction*, 2nd edition, Malden, MA: Polity Press.
United States v. Brignoni-Ponce, 422 US 873 (1975).
United States v. Martinez-Fuerte, 428 US 543 (1976).
United States ex rel. Turner v. Williams, 194 US 279 (1904).
Vaughan, J. (2006) "Attrition Through Enforcement: A Cost-Effective Strategy to Shrink the Illegal Population." *Center for Immigration Studies*, www.cis.org/Enforcement-IllegalPopulation.
Walzer, M. (1983) *Spheres of Justice: A Defense of Pluralism and Equality*, New York: Basic Books.
Wellman, C. (2008) "Immigration and Freedom of Association." *Ethics* 119: 109–141.
Yeng, S. (2013) *Biopolitics of Race: State Racism and U.S. Immigration*, Blue Ridge Summit, PA: Lexington Books.

36

MIXED-RACE

Jared Sexton

> Under the best of circumstances, mixed race identity can provide a useful optic on power, a privileged standpoint from which important aspects of social relations can be absorbed, analyzed, and understood.
> —George Lipsitz, "Noises in the Blood"

To write about mixed-race, however designated, is above all to address questions of power. It is to come to terms with power's emergence and operation at various scales, in different registers, and through multiple forms in the production, sorting, and grouping of populations in vertical array. It is to think about the collective organization and deployment of violence, the political economy of goods and services, and the libidinal economy of pleasure and pain; and it is about the symbolic order and semiotic activity that together describe, explain, motivate, and justify these elements and aspects of social formation. To broach the matter of mixed-race without articulating the discourse in terms of such *situatedness* is to evade the issues of greatest import and, through that evasion, to de-historicize and de-politicize the history and politics responsible for the suffering exacted in its name.

The rise of multiracialism in the post–civil rights era United States has been characterized especially, but not exclusively, by a general evasion of these considerations. This is not to say that scholars in the academic field of multiracial studies and activists involved with the multiracial movement since the 1980s have not understood their collective endeavor to be, among other things, a reckoning with historical dynamics and political realities. Indeed, the discourse of multiracialism has, across two generations now, claimed to *intervene* upon the history and politics of race and racism in the United States and beyond, and, furthermore, to intervene against the purported *exceptionality* of a racial order unlike any other in the world and defined by the most extreme standard of classification: the one-drop rule of hypo-descent.

Hypo-descent is a concept coined by the anthropologist Marvin Harris (distinguished for his quasi-Marxist theory and method of "cultural materialism") in his 1964 *Patterns of Race in the Americas*. There, Harris writes:

> In the United States, the mechanism employed is the rule of hypo-descent. This descent rule requires Americans to believe that anyone who is known to have had a Negro ancestor is a Negro. We admit nothing in between.... "Hypo-descent"

means affiliation with the subordinate rather than the superordinate group in order to avoid the ambiguity of intermediate identity.

(quoted in Jordan 2014: 120n12)

Crucially, for Harris, the avoidance of "intermediate identity" does not represent, as it were, an inherent and necessary aversion to ambiguity among the architects of racialization, such that any departure from hypodescent thereby undermines this fundament of the social order. Rather, as he makes clear throughout his comparative study, the rules of racial definition of a given society, or region, are driven by largely strategic considerations. Kalvero Olberg, then a senior research associate at Cornell University and best known for introducing the concept of "culture shock" to a general audience, summarized Harris's position in a review for *American Anthropologist*:

> The definition of race in the Americas, the author states, has little or nothing to do with race as defined by the physical anthropologist. While physical traits play a part, race classifications are in terms of economic, political, and social realities. The author makes a telling point by showing that discrimination is not the result of race prejudice but the other way around. As color prejudice is shared by the members of racially mixed groups, this can scarcely be considered a cause of discrimination. When a superordinate group wishes to hold another group in subjection through full scale economic, social, and political discrimination, a body of beliefs and attitudes prejudicial to the members of this group is invented to support discriminatory practices.
>
> (Olberg 1965: 797)

What Olberg highlights in Harris's work is a political, or political economic, conception of the rules of racial definition rooted in large-scale historical developments and bearing little or no motive relation to "physical traits" or what Harris, in turn, calls "biological facts." The important point not to be missed here, however, is that Harris does not offer an evaluation in preference of hypo- or hyper-descent (or, for that matter, cognatic-descent) rules of definition. Rather, he attempts to describe their operation and analyze their causes and consequences. What he finds, in a concise survey of the Americas, is that hierarchical social orders have been established and continue to be maintained *across* the relative permeability of racial borders or proliferation of racial categories. Polarities of hierarchy accommodate greater or lesser degrees of contact.

Duana Fullwiley aptly illustrates the point in a 2008 interview for *Harvard Magazine*. A medical anthropologist at Stanford, she is discussing fieldwork conducted on sickle-cell disease in Senegal for her critically acclaimed book (Fullwiley 2011) when she remarks:

> I am an African American . . . but in parts of Africa, I am white. . . . I take a plane to France, a seven- to eight-hour ride. My race changes as I cross the Atlantic. There, I say, "*Je suis noire*," and they say, "Oh, okay—*métisse*—you are mixed." Then I fly another six to seven hours to Senegal, and I am white. In the space of a day, I can change from African American, to *métisse*, to *tubaab* [Wolof for "white/European"].

Crucially, she adds: "This is not a joke, or something to laugh at, or to take lightly. It is the kind of social recognition that even two-year-olds who can barely speak understand" (Rosenberg 2008). Fullwiley does not share this anecdote in order to delight in the contingency of rules of racial definition or to suggest the absurdity of US racialization in particular. Rather, in revealing how apparent ambiguity results in differing and divergent racial designations in transit from North America to Europe to Africa, she demonstrates that the relative meanings and values attached to whiteness and blackness and their admixture are not upended simply because those meanings and values are differently assigned to different bodies in different geographic settings. In other words, she may be considered African American, or black, in the United States, *métisse*, or mixed, in France, and *tubaab*, or white, in Senegal; but her migration across categories does nothing to alter the status and function of those categories. "Black," "mixed," and "white" continue to name positions in and as hierarchy.

We are not saying anything particularly new here, but it bears repeating in light of the resurgent interest in multiracialism following the 2008 election of US President Barack Obama (Carter 2013; Elam 2010; DaCosta 2008; Hochschild, Weaver and Burch 2012). I attempted a similar argument in my earlier study of the phenomenon (Sexton 2008), where I drew, in part, upon interdisciplinary research in Latin American studies to contradict a powerful tendency in the United States to view ideologies and practices of *mestizaje, mestiçagem,* or *metissage* as propaedeutic. The subsequent scholarly literature on that score has only deepened and reinforced the critique (Andrews 2010; Cottrol 2013; Gates 2011; Hernández 2012; Nascimento 2007; Nobles 2005; Sue 2013; Telles 2014; Telles and Sue 2009; Vargas 2010; Wade 2004; Wade et al. 2014). What we see presently are broad countervailing regional trends toward increasing color-blindness in North America, convergent with the rise of the New Right and popular conservatism in US and Canadian politics (Farney and Rayside 2007; Thompson 2007), and increasing color-consciousness in Central and South America, where movements among Afro-Latinos and indigenous peoples have pushed against official discourses of racial democracy and, alongside popular resistance to neoliberal globalization, for fundamental changes in law and policy (Rahier 2012; Rice 2012; Silva 2009; Webber and Carr 2013). Something similar can be said about comparative studies of mixed-race in Europe, in the larger Atlantic world, and even at the global scale (Haritaworn 2012; King-O'Riain et al. 2014; McNeil 2009; Song 2012). So, while the *fin de siècle* announcement of multiracialism has reshaped policy debates in the United States and elsewhere from census counting to student services to public health, one would be hard-pressed to conclude that its effect has been salutary, if one is interested primarily in social justice (Sundstrom 2008). This is especially the case as the new biological sciences—from genomics to bioinformatics—have, in public-private partnership with state and capital, served to "re-create race in the twenty-first century" (Roberts 2013; see also Bliss 2012; Happe 2013; Kahn 2013; Koenig, Lee and Richardson 2008; Morning 2011; Philips, Odunlami and Bonham 2007; Reardon 2009; Wailoo, Nelson and Lee 2012).

A 2015 symposium at NYU's Asian Pacific American Institute helped to concentrate our collective effort by asking: "What's Radical About 'Mixed Race'?" Not, what is interesting or distracting, comforting, or disturbing, but rather what is the relation of mixed-race to radicalism in general and to radical traditions in particular? On the one hand, we could say there is nothing radical about mixed-race, if we assume that such radicality stems from the novelty of the matter or the discourse that nominates it. As a point of reference we have, for instance, Hortense Spillers's (2011) observation, in a terse commentary titled "Mama's Baby, Papa's Too," responding to the 2011 *New York Times* "Race Remixed" series spearheaded by Susan Saulny, now a national correspondent for ABC News. The yearlong series set out to "explore the growing number of mixed-race Americans" and reported, among other things, that mixed-race people, especially those attending college, "use the strength in their growing numbers to affirm roots that were once portrayed as tragic or pitiable" while "leading a sea of change in how we think about race and ethnicity." In her commentary Spillers writes that, contrary to the upbeat breaking news rhetoric of the publication of record, "racial ambiguity is . . . a new-world thematic—probably about seven centuries old by now." For those doing the math, that takes us back to something approaching the fourteenth century CE and to an examination of the social, political, and economic developments unfolding in historical outline within and between Africa, Asia, and Europe. As there is not yet anything but speculation about the existence of the Americas in this hub of early global encounter, we see that the racial thematics of the "new world" begin in and as transformations well prior to the Columbian advent.

Three massive shifts deserve mention in this respect. First, the shift in the principal vector of trade in enslaved Africans, from the trans-Saharan and Indian Ocean basin toward the newer transatlantic circuit—what historian Patrick Manning (1990) calls, respectively, the "Oriental" and "Occidental" slave trades—whose pivot entailed an intensification of the internal slave trade throughout most of the African continent. It is crucial to note that the transatlantic Occidental slave trade launched its maritime enterprise along a North-South axis, centered about the Mediterranean region, in the fifteenth century, well before European imperial expansion to the Americas (Green 2012; Hunwick and Powell 2002; Segal 2001). Second, the related shift in mode of production from feudalism toward mercantilism in Europe, including the systematic enclosure of the commons so crucial to the incipient stage of capitalism in the early modern period (Solow 2014; Wood 2002). Third, the stirrings of Renaissance humanism throughout European intellectual life, unleashing historical, philosophical, theological, and scientific debates that would reconfigure long-standing notions of slavery and freedom for the subsequent formulation and eventual consolidation of the idea and practice of racial differentiation (Brotton 2006; Goldenberg 2005; Isaac 2004). We thus begin to understand, following the lead of Elizabeth Donnan's four-volume documentary history of the transatlantic slave trade, whose landmark research Spillers consults in the course of writing her most famous essay, that by the mid-1400s at least "the magic of skin color is already installed as a decisive factor in human dealings" (Spillers 2003: 212). In this zone of convergence—where the European's relation to the African is mediated by long-standing relations with the Arab and Berber peoples of the Maghreb—slavery as a legal, political, and economic institution becomes progressively *circumscribed* to the populations of sub-Saharan West and Central Africa and *racialized* as black and, concomitantly, the status of the enslaved is *degraded* relative to its pre-modern and ancient variants across most of the inhabited world (Black 2015; Blackburn 1997; Lovejoy 2012). "Slavery," as Toby Green notes, "has been a universal human institution and remains widespread, but Atlantic slavery holds *an unusual importance* for thinking about modernity, foreshadowing as it did racial consciousness and the industrialization of global economies" (2012: 4, emphasis added).

On the other hand, there is nothing more radical than mixed-race, provided we approach the questions it raises *in the abstract*. Rainier Spencer has argued this point since the late 1990s, notably in his *Spurious Issues* (1999), where he writes: "the multiracial idea, considered in the abstract, can possess a measure of subversive power" (168), it "can invalidate race and then of necessity itself" (126). Insofar as it becomes a term of social identity, however, it "would have precisely the opposite effect" (126). Thomas Holt (2004) suggested as much more recently in his contribution to the American Anthropology Association's public education project "Understanding Race and Human Variation," funded by the National Science Foundation and the Ford Foundation. For Holt,

> [The] very possibility of the mixture of races frames—indeed has always framed—the larger problematic of race as such. That [theoretical] possibility forms one of its essential components, at once enabling and destabilizing racial thought and racial regimes. All of the things taken for granted about race are brought into question when races [ostensibly] mix—not least of them the physical-biological reality of race itself (i.e., what is race?); as well as whether and to what extent race is best understood as biology or culture; and, indeed, what motivates racism (i.e., the relation between racial identification and racism).
>
> (2004: 2)

The Critical Mixed Race Studies (CMRS) association and its academic journal stand in *prima facie* agreement. The official website describes the project as "the transracial, transdisciplinary, and transnational critical analysis of the institutionalization of social, cultural, and political orders based on dominant conceptions of race." But that analysis is hamstrung by the assumption that emphasizing "the *mutability* of race and the *porosity* of racial boundaries" ensures the "critique of local and global . . . injustices rooted in systems of racialization." That is to say, it assumes that dominant conceptions of race do not already acknowledge—when they do not emphasize and employ—"the mutability of race and the porosity of racial boundaries" to institutionalize unjust social, cultural, and political orders. It assumes, more importantly, that what is most important about a racial order is the relative mutability or porosity of its boundaries rather than the structural violence of "permanent group hierarchy" (Fredrickson 2002: 6).

That the idea of mixed-race raises questions about the larger problematic of race as such does not guarantee that those questions will be posed in the most adequate way or, moreover, that they will not solicit a reactionary quest for resolution. What I have referred to as "racial suture" (2008: 18–26) can, and often enough does, give rise to a rage for order that closes down thinking in the name of a certain knowledge. In fact, it would seem that regimes of racialization have always worked with and through mutability and porosity, through figures of mixture as much as through figures of purity. Borrowing from psychiatrists Maurice Dide and Paul Guiraud (Magin-Lazarus 1995), Fanon described this phenomenon at midcentury as the fluid metaphysics of the "delirious Manicheanism" of race. In the last generation, one might revisit works ranging from Spiller's (2003) "Notes on an Alternative Model—Neither/Nor" (addressing the idea-forms of the "mulatto/a" in the post-Reconstruction era literature of racial passing, originally published in 1987) to Robert Young's *Colonial Desire* (1995) (addressing the mixed-race obsessions of purportedly anti-miscegenationist Anglo-Saxons in pursuit of global empire) to Teresa Zackodnik's *The Mulatta and the Politics of Race* (2004) (addressing the ingenious uses to which black women creative writers have put the figures of mixed-race in a deconstruction of the patriarchal anti-blackness of slavery and segregation) to Daniel Sharfstein's *The Invisible Line* (2011) (addressing the mythology of the one-drop rule as a component of the nineteenth- and twentieth-century US racial order). An extended quote from Sharfstein suffices to sharpen the focus:

> Ideologies of- racial purity and pollution are as old as America, and so is interracial mixing. Yet the one-drop rule did not, as many have suggested, make all mixed-race people black. From the beginning, African Americans assimilated into white communities across the South. Often, becoming white did not require the deception normally associated with racial "passing"; whites knew that certain people were different and let them cross the color line anyway. These communities were not islands of racial tolerance. They could be as committed to slavery, segregation, and white supremacy as anywhere else, and so could their newest members—it was one of the things that made them white. The history of the color line is one in which people have lived quite comfortably with contradiction.
> (Sharfstein 2007: 594)

Commitment to slavery, not judgments of appearance or lineage, as "one of the things that made them white": is there not a structural homology today in the (active or passive) commitment to hyper-segregation, disciplinary welfare, punitive schooling, police profiling, and mass imprisonment, or to the menu of ideological accompaniments to the ongoing repression of black freedom movement? "White" no longer means the same thing post–civil rights, of course, or rather, the same thing no longer means simply "white." But, as Sharfstein cautions, whiteness as the historical formation of an internally differentiated social category should not be hypostasized. There are other possibilities afoot as what Charles Gallagher (2004) terms "racial redistricting" expands the boundaries of whiteness in our time, while lending ever-greater salience to any and every indication of non-blackness (Lee and Bean 2007; Yancey 2003).

Spillers, then, pushes us to this consideration: "[To] call oneself mixed-race, or black and white, or something and something else, means *what*? What work is that supposed to do for you?" Her reply is astute:

> We very much doubt that the fury here is that there are not enough boxes on the census form, or a deficit of classificatory items, or the prohibition to check more than one, or even the thwarted desire to express racial pride, but, rather, the dictates of a muted self-interest that wishes to carve its own material and political successes out of another's hide.... In other words, if "racial ambiguity" or *looking* that way, can be amplified and translated into a legitimate *political* interest (as it is increasingly becoming a *commercial* one), then the padded new racism that comes about as a result will gladly declare a new class of winners.

One must keep in mind that these are not observations made from lack of charity or broad learning, as too many defenders of multiracialism presume when fielding criticism from black scholars. I think that the "self-interest" Spillers infers here is muted not only for the audience that is expected to hear the multiracial claim but for the one who utters it as well. That is to say the differentiation and distanciation at work in the articulation of mixed-race may be driven by sources, aims, and objects that remain obscure even, or especially, to the *subject* of multiracialism. This obscurity would be essential to sustaining the leaps of logic required to massage or manage the unavoidable contradictions, to deflect otherwise pressing questions, and to bring the multiracial claim, and its cohorts, into a sort of coherence.

Most acutely, there is philosopher Lewis Gordon, who 20 years ago, between the publication of several canonical anthologies edited by psychologist Maria Root (1992, 1996) and philosopher Naomi Zack (1993), raised the bar, or threw down the gauntlet, in his 1995 *Social Identities* article, "Critical 'Mixed Race'?" In this article, as well as in his *Existentia Africana* (2000), Gordon commented at length on the foundational work of Zack (1993), whose first book remains the standard introduction to the issues at hand and the only sustained philosophical meditation on mixed-race until Ronald Sundstrom's *The Browning of America and the Evasion of Social Justice* (2008). Gordon's contention—"there is no way to reject the thesis that there is something wrong with being black beyond the willingness to 'be' black"—is derived from his extensive engagement with Fanon's thought on the power and pervasiveness of anti-blackness, or "negrophobogenesis." Nevertheless, Gordon's arguments have hardly been addressed, let alone persuasively challenged, within the subsequent literature on multiracialism. Neither has Gordon's corollary call for a *critical* mixed-race theory that operates by way of a "suicidal irony" in ethical pursuit of what he terms "a blackened world," about which more in a moment. Instead, multiracial studies or its rebranding as CMRS proceeds, in the main, as if the article and its follow-up (Gordon 2000) were never published, to say nothing of the larger body of work of which it is a part. Gordon's many books and articles on the concept of the anti-black world represent elements of a cogent and far-reaching critique of the political *impetus* or *impulse* behind the emergence of multiracialism in the historic instance, including the work of David Brunsma (2005), Kimberly DaCosta (2007), Heather Dalmage (2004), Angelique Davis (2007), Michelle Elam (2011), David Hollinger (2005), Ralina Joseph (2013), Minelle Mahtani (2012), Minkah Makalani (2003), Melissa Nobles (2000, 2005), Rainier Spencer (2006, 2011), Kim Williams (2005, 2008), and many more. These scholars represent a countercurrent to the mainstream of CMRS and, as to be expected, such currents mingle at points, generating still underexplored eddies and vortices (McKibben 2014).

At this point, we might ask, in a Fanonian register, does this leave multiracialism with no viable option but "to turn black or disappear?" Is this really the price, as it were, of being ethical in an anti-black world? Is this not just another enforcement of hypo-descent from below, the much-decried bane of the multiracial experience? The charge is spurious (in the sense that it appears to be but is not actually valid), but it has its purposes. If I might be indulged a brief reply to critics in hopes that is it illustrative of a more general procedure, I will recall that *Amalgamation Schemes* was first reviewed some years ago in a special issue of *The Black Scholar* (Nishime 2009). Amid a hurried appraisal, the reviewer gets something right, albeit for the wrong reason, when claiming that the book "sets up a tautology where multiracial studies is defined as anti-black and if it is not anti-black then it is not multiracial studies." The judgment is hasty, not least because I am interested in the broader phenomenon of *multiracialism*, "inclusive of the political initiatives of the multiracial movement, the academic field of multiracial studies, and the media discourse about 'race mixture' in contemporary culture and society" (2008: 1). I might continue defining multiracial studies as axiomatically anti-black, which is to say at the level of its guiding assumptions and premises, if that is as plainly as the point needs to be made for fulsome discussion and debate to happen. Rather, one might better say, as I attempted in the earlier book, that anti-blackness is irreducible for the formation of *any* instance of multiracialism, academic or otherwise, and insist, moreover, that anti-blackness is not nearly as transparent a concept as one might think. The curious fact is that the review uses the notion of tautology to accuse the critique of multiracialism of a definitional police operation: "if it is not anti-black then it is not multiracial studies." If we unpack the triple negative, then the charge might sound like this: *there is no such thing as pro-black multiracial studies.*

In other words, the reviewer finds this particular black scholar, not unlike many fellow critics, refuses to recognize multiracial friends and allies due to a too black assumption that, if one identifies as black, then one has no multiracial friends and allies by definition. In this self-enclosed racial paranoia, the fantasy of global persecution prevents the black-identified from accepting multiracial acceptance and much-needed coalition as well, but it also, tragically, prevents one from recognizing the lives of others. In academic circles, the diagnosis is "failure to conduct sufficient research" and the prescription for recommended reading involves recourse to supposedly better titles in multiracial studies and adjacent fields where illumination and reassurance await. Uncanny advice, for the main criticism on offer is that the sample is not representative (despite some 70 pages of notes and works cited). In this, the initial review is paradigmatic of the text's larger critical reception (Comer 2012; Spickard 2009; Wachter-Grene 2011; cf. Cantanese 2011). None establishes (though at least one asserts) any misreading or misunderstanding of the primary and secondary sources under consideration and none claims the argument is unsound *as far as it goes*. The problem, rather, is that the critique of multiracialism takes aim at a "couple of not-very-thoughtful activists" and "weaker writers . . . tangential to the multiracial literature," and that when it does address leading figures it "cherry-picks . . . evidence," and so on (Spickard 2009). More telling is the objection that the critique leaves multiracialism "nowhere" to go, which is to say it is a *critique* and not a friendly reminder or a note of caution. The anxiety accompanying the reading, then, is about the parameters of a general implication: "We are not *all* like that and those of us that are aren't *that* bad." Such responses misrecognize the distinction between, say, a discourse analysis and a social or political psychology, much less a psychologizing or moralistic character judgment (Cuéllar 2010; Paltridge 2012; Parker and Cuéllar 2014). They express a collective concern about where to cut the border, where to draw the line, and how to maintain it, how to say who is and who is not, who's in and who's out. This is not an empirical problem regarding the breadth of the literature review or the diligence or fairness of the criticism, however, but a structural problem regarding the disavowed logic, or what Fanon would call the affective "pre-logic," of an entire discursive formation. In fact, this is precisely the argument developed in chapter 3 of *Amalgamation Schemes* and one is only mildly surprised to see it replicated at a remove, since the reviewers participate in the discourse under examination. To wit: "Unable to produce an absolute refutation of the charges levied against it—as if that were the point—multiracialism instead celebrates the arrival of a critical mass or the achievement of safe distance" (Sexton 2008: 170).

What I am saying, in short, is a pro-black multiracial studies, one "that is not anti-black," a genuinely *critical* mixed-race studies oriented by a suicidal irony, would be nothing other than an aspect of black studies itself; and multiracialism, by extension, an aspect of black freedom movement more generally. Far from setting up a tautology for those investigating the politics of mixed-race, we are referencing a *heuristic* that gives the lie to that line of demarcation drawn, loud and uncertain at present, between CMRS and the field of black studies it is meant to enlist and enlighten. Against the compulsive ascription of "a kind of parochialism in the discourse of African Americans in the United States" (Chandler 2006: 42) on matters of mixed-race, we might affirmatively describe and promote black studies as that open secret whose object is the radical "critique of western civilization" and whose aim is to extend and deepen *everyone's* "critical and imaginative relation to the terms *abolition* and *reconstruction*" (Moten 2008: 1745).

Indeed, such work is already intimated, for instance, in the writings of sociologist Kimberly DaCosta and literary critic Michelle Elam. DaCosta (2008) spoke to the question of Barack Obama's racial designation for the BBC News during the US presidential election season of 2008. In surveying the range of positions in response to queries about whether Obama is black or mixed-race, DaCosta writes:

> [The] question whether Obama is black or mixed-race reflects a basic misunderstanding of the experience of those of us who have grown up in interracial families, particularly those of us of African descent, born in the post-Civil Rights period. It was in our families where we first felt love and protection as well as the first sting of racial prejudice. And many of us forged a black identity, *one that was not at odds with being mixed-race*, but arose out of our experiences as mixed people: from an awareness that the racial dilemma we were born into has its deepest roots in anti-black prejudice. For us, being black and mixed-race are not mutually exclusive.
>
> (emphasis added)

Elam (2010), in a similar vein, addressed the question of multiracial identification in a piece for the *Huffington Post* on the occasion of the 2010 decennial census. She enjoined an erstwhile multiracial constituency to consider the (unintended) political effects of their forms of official public identification and suggested that there are "better venues in which to both represent our multisplendored selves and more productively ally with social justice efforts." The both/and logic of DaCosta's and Elam's public commentaries represent a profound challenge to the politics of multiracialism insofar as its displaces the presumed conflict between black and multiracial, but does so by at once cancelling and retaining the difference.

The strategy is akin to that established in Stuart Hall's well-known essay, "What Is This 'Black' in Black Popular Culture?" His reading of that essay opened a three-day symposium on black popular culture convened by Michelle Wallace in 1991 at The Studio Museum of Harlem and the Dia Center of the Arts. Hall's contribution appeared shortly thereafter in the panoramic 1992 *Black Popular Culture* anthology edited by Gina Dent for the Dia Art Foundation's award-winning Discussions in Contemporary Culture book series and it has since been reprinted at least a half dozen times. Hall spoke most famously on that historic occasion about what he termed "the end of innocence of the black subject or the end of the innocent notion of the essential black subject" (Hall 1996: 447). The phrase was meant to indicate the "plurality of antagonisms and differences that now seek to destroy the unity of black politics, given the complexities of the structures of subordination that have been formed by the way in which we were inserted into the black diaspora" (Hall 1996: 447). Hall, of course, does not lament this development, but rather celebrates the possibilities of a disunited black politics, so to speak, a politics expansive and multidimensional enough to accommodate the "continuous [dislocation] of one identity by another, one structure by another" (Hall 1996: 447).

The spirit of Hall's "conjunctural" politics is taken up at great length in Tommie Shelby's 2005 book, *We Who Are Dark: The Philosophical Foundations of Black Solidarity*, a work that advances a post-nationalist conception of black solidarity that is transnational, feminist, queer, and socialist at least, wherein "black interests are not limited to racial justice but also include any progressive agenda that a group of blacks attempts to advance *qua* black people" (Shelby 2005: 158). This revised and expanded conception of black solidarity is enabled by a pivot away from a notion of blackness as collective identity and toward a notion of blackness as common oppression and commitment to resisting it. He adds, with respect to the notion of black identity, that "from the standpoint of black solidarity, each should be allowed, without molestation, to interpret 'blackness' however she or he sees fit (provided the interpretation does not advocate anything immoral and is consistent with the principles and goals of antiracism)" (Shelby 2002: 254). So much goes for the question of multiraciality as well, where one might thus articulate blackness with or within a claim to mixed-race heritage or identity without contradiction. Black and multiracial without contradiction or compromise, "provided the interpretation [of blackness] . . . is consistent with the principles and goals of antiracism." That's the rub, then, the central point of contention. This is not a politics of authenticity giving rise to litmus tests, enforcing codes of silence and invisibility on identity formations considered impure, wayward, illegitimate, and so on. Rather, it is a politics of solidarity in which the terms of debate regard the nature and direction of political struggle.

I take up the matter of mixed-race in the present chapter from this particular angle—rather than trying to provide an omnibus account—because I come to the questions raised therein by way of intramural debates about the disunited black politics Hall diagnosed and about the vexed political coalitions attendant to "the browning of America" post-civil rights. My comments here represent an attempt to understand a convergence of historical developments that often enough lack a strong critical sensibility. This blunted critical sensibility can even be found among progressive historians like the late Peggy Pascoe, whose award-winning and definitive study of the legal regulation of interracial marriage in the United States, *What Comes Naturally*, conflates overlapping circumstances with shared structural positioning while seeking to prove that "miscegenation law was a national—and multiracial—project" (Pascoe 2009: 14). While Pascoe correctly notes that "miscegenation law was clearly a project of white supremacy rooted in notions of white purity" and, further, that it was "written to prohibit Whites from marrying Blacks, Asian Americans, and Indians but not to prohibit Blacks from marrying Asian Americans, or Asian Americans from marrying Indians"; there is no need to conclude thereby that "the structure of the laws was an attempt to place non-Whites in *structurally similar* subordination to Whites, as if all non-Whites inhabited *the same social world* and embodied *the same threat* to whiteness" (Pascoe 2009: 8, emphasis added). One could raise the immediate objection that Blacks, Asian Americans, and Indians were considered to pose *different* and perhaps even *differential* threats to whiteness—quantitatively or qualitatively—but that *all* such threats were sufficient to warrant prohibition. On that note, Pascoe's research demonstrates clearly that while Blacks were not the *only* target of miscegenation law (i.e., the law's reach was national and multiracial), they were never *not* the target of such legal bans, regardless of demographic variations from state to state. The regulation of Asian Americans and Indians, by contrast, was regionally specific and in some cases made provisions their allowance (even if such provisions were unjust and pursuant to conquest and/or forced assimilation). Given that miscegenation law was, for Pascoe, central to the making of race in the United States (and elsewhere), we see the peculiar role played by anti-black miscegenation law to that end, something that the subsequent patterns of interracial marriage and dating have borne out in the post-*Loving* moment.

I raise the above point about Pascoe's text as one example of how studies of white supremacy, including those of the highest caliber, can and should be supplemented by an analysis of the dynamics of anti-blackness. This fundamental reframing of the study of race, philosophical and otherwise, is too often rejected by those who misconstrue the conceptual framework as a stricture on the topics and themes available for investigation. Can one examine the lived experience of multiracial Latino-Asian Americans in contemporary California or the nineteenth-century history of Anglo-Indians on the subcontinent through the lens of anti-blackness? Absolutely, as readily as one could explore the political mobilization of the Garifuna in Central America or the shifting significance of the social category "colored" in post-apartheid South Africa. If one is not only interested in yielding ethnographic data or phenomenological description—or, even in those cases, if one wants to generate better results—then one must attend to the broadest context of social relations available and, as indicated in the epigraph, allow the study to become a genuine "optic on power." This is not only a plea for a more capacious relational research program, but also a rejoinder to the sort of parceling out of oppression that tends to inform approaches to comparative racialization, a problem traceable across a wide literature from Omi and Winant (2014) to Gines (2013). In this sort of approach, slavery is something experienced by a segment of the African Diaspora, settler colonialism and genocidal conquest by the indigenous peoples of the Americas, exclusionary immigration policy and imperial warfare by Asians, and so forth. A problem arises immediately for this typology when one considers that New World Africans have experienced *all* such forms of oppression: slavery, settler colonialism, genocidal conquest, exclusionary immigration policy, imperial warfare, and so on (Sexton 2015).

What the study of the African Diaspora and the unavoidably central place of racial slavery in its formation presents—theoretically and conceptually—is the demand to devise a framework for thinking about power in the most comprehensive manner, from the everyday to the extreme and, crucially, at the point where they fatally combine. Gordon (2000) suggested something along these lines when he remarked as follows:

> I would say that the insight of some of the leaders in previous generations of mixed-race people [in and beyond the US context] is that they knew that no justice was to be attained in any contemporary society through the affirmation of a white [or lightened] identity. They knew they were mixed, but they also

knew that, when it comes to political action and the fight for social change, one has to work with those dimensions that will effect social change.

(116)

The politically effective dimension: where DaCosta and Elam adumbrate a discourse of black identity "not at odds with being mixed-race," a gesture that might read as indemnifying against allegations of essentialism or "monoracialism," Sika Dagbovie-Mullins (2013) advances a formulation of mixed-race identity based in what she calls "black sentience" in response to the "brand new fetish" of multiracialism. For Dagbovie-Mullins:

> Black sentience intimates a mixed-race subjectivity that includes a particular awareness of the world, a perception rooted in blackness. It suggests a connection to a black consciousness that does not overdetermine one's racial identification but still plays a large role in it. The emergence of multiracial organizations that promote multiple-race classification options on census and other forms promotes and politicizes a multiracial identity that, I argue, tends to diminish blackness. Many black/white mixed-race people who reject multiracial classification advance a black subjectivity—a black-sentient consciousness, skeptical of what they see as elitism associated with projecting a biracial identity. A black-sentient mixed-race identity reconciles the widening separation between black/white mixed-race and blackness that has been encouraged by contemporary mixed-race politics and popular culture.
>
> (Dagbovie-Mullins 2013: 2–3)

While Dagbovie-Mullins inadvertently reproduces an element of the negrophobia attendant to multiracialism when describing, elsewhere in her book, "black sentience" as enabling a form of identity that "resists racial scripts," one in which "black consciousness does not completely dictate identification" (2013: 123); a crucial part of her formulation is that black sentience does not require a black identity, at least not in the common sense of the term. Rather, "a perception rooted in blackness" serves to ward against elitism and to actively resist the prevailing tendency "to diminish blackness." Put somewhat differently, this is an ethical disposition that holds onto blackness and affirms it, not as a matter of cultural practice, but as a critical sensibility, an attachment to "a lived critique of the assumed equivalence of personhood and subjectivity" (Moten 2003: 242). Personhood, in the usual meaning of the term, indicates the achievement of or aspiration to some minimal distance toward black identity, as if that were some kind of achievement. This problematic definition of personhood would include as well those qualifications that serve or seek to mitigate "the dual significance of blackness as both sin and *suffering*" (Gordon 2000: 98). The ethical dimension of mixed-race, then, would condition any and all ontological, epistemological, and aesthetic claims and concerns as they are forged within the shadow of the overriding opposition to anti-blackness (and this is ipso facto an opposition to white supremacy in all of its forms and even opposition to hierarchy as such.)

The literature on multiracialism by and large acknowledges that anti-blackness is at least compatible with mixed-race claims and most allow that some do, in fact, articulate anti-black multiracial identities, but as a rule scholars and activists nonetheless maintain that anti-blackness is contingent to multiracialism and therefore consciously (easily?)

avoidable and, again, certainly not representative. Not only do such arguments overlook the way in which, as Minelle Mahtani recently noted at the abovementioned NYU symposium, the discourse of multiracialism is governed by "the grammar of good intentions" (Ryan 2003) and punctuated by symptomatic oaths of moral obligation; they also miss the crucial fact that *black* identities are compatible with anti-blackness as well and so share with mixed-race—and all other non-black identities—a common ethical challenge, if with radically divergent stakes. This intramural, even intrapsychic black struggle against anti-blackness—addressed by towering figures from Ida B. Wells and W.E.B. Du Bois to Malcolm X and Toni Cade Bambara—represents not only a searing critique and refusal of an anti-black world, but also an archive of examples of ways to affirm blackness, to love the *flesh* as it is embodied by those marked by racial blackness. Though it also functions as a form of defense and defiance, "black is beautiful" is in the first instance a solicitation to black folks to turn *toward* blackness as an ethical decision. But it is, at once and beyond that, a solicitation to the world. Black Power, the social movement that provides "American mixed-race" with its principal frame of reference and source of moral anxiety, re-politicized blackness and, at its best, re-energized it as a radical political identity. This identity was capacious enough to encompass differences among its constituency of gender and sexuality, color and complexion, class and nation, ethnicity and religion, education and language, age and ability, among others. All of these differences were sites of serious, sometimes lethal, conflict and many such differences—or rather an inability to engage them all as matters of *equality*—undermined the movement's prospects and potential. But the history of black movements, as models of struggle not dependent upon interest-based coalition or strategic alliance as a means of negotiating difference, opens out into the political culture of radical politics in general. To state things more strongly, the history of black movements demonstrates not only the sustenance of radical tradition across several centuries, but also an incessant drive to radicalize its radicalism.

To be sure, black women, feminist-identified or not, and poor black women especially have been the leading social force of this movement within movements, but within the last two generations at least the gender conflict between black men and women and the class conflict between poor and working-class blacks and the black "*lumpenbourgeoisie*" (as E. Franklin Frazier would have it) has expanded, *pace* Hall, into a whole series of (long-standing but newly articulated) intersecting differences, most acutely regarding interrogations of black sexualities, genders, and abilities. The development of the concept of "misogynoir"—a portmanteau term naming the particular anti-black sexism targeting black women—by queer black feminist scholar Moya Bailey (2013) is a principle instance of this shift. In this light, we can see how forms of hetero-patriarchal blackness might also be considered anti-black because they claim forms of being black *plus* some normative striving: black but also man, but also heterosexual, black but . . . Not *just* black, but *also*. This sort of intersectional identification, when it is claimed in order to attenuate the social costs of anti-blackness, should not be confused with the critical practice of identifying intersectional identities that compound or condition such costs, that is, black and woman, disabled, queer. In point of fact, one could make the argument that, politically speaking, black women are blacker than black men, that black trans, queer, and genderqueer folks are blacker than presumptively heterosexual or cis-gendered blacks, and so on—even as we acknowledge that such ontic internal differentiation of the political ontology of racial blackness throws into permanent crisis the very terms of that gendered, sexual, classed differentiation (Warren 2013).

If we conceive of blackness in this way, as a "political blackness" (Guinier and Torres 2003), we might affirm and amplify not only the capaciousness (rather than the curtailment) of blackness in the historical movement of black people in the United States (including those of mixed heritage), but also affirm and amplify the capaciousness (rather than the curtailment) of blackness, for example, in the historical movement of Africans, West Indians, and Asians *as black people* in the UK of the 1960s, '70s, and '80s (Sinvanandan 1990). This is not to romanticize the latter example, of course, given that its dissolution was linked to a submerged coalitional model of political struggle. What is of greatest interest is the fact that a multiracial demographic, as it were, could mobilize under the banner of blackness in order to *maximize* its radical political power. Gordon (2000) suggests as much, in a pointed response to the emerging multiracial movement of the 1990s:

> Why not apply the one-drop rule with a vengeance by claiming any black ancestry? Why not simply "blacken" or "color" as much of the U.S. as possible? . . . Why darken the world? Because lightening our racist world will be perceived as a positive thing, which will increase the probability of differentiating the lighter from the light—in short, a new set of black folks. Whereas, to do the negative thing, to do more than darken it, to *blacken* it, will surely be perceived as an act calling for decisive action.
>
> (116)

Blackening the world might *begin* by reframing the issues of greatest political concerns with respect to those most blackened by their effects. So when addressing the matter of mixed-race, we talk centrally about multiracial blacks, as it were. And from that vantage we are able to speak to and about a universe of overlapping struggles: black Asians (or "blasians") and Afro-Latinos to illuminate the dynamics of "the racial middle" (O'Brien 2008), black Indians on indigenous struggles throughout the Americas, black immigrants with respect to nativism and xenophobia worldwide, black women pursuing the evolution of feminist theory and practice transnationally, black workers in international resistance to neoliberal capitalism, black students addressing the crisis of public education, and so forth. "Black X": because to think the terms of political analysis and political mobilization through a black (or blackened) lens is to think from the point of constitutive exclusion from those very terms, which is to say freedom from those very terms insofar as that exclusion is affirmed. Not unlike the visual archive of the ongoing Black Lives Matter movement, wherein we see a mounted placard bearing the affirmative defiant words:

ALL BLACK EVERYTHING.

References

Andrews, G. (2010) *Blackness in the White Nation: A History of Afro-Uruguay*, Chapel-Hill: University of North Carolina Press.

Bailey, M. (2013) "New Terms of Resistance: A Response to Zenzele Isoke." *Souls: A Critical Journal of Black Politics, Culture, and Society* 15, no. 4: 341–343.

Bennett, P. (2011) "The Social Position of Multiracial Groups in the United States: Evidence from Residential Segregation." *Ethnic and Racial Studies* 34, no. 4: 707–729.

Black, J. (2015) *The Atlantic Slave Trade in World History*, New York: Routledge.
Blackburn, R. (1997) *The Making of New World Slavery: From the Baroque to the Modern, 1492–1800*. New York: Verso.
Bliss, C. (2012) *Race Decoded: The Genomic Fight for Social Justice*, Stanford: Stanford University Press.
Boof, Kola. (2011) *The Sexy Part of the Bible: A Novel*, New York: Akashic Books.
Bratter, J. (2007) "Will 'Multiracial' Survive to the Next Generation? The Racial Classification of Children of Multiracial Parents." *Social Forces* 86, no. 2: 821–849.
Brotton, J. (2006) *The Renaissance: A Very Short Introduction*, New York: Oxford University Press.
Brunsma, D. (ed.). (2005) *Mixed Messages: Multiracial Identities in the 'Color-Blind' Era*, Boulder: Lynne Rienner.
Cantanese, B. (2011) "Amalgamation Schemes: Antiblackness and the Critique of Multiracialism (review)." *Journal of American Ethnic History* 30, no. 4: 117.
Carter, G. (2013) *The United States of the United Races: A Utopian History of Racial Mixing*, New York: New York University Press.
Chandler, N. (2006) "The Figure of W.E.B. Du Bois as a Problem for Thought." *CR; The New Centennial Review* 6, no. 3: 29–55.
Comer, N. (2012) "*Amalgamation Schemes: Antiblackness and the Critique of Multiracialism.* By Jared Sexton." *Black Diaspora Review* 3, no. 1: 52–53.
Cottrol, R. (2013) *The Long, Lingering Shadow: Slavery, Race, and Law in the American Hemisphere*, Athens: University of Georgia Press.
Cuéllar, D. (2010) *From the Conscious Interior to an Unconscious Exterior: Lacan, Discourse Analysis and Social Psychology*, eds. Danielle Carlo and Ian Parker, London: Karnac Books.
DaCosta, K. (2007) *Making Multiracials: State, Family, and Market in the Redrawing of the Color Line*, Stanford: Stanford University Press.
———. (2008) "Viewpoint: Is Barack Obama Black?" *BBC News*, November 18. http://news.bbc.co.uk/2/hi/americas/us_elections_2008/7735503.stm.
Dagbovie-Mullins, S. (2013) *Crossing B(l)ack: Mixed-Race Identity in Modern American Fiction and Culture*, Knoxville: University of Tennessee Press.
Dalmage, H. (ed.). (2004) *The Politics of Multiracialism: Challenging Racial Thinking*, Albany: State University of New York Press.
Davis, A. (2007) "Multiracialism and Reparations: The Intersection of the Multiracial Category and Reparations Movements." *Thomas Jefferson Law Review* 29: 161–188.
Duster, T. (2003) *Backdoor to Eugenics*, 2nd edition, New York: Routledge.
Elam. M. (2010) "Think Twice, Check Once." *Huffington Post*, May 8. www.huffingtonpost.com/michele-elam/2010-census-think-twice-c_b_490164.html.
———. (2011) *The Souls of Mixed Folk: Race, Politics, and Aesthetics in the New Millennium*, Stanford: Stanford University Press.
Evans, F. and L. Lawler (eds.). (2012) *Chiasms: Merleau-Ponty's Notion of Flesh*, Albany, NY: State University of New York Press.
Fanon, F. (2008) *Black Skin, White Masks*, trans. Richard Philcox, New York: Grove Press.
Farney, J. and D. Rayside (eds.). (2007) *Conservatism in Canada*, Toronto: University of Toronto Press.
Fredrickson, G. (2002) *Racism: A Short History*, Princeton: Princeton University Press.
Fullwiley, D. (2011) *The Encultured Gene: Sickle Cell Health Politics and Biological Difference in West Africa*, Princeton: Princeton University Press.
——— (2015) "Race, Genes, Power." *British Journal of Sociology* 66, no. 1: 36–45.
Gallagher, C. (2004) "Racial Redistricting: Expanding the Boundaries of Whiteness," in Heather Dalmage (ed.), *The Politics of Multiracialism: Challenging Racial Thinking*, Albany: State University of New York Press, pp. 59–76.
Garrod, A., R. Kilkenny, and C. Gomez (eds.). (2013) *Mixed: Multiracial College Students Tell Their Life Stories*, Ithaca: Cornell University Press.
Gaskins, P. (ed.). (1999) *What Are You? Voices of Mixed-Race Young People*, New York: Henry Holt.
Gates, H. (2011) *Black in Latin America*, New York: New York University Press.

Gines, K. (2013) "Introduction: Critical Philosophy of Race Beyond the Black/White Binary." *Critical Philosophy of Race* 1, no. 1: 28–37.

Goldenberg, D. (2005) *The Curse of Ham: Race and Slavery in Early Judaism, Christianity, and Islam*, Princeton: Princeton University Press.

Gordon, L. (1995) "Critical 'Mixed Race'?" *Social Identities* 1, no. 2: 381–395.

———. (2000) *Existentia Africana: Understanding Africana Existential Thought*, New York: Routledge.

———. (2015) *What Fanon Said: A Philosophical Introduction to His Life and Thought*, New York: Fordham University Press.

Green, T. (2012) *The Rise of the Trans-Atlantic Slave Trade in Western Africa, 1300–1589*, New York: Cambridge University Press.

Guinier, L., and Torres, G. (2003) *The Miner's Canary: Enlisting Race, Resisting Power, Transforming Democracy*, Cambridge, MA: Harvard University Press.

Hacking, I. (2005) "Why Does Race Still Matter?" *Daedalus* 134, no. 1: 102–116.

Hall, S. (1996) "What is this 'Black' in Black Popular Culture?" in D. Morley and K. H. Chen (eds.), *Stuart Hall: Critical Dialogues in. Cultural Studies*, New York: Routledge, pp. 468–478.

Happe, K. (2013) *The Material Gene: Gender, Race, and Heredity after the Human Genome Project*, New York: New York University Press.

Haritaworn, J. (2012) *The Biopolitics of Mixing: Thai Multiracialities and Haunted Ascendancies*, London: Ashgate.

Harms, R., Freamon, B., and Blight, D. (eds.). (2013) *Indian Ocean Slavery in the Age of Abolition*, New Haven: Yale University Press.

Hernández, T. (2012) *Racial Subordination in Latin America: The Role of the State, Customary Law, and the New Civil Rights Response*, New York: Cambridge University Press.

Hochschild, J., Weaver, V., and Burch, T. (2012) *Creating a New Racial Order: How Immigration, Multiracialism, Genomics, and the Young Can Remake Race in America*, Princeton: Princeton University Press.

Hollinger, D. (2005) "The One Drop Rule and the One Hate Rule." *Daedalus* 134, no. 1: 18–28.

Holt, T. (2004) "Understanding the Problematic of Race Through the Problem of Race Mixture." Paper presented at "Race and Human Variation: Setting an Agenda for Future Research and Education," Alexandria, VA, September 12–14.

Hunwick, J., and Powell, E. (eds.). (2002) *The African Diaspora in the Mediterranean Lands of Islam*, Princeton: Princeton University Press.

Ifekwunigwe, J. (ed.). (2004) *'Mixed Race' Studies: A Reader*, New York: Routledge.

Isaac, B. (2004) *The Invention of Racism in Classical Antiquity*, Princeton: Princeton University Press.

Jordan, Winthrop. (2014) "Historical Origins of the One-Drop Racial Rule in the United States." Edited by Paul Spickard. *Journal of Critical Mixed Race Studies* 1, no. 1: 89–132.

Joseph, R. (2013) *Transcending Blackness: From the New Millennium Mulatta to the Exceptional Multiracial*, Durham: Duke University Press.

Judy, R. (Forthcoming) *Thinking in Disorder: Essays of Poetic Socialities in Radical Humanism*, New York: Fordham University Press.

Kahn, J. (2013) *Race in a Bottle: The Story of BiDil and Racialized Medicine in a Post-Genomic Age*, New York: Columbia University Press.

Khanna, N. (2011) *Biracial in America: Forming and Performing Racial Identity*, Lanham: Lexington Books.

King-O'Riain, R. et al. (eds.). (2014) *Global Mixed Race*, New York: New York University Press.

Koenig, B., Lee, S., and Richardson, S. (eds.). (2008) *Revisiting Race in a Genomic Age*, New Brunswick, NJ: Rutgers University Press.

Korgen, K. (ed.). (2010) *Multiracial Americans and Social Class: The Influence of Social Class on Racial Identity*, New York: Routledge.

Lee, J., and Bean, F. (2007) "Reinventing the Color Line: Immigration and America's New Racial/Ethnic Divide." *Social Forces* 86, no. 2: 561–586.

Lipsitz, G. (2003) "Noises in the Blood: Culture, Conflict and Mixed Race Identities," in M. Coronado et al. (eds.) *Crossing Lines: Race and Mixed Race Across the Geohistorical Divide*. Santa Barbara, CA: Multiethnic Student Outreach.

Lovejoy, P. (2012) *Transformations in Slavery: A History of Slavery in Africa*, 3rd edition, New York: Cambridge University Press.

Magin-Lazarus, C. (1995) "Maurice Dide (1873–1944): A Forgotten Hero of French Psychiatry." Trans. Françoise Gaillard. *History of Psychiatry* 6: 539–548.

Mahtani, M. (2014) *Mixed Race Amnesia: Resisting the Romanticization of Multiraciality*, Seattle: University of Washington Press.

Makalani, M. (2003) "Rejecting Blackness and Claiming Whiteness: Antiblack Whiteness in the Biracial Project," in A. Doane and E. Bonilla-Silva (eds.), *White Out: The Continuing Significance of Racism*, New York: Routledge, pp. 81–94.

Manning, P. (1990) *Slavery and African Life: Occidental, Oriental, and African Slave Trades*, New York: Cambridge University Press.

McKibben, M. (2014) "The Current State of Multiracial Discourse." *Journal of Critical Mixed Race Studies* 1, no. 1: 183–202.

McNeil, D. (2009) *Sex and Race in the Black Atlantic: Mulatto Devils and Multiracial Messiahs*, New York: Routledge.

Morning, A. (2011) *The Nature of Race: How Scientists Think and Teach About Human Difference*, Berkeley: University of California Press.

Moten, F. (2008) "Black Op." *PMLA* 123, no. 5: 1743–1747.

Nascimento, E. (2007) *The Sorcery of Color: Identity, Race, and Gender in Brazil*, Philadelphia: Temple University Press.

Nemoto, K. (2011) "Interracial Romance: The Logic of Acceptance and Domination," in S. Seidman, N. Fischer, and C. Meeks (eds.), *Introducing the New Sexuality Studies*, 2nd edition, New York: Routledge, pp. 221–228.

Nishime, L. (2009) "Review of *Amalgamation Schemes*." *Black Scholar* 39, no. 3/4: www.mixedracestudies.org/wordpress/?p=4919.

Nobles, M. (2000) *Shades of Citizenship: Race and the Census in Modern Politics*, Stanford: Stanford University Press.

———. (2005) "The Myth of Latin American Multiracialism." *Daedalus* 134, no. 1: 82–87.

O'Brien, E. (2008) *The Racial Middle: Latinos and Asian Americans Living Beyond the Racial Divide*, New York: New York University Press.

O'Hearn, C. (ed.). (1998) *Half and Half: Writers on Growing Up Biracial and Bicultural*, New York: Pantheon.

Olberg, Kalvero. (1965) "Patterns of Race in the Americas. Marvin Harris." *American Anthropologist* 67, no. 3: 796–798.

Omi, M., and Winant, H. (2014) *Racial Formation in the United States*, third rdition, New York: Routledge.

Pabst, N. (2003) "Blackness/Mixedness: Contestations Over Crossing Signs." *Cultural Critique* 54 (Spring): 178–212.

Paltridge, B. (2012) *Discourse Analysis: An Introduction*, 2nd edition, New York: Bloomsbury.

Parker, I., and Cuéllar, D. (eds.) (2014) *Lacan, Discourse, Event: New Psychoanalytic Approaches to Textual Indeterminacy*, New York: Routledge.

Pascoe, P. (2009) *What Comes Naturally: Miscegenation Law and the Making of Race in America*, New York: Oxford University Press.

Philips, E., Odunlami, A., and Bonham, V. (2007) "Mixed Race: Understanding Difference in the Genome Era." *Social Forces* 86, no. 2: 795–820.

Piper, A. (1992) "Passing for White, Passing for Black." *Transition* 58: 4–32.

Prasad, C. (ed.). (2006) *Mixed: An Anthology of Short Fiction on the Multiracial Experience*, New York: W. W. Norton.

Rahier, J. (ed.) (2012) *Black Social Movements in Latin America: From Monocultural Mestizaje to Multiculturalism*, New York: Palgrave Macmillan.

Reardon, J. (2009) *Race to the Finish: Identity and Governance in an Age of Genomics*, Princeton: Princeton University Press.

Reyes, A. (2012) "On Fanon's Manichean Delirium." *Black Scholar* 42, nos. 3–4: 13–20.

Rice, R. (2012) *The New Politics of Protest: Indigenous Mobilization in Latin America's Neoliberal Era*, Tucson: University of Arizona Press.

Roberts, D. (2013) *Fatal Invention: How Science, Politics, and Big Business Re-Create Race in the Twenty-First Century*, New York: New Press.

Root, M. (2001) *Love's Revolution: Interracial Marriage*, Philadelphia: Temple University Press.

Root, M. (ed.). (1992) *Racially Mixed People in America*, Thousand Oaks, CA: Sage.

―― (ed.). (1996) *The Multiracial Experience: Racial Borders as the New Frontier*, Thousand Oaks, CA: Sage.

Rosenberg, J. (2008) "Race in a Genetic World." *Harvard Magazine* (May): 62–65.

Ryan, S. (2005) *The Grammar of Good Intentions: Race and the Antebellum Culture of Benevolence*, Ithaca: Cornell University Press.

Segal, R. (2001) *Islam's Black Slaves: The Other Black Diaspora*, New York: Farrar, Straus and Giroux.

Sexton, J. (2008) *Amalgamation Schemes: Antiblackness and the Critique of Multiracialism*, Minneapolis: University of Minnesota Press.

Sharfstein, D. (2007) "Crossing the Color Line: Racial Migration and the Emergence of the One-Drop Rule, 1600–1860." *Minnesota Law Review* 91: 592.

―― (2011). *The Invisible Line: Three American Families and the Secret Journey From Black to White*, New York: Penguin.

Shelby, T. (2002) "Foundations of Black Solidarity: Collective Identity or Common Oppression?" *Ethics* 112, no. 2: 231–266.

――. (2005) *We Who Are Dark: The Philosophical Foundations of Black Solidarity*, Cambridge, MA: Harvard University Press.

Silva, E. (2009) *Challenging Neoliberalism in Latin America*, New York: Cambridge University Press.

Sinvanandan, A. (1990) *Communities of Resistance: Writings on Black Struggles for Socialism*, New York: Verso.

Solow, B. (2014) *The Economic Consequences of the Atlantic Slave Trade*, Lanham: Lexington Books.

Song, M. (2012) "Making Sense of 'Mixture': States and the Classification of Mixed People." *Ethnic and Racial Studies* 35, no. 4: 565–573.

Spencer, R. (1999) *Spurious Issues: Race and Multiracial Identity Politics in the United States*, Boulder: Westview Press.

――. (2006) *Challenging Multiracial Identity*, Boulder: Lynne Rienner.

――. (2011) *Reproducing Race: The Paradox of Generation Mix*, Boulder: Lynne Rienner.

Spickard, P. (2009) "Amalgamation Schemes: Antiblackness and the Critique of Multiracialism (review)." *American Studies* 50, nos. 1–2: 125–127.

Spillers, H. (2003) "Notes on an Alternative Model—Neither/Nor," in *Black, White and In Color: Essays on American Literature and Culture*, Chicago: University of Chicago Press, pp. 301–318.

――. (2011) "Mama's Baby, Papa's Too." *Feminist Wire*, February 25. http://thefeministwire.com/2011/02/mamas-baby-papas-too/.

Sue, C. (2013) *Land of the Cosmic Race: Race Mixture, Racism, and Blackness in Mexico*, New York: Oxford University Press.

Sundstrom, R. (2008) *The Browning of America and the Evasion of Social Justice*, Albany, NY: State University of New York Press.

Taylor, P. (2013) *Race: A Philosophical Introduction*, 2nd edition, Cambridge: Polity Press.

Teele, J. (ed.). (2002) *E. Franklin Frazier and Black Bourgeoisie*, Columbia: University of Missouri Press.

Telles, E. (2014) *Pigmentocracies: Ethnicity, Race, and Color in Latin America*, Chapel Hill: University of North Carolina Press.

Telles, E., and Sue, C. (2009) "Race Mixture: Boundary-Crossing in Comparative Perspective." *Annual Review of Sociology* 35: 129–146.

Thompson, M. (ed.). (2007) *Confronting the New Conservatism: The Rise of the Right in America*, New York: New York University Press.

Vargas, J. (2010) *Never Meant to Survive: Genocide and Utopias in Black Diaspora Communities*, Lanham: Rowman & Littlefield.

Wachter-Grene, K. (2011) Amalgamation Schemes: Antiblackness and the Critique of Multiracialism (review). *Callaloo* 34, no. 1: 208–210.

Wade, P. (2004) "Images of Latin American Mestizaje and the Politics of Comparison." *Bulletin of Latin American Research* 23, no. 3: 355–366.

———. et al. (eds.). (2014) *Mestizo Genomics: Race Mixture, Nation, and Science in Latin America*, Durham: Duke University Press.

Wailoo, K., Nelson, A., and Lee, C. (eds.). (2012) *Genetics and the Unsettled Past: The Collision of DNA, Race, and History*, New Brunswick, NJ: Rutgers University Press.

Warren, C. (2013) "Onticide: Toward an Afro-pessimistic Queer Theory." Paper presented at the Annual Meeting of the American Studies Association Annual Meeting, Washington, DC, November 21.

Webber, J. and B. Carr (eds.). (2013) *The New Latin American Left: Cracks in the Empire*, Lanham: Rowman & Littlefield.

Whitmarsh, T. and D. Jones (eds.). (2010) *What's the Use of Race: Modern Governance and the Biology of Difference*, Cambridge, MA: MIT Press.

Williams, K. (2005) "Multiracialism and the Civil Rights Future." *Daedalus* 134, no. 1: 53–60.

———. (2008) *Mark One or More: Civil Rights in Multiracial America*, Ann Arbor: University of Michigan Press.

Wood, E. (2002) *The Origin of Capitalism: A Longer View*, New York: Verso.

Wright, R. et al. (2003) "Crossing Racial Lines: Geographies of Mixed-Race Partnering and Multiraciality in the United States." *Progress in Human Geography* 27, no. 4: 457–474.

Yancey, G. (2003) *Who Is White? Latinos, Asians, and the New Black/Nonblack Divide*, Boulder: Lynne Rienner.

Young, R. (1995) *Colonial Desire: Hybridity in Theory, Culture, and Race*, New York: Routledge.

Zack, N. (1993) *Race and Mixed Race*, Philadelphia: Temple University Press.

———. (ed.). (1995) *American Mixed Race: The Culture of Microdiversity*, Lanham: Rowman & Littlefield.

———. (1996) *Bachelors of Science: Seventeenth-Century Identity, Then and Now*, Philadelphia: Temple University Press.

———. (2002) *Philosophy of Science and Race*, New York: Routledge.

———. (2003) *Thinking About Race*, 2nd edition, Belmont, CA: Wadsworth Cengage Learning.

———. (2010) "The Fluid Symbol of Mixed Race." *Hypatia* 25, no. 4: 875–890.

———. (2011) *The Ethics and Mores of Race: Equality After the History of Philosophy*, Lanham: Rowman & Littlefield.

———. (2015) *White Privilege and Black Rights: The Injustice of U.S. Police Racial Profiling and Homicide*, Lanham: Rowman & Littlefield.

Zackodnik, T. (2004) *The Mulatta and the Politics of Race*, Jackson: University Press of Mississippi.

37
RACISM, STATE VIOLENCE, AND THE HOMELAND

Falguni A. Sheth[1]

Introduction

Many of us who contemplate race and racial divisions in the United States are accustomed to thinking of them primarily in terms of whites and blacks. In part this is because of the political and moral legacy and gravity of slavery on the Western/American historical consciousness. For long parts of US history, it would be appropriate to assume that the racial divide applied to white and non-white citizens/members within a society. Charles Mills names this divide the Racial Contract (RC), which he understands as the counterpart to the Social Contract, the moral code and set of political obligations that undergirds liberal societies (Mills 1997: 9–11). As Mills suggests, "The Racial Contract is an exploitation contract that creates . . . national white racial privilege" (31).

By extension, political obligations under the Social Contract involve a tacit distinction between national and extra-national contexts: our obligations appear to be first and foremost to our fellow citizens; all others—immigrants, foreigners, and refugees—can wait. During times of peace, prosperity, and minimal global mobility, this distinction could be accepted with fewer concerns: we should have obligations to our fellow citizens. But in contemporary times—times of war, high unemployment, decimated social structures, and high global mobility—it is not clear whether all residents within a society are considered to belong to that society, let alone have the rights and entitlements of members, that is, those who are considered to "rightfully belong" to that society. To further complicate the picture of the racial divide, at various moments, the violent implications of the Racial Contract can be diluted for middle- and upper-class populations of color, in that they are not always as starkly subject to the deprivation of rights and protections as poorer populations, white and non-white. Moreover, the question of our political obligations to members of other societies also arises in relation to the scope of the racial divide: can we understand the RC in relation to a "white supremacist" government that wages war in the name of national security, especially when that war involves tens of thousands of deaths of civilian "foreigners"? "White supremacy" is a technical term utilized to illustrate the dominance and hegemony of European colonialism, and its ensuing white settler society, which has historically dominated political government and other power structures (Mills 1997: 27ff). How should we understand the status of both registered non-citizen migrants along with undocumented migrants in the RC? In considering these questions, we are confronted with the additional complexity, not only of racism, but of wealth, as well as the relationship between racism and xenophobia within a nationalist framework.

Insofar as the RC refers to a white/non-white divide within the neat context of a nation or society, it is conceptually limiting. There is a certain applicability of the RC to a range of other non-white populations, on both sides of the racial-political hierarchy of persons and sub-persons. For example, we could consider the following practices to be part of the RC: the intensive war against black Americans as conducted by both white and non-white police officers; the war against undocumented migrants in the United States; the continuation of the War on Terror as exemplified through drone strikes into Pakistan and the Horn of Africa (Djibouti, Yemen, and Somalia); and the December 2014 admission of the US Senate Select Committee on Intelligence (SSCI) of the widescale physical and psychic degradation of suspected terrorists—as engaged "off-site" (by the United States) by both white and non-white agents for the CIA and the US government ("SSCI Torture Report" 2014). All of these actions were initiated or continued and facilitated over the course of the last two US presidential administrations, and will likely intensify through the 2016–2020 US presidential administration, as understood through the President Donald Trump's own campaign promises.

In these examples, the stark racial divide between whiteness and non-whiteness does not map squarely onto the contemporary US Racial Contract. That unruliness suggests that white supremacy refers less to skin color than ever before, and instead is a reference to the dynamics of institutional, legal, and economic power. Despite this caveat, the complexity of the RC can be sustained by dematerializing the political-racial hierarchy further, and insisting upon the possibility that a range of non-whites, depending upon a range of factors—from sexuality, gender, class, ethnicity, caste (understood as political/social status)—can be both "persons" as well as sub-persons in the nomenclature of the RC.

As such, in the current epoch, the RC is in need of careful reformulation with regard to new divisions between the racially dominant and the racially vulnerable. I don't wish to erase the racial salience of systemic inequality of the RC; rather I wish to highlight the racial complexity of systemic exploitation and oppression. In that vein, I want to consider a different framework in relation to the RC: the Homeland, through which I hope to illustrate a revision of the racial divide that will reflect its salience in the current moment.

The Homeland

The Homeland has become a refreshed racial imaginary for the United States. It came into visibility in the various state-led, media-driven, and racial-cultural responses to the events of 9/11. The term itself was officially inaugurated in the US political context through the creation of the Department of Homeland Security in 2002, which was to oversee all things related to the War on Terror and immigration. There was, of course, a strong association between those two. "Homeland" calls to mind *Heimat*, with all of its affective associations, ethnic ties, and cultural unity, as linked with Austria and Germany during the 1920s and '30s (Blickle 2002). *Heimat*, broadly echoing the notion of Home and cultural unity, evokes a similar sense of the norms and superiority of the US Homeland, even as the first director of the Department of Homeland Security, Tom Ridge, purported to be unaware of the unsavory associations of Homeland. (Becker

2002). The Homeland allows for the possibility of understanding the RC as it applies to persons and sub-persons, and non-persons as well. The category of non-persons would pertain to those who don't have *de jure* legal standing as members in US society, such as undocumented Latino migrants or peoples of Muslim/Middle Eastern/South Asian (MEMSA) descent. Among the latter example of non-persons, I would include those who are detained in the United States because they are, legally, pre-emptively understood as "terrorists," that is, without being assigned criminal charges or trials as these procedures apply to US citizens; also included would be those understood as "Muslim" nationals of countries against which the United States is engaging in a drone war: Pakistan, Yemen, Syria, and so forth, which do not have the right of appeal or legal recognition/protection of human rights within the context of the United States. The contours of the Homeland also allows us to see a slightly different dimension of white supremacy, as it accommodates and absorbs certain non-whites in the name of a united America.

Since its explicit invocation, the conceptual architecture of the Homeland has remained vivid, illustrating certain political antagonisms between populations who might otherwise be allied. These antagonisms revealed a new configuration of "white supremacy," in which the membership of populations of color has become more frequent. The associations between (seemingly) non-Muslims and Whites have become part of a national imaginary of patriotic unity. The category of non-Muslims includes Black, Latino and non-Muslim South Asians as part of a national agenda to "conquer" Muslim men suspected to be terrorists. In this seemingly color-blind configuration, "true Americans" are united in their support of certain jingoist agendas like the War on Terror, in which the casual genocide of Iraqi and Afghani civilians, and Pakistani and Yemeni civilians become a byproduct of "National"/"Homeland" Security. The image of patriotic unity has shifted in terms of colors and hues; it encompassed various strata and political ranks—from Congress politicians to ordinary Democrats and Republicans, academics, feminists, and anti-racist activists. The contours of support for the War on Terror ebbs and flows depending up on various factors, including whether it is an election year.

As well, there has been a sustained renewal of an anti-immigrant agenda which also calls into question the narrow racial formation of white supremacy: At the federal and state levels, we have seen not only white, but multiple Black, Latino, and Asian officials who have for six years led a charge against undocumented migrants appearing as mostly Latino. For example, Louisiana's governor of South Asian descent, Bobby Jindal, Florida Senator Ted Cruz, and US President Obama, under whose administration, the Department of Homeland Security deported over two million immigrants in fewer than six years (Gonzalez-Barrera and Krogstad 2014). And finally, most recently, there has been a renewed attention to white police violence as directed against young black boys, girls, men and women, even as there have been many non-white police officers who are implicated in incidents of political violence.

Since the war on Terror, there appears to be an expectation that patriotic, and even progressive, members will uphold certain xenophobic practices as less troubling than racism. This expectation, in turn, complicates the other assumption of the RC that I mentioned earlier, namely that national racial privilege is mostly held by whites, who are automatically considered members regardless of their citizenship status. In a society in which there is simultaneously (1) the rising visibility of non-white elites, as we are increasingly seeing over the last decade; (2) a non-partisan "American" commitment to engaging in a War on Terror against Muslim/Middle East/South Asian nations; (3) an "American" debate over the legitimacy of undocumented migration, the contours of Americanness (which has historically meant phenotypical or genealogical "whiteness" both in terms of power and in terms of racial membership) are slowly changing to accommodate a multiracial national membership. Thus, the privileging of commitments to challenge racism over commitments to challenge xenophobia is justified in terms of national security and the need to protect the Homeland. This is why the initial reading of the RC must be augmented by a consideration of the Homeland (in which racial alliances must be considered in light not only of domestic social relations and culture, but international relations as well).

The Rhetoric of "Security" and the "Crisis" of Immigrants and Refugees

The impact of the Homeland can be further illustrated through a marked antagonism towards accepting immigrants and refugees. Since 2015, increasing attention has been directed toward the mass migration of human beings from a range of regions to Europe. In particular, the last year has found an unceasing focus not only on "the refugee crisis," but on how to "arrest" it. Of course, the concern over mass migration of Middle Eastern (framed currently as Syrian) migrants to Europe and North America dovetails with corresponding migration and concern over African and Asian migrants, who are leaving their residences for a variety of reasons, whether civil strife, economic desperation, climate change, or other issues.

This phenomenon overlaps with the continual War on Terror, initiated by the United States in the aftermath of 9/11. The United States framed its war as a defense (and an attack) against "terrorism." This war was described in a range of discourses (though not always explicitly) as a war against Islam, against Muslim extremists, and jihadists. However, as a cursory review of the last 15 years will show, it affected a much broader range of Muslim/South Asian/Middle Eastern populations globally, whether in North America, Europe, or Australia. The War on Terror, and its corresponding policies—from pre-emptive policing, warrantless wiretapping, stricter migration policy, and the highest rate of deportations since the nineteenth century (under the Obama administration), was framed as a way to regain the security that the United States lost through the events of 9/11: secure borders, internal safety and, presumably some sort of economic/political/social security within the homeland. This notion of security is not only significant, it is contagious. Indeed, in the post-9/11 era, swaths of Europe and Asia, from the UK to the Netherlands, Denmark, to India, have taken up the concept of security as the basis to engage in creative domestic policing and foreign policy.[2] As Gregory White (2011) points out, the concept of security as popularized in the aftermath of the declaration of the War on Terror was taken up similarly as a notion framing the concerns of the European Union with regard to climate-induced migration.

Are these concerns warranted? According to the Migration Policy Institute, in 2014 the United States had 42.4 million immigrants, constituting 13.3% of the total US population. It is not the largest proportion of immigrants that the United States has ever had, nor the lowest. For example, immigrants constituted 14.8% of the population in 1890 and 14.7% in 1910. The raw number is the highest number of immigrants. This number includes both authorized and unauthorized residents who are not US citizens at birth. Migrants from India constituted the largest number of immigrants, at 147,500; they were followed by immigrants from China (131,800), Mexico (130,000), Canada (41,200) and the Philippines (40,500). Yet, to believe the political rhetoric during the US 2016 election year, the biggest threat to the United States came from Mexican/Central/Latin American immigration, and "Muslim" immigrants, a generally amorphous category not substantiated through much hard evidence, if any.

According to Eurostat, the "statistical office" of the European Union, 3.4 million people migrated to Europe in 2014, 1.6 million of whom were not citizens of EU member states. In 2015, according to the International Organization for Migration, approximately 1.3 million people were estimated to have crossed into Europe in 2015, one million by sea and almost 35,000 by land. These numbers vary highly: Frontex, the European Union's external border force, estimates that over 1.8 million people have crossed into Europe. The European Union asserts that, during the same year, 1.3 million asylum claims had been filed. In the EU-28 + Norway and Sweden, 215,000 Syrians were registered as refugees as of November 2014 (Migration Policy Centre 2016). Unclear on the numbers for 2015, but the seeming "threat" was expressed in very loud terms.

At least with regard to Europe, it is difficult to ascertain the correspondence between the hype surrounding the seeming influx of Syrians with the data. In the United States, it is clear that the hype over migration from Mexico and Latin/Central America is in fact overinflated; Indian and Chinese immigrants constitute more than twice the number of Mexican immigrants entering the United States. Yet, there is something about the perception and reception of these migrants that shapes public policy and public response to these migrants. As Michel Foucault makes us aware, "truth" is hardly about objectivity, but rather about the production of certain realities (Foucault 1982).

Most Syrian migrants are attempting to claim refugee status, and yet, Hannah Arendt's 1951 lament—that a human rights framework was insufficient in prodding European nations into undertaking their obligations to provide shelter and protection to Jewish and Eastern European migrants during World War II—still remains relevant. Claims to give entry to Syrians at a faster rate, to increase the entry quotas, to accommodate them in a more humane fashion as they await entry in detention camps—on human rights grounds—has generally been ineffectual, as nations claim scarcity of resources, cultural differences, religious tensions, fear of sexual assault, and a myriad of other political and social concerns (Smith and Kingsley 2016; Thomson Reuters Foundation 2016). If the general commentary about the exit of the UK from the European Union (Brexit) is to be believed, nations would rather pull out of a federated sovereignty such as the EU rather than be told how to accept immigrants. Yet, the fact remains that it is difficult to reconcile how nations can turn away from an ethical appeal to help observe human rights as these human beings die a slow death.

One way to understand the application of the Homeland's racial imaginary to a liberal society that values democracy, and human rights is through the language that heads of state use to illustrate their commitment to such concepts, such as security and sovereignty. In the *Security, Territory, Population* lectures, Michel Foucault describes security as the oversight over a population—in relation to sovereignty as "exercised within the borders of a territory" and discipline, which is implemented "on the bodies of individuals" (Foucault 2007: 11). Security, as Foucault gradually teases out the concept, is expressed through mechanisms that neither prohibit nor prescribe (which is what is done by law and discipline, respectively). "With the establishment of these mechanisms of security, there is a considerable activation and propagation of the disciplinary corpus" (Foucault 2007: 7), but by drawing on both law and discipline security, tries to "work within reality, by getting the components of reality to work in relation to each other, thanks to and through a series of analyses and specific arrangements" (Foucault 2007: 47). These mechanisms seem to overlap with regulatory power. Mechanisms of security are designed to "respond to reality in such a way that this response cancels out the reality to which it responds—nullifies it, or limits, checks, or regulates it. I think this regulation within the element of reality is fundamental in apparatuses of security" (Foucault 2007: 47).

In this light we can see that security is hardly a neutral concept: it is crucial to the notion of governmentality: governing so as to arrive at "the right disposition of things to a suitable end" (Foucault 2007: 96). A suitable end, then, is distinct from the end of sovereignty, which is the making of decisions for "the common good and salvation of all" (Foucault 2007: 98). From this crucial distinction, we can elicit the role and telos of security in the context of the "refugee crisis" namely in relation to state racism.

Perhaps not so strangely, security is also a crucial term in considering the "refugee crisis," although it takes on a somewhat different but related meaning in the contemporary moment. In particular, the immigration "crisis," whether in relation to the influx of Syrian refugees, Muslim or Latino migrants to the United States, or climate-induced migration, is articulated as the fear of losing sovereign control over the right to control one's borders and of endangering the security of a nation's citizens. In fact, this is one of the reasons that the UK appears to have exited the EU—because they don't want to have their borders in relation to Muslim or Syrian or non-EU migrants regulated by the EU rather than by UK government.

The discourse of security, in the post-9/11 US context of the Homeland can be marked through concerns about terrorist threats, not just externally but "within our midst." It encompasses the fear that someone who lives next to us, or with whom we work or socialize might suddenly rise up to endanger us. It is marked by the concern that more immigrants will lead to depressed wages, rising unemployment for deserving residents and citizens. It is indicated through the fear of illegal drivers, illegal residents, increasing crime on the part of illegal migrants. The production of these fears and anxieties have led to policies that are believed, in Foucault's words to "nullify, limit, check or regulate" those realities: from pre-emptive policing (otherwise known as racial profiling); warrantless wiretapping; removing safeguards to privacy in the name of anticipating potential terrorist attacks; to material support statutes designed to track the inflows and outflows of relatively large sums of money; or to inhibit money laundering (as this is ascribed to Somali migrants who are channeling money home through Al-Shabab much more so than by global banks or drug cartels). It includes racial profiling of darker populations through immigration laws, which makes it difficult, if not illegal, for non-citizens to reside in the United States without having residency papers in their possessions at all times; however, it should be noted that such laws are meeting effective challenges in the federal courts (Rau 2012). It encompasses new requirements to prove legal residencies or citizenship before being entitled to receive a driver's license (Perron 2016). US citizens, by contrast, are not required to carry proof of citizenship upon their persons.

The concern over security has led to more stringent immigration policies against countries thought to harbor more anti-democratic/anti-US/anti-liberal sentiments:

mostly countries with predominantly Muslim populations, such Pakistan, Afghanistan, Indonesia, Somalia, and so forth. The fear of threats to the "internal security" of the United States has also been extended to increased measures to deter migrants entering from the South (presumably in efforts to check Mexican/Central American migration).

These measures—security apparatuses—are designed to nullify the threat of terror and the "onslaught" of migration (whether these are "realities" or "chimeras"). Perhaps terror and migration were once separate fears, initially emerging in the context of the post-9/11 United States, but they appear to have converged in a larger concern about security writ large. However, since 9/11, such security discourses and apparatuses have spread, like contagion, to other parts of the world, as other countries have followed and taken up the security discourses popularized through post-9/11 US security measures.

By expressing their resistance to the ethical mandate in the language of security, in effect, these states express the absence of recognition of these migrants as humans, as members of nations; indeed, they affirm that these migrants are barely human, bare life, in the lingo of Giorgio Agamben, and thereby constitute that part of life that is allowed to die (Agamben 1998). But perhaps in distinction to Agamben, the decision over abandoning life outside the gates of the city, so to speak, is articulated through the frame of security—couched in terms of sovereignty—but is in fact delivered through the apparatus of governmentality: governing/managing towards suitable ends rather than towards the common good.

Which suitable ends would those be? In light of the previous argument, I suggest that those ends have to do with the racial and political management of sub-persons and non-persons through legal technologies of security, immigration policy, and a constant attention to the racial hierarches erected through the conceptual and legal framework of the Homeland. The Homeland encompasses those broad hierarchies of the Racial Contract; it also adds a dimension that highlights the multiple layers of racial hierarchies that accompany war, jingoism (understood as extreme chauvinism or nationalism marked especially by a belligerent foreign policy; Merriam-Webster 2012), and patriotism. There is, if you will, a new racial divide, but it transcends the long-standing racial boundaries embedded in the political history of the United States—in the history of slavery, lynchings, Jim Crow, the Treaty of Guadalupe Hidalgo (in which the United States annexed large swaths of Mexico, giving rise to what we now understand as the Southwestern United States), the Bracero Program, Chinese Exclusion, Japanese Internment, the Hindu Conspiracy Trials, among other policies that gave rise to the original racial contract—the original racial imaginary.

State Violence

Those suitable ends become the telos of the racial imaginary of the Homeland: how best to manage sub-persons and non-persons for the purposes of governing. This is where a perspective on the purpose of the state becomes an important link to understanding the relationship between racial management and the Homeland: state violence. State violence need not be understood in purely active, vivid, or isolated moments of spectacular violence such as droning, bombings, or police brutality. Certainly, these would be examples of state-led violence. However, here I want to suggest a slightly different take on state violence, namely that which takes place in the form of legal procedures, or what might be called legal technologies. Within liberal political thought, legal procedures are considered important political safeguards of individual rights. This is one of the reasons that the Social Contract is considered to be an important foundation for liberal societies: because it appears to guarantee the rights, recognition, and obligations of individuals in those societies. And yet, as Mills shows us through his illumination of the Racial Contract, such political frameworks work in favor of some populations precisely as they work against other—darker—populations.

As I have tried to illustrate, we can dematerialize this relationship such that we understand the application of sovereign management to work against those who are politically vulnerable for a range of reasons (race, citizenship, class, or other privations of protections or privilege). As a result, laws and legal procedures—seen as neutral and protective of all members of society in the context of liberal political thought—take on a different light in the context of understanding the state as engaging in the practice of sovereign racial management. In previous work, I have located such practices under the category of legal technologies (Sheth 2009: chapter 1) which unruly or threatening populations are "processed" through seemingly neutral procedures. Here, I want to augment the idea of legal technologies by suggesting that these can also be adapted/expanded to make unruly populations politically vulnerable, that is, exposed to state-led hostility, designed to further outcaste such populations as criminal or morally deviant or otherwise ideologically, politically, socially, or even physically "quarantined." This may be similar to social death, as Orlando Patterson and others have argued (Patterson 1982; Cacho 2012). However, whereas social death can be produced through multiple channels, here I want to emphasize the state-led emphasis on producing the outlaw or the criminal through the legal processing of unruly populations into populations who are made vulnerable, that is deprived of rights, legal recognition, and standing—through the application of laws, legal categories, and procedures that further formulate and cement the Homeland in ways that reproduce the racialized or enfranchised hierarchies between persons, sub-persons, and non-persons. Examples of this can be seen in the legally changing divisions in membership in US society: from enhancing the difficulty of obtaining citizenship, to the procedural criteria which make it more or less difficult by which certain residents of US society can transition into membership (naturalization, or legal residency, or different visa statuses). Other examples include the legal procedures instantiated in the 2001 USA Patriot Act, passed shortly after 9/11 (but written well before), by which certain populations, such as Muslims/Middle Easterners/South Asians are efficiently (and legally) pipelined into being pre-emptively policed, racially profiled, put on TSA watchlists at airports, and so forth, on the grounds that there is good reason to consider them to be terrorist threats. These procedures, prima facie, appear to be neutral, but take on a new light when considered in relation to the discourse of "security" (see the second section of this chapter).

These, among many other legal processes (including the absence of grand jury indictments of police officers who have been recorded as killing black men in the course of duty), could be—with proper accounting of those procedures—considered to be part and parcel of the state's racial management of sub-persons and non-persons. This, in brief, is a description of state-led violence in relation to the racial imaginary of the Homeland.

Conclusion

Even though it is seductive to believe the promises of liberal political theory and the seeming universality of the Social Contract, these promises are at odds with the history of systematic racism in the United States. Moreover, the Racial Contract does not extend neatly to the divide between whites and blacks, but extends in complex, unruly ways to populations of color on both sides of the racial divide. The framework of the Homeland, as a structure that involves citizens and non-citizens of different ethnicities and races, helps to illuminate the multiracial white supremacy that is much more of an accurate depiction of the multipronged racial divide that undergirds the United States as of this writing. The Homeland, which has reframed some US populations of color as part of the in-group in the US racial imaginary, also—through legal and political measures—argues for the rejection and exclusion of immigrants, and refugees on the grounds of security considerations. As I hope I have shown, this is a language deployed by the state to justify its unethical neglect—indeed even violent practice—in relation to its liberal and human rights obligations to care for human beings in need. This rejection, and its justification, is one version of state racism, and indeed can be seen as a form of state violence deployed through various legal and political measures described in the previous section.

Notes

1 Sincere thanks to Marcellus Andrews, Mickaella Perina, Robert E. Prasch III, and Paul Taylor for their extensive and generous interlocutions.
2 See India's Prevention of Terrorism Act (POTA) of 2002, repealed in 2004; the UK POTA 2005, the Anti-Terrorism Crime and Security Act of 2001.

References

Agamben, Giorgio. (1998) *Homo Sacer: Sovereign Power and Bare Life*, Stanford: Stanford University Press.
Becker, Elizabeth. (2002) "Prickly Roots of 'Homeland Security.'" *New York Times*, August 31, National edition, sec. Washington Talk.
Blickle, Peter. (2002) *Heimat: A Critical Theory of the German Idea of Homeland*, Rochester, NY: Camden House.
Cacho, Lisa Marie. (2012) *Social Death: Racialized Rightlessness and the Criminalization of the Unprotected*, Nation of Newcomers: Immigrant History as American History, New York: New York University Press.
Foucault, Michel. (1982) *The Archaeology of Knowledge*, New York: Pantheon Books.
———. (2007) *Security, Territory, Population: Lectures at the College de France 1977–1978*, New York: Picador Press.
Gonzalez-Barrera, Ana, and Krogstad, Jens Manuel. (2014) "U.S. Deportations of Immigrants Reach Record High in 2013." *Pew Research Center*, October 2. www.pewresearch.org/fact-tank/2014/10/02/u-s-deportations-of-immigrants-reach-record-high-in-2013/.
Migration Policy Centre. (2016) "Focus on Syrians." Accessed June 10. www.migrationpolicycentre.eu/migrant-crisis/focus-on-syrians/.
Mills, Charles. (1997) *The Racial Contract*, Ithaca: Cornell University Press.
Patterson, Orlando. (1982) *Slavery and Social Death: A Comparative Study*, Cambridge, MA: Harvard University Press.
Perron, Darren. (2016) *Tips to Speed Up Your Next Visit to the Vt. DMV*. www.wcax.com/story/33017676/tips-to-speed-up-your-next-visit-to-the-vt-dmv.
Rau, Alia Beard. (2012) "Arizona Immigration Law: Supreme Court Upholds Key Portion of Senate Bill 1070 Read More: http://archive.azcentral.com/news/politics/articles/2012/06/03/20120603arizona-immigration-law-supreme-court-opinion.html.
"Senate Select Committee on Intelligence: Committee Study of the Central Intelligence Agency's Detention and Interrogation Program." (2014) Declassified Executive Summary. Washington, DC: U.S. Senate. www.amnestyusa.org/pdfs/sscistudy1.pdf.

Sheth, Falguni A. (2009) *Toward a Political Philosophy of Race*, Albany: State University of New York Press.
Smith, Helena, and Kingsley, Patrick. (2016) "Far-Right Group Attacks Refugee Camp on Greek Island of Chios." *Guardian Online*, November 18, sec. World. www.theguardian.com/world/2016/nov/18/far-right-group-attacks-refugee-camp-greek-island-chios.
Thomson Reuters Foundation. (2016) "Rights Groups: Rape so Prevalent Female Refugees, Migrants Taking Contraceptives Before Journey." *Japan Times*, December 1, sec. World/Social Issues. www.japantimes.co.jp/news/2016/12/01/world/social-issues-world/rights-groups-rape-prevalent-female-refugees-migrants-taking-contraceptives-journey/.
White, Gregory. (2011) *Climate Change and Migration*, Oxford: Oxford University Press.

INDEX

Page numbers in italic refer to a figure on the corresponding page. Page numbers in bold refer to a table on the corresponding page.

abjection 293–295
abstract liberalism 499
Achebe, Chinua 70
Acta Anthropologica Sinica 174
active ignorance 250–251
adaptive evolution 428–440
Addams, Jane 83–84
Adivasis 189
aesthetic racialization 366, 391–392; appropriation and transculturation 374–375; beauty and the sublime 376; critical race feminist aesthetics 369–370; Du Bois's and Fanon's views of aesthetic experience 367–369; in everyday life 375–376; Kara Walker's art 370–373, *370–372*; lighting in filmmaking 395–397; post- and decolonial theory 366–377
aesthetics 365; beauty and the sublime 376; racial heritage of 365–366; and taste 391
affective disorders 292–293
affective/volitional accounts of racism 415–416
Africa: Hegel's conception of its history 46–48; 'Out of Africa' thesis 176
"Africana" 140
Africana intellectual history 144
Africana philosophy 91, 141–149; as creolizing practice 148–149; de-intellectualization of Africana thought 142; development 53–54; excluded moderns 18–25
African-descended thinkers, as excluded moderns 18–25
Africanness, linking to blackness 140–141
"Afrocentrists" 19–20
Afro-melancholia 144–145
"Afromodern" 142
Afropessimism 146
Agamben, Georgio 113; *homo sacer* 115–116; state of exception 113–118
agent-based accounts of racism 412–419; affective/volitional accounts 415–416; behavioral accounts 413–415; doxastic accounts 412–413

agokwa 155
Albert, Kurt 103
Alcoff, Linda Martín 58n38, 242–243
Alexander, Michelle 194
Algren, Nelson 94
"alief" 272
alienated familiar 249, 253
alleles 307–312, 309–310, **311**, *312*
Allen, Grant 219
ally status, reinforcing through jokes 381–382
Ambedkar, B. R. 188, 191
ambivalence 299
American experimentalism: Du Bois, W.E.B. 221–226, 229–231; James, William 216–218; "social Darwinism" 218–221; Spencer, Herbert 218–221
American philosophy: excluded moderns 18–25; as "Idol of the Theater" 17–20
American race canon 76
American racial canon 75–82
Amo, Anton Wilhelm 131, 146; "Afer" 133–134; "On the Apathy of the Human Mind" 131–132; *De Jure Maurorum in Europa* 132
analytic metaphysics 203–205; Andreasen's Cladism 212–213; Appiah's reduction of race to racial identity 206–207; Corlett's reductionism 208–209; Garcia's opposition to racial and ethnic identities 209–210; Glasgow's reconstructionist account of race 210–211; Zack's radical eliminativism 207–208
ancestry, and patriarchy 156–158
Andreasen, Robin O. 212–213
Anglo White privilege 254–255
Anglo-American feminists, intersectionality 344–345
animal breeding: "Buffon's rule" 325–326; Darwin's interest in 327
Anishinaabe/Neshnabé society 154
anthropocene 465; as era 467–468
anthropology: Boasian school of anthropology 5–6; Chinese research in 174–177

INDEX

anthropos 463–464
antiblack racism 147, 391–394; and mixed-race 531–533
antiblackness 142
anti-caste activists 186–187
anti-realism 314–315
anti-Semitism: Baden Decree 62; generic generalizations about *them* 282; and Heidegger 62–65; Jewry 64; Judeophobia 63; *weltjudentum* 63–64
anti-Semitism, of canonical philosophers 9–10
APE (Associative-Propositional model of Evaluation) 266; explicit prejudice 271–273; implicit bias 270–271
Appiah, K. Anthony 48–49, 286; reductionism of 206–207
appropriation 374–375
arc of history metaphor 372
Arendt, Hannah 69; racism of 70–72
Aristotle 204; characterization of "man" 424–428; views on natural slavery 7–8
"Aryan myth" 187–189
Aryanism 196n44
Ascher, Saul 9
Ashheim, Steven 65
Asian existentialism 96–97
Atiy-Yuyah 466
attitudes: control over implicit attitudes 268–270; "Driven Underground" 268–270; implicit 264–266; "sequential priming" 267; "True Attitudes" 266, 268; unawareness of implicit attitudes 268
"Austrian school" 222–223
automaticity 267
autrui 66
aversive racism 267, 410
awareness 268–270
Azalea, Iggy 374–375

Bacon, Francis 15–16
Baden Decree 62
Ballou, Hosea 134
Banaji, Mazarin 267
Banneker, Benjamin 79, 146
baozhong 170
Barkley, Charles 285
Barrett, William 89
Bartky, Sandra Lee 453
Bashar 470
Beale, Francis 337
Beattie, James 8
beauty 376
Beauvoir, Simone de 93–94, 99n16; "critical phenomenology" 234–235
Beijing Man 175–176
Being and Nothingness (Sartre, 1943) 91
Bell, Derrick 350; *Faces at the Bottom of the Well* 356–357; racial realism 353–357; "Racial Remediation: An Historical Perspective on Current Conditions" 355; *And We Are Not Saved: The Elusive Quest for Racial Justice* 355–356
Benedict, Ruth 6–7
beneficial internal epistemic friction 252
"benevolent" forms of racism 416–417
Benjamin, Walter 35, 114
Bentley, Jerry 129
"berdache" 165n1
Bernasconi, Robert 36–37, 64, 66, 357–358
Bernier, François 5, 169
Berreman, Gerald D. 185–186
Bethencourt, Francisco 7
Bhabha, Homi 299
bias: black-white IAT 261–264, *262–263*; explicit prejudice 271–273; implicit bias 264–266; jokes and implicit bias 383–388; "shooter bias" 269
bigotry, of Hume 22
biogenomic race 306
biological concept of race 5
biological race 306–307
"biologism" 64
biology: biological implications of human genetic variation 312–313; Galápagos-writ-large scenario 305–306; philosophical implications of human genetic variation 313–315; sociobiology 428
biopolitics 7
biopower 118–120
birth control 330–331; *see also* eugenics
"blaccent" 374–375
black *noir* 255
Black Notebooks 63
Black Panther Party 108; Dalit Panther group 187
"Black Power" 43–44
Blackface 299, 386–387
BlackLivesMatter protests 491–492, 531–533
blackness 95, 181; linking to Africanness 140–141; mixed-race identity 526–533; "Negro" categorization of the black race 225–226; pro-black multiracial studies 526–528
black-white IAT 261–264, *262–263*; implicit bias 264–266
Blake, Michael 509
blindness 249–250; color-blindness 492–493; white racial blindness 388
Blumenbach, J. F. 6
Boas, Franz 5–6
Boasian school of anthropology 5–6
Bodin, Jean 8
Bogin, Ruth 134
Bracken, Harry 10
Brahmins 184
the brain, evolution of 435–436
breeding: "Buffon's rule" 325–326; Darwin's interest in 327

550

INDEX

Broca, Paul 6
Brown, Michael 114, 256, 393
Brown v. Board of Education 351
Bruckner, Jacob 11
"Buffon's rule" 325–326
Burruz, Stephanie Rivera 99n17
Burton, Jonathan 194n3
Butler, Judith 238, 298–299

Caliphates 140–141
Calvinism 134
Cameron, David 114
camps 113–118; and ghettos 114–115; and modern sovereignty 116–117
canonical philosophers 78–82; American racial canon 75–82; excluded moderns 18–25; racism of 9–10; racism of, handling in the classroom 15
canons 75
Cappetti, Carla 99n13
Card, Claudia 448
Carmichael, Stokely 7
Carter, Robert 354–355
Cassirer, Ernst 147
caste 183; "Aryan myth" 187–189; "Harijan" 184–185; Hinduism's influence on racial philosophy 190–191; "racist casteism" 194; "Scheduled Castes" 185; and slavery 187; violence in 184
categories of race 306–307
Caygill, Howard 67
Césaire, Aimé 22, 71
Chakana 465–466
challenging generics 286–287
character 446; taking responsibility for 457
characteristic generics 279
chattel slavery 21
Cheng, Anne Anlin 299
Cheyette, Bryan 71
Chiang, Kaishek 174
China: Beijing Man 175–176; concept of 'race' in 169–170; Daoism 471–472; eugenics 172–173; genealogies 170; 'Han chauvinism' 174; 'Han race' 170–171; Japan's victory over 169; minority nationalities in 174; racial politics 172; Ren 468–469; Yellow Emperor 170; *zhonghua minzu* 174; *zu* 170
China's Destiny (Kaishek) 174
Chinese Committee for Racial Hygiene 172–173
Chinese Eugenics Institute 172–173
chromosomes 307
Civil Rights 355
Cladism 205–206; Andreasen's Cladism 212–213
clans 154
Clarkson, Thomas 8
classes of "idols" 16–17
classical racism 408–409

Cleaver, Eldridge 398
closet racism 408
CLS (Critical Legal Studies) 355
CMRS (Critical Mixed Race Studies) association 524–525
Coates, Ta-Nehesi 228
coercion and power in liberal society 327–330
cognitive therapy for racial ignorance 253
Cohen, Ted 385
collectivism of Du Bois 226–227
Collins, Julia 194
colonialism 141–142; *Discourse on Colonialism* (Césaire) 71; and freedom 143; US settler colonialism 154–156
coloniality 462–463
colonization 293–294, 297; dehumanization of 296; racialization of 295
color-blindness 492–493; disruptive defense of post-racial ideal 502–503; historical objection against post-racial ideal 501–502; liberal defense of post-racial ideal against ideological objection 498–501; objections against post-racial ideal 495–498; vicious nature of post-racialism 503–504
Combahee River Collective's founding statement 337–338
Communist Party, Du Bois's membership in 228
concept of race, origins of 5–6
conceptual jurisdiction: of freedom 33–35; of nature 47
Conrad, Joseph 70
"constitutive luck" 448
construction of the philosophical canon 10–11
constructionism 205
Continental philosophy 349
control over implicit attitudes 268–270
conventionalism 314–315
convivencia 471
Cooper, Anna Julia 81–82
core tenets of twentieth-century eugenicists 323–324
Corlett, J. Angelo, reductionism of 208–209
cosmologies 462; *Bashar/Insan* 470; *Chakana* 466; Ren 468–469; *Runa* 470–471; universals 469–470
cosmopolitanism, and racism 36–37
Coste, Pierre 10
Cox, Oliver Cromwell 7, 186
CPR (Critical Philosophy of Race) 357–358, 359n1; and CRT 357–358
creolization 147–149
Criminal Tribes Act of 1871 189
critical frameworks for aesthetics and race: critical race feminist aesthetics 369–370; Du Bois's and Fanon's views of aesthetic experience 367–369; post- and decolonial theory 366–377
"critical phenomenology" 233–235; Alcoff, Linda Martín 242–243; discriminatory treatment, ending 241–242; intersubjective communication

240; "natural attitude" 235–238; "zone of indeterminacy" 238
Critical Philosophies of Race 350
critical race feminist aesthetics: aesthetic sustenance and pleasure 373–374; appropriation and transculturation 374–375; beauty and the sublime 376; in everyday life 375–376
critical theory 102–103; Davis, Angela 105–108
"critical whiteness studies" 480
Critique of Practical Reason (Kant), "transition" 33
CRT (Critical Race Theory) 349; *alienated familiar* 249; Bell, Derrick 350; and CPR 357–358; focus on laws 7; idealist shift of 350–353; influence on scholarship 357–359; institutionalization of 351; and psychoanalysis 298–300; racial realism of Bell 353–357; simply alien 249; Western philosophy, role in spread of racist ideas 3–4; white ignorance 253
Crummell, Alexander 79, 84
Cugoano, Quobna Ottobah 8, 136–138, 146
"cultural code" 63
cultural racism 409
culture: Fanti culture 136–138; "ratcheting" 437; and "transition" 34–35; treating as pollutant 147
Curry, Tommy 79–80

Dagbovie-Mullins, Sika 531
Dalit Panther group 187
Dalits 184–185
Darwin, Charles 170; adaptive evolution 428–440; Galápagos-writ-large scenario 305–306; interest in animal breeding 327; natural selection 442n4; pragmatism 216–218; "social Darwinism" 218; "survival of the fittest" 218
Davis, Angela 102–103, 105–106, 108–109
De Jure Maurorum in Europa 132
Deer, Sarah 159
defining racism 407–411
DeGraffenreid v. General Motors 339–340
dehumanization of colonization 296
de-intellectualization of Africana thought 142
Delany, Martin R. 86
Delbanco, Andrew 491
delegitimization of Indigenous political representation 162–163
Delgado, Richard 349
Deloria, Vine, Jr. 157–158
Department of Homeland Security, the 540–542
deploying white power 481–482
Descartes, Rene 129–132; "natural attitude" 237–238
descriptive generics 284–286
deserved suffering 145
detrimental internal epistemic friction 252–253
Deutscher, Penelope 93–94
development: *Entwicklung* 53–55; *massa damnata* 54
development of human sociality 428–440
Diamond, Jared 45–46

differences in proponents of eugenics 322–324, 330–332
Dikötter, Frank 177n1
Dilthey, Wilhelm 222, 225
Diné Marriage Act 157
Dirks, Nicholas 187
disabilities, prenatal genetic testing 329
disciplinary decadence 146
discrimination: and the ethics of immigration 507–511; intersectionality 338–341; perpetuating through jokes 381–382
disruptive defense of post-racial ideal 502–503
division of labor, caste system 191–192
DNA: genome 307; mitochondrial Eve 313
Dolezal, Rachel 447
Dongyi 469
Dossa, Shiraz 70
Dotson, Kristie 256–258, 345
double consciousness 251–252
Douglass, Frederick 144
doxastic accounts of racism 412–413
Drabinski, John 68
Dravidians 187–189
Du Bois, W.E.B. 5, 84, 140, 144, 221–226, 248; member of Communist Party 228; Negro Academy 226; pragmatism of 84–86, 229–231; racial "tendencies" 229; Schmoller's influence on 222–223; Talented Tenth 226; view of aesthetic experience 367–369
Duffy gene 311
Dumont, Louis 191
Duster, Troy 322
Dutch Sri Lanka, caste-race groups 184
Dyer, Richard 395
dynamic images 394

Eaglestone, Robert 69
economics: Frankfurt School critical theory 102–103; Schmoller, Gustav von 222–223
Edwards, Jonathan 134
Eisenmenger, Johann Andreas 9
Eisenstadt, Oona 68–69
eliminativism 205; ontological position of as post-racialism 494; Zack's radical eliminativism 207–208
Ellison, Ralph 94–95, 248
emotions: and race 450–455; and responsibility 448–450
empirical concept of race 30–31
empiricism 10; pseudo-concepts 40n16
Encyclopedia Africana 140
Entwicklung 53–55
environmental racism 331–332
epigenetics 331–332
epistemic death 254–255
epistemic hiding 249
epistemic injustice 247; hermeneutical injustice 248–249; racial ignorance 248

INDEX

epistemic resistance 248; double consciousness 251–252; internal epistemic friction 252; micro-resistance 258–259

epistemic violence 256–259; testimonial quieting 257; testimonial smothering 257

epistemologies of ignorance 247

Equiano, Olaudah 8, 26n5

ethics: "Herrenvolk Ethics" 38; of immigration 507–511; of Nazism 38

Ethiopia: Ge'ez 129; Yacob, Zera 127–131

ethnic versus racial differentiation 50–51

eugenics: in China 172–173; core tenets of twentieth-century eugenicists 323–324; Galton, Francis 321; liberal eugenics 321–322; negative eugenics 323; positive eugenics 322–323; power and coercion in liberal society 327–330; proponents of, differences in 322–324, 330–332; as pseudo-science 25–26n1; State intervention 328–329

Evans, Richard J. 280–281

evolution: adaptive evolution 428–440; biological implications of human genetic variation 312–313; Galápagos-writ-large scenario 305; natural selection 442n4; Neo-Lamarckism 170–171; "survival of the fittest" 218

excluded moderns 18–25

existentialism 89, 97n2; Africana philosophy 91; Asian existentialism 96–97; in feminism 95–96; Gordon, Lewis 91–95; as method of inquiry 88–90; Mexican existentialism 96

experimentalism 217; Du Bois, W.E.B. 221–226; "social Darwinism" 218–221

explicit prejudice 267, 271–273; versus implicit attitudes 270–271

Eze, Emmanuel C. 16, 31

Fabre, Michel 95

facticity 329

family planning 330–332; *see also* eugenics

Fanon, Frantz 10, 22, 91–92, 95, 291; "critical phenomenology" 233–235; "Negrophobia" 292–293; view of aesthetic experience 367–369

Farías, Victor 62

Farred, Grant 25

favelas 115

Faye, Emmanuel 62

Fazio, Russ 267

Feldman, Ron H. 70

Femenías, María Luisa 96

feminism: Anglo-American 344–345; Combahee River Collective's founding statement 337–338; critical race feminist aesthetics 369–370; existentialism in 95–96; intersectionality 110–111, 335–336; new directions in intersectional feminism 345–346; and phenomenology 239; proto-intersectional thought 337

Ferguson, Adam 8

Ferguson, Missouri 114, 256, 406

Fichte, Johann Gottlieb 9

film: black *noir* 255; lighting in 395–397

Firmin, Anténor 144

First People of India 189

first use of concept of race 5

Flory, Dan 255

Flower MacCannell, Juliet 295–296

Foucault, Michel 113, 328; biopolitics 7, 118; biopower 118–120; *The History of Sexuality, Volume 1* 118–119; "Inaugural Lecture" 55; security 543

Frankfurt School 102–103

freedom 143; conceptual jurisdiction of 33–35; *Entwicklung* 53–55; Haynes's view on 135; Hegel's "idea of freedom" 45–46; Kant's "transition" to 32–33; state of exception 113–118; and *Untermenschen* 38

Fricker, Miranda 247, 482

Friedman, Maurice 89–90

Fuller, Chris 186

Fullwiley, Duana 521–522

Galápagos-writ-large scenario 305–306

Galton, Francis 321

Gandhi, Mahatma 182; "Harijan" 184–185

Garner, Eric 121, 123n12

Gassendi, Pierre 5

Gaza 114

Ge'ez 129

Geisteswissenschaften 222

Gendler, Tamar 272

gene-culture co-evolution 431

generalizations 277–279; generic generalizations 277–278; qualified generalizations 278–279

generic generalizations 277–278; about *us* 283–285; challenging 286–287; construction of *us* and *them* 285–286; descriptive generics 284–286; normative generics 284–286; versus qualified generalizations 278–279; of *them* 281–283

genetics: biological implications of human genetic variation 312–313; epigenetics 331–332; human genetic variation 307–312, 309–310, **311**, **312**; philosophical implications of human genetic variation 313–315; prenatal genetic testing 329; reprogenetic technologies 329–330; *see also* eugenics

genome 307

Ghana 131

ghettos, and camps 114–115

Gilman, Sander 63

Gilroy, Paul 39n2

Gines, Kathryn 70, 337

Glasgow, Joshua 417–419; reconstructionist account of race 210–211

Gleichschaltung legislation 62

INDEX

Gobineau, Joseph-Arthur 5
Goldberg, David Theo 58n38, 482
Gooding-Williams, Robert 251
Gordon, Jane Anna 147
Gordon, Lewis 89–95, 133–134, 296, 526
Graham, Lindsey 504
Gramsci, Antonio 19, 482
Grant, Linda 284
Great Britain, criticism of slavery in 8
Greenwald, Anthony 267
Grinberg, Sylvia 115
Grotius, Hugo 8
group membership 455–458
groupism 432
Grünberg, Carl 103
Guantanamo Bay 114
Guenther, Lisa 233
Guha, Sumit 190–191
guizhong 170

Habermas, Jürgen 109
Hall, Stuart 181
Hallen, Barry 25
Hamilton, Charles, V. 7
'Han chauvinism' 174
Hansberry, Lorraine 92–93, 98n6
Harbin, Cassandra Byers 257–258
"Harijan" 184–185
Harris, Leonard 256
Harris, Marvin 520–521
Hatäta 127
Haynes, Lemuel 128–131, 134–135, 146
hearsay 347n2
Hegel, Georg Wilhelm Friedrich: *Entwicklung* 53–55; "natural spirit" 46–49, 57n25; non-existence of racialism 51–55; racial chauvinism 44–46; racial versus ethnic differentiation 50–51; racialism 48–49, 57n23; representative discussions on racialism 56n6; spirit 59m47
Heidegger, M.: lack of "biologism" 64; "The Self-Assertion of the German University" 62; *Technikkritik* 65–66; views on technology 324–325; völkisch thought 62
hereditary slavery 8
heredity *see* biology; eugenics; genetics
hermeneutical death 255
hermeneutical injustice 248–249
hermeneutics 224–225
heterozygosity 309
Heywat, Walda 127
Hierro, Graciela 96
Higashida, Cheryl 93–94
Hill Collins, Patricia 252, 344
Hilterism 66–67
Hinduism: caste 183–186; influence on India's racial philosophy 190–194; "Ram Rajya" 192

Hispanics, generic generalizations about *them* 282
historical objection against post-racial ideal 501–502
historical reception of intersectionality 341–345, *342*
historical theme of racial realism 353–354
Hitlerism 66–69
Hollinger, David 493–494
Holy Qur'an 470
Holy Roman Empire, slavery in 133
Honneth, Axel 109
Horkheimer, Max 103
Horton, James Africanus Beale 22–24
huacas 471
huangzhong 170–171
human beings: and anthropocene era 467–468; *anthropos* 463–464; Aristotle's characterization of "man" 424–428; development of sociality 428–440; genetic variation 307–312, *309–310*, *311*, *312*; as problems 145; and solidarity 440–442; "subpersons" 385–386
Hume, David 8, 10, 22
humor 380; ally status, reinforcing through jokes 381–382; Blackface 386–387; and implicit bias 383–388; and racial insensitivity 388–389; white racial blindness 388
Husserl, Edmund 62, 233; "natural attitude" 235–238; "zone of indeterminacy" 238
Hutcheson, Francis 8
Huxley, Julian 5
hyperagency 329
hypo-descent 520–521
Hyppolite, Jean 55

IAT (Implicit Association Test) 267; black-white IAT 261–264, *262–263*; implicit bias 264–266
ICRA (Indian Civil Rights Act) 157
ICWA (Indian Child Welfare Act) 161
idealist perspective on CRT 352
ideals of post-racialism 494–495
identification of races 5–6
identity 455–458; hermeneutic accounts of 344; intersectional model of *342*
ideological objections against post-racial ideal 495–498
Ignatiev, Noel 480
ignorance: epistemologies of 247; *meta-ignorance* 250–251; racial ignorance 248; white ignorance 253
illegality, state of exception 113–118
immigration 507; ethics of 507–511; and the philosophy of race 511–517; RC 539–540
implicit bias 392; APE 266; black-white IAT 264–266; control over 268–270; versus explicit attitudes 270–271; explicit prejudice 271–273; and jokes 383–388; and memory 266; "True Attitudes" 268; unawareness of 268
implicit social cognition, unconsciousness 267
incorrigible social meaning 385–.386

INDEX

India: Adivasis 189; "Aryan myth" 187–189; caste 183; Dalits 184–185; Gandhi, Mahatma 182; Hinduism's influence on racial philosophy 190–194; paternalism 182; Portuguese Goa, seventeenth-century history of 183; racism in 181–182; "racist casteism" 194; "Scheduled Castes" 185; "varnas" 184

Indigeneity 152–154; delegitimization of Indigenous political representation 162–163; and patriarchy 152–153; and sovereignty 162; US Dawes Act 157; and US settler colonialism 154–156

injustice: advantaging of whites 483–485; hermeneutical injustice 248–249; testimonial injustice 248

inquiry, existentialism as method of 88–90

Insan 470

insensitivity, resisting 251–256

instinctual repression 105

Institutes (Justinian) 133

institutional racism 7, 10, 410–411, 417–419; excluded moderns 18–25

institutionalization of CRT 351

instrumental objections against post-racial ideal 495–498

insurrectionary practices 255

internal epistemic friction 252

International Herbert Marcuse Society 105–106

internationalism 6

intersectionality 335–336; Anglo-American feminist reframing of 344–345; Combahee River Collective's founding statement 337–338; Davis, Angela 109–111; *DeGraffenreid v. General Motors* 339–340; hermeneutic accounts of identity 344; historical reception 341–345, 342; new directions in 345–346; operative intersectionality 343; origins of 110–111; proto-intersectional thought 337; tracing 336–341

intersubjective communication 240

"inversion of perspectives" 253–254

Isaac, Benjamin 478

Israel, Jonathan 37–38

Jacobs, Margaret 161

James, C.L.R. 94

James, William 216; nature versus nurture 220–221; role of the individual 220; "social Darwinism" 221; view of race 216–218

Jameson, Russell 8

Japan's victory over China 169

Jaspers, Karl 62

"jatis" 184

Jay, Martin 103

Jefferson, Thomas 26n5, 78–79, 398–400

Jenner, W.J.F. 174

Jewry 64

Jia, Lanpo 176

jianmin 170
jianzhong 170
Jim Crow segregation 71
Johnson, Sir Harry 195n9
jokes 380; Blackface 386–387; culpability 388; and implicit bias 383–388; perpetuating discrimination through 381–382; and racial insensitivity 388–389; securing ally status with 381–382; white racial blindness 388
Joseph, David 406
Judaism, anti-semitism of canonical philosophers 9–10
Judeophobia 63
"judgement of experience" 30–31
Justinian 133

"kaffirs" 182
Kafka, Franz 90
Kant, Immanuel: conceptual jurisdiction of freedom 33–35; cosmopolitanism 36–37; "culture" 34–35; deduction in 40n9; "Determination of the Concept of a Human Race" 32; "Of the Different Races of Human Beings" 32; ethic of Nazism 38; "germs" 30; and Hegel's *Entwicklung* 53–55; "Idea for a Universal History with a Cosmopolitan Aim" 33–34; "judgement of experience" 30–31; origin of scientific concept of race 5–6; racial chauvinism of 29; racial essentialism 6; "second thoughts" on "race" 35–36; "Toward Perpetual Peace" 35; "transition" from nature to freedom 32–33; *Untermenschen* 38; "On the Use of Teleological Principles in Philosophy" 32; views on slavery 9
"Kantianism simpliciter" 38
Kaplan, Cora 136
Kateb, George 70
Kaufman, Walter 89
Kawabata, Yasunari 97
Kawsay 466
keime 30
King, Martin Luther Jr.: arc of history metaphor 372; "I Have a Dream" speech 28, 43; *Where Do We Go From Here: Chaos or Community?* 43–44
King, Richard H. 69, 99n15
Kinsey, Charles 393
Kleingeld, Pauline 8, 35–37, 39
Knox, Robert 5, 23–24
Kristeva, Julia, abjection 293–295
Kshatriyas 184
Kuku, Diepiriye 182

La Peyrère, Isaac 10
Lacan, Jacques, and race theory 295–298
laissez-fair racism 409
Lane, Christopher 298
Lang, Berel 64
Langer, Susanne 392
Las Casas, Bartolomé 142

INDEX

Le Cato, N.J.W. 194
LEEP (Law Enforcement Exchange Program) 114
legal reasoning, hearsay 347n2
less-than-conscious racism 409
Levinas, Emmanuel 9, 66–68; Zionism 68–69
LGBTQ 158–159
Li, Chi 172
Liang, Boqiang 172
liangmin 170
liberal defense of post-racial ideal against ideological objection 498–501
liberal eugenics 321–322; power and coercion in liberal society 327–330
liberty, Haynes's view on 135
liezhong 170
lighting in filmmaking 395–397
linguistic colonization 163
linguistics, slippage 286–287
Linschoten, John Huighen van 183
"location problem" of racism 416–417
Locke, Alain 40n13, 78, 83
Locke, John 8, 117–118, 127, 129–130
locus 307
logic, philosophies of 148
Lord Cromer 282–283
Löwith, Karl 65
Lu, Xun 97
luck 447–448; "symmetry response" 453–454
lynching 83–84
Lysenko, Trofimo 173

Macey, David 95
machenschaft 64
Magubane, Bernard M. 26n1
majority generics 279
Maldonado-Torres, Nelson 68
"man camps" 159
Manchus 169, 171
Manitoba First Nation 406
Manuel, Mita Luz de 96–97
Mao Zedong 174
Marcuse, Herbert 102–105
mark of the plural 277; generic generalizations 277–278
Markandaya, Kamala 97
marriage: Diné Marriage Act 157; monogamous heterosexual marriage 156–157; and patriarchy 156–158; positive eugenics 322–323; prenatal genetic testing 329
Marshall, John 129
Martinez, Julia 157
Marxism 220; social change 103–105
masintin 472
massa damnata 54
Maupertuis, Pierre-Louis Moreau de 326
Mbembe, Achille 392

McCarthy, Thomas 35
McGary, Howard 494
McGee, Brian 105
Medina, José 447
Meiners, Christoph 11
memory, and implicit bias 266
Menon, Dilip 193
mens rea racism 408–409
Merleau-Ponty, Maurice 238–239; intersubjective communication 240
meta-ignorance 250–251
metaphor of blindness 249–250
"metaphysical racism" 72
metaphysics 204; analytic metaphysics 203–204; of race 313–315; the soul 425–426
Methodenstreit 223
Mexican existentialism 96
micro-aggressions 257–258
micro-invalidation 258
micro-practices of resistance 248
micro-resistance 258–259
miezhong 170
miezu 170
Millar, John 8
Miller, David 509
Mills, Charles 4, 37–38, 149, 253
minority nationalities in China 174
minzu 170–171
mitochondrial Eve 313
mixed-race identity 520–521; CMRS association 524–525; Gordon, Lewis 526; multiracialism 526–527; radicality of 522–525
MODE (Motivation and Opportunity as Determinants) 267; "True Attitudes" 268
"modern" 140–141
Modern Racism Scale 261
modern sovereignty 116–117
modernity: aesthetic underpinnings of 366–377; "Afromodern" 142; Euromodernity 142, 144–145; excluded moderns 18–25
Modi, Narendra 193
Monahan, Michael 147
'Mongoloid race' 175–176
Montegu, Ashley 5
Montesquieu 8
moral emotions: and race 450–455; and responsibility 448–450
moral luck 447–448
Morrison, Toni 27
Mosse, George 62
Müller, Max 187–189
multiracialism 520, 526–533
Murillo, Edwin 96

Nagel, Thomas 447
Namboodiripad, E.M.S. 196n42

INDEX

Nanman 469
National Socialism 62
Native Americans: ICRA 157; Indigeneity 152–154; state of exception 117; and US settler colonialism 154–156
"Nativism" 141
"natural attitude" 235–238
natural selection 442n4
"natural spirit" 46–49; of Hegel 51–55, 57n25
nature 464–465; conceptual jurisdiction of 36, 47; and "natural spirit" 46–48
nature versus nurture 220–221
Natürgeister 49
Naturwissenschaften 222
Nazism 38, 119; deploying white power 481–482; eugenics 322; and Heidegger 62–65
negative eugenics 323
"Negro" categorization of the black race 225–226
"Negrophobia" 292–293
Neo-Lamarckism 170–171
new directions in intersectionality 345–346
New Divinity 134
new forms of racism 409–410
New Zealand, Treaty of Waitangi 152
non-analytic metaphysics 204
non-existence of Hegel's racism 51–55
Norman Conquest 119
normative generics 284–286
Norton, Anne 70
not-out-of-Africa thesis 142
nucleotides 307
Nzema people 131

Obama, Barack 491
objections against post-racial ideal 495–498; historical objection against post-racial ideal 501–502
obscuring of violence 162
obsessional neurosis 292–293
okitciakwe 155
Olberg, Kalvero 521
one-drop rule 152
ontology 463
operative intersectionality 335–336, 343
oppression: Combahee River Collective's founding statement 337–338; double consciousness 251–252; epistemic death 254–255; epistemic resistance 248, 254; and group membership 455–458; insurrectionary practices 255; intersectionality 335–336; new directions in intersectional feminism 345–346; proto-intersectional thought 337; and US settler colonialism 161–165; white supremacy 475–477
Oriental philosophy 10
origin of scientific concept of race 5–6
Ortega, Mariana 95–96, 253
'Out of Africa' thesis 176

Outlaw, Lucius 106
overt racism 408–409

Pakistan, slavery in 190
Paley, William 8
Pan, Guangdan 172–173
Parents Involved in Community Schools v. Seattle School District No. 1 498
Paris terrorist shootings (2015) 405
Park, Peter 11
Pascoe, Peggy 529–530
passive ignorance 250–251
patriarchy 152–154; delegitimization of Indigenous political representation 162–163; Diné Marriage Act 157; and Indigeneity 154–156; through children 160–161; through language 158–159; through marriage and ancestry 156–158; through sexual violence 159–160
Patrik, Linda E. 90
Peller, Gary 351–352
periodization: of race 477–478; of whiteness 478–481
Periyar 188
perpetuating discrimination through jokes 381–382
phenomenology 62; Alcoff, Linda Martín 242–243; discriminatory treatment, ending 241–242; of Fanon 233–235; intersubjective communication 240; Merleau-Ponty 239–241; "natural attitude" 235–238; "zone of indeterminacy" 238
philosophical accounts of racism: affective/volitional accounts 415–416; agent-based accounts 412–419; behavioral accounts 413–415; doxastic accounts 412–413
philosophical canon, construction of 10–11
philosophical historiography, Western philosophy, role in spread of racist ideas 3–4
philosophical implications of human genetic variation 313–315
philosophies of existence 97n2
philosophy: American racial canon 75–82; as "Idol of the Theater" 17–20
phobia 292–293; and abjection 293–295
Phule, Jotiro 187–188
pigmentocracy 484–485
Pippin, Robert 46
Pitkin, Hannah 70
Pitts, Andrea 252
plural generics 280
political animal, Aristotle's characterization of man as 424–428
political philosophy 148–149; RC 539–540; slavery 7–8
politics, racial politics in China 172
polygenesis 6, 10
Popkin, Richard 10, 19
population control 330–332; *see also* eugenics
Portuguese Goa, seventeenth-century history of 183

positive eugenics 322–323
post-racialism 491; #BlackLivesMatter protests 491–492; color-blindness 492–493; disruptive defense of 502–503; eliminativism as 494; historical objection against post-racial ideal 501–502; ideals of 494–495; ideological objections against 495–498; liberal defense against ideological objections 498–501; objections against post-racial ideal 495–498; versus post-racism 492; viciousness of 503–504
post-racism 492
power and coercion in liberal society 327–330
pragmatism 83–84, 216; Du Bois, W.E.B. 84–86, 229–231; James's view of race 216–218
prejudice 29; explicit prejudice 267, 271–273; intersectionality 340–341; "judgement of experience" 30–31; perpetuating discrimination through jokes 381–382; *see also* intersectionality
prenatal genetic testing 329
primitivism 70, 141
private prisons 123n11
privilege 450–452
pro-black multiracial studies 526–528
problematization 113
problems, human beings as 145
proponents of eugenics, differences in 330–332
propositional processing 270–271
proto-intersectional thought 337
proximate causation 442n4
pseudo-concepts 40n16
pseudo-science 25, 26n1; of eugenics 323; in modern philosophy 23–24
psychic space, colonization of 296–298
psychoanalysis 290; melancholia 299; "Negrophobia" 292–293; phobia and abjection 293–295; and race theory 298–300; and social conditions 290–292; sublimation 291–292
public meaning 385–386

Qi 471–472
Qi, Sihe 173
qualified generalizations 278–279
Quecha, *Runa* 470–471

Rabinbach, Anson 62
race 141, 205–206; Andreasen's Cladism 212–213; Appiah's reduction of race to racial identity 206–207; biogenomic race 306; as biological concept 5; biological race 306–307; canonizing race theory 78–82; and caste 183; in China 169–170; *Cladism* 205–206; as concept, first use of 5; constructionism 205; Corlett's reductionism 208–209; Du Bois, W.E.B. 221–226; eliminativism 205; as empirical concept 30–32; and eugenics 325; Glasgow's reconstructionist account of 210–211; 'Han race' 170–171; immigration and the philosophy of race 511–517; James's view of 216–218; "judgement of experience" 30–31; Kant's "second thoughts" on 35–36; and luck 447–448; metaphysics of 313–315; 'Mongoloid race' 175–176; and moral emotions 450–455; "Negro" categorization of the black race 225–226; periodization of 477–478; pragmatism 216; racial "tendencies" 229; reductionism 205; social race 307; unreality of 205–206; 'yellow race' 168–169; Zack's radical eliminativism 207–208
racial chauvinism: of Hegel 44–46; of Kant 29
racial essentialism 6
racial identity 205–206
racial ignorance 248, 250–251; *alienated familiar* 249; treating 253; white ignorance 253
Racial Integrity Act 152
racial micro-aggressions 257
racial solidarity 423–424
racial "tendencies" 229
racial theories 168; in China 173
racialism: disruptive defense of post-racial ideal 502–503; *Entwicklung* 53–55; of Hegel 48–49; historical objection against post-racial ideal 501–502; ideals of post-racialism 494–495; of Kant, representative discussions on 39n4; non-existence of Hegel's 51–55; objections against post-racial ideal 495–498; post-racialism 491; racial versus ethnic differentiation 50–51; radicality of mixed-race 522–525; vicious nature of post-racialism 503–504
racialized aestheticization 366, 391–392; aesthetic sustenance and pleasure 373–374; appropriation and transculturation 374–375; beauty and the sublime 376; critical race feminist aesthetics 369–370; Du Bois's and Fanon's views of aesthetic experience 367–369; in everyday life 375–376; Kara Walker's art 370–373, 370–372; lighting in filmmaking 395–397; post- and decolonial theory 366–377
racism 406–407; aesthetic racialization 391–392; antiblack racism 147, 391–394; of Arendt 69–72; aversive racism 267, 410; "benevolent" forms of 416–417; classical racism 408–409; closet racism 408; and cosmopolitanism 36–37; cultural racism 409; defining 407–411; deploying white power 481–482; environmental racism 331–332; epistemic violence 256; explicit prejudice 271–273; first use of term 6–7; in India 181–182; institutional racism 410–411, 417–419; jokes 383–388; "location problem" 416–417; Modern Racism Scale 261; "Negrophobia" 292–293; new forms of 409–410; as normative concept 407–408; perpetuating discrimination through jokes 381–382; philosophical accounts of 411–419; tolerant racism 408–409; unacknowledged racism 409; white racial blindness 388; white supremacy 475–477

INDEX

racisms 7
"racist casteism" 194
radicality of mixed-race 522–525
"Ram Rajya" 192
Ramasamy, E. V. 188
rape: 2013 Violence Against Women Act 164; patriarchy through sexual violence 159–160
Rapin, René 10
"ratcheting" 437, 443n6
raza 141, 325
RC (Racial Contract) 539; the Homeland 540–542; and state violence 545–546
realism 314–315
realist objection against the post-racial ideal 501–502
reason, "unreasonable reason" 146
reconstructionism, Glasgow's reconstructionist account of race 210–211
reductionism 205; Appiah's reduction of race to racial identity 206–207; in Corlett 208–209
refugees: the Homeland 540–542; rhetoric of security 542–545
religion, influence on India's racial philosophy 190–194
Ren 468–469
repression, sublimation as alternative 291–292
reproduction: "Buffon's rule" 325–326; prenatal genetic testing 329
reprogenetic technologies 329–330
resisting insensitivity 251–256
responsibility: and emotions 448–450; and identity 455–458
"revised views" of Kant on "race" 35–36
rhetoric of security 542–545
Rich, Adrienne 239
Richards, Katharine C. 96
Rifkin, Mark 116
Risley, Sir Herbert 187
Roberts, Dorothy 329–330
Roberts, Rita 135
Robeson, Paul 22
Rockmore, Tom 64
Roelofs, Monique 391
Rojas, Fabio 350–351
Rong, Zou 171
Roof, Dylann 405
Roos, Jerome 114
Rose, Nikolas 328
Rothberg, Michael 71
Runa 470–471
Ruray 466

Sánchez, Carlos Alberto 96
Sancho, Ignatius 21, 26n5
Sandel, Michael 329
Santa Clara Pueblo v. Martinez 157
Sartre, Jean-Paul 10, 89, 91, 94, 98n4; *facticity* 329

Saul, Jennifer 259, 265–266
"Scheduled Castes" 185
Schmitt, Carl 113–114
Schmoller, Gustav von 222–223
scholarship, CRT influence on 357–359
science 168; Euromodern 145–146; James's view of race 216–218; and technology 324–325
scientific concept of race, origin of 5–6
scope of whiteness 478–481
Scottish Enlightenment, criticism of slavery 8
"second thoughts" of Kant on "race" 35–36
security: the Homeland 540–542; rhetoric of 542–545; and state violence 545–546; state violence 545–546
segregation 71, 354
Sekyi, William Essuman Gwira 27n7
Self-Respect Movement 188
Sepulveda, Juan Ginés de 142
"sequential priming" 267
Seshadri-Crooks, Kalpana 295, 299
settler colonial erasure 161–162
sexual violence: 2013 Violence Against Women Act 164–165; as means of patriarchy 159–160; obscuring of violence 162
shantytowns 115, 122n4
Sharp, Granville 8
Sherman Institute 160
Sheth, Falguni 116
"shooter bias" 269
Sikka, Sonia 65
silencing, types of 257
simply alien 249
singular generics 280
Slabodsky, Santiago 68–69
slavery 7–9, 141–142; Aristotle's views on 7–8; in British society 8; canonical philosophers' defense of 3–4; and caste 187; chattel slavery 21; and excluded moderns 21; hereditary slavery 8; in Holy Roman Empire 133; Kant's views on 9; in Pakistan 190; "Space Traders" 356–357; transatlantic slave trade 523–524
SLC24A5 313
slippage 286–287
Smith, Adam 8
Smith, Andrea 159
smoothing over 401
social conditions and psychoanalysis 290–292
Social Contract 539, 546
"social Darwinism" 218–220; Weber, Max 225
social death 254–255
social development of *Homo sapiens* 428–440
social race 307
sociobiology 428
Socratic method 287
solidarity 440–442; racial solidarity 423–424
Solórzano, Carlos 96

INDEX

Soosairaj, Bama Faustina 196n49
"South Asia" 194n4
sovereignty 116–117; and *homo sacer* 122n2; of Indigenous peoples 162
"Space Traders" 356–357
Spelman, Elisabeth 98n7
Spencer, Herbert 170, 218–219
Spivak, Gayatri 256
Sri Lanka, caste-race groups in Dutch Sri Lanka 184
state of exception 113–118; and Native Americans 117
state violence 545–546
state's rights, ethics of immigration 507–511
stereotype lift 284
stereotyping 6, 280; challenging generics 286–287; construction of *us* and *them* 285–286; generic generalizations about *them* 281–283; generic generalizations about *us* 283–285; jokes 385
Stern, Fritz 62
Stone, Dan 69
striking property generics 279
structural racism 410–411
sublimation as alternative to repression 291–292
Sublimis Deus 8
"subpersons" 385–386
suffering, *deserved suffering* 145
suicides in Manitoba First Nation 406
Sumak Kaway 466
Sumner, Claude 128–129
Sun, Yatsen 171
"survival of the fittest" 218; adaptive evolution 428–440
symbiosis 439–440
"symmetry response" 453–454
"systemic luck" 448

Talented Tenth 226
TallBear, Kim 156–157
Tang, Caichang 170
taste 391
Taylor, Paul 84–85, 127, 492
Technikkritik 65–66
technologies of the self 328
technology: application of in reproduction 326; characteristics of modern technology 324–325; Euromodern science 145–146; reprogenetic technologies 329–330
terrorism, the Homeland 540–542
testimonial injustice 248
testimonial quieting 257
testimonial smothering 257
tezheng 174
them, generic generalizations about 281–283; construction of *us* and *them* 285–286
theodicy 144
theonaturalism 141

theory of evolution: biological implications of human genetic variation 312–313; development of human sociality 428–440; Galápagos-writ-large scenario 305–306; "survival of the fittest" 218
theory of recognition 109
theory of unilinear evolution 170–171
theses on human genetic variation 307–312, 309–310, 311, *312*; biological implications 312–313; philosophical implications 313–315
Thind, Bhagat Singh 188–189
thought 140; Africana *thought* 141–143; de-intellectualization of Africana thought 142; European *thought* 142
Tlumak, Jeffrey 128–129
tolerant racism 408–409
"Toward Perpetual Peace" 35
tracing intersectionality 336–341
transatlantic slave trade 523–524
transculturation 374–375
treating, racial ignorance 253
Treaty of Waitangi 152
Treitschke, Heinrich von 222
"True Attitudes" 266–268
Trump, Donald 540
Tuck, Eve 157–158
Tuck, Richard 130
Tukhanen, Mikko 299
Turner, Darwin 94
Turner, Lou 95, 99n15
Two-Spirit persons 158–159
Tyrell, James 8

Übergang 32
Ulrich, Duke Anton 131
unacknowledged racism 409
unawareness of implicit attitudes 268
UNESCO Statement on Race 5
universals 469–470
"unnatural lottery" 448
unreality of race 205–206
"unreasonable reason" 146
Untermenschen 38
Untouchables 184–185
us, generic generalizations about 283–285; construction of *us* and *them* 285–286
US Dawes Act 157
US immigration policy: ethics of immigration 507–511; and the philosophy of race 511–517; RC 539–540; rhetoric of security 542–545; and state violence 545–546
US settler colonialism 154–156; delegitimization of Indigenous political representation 162–163; obscuring of violence 162; and oppression 161–165; settler colonial erasure 161–162
USA Patriot Act 114

INDEX

Vaishya 184
"varnas" 184
Verstehen 225
vicious nature of post-racialism 503–504
vincularidad 462
violence: Dylann Roof 405; epistemic violence 256–259; Fanon's view of 297–298; Ferguson, Missouri 406; micro-aggressions 257–258; Paris terrorist shootings 405; racial micro-aggressions 257; state violence 545–546
Violence Against Women Act (2013) 159–160, 164
virtue 446
Viswanath, Rupa 192
Voegelin, Eric 10, 325
Volk 171
völkisch thought 62–63, 65
völkisch tradition 61
Volkov, Shulamit 63
volksgemeinschaft 63
Voting Rights Act 496

Wacquant, Loïc 119
Walker, Alice 373–374
Walker, David 24, 78–79
Walker, Kara 370–373, *370–372*
Walker, Margaret Urban 458
Wallace, Alfred Russell 219
Walzer, Michael 508
Wang, Fuzhi 169
War on Terror, the Homeland 540–542
Watts, Jerry Gafio 95
Weber, Max 222, 224–225
Wellman, Christopher Heath 509
Wells-Barnett, Ida B. 83–84
weltjudentum 63–64
West, Cornel 55n2
Western philosophy, role in spread of racist ideas 3–4
Wheatley, Phillis 373
White, Richard 156
"White Australia Policy" 508
white ignorance 253
white privilege 450–452; advantaging of whites 483–485
white racial blindness 388; antiblack racism 391–394; racial insensitivity 388–389
white supremacy 475–476, 539–540; deploying white power 481–482; Dylann Roof 405; as existent and oppressive 476–477; periodization of race 477–478; periodization of whiteness 478–481
whiteness 295–296, 299; "critical whiteness studies" 480; periodization of 478–481; *pigmentocracy* 484–485
Williams, Bernard 447
Wilson, Darren 114, 393
Wilson, E. O., development of human sociality 428–440
Wilson, Russell 285
Wolff, Christian 131
Wolin, Richard 66
Wollstonecraft, Mary 136
Wood, Allen 37
Woolman, Joanna 161
Wright, Richard 93–95, 98n9
Wu, Rukang 176
Wynter, Sylvia 53–54, 472n1

Xirong 469

Yachay 466
Yacob, Zera 127–131, 138
Yancy, George 235
yanintin 472
Y-chromosomal Adam 313
Yellow Emperor 170
'yellow race' 168–169
yin and *yang* 471–472
youlishi de zhongzu 170
Young, Julian 64
Young-Bruehl, Elizabeth 70
"younger historical school" of economists 222–223
youzhong 170
Yucang, Chen 172

Zack, Naomi, radical eliminativism of 207–208
Zaidi, A. S. 282
"Zarpies" 281
Zhang, Junjun 172
Zhang, Junmai 173
Zhao, Tongmao 174
zhonghua minzu 174
Zionism 70; of Levinas 68–69
"zone of indeterminacy" 238
zu 169–170
zupu 170